WOMEN EDUCATORS IN THE UNITED STATES, 1820–1993

A Bio-Bibliographical Sourcebook

Edited by

MAXINE SCHWARTZ SELLER

Greenwood Press
Westport, Connecticut • London

Library of Congress Cataloging-in-Publication Data

Women educators in the United States, 1820–1993 : a bio-
  bibliographical sourcebook / edited by Maxine Schwartz Seller.
      p.   cm.
  Includes bibliographical references and index.
  ISBN 0–313–27937–3
  1. Women educators—United States—Biography.   2. Education—
United States—History—19th century.   3. Education—United States—
History—20th century.   I. Seller, Maxine.
  LA2311.W65   1994
  371.1'0092'2—dc20
  [B]   93–28033

British Library Cataloguing in Publication Data is available.

Library of Congress Catalog Card Number: 93–28033
ISBN: 0–313–27937–3

First published in 1994

Greenwood Press, 88 Post Road West, Westport, CT 06881
An imprint of Greenwood Publishing Group, Inc.

Printed in the United States of America

The paper used in this book complies with the
Permanent Paper Standard issued by the National
Information Standards Organization (Z39.48–1984).

10 9 8 7 6 5 4 3 2 1

Contents

Introduction and Overview

Women Educators in the United States, 1820–1993 profiles sixty-six women who made significant contributions to American education from the early nineteenth century to the late twentieth century. Although it is a reference work, it does not include all of the women educators who deserve to be remembered; there are far too many. Nor does it include only the most celebrated, although many well-known names do appear. Rather, my intention as the editor has been to assemble biographies that will introduce the reader to the broad range of women who have influenced American education and to the wide variety of fields in which they worked. Thus, each educator profiled here is important in her own right but is also representative of many others who have made similar and often equally important contributions.

USING WOMEN EDUCATORS IN THE UNITED STATES

Each biography opens with an introductory paragraph summarizing its subject's importance and concludes with two selective bibliographies, "Works by——," listing major works by the subject, and "Works about——," listing major works about the subject. A general bibliography about women and education in the United States has also been included.

As is customary in a reference work, the biographical entries are arranged alphabetically by the last name of the subject. However, an appendix has also been included that lists the women chronologically in order of their birth. This appendix is divided into four chronological blocks: (1) Pioneers, 1820–1870; (2) Expanders and Reformers, 1870–1920; (3) Losses and Gains, 1920–1960; and (4) Pursuing Equality and Excellence, 1960–1993. It has been added to facilitate use of *Women Educators in the United States* with courses in women's history and in the history of education, and to help readers place each educator in a meaningful historical context.

Each of the sixty-six biographies was written by a scholar with special expertise on this particular educator, the period in which she lived, and the educational field in which she worked. Biographies of living educators were often based on interviews as well as written sources. The biographies vary in length and style, reflecting the individuality of their authors. However, each biography includes basic information about the subject's family background, her education, her career, and the people and events that influenced her. As this is a reference work on *women* educators, the authors were also asked to explore the impact of gender in the lives of their subjects. Contributions to education are stressed, but women educators' activities and achievements in other fields are also described.

A RANGE OF WOMEN

Like the much larger population of women educators from whom they are drawn, the educators profiled in this volume came from many different religious and social backgrounds. They lived and worked in the Northeast, the South, the Midwest, and the West. Most were white, but some were African-American, Native American, Asian-American, and Hispanic. Two were born into slavery, eight were immigrants, and one was born in Puerto Rico. Some had access to tutors, foreign travel, and elite colleges and universities. Others attended one-room schools in rural areas or segregated schools in the South and struggled to acquire higher education at small religious institutions, normal schools, or public universities. Their political and ideological commitments, including their views on women's roles, ranged from conservative to radical.

Their contributions to American education varied as much as their backgrounds. Most began as teachers, and, regardless of later accomplishments, some continued to see themselves primarily as teachers throughout their lives. Some left the classroom for educational administration, making their contributions as innovative principals, superintendents, state supervisors, deans, or college presidents. Others founded influential schools or colleges, wrote widely used textbooks, conducted important research, or created organizations to promote educational goals. Some worked partly, or entirely, outside the traditional classroom setting, educating through women's clubs, newspapers, magazines, labor unions, art museums, and theaters. Their areas of expertise included rural education, early childhood education, reading education, science education, vocational education, music education, sex education, adult literacy, worker's education, medical and nursing education, and the education of the blind. Many devoted their lives to the education of "minorities" (often, but not always, their own) or to the education of women.

Influenced by mothers, older sisters, and teachers, many wanted to be educators from early childhood and began to teach while still in their teens. Alice Freeman Palmer became president of Wellesley College at the age of twenty-six, scarcely older than many of her students. Others came to education later in life, after pursuing political or other interests or raising a family. Mary Calderone was over sixty when she created the influential and controversial Sex Information and Education Council of the United States (SIECUS).

Most entered the field of education because they needed money and there were few other "respectable," paid occupations for women in the nineteenth and, indeed, well into the twentieth centuries. Love of learning and teaching was another motive. In addition, there were often ideological motives, as many women considered their careers in education a form of religious, social, or political activism. Zilpah Grant Banister and Mary Lyon, founders of influential nineteenth-century schools for girls, were evangelical Christians as eager to save students' souls as to educate their minds. Frances Jackson Coppin, Mary Church Terrell, and Nannie Burroughs saw their careers as contributions to the "uplifting" of the African-American community. An ardent socialist, Russian Jewish immigrant Fannia Cohn developed workers' education to strengthen the labor movement and promote economic justice.

COMMON THEMES

Each of these educators was unique. Yet, when the biographies are viewed as a group, common themes emerge. One common theme was the passion and determination with which women educators pursued their own educations, sometimes traveling to different states, even different countries, for educational opportunities and completing advanced degrees late in their careers. Educator, activist, and feminist Anna Cooper received her doctorate in French literature and history from the University of Paris, Sorbonne, at the age of sixty-five. Other common themes were their giftedness as learners and teachers, their ability to inspire the confidence and support of others, and the ingenuity with which they overcame personal and professional difficulties. For example, Caroline Putnam broke through isolation and mitigated the hostility of the white community surrounding her school for African Americans in post–Civil War Virginia by becoming town postmistress and placing the post office in her schoolhouse.

Another common theme was the energy and versatility that enabled many women educators to pursue multiple careers sequentially or simultaneously. Sister Mary Madeleva Wolff was an internationally honored poet as well as the innovative president of St. Mary's College. Mary McLeod Bethune founded a school for African-American girls and directed its development into a coeducational college, but she also played a leadership role in several national women's organizations, lectured, wrote newspaper columns, and advised President Franklin Roosevelt's administration on matters concerning youth, education, and African Americans. Miriam Colón combined a demanding and successful career as a stage, film, and television actress with the creation and management of a bilingual Puerto Rican theater and theater school.

One thing all of these educators shared, of course, was the fact that they were women, and the impact of this factor is explored in many of the biographies. In the lives of a minority, gender issues sometimes seemed unimportant. Chinese-born Sucheng Chan found that being foreign-born and having a physical disability (she had had polio as a child) presented more obstacles than being female. Tribal identities were more important than gender for the Native American educators, whose first concern was the welfare, even the survival, of their people. For similar reasons, race was usually more salient than gender for the African-American educators, but many were also outspoken feminists. Anna Cooper complained that in the African- American community men did not support women's aspirations for higher education and rejected women's help in addressing "the great questions of the world."[1] Frances Jackson Coppin wrote a regular "Women's Department" column in the national newspaper of the African Methodist Episcopal church promoting equal educational and professional opportunities for women.

Being female made it more difficult for most of the educators profiled here to acquire their own educations and to pursue their chosen careers. Many biographies document the problems caused by gender stereotypes, restrictive social expectations, and discrimination. The biographies also document the strategies women educators developed to overcome these problems. For example, in the antebellum decades "respectable" women were confined to the home and literally silenced if they ventured outside it. Educational leaders like Emma Willard, Catharine Beecher, and Mary Lyon accomplished their goals in this restrictive environment by persuading influential men (usually ministers) to provide "cover" for their fund-raising, organizing, and other public activities. Shut out of the traditional "male" professions in the late nineteenth and early twentieth centuries, women created new professions for themselves in "female" areas or upgraded traditional women's professions; chemist Ellen Swallow Richards developed home economics, Adelaide Nutting brought nursing education to the university campus, and Jane Addams and Sophonisba Breckinridge turned women's traditional charitable activities into the profession of social work. Isolated by male administrators and colleagues, academic and professional women of the nineteenth and early twentieth centuries created female networks to help one another and to nurture the careers of junior colleagues—and continue to do so.

One of the most difficult gender-related problems for women educators has been conflict between family and career. Religious and secular ideologies assigned women to domestic, rather than public, life. The biographies show that most middle-class white educators and, to a lesser extent, working-class and minority women faced social pressure to forgo higher education or paid employment and stay at home to fulfill their traditional obligations as daughters, sisters, wives, and mothers. The problems of combining family and career were logistical as well as ideological, as the time and energy demands of working both inside and outside the home were formidable. It is not surprising, therefore, that thirty-four of the sixty-six women profiled (over half) never married, a proportion greater than that of their contemporaries of comparable social status and education. Seven married late, when their careers were already well established, and an additional ten began their careers after being widowed, separated, or divorced. Only fourteen of the sixty-six combined marriage (and often motherhood) with professional life for significant periods of time.

The biographies demonstrate the many ways in which the conflicts between marriage and career were played out in women's lives. In 1887 Alice Freeman Palmer's new husband pressured her to the point of physical illness to give up the presidency of Wellesley College, a sacrifice to the ideals of "true womanhood" that she made with great ambivalence and to which she was never fully reconciled. Emily Ingham Staunton, founder (with her sister) of Ingham University in the mid-nineteenth century, was more fortunate. Her husband supported her leadership role at Ingham and became an invaluable colleague in her work. The problems of career and family did not disappear with time. Wife and mother of two, Joyce Tsunoda pursued her career as a successful community college administrator and provost in the 1980s with household assistance from her mother as well as her husband. One of Johnnetta Cole's stated goals as president of Spelman College was to encourage her students to follow her example in struggling for both personal and professional fulfillment.

HISTORICAL CONTEXT

The Pioneers, 1820–1870

Common themes recur in the lives of women educators from the early nineteenth century to the late twentieth century. Nevertheless, the historical contexts in which women educators worked changed over time, as did the tasks they addressed. To understand the individual biographies more fully, therefore, it is useful to survey, albeit in broad outline, the history of women as educators in the United States.

Although the careers of the women profiled in this volume began around 1820, American women's educational activities began much earlier. In colonial America, Native American and African-American women and women from various European backgrounds taught their daughters and other younger women the domestic, herbal, and craft skills, and other things necessary for individual and group survival. In the English colonies, white women, often widows, kept "dame schools" for very young children, occasionally served as family tutors, and, beginning in the mid-eighteenth century, conducted boarding schools for "young ladies." The few African Americans who were able to acquire literacy under slavery passed this precious knowledge on to others, often secretly and at great risk to their own safety. It was not until the half century beginning about 1820, however, that it became possible for a significant number of American women to pursue publicly recognized—indeed, publicly honored—careers as educators.

The emergence on the public scene of women as educators took place when it did because of two simultaneous and interdependent developments—the opening of higher education to women and the popular acceptance of teaching as an important and desirable "female" occupation. Underlying both was an ideological development, the emergence of a widespread belief that women were naturally more religious and more virtuous than men and therefore had a special social, moral, and educational mission. Women were to be educated so that they could exert their influence over their husbands, their children, and, through teaching, the children of others to uplift and purify American society. By mid-century, economics as well as ideology supported the emergence of careers for women in education. The new tax-supported common schools needed large numbers of inexpensive (therefore female) teachers, and increasing numbers of women needed a source of income.

Women could not become educators until they were educated. In colonial America only exceptional women were fortunate enough to acquire more than basic literacy. Widespread and systematic improvements began around 1820, however, when district schools of New England began to admit girls on an equal basis with boys and when a new generation of private schools offered young women secondary and, in some cases, even college-level education comparable to that available to their brothers. In the decades that followed, white girls were accepted into the new common (public) elementary schools. Despite considerable opposition, women were also accepted into many high schools and, beginning with Oberlin (which also admitted African Americans) in 1833, into some colleges and a handful of medical schools, though often not on an equal basis with men. By 1870 the majority of all high school graduates and 21 percent of all college students were women.[2] A pool of educated women had been created from which women educators could emerge.

As the biographies in this volume demonstrate, women were the creators as well as the beneficiaries of expanded educational opportunities in the mid-nineteenth century. Emma Willard and her sister Almira Hart Phelps, Catharine Beecher, Zilpah Grant Banister and her friend and colleague Mary Lyon, Grant's student Emily Ingham, and other early white women educators founded precedent-setting private schools for women, proving to a skeptical public that women could do serious academic work. These pioneer educators trained hundreds of "daughter" teachers who created and staffed academies, public schools, even colleges throughout the nation.

Similar pioneering work was done in racially segregated minority communities by African-American educators such as Sarah Mapps Douglass, abolitionist and founder of an important school for African-American girls in antebellum Philadelphia, Fanny Jackson Coppin, principal of the prestigious coeducational Institute for the Education of Colored Youth, and Native American educator Caroline Bushyhead Quarles, a teacher in bilingual Cherokee tribal schools. African-American women educators had the double burden of proving to an often skeptical or even hostile public that their race as well as their gender could learn. In the immediate post–Civil War years hundreds of white and African-American women from the North went South under the auspices of the Freedman's Bureau or missionary societies to help newly freed African Americans in their struggle for literacy. A few white educators like Caroline Putnam and Sarah Dickey remained for decades, braving social ostracism or worse from the white community to provide schools for blacks whose educational needs were neglected by local and state governments.

Early and mid-nineteenth century women pioneered in informal as well as formal education. Some became authors and editors, educating through the now cheaper, more readily available printed materials. Others used the many nineteenth-century social and moral reform movements (some of which were seen as compatible with women's expanding social roles) as their forum. Willard, Beecher, and others were important educators of adults as well as children. Their publications and lectures were instrumental in creating and popularizing the new ideologies that raised the status of women in the home and provided a rationale for their employment as classroom teachers. Controversial civic educator and reformer Lydia Maria Child wrote educational materials for children and adults advocating the rights of Native Americans, women's rights, and the abolition of slavery. Also controversial, health reformer and feminist Marie Zakrzewska ("Dr. Zak") opened a women's hospital to provide clinical education for women physicians.

In the closing decades of the century women were still considered intellectually inferior by many and relegated, at least in theory, to domestic life by most. Yet by 1870 nearly two-thirds of all the teachers in the nation's schools were women.[3] A pioneer generation of women educators had opened the way for themselves and others to pursue careers in education not only as teachers but also, in smaller numbers, as lecturers, social reformers, editors, authors, professors, and physicians.

Expanders and Reformers, 1870–1920

A predominantly rural "developing" nation in the early 1870s, by 1920 the United States had become an urban, industrial giant. Education changed too, in response to the needs of an increasingly complex society with an increasingly diverse population. By the turn of the century, schooling in most of the industrial states had become compulsory for children up to the age of fourteen. Public and parochial schools increased in number, kindergartens were introduced, and high schools multiplied. "Progressive" educators experimented with a freer, more humane pedagogy that was related to children's interests and to their communities. Educators also experimented with bureaucratic forms of school organization, while a new institution, the research university, revolutionized higher and professional education. Supported by networks of female colleagues and a powerful women's movement (culminating in the passage of the women's suffrage amendment in 1919), women educators played important roles in all of these changes.

Many women educators of the late nineteenth and early twentieth centuries focused their efforts on "minority" populations, often providing social services as well as schooling and assuming advocacy roles in their behalf. Frontier missionaries like Sister Blandina Segale and Harriet Bedell addressed the needs of Native Americans and others on the western frontier and in other sparsely settled areas. Networks of educated and dedicated African-American women, including Anna Cooper, Lucy Laney, Nannie Burroughs, and Mary McLeod Bethune, created schools for African Americans, resisting pressure from many whites and some African Americans to provide low-level "industrial" training in favor of solid academic and vocational education.

Women were also instrumental in the education and Americanization of the millions of Eastern and Southern European immigrants who poured into the impoverished "ghettos" of industrial cities at the turn of the century. Working in public schools, settlement houses, parochial schools, and a variety of ethnic and other organizations, women educators, like their male counterparts, differed in their approach to the immigrant "problem." Julia Richman, the first Jewish principal in New York City, introduced health care and other social services to the schools and earned a national reputation (and the hostility of much of the Russian Jewish immigrant community) for vigorous "Americanization." Jane Addams, founder of the influential Hull House settlement of Chicago, represented the minority of educators who sought to preserve the rich elheritage of immigrant cultures. Parochial school educators like Mother Mary Regis Casserly had yet another aim, the preservation of the Catholic traditional faith.

As school populations—and budgets—soared, male-controlled school bureaucracies designed for "efficiency" curtailed the autonomy of the classroom teacher. Margaret Haley, organizer of the first teachers' unions in Chicago, was one of a number of women educators who fought, though often unsuccessfully, for the interests of the children as well as the teachers. Throughout the nation, women teachers and administrators, including Ella Flagg Young, superintendent of schools in Chicago, and Mary Bradford, state superintendent of public instruction in Colorado, developed and implemented "progressive" curricula and child-centered pedagogy.

Women educators were active outside, as well as inside, the classroom, editing or writing for a wide range of publications and working with (and in some cases helping to create) organizations such as the Women's Christian Temperance Union, the Baptist Women's Convention Auxiliary, the National Council of Jewish Women, the National Association of Colored Women, the Association of Collegiate Alumnae, the American Association of University Women, the National American Woman Suffrage Association, the National Education Association, and the National Association for the Advancement of Colored People. Through these and other organizations, many women educators played an active role in educational and political campaigns for racial justice, temperance, peace, and women's suffrage.

Women's ability to function as educators at the turn of the century depended, as it had earlier, on their own access to education. Therefore, many women educators of the late nineteenth and early twentieth centuries, like many of their predecessors, focused their energies on the higher education of women, viewing this as a reform in itself, as well as a means toward other improvements in womens' status and in society. Under the guidance of presidents like Alice Freeman Palmer of Wellesley and Martha Carey Thomas of Bryn Mawr, new women's colleges offered outstanding education to elite women and faculty positions to a growing cadre of women scholars. Most women were educated in coeducational institutions, however, where newly appointed deans of women like Marion Talbot at the University of Chicago and Lucy Sprague Mitchell at the University of California Berkeley helped carve out academic and social space for female students and faculty on often hostile, male-controlled campuses.

In 1920 there were reasons to see a promising future for women in the field of education. The percentage of women among college students had risen from 21 percent in 1870 to 47.3 percent, and women were a quarter of college faculty and 86 percent of classroom teachers.[4] Still, women were a small minority of the growing numbers of educational administrators at all levels, and in higher education women students and faculty were "ghetto-ized" in the less prestigious and remunerative fields. Ominously, a backlash to women's progress in many areas of public life, including education, was under way. Leading physicians, social scientists, and male educators argued, with pseudoscientific evidence, that women had less intellectual and leadership ability than men. Some warned that higher education and careers would prevent the "best" (white, middle-class) women from becoming wives and mothers, thus endangering the future of the (white) race.

Losses and Gains, 1920–1960

The half century between the passage of the women's suffrage amendment and the rise of a new wave of feminism was a time of losses as well as gains. The number of women students and educators continued to grow, but the

gap between women's position in education and that of men, which had
been narrowing for a century, widened in many areas. Between 1920 and
1950 the percentage of women among holders of bachelor's or first professional degrees fell from 34 percent to 24 percent. Between 1930 and 1950
women's share of doctorates fell from 18 percent to 10 percent, and their
share of positions as college faculty and presidents fell from 32 percent to
23 percent. Women holding elementary school principalships fell from 55
percent of the total in 1928 to 22 percent in 1968.[5]

One reason for these relative losses was the decline of organized feminism
after the suffrage victory of 1919 and, in an era of increased emphasis on
"normal" heterosexuality and individualism, a weakening of women's support networks. Probably a more important reason was the fact that men were
given preference in higher education and employment during the Great Depression of the 1930s because they were seen as primary breadwinners and
again, after World War II, because they were veterans. The federal government paid for the education of hundreds of thousands of World War II
veterans, few of them women. Moreover, during these years psychiatrists,
social scientists, and commercial interests, aided by the expanding media,
urged women to seek fulfillment in marriage and motherhood rather than
in "selfish," even "unnatural," careerism.

Although their proportions fell relative to their male counterparts, women
continued to pursue careers at all levels of education. In the universities,
some women fought back at their critics. Willystine Goodsell, a faculty
member at Teachers College, Columbia University, gathered empirical evidence (much of it produced by women psychologists) to refute charges of
female intellectual inferiority. Other academic women studied child development and developed early childhood education and day care, addressing
the needs of a still relatively small but growing number of women who
wanted both careers and families. Progressive educators like Santa Fe superintendent of schools Nina Otero-Warren, California commissioner of
rural and elementary education Helen Heffernan, and Hopi educator Polingaysi Qóyawayma continued the campaign for child-centered, community-
related schools. Progressive education was not limited to the schoolroom,
however; museum curator Katharine Kuh devised new, participatory
methods to educate adult museum goers about modern art.

Although women in general lost ground relative to men in the interwar
years, women from some minority and working-class groups gained. Their
own leadership positions protected by a religious tradition of single-sex education, Catholic college presidents like Mother Joseph Butler and Sister
Mary Madeleva Wolff improved the availability and quality of education for
a new generation of Catholic women. New educational opportunities for
women workers, many of them the daughters of Southern and Eastern European immigrants, were created by educators as diverse as garment worker
and union official Fannia Cohn and Bryn Mawr College administrator Hilda

Worthington Smith. African-American women continued to pursue higher education in larger numbers than their brothers, knowing that jobs awaited them as teachers in segregated schools. New African-American educators like Lucy Diggs Slowe, dean of women at Howard University, joined distinguished older colleagues like Nannie Burroughs and Mary McLeod Bethune as advocates for African-American women.

Pursuing Equality and Excellence, 1960–1993

In the 1960s and 1970s the civil rights movement among African Americans, ethnic revivals among many other groups, and a revitalized feminist movement revolutionized American education. This revolution included the Brown decision, which outlawed racially segregated schools, movements for bilingual and multicultural education, the "education for all handicapped" act, and Title IX of the Educational Amendments of 1972, which outlawed sex discrimination in most educational institutions. In addition, educational institutions receiving federal funds were required under controversial affirmative action policy to seek out women and minorities for faculty and administrative positions. Meanwhile, existing colleges and universities were expanded, and a network of community colleges was created. The result of all these changes was the opening of new educational and career opportunities for women of all backgrounds.

By the 1980s women's participation in higher education at the bachelor's and master's levels equaled or exceeded that of men, women were making dramatic inroads into law and medicine, and women's share of faculty and administrative positions had begun to grow, albeit modestly. Equality remained elusive, however. Women students and faculty, especially minorities, remained disproportionately concentrated in community colleges and other less prestigious institutions rather than in research universities. They also remained disproportionately concentrated in lower-paid, stereotypically female fields such as teaching, library science, and fine arts rather than engineering, physical sciences, and mathematics.

Late twentieth-century women, like their predecessors, were the creators as well as the beneficiaries of educational change. Minority women were especially active as agents of change in the educational movements for civil rights and cultural pluralism. African-American teacher Septima Clark worked with the Southern Christian Leadership Council to teach disfranchised adults a curriculum of literacy specifically directed toward their political empowerment. Yakima educator Martha Yallup and Crow educator Janine Pease-Windy Boy developed colleges that prepared Native Americans to live successfully in "mainstream" America without abandoning their rich tribal heritages. Preservation of her people's language and culture was also an educational goal for Mexican-American Dolores Gonzales, a pioneer in bilingual education. A productive and respected scholar and administrator,

Sucheng Chan was instrumental in establishing the legitimacy of Asian studies on the university campus. Anthropologist Johnnetta Cole worked at the intersection between race and gender, translating her social and scholarly commitments to the African-American community and to women into her activities as president of Spelman College.

"Mainstream" and minority women educators were active in a variety of late twentieth-century educational reforms, including the movements for ethnic and women's studies, the "excellence" movement to increase educational achievement, and the movement to restructure schools by providing teachers with more decision-making power. At the University of Chicago Helen Mansfield Robinson continued her long-established career of developing and disseminating ways to improve reading education. Peggy McIntosh worked to incorporate the new scholarship on gender and ethnic "diversity" into the high school and college curriculum. In the tradition of earlier progressive reformers, Harlem public school principal Deborah Meier drew on the initiative and professional abilities of teachers as well as on the interests of students to "restructure" inner-city schools. Late twentieth-century educators also participated in the making of educational policy and in government service at many levels; for example, Janine Pease-Windy Boy was a delegate to the 1992 White House conference on Indian education and teacher-educator Mari-Luci Jaramillo served as ambassador to Honduras.

By the early 1990s, when this book was compiled, the number of women educators was greater than at any time in the past. The range of fields in which they worked was greater, too, including relatively new technological areas such as the development of educational computer software for children and adults, new teaching techniques (such as whole language reading and writing instruction), and new areas of study, such as gay and lesbian studies. The full significance of the contributions of the educators of the 1990s, however, awaits documentation at a later time.

In conclusion, I would like to thank Greenwood Press for their commitment to this project and my assistant Barbara Shircliffe for her excellent editorial work. I would also like to thank the many knowledgeable colleagues who made helpful suggestions; I wish there had been space to include all of the educators they brought to my attention. Most of all, I would like to thank the authors, whose outstanding scholarship and generous cooperation made this project possible.

NOTES

1. A. [Cooper], *Voice from the South*, in Dorothy Sterling, ed., *We Are Your Sisters: Black Women in the Nineteenth Century* (New York: W. W. Norton, 1984), 435–36.

2. Barbara Miller Solomon, *In the Company of Educated Women: A History of Women and Higher Education in America* (New Haven, CT: Yale University Press, 1985), 63.

3. Geraldine Joncich Clifford, "Man/Woman/Teacher: Gender and Career in American Educational History," in Donald Warren, ed., *American Teachers: History of a Profession at Work* (New York: Macmillan and the American Educational Research Association, 1989), 294.

4. Solomon, 63, 113; Clifford, 294.

5. Solomon, 133; Cynthia Fuchs Epstein, *Women's Place: Options and Limits in Professional Careers* (Berkeley: University of California Press, 1971), 7, 60.

Women Educators
in the
United States,
1820–1993

Laura Jane Addams

Mary Lynn McCree Bryan

Jane Addams (1860–1935) was a legend in her lifetime. Cofounder, in 1889, of the world-famous social settlement, Hull House, she guided it as well as the American settlement movement when both were at the forefront of national reform efforts in child labor, infant welfare, education, housing, health care, immigrant education and protection, and women's rights and suffrage. Considered one of the first generation of college women, Addams knew the value of education in her own life and worked tirelessly to bring meaningful education to all. Like John Dewey, a progressive, Addams turned the settlement into a laboratory for educational experimentation that dovetailed with Dewey's theories. She and the residents at Hull House pioneered in the development of educational experiences useful to immigrants and adults. Particularly noteworthy elements of the settlement program in this regard were the Labor Museum and a manual training program, which was important in the development of vocational education. Instrumental in creating a new profession of social work and in seeing its first professional school established at the University of Chicago, Addams and her network of associates were also at the forefront of the effort to abolish child labor and to demand national compulsory education. A prolific writer and frequent public speaker, Addams published thirteen books and hundreds of newspaper and journal articles to promote her reform perspective. Dedicated to the ideals of peace and social justice, Addams became the leader of the first modern women's peace movement. She was the primary organizer of the Woman's Peace Party and the Women's International League for Peace and Freedom in 1915, and she served as an active president of the Women's International League until 1929. In addition to fourteen honorary degrees and countless other honors in America, she was recognized by the governments of Germany and Greece for humanitarian relief immediately after World War I, and in 1931 was the first American woman to be awarded the Nobel Peace Prize.

Laura Jane Addams (September 6, 1860–May 23, 1935) was the eighth of nine children born to Sarah Weber (1817–1863) and John Huy Addams (1822–1881). Her parents had met while John Addams, formerly a school-teacher, was learning the miller's trade at her brother-in-law's mill in Ambler, Pennsylvania. On their wedding trip in July 1844, they journeyed to the Midwest and settled in the village of Cedarville, Illinois, just a few miles north of Freeport. John Addams quickly built a solid reputation as a fair and astute businessman, a social and cultural leader, and a successful Illinois Republican political figure. He established a prosperous milling business on Cedar Creek and began to purchase and to farm land surrounding the village. In addition to organizing the Second National Bank of Freeport, helping to bring the railroad to Stephenson County, and representing his district in the state legislature, 1855–1872, this friend of Abraham Lincoln was instrumental in starting the Cedarville public school and founding two Sunday schools. With his own collection, he began one of the first lending libraries in the state.

As the fortunes of John Addams grew, so did his family. By September 6, 1860, when Jane Addams was born, four Addams children were living. They were a son, John Weber, and three daughters, in birth order, Mary Catherine, Martha, and Sarah Alice. Compared with the information available about John Addams, little is known about Sarah Addams. She seems to have been a dedicated wife and mother, respected in her community for her help to others. Perhaps, like John Addams, she believed strongly in higher education for all of her children.

Two years and four months after Jane was born, Sarah Addams died soon after giving birth to a stillborn son. Jennie, as Jane was called, was now motherless and the youngest child in the Addams family. She looked to her oldest sister, Mary, who was sixteen, to assorted household help, and to her father for guidance through her early childhood years. Not surprisingly, she would always feel extremely close to Mary and to her father, whom she adored.

When she was nine years old, her world changed dramatically. John Addams remarried on November 17, 1868. His choice was Anna Hostetter Haldeman, the widow of William Haldeman, who had been a miller in Freeport. Anna brought with her into the Addams household two sons, Henry Winfield Haldeman, who was away in Germany studying medicine and music, and George Bowman Haldeman, who was a little younger than Jane. About this time all of Jane Addams's siblings left. Sarah Alice and John Weber went to college. Mary Catherine Addams, on whom Jane had relied as surrogate mother, spent time traveling and visiting relatives and by 1871 had left the household permanently to begin her own married life as the wife of John Manning Linn, a Presbyterian minister. With her father away in Springfield in the legislature, Jane Addams faced her stepmother and stepbrother alone.

The new Mrs. Addams was a dominating figure. She was well-read and witty, loved music and poetry, and knew her own mind. She was delighted to be Mrs. Addams, adored educated society, and demanded achievement from all of the children in her care. While Anna doted on her sons, there is little evidence that the relationship between Jane Addams—or indeed, any of the other Addams children—and Anna was anything but respectful. Jane Addams and George Haldeman became playmates. They attended Cedarville public school, competed in educational activities, played childhood games together, explored the northern Illinois countryside, collecting snakeskins and Native American artifacts, and became each other's primary peer companion. The first letters that Jane Addams wrote date from the time Anna became her stepmother.

With the conclusion of her local schooling, where Jane consistently received high grades in writing and reading and poor grades in spelling, Jane Addams looked forward to college. She had hoped to go away from home and to attend Smith College, just opened in 1871 in Massachusetts, but her father and stepmother decreed that she would follow her sisters and attend Rockford Female Seminary in Illinois. George went to Beloit College in Wisconsin.

The four years Jane Addams spent at Rockford were signal. Here she began to feel the scope of her intellectual capabilities and to hone them. She took the most challenging curriculum offered. The goal of the school was to prepare young women to be wives, missionaries, or teachers. In addition to studying biology, astronomy, chemistry, and taxidermy, she undertook Greek, literature, religion, composition, and math. She led an active social life, too, participating in clubs, debates, and public class exercises and serving as the editor of the school magazine. During this time she discovered her leadership skills as well as her ability to make friends and to inspire admiration. She graduated valedictorian of her class in 1881 and returned the next year to receive one of the first baccalaureate degrees granted by the institution. During her freshman year at Rockford Jane Addams befriended Ellen Gates Starr, a classmate from Durand, Illinois, with whom she later founded the social settlement known as Hull House.

The years between 1881 and 1889 were filled with pain, personal growth, and continuing education. Shortly after she graduated from Rockford, her father died unexpectedly from a ruptured appendix. It was an emotional blow from which she could not quickly recover. According to plan and with her father's previous blessing, she entered the Women's Medical College of Philadelphia, as her sister Sarah Alice had done. She matriculated in the fall of 1881, but by the spring of 1882 she had decided that medical school was not what she wanted.

The emotional burden of her father's death was still overwhelming. After being treated for nervous prostration in S. Weir Mitchell's clinic in Philadelphia, Jane Addams returned to Cedarville. Her continuing poor health, including debilitating back pain, caused her to undergo surgery to correct a spinal curvature with which she had been afflicted since childhood. Performed by her stepbrother Henry Haldeman, who had received medical training in Germany before marrying her sister Alice in 1875, the surgery required that Addams spend the winter of 1882 in bed at their home.

By the fall of 1883, she had recovered her physical and emotional equilibrium sufficiently to undertake a major tour of Europe with her stepmother and four other women. Addams spent the next two years learning the languages of the Continent, attending lectures, reading the literature and history of the places she was seeing, listening to the music, and viewing the art. Occasionally her letters contain commentary on deplorable social conditions. She spent much of the following two years, 1885–1887, in the company of her stepmother, with summers in Cedarville and winters in Baltimore, where her stepbrother George was in graduate school at Johns Hopkins University. Continuing her program of self-education, she attended lectures, exhibits, and musicales in Baltimore, and she spent time helping at an orphanage for African-American children and working with elderly women.

In 1887, Jane Addams went back to Europe. This time she was accompanied by Sarah Anderson, her favorite Rockford Seminary teacher, and by Ellen Gates Starr. More reading, sightseeing, and investigation of European culture were finally interrupted by another milestone occasion. In June 1888, Sarah Anderson and Jane Addams visited the prototype social settlement Toynbee Hall, located in the slums of the East End of London. Founded by Samuel and Henrietta Barnett in 1884, it was an attempt to create communication between the working class and the upper class. The hope was to bring from that dialogue an understanding and some solutions to the social and economic problems workers faced and to give those in need an opportunity to help themselves. At its heart was education. It permitted the educated to use their knowledge in a direct and pragmatic way to seek solutions to society's ills; it permitted those without formal education to learn. "It is a community of University men who live there, have their recreation, clubs and society all among the poor people yet in the same style they would live in their own circle. It is so free from 'professional doing good,' so unaffectedly sincere and so productive of good results in its classes and libraries, etc. that it seems perfectly ideal," wrote Addams after her visit.[1]

Jane Addams had experienced a significant manifestation of Christian socialism and found it to her liking. She knew what she wanted to do. Though not mission work nor school teaching, the settlement idea clearly had elements of both vocations, for which her days at Rockford Seminary had prepared her. As she and Sarah Anderson left for America, she encouraged Ellen Starr, chaperoning two young women on a tour of Europe, to include Toynbee Hall in her itinerary.

By January 1889, Addams and Starr had decided that they would create an institution in Chicago similar to Toynbee Hall. In the last years of the nineteenth century and during the first decades of the twentieth century, urban America was characterized by growing industrial development spurred by the progress of technology and an unlimited supply of cheap labor provided by immigrants. Slums grew almost overnight and became havens of social inequality, poverty, sickness, filth, and hopelessness. As in London, the conditions in which people were forced to live and work required reform. Jane Addams believed Toynbee Hall could provide the inspiration and the model.

In September 1889, Jane Addams, Ellen Gates Starr, and Mary Keyser, who had been a nurse and housekeeper for the Addams family, opened the doors of what was to become Hull House at 800 South Halsted Street. It was the first settlement house in Chicago, the third in America, and it was destined to become world-famous. Jane Addams and Ellen Gates Starr had spent the early part of 1889 obtaining the support of leading men and women of the city for their unique social experiment. While Toynbee Hall had only male residents, Addams and Starr hoped to interest other well-educated, financially self- sufficient young women in coming to settle (thus the term *settlement*) with them. Their home was to be a large, gracious old house known to their German, Italian, Irish, French, and Russian Jewish neighbors as Mr. Hull's house. Charles J. Hull had built it as a summer home in 1856, and, not surprisingly, Addams kept a version of that name.

Eventually hundreds of men and women of all ages, idealistic and hoping to make a difference, joined the effort. Taken together and through time, they form an impressive network of mutually supportive, reform-minded leaders who helped bring beneficial change to America. Among them were Florence Kelley, founder of the National Consumers League; Alice Hamilton, pioneer in industrial medicine and the first woman on the Harvard medical faculty; and Grace Abbott and Julia Lathrop, the first two heads of the U.S. Children's Bureau. Edith Abbott and Sophonisba Breckinridge were leaders in developing America's first social work school at the University of Chicago. Others were Jeanette Rankin, first woman in Congress; Paul Douglas, U.S. senator from Illinois; Robert Weaver, first African American in a U.S. cabinet; and Frances Perkins, the first woman in a U.S. cabinet.

The settlement program proceeded along two complementary lines. Hull House, through its residents and volunteers, provided programs and services focused on helping individual neighbors improve the quality of their lives. At the same time they worked with neighbors to investigate problems common to all and to seek solutions. By the turn of the century Addams was the acknowledged leader of the growing American settlement movement at a time when it was at the forefront of all major reform efforts sweeping the country. Inspired by the energetic, articulate, and pragmatic Miss Addams, the residents at Hull House led the fight for a better environment; for parks, playgrounds, and clean, well-lighted streets; for improved housing; and for health care. Working in support of labor and unions, they pushed for improved working conditions and fair wages for men and women workers.

They lectured and lobbied for women's rights and women's suffrage, too. Of paramount importance was the program that Addams and her coworkers established for educating the immigrant population they served. Also very significant was their dedication to the fight for compulsory education and the end of child labor.

From the first activity, a kindergarten begun in September 1889, programs associated with the settlement exploded with innovative efforts to provide social and educational opportunities for the male and female immigrant population of all ages. The original settlement house, eventually augmented by twelve other buildings covering a city block, became a huge educational institution. The progressive ideas of Addams, for the most part consistent with those of fellow progressive John Dewey, were put into practice. Dewey lived at the settlement for a while to observe. "My indebtedness to you for giving me an insight into matters there is great. . . . Every day I stayed there only added to my conviction that you had taken the right way," wrote John Dewey to Addams after his stay. Dewey often referred to Hull House as the laboratory in which his theories became reality.[2]

Addams's perspective on education was rooted in the idea of self-expression, learning through play, and participatory involvement. She believed that schools were meant to be transmitters of American culture, which she defined as "a knowledge of those things which have been long cherished by men, the things men have loved because through generations they have softened and interpreted life, and have endowed it with value and meaning."[3] She believed that they were unable to accomplish this for the immigrant community, primarily because the culture they taught was without relationship to daily experience. In an address to the National Education Association in 1897, Addams argued that schools needed "to give the child's own experience a social value"[4] by providing a curriculum that would lead to an understanding of the industrial world in which the immigrant student, child or adult, would work and live. She came to see that the settlement should do no less. "The educational efforts of a settlement should not be directed primarily to reproduce the college-type culture but to work out a method and an ideal adapted to adults who spend their time in industrial pursuits."[5]

Though the Hull House program shifted throughout the years to reflect the growth of Addams's educational philosophy and to meet neighborhood need, there were basic educational elements that never changed. There were always a nursery, well-baby clinic, and kindergarten, which eventually became a lab school for the National College of Education, Evanston, Illinois. There were classes, clubs, playgrounds, and summer camps that stressed play and learning in social settings for school-aged children. Offerings in domestic science prepared students in cooking, sewing, and housekeeping. College extension classes, reading parties, lecture series, and summer school for neighborhood women at Rockford College, so much a part of the early settlement efforts, gave way by the turn of the century to a more practical curriculum. Many neighbors simply wanted to learn how to speak, read, and write English. They needed classes in citizenship, too. A manual training program, soon to be called vocational education, was offered in the settlement shops. It provided job training in everything from typewriting, sewing, and millinery to shoe repair and printing.

The settlement's attempt to afford access to beauty and culture and to preserve immigrant culture was continual. There were dancing classes, drama classes and presentations, art and music lessons with exhibitions and recitals. One of the unique educational experiments at the settlement was the Labor Museum. Opened in 1900, its exhibits and the opportunity it afforded immigrants to practice the hand methods of production associated with the lands from which they came helped to preserve traditional crafts and to teach generations born in America about the beauty of their heritage. Here was industrial education at its best and with an intergenerational focus. "In the narrow confines of one room," Addams wrote, "the Syrian, Slav, Latin, and the Celt, show the continuity of industrial development which went on peacefully year by year among the workers of each nation, heedless of differences in language, religion and political experiences."[6]

She served both on the ad hoc citizens school committee formed in 1893 to reform the Chicago public schools and on the Chicago Board of Education, 1905–1909, as the appointee of a reform mayor. However, Addams was not successful in achieving reform in methodology or curriculum. Though she tried, she was not successful, either, in luring to the settlement one of the progressive schools started in Chicago in the late 1890s.[7] The settlement did, however, draw considerable attention to her efforts on behalf of education by investigating and reporting on such vital educational issues as school conditions in her neighborhood, the causes of truancy, the horrors of child labor, and cocaine addiction among youth. Her dedication to achieving the end of child labor and nationwide compulsory education was centered in the National Child Labor Committee, which she helped found in 1904. Her continuing efforts to make education more practical led to her participation in the National Society for the Promotion of Industrial Education. It was instrumental in achieving passage of the Smith-Hughes Act in 1917, which supported vocational education in high school.

In helping to develop the methods of practice associated with social settlement, Addams was instrumental in creating the new profession of social work. Loosely allied with the University of Chicago's unique department of sociology, the evolving profession eventually had its own curriculum and school. Recognized as the first school of its kind in America, the Graduate School of Social Service Administration at the university was created in part from the Chicago School of Civics and Philanthropy, started in 1903 by Graham Taylor, Addams, and other settlement leaders to offer training for social workers.

As she did with all of her reform ideas, Addams shared her educational perspective and reform experiments with other settlement leaders, who tried to replicate them, with other reformers and national leaders, with educators, and with America. As a sought-after public speaker as well as a prolific writer, Addams never lacked for platforms from which to explain and popularize her ideas. She was teacher to a whole generation of Americans. She wrote or edited thirteen books, most of which were widely read, and the collection of her papers contains more than 1,000 articles, speeches, and radio addresses, many of which focus on issues related to education.

Improving public education and creating more exciting educational opportunities for all Americans remained a lifelong commitment of Jane Addams. However, with the beginning of World War I, her focus turned primarily to the cause of world peace. Her dedication to the ideals of peace and social justice began early. It was a natural extension of her reform perspective. Living in the Hull House neighborhood had permitted her to see that people of different ethnic backgrounds, with historical traditions of antagonism between their home countries, could learn to appreciate and respect one another through education and social intercourse. She believed that the nations of the world could develop that same response to one another. "Justice between nations as between man must be founded upon understanding and good will," wrote Addams in 1929.[8]

In January 1915, shortly after the war began, Addams and Carrie Catt, together with a group of women from throughout the country, met in Washington, D.C., and founded the Woman's Peace Party in America. Addams became its public voice, urging President Wilson and congressional leaders to keep America out of war. She was chosen president of an international gathering of women held at The Hague, Netherlands, during April and May 1915 to promote a mediated settlement to the hostilities. Though their efforts were not successful, women from belligerent and neutral European countries and from America continued to pronounce their commitment to peace throughout the war. They met in Zurich, Switzerland, at the war's close and founded the Women's International League for Peace and Freedom, of which the Woman's Peace Party became the U.S. section. Jane Addams was selected president, an office she held until 1929, when she became honorary president until her death. Addams worked steadfastly against military preparedness and compulsory military training in schools and for civil liberties, the fair treatment of conscientious objectors, disarmament, mediation of international disputes, and the League of Nations.

During the war, Addams continued to speak out in America on behalf of world peace. She severely disappointed thousands of American citizens who followed their country into war and thought Addams, the model of American womanhood, should have done the same. Addams made her contribution to America's war effort by speaking throughout the country for the U.S. Food Administration, encouraging preservation and conservation of food. For many it was not enough. She found herself castigated as unpatriotic and attacked as a dangerous woman supporting the cause of socialism and communism.

By the 1920s, World War I and its red scare aftermath were fading in memory. Once again, Jane Addams's name was among the pantheon of America's most famous women. She added several more honorary degrees to those she had previously received, making fourteen in all. She was often mentioned in annual lists of America's twelve greatest living women. Buildings, children, and characters in novels were named for her; poems were dedicated to her. She received the M. Carey Thomas Award, the Pictorial Review Magazine Award, and the American Education Award, presented by the Associated Exhibitors, National Education Association. The apex of her life and career came in 1931, when she became the first American woman to receive the Nobel Peace Prize, which she shared with Nicholas Murray Butler.

Though ill health had plagued her most of her life, she left a prodigious record of influence and achievement. Shortly after participating in the Women's International League for Peace and Freedom twentieth anniversary celebration in Washington, D.C., she entered Passavant Hospital in Chicago for removal of an intestinal obstruction. A cancerous growth was removed, but Jane Addams died three days later, May 23, 1935. After a funeral service at Hull House her body was taken to Cedarville and buried in the Addams family plot.

NOTES

1. Autographed letter signed (ALS). Jane Addams to Sarah Alice Addams Haldeman, June 14, 1888, London, England, in Mary Lynn Bryan, ed., *Jane Addams Papers*, microfilm edition (Ann Arbor, MI, 1984–1986), 2–968.

2. ALS. John Dewey to Jane Addams, January 27, 1892, Ann Arbor, MI, in *Jane Addams Papers*, 2–1298.

3. Jane Addams, "Public Schools and the Immigrant Child," National Education Association, *Journal of Proceedings and Addresses* (1908), 99.

4. Jane Addams, "Foreign-Born Children in the Primary Grades," National Education Association, *Journal of Proceedings and Addresses* (1897), 105.

5. *Hull-House Year Book, 1906–1907* (Chicago: Hull House, 1907), 8.

6. Jane Addams, *First Report of the Labor Museum at Hull-House, Chicago, 1901–1902* (Chicago: Hull House, 1902), 9.

7. Francis W. Parker School, underwritten by Anita McCormick Blaine, and the Dewey School, located at the University of Chicago.

8. Typed letter signed. Florence C. Floore to Jane Addams, February 25, 1929, Cleburne, TX, in *Jane Addams Papers*, 20–861.

WORKS BY LAURA JANE ADDAMS

Democracy and Social Ethics. New York: Macmillan, 1902.
Newer Ideals of Peace. New York: Macmillan, 1907.

The Spirit of Youth and the City Streets. New York: Macmillan, 1909.
Twenty Years at Hull House. New York: Macmillan, 1910.
A New Conscience and an Ancient Evil. New York: Macmillan, 1912.
Peace and Bread in Time of War. New York: Macmillan, 1922.
The Second Twenty Years at Hull House. New York: Macmillan, 1930.
The Jane Addams Papers, Mary Lynn McCree Bryan, ed. Ann Arbor, MI: University Microfilms International, 82 reels and guide, 1984–1986.
Jane Addams on Education (Classics in Education, No. 51), Ellen Condliffe Lagemann, ed. New York: Teachers College Press, Columbia University, 1985.

WORKS ABOUT LAURA JANE ADDAMS

Bryan, Mary Lynn McCree, and Allen F. Davis. *One Hundred Years at Hull House.* Bloomington: Indiana University Press, 1990.

Bussey, Gertrude, and Margaret Tims. *Pioneers for Peace, Women's International League for Peace and Freedom 1915–1965.* London: WILPF, British Section, 1980.

Conway, Jill. *The First Generation of American Women Graduates.* New York: Garland, 1987.

Davis, Allen F. *American Heroine, the Life and Legend of Jane Addams.* New York: Oxford University Press, 1973.

Deegan, Mary Jo. *Jane Addams and the Men of the Chicago School 1892–1918.* New Brunswick, NJ: Transaction Books, 1988.

Degen, Marie Louise. *The History of the Woman's Peace Party.* Baltimore: Johns Hopkins University Press, 1939.

Farrell, John C. *Beloved Lady, A History of Jane Addams' Ideas on Reform and Peace.* Baltimore: Johns Hopkins University Press, 1967.

Linn, James Weber. *Jane Addams, a Biography.* New York: D. Appleton-Century, 1935.

Zilpah Polly Grant Banister

Rita S. Saslaw

Zilpah Polly Grant (1794–1874) was one of the major forces in promoting the education of women in the United States. Her name is often
mentioned along with Emma Willard, Catharine Beecher, and Mary
Lyon in resources dealing with nineteenth-century education for girls,
and yet she stands in the shadow of her closest friend and most distinguished colleague, Mary Lyon. Grant's early life, plagued with poverty
and illness, was filled with a faith that sustained her throughout her long
life. This strength of religious belief and the teachings of the Reverend
Joseph Emerson most influenced Zilpah Grant's ideas on education, and
her close relationship with the better-known Mary Lyon promoted her
often unique educational ideas.

> I generally remained in the schoolhouse, after dismissing the
> school at the close of the afternoon, to ask myself whether for that
> day I had done as well as I could, and wherein I could do better
> in the future; also what advancement in application to study or
> improvement in conduct, I should seek for the school.... The
> next day I acted on the conclusions to which I had the day before
> come.[1]

Zilpah Polly Grant was born on Chestnut Hill in South Norfolk, Connecticut, on May 30, 1794. She was the third daughter of Joel and Zilpah Cowles
Grant. Joel Grant, a farmer, was known for his Scotch thrift, his strength,
and his intelligence while his somewhat reserved wife was known for "her
lips full of sacred hymns and loving kindness, and her mind ever full and
still freshly filling itself with the Bible."[2] Her mother read a book, undoubtedly the Bible, as she did the ironing and the spinning. The Grant family
had lived in the area served by the Connecticut Western Railroad and close
to the Hartford and Albany Turnpike for at least fifty years. As a family,
they were known for their "Scotch grit and toughness" as well as "intellec-

tual grace and strength."[3] Grant inherited many of the family characteristics, and these same terms were often used to describe her. The first tragedy in Grant's life occurred with the accidental death of her father when she was only two years old. Her mother was left with five children but managed to maintain the family farm with the assistance of her brother, Samuel, and her eldest son, Elijah. The young Zilpah lived for twenty years with a woman who showed strength of character, stamina, and love for her children and served as a religious and intellectual role model for her youngest child, Zilpah.

The formal education of this pioneer in the education of women was limited. She attended the local district school a few weeks each year. These schools were held in barren, poorly lit rooms with long benches for the students. Curricula differed from school to school, but all included spelling, grammar, history, and English literature. Students learned the subject matter well, and, as in the case of Grant, some went on to become teachers themselves. No written record remains of her progress in her early schooling, but from the level of competence that she exhibited in her later life, we can assume that she learned well and quickly. Rev. John Cowles describes the maturing Grant: "In person she was early developed, tall, erect, and well proportioned, her head firmly on her shoulders. Her countenance was comely with the triple expression of kindness, dignity, and power. Her hair was like the raven; her luminous black eyes were full of life and intelligence."[4]

Gail Hamilton, who called Grant an American queen, gives the following description:

My queen was a Puritan...when she was only five years old, pangs of conscience wrung her because she had chosen not to go to an afternoon meeting with her mother. Such a Puritan as this; that at twelve, she had great solicitude regarding her guilt in the violation of perfect law. . . . Such a Puritan, that her sense of sin was overpowering.[5]

This quality of desire for perfection combined well with her deep religious faith to make an outstanding teacher.

Zilpah Grant followed in the footsteps of her sisters, Jerusha and Nancy, and began a teaching career at the age of fourteen or fifteen in East Norfolk in the district of Paug, where she taught in the summer and went home to study and help her mother in the winter. Even in her early career, she insisted that all students must progress and that they show this progress in an orderly classroom. Here, too, she exhibited her constant concern about her own and the students' religious state. She taught in these local district schools for twelve years, summer and winter, and became known locally for her ability as an educator.

Several events occurred during these twelve years that had a lasting effect on the life of Zilpah Grant. The teaching experience taught her to be a reflective teacher as she was always certain that she and her students could do better tomorrow. A recurring illness that resulted in a general weakness had an even more profound effect, as she was told that she could not recover. Illness plagued her entire life and teaching career but also served to strengthen her religious faith. During this time period she was baptized and joined the Congregational church. She also met two men who would greatly affect her future life, the Reverend Frederick Marsh and the Reverend Ralph Emerson. Through Marsh she "became an intelligent and shining Christian," and through Emerson she met his brother, Rev. Joseph Emerson, at whose Massachusetts school she perfected her teaching skills.[6]

In 1820, her twelve-year stint in the district schools of Connecticut ended. This move to the Byfield Female Seminary of the Reverend Joseph Emerson was not an easy one for Zilpah. Her mother had remarried, but Zilpah was still forced to convince her family that this move for more education would not separate her from her less-educated family and friends, who wished that she marry and remain in the area. In addition she had to convince them that she would be able to care for herself during periods of poor health, which in her case were frequent. Finally, with the help and best wishes of her pastor, Rev. Ralph Emerson, her Uncle Samuel, and her brother, Grant took her life savings of fifty dollars and left on the adventure of her young life.

From Rev. Joseph Emerson she learned the benefits of the Bible as a useful educational tool. She learned this through weekly prayer meetings and daily careful reading and study of the Bible. Emerson taught Grant that three-fourths of the Bible was history and that if "God dictates it, history must be important."[7] Emerson further taught that the sexes were mutually dependent and that females were the foundation of society. Grant maintained contact with him for the rest of his life and often stated that Emerson was the most significant of her mentors. Mary Lyon, whom she also first met at Byfield, was her dearest and closest friend and undoubtedly the most important contact that she made in her time in the seminary. This close friendship lasted until the untimely death of Mary Lyon in 1849 and was marked by regular, oftentimes weekly, correspondence during periods of separation.

Zilpah Grant's first teaching experience after her year with Emerson was in Winstead, Connecticut, at an exclusive girls' school located in a room in a private home. In 1823, Grant briefly returned to Emerson's seminary, which had been moved to Saugus, Massachusetts. She remained there for only one year, renewing her friendship with Lyon and Emerson. She was then called to serve as preceptress for a new school, the Adams Female Academy in Derry, New Hampshire. In this position, Grant could be called the first head of a college for women in the United States because Adams, unlike the earlier Troy Seminary, issued diplomas.

Here, and later at Ipswich, working with Mary Lyon during the summers, she began to practice her special brand of education with the Bible as a centerpiece. She was convinced the Bible should be used in the common schools as well. At entry, students were expected to "read prose with a good degree of correctness and to spell with considerable accuracy." At the school they learned reading, spelling and defining, arithmetic, geography, and English grammar. The day began with the study of the historical part of the Old Testament. "In this study they gained more useful knowledge and more mental discipline than in any other."[8] An example of a lesson might be: Where is the first mention of a cemetery in the Bible? Then students would locate the site on a map of ancient and modern Palestine, combining the subjects of Bible study, history, and geography. Grant did not believe that the education of girls should consist only of the fine arts but did allow for instruction in drawing and painting once all of the students' other work had been mastered.

Grant did not have an instrumental view of education but encouraged the preparation of girls for their work and for learning how to learn and learning on their own. She did not use competition or emulation as a motivator. She struggled always to increase self-control and stressed doing the best that one could do. Grant, a product of the Enlightenment as well as Puritan thought, taught lessons in logic as well as the importance of biblical history. She taught patriotism, service to society, charity, and benevolence. Her greatest concern was always with the living soul, and the students often reported in their letters to their former teacher their attempts to achieve moral improvement.

During her service at Derry, Zilpah Grant suffered another personal tragedy. In the opening months of school, she was notified of the death of her mother by suicide. This event caused an already pensive person to examine her behavior and her moral self-worth even more carefully.

Always most important to Grant was religious and moral education. She kept the Board of Trustees informed of her efforts in this area. "Within the last ten days I have spent two hours and forty minutes in lessons and instruction of a moral and religious nature. With the young ladies, one at a time . . . I have spent one hour and eight minutes."[9] Grant made every effort to infect her students with the self-discipline that she possessed in full measure. All rules being considered were shared with the student, who would make a pledge to honor the rules. The self-discipline was a part of her "self-reporting system" and an integral part of her educational plan. Students were to document their own transgressions from the rules, but Grant seemed to understand human behavior and did not expect students to report breaking the rules when violations were numerous, only after "they have been led to control themselves so as to succeed."[10] Grant believed that students would make every effort to avoid breaking a law they had voted for.

Her strong religious belief caused the final separation between the Adams Academy and Zilpah Grant. When she came to Derry, Grant informed the trustees that she intended to spend one-seventh of the instructional time on the Bible, but "this instruction was like the coming of an army with banners."[11] In 1827 the trustees informed her that music and dance would become a regular part of the course of instruction. While Grant did not oppose music, she objected strenuously to the teaching of dance. The trustees objected to the Calvinistic nature of the school under Grant's influence and claimed that they had established Adams on liberal principles. With great sadness, Grant left Adams, and to Lyon she wrote, "I was not aware of the strength of my attachment." Grant decided to return to Byfield and search for a new position because she did not want to harm the school that she loved and that had been such an important part of her life for five years.[12] The irony of this situation was that two years later the trustees unanimously asked Grant to return, but by that time, she was too involved in her new school at Ipswich.

A leading group of businessmen in Ipswich saw the founding of a seminary for girls as an economic opportunity and as a chance to draw settlers to the town. This idea was working in other towns such as Oberlin, where the reputation of the school encouraged people to migrate. Forty students moved to Ipswich from Derry along with Zilpah Grant and Mary Lyon. The school building had been erected in 1825 with the idea that the enterprise could be profitable and bring a return to the contributors. The building was leased to Grant without charge, but it was up to her to raise all the other revenue needed through tuition and contributions.

The Ipswich Seminary, modeled after the Adams Seminary, was successful despite the fact that Grant and Lyon were very ill. Both suffered from typhoid fever, and Grant walked on crutches from a serious accident in a calisthenics class at Adams. As students and teachers boarded with neighboring families, close supervision and relationships with Grant and Lyon were not as easy as they had been at residential Adams.

Course work at Ipswich and Derry was more similar than different. Natural philosophy and astronomy, offered in the third year at Derry, appear not to have been taught at all at Ipswich. The greatest differences in the offerings of the two schools were in the heavy emphasis on classes in history, science, and theology at Ipswich. Analysis of poetry was added to the reading instruction. Teacher training courses were offered during the second and third years at both schools. Music, reading, composition, and calisthenics were also included. While science courses were included, foreign language was not, an arrangement continued by Mary Lyon at Mount Holyoke. This variety of subject matter reflected the ideas of both Zilpah Grant and Mary Lyon but does seem to violate one of Grant's teaching principles, that students should thoroughly study only two or three subjects at a time and review them carefully.[13]

Grant believed that her ideas on education should be shared with her students with the idea that they could pick and choose among them, selecting those that they saw reason to use. She insisted that a student not move to new material until the old work was mastered. Students were to be treated with affection, and material was always to be made interesting. The student would obey the teacher and continue to learn on her own if she had learned to govern herself and to exercise her own judgment.[14] This practiced self-control appears to be as important a cornerstone to Grant as was the moral and religious education. Grant included the girls in the development of the rules, in the keeping of records on their own behavior and progress, and in keeping fit through calisthenics set to music. Borrowing from her mentor, Emerson, she used probing questions to help students develop higher-order thinking. She maintained a low pupil-teacher ratio of fifteen to one.

It is not surprising that Grant was asked to describe her school for the public. In August 1833, Grant received a letter from Jacob Abbott asking her to write accounts of Ipswich Academy for *Annals of Education*. She wrote several articles describing instruction, especially in her Bible class. She further promoted her educational ideas and key ideas on patriotism by forming the Society for the Education of Females in Ipswich Seminary. This group promoted the development of education in the West by giving students loans to pay for their education as teachers and by paying for their moves to the West when they began to teach. From 1830 to 1835, fifty-three teachers were employed in the West and the South through the auspices of this group, and almost every tuition loan was repaid. Grant was also active in the small Ohio towns of Austinburg, Chillicothe, Granville, and Marietta. Even in these western operations her major concern was with the number of students who had "consecrated themselves to the Lord."[15]

The success of the school at Ipswich can be measured in many ways, only one of which is the number of saved souls. Another measure of success is Grant's own figures provided in an 1838 article in the *American Quarterly*. To that date:

1,675 young ladies had attended Derry and Ipswich;

21 were foreign missionaries with the American and Baptist Board;

400 were teachers in New England and the West; and

88 were teachers in impoverished areas of the West and South.[16]

In sheer numbers, Grant's school would be judged a success.

Success for Zilpah Grant could also be measured by the many invitations that she received to teach or head schools. One already mentioned was the invitation to return to Adams Seminary on her own terms. Other invitations came from Greenfield and Andover. Catharine Beecher, at the time head of the Hartford, Connecticut, Female Seminary, invited Grant to join her as principal of the institution. Beecher also invited Grant on her own terms, as she promised student uniforms so that middle-class girls, who were the special interest of Grant, would also be able to attend. It was not the munificent salary of $1,000 that tempted her to accept the offer, but the "literary and religious privileges of Hartford."[17] This invitation from the most prominent educator of the time, who through the National Board of Education provided many teachers for the West, was taken very seriously by Zilpah Grant. She refused the position because of her delicate health but, more importantly, because she did not wish to leave Mary Lyon, "after having labored with her harmoniously and successfully for six years."[18]

Grant's relationship with Mary Lyon bears investigation. How did the two women work together and feel about each other? We will never fully know the answer to the question because Zilpah Grant often kept what she thought hidden from view, and while Grant kept all of Mary Lyon's letters to her, Lyon kept none of Grant's frequent responses. Zilpah Grant contributed the Lyon letters and also helped to gather other material for the first biography of Mary Lyon, written by Edward Hitchcock in 1852. These letters tell the tale of two devoted friends who maintained close contact as friends and colleagues from 1821 to the death of Mary Lyon in 1849.

The two women parted in education in 1835, when Mary Lyon left Ipswich and her dear friend, Zilpah Grant, and moved to South Hadley, Massachusetts, where she eventually founded Mount Holyoke. Grant had assisted her in raising funds and support for the new venture and seemed to show no resentment of her younger colleague's setting out without her to form a new school, where Lyon could concentrate on education of poor girls for the professions of teaching and missionary work. Lyon questioned, more than once, the need for two principals at Ipswich. "Is it not your solemn duty and mine to review the question whether my services are needed as much in our beloved seminary as in some other part of the Lord's vinyard?" In a most poignant letter written to Grant in March 1833, Lyon sets the stage for continued friendship and collegiality when both find themselves working in different places. "I am very glad, my dearest friend, that you propose to endeavor to learn that you can do without me."[19] Grant's answer, of course, is missing. There is also little doubt that Grant could have joined Lyon in South Hadley if she wished, as four of Grant's teachers and many of her students did.

Indeed, Zilpah Grant did go on without her trusted colleague. In the four years she remained at Ipswich she managed to maintain standards and inaugurated her plan for providing teachers for the West. Her health again became a serious problem, and without Mary Lyon, who had so often helped her in times of illness, she decided to retire. She was forty-five years old and had spent thirty years in teaching. In retirement, Grant maintained contact with Lyon. After the death of Mary Lyon, Grant continued to work with and visit Mount Holyoke, where up to the time of her own death she reinforced their joint ideas.

Grant moved to Deedam, Massachusetts, where she rested and recovered from the illness that forced her to leave Ipswich. As one of her biographers states: "The love of her life was absorbed in her work and her purpose. But it is to be noted that the moment she had time to look at a man the man was there!"[20] Grant met William Bostwick Banister, a man of intellect and culture. He had been an attorney and state senator, and like Grant, he was a Puritan who possessed a dignity and grace that matched her own. They were married on September 7, 1841. As his third wife, she became the mistress and hostess of his large home and stepmother to his two adult daughters. Here, too, she wrote a set of "Rules for a Happy Home." In this phase of her life she continued her strong religious belief, accepting the biblical ideas of marriage that required obedience to her husband. "Where there are only two there can be no majority, and the supremacy must rest on one," and her logical nature stated, "Since the wife must see that she reverence her husband, she must see that she do not marry a man whom she cannot reverence."[21]

For the twelve years of their marriage, the couple continued to study God's word and to lead a productive life. Like many other middle-class married women, Grant turned to benevolence, founding the General Charitable Society of Newburyport. She also served on the board of managers of Catharine Beecher's American Women's Educational Association and lectured in Hartford to the prospective western teachers. She toured colleges and seminaries to recruit teachers for the West and in 1856 wrote a pamphlet, *Hints on Education*, describing her ideas on education.

William Banister died in 1853, leaving her with property and a certain amount of wealth. She was able to spend 1860 in Europe, but this life-style soon ended, as she found herself destitute because of mismanagement of her funds by a business friend. She continued to live with dignity in rented rooms in Newburyport, using the little money that she had saved from her own work to support certain charities. She continued writing letters to her friends and former students, conducting her Bible class, and visiting with her family and friends.

Zilpah Grant died on December 3, 1874. She had dedicated her entire life to education and the betterment of society. The mark she left on those more famous than she cannot be forgotten. Harriet Marr selected words from a letter written by Catharine Beecher sometime before Grant's death as an epitaph:

She has been for years my chief resort for counsel and sympathy, and to me seems more like Jesus Christ than earthly friends I ever knew. She has a strong, quiet, self-reliant common sense, a most elevated habit of communion with our Lord, and a most tender and comforting sympathy in everything that interests the thoughts and feelings of her friends, and she is so well balanced and so clear and discriminating in intellectual and moral perception that I always grew wise by communicating with her.[22]

One can almost hear Mary Lyon repeat the words that she had written to her dear friend at an earlier time: "My heart vibrates with tender emotions as the time draws near when I hope again to sit by your side, enjoying your society as I have in former times."[23] It is impossible to separate the educational ideas of Mary Lyon and Zilpah Grant. Fame eluded Grant only because Ipswich Seminary never achieved the fame of Mount Holyoke College, but Grant's heritage became a permanent part of the education of women as Mount Holyoke graduates took the ideas to the West.

NOTES

1. Z.P.G. Banister, *Hints on Education: Extracts from Letters Written in 1856* (Boston: Crocker and Brewster, 1856), 16.
2. Rev. John P. Cowles, "Miss Z. P. Grant—Mrs. William B. Banister: Memoir," *American Journal of Education* 50 (September 1880): 611.
3. Ibid.
4. Ibid., 614.
5. Gail Hamilton, "An American Queen," *North American Review* 143 (October 1886): 331.
6. Cowles, 615.
7. Lucinda T. Guilford, *The Use of a Life: Memorials of Mrs. Z. P. Grant Banister* (New York: American Tract Society, 1885), 20–21.
8. Ibid., 51–59.
9. Ibid., 20–21.
10. Ibid., 110.
11. Hamilton, 336.
12. Guilford, 19.
13. Harriet Webster Marr, "Study of Zilpah Polly Grant Banister, Noted Educator of Ipswich Seminary," *Essex Institute Historical Collections* (October 1952): 352–53.
14. Leonard W. Labaree, as recorded by Eliza Paul Capen in "Zilpah Grant: The Art of Teaching: 1829," *The New England Quarterly* 20 (September 1947): 350–56.
15. Guilford, 193.
16. Ibid., 204.
17. Marr, 358.
18. Marr, 358–59.
19. Ibid., 361.
20. Hamilton, 340.
21. Ibid., 340.
22. Marr, 364.
23. Hitchcock, 109.

WORK BY ZILPAH POLLY GRANT BANISTER

Hints on Education: Extracts from Letters Written in 1856. Boston: Crocker and Brewster, 1856.

WORKS ABOUT ZILPAH POLLY GRANT BANISTER

Cowles, Rev. John P. "Miss Z. P. Grant—Mrs. William B. Banister: Memoir." *American Journal of Education* 50 (September 1880): 611–24.

Gilchrist, Beth Bradford. *The Life of Mary Lyon.* Boston: Houghton Mifflin, 1910.

Goodsell, Willystine. *Pioneers of Women's Education in the United States: Emma Willard, Catharine Beecher, Mary Lyon.* New York: AMS Press, 1931.

Guilford, Lucinda T. *The Use of a Life: Memorials of Mrs. Z. P. Grant Banister.* New York: American Tract Society, 1885.

Hamilton, Gail. "An American Queen." *North American Review* 143 (October 1886): 329–40.

Hitchcock, Edward. *The Power of Christian Benevolence Illustrated in the Life and Labor of Mary Lyon.* Philadelphia: Thomas Couperthwait, 1852.

James, Edward T., ed. *Notable American Women, 1607–1950.* Vol. 2. Cambridge: Belknap Press of Harvard University Press, 1971.

Labaree, Leonard W. "Zilpah Grant and the Art of Teaching: 1829," as recorded by Eliza Paul Capen. *The New England Quarterly* 20 (September 1947): 347–64.

Lansing, Marion, ed. *Mary Lyon through Her Letters.* Boston: Books, 1937.

Marr, Harriet Webster. "Study of Zilpah Polly Grant Banister, Noted Educator of Ipswich Seminary." *Essex Institute Historical Collections* (October 1952): 348–64.

structor in English but left in 1907 for graduate work at Columbia. From 1908 to 1911, Barrows worked as a social investigator with the Russell Sage Foundation, collaborating with Mary Van Kleeck in extensive studies of working women in the millinery and garment trades in New York City. Her work with the Russell Sage Foundation, essentially interviewing working women in their homes and shops, stimulated her concern and respect for working people; she also became outraged over the intolerable living and working conditions that prevailed in the city. During these years, Barrows became committed to progressive urban reform.

In 1911, Barrows turned again to education, becoming director of a vocational guidance survey sponsored by the New York Public Education Association (PEA), a private group promoting progressive educational reforms. In 1912, the PEA broadened the scope of its survey to include other aspects of vocational education besides guidance. At the time, the vocational guidance movement seemed to most educators to be a rational means of directing children of working age into the employment market. By contrast, the unconventional Alice Barrows believed that vocational guidance contributed to the child labor problem by pushing children out of the schools and into dead-end jobs. As she put it in her vocational guidance report for the PEA, "There are no jobs for children under sixteen which they ought to take." By contrast, Barrows promoted a broad vocational training in which children were not trained to operate specific factory machines but learned the "mechanical principles . . . found in nearly all machines."[1] Thus, students would be prepared for any number of jobs in a complex industrial society. This theme—that education should broadly, rather than narrowly, prepare for life—lay at the heart of Barrows's views about the humanistic and democratic functions of the schools.

Alice Barrows's work in vocational education had familiarized her with the innovative schools of Gary, Indiana, where Superintendent William A. Wirt had introduced an elaborate program of industrial training. In fact, Wirt's Gary plan had begun to attract national attention by 1912, when he delivered the keynote address at a vocational guidance convention in New York City. Barrows was especially enthusiastic about the vocational aspects of the Gary plan because Wirt opposed narrow and specialized job training. Rather, he asserted the importance of developing fundamental industrial skills that could be utilized in a variety of trades—the same kind of program Barrows advocated in her final report on the Vocational Educational Survey in 1914.

By 1914, Barrows had become an admirer of Wirt and embraced the Gary plan. In its idealized form, the Gary plan divided a school's student body into two platoons, X and Y. During the morning hours, platoon X filled all the traditional classrooms, studying academic subjects, while platoon Y was divided into smaller groups for a succession of specialized activities, such as art, music, dancing, and dramatics; they used the athletic fields, gymnasiums, swimming pools, workshops, libraries, and science laboratories; they met in the auditorium for movies, plays, group singing, and special programs; or they went on field trips into the community. After lunch, the two platoons switched, platoon Y moving to the academic classrooms and platoon X taking the specialized activities. The Wirt plan also emphasized bureaucratic efficiency. Flexible scheduling and rotation of pupils from class to class and activity to activity made it possible to use every room, facility, and piece of equipment constantly throughout the school day (and in the evening as well, since the Gary schools had an extensive program of adult education). The addition of the specialized facilities made it possible to squeeze into a single school building twice as many students as had originally been intended. At the same time, the plan could be presented to parents and the community as providing enriched education, as few American public schools had such diverse programs and facilities at the time. Consequently, the Gary plan appealed both to "administrative progressives," who focused on its efficiency and financial savings, and to "social progressives," like Alice Barrows, who lauded its creative and humanistic features.[2]

Between 1914 and 1918, Barrows worked as secretary to William Wirt, who had been hired as an educational consultant by the New York City mayor, John Purroy Mitchel. An efficiency-minded reformer, Mitchel seized upon the Gary plan, as a means of both reforming the enormous New York City school system and cutting the ballooning costs of New school construction. Wirt commuted to New York City one week a month for three years to supervise the introduction of the Gary plan. Barrows's job involved working with Mitchel's political advisers and school officials in the transition effort in several experimental schools. But she also spent much of her time publicizing the platoon school plan and establishing broad support for the new school reform.

Barrows was a natural choice for this effort: through her vocational education work, she had already developed important contacts in the Mitchel administration, the New York City Board of Education, and the school bureaucracy. Moreover, she had a wide circle of friends among the city's intellectuals, educators, social workers, writers, journalists, reformers, and radicals. She brought to her task a tremendous fund of creative energy, orchestrating a massive propaganda campaign for the platoon school over three years. She wrote pamphlets and articles, gave innumerable speeches, sponsored meetings, organized parents' groups, mobilized civic leaders and reformers, fought obstructionist school officials, and lobbied the politicians. She recruited to the Gary cause writers and reformers such as Rheta Childe Dorr, Agnes de Lima, Alyse Gregory, Frances Perkins, Henrietta Rodman, Floyd Dell, and Randolph Bourne (who later wrote a book on the Gary schools). Barrows also persuaded editors of *The Survey*, *The New Republic*, *The Masses*, and other magazines to publish laudatory articles on the Gary plan. She arranged publication of pro-Gary pamphlets and leaflets in Yiddish, Italian, and German in order to reach immigrant neighborhoods. Barrows was convinced that only persistent publicity would build the necessary support for the platoon school plan. She also kept Wirt informed of her progress through long letters filled with details of school activities in New York City.

Alice Barrows the propagandist was deeply committed to the Gary plan. To her, the plan represented "the biggest thing in democratic educational reconstruction in the country"—a real effort at "free" schooling in an era when urban schools had become rigidly bureaucratized. The platoon plan, Barrows contended in 1917,

was part of a nation-wide movement for democracy and progress in public education. It makes the school exist for the child, not the child for the school system. It humanizes instruction and permits the child, for the first time, to be treated naturally and as a human being. It develops the child's individuality. It educates all his faculties.[3]

Barrows promoted the Gary plan as a child-centered school reform.

Many New Yorkers did not share Alice Barrows's enthusiasm for the Gary plan. By 1915, the Mitchel administration was running into opposition to its school reform program. The school board and the school bureaucracy resisted what seemed like political meddling in school matters. Tammany Hall Democrats, seeing an issue with which to flay the independent John Purroy Mitchel, launched a propaganda campaign of their own to discredit the Gary plan in the city's working-class neighborhoods, where they established anti-Gary mothers' groups. Tammany's chief argument was that the Gary plan, through its vocational education features, channeled children into industrial jobs and limited their educational opportunities. Much of the city's press came out against school reform.

Barrows picked up the pace of the pro-Gary public relations campaign in 1916 and 1917, organizing parents in a newly formed Gary School League with many neighborhood branches. The issue peaked during the 1917 municipal election campaign, which turned into a plebiscite on the Gary plan. Two weeks of rioting against the Gary plan by 30,000 elementary school children in late October 1917, mostly instigated and coordinated by adults, ultimately undermined Mayor Mitchel's school reform and brought Tammany to power. New York's new mayor, John F. Hylan, ended the Gary experiment, but Barrows persisted. Borrowing from the organizational techniques of antiwar socialists, Barrows spent six months after the election organizing neighborhood units of a new group she called the People's Educational Council, hoping to press forward with educational reform. This effort disintegrated by mid-1918 for lack of funds, but Barrows's use of a socialist community-organizing technique suggests her own political movement toward the Left.

The Gary school campaign in New York City was merely a warm-up for

Alice Barrows. Committed to social change through the schools, she accepted a position in the City Schools Division of the U.S. Bureau of Education in 1918. She promptly launched a nationwide platoon school campaign, this time backed by the resources of the federal government. Her job—first as a specialist in social and industrial relations in education and later as an expert on school building problems—was one of making surveys of urban public school systems and recommending desirable curricular and building changes. Over the next decade, she made detailed surveys of schools in Memphis, Tennessee; Passaic, New Jersey; Lexington, Kentucky; Mount Vernon, New York; Portland, Oregon; Wilmington, Delaware; Wheeling, West Virginia; Alexandria, Virginia; and numerous other cities. In each case, her published report laid out the educational and financial advantages of the platoon school system over traditional curricular and building arrangements.

From her position in the U.S. Bureau of Education, Barrows became the most forceful and the most aggressive promoter of the platoon school plan during the 1920s. Field service reports to the City Schools Division of the Bureau of Education show that Barrows traveled more often and for longer periods of time than any other staff member. She made more surveys, published more reports, and gave more speeches, as well. During the Portland, Oregon, survey, for instance, Barrows gave fifty speeches on the platoon school in twenty-four days. During several summers, she taught courses on the platoon school to teachers at the University of Oregon. She also promoted the platoon plan in articles for *The New Republic* and *School Life* (the Bureau of Education's official monthly journal) and in her voluminous correspondence with school officials around the nation.

In 1922, under the auspices of the Bureau of Education, Barrows organized the first of several annual conferences on the platoon school plan. These meetings led to the formation in 1925 of a new and independent professional organization with the unwieldy name of the National Association for the Study of the Platoon or Work-Study-Play School Organization. For the next six years, while holding down her full-time government job, Barrows served as the new association's executive secretary and as founder, editor, and frequent contributor to its quarterly journal, *The Platoon School*, virtually a second full-time job.

By the end of the 1920s, the seemingly tireless efforts of this prodigious activist for educational change brought real and positive results. More than 200 cities adopted the platoon school system for some or all of their elementary schools by 1930. Detroit had 110 schools on the work-study-play plan in 1928, and Pittsburgh had 75. Other major cities implementing the plan included Philadelphia, Cleveland, Los Angeles, Hartford, Memphis, Portland, Kansas City, Dallas, Seattle, Cincinnati, Toledo, Akron, and Birmingham. The financial pressures imposed upon cities and school systems by the Great Depression highlighted the financial savings of platoon schools. One writer in 1934 contended that the platoon school perfectly embodied "the spirit of the new deal in education."[4] Thus, despite the setback in New York City in 1917, Alice Barrows and her "platooniacs" scored important successes in the 1920s and 1930s.

The Gary plan and its successor, the platoon school plan, had a significant impact on the development of urban education in the twentieth century. By mid-century, few of the nation's schools had escaped its influence. Auditoriums, gymnasiums, playgrounds, laboratories, workshops, and special facilities for music, dramatics, art, home economics, and other activities had become standard equipment in American schools. The platoon arrangement, demanding efficient and flexible use of space, permitted overcrowded school systems and financially strapped municipalities to accommodate larger numbers of children without expensive building programs. At the same time, in necessitating wider use of school facilities, the platoon school provided a diversity of educational activities and a richer instructional program. It met all the requirements of the efficiency-minded structural reformers, but it also promised to forge, as Alice Barrows often noted, the kind of social reconstruction urged by such progressive educators as John Dewey and, later, George S. Counts.

During the 1920s and 1930s, while turning a bureaucratic government job into a pulpit for educational activism, Alice Barrows's political sentiments had moved decidedly toward the Left. She was already a bit of a radical reformer by the end of the Gary experiment in New York City, undoubtedly influenced by the cultural and political radicals in the Greenwich Village crowd with whom she associated during the first decade of the century. Barrows's politics became startlingly evident in 1919, when she created an uproar in Passaic, New Jersey, where the Bureau of Education had sent her to make a survey of adult education needs. Instead of beginning with the school bureaucracy, Barrows spent two weeks at the office of Robert W. Dunn, the left-wing organizer of the Passaic local of the Amalgamated Textile Workers of America. Her purpose was to determine from the workers themselves what kind of adult education programs they wanted. In the process, she uncovered and publicly condemned an extensive industrial espionage system designed by the textile industry to suppress union activities. Industry representatives denounced her in the newspapers as a "misguided zealot" who would turn the schools of Passaic into breeding places for "Bolshevists," while the city's mayor labeled her an undesirable "foreign influence." Barrows quickly responded by defending the schools as agencies of the people and renewing her attack on the espionage system as a Red Scare "reign of terror."[5] The U.S. commissioner of education hustled Barrows back to Washington, and the excitement in Passaic soon died down. However, the Passaic incident illustrated Barrows's emerging commitment to the Left and to what she called the "socialized school"—schools that "belong to the people . . . and grow and change in accordance with their needs."[6]

The shift in Barrows's thought became even more pronounced in the

1930s, a shift punctuated by a widely publicized break with her educational mentor, William Wirt, in 1934. For twenty years, Barrows had worked closely with Wirt, despite the fact that he was a conservative elitist who never shared her vision of the platoon school as an instrument of social change. During the 1920s, Barrows had brought Wirt into several of her school surveys, and he was centrally involved in the affairs of the new platoon school organization. As the New Deal got under way in 1933, Barrows even floated Wirt's name around Washington as a candidate for U.S. commissioner of education. In 1934, Barrows gave a dinner party at her home for the increasingly eccentric Wirt, who was visiting Washington as an educational consultant. Later, Wirt publicly charged that Barrows's other dinner guests, several lower-level New Dealers, plotted to supplant the Roosevelt administration with a communist dictatorship. The right-wing press sensationalized these charges, leading to a congressional investigation of the affair. Although the investigation vindicated Barrows and her friends, Wirt had become an instant hero to New Deal opponents while Barrows emerged as the darling of the New Deal left-wingers.

In fact, by the mid-1930s Barrows had been caught up in the heady optimism of the early Roosevelt presidency. As one of her friends suggested, she became convinced that the good society could be achieved through rational planning. It is also probable, as Edmund Wilson noted of her in a 1934 *Scribner's* article, that Barrows had come to the conclusion that "a new deal in education [was] impossible without a new social-economic system."[7] Always an activist, she was captivated by the reform spirit of New Deal Washington and soon became involved in many political and ideological causes besides education. Barrows had been involved in the technocracy movement from its origins in New York in 1918, and she continued on the fringes of this movement to link modern technology with social engineering in the 1930s. She vigorously opposed Congressman Martin Dies and his House Un-American Activities Committee, and she spoke out for civil liberties for radicals and civil rights for blacks. She became a leader of the Washington branch of the American League for Peace and Democracy, a communist-front group opposed to fascism and capitalism. She actively supported Loyalist Spain and organized consumer boycotts against Japan protesting the 1937 invasion of China.

Barrows pursued these radical activities more persistently after her retirement from the Office of Education in 1942. She assumed leadership positions in several alleged communist-front organizations: director of the Congress of American-Soviet Friendship (1942–1943); public relations director of the National Federation of Constitutional Liberties (1943–1944); public relations director of the Abraham Lincoln School in Chicago (1944–1945); national director of the Arts, Sciences, and Professions Division of the Progressive Citizens of America (1946–1948); and a sponsor of the Cultural and Scientific Conference for World Peace (1949). These associations earned her a spot on several lists of dangerous radicals during the postwar era. During the 1948 presidential campaign, she worked hard for Henry Wallace's Progressive party ticket. She opposed the cold war policies of the Truman administration, and, as the anti-communist hysteria of the late 1940s and early 1950s heated up, she championed the civil liberties of radicals, communists, and others victimized by McCarthyism. Hauled before the Senate Internal Security Subcommittee in 1953, Barrows invoked the Fifth Amendment when asked if she had ever been a communist. She also proceeded to lecture the committee members on the meaning of liberty, world peace, and human freedom and dignity. Barrows filled up her last years organizing demonstrations and writing letters to newspapers, congressmen, senators, and presidents in defense of civil liberties. By the time of her death in October 1954, Alice Barrows had established a long record on behalf of progressive social change in the United States.

During her ideological and political pilgrimage from progressive reform to the extreme Left, Alice Barrows worked to transform the public schools into creative and humanistic institutions. Her social thought changed over time, but she never wavered from her conception of the school as an agent of social democracy. She was an activist and an organizer, accustomed to working from the bottom up. Like most other professional women of her time, who were excluded from the seats of power, she was never a manager or a policymaker or a decision maker. Her role was that of the gadfly, of the publicist or critic who had the freedom to stand outside the offices of the great and powerful and persuade or encourage them to action; or to organize community interest groups demanding changes from the power structure. She recognized quite early that education could empower the people and facilitate the building of the good society. Throughout her professional life, Alice Barrows never wavered in her commitment to those idealistic social goals.

NOTES

1. Alice P. Barrows, *Report of the Vocational Guidance Survey* (New York: Public Education Association, 1912), 13; Alice P. Barrows, Autobiography, 123–25, unfinished typescript, Alice P. Barrows Papers, University of Maine, Orono.

2. The "administrative progressives" were first introduced in David B. Tyack, *The One Best System: A History of American Urban Education* (Cambridge, MA: Harvard University Press, 1974), 127, 196. The contrasting ideas of the "social progressives" are emphasized in Ronald D. Cohen and Raymond A. Mohl, *The Paradox of Progressive Education: The Gary Plan and Urban Schooling* (Port Washington, NY: Kennikat Press, 1979), 3–9.

3. Alice P. Barrows, "Statement in Reply to Judge Hylan's Attack on the Gary Schools," 1917, typescript, William A. Wirt Manuscripts, Lilly Library, Indiana University, Bloomington.

4. Merle C. Prunty, "Platoon Schools Meet the New Deal," *The Platoon School* 8 (September 1934): 5.

5. *New York World*, February 22, 1920; *Passaic Daily News*, February 23, 1920, February 24, 1920, clippings in Alice P. Barrows Papers, University of Maine, Orono.

6. Alice P. Barrows, *The Problem of Adult Education in Passaic, N.Y.*, (Washington, DC: U.S. Bureau of Education, Bulletin No. 4, 1920), 16, 21, 25.

7. Edmund Wilson, "Miss Barrows and Doctor Wirt: An Inside Story of a Famous Episode," *Scribner's Magazine* 96 (August 1934): 104.

WORKS BY ALICE P. BARROWS

(Between 1914 and 1922, Barrows's writings were published under her married name, Alice Barrows Fernandez.)

"How Girls Learn the Millinery Trade" (with Mary Van Kleeck). *The Survey* 24 (April 16, 1910): 105–13.
Report of the Vocational Guidance Survey. New York: Public Education Association, 1912.
"The Meaning of the Wirt Plan." *New Republic* 7 (July 1, 1916): 221–23.
The Problem of Adult Education in Passaic, N.J. Washington, DC: U.S. Bureau of Education, Bulletin No. 4, 1920.
"The Work-Study-Play, or Balanced-Load Plan." *New Republic* 40 (November 12, 1924): 16–17.
"Modern Cities and Children." *The Platoon School* 3 (June–August 1929): 79–81.
Functional Planning of Elementary School Buildings. Washington, DC: U.S. Bureau of Education, Bulletin No. 19, 1936.
"P.W.A. and the Public Schools." *The Nation's Schools* 22 (December 1938): 14–17.
"New School Buildings for Old." *American Teacher* 24 (April 1940): 22–24.

WORKS ABOUT ALICE P. BARROWS

Cohen, Ronald D., and Raymond A. Mohl. *The Paradox of Progressive Education: The Gary Plan and Urban Schooling.* Port Washington, NY: Kennikat Press, 1979.
Moehlman, Arthur B. "Alice Prentice Barrows." *The Nation's Schools* 30 (September 1942): 13.
Mohl, Raymond A. "Urban Education in the Twentieth-Century: Alice Barrows and the Platoon School Plan." *Urban Education* 9 (October 1974): 213–37.
———. "Schools, Politics, and Riots: The Gary Plan in New York City, 1914–1917." *Paedagogica Historica* 15 (June 1975): 39–75.
———. "Alice Barrows: Crusader for the Platoon School, 1920–1940." *Elementary School Journal* 77 (May 1977): 351–57.
Wilson, Edmund. "Miss Barrows and Doctor Wirt: An Inside Story of a Famous Episode." *Scribner's Magazine* 96 (August 1934): 102–4.

Harriet M. Bedell

Karen K. McKellips

Harriet M. Bedell (1875–1969) devoted her life to the education of Native Americans. As a mission teacher for the Protestant Episcopal church, she became known as an authority on Native American life through the material written by and about her during her many years in the mission field. Her mission work began with her arrival at a Cheyenne mission school in Oklahoma in 1907, continued at Native American missions in Alaska, and ended with her service as a missionary to the Mikasuki Seminoles in Florida. Committed to the belief that education and Christian conversion were essential to the welfare and even the survival of Native Americans in modern America, she attempted to equip the people she served with the knowledge and skills to participate fully in American life. Yet she saw value in certain aspects of indigenous culture and, in a limited way, supported the Native American groups with which she worked in keeping alive some of their traditions. She thus stands as an interesting example of the type of teacher, charged with the task of "Americanizing" the American Indian, who nevertheless was unable either to fully integrate the people she served into mainstream American culture or to win acceptance for them and their culture as a separate but equal people.

Bedell was born in Buffalo, New York, March 19, 1875, the oldest child of Horace Ira and Louisa Sophia (Oberist) Bedell, natives of New York. Two siblings died as infants, but Harriet shared her childhood with her sister Sarah and brother Alfred. During her early childhood, the family was moderately well-to-do as her father operated an excursion boat on the Niagara River, had investments in cargo boats, and speculated in stock. Her mother's family were Swiss immigrants of the professional class.

Horace Bedell drowned in 1885 after having lost most of his money, even that obtained from mortgaging the family home, in the stock market crash in 1884. Louisa and the children were then forced to live very frugally, with Louisa taking in boarders to help support the family.

Harriet graduated from the State Normal School at Buffalo in 1894 and taught for a year in a one-room country school. In 1895 she began teaching in the Doyle School, a public school in a Polish neighborhood in Buffalo, becoming a preceptress, or assistant principal, in 1900. During this time she did Sunday school work on the Seneca Indian Reservation in Lawtons.

A devout member of the Protestant Episcopal church, she decided to volunteer as a missionary teacher in China. In 1906 she entered the New York Training School for Deaconesses to prepare for mission service. She studied the Bible, Episcopal theology and ritual, and such practical studies as bookkeeping, sewing, and hygiene. She also took a year of nurses training at General Hospital in Buffalo.

Bedell's mother was opposed to her going to China, and the church had need for missionary teachers for Indian schools. Bedell agreed to serve for a year in a home mission field before taking up foreign service, but once she began, she never left Native American mission work.

Bedell's Indian service began with her arrival at Whirlwind Mission in Oklahoma in 1907. The mission school, later known as St. Luke's, had begun as a government day school in 1897 on what had been the Cheyenne-Arapaho Reservation in Oklahoma Territory before the assignment of individual allotments of land to the people of these tribes. Closed in 1901, it reopened in 1904 as a mission school designed to serve only Cheyenne children in poor health. The priest in charge at that time had quarreled with the Indian agent, and his bishop transferred him, so that when Bedell arrived, there were only Cheyenne people there. The mission was nine miles from the nearest white settlement, the small town of Fay, and many miles from the Indian Agency. The only English speaker was a Cheyenne deacon, and the Indians living near Whirlwind had had very little exposure to the white people's form of education. Conditions were primitive and life difficult, yet Bedell adjusted quickly, developing and implementing a program of education in keeping with the approved philosophy of the day, a program that attempted to eliminate the "Indianness" in Indian people through a combination of education and Christian conversion.

The mission school at Whirlwind had displeased the Indian agent prior to Bedell's arrival and had been blamed for encouraging the Cheyenne to camp around it rather than disperse to their individual land allotments. Bedell was careful to report regularly to the Indian agent, keeping him informed regarding what was being done at the school to promote the Indians' adoption of a white life-style. She voluntarily kept him informed regarding the behavior of individual Indians, both adults and school students, reporting drunkenness, adultery, refusal to send children to school, and failure to work their land, as well as reporting the actions of those behaving in ways the agent approved. Her educational program included both academic subjects and the industrial education prescribed by the government as essential for Indian education.

The isolated Indian school did not have the proper equipment or facilities for teaching the forms of industrial education found at such boarding schools as Carlisle or Chilocco; therefore, Bedell had to make do by assigning the boys to assist the agency farmer, (a government employee charged with teaching the Cheyenne people how to farm) in such tasks as building and repairing windmills. She had the girls take turns living with her at the mission house and taught them the skills of a white housewife while they were there.

Efforts were made to supply other missionaries to work with her, but those found seemed unable to adjust to the difficulties of the work and stayed brief times. Bedell was the only white person at the mission for most of her tenure there, and those who served with her were never as influential in the structure and implementation of the program as she was.

Her work was exhausting and went far beyond teaching. She served as nurse to the sick and spiritual leader to the tribe, as the priest in charge visited only a few times a year. She helped the Indian women market their beadwork and wrote letters for the men, including one about the wishes of Cheyenne leaders, which they delivered to Washington in 1912. She was given a Cheyenne name, Vicsehia, meaning birdwoman, because of her humming as she went about her work.

Bedell did not confine herself to the mission property. She traveled to various Indian camps in the area and to the government boarding school at Chilocco, which in 1914 enrolled 500 students from 40 tribes and at which she conducted religious instruction. A tent was purchased, painted with her Cheyenne name and a Christian cross, and she traveled throughout the area attending Indian gatherings, erecting her tent among the tepees of several Southern Plains Indian tribes. During this period, Bedell began writing for Episcopal publications, both those for adults and those for children.

Bedell strove to maintain cordial relationships with the various government employees working with Indians in Oklahoma. This effort was made difficult by the frequent changes in personnel and shifts in government policy during her tenure. Her letters to and from her bishop and government officials and the opinions expressed in her published writing show a tendency to tailor her statements to match the attitudes of whoever would be reading the material, especially as sentiment again grew to close the Whirlwind School.

In the summer of 1913, Bedell returned to her home in Buffalo for her first visit since beginning her mission work. During her time at Whirlwind, she had written frequently to various church groups in the East, encouraging donations of money and items useful at the mission, like clothing, books, and household goods. While at home, she visited many parishes, speaking in Indian costume and raising funds for her work.

At this time correspondence between her bishop and the Indian agent discussed closing the school in compliance with the government policy of removing Indian children from the influences of their families in an attempt to speed their adoption of non-Indian culture. Bedell argued against the move, citing the cruelty of taking children from their homes and her belief that only when Indian children were shown how to change conditions and behavior in their own homes would training in the white people's way of life have any permanent effect. These beliefs were in conflict, however, with government policy and the beliefs of the current Indian agent, who stated that all Indian camps were wrong and that since the public schools of Oklahoma had begun accepting Indian students, a combination of government boarding schools and attendance in state public schools should provide Indian education. His arguments were supported by references to a rising incidence of the use of peyote and the continued tendency of Oklahoma Plains Indians to live in tepee camps rather than dispersing to individual allotments of farmland to which each family had been assigned by the government.

In June 1916, Bedell went for a visit to the Church Mission House in New York, expecting to return to Whirlwind School and resume her post in late summer. However, the decision was made to close the school, and Bedell was reassigned to Alaska.

Bedell arrived at St. Mark's Mission in Nenana, Alaska, about sixty miles from Fairbanks, on October 5, 1916. This mission station was larger and better equipped than Whirlwind Mission had been at the time of her arrival there, and the staff included several women. She taught children from 9:00 to 3:00 and adults at night. While her first summer in Oklahoma had seen temperatures of 115 degrees, winter at Nenana meant temperatures of 60 degrees below zero. She made the necessary adjustments, traveling about the area by dogsled. She requested transfer to a more remote post and was assigned to St. Stephen's Village, an isolated Indian village where she was once again the only missionary. This time she was the only white woman within one hundred miles.

Arriving at St. Stephen's Village in August 1917, she found herself, as at Whirlwind, responsible for much more than just teaching. She raised and preserved food to improve the Indians' diet and served as nurse and religious leader. On one occasion she and two Indian men transported a sick child by dogsled 160 miles in −50-degree temperatures to the nearest hospital.

In 1922 Bedell was selected by the Protestant Episcopal church to be made a deaconess. The service of consecration was performed at the general convention in Portland, Oregon. Following the ceremony, she visited her home in Buffalo and toured extensively, raising money for her mission, speaking to 130 groups in 62 towns. In August 1923, she was back at St. Stephen's Village. She continued to correspond with groups supporting her work and in the summer of 1926 took a furlough in the eastern states, raising money to be used to establish a boarding school at Tanana Crossing. The money raised was sufficient to begin construction of the school. The mission house at St. Stephen's Village was dismantled and moved by raft to Tanana Crossing, with Bedell pitching her tent on the raft and accompanying the building material to its new location. The resulting Rowe Hall was opened in September.

At first, donations sufficient to maintain the school came from her supporters. However, the economic effects of the Great Depression soon began to be felt. By September 1931, donations had practically ceased, and Bedell once again returned to the continental United States to attempt to raise money. Unable to collect even enough to pay her own tour expenses, Bedell began working at All Saint's Mission in New York City, and the Rowe Hall project was abandoned.

The Episcopal church maintained a speaker's bureau list of missionaries available to speak, and Bedell's name was included for many years. While working in New York City, she responded to a request from several cities in Florida to speak about her Alaskan experience. While there, she visited a Seminole village and once again found an Indian group she could help. Appalled by what she considered degradation of the Seminoles, their being treated as wild animals in a tourist attraction, and by the poverty and lack of Christian belief, she requested to be allowed to reopen the Glades Cross Mission, which had been established by the Protestant Episcopal church in 1898 but abandoned in 1914. Permission was granted, and support of the Church Service League was promised. For the third time, Bedell was among a group of Indian people living in poverty, isolated from mainstream American life, most speaking little, if any, English. The Mikasuki Seminoles with whom she worked lived deep within the Everglades in scattered camps mainly accessible by canoe. Just as the Cheyenne in Oklahoma and the Alaskan Indians with whom Bedell worked had been deprived of their traditional hunter life-style by the disappearance of game, so the hunter-gatherer lifestyle of the Seminoles was being destroyed by the draining of the wetlands and the activities of land speculators.

The Indian agent and Barron Collier, the white entrepreneur who owned much of Collier County, welcomed Bedell and her work. She rented a house in the company-owned town of Everglades, and from this base visited the Mikasuki villages. She found the people less welcoming than at her other posts. For months they did not respond to her, refusing to speak to her or shake her hand. She was finally able to make contact by offering to buy items such as carvings and clothing that they made. As she had in Oklahoma, she became a contact between the Indians wishing to sell handicrafts and those who wished to buy them, securing a fair price for the items and expanding their markets beyond the roadside stands and tourist curio shops. She also established a small Indian village at the edge of the town of Everglades where she cared for sick Indians who had come for medical help. She began holding devotional services at various Indian villages as well as for whites. Everglades had a community church serving several denominations where she took charge of Protestant Episcopal devotional services, and she conducted Sunday school for white parishioners at other towns in the area. She taught sewing classes at the Collier City High School and spoke often to groups throughout Florida. Correspondence continued with benefactors throughout the country. She worked to improve sanitation and nutrition within the Indian villages. Gradually she was accepted, and then welcomed, into the Seminole camps. She refused to leave her work to attend the funerals of her mother and sister, who died during the early years of her service in Florida.

The Florida Seminoles are said to be the only Indian group never to have surrendered to, or signed a treaty with, the U.S. government. During World War II, the Seminoles independently declared war on the Axis powers and had Bedell sign their ration cards for them, still not trusting any document prepared by the U.S. government but trusting her to do it for them.

In 1943, Bedell's status with the church changed as she retired as a diocesan missionary but remained as a parish worker, technically a volunteer living on her retirement pension rather than being paid as an active missionary. She did not abandon her work. Following a hurricane in 1947 that flooded the town of Everglades, her major project became the establishment of a mission Indian village with Seminole-style chickee dwellings on the Tamiami Trail. The village included one chickee with a small room for her. Young Seminole couples lived at the village, where she instructed them in adapting to white ways much as she had the Cheyenne girls in the mission house in Oklahoma.

Bedell was a strong supporter of the establishment of Everglades National Park, hoping that it would help preserve the environment and provide work and tourist markets for the Seminoles. When the park was dedicated in 1947, President Harry S Truman delivered the address, and Bedell gave the invocation.

In spite of her advancing age, Bedell continued her Everglades mission work until Hurricane Donna in 1960 totally destroyed Glades Cross Mission. She had taken refuge in a friend's home in Ochopee during the storm. Returning to the area, she found that the Indian village had survived fairly well but that her personal home in Everglades had been devastated, as had most of the mission property scattered throughout the area. Her personal possessions, including her beautiful, handmade Indian clothing and beadwork, some brought from Oklahoma, her books, and her papers—all were gone. She moved into the Bishop Gray Inn, an Episcopal home for retired religious, in Davenport, Florida, and her property was given to the church. She continued to speak to groups in the Davenport area, to prepare Sunday school lessons, and to help care for the sick at the inn. On January 8, 1969, at the age of ninety-three, she died at Bishopscourt, Lakeland, Florida.

Bedell was one of numerous, highly committed missionary women of her era who devoted their lives to teaching and serving American Indian people.

Her influence was perhaps more important than most because of her publications in missionary magazines, voluminous correspondence, and frequent speaking tours with accompanying newspaper publicity, all designed to raise support for her work. These activities served to convey her view of Indian people and their culture and to stimulate others to share in her beliefs as to what was best for their welfare. Beginning her work at a time when many thought there was nothing of value in Indian culture and that the best path was to eliminate, through education and Christian conversion, all vestiges of Native American life, Bedell herself often expressed her belief that there were aspects of that life that were good and should be allowed to survive. Following attendance at a Cheyenne ceremony in which peyote was used, she deplored the peyote use but saw parallels between some aspects of the ceremony and Christian religious practice. She was offended by those who made fun of Indian names, pointing out that European names originally had concrete meanings and giving the example that her bishop, Rev. Francis K. Brooke, was not really a brook. It did not escape her notice that the hurricane that destroyed much of her mission did not destroy the Seminole chickee dwellings because of their design. She carried on a spirited correspondence with government and church officials, insisting that Plains Indians were more likely to adopt white standards of housekeeping, industrial trades, and farming if they were taught such things on their own land rather than in the artificial environment of a boarding school.

However, she also believed that unless American Indians adapted, they were doomed to a poverty-stricken, marginal existence or perhaps to extinction. She saw hunger at all three of her mission stations, linked to the disappearance of wild game. A major focus of her work was the development of cottage industries where the crafts of these people could be produced and marketed in such a way as to prevent exploitation, with the products crafted by the women being most important.

Her status as a woman had other effects upon her work. It seems more than coincidence that throughout her career she worked primarily alone, especially in the early years when a woman's place on the mission field was more restricted. In a letter to her bishop regarding the closing of Whirlwind Mission, the Indian agent severely criticized Bedell, saying that she was unwilling to take a "subordinate place" and that she dominated whoever was nominally in charge. He recommended that she find "other work." In explaining her transfer to Alaska, an Episcopal journal article indicates that since others had come to work at the Cheyenne mission, she felt free to go elsewhere, an explanation at odds with the facts of the situation since Bedell had worked diligently to keep Whirlwind School open and herself in charge. Her move to St. Stephen's Village, where she was alone, was a move she instigated herself, as was her choice of Glades Cross Mission, which had been abandoned while other Florida mission facilities had not.

First and foremost, Bedell was a Christian missionary. While her efforts to improve standards of living and provide both academic and vocational education were immense, Christian conversion of the Indians with whom she worked was always the ultimate focus of her work, as can be seen in all that was written by or about her. Assessing the lasting successes in the various aspects of her work is difficult as is true regarding most missionary and educational work of the past 500 years, wherein the goal was to persuade Native American people to accommodate themselves to a dominant, European-based culture. All three of her mission posts were closed, at least temporarily, when she left—Whirlwind Mission School, Rowe Hall, and Glades Cross Mission. Her impact on the lives of the American Indians at those places and on the thinking of those within mainstream society who read her articles, heard her speak, and supported her efforts and her work is difficult to measure but is most likely quite significant.

WORKS BY HARRIET M. BEDELL

"Among the Indians of Oklahoma." *Spirit of Missions* 74, no. 4 (April 1910): 271–74.
"The Year at St. Luke's, Whirlwind." *Spirit of Missions* 75, no. 9 (September 1910): 776–78.
"An Indian Dance in Oklahoma." *Spirit of Missions* 75, no. 12 (December 1910): 1003–5.
"United Offering Days Among Our Indians in Oklahoma." *Spirit of Missions* 78, no. 4 (April 1913): 271–73.
"At Whirlwind, Oklahoma." *Spirit of Missions* 80, no. 2 (February 1915): 136.
"How Many Sleeps Till Christmas?" *Spirit of Missions* 81, no. 2 (February 1916): 100–101.
"Everyday Life on the Arctic Circle: Isolation—Darkness—Cold—But All 'So Worthwhile.' " *Spirit of Missions* 89, no. 12 (December 1924): 774–75.
"Stephen's Village Moves to Tanana." *Spirit of Missions* 94, no. 2 (February 1929): 111–12.
"South Florida Resumes Seminole Mission." *Spirit of Missions* 98, no. 10 (October 1933): 543–44.

WORKS ABOUT HARRIET M. BEDELL

Archives and Manuscript Division, Oklahoma State Historical Society. *Cheyenne and Arapaho Agency Records*. Roll no. CAA 89. Oklahoma City, 1986. Microfilm.
" 'Aristocrats of Florida'—Seminoles, Deaconess Bedell Serves Vast Everglades." *Spirit of Missions* 104 (September 1939): 21, 34.
Botkin, Sam L. *The Episcopal Church in Oklahoma*. Oklahoma City: American-Bond Printing, 1958.
———. "Indian Missions of the Episcopal Church in Oklahoma." *Chronicles of Oklahoma* 36, no. 1 (Spring 1958): 40–47.
Brooke, F. K. "The Bishop's Journal." *The Oklahoma Churchman* 21, no. 3 (October 1916): 3.

Hartley, William, and Ellen Hartley. *A Woman Set Apart*. New York: Dodd, Mead, 1963.

McKellips, Karen. "Harriet Bedell, Episcopal Authority on Life Among the Indians." In Wayne Willis, ed., *Proceedings of the Forty-Second Annual Meeting Southwestern Philosophy of Education Society*, 97–105. Morehead, KY: Morehead State University, 1992.

Reedy, James J. "Whirlwind Indian Day School." *The Indian School Journal* 4, no. 4 (April 1909): 17–19.

Catharine Beecher

Sally H. Wertheim

Catharine Beecher (1800–1878) was a prolific author and educator who advocated the importance of the professionalization of women's domestic and educator roles, seeing women's self-sacrifice as integral to self-fulfillment. Beecher did not support the first movement for women's rights. Instead she advocated what she believed to be the most important role for women, to work as mothers and as teachers in the new and rapidly expanding common schools. In these indirect ways women would exert their influence on the developing nation.

Catharine Beecher was born in 1800 in East Hampton, Long Island. She was a woman of her time and must be understood in the context of her time, a period of change. Development of nationalism and patriotism was paramount to the new nation's existence. The immigrants of the 1830s and 1840s were looked upon with suspicion and fear. The Catholic population grew rapidly from the time John Carroll became bishop in 1789, threatening the established Protestant structure of the land. Protestantism began to splinter into many new sects, such as the Mormons and the Shakers. Suffrage, extended to the common man, tended to become a threat to the existing political, elitist structure. Industrialization and urbanization were on the rise. This era of ferment gave rise to many reform movements, focusing on such causes as abolitionism, women's rights, temperance, prison reform, and education. Often the same reformers were the leaders of the different causes. Beecher saw the growing need for a common type of schooling for all people in response to the many changes that were taking place. The school could become the unifying, homogenizing element in the culture that would deal with the problems created by the vast changes of the times. This was not to be a school only for the common man, but a school for all, publicly supported and publicly controlled.

Beecher's father was Lyman Beecher, a Calvinist minister and spokesman for resurgent Evangelicism, who lived from 1775 to 1863. He was born in Litchfield, Connecticut. Her mother Roxana Foote, was part of a very prominent Episcopalian family descended from the Puritans. She was born in Guilford, Connecticut, in 1775 and died at the age of 41 in 1816, when Catharine was sixteen years old. Catharine Beecher was the oldest of thirteen children and often was referred to as the favorite child of her father. She was described as having a superior intellect and as one adept at using power.

When Catharine was nine years old, the family moved to Connecticut. Though she attended Pierce's Litchfield school, probably the most important education she received was from the various members of the Beecher family. The Beecher family was known to have a sense of urgency and mission. They worked hard to become part of the national elite. Her siblings, such as Harriet Beecher Stowe and Henry Ward Beecher, shared her fame and helped establish the family as an important part of the society working to establish the concepts of popular democracy. Following the move to Connecticut, her education was more formalized by her attendance at Pierce's school. After her mother's death, her father remarried a second wife, Harriet Porter. Out of thirteen children, there were nine surviving siblings, four of them from Lyman Beecher's second marriage.

Catharine Beecher's fiancé, Alexander Fisher, a gifted Yale professor, was killed in a shipwreck off the Irish coast in 1822, and she never married. She devoted her life to the major careers of writing and teaching. At the age of seventy-eight Beecher died in her sleep of a stroke in 1878, a year after she had moved to Elmira, New York. She was still very active and busy making plans for the future. Just a few days before she died, she had begun some correspondence with publishers and educators concerning future projects. It seemed to her biographers that she was almost frenetic about the many activities she tried to pursue late in her life. Her obituary characterized her as a person focused on instruction and improvement. She exhibited the directness and positiveness of her father.

Catharine Beecher devoted much of her life to articulating and carrying out her philosophy of women's education, a philosophy that was integrated with a feminist social vision. It centered around the important work of mothers and teachers as educators. She felt strongly and wrote that it was important for mothers and teachers to be engaged in the business of education as they nursed and reared their children in order to assure that each succeeding generation was perfectly taught and formed. She saw this mission as the true profession of a woman and was concerned that neither mothers nor teachers had been properly prepared and educated for this profession. Given that belief, she set about devoting her life to providing for the education of both mothers and teachers. She did the former through her work with home economics and the latter through her work in promoting women to be teachers for the common schools and setting up educational programs to prepare them for this important work.

Following the tragic death of her fiancé in 1822, Beecher opened a school for young women in Hartford in 1823, working with her sister Mary. This school became the Hartford Female Seminary. Beecher then published a moral philosophy text in 1831, which became the first of a long group of her works that influenced American thought. The Hartford Female Seminary provided one of the few places where women could go for education beyond the elementary level. The Beechers taught grammar, geography, rhetoric, philosophy, chemistry, ancient and modern history, arithmetic, algebra, geometry, moral philosophy, natural theology, and Latin, very parallel to the curriculum found in men's higher educational institutions.

Following this venture and in conjunction with her father's work to provide missionary services in the West, Beecher went to Cincinnati in 1832 and began a school there called the Western Female Institute, reflecting some of her earlier work at Hartford. This was the period of the beginnings of the common school movement, and she actively promoted and embraced the concept of a common school. Some of her ideas grew out of the Evangelical movement which was so prominent during this period, when societies were established to train ministers, to print Bibles, and to advance the Sunday school movement. Beecher saw her own role as stressing the importance of having female teachers staff these fledgling institutions. As she began to give her attention to the common school cause, she saw it, as did others of the time, as a crusade. Not only was she supporting the schooling movement; she was developing a new vocation of teaching for women. Women's role would be to promote national unity through their influence on children as their teachers.

In 1835 Beecher published *An Essay on the Education of Female Teachers*. This work grew out of a lecture she delivered for the Lyceum in New York and provided information on the training of women for teaching in the common school. When women were teachers, the existing perception of the female as a plaything of men would be changed. Qualities of mind would be developed to prepare women for their new duties. The curriculum would be designed to cultivate the intellect. Mathematics would be taught to produce skills of investigation and reasoning. Women would be taught perseverance and accuracy. All of these subjects would lead to "virtuous" intelligence, undergirded by a reverence for Christianity and moral virtue. Each seminary would have a model school where the local children would receive moral and intellectual training. This training would elevate the role of teachers, making teaching a special profession for women that they would pursue prior to taking on their domestic duties. This new role would eliminate the extremes of class and caste that oppressed women, creating a middle-class, unified social system.

Beecher joined a group of "educators" who came from different professions to band together to promote the common school movement. Notable among these professionals were people like Horace Mann, Henry Barnard,

Calvin Wiley, Samuel Lewis, Calvin Stowe (a member of her family), and Albert Picket. Many of these people were ministers, attorneys, or editors. All of them believed that education was essential in order to support a republican form of government. Their thoughts reflected the Evangelical movements of the time, emphasizing the importance of religion, morals, volunteerism, and politics. They gave each other support and wrote frequently to advance the common school. In these ways her efforts worked to bring a clear and strong Protestant influence to the common school. This emphasis on Protestantism in the schools caused political problems with the developing Catholic immigrant community, one of the factors that, over time, in 1884, resulted in the formation of a separate system of Catholic parochial schools. Beecher was also a part of a national benevolent movement to raise funds for the common schools and for the education of teachers.

One of Beecher's major visions was to create a group of endowed teacher-training seminaries for women at key places throughout the West, supported by eastern money. To interest benefactors, she was quick to point out the importance of women and the influence that they could exert. For example, she noted the role women played in the education of their own children and how they were involved in most benevolent enterprises, particularly those related to developing morals or manners. Through their work in the home and now in the school, women could play a very important role in creating the necessary unity and morality that the new government would require. Beecher saw women as particularly well-equipped for these types of responsibilities. However, she pointed out the importance of a proper education. Properly trained, the women could influence the men and provide excellent role models for the children.

Many of these ideas were originally discussed in her famous book, *A Treatise on Domestic Economy*, published in 1841. This book is both a theory of domestic management and a theory of female education. Beecher stressed that females must be educated in order to carry out their domestic role. Beecher discussed four female virtues: domesticity, piety, purity, and submissiveness. This was the first textbook in the field of home economics to be recognized by a state board of education, the Massachusetts Board of Education in 1843. Beecher is credited with founding home economics as a professional subject. Many felt that these subjects could not be taught through books, but Beecher was quick to point out the analogy of chemistry, which is learned in the same way. Beecher believed that domestic education and equality of roles must be based in reason, requiring a formal type of education.

Beecher went on to complete ten publications dealing directly with the subject of home economics, which she referred to as domestic science. One of her later works, *The American Woman's Home*, which was coauthored with her sister, Harriet Beecher Stowe, was a good example of the type of daring that she constantly displayed. In this work her architectural plans for the home included such things as a movable storage wall and were quite progressive for the time.

Her books provided a well-balanced foundation of subject matter for students of home economics. She included such topics as economics, home management, family relationships, child development, nutrition, housing equipment, and home furnishings. She consistently advocated the idea that science was basic to an intelligent study and understanding of the home. Subsequent leaders in the field credit Beecher with providing the outline and foundation of a scholarly plan for a home economics curriculum that has been sustained over time and for founding home economics as a professional field of study.

Adding to her myriad interests, Beecher also devoted her energy and thought to the area of preventive medicine. Since many women were faced with ill health at that time, she developed ways to improve the health of women in her book *Letters to the People on Health and Happiness*, published in 1855. She introduced calisthenics into each school and college that she founded and urged public school administrators to follow suit. She and her sister Harriet urged that women be trained as "home physicians" to focus on preventive medicine and public health. In 1871 they circulated notification of their intent to start such a program of medical training under the auspices of the Women's Educational Association but had little response.

Beecher also wrote several books on religion and was a leader in reinterpreting Calvinism. Unlike her father, she believed that conversion was unnecessary and that by living an upright life, one was assured of salvation. She early denied the essential depravity of human nature and used her work in education to demonstrate the essential goodness of the child. She was committed to educating children to lead Christian lives and so wrote several books on religious education.

Another of Beecher's efforts was raising funds to support an agency that would coordinate the work of locating western schools in need of teachers, recruiting women willing to serve in them, and then coordinating the two. Due to her influence, a group of women set up the American Women's Educational Association in 1852 to provide endowments for the colleges Beecher established. Further, the aim of the group was ultimately to create teaching positions for women to make them financially independent. Beecher's ideas on behalf of common schools, especially those where female teachers taught, were quite influential and can be found in Horace Mann's second annual report in a discussion about the special qualifications of females as teachers. It was generally assumed that the early normal schools in Massachusetts would be attended by females.

In order to assess Beecher's contributions to the field of education, it is important to consider the conditions at the time. Notable is the fact that women were denied political rights and consequently were in a subordinate position. Furthermore they were completely dependent upon their husbands economically. Unlike many women's movement advocates, Beecher differentiated women's roles from those of men's; however, she viewed the domestic and the public spheres, women and men, as working together to advance society. She also felt any women's movement should progress from the domestic to the public and consequently from women to men. Women's traditional duties were valuable, deserved respect, and must be underpinned by reason. Beecher felt she would probably have difficulty reaching her goals if men were not included in her education plan. She believed men also needed to be educated so that they would respect and accept women's roles.

Catharine Beecher often conveyed confusing messages concerning her beliefs about women. Though she was actively involved in many causes, her major accomplishments were in the field of women's education, in its broadest sense, with an ultimate goal of professionalizing women's domestic roles and overcoming their marginal status. She was not a strong supporter of women's political rights and equality and was against the women's suffrage movement of her time. She did, however, advocate a professional role for women, mainly a domestic one, and worked to overcome women's marginal status through education.

One of Catharine Beecher's major contributions to women's education was her social vision, which emphasized the importance of home and family. She felt women should be ready to put the needs of others ahead of their own needs. Women should see self-sacrifice as self-fulfillment. These ideals very much reflected her own personal experience. She placed the domestic environment of women within the context of a larger society and emphasized its social and political significance. She related these ideas to the newly emerging democratic nation and saw them as primary to the successful operation of this new form of government. She made women's roles central to national life. The home should be a place where activities abound that are noncommercial and apart from the rest of the society but directed toward improving that society.

In order to achieve these goals, Beecher advocated a very broad, liberal education for women. She did not forget the need for developing the whole person and included physical education in her program. She believed that women's studies must be rigorous and extensive, using the same textbooks that men's colleges required. Very modern in her thinking, her emphasis was on developing skills such as critical thinking and problem solving rather than having students amass and memorize information. She was also quick to point out that women needed the ability to exercise independent judgment in practical matters; this was what professionalized their work.

The concept of professionalism was central in all of Beecher's writings and philosophy. Beecher's approach, the combination of theoretical and practical training, resulted in giving women the expertise to make critical judgments in their areas of influence, teaching and domestic matters. Professionalism, in Beecher's terms, was based on issues of knowledge in education, not necessarily on the issue of pay for women.

Though it may appear, as one superficially studies Beecher's ideas, that she believed in an unequal role for women, she did not see "equal" as needing to be identical to the position of men. She actually believed that women were equal; however, she saw this equality being played out within their own sphere of influence, the domestic scene. Her concept of equal implied a "different but equal" theory. Women's contributions to the development of a good society allowed them to be equal, while operating from a subordinate position.

Beecher's ideas rested on the important function that women performed as educators and socializers of children. She noted that the formation of a child's character, both intellectual and moral, is a very important woman's function. Women achieved their influence and goals through others, men who themselves went on to affect the society, but only as a result of the education they received at the hands of women. The women that carried out this important role needed to be autonomous, rational, and thinking people. They could not be mere technicians who had not been formally educated.

Beecher's contributions to advancing women's education are major, particularly because of her emphasis on professionalism. Though men and women currently may not subscribe to Beecher's belief in equal but separate spheres for the sexes, they can appreciate the importance of her efforts to ensure women their share of important roles and top positions in an occupational hierarchy during her lifetime. She advanced and enhanced women's societal position, using the panacea of the time, education, as the most important tool.

WORKS BY CATHARINE BEECHER

Suggestions Respecting Improvements in Education. Hartford, CT: Packard and Butler, 1829.
An Essay on the Education of Female Teachers. New York: Van Nostrand and Dwight, 1835.
The Moral Instructor for Schools and Families. Cincinnati: Truman and Smith, 1838.
A Treatise on Domestic Economy for the Use of Young Ladies at Home and at School. New York: Harper, 1841. Rev. 1856.
Letters to the People on Health and Happiness. New York: Harper, 1855.
Religious Training of Children in the School, the Family and the Church. New York: Harper, 1864.
Educational Reminiscences and Suggestions. New York: J. B. Ford, 1874.

WORKS ABOUT CATHARINE BEECHER

Biester, Charlotte. "Prelude—Catharine Beecher." *Journal of Home Economics* 51 (1959): 549–51.
Burstyn, Joan. "Catharine Beecher and the Education of American Women." *New England Quarterly* 47 (1974): 386–403.

Cremin, Lawrence A. *American Education: The National Experience*. New York: Teachers College Press, 1980.

Cross, Barbara M. ed. *The Educated Woman in America: Selected Writings of Catharine Beecher, Margaret Fuller, and M. Carey Thomas*. New York: Teachers College Press, 1965.

Harveson, Mae Elizabeth. *Catharine Esther Beecher: Pioneer Educator*. Philadelphia: University of Pennsylvania, 1932.

Martin, Jane Roland. *Reclaiming a Conversation*. New Haven, CT: Yale University Press, 1985.

Sklar, Kathryn Kish. *Catharine Beecher: A Study in American Domesticity*. New Haven, CT: Yale University Press, 1973.

Woody, Thomas. *A History of Women's Education in the United States*. 2 vols. New York: Octagon Books, 1966.

Mary McLeod Bethune

Olga Skorapa

Mary McLeod Bethune (1875–1955) founded Bethune-Cookman College, worked as head of the Division of Negro Affairs in the National Youth Administration, and created a coalition of African-American Women's Clubs, the National Council of Negro Women, with over 800,000 members. She worked for social justice throughout her life, focusing primarily on improving the lives of the women and children of her race. While living in Washington, D.C., during the New Deal, Bethune forged a coalition of African Americans who worked in the government advising the president of the group's conclusions. Her final public act was to serve as "Official Representative of American Negroes" to the meeting that created the United Nations in San Francisco in 1945. Bethune called upon her religious conviction to further these goals. She also worked to preserve the historical record of her own accomplishments and those of other African Americans. While she might be remembered as politician or administrator, Bethune's contribution to education is essential to understanding both her work and how she perceived herself.

As an educator, Bethune was not primarily a classroom teacher or a theoretician, although she both taught and theorized. Instead, she used her status as a public figure to educate the American people concerning issues of race, racism, poverty, education, and women's rights. Bethune-Cookman College was not important for its pedagogical innovation or the scholarly accomplishments of its faculty. The school's continued existence in the face of tremendous racism and poverty among the black community of Daytona, Florida, distinguished both its graduates and its founder. When she left Daytona to live in Washington, D.C., Bethune changed the focus of her teaching from the students who attended her school to the African-American women who were members of the National Council of Negro Women, which she founded, and to the wider American public. She also educated the African Americans who worked in the New Deal in the value of their collective voice. She was unpar-

alleled in building unlikely coalitions to empower African Americans and
people of conscience.

Mary McLeod Bethune was born in Mayesville, South Carolina, on July 10,
1875. Though their fifteenth child, she was the first of the seventeen children
of Samuel and Patsy McIntosh McLeod to be born after emancipation. Her
parents continued to work on the same farm on which they had been slaves,
sharecropped, and planted their own land. When a school for black children
opened in Mayesville, Mary Jane McLeod was chosen, of all her siblings, to
attend. From 1886 to 1887, the young girl learned to read and write and
cipher under the tutelage of Emma Wilson, who remained for Bethune a
role model and an inspiration throughout her life. Soon exhausting the limited resources of the school, Mary headed for Scotia Seminary in Concord,
North Carolina. There she completed the course of study, financed in part
with the help of a Quaker woman, Mary Crissman, who agreed to finance
Mary's college education as well. At Chicago's Moody Bible Institute in
1895, the education of Mary McLeod was completed. Dedicating her life to
serving God, the young woman prepared for missionary work in Africa only
to be told there was no work for blacks in the missions in Africa.

Instead of foreign service, Mary McLeod began a career educating African-American children, first back in Mayesville for a year and then at Haines
Institute in Augusta, Georgia, and other schools around the South. Haines
was a model of black education in the South, and its founder, Lucy Craft
Laney, proved to be instrumental in the professional education of the young
teacher. Mary McLeod also met and married Albertus Bethune at Haines in
May 1898. Though their relationship was never smooth, their son and only
child, Albert McLeod Bethune, was born in February 1899. After several
months, during which Mary Bethune stayed home with the baby, the Bethune family moved to Palatka, Florida, so that Mary might begin teaching
once again. By this time, her husband, who had been teaching at Haines,
gave it up entirely and instead worked at a variety of other jobs.

Palatka proved unsuitable to Mary Bethune's considerable talents, for she
wanted to create her own school. This happened in October 1904 in Daytona, Florida, when she founded Daytona Literary and Industrial Institute
for the Training of Negro Girls. Relying first on the African-American community for support and then reaching out to the wealthy white Daytona
vacationers for assistance, through great effort and a widening circle of important acquaintances, Bethune and her school prospered. Unlike her school,
Mary Bethune's marriage did not. As the couple were unable to resolve their
domestic difficulties, Albertus Bethune returned to his home in South Carolina in 1908, leaving their young son in the care of his wife. He died there
in 1919.

Bethune's founding of her school was her chance to put into action her
religious visions. In this endeavor, the secular and religious education of

women was paramount. Her concern for women's education identifies Bethune with contemporary feminist educators and is demonstrated in her work both at the turn of the century and beyond. Against her wishes, Bethune-Cookman Collegiate Institute (the institution that grew from her school in Daytona) became coeducational under the auspices of the Methodist church in July 1923, a circumstance Bethune had to accept in order to receive the necessary financial support offered by the Methodists.[1] She attempted unsuccessfully to reverse that circumstance later on in her presidency.

While Bethune was teaching her young girls the basics of reading, writing, and arithmetic, she was also teaching them service to their community and the means to make a living. The first hospital for blacks in Daytona grew out of Bethune's school because no hospital would accept African-American patients. The first practical nursing school in Florida began there as well. Bethune built a truck garden on the vacant lot across the street and sold the produce. She built a normal school at the institute to facilitate her efforts to teach literacy to the workers in the turpentine camps near Daytona. Using the model of Fisk University's Jubilee Singers, Bethune formed her students into a choir, which sang in the hotels of the elite whites who vacationed in Daytona. She used this introduction into "polite" society as a means to make the acquaintance of the rich, a strategy she parlayed into a national political career.

To see her school as merely her stepping-stone to the wider world, however, would be a mistake. It also represented a means for others to follow the path of its founder into the wider culture if they followed her strict supervision. This path grew wider and ran further into the mainstream of white culture as Bethune became more widely known and "acceptable" in white society. The school simultaneously expanded to meet the wider opportunities available to Bethune and to the African-American community during the first half of the twentieth century.

As Bethune's institution grew from an industrially oriented grade school to a high school to a junior college and finally to the four-year college it is today, it gradually lost some of its revolutionary features. These features— Mary Bethune selling pies on the street and soliciting money door-to-door; the time contribution of the workers who built the school; the haphazard economic and physical structure of the school; the direct participation of the community in the daily tasks of running the school; the more industrial aspects of the curriculum such as farming, animal husbandry, making and selling sugarcane syrup, and laundering; the singing Sunday school for the community; and the adult literacy school at the turpentine camp—all ended as the institution was gradually transformed. Its functions became less distinguishable from the widely accepted functions of an academic environment as its students gradually could look forward to more respectable positions in the larger community. Nursing, business, and teaching gradually took the place of basic literacy, agriculture, and hygiene. With these changes, Bethune herself came to relinquish some of her control. By the time Daytona Literary and Industrial Institute for the Training of Negro Girls became Bethune-Cookman College the curriculum, too, was transformed.

In addition to managing her school, Bethune began a national career through her work with the Red Cross, the African Methodist Episcopal church (she always participated in the general conference), and the African-American women's club movement. She found financial, as well as moral, support in the white community, to which she appealed for financial assistance and advice. Through this interaction with the elite white capitalists who spent their winters in Florida, Bethune found funding for her school and met Eleanor Roosevelt and many other rich and powerful women and men. By 1914, Bethune was advising the Red Cross at the federal level.

Mary McLeod Bethune began her involvement in the women's club movement, working with the club that was part of her African Methodist Episcopal church in Daytona. From there she went on to lead the consortium of Florida black women's clubs. Always using her power to create more, Bethune soon parlayed that role into a national position and began the long drive to create a national coalition of black women, which yielded her a large measure of both power and influence. This dream was realized on December 5, 1935, with the formation of the National Council of Negro Women (NCNW).

Because the various African-American women's clubs were often at odds, particularly at the national level and apparently as a result of regional and class conflict among the organizations, Bethune's creation of the NCNW was problematic within the existing institutions of the African-American women's club movement.[2] When Mary McLeod Bethune formed the NCNW in 1935, she brought together many of the people and ideas that had motivated her life: black women, political power directed toward the improvement of her race and sex, and her commitment to helping the race through education. Bethune was anxious to consolidate the diffuse power of African-American women throughout the country into a political constituency. Rejecting the National Association of Colored Women (NACW) as too narrow (and elitist) for her vision, she moved to develop her own power base. This is ironic considering that she had in the past headed the NACW, which was the most formidable rival to her new organization. Her decision was not without negative consequences, related to her usurping the power of the organization over which she had presided. By this time in her life, however, Bethune was accustomed to wielding power, and these consequences ultimately proved small to her.

Among Bethune's other affiliations in the women's club movement, she was president of the National Association of Colored Women, president of the Florida State Federation of Colored Women's Clubs, and honorary vice president of the National Council of Women of the U.S.A. (an integrated, mostly white group). In addition, she was a member of the League of Women Voters and the Florida State Teachers Association.

Besides her work with women, Bethune was active in a number of organizations that were primarily interested in the problems of race. She served as vice president of the National Association for the Advancement of Colored People (NAACP), the National Urban League, the Commission for Interracial Cooperation, and the Commission for International Cooperation. She was also a member of the board of directors of the Southern Conference Educational Fund and Highlander Folk School and a sponsor for Planned Parenthood Federation of America.

Bethune served as adviser for a child welfare conference held by Calvin Coolidge in 1928 and in 1933 advised the planning commission created by the U.S. Office of Education. In 1935 she was awarded the Springarn Medal by the NAACP, which brought her national media attention and set the stage for her appointment under Roosevelt to the federal government as assistant to the director of the National Youth Administration (NYA) in charge of minority affairs. Changing the name to "Director of Negro Affairs," she held that post until the NYA was dismantled at the beginning of U.S. involvement in World War II.

Initially serving on a panel of advisers to the Roosevelt administration on the problems of youth, Mary McLeod Bethune was recommended by her associates for the newly created post of assistant to the director. Bethune moved to Washington, D.C., in 1936 to work for the administration. This move also facilitated her leadership of the NCNW and her bringing together various African Americans among the New Dealers to form an unofficial advisory group. This coalition was called variously the "black cabinet," the "black brain trust," and the "Federal Council on Negro Affairs."[3]

Her understanding of the intertwining oppression of race and class and their potential to serve as catalysts for change helped make Bethune an able administrator and champion of African Americans in the Roosevelt administration. The confounding nature of oppression in all its various guises gave the division director impetus for alleviating misery in whatever venue she found herself. Within the NYA, however, Bethune worked most diligently to incorporate blacks into the federal programs both as administrators and as recipients of the governmental "largesse."

Bethune served as division director from 1936 until 1943, when the NYA was "terminated" by Congress.[4] During that time, she used her office to create a political power structure for black leadership to express its needs and desires to the president, the government, and the nation as a whole. During her tenure as director of the division of Negro affairs, Bethune used both the duties of her office and the prestige that it gave her to promote a variety of causes in which she was interested, among them the black cabinet. While the interests of black women were often preeminent in her life, as demonstrated in both her actions and her writings, the NYA focused Bethune's attention on the plight of all African Americans in the throes of the Depression. Viewed from this central focus, Bethune appears to personify the liberal perspective working within the system to reform society. As she gained power, her earlier radical activities—her direct, interactive praxis in creating a school; teaching young women of her race literacy and the means to earn a living and to be proud of themselves; standing against the Ku Klux Klan; building a hospital; teaching the turpentine workers of Palatka, Florida; begging door-to-door to make money for the rent on the school; making pies to sell on the street; finding workers who would donate their skills to help educate young women—appeared less functional in working toward the liberation of her race. She found she could use the system better to achieve her goals. Bethune's definition of that liberation appeared to change as well.[5] For her, blacks' participation in the wider culture as equals replaced her desire to create a separate place unique to the members of her race.

Bethune also used her position to spread the gospel of black liberation among the other government agencies and the state programs created by the NYA. Within those state programs, Bethune required black representation and management, thus giving many talented individuals a chance to develop skills needed to pursue their own political agendas, like creating political bases in the states. This network helped to provide the superstructure for developing leadership leading to the incipient civil rights movement.

Working with the NYA, Bethune widened federal programs targeted to African Americans during the New Deal. She interpreted her role to mean attempting to provide equal opportunity not only of race but also of sex, for she saw the two as intersecting and "parallel." In an undated speech, Bethune wrote:

It is one of the peculiar accidents of our social life and of the mental and emotional relation between groups that are distinguished by any mark, that there should grow up around these differences certain imputations which depend on their advantage of statement upon the most articulate group . . . .

That the measurements used for the anatomical differences are subject to severe strictures which disqualify them as scientific evidences; that the revolution of thinking on the question has affected more startling changes in accomplishment than any revolution in physical structure could hope to bring about.[6]

Bethune did not comment on how gender and race together affected black women, but she worked all her life to alleviate the injustices they suffered.

Throughout her professional life, Bethune also was involved in the creation of archives of historical material. She collected and attempted to preserve materials relating not only to her life and work but to those of her race as well. Both the NCNW and Bethune-Cookman College house archives, begun by Bethune, document her life. In preserving the history of African-American people, Bethune was also working to complete an idea of herself as well as an idea of her race. She began this project almost as she began Daytona Literary and Industrial Institute for the Training of Negro Girls in 1904. Of necessity, as she was constantly asking for money, Bethune built an image of herself and her work in concert with what she was "supposed" to be. This included the constant retelling and embellishment of the story of her school, "The School Founded on a Garbage Dump," which began "with $1.50 in her pocket." Bethune's creation of an "acceptable" persona dictated both how the world would "know" her in the past and how she is remembered today, an intentional mystification of herself that no longer serves to inform the present. Issues concerning Bethune's personal life—her relationships, her disappointments, her sexuality, her political convictions—are hidden due to her choice to keep her personal life and papers inaccessible to scholars. In fact, the hidden nature of her private life facilitated the creation of a public image that could "educate" a world unready for an African-American woman as strong, wise, and resolute as Mary McLeod Bethune.

This persona often led her detractors in her own day and the present to criticize her as being too accommodationist. To them she appeared to stoop to stereotypical actions to get what she wanted. While these strategies may not have endeared her to the more radical of her critics (Nikki Giovanni and Dick Gregory ridiculed her posthumously in 1974 at the dedication of the Mary McLeod Bethune Monument in Washington, D.C.), her means were tailored to accomplish the most she could while constrained by the conflicting and overlapping categories of race and sex.[7] Bethune did all she could to help poor African-American women and children, "by any means necessary." This did not, however, include acceding to the indignities of Jim Crow segregation.

An important aspect of her public persona was built on her refusal to accept second-class treatment on the basis of race or sex. She was always quick to point out the inequities of Jim Crow discrimination that kept her from doing what she wanted to do in the way that she wanted to do it. She used the power she had accrued in her position as a political leader to influence the people who assumed segregation was acceptable. Whether refusing to ride the freight elevator because the main elevator was denied to her or buying tickets for the train at the "whites only" window, Bethune refused to abide by segregation in public places. She also told and retold her victories, thus creating the text of her life, a text that spoke of her personal courage and unwavering resolve. In these battles, Bethune used her position to open the doors for other African Americans to enter after her and to cause white Americans to think about the direct effects of bigotry.

For Bethune, the crowning accomplishment of her life came when she served as official representative for American Negroes (with W.E.B. Du Bois and Walter White) to the conference that drafted the charter of the United Nations in 1945. Continuing her political involvement in the black community from 1935 to 1945 through a weekly column in the African-American newspaper *The Chicago Defender* and many appearances and appointments, Bethune stayed active into her final years. She died May 18, 1955.[8]

Bethune's life was a series of struggles to the top of many groups, developing many friends and enemies on her way. Because of the times in which she lived, like Martin Luther King, Jr., she was the continued object of scrutiny by the Federal Bureau of Investigation and various security organizations concerned with the patriotism of someone working so diligently to change fundamentally the racial caste system. Bethune's tireless actions in the face of harassment from the government and the society at large serve as a model to us in the twentieth century, a model of action in the face of adversity.

NOTES

1. Clarence Genu Newsome, "Mary McLeod in Religious Perspective: A Seminal Essay," Ph.D. diss., Duke University, 1982, 158.

2. Rackhan Holt, *Mary McLeod Bethune, A Biography* (Garden City, NY: Doubleday, 1964), 174–75.

3. Holt, 198.

4. Elaine M. Smith, "Mary McLeod Bethune and the National Youth Administration," in Mabel E. Deutrich and Virginia C. Purdy, eds., *Clio Was a Woman: Studies in the History of American Women* (Washington, D.C.: Howard University Press, 1980), 149–69.

5. These are all mentioned in Bethune's biographies as enterprises she began while creating her school in Daytona. See Holt, 63, 65, for example.

6. Mary McLeod Bethune, "An Introduction," in Gerda Lerner, ed., *Black Women in White America: A Documentary History* (New York: Random House, 1972), xxxv–xxxvi.

7. "Memories of Mary McLeod Bethune," *The Washington Post*, July 13, 1974.

8. Holt, 44, 290–95.

WORKS BY MARY McLEOD BETHUNE

Chicago Defender. Weekly Column, 1935–1945.
Pittsburgh Courier. Weekly Column, 1935–1945.

WORKS ABOUT MARY McLEOD BETHUNE

Blackwell, Barbara Grant. "The Advocacies and Ideological Commitments of a Black Educator: Mary McLeod Bethune, 1875–1955." Ph.D. diss., University of Connecticut, 1979.

Fitzgerald, Tracey A. *The National Council of Negro Women and the Feminist Movement, 1935–1975*. Washington, DC: Georgetown Monograph in American Studies, Georgetown University Press, 1985.

Giddings, Paula. *When and Where I Enter: The Impact of Black Women on Sex and Race in America*. New York: Morrow, 1984.

Holt, Rackham. *Mary McLeod Bethune: A Biography*. Garden City, NY: Doubleday, 1964.

Newsome, Clarence Genu. "Mary McLeod in Religious Perspective: A Seminal Essay." Ph.D. diss., Duke University, 1983.

Peare, Catherine Owens. *Mary McLeod Bethune*. New York: Vanguard Press, 1951.

Smith, Elaine M. "Mary McLeod Bethune and the National Youth Administration." In Mabel E. Deutrich and Virginia C. Purdy, eds., *Clio Was a Woman: Studies in the History of American Women*. Washington, DC: Howard University Press, 1980.

Mary Carroll Craig Bradford

Lynne Marie Getz

> Mary Carroll Craig Bradford (1856/1862?–1938) was a Colorado educator, club woman, and suffrage leader. She was a teacher and county superintendent and served as state superintendent of public instruction for six terms. During World War I she was president of the National Education Association. She campaigned in Colorado and other states for women's suffrage and was an active organizer for the Democratic party.

Mary Carroll Craig was born in New York City on August 10, either 1856 or 1862.[1] Her father, James Barnes Craig, was a native of Lexington, Kentucky, and a well-regarded international lawyer in New York. Her mother, Anna Turk Carroll Craig, could trace her family back to Charles Carroll of Carrollton, Maryland, a signer of the Declaration of Independence. The Craigs provided a sheltered, yet cosmopolitan upbringing for their daughter, who never attended a formal school but who traveled with them around the world. Tended by governesses and taught by private tutors, Mary received her only formal education at the University of Paris.

In 1876 Mary Craig married Edward Taylor Bradford (1848–1901), whose family also boasted a distinguished lineage, being direct descendants of Governor William Bradford of Massachusetts. Edward's father had served as paymaster general of the navy, and young Bradford entered that service, graduating from Annapolis in 1869 and serving as an aide on Admiral Farragut's flagship. After their marriage the Bradfords settled in Brooklyn, New York.

In 1878 Bradford resigned his naval commission and moved to Leadville, Colorado, to pursue a mining venture. Joining her husband in Colorado and finding him nearly penniless, Mary Bradford responded with great fortitude to her changed circumstances. While raising a son and two daughters (another son died in childhood), Mrs. Bradford wrote articles for publication and taught school in Leadville. Her husband's endeavors in mining never produced the hoped-for rewards, and in 1890 the Bradfords moved to Colorado Springs, where Mr. Bradford continued to speculate in mining property and tinkered with mining inventions.

In 1893 Mary Bradford involved herself in the suffrage movement, an activity that propelled her into public life and established her reputation as an organizer and orator. She helped to organize a local group under the name of the Colorado Springs Equal Suffrage Association, of which she was elected president. This group was absorbed by the Colorado Equal Suffrage Association, a bipartisan organization working for the passage of a suffrage bill in the 1894 general election. The success of this suffrage measure for women was due in no small part to actions taken by Colorado women. In the 1893 school elections, women turned out in droves to vote, thus showing their desire to use the franchise. Then in 1894 they played a major role in party politics, demonstrating both ability and sincerity in their participation. Mary C. C. Bradford was a leading participant in these efforts.

After moving to Denver in late 1893, Mrs. Bradford organized the Colorado Women's Democratic Club at a meeting held in her home. The Democratic women devoted themselves not only to the cause of women's suffrage but also to uniting the Colorado Democratic party, which at the time was split between Silver and Cleveland Democrats. Membership in the Colorado Women's Democratic Club increased rapidly, and the National Democratic Committee recognized it as the only undivided Democratic organization in the state. On behalf of the club Mary Bradford canvassed the entire state, urging both factions to set aside their differences for the good of the party. The club's efforts resulted in a United Democratic state convention. Mary C. C. Bradford's contributions were recognized when the convention chose her as the candidate for state superintendent of public instruction, making her the first woman ever nominated for a state office in Colorado. Although she lost in the general election, she was now a recognized public figure, and women now had the vote in Colorado.

Mary C. C. Bradford continued to participate actively in Democratic politics and the national suffrage movement. She was well known by national suffrage leaders for her oratorical skills and willingness to spend weeks on the road campaigning in other states. For Bradford the vote for women was a means for achieving social goals, not an end in itself. By taking an active part in politics women could effect progressive reforms on issues that mattered to them: education, child labor regulation, conservation, juvenile law, and property rights for women. These issues were consistently raised by Bradford in her political and club activities. In defending women's suffrage fifteen years after its enactment in Colorado, Bradford claimed that "the sanest, most progressive, most humane, most scientific laws" had been passed since women had gained the vote, thus demonstrating that "a State becomes more truly civilized when the wishes of both men and women become in-corporated in the statutes." In making this argument Bradford revealed her view of the sexes as essentially different, yet complementary:

Man and woman are not alike; they are equal but not identical. Man represents mental force, woman spiritual force. Masculine civilization is splendid, dominant, aggressive, creative, but it is also sordid and brutal. Feminine civilization would be beautiful, tender, self-sacrificing, strong in moral and spiritual energy, but somewhat lacking in qualities wherein men are great. A purely masculine civilization would be a misfortune. Fortunately a purely feminine civilization is impossible, for it would be equally unfortunate.[2]

In 1902 Mary C. C. Bradford organized the Jane Jefferson Democratic Club, a statewide organization for women that participated in Democratic campaigns on the county, state, and national levels. The club lobbied for passage of legislation affecting women and children, supported women can-didates, and corresponded with national political leaders regarding issues of concern to them. Bradford served as president of the club from 1913 to 1921, a tenure coinciding with the presidency of Woodrow Wilson. As a Democratic party organizer Bradford was a frequent correspondent with Wilson, and she used the weight and influence of the Jane Jefferson Club in her appeals to him. She defended Wilson's wartime policies against the verbal attacks of more militant feminists and let the president know that her active support and that of the Jane Jefferson Club in Colorado were predi-cated on their faith that he would push vigorously for women's suffrage and a child labor law.[3]

Political work also entered the activities of yet another organization with which Mary Bradford was affiliated. Bradford had become a member of the Denver Women's Club in 1894 and in 1895 became a charter member of the Colorado Federation of Women's Clubs. She served as the federation's president from 1902 to 1904. The Federation of Women's Clubs endorsed women candidates and actively lobbied for legislation affecting women and children. The state federation also sponsored a State Travelling Library until 1903, when the Colorado legislature authorized a State Travelling Library Commission to take over the work being done by the clubwomen. The governor appointed Mary Bradford as a member of this commission.

While Bradford used political work and club activities as vehicles for social reform, she saw the schools as the greatest agent of improvement in society. After the death of her husband in 1901, Mary Bradford taught school in Denver and served as county superintendent of Adams County (1902–1904) and Denver County (1909–1912). In 1912 she was elected state superinten-dent of public instruction and served six terms in that office (1913–1920 and 1923–1926). As an educator Mary Bradford shared the goals, means, and rhetoric of the progressive education movement, embracing the ideals of centralized administration, consolidation and standardization of rural schools, and Americanization of students outside of the mainstream. Under her guidance progressive education came to Colorado.

When Mary C. C. Bradford became state superintendent of public instruction, that office had no power to standardize the schoolwork of the various districts of the state. In the rural school districts one-room schools managed by poorly paid and ill-prepared teachers were the rule. Improvement of the rural schools became Bradford's primary goal as state superintendent, and her favored methods of doing so were consolidation, standardization, and increasing both the requirements and compensation for rural teachers.

Although Bradford did not formulate an original theory or plan of consolidation, she became an indefatigable promoter of the plans of other Colorado educators. She traveled throughout the state speaking to school and community leaders about the benefits of consolidation. She addressed teachers' meetings and held workshops through the Colorado Teachers' Association and regularly wrote on the topic in the *Colorado School Journal.*

Hand in hand with consolidation went standardization. Bradford initiated a statewide standardization plan in 1914, which entailed evaluations of each school according to a scale set by the state. Schools were judged on the merits of their physical plant, library and music facilities, classroom space, playground and landscaping, status of the school as a community center and the teacher as a community leader, and the lodging, certification, and salary of the teacher. If the school met the standard of requirements, it received a tablet with the rating of "Approved" or "Superior" on it and the title of "State of Colorado Standardized School." As was typical with Bradford's methods in general, public relations played a large role in carrying out the plan. She declared "Standardization Days" in Colorado, on which the people of a community were to gather at the schoolhouse, bring a picnic basket, sing patriotic songs, and listen to speeches on school betterment. Bradford was in great demand to attend these and other events connected with the standardization of the schools.

Like other progressive educators Mary Bradford relied heavily upon scientific "experts" to provide methods of improving the schools. To determine where students should be placed in the newly graded and standardized schools, Bradford implemented a program of mental testing. To ensure that Colorado teachers would have the benefit of the latest scientific tools, she collected samples of intelligence and standardized tests from universities around the country. She sent tests out to all schools in 1919, instructing teachers to administer group tests and to assign students to classes on the basis of the results. To train teachers in the use and administration of the tests, she held group meetings with county superintendents and sent the rural school supervisor to visit the more isolated schools. While the use of intelligence tests, especially in the hands of poorly trained administrators, held much potential for abuse, these dangers would become more apparent to later educators. For Bradford and her generation the tests represented a means of making education more efficient and modern.

As state superintendent of schools, Mary Bradford's greatest contribution was to improve the quality of instruction in the rural schools. By consolidating school districts and centralizing school administrations in single county units, she brought the rural schools more under the guidance of professional educators, and rural schoolchildren enjoyed a richer educational experience. Bradford also supported more stringent requirements for teachers and helped to implement a new certification law, which passed in 1923. Throughout her tenure as state superintendent she called for higher salaries for teachers.

In 1917 Mary C. C. Bradford was elected president of the National Education Association (NEA). For Bradford it was indisputably clear that the schools should be engaged in national service, and under her leadership the NEA wholeheartedly enlisted the nation's schools in the war effort. She proposed that schools adopt a "war-modified education," which meant

an education sensitive to the needs of national development. War-modified education helps the child to train himself spiritually as the patriot and lover of his kind. War-modified education results in a surrender of personal rights in favor of the greatest of all rights—that of free cooperation in the service of the spirit of America.[4]

Bradford saw the war as an opportunity for standardizing and centralizing the nation's schools in much the same way as she was doing in Colorado. She called for the creation of a national department of education and a uniform course of study. Problems that had been the concern of local and state officials, such as rural education, preparation and compensation of teachers, immigrant education, adult illiteracy, and compulsory attendance, should be addressed on a nationwide scale by national organizations of educators. Above all, the schools should train all American children, and immigrants as well, to be good citizens.

Bradford urged schools across the nation to adopt a modified curriculum to meet these challenges. Citizenship and American ideals, she believed, could be taught in many subject areas as well as through community service. The teaching of history and geography should demonstrate the essential differences between the "military minded nations" and "those peoples who believe in individual freedom and the greatest good to the greatest number." In these courses the "moral issues of the war should be stressed." Even in the teaching of English, "genuine patriotism" could be evoked "by showing the growth of constitutional liberty as evidenced in the growth of the English language and supremely in English literature." Vocational education should be devoted to practical and immediate service, such as Red Cross work and nursing. Students should also be taught the value of temperance for "straight thinking" and conservation.[5]

As state superintendent of Colorado schools, Mary Bradford was in a position to implement many of her own recommendations, and the Colorado schools did become centers of Red Cross work, war bond campaigns, and Americanization programs. She disapproved of the teaching of German in the high schools and insisted that all instruction in the elementary schools should be in English. In a state with large numbers of immigrants and many Spanish-speaking citizens of Mexican descent, these directives had a profound impact. Like many other progressives caught up in the war fervor, Bradford equated culture with patriotism and assumed that uniformity of customs and language was the only sure guarantee of national unity. In a circular letter to all Colorado school districts Bradford recommended an especially insidious plan of Americanization that had been practiced in the Denver school system. Under this scheme children would instruct their parents at home in "American standards of living and in the use of the English tongue." The progress of the parents would be judged by the teacher during home visits, made "in friendly cooperative fashion," with the child receiving credits "when progress in the home is plainly visible."[6]

After her term as president of the NEA, Bradford remained active in that organization through the 1920s. She served as chair of several committees, including the Committee of One Hundred on Classroom Teachers' Problems in 1924. She was also a member of the World Federation of Education Associations and was elected to the Board of Directors of the federation in 1926. Upon her retirement as state superintendent in 1927, Mary Bradford largely withdrew from public life. She died on January 15, 1938, at her home in Denver. She was survived by one daughter, Adele Bradford Hatton, and a grandson, Bradford Hatton.

Although Mary C. C. Bradford was not an innovator in either women's suffrage or progressive education, she made a significant impact in both movements as a vigorous crusader and communicator. Energetic, articulate, and self-righteous, Mary Bradford fought on the front lines of the political process and the educational system. She went to the people, even visiting isolated mountain towns in the dead of winter, to organize Democratic party cells or to explain school consolidation to a suspicious community. She was not one of the people, however, but rather self-consciously viewed herself as a daughter of aristocrats working as a missionary among heathens whose sins included inefficiency and a lack of culture. She prided herself upon bringing rationality to the administration of schools in Colorado, and certainly, by the measure of the progressive reform movement, she was a very successful reformer indeed.

NOTES

1. The earliest biographical information on Bradford (*Woman of the Century*, Frances E. Willard and Mary A. Livermore, eds., [New York: Mast, Crowell, and Kirk-

patrick, 1893]) gives her birthdate as August 10, 1856, and states that she had been married at the age of nineteen. Later biographical statements give Bradford's birthdate as 1860 (*The National Cyclopaedia of American Biography*, 1927, B, 207) or 1862 (Denver *Post*, January 15, 1938). Her husband's obituaries indicate that the couple was married in 1876 (Denver *Times*, December 26, 1901; Denver *Republican*, December 26, 1901), which gives credibility to the earlier date of her birth.

2. Mary C. C. Bradford, "Equal Suffrage in Colorado from 1893 to 1908," 1908, pamphlet file, Western Historical Collection, Norlin Library, University of Colorado Libraries, Boulder.

3. Minutes, July 19, 1916, Colorado Federation of Jane Jefferson Clubs Collection, Colorado Historical Society, Denver.

4. *Addresses and Proceedings of the 56th Annual Meeting of the National Education Association, Pittsburgh, Pennsylvania, July 29–July 6, 1918* 56 (1918): 36.

5. Mary C. C. Bradford, "War-Modified Education," "Suggestions for Training for Citizenship," and "The Value of Scientific Temperance Teaching in the Public Schools," bulletins for teachers, 1918, State Superintendent of Public Instruction, Box #50125, Department of Education Records, Colorado State Archives, Denver, Colorado.

6. Mary C. C. Bradford, "Suggestions for Training For Citizenship."

WORKS BY MARY CARROLL CRAIG BRADFORD

"Equal Suffrage in Colorado from 1893 to 1908." N.p., 1908. Pamphlet File, Western History Collection, University of Colorado Libraries, Boulder.
Correspondence, State Superintendent of Education, 1913–1920, 1923–1926, Department of Education Records, Colorado State Archives, Denver.
Biennial Reports of the State Superintendent of Public Instruction. Denver: Colorado Department of Public Instruction, 1914, 1916, 1918, 1920, 1924, 1926.
History and Chronology of the Colorado State Federation of Women's Clubs, 1895–1932. Denver: Colorado Federation of Women's Clubs, 1932.
Colorado Federation of Jane Jefferson Clubs Collection, Colorado Historical Society, Denver.

WORKS ABOUT MARY CARROLL CRAIG BRADFORD

Baker, James H., and LeRoy R. Hafen. *History of Colorado.* Denver: Linderman, 1927.
Bluemel, Elinor. *One Hundred Years of Colorado Women.* Denver: Colorado Imprints, 1973.
Brown, Joseph G. *The History of Equal Suffrage in Colorado, 1868–1898.* Denver: Colorado Equal Suffrage Association, 1898.
National Cyclopedia of American Biography. New York: James T. White, 1927.
Ohles, John F., ed. *Biographical Dictionary of American Educators.* Westport, CT: Greenwood Press, 1978.
Semple, James A. *Representative Women of Colorado.* Denver: n.p., 1911.
Willard, Frances E., and Mary A. Livermore, eds., *Woman of the Century.* New York: Mast, Crowell, and Kirkpatrick, 1893.

Sophonisba Breckinridge

John L. Rury

Sophonisba Breckinridge (1866–1948) was among the founders of the field of professional social work and a leading social work educator in the opening decades of the twentieth century. Her life was filled with many accomplishments, but her numerous academic and professional achievements grew out of a commitment to social justice and service to society that was rooted in her childhood experiences. Like other prominent women of her time, she did not have clearly defined opportunities for a professional career. Rather, Sophonisba Breckinridge was compelled to help create her own profession. In doing this she made a lasting contribution to the emerging urban civilization that took form in the decades following 1900.

Sophonisba Breckinridge was born into a prominent Kentucky family in 1866, immediately following the Civil War. Her great-grandfather, John Breckinridge, had been a senator and attorney general of the United States under Jefferson. Her father, William Campbell Preston Breckinridge, was a prominent lawyer who had been a colonel in the Confederate army and later served for a time in Congress. Unlike other leading southern men at this time, William Breckinridge was a supporter of women's education. He was a liberal who endorsed greater rights for blacks and other social reform causes, within limits, and encouraged his children to sustain the family's tradition of involvement in social and political affairs. "This name has been connected with good intellectual work for some generations," he wrote Sophonisba in 1902; "you must preserve this connection for the next generation." This was an admonition that she evidently took quite seriously (although, because Sophonisba never married, she did not "preserve" this family tradition in quite the way her father may have preferred).

One measure of William Breckinridge's commitment to women's education was his willingness to send "Nisba," as she was known to family and friends, to college at Wellesley, then a newly established women's school dedicated to the principle of high quality instruction in the liberal arts. Founded by Henry Durand in 1875, Wellesley was one of a handful of small colleges dedicated to giving young women an education essentially similar to that given men. Unlike their counterparts in the South, students at Wellesley studied classical languages and the sciences and shared quarters with classmates from across the country. While a student there, Nisba reportedly excelled at mathematics. When she graduated in 1888, Breckinridge had received an exceptional education which prepared her well for the challenges that lay ahead.

Like many of the college-educated women of her generation, Sophonisba Breckinridge never married. For middle-and upper-class women, however, there were few clear-cut professional careers to pursue, and Breckinridge went through a difficult series of transitions before she entered upon her life's work in social work and education. As was typical of young, unmarried, women college graduates at the time, she became a teacher, teaching mathematics in school for several years in Washington, D.C., while her father was in Congress. When he returned to Kentucky in 1894, she did so too, partly to help maintain the household (her mother had died in 1892) but also to study law in her father's office. This was a troubled time for her, as she sought to gain entry to a male-dominated profession against the wishes of her family. But she would not be dissuaded, and later that year she became the first woman to successfully complete the Kentucky bar examination. The South was not ready for female lawyers, however, and Breckinridge encountered great difficulty in getting a law practice established in Kentucky. Before long she was quite discouraged.

A turning point in Breckinridge's life came shortly after this, when a former Wellesley classmate invited her to live in a suburb of Chicago. Upon arriving, Breckinridge became secretary to Marion Talbot, dean of women at the University of Chicago. Here she found herself at yet another recently established institution of higher education; but under the leadership of William Rainy Harper, this one was dedicated to superior achievement in the areas of graduate study and research. Established in 1892 with a large endowment from John D. Rockefeller, the University of Chicago was a source of considerable innovation in higher education at this time. Harper had recruited an outstanding faculty, a significant number of whom were supportive of advanced graduate training for women. In persuading Talbot to come to Chicago, moreover, Harper had made a commitment to educating women at the new institution. Once again, Breckinridge found herself in a highly stimulating educational environment.

She wasted little time taking advantage of it. With Talbot's support, Breckinridge won a fellowship in political science and began a program of graduate studies. In 1901 she became the first woman to receive a Ph.D. in political science and economics, and she immediately enrolled in the university's newly established law school, graduating three years later with a J.D. degree. In 1902 she became assistant dean of women, helping Talbot with her duties as an advocate for women at the university. Two years later, after finishing her law studies, Breckinridge joined the faculty of the university in Marion Talbot's newly created Department of Household Administration, where she taught courses in economic and legal issues associated with family life. Like other talented women scholars of her day, Breckinridge was able to find employment in higher education only in the field of home economics. Fortunately, under Talbot's leadership, her department permitted a great deal of individual initiative in selecting topics for research and teaching. Chicago provided a most stimulating setting for her interest in issues of social and economic justice. By 1906, at the age of forty, she was becoming established in a new career of scholarship, teaching, and social activism.

Over the next decade Breckinridge plunged headlong into a wide variety of social and political reform activities, all undertaken while maintaining her positions at the University of Chicago. Shortly after finishing her studies, she became associated with Hull House and the circle of reformers who revolved around Jane Addams and her many reform campaigns. Living at Hull House, Breckinridge was exposed directly to the difficult living conditions in the immigrant communities on Chicago's west side. She was also a party to the constant array of activities and educational programs held at Hull House. This experience was to have a major influence on her subsequent career. She was a resident, on and off, of Hull House for the next twenty years (generally during her vacations from the university).

Like other progressive women of her generation, Breckinridge was also active in a host of political and economic reform organizations. Many of these concerned women's rights. As a scholar concerned with women's lives, she assisted the Women's Trade Union League, a reform organization dedicated to improving the condition of women workers. Using her legal training, she helped write legislative bills to protect women working in industry. She was also a participant on the picket lines during garment workers' strikes in 1911 and 1915. She was elected a vice president of the National Women's Suffrage Association in 1911, at the national convention in Louisville, representing southern women in yet another popular progressive reform. She served as president of the Women's City Club of Chicago and was active in the American Association of University Women. Along with Jane Addams, she became an avid supporter of the Progressive party in 1912 and campaigned to endorse its support of women's issues. She was among the founders of the Woman's Peace party in 1915, serving as treasurer, and later participated in the International Women's Conference held at The Hague.

Breckinridge was also active in a range of other progressive reform causes. She served as a city health inspector, wrote reports for the juvenile court, became involved in the campaign for child labor legislation, and joined both the National Association for the Advancement of Colored People (NAACP) and the Urban League soon after they were established. She was an important figure in establishing the Cook County Bureau of Public Welfare. Like other progressive reform figures of her day, she did not limit her interests to a single set of professional concerns. To her mind, social justice was a compelling vocation, no matter what the particular issue at hand.

One of Breckinridge's principal areas of interest, however, continued to be the deplorable living conditions endured by immigrants in the city's working-class neighborhoods. She was one of the founders (in 1908) of the Immigrant Protective League, an organization dedicated to upholding the legal, social, and economic rights of immigrants in Chicago. She spent a great deal of time examining tenement conditions, often reporting on them to city authorities. These investigations, extending for nearly two decades, became the source for a series of detailed studies. These books established her reputation as an authority on the problems of family life in urban working-class communities.

In 1907, just a few years after finishing law school, Breckinridge became director of research at the Chicago School of Civics and Philanthropy, an independent training institute for social workers that had been founded four years earlier. There she enlisted Edith Abbot, a friend from graduate school, to assist her in expanding the school's Department of Social Investigation. Supported by a generous grant from the Russell Sage Foundation, Breckinridge, Abbott, and their students conducted firsthand investigations of life on Chicago's west side that resulted in *The Delinquent Child and the Home* (1912), *Truancy and Non-Attendance in the Chicago Schools* (1917), and *New Homes for Old* (1921). These studies were characteristically detailed and filled with relevant statistics, but unlike academic sociological studies, they were aimed at the resolution of pressing social problems. These publications and others associated with the circle of reformers around Hull House helped to make Chicago a focal point of research and teaching about social problems.

The School of Civics and Philanthropy, however, led a somewhat precarious existence as an independent institution. Unattached to a degree-granting college or university, it lacked the comprehensive program of instruction that the emerging field of social work required. Breckinridge recognized this and began to work toward its affiliation with the University of Chicago, where she continued to hold administrative and academic appointments. In 1920 the school formally became the University of Chicago's Graduate School of Social Service Administration, the first professional school of social work to be affiliated with a university in the United States. Breckinridge became associate professor of Social Economy, with appointments in both the Graduate School of Social Service Administration and the Department of Household Administration.

Together with Edith Abbott, who became dean in 1924, Breckinridge worked to broaden the training given professional social workers. At the same time that the school emphasized technical training in a wide range of fields (from nutrition to counseling psychology), it also required students to have a broad familiarity with a host of social problems. Her many years in the field, observing social problems firsthand, had taught Breckinridge that important social problems did not develop in isolation. If professional social workers were to be effective, they had to be able to contend with a range of issues concurrently.

At the University of Chicago School of Social Service Administration students learned that both theory and practice were critical elements of their profession. Breckinridge knew the value of research and theory, having devoted so much time to writing in her own career. "Miss Breckinridge," a former student wrote, "never failed in her efforts to have the student relate the specific social work job to the broad concepts and implications of social work service."[1] But she also recognized the importance of direct experience. The assignment of practicums at the school, long a tradition at the old professional schools where students worked in the field, was maintained in the new university setting, and the Graduate School of Social Service Administration became a pioneer in making faculty appointments to supervise field experience. With this combination of demanding course work in a variety of disciplines and practical exposure and hands-on training in the field, Chicago's Graduate School of Social Service Administration set new standards for professional education in social work. It immediately became known as a leading institution in the field and continues to exert influence as a major center of social research and social work education today.

Breckinridge continued to write and conduct research in these years, much of it organized around the courses she taught in the new college. Of particular significance was her compilation of case records for use in classes. Understanding the importance of the case method in law schools, she recognized its value to social work education as well. She developed a distinctive method of teaching with cases to help students understand the complexity of problems social workers encounter and to develop the skills of analysis and decision making they would need as practitioners. Her book of case records, the first of its kind in the field, became a classic and remained a standard text for more than two decades.

Breckinridge's stature as a scholar and educator proceeded apace, both within the university and among her professional peers. In 1925 she was made professor of Social Economy, and in 1929, at age sixty-three, she became the Samuel Deutsch Professor of Public Welfare Administration. She was a founding editor of the *Social Service Review*, a leading professional journal in social work established in 1927, a role she continued to play until her death. In the thirties she was accorded a number of honors, perhaps the most telling of which was her election to the presidency of the American Association of Schools of Social Work in 1934, at a time of great ferment in the profession. In this capacity she helped oversee the establishment of standards for training an entire generation of social workers as they prepared to enter rapidly expanding state and federal social service programs.

In addition to her many scholarly and professional accomplishments,

Breckinridge was a compassionate and inspiring educator. Following her death, students from across the country volunteered accounts of her contributions to their education and their professional lives. One told a story about Breckinridge's secretly giving a poor student a ticket home for Christmas; others related accounts of how she invited them for dinner on holidays; yet others described how she taught them the importance of research and practical wisdom in the profession of social welfare. Students and colleagues alike spoke of her uncompromising standards of excellence, whether it was in matters of scholarship, teaching, or professional conduct.[2]

Breckinridge's interest in family issues continued to dominate her professional life throughout her career. Her interests in women and children were connected, she believed, with her concern with the family and the importance of creating stability in family relationships. In this regard she was not an advocate of radically changing women's roles. Women, she believed had vital functions to play within the family, roles that deserved more support from the rest of society than they typically received. She was a participant in all three White House conferences on children held between the two world wars and argued forcefully for the establishment of minimum wage standards to enable "the mother to specialize in the exercise of the maternal function." The family, she felt, was a vital building block of society and was subjected to great pressure in the face of social and economic deprivation.

Like most other progressives of her age, Breckinridge was a firm believer in the responsibility of the state for the amelioration of complex social problems. In her books and articles she often advocated a stronger role for the state in the care of children and other social problems. This was not a widely accepted view in the 1920s, but with the arrival of the New Deal after 1932, interest in her ideas underwent a revival. In the words of one associate, "She rejoiced when federal aid for relief was granted in 1932," and she worked "indefatigably" to send welfare workers across the country during the depression.[3] Enrollments in the Graduate School of Social Service Administration—and similar programs at other universities—grew dramatically at this time. With the development of welfare programs at the federal level, social work became a much better-established profession. The field that Breckinridge had given shape to had finally achieved a measure of maturity.

Although she retired from her faculty position in 1942, Breckinridge remained active until her death in 1948, at the age of eighty-two. Through her work as a researcher and writer, educator, and community activist, she had helped to establish the modern profession of social work. In doing this she had also advanced the status of women faculty members at Chicago and other universities. At the same time, she continually reminded her colleagues in higher education of their responsibilities to the larger community, particularly the poor and dispossessed. Altogether, it appears that she lived a life worthy of her father's admonition to carry on the family's good work. The institutions she helped to build and the professional field she helped to shape are a legacy to the generations that followed her.

NOTES

1. *Social Service Review* 22, no. 4 (December 1948): 422.
2. Ibid., 421–22.
3. Ibid., 421.

WORKS BY SOPHONISBA BRECKINRIDGE

The Modern Household (with Marion Talbot). Boston: Whitcomb and Barrows, 1910.
The Delinquent Child and the Home. New York: Charities Publication's Committee, 1912.
Truancy and Non-Attendance in the Chicago Schools (with Edith Abbott). Chicago: University of Chicago Press, 1917.
New Homes for Old. New York: Harper, 1921.
Family Welfare Work in a Metropolitan Community. Chicago: University of Chicago Press, 1924.
Public Welfare Administration. Chicago: University of Chicago Press, 1927.
Marriage and the Civic Rights of Women. Chicago: University of Chicago Press, 1931.
Women in the Twentieth Century. New York: McGraw-Hill, 1931.
The Family and the State. Chicago: University of Chicago Press, 1934.
The Tenements of Chicago (with Edith Abbott). Chicago: University of Chicago Press, 1936.
The Illinois Poor Law and Its Administration. Chicago: University of Chicago Press, 1939.

WORKS ABOUT SOPHONISBA BRECKINRIDGE

Lasch, Christopher. "Sophonisba Breckinridge." In Edward T. James, ed., *Notable American Women, 1607–1950: A Biographical Dictionary.* Cambridge: Belknap Press of Harvard University Press, 1971.
McCarthy, Kathleen D. *Noblesse Oblige: Charity and Cultural Philanthropy in Chicago, 1849–1929.* Chicago: University of Chicago Press, 1982.
Social Service Review (December 1948, March 1949, September 1949).
Solomon, Barbara Miller. *In the Company of Educated Women: A History of Women and Higher Education in America.* New Haven, CT: Yale University Press, 1985.

Nannie Helen Burroughs

Marcia G. Synnott

Nannie Helen Burroughs (1879–1961) was the founder of the National Training School for Women and Girls in Washington, D.C., and one of the leading Baptist women organizers, clubwomen, and social feminists of her generation. An inspiring orator and forceful personality, she can be compared with other black women founders of educational institutions, such as Mary McLeod Bethune, Charlotte Hawkins Brown, and Lucy Craft Laney. Although called the female Booker T. Washington by many of her contemporaries, she was far more militant on racial issues. Her outspoken feminism anticipated many of the arguments against male chauvinism that appeared during the 1960s and 1970s. To her biographer, Dr. Earl L. Harrison, Burroughs was "brilliant," "stubborn," and "gentle," as long as she was not "rubbed the wrong way."[1]

Nannie Helen Burroughs was born in 1879 in Orange, Virginia, the elder of two daughters of John Burroughs and Jennie (Poindexter) Burroughs. Following the Civil War her maternal and paternal grandfathers, born into slavery, became, respectively, a skilled carpenter and a landowning farmer. After her sister and father, who was a farmer and preacher, died, Burroughs moved with her mother, a cook, to Washington, D.C., in 1883. In later years, she supported her mother until her death. At the M Street High School, Burroughs organized the Harriet Beecher Stowe Literary Society and graduated with honors in business and domestic science in 1896. Racial discrimination prevented her from obtaining a position either in the district's public schools as a domestic science teaching assistant or in the federal civil service. Therefore, she moved, first to Philadelphia, where she served as associate editor of the Baptist *The Christian Banner*, and then to Louisville, Kentucky, where, from 1900 to 1909, she was bookkeeper and editorial secretary of the Foreign Mission Board of the National Baptist Convention. She studied business, receiving in 1907 an honorary A.M. from Eckstein-

Norton University. She also organized a Women's Industrial Club, which served inexpensive lunches to working women and provided evening classes in office and domestic skills; it developed into a vocational and trade school for African-American women.

God was an everyday reality to Burroughs and the Baptist religion was the central core of her life. At the 1900 meeting of the National Baptist Convention (NBC) in Richmond, Burroughs helped found the Women's Convention Auxiliary and traveled extensively as its corresponding secretary from 1900 to 1939. The convention became "the largest body of Negro Christian women in the world," despite the efforts of NBC officers to replace it with a Woman's Home and Foreign Mission Board. Addressing the First Baptist World Alliance meeting in London in 1905 on "Women's Part in the World's Work," Burroughs subsequently proposed, at the September 1906 Women's Convention Auxiliary meeting, that a National Woman's Day for the churches be observed on the fourth Sunday in July. It was inaugurated in 1907 to raise money for foreign missions, and she used the occasion to write speeches and to encourage other women to develop public speaking and leadership skills. To provide black women with educational and missionary materials, so that they could become church and civic leaders, Burroughs, a columnist for the *Afro-American* and the *Pittsburgh Courier*, also launched and edited *The Worker* in 1912. Its circulation topped 100,000 after it was relaunched in 1934, with the assistance of Mrs. Una Roberts Lawrence and the Women's Missionary Union.[2]

At the 1901 Women's Convention Auxiliary Meeting, Burroughs introduced the idea of a National Training School for Women and Girls, offering both an academic and an industrial education. A site committee was appointed in 1904, consisting of three ministers of the NBC, including President E. C. Morris and three representatives of the Women's Convention Auxiliary, Mrs. S. Willie Layten, Mrs. Julia M. Layten, and Burroughs. Before the September 1907 meeting of the NBC in Washington, D.C., Burroughs found a suitable six-acre lot with an eight-room house, fruit trees, a well, a stable, and a barn on a gullied hill in Lincoln Heights, at 50th and H streets, Northeast. The certificate of the title, taken in the names of Burroughs and two other committee members, omitted the word "Baptist," since the school was "non-sectarian," admitting students of all religious faiths, "including Roman Catholics." But its students should live "a consistent Christian life and actively participate in denominational and school religious activities."[3]

Dedicated on September 14, 1907, the National Training School for Women and Girls, Inc. (NTS) did not open until October 19, 1909, after Burroughs, who raised most of the money, paid off the balance of the $6,000 purchase price, plus a $500 lawyer's fee. Self-described as "the first united effort of the part of Colored women to found an institution for the mental, moral, and spiritual culture of their sex," the school adopted as its motto:

"We specialize in the wholly impossible." Burroughs served as its first president until her death and lived on campus. She never married but was close to Alice Smith, an NTS student who later became her assistant. Burroughs believed that separate schooling for girls in their adolescent years provided the best training for "the most effective service in slum, social settlement, reformatory and missionary work." Her creed was "the three Bs—the Bible, the bath, and the broom: clean life, clean body, clean house."[4]

For admission, students had to be at least fifteen years of age and ready for sixth grade, pass English and mathematics entrance examinations, be rated satisfactory in "deportment," and submit a certificate indicating healthy eyes and teeth. Much like conservative preparatory schools, NTS imposed strict discipline, requiring every student to bring a Bible, purchase a songbook, and attend the mandatory daily chapel, Sunday school, and Sunday vespers. Students were chaperoned off campus and their correspondence and packages were inspected. Since there were no scholarship funds, students relied on "self-help" and worked during vacations. The school employed a small number of students in the laundry year-round and additional students during the summer in the garden and other campus jobs. Expenses for room, board, and tuition averaged $44.00 for the first month and then about $17.50 every four weeks thereafter.

NTS offered both literary and vocational courses, assigning standard texts for its first and second preparatory and junior normal students (grades 6–8), its four classes of secondary normal students, and its advanced teachers' preparatory program. Vocational courses were offered in missionary training and social service, practical nursing, domestic science and home economics, plain sewing, dressmaking and tailoring, millinery, music, printing, public speaking, beauty culture, gardening, and laundering. Prizes were awarded to the best student both in academic subjects like Latin and in vocational skills like domestic science. NTS students were trained to serve both at home and abroad, as practical nurses in the United States to teach proper hygiene, sanitation, and disease prevention to migrants from rural areas to urban centers and as Baptist missionaries in Africa and other foreign areas.

Believing that "cooking and homemaking" were "man's greatest need and basic civilizer" and that well-trained homemakers were "household engineers," Burroughs professionalized domestic service, thereby preparing students for both the successful management of their own homes and a vocation. Recognizing existing job market realities for African Americans, the school touted class and race-defined jobs, for example, beauty culture, "a splendid course adapted to meet the requirements of ladies' maids." Laundering, then in the process of commercialization, was seen as a new employment opportunity.[5]

The school emphasized "the full development of true womanhood," adhering to the nineteenth-century Victorian ideal that women should be pious, pure, and domestic. But rather than teaching submission, the students were exhorted to develop a "purposeful—determined—aggressive spirit." Indeed, NTS endeavored "to build the fibre of a sturdy, moral, industrious and intellectual woman" and prepare her for leadership "by emphasizing honor, orderliness, precision, promptness, courage." Burroughs also instilled racial pride by requiring all students to take one course in African-American history and culture. She was active in the National Association for the Advancement of Colored People and worked with other clubwomen to memorialize Frederick Douglass's Anacostia home. A life member of the Association for the Study of Negro Life and History, she presented a paper in 1927 on "The Social Value of Negro History," sharing the platform with scholar Carter Godwin Woodson, founder of the *Journal of Negro History*.[6]

Opening with 5 students and 8 assistants, NTS's enrollment rose to 31 students during its first year and ultimately to 150 students. By 1934, NTS had trained over 2,000 girls and women. Its physical plant expanded to eight buildings: Domestic Science Hall; Walker Hall, which had dormitories and classrooms (named for Mrs. Maggie L. Walker, a Richmond banker and member of the school's investment and advisory board); Pioneer Hall (named for outstanding African Americans); Burdette Home for domestic science and household management classes; Whitfield Hall (named for NTS field secretary and fund-raiser Mrs. Ella Ewell Whitfield); the Laundry Building, which also housed the printery and business classroom; Community Service Center with a library of over 6,000 books and the Community Shop; and Sunlight Laundry, a public laundry. Burroughs also solicited funds for a $25,000 Trades Hall (1928), raising some money by a benefit concert at which the Hampton Normal and Agricultural Institute choir performed before an audience that included President and Mrs. Calvin Coolidge. White-supported organizations, such as the Woman's Missionary Union of the Southern Baptist Convention, the American Baptist Home Missionary Society, the Emmeline Cushing Estate, and the Phelps- Stokes and Slater funds, also made contributions to the National Training School.

Keenly aware of the necessity of keeping in close contact with the mass of African Americans and of developing self-help among them, Burroughs used her school as a center for community organizations. In 1923, the International Council of Women of the Darker Races held its annual convention at the NTS. During the Great Depression, Burroughs established the self-help Cooperative Industries, Inc., which opened a medical clinic and convenience store and had facilities for farming, canning, and hairdressing. She also developed plans for a children's department to instruct girls eight to twelve years of age while their mothers were working.

Beginning in 1915, the National Training School became embroiled in a lengthy controversy over its management and financial control, as a result of the National Baptist Convention's own lack of a convention-approved charter on file. After the latter legally became the National Baptist Convention of the United States of America, Inc. (NBC, Inc.) in September 1920, assertive Texans, notably, President Lacy K. Williams, assumed leadership. Reviewing all charters, they insisted that all boards were dependent entities; for example, that the Women's Convention was nothing more than an auxiliary society. NTS's charter was judged "wholly defective," because it failed "to put the school under the management and control" of either the Women's Convention Auxiliary, from which it received support, or the National Baptist Convention, Inc., which claimed it always possessed the right "to regulate its management." Burroughs insisted, however, that "full control of the institution" rested with the self-perpetuating Board of Trustees, consisting of eighty "persons of good standing in regular Baptist churches," a majority of whom were women. She personally never claimed title to the school: "This is God's Hill," given to her "and to the Negro Baptist Women of America" for the world's black women. Burroughs also questioned the NBC, Inc.'s financial ability to support the NTS, given the former's heavy debt on a publishing plant. In 1927, NTS amended its charter, changing its name to the National Seminary and Trades School for Girls and reduced the number of trustees from eighty to twenty-three. Bylaw Nine, which was incorporated in the charter, vested property rights in the Women's Convention Auxiliary.[7]

The controversy subsided for a time, partly because financial problems closed NTS from about 1935 to 1938. Then, on June 22, 1938, at Tuskegee Institute, NBC, Inc.'s Board of Directors, resenting Burroughs's continuing drift away from its control, resolved to "withdraw all connections, allegiance, and support from the said training school at Washington, D.C.," and recommended that the Women's Convention Auxiliary do likewise. Support should henceforth be given to the NBC, Inc.'s new training school in Nashville, built by southern white Baptists for black Baptists and affiliated with the American Baptist Theological Seminary. Arriving late and ill, Burroughs was unable to defend the school and herself until NBC, Inc.'s annual meeting in September 1938. NTS was "the life work *of* women *by* women and *for* women," she asserted, pointing out that the NBC, Inc. was a "man's organization." Having "worked, sacrificed, stood all sorts of misrepresentations and downright libel," she would deed NTS to the Women's Convention Auxiliary, but NBC, Inc.'s male officials would not permit it to incorporate and thus hold title.[8]

In November 1938, some 250 friends and trustees from twenty-one states attended a conference at NTS, which approved the trustees' votes to change its name to the National Trade and Professional School for Women and Girls, Inc.; to have a twenty-four-member board; and to launch a national fund-raising campaign. Burroughs received support from friend and former teacher Mary Church Terrell. But in 1939, Burroughs was not reelected to the Board of Directors of the Women's Convention Auxiliary and hence could not effectively continue as its corresponding secretary, although the convention issued a statement pledging "unstinted support" to NTS and praised her work in missions and Christian education, in launching *The Worker*, in building the Women's Convention program, and in interracial cooperation. Following a change of leadership, the NBC, Inc. formally endorsed the NTS in 1947. Burroughs was elected president of the Women's Convention Auxiliary in 1949 and served until her death; from 1950 to 1955, she was a member-at-large of its Executive Committee. In 1953, inadequate income and physical plant forced NTS to suspend operation temporarily; and in 1956, it ceased academic-year instruction, offering only summer classes. The site had expanded to thirteen acres and had nine buildings, including a $200,000 dormitory (1956) and a memorial chapel (1960).⁹

Burroughs, who attended the Nineteenth Street Baptist Church in Washington, D.C., and supported the social gospel program of the Reverend Walter Henderson Brooks, was also active in several civic and political organizations. She chaired the Citizenship Department of the National Association of Colored Women (NACW), which in 1896 had united the three largest federations and many local clubs into the first national black organization. She founded, and was president of, the National Association of Wage Earners, serving with Mary McLeod Bethune and Maggie Lena Walker. President of the National League of Republican Colored Women, Burroughs supported that party's candidates in 1928 and 1932 and was appointed by President Herbert Hoover to a committee on Negro housing at the 1932 White House conference.

With Jessie Daniel Ames, founder of the Association of Southern Women for the Prevention of Lynching and director of Woman's Work for the Commission on Interracial Cooperation (CIC), Burroughs sought ways of helping black women organize citizenship groups for membership in the National League of Women Voters. She thought that southern white women, motivated "by an overpowering sense of everyday duty, and a new sense of the value and dignity of human personality," held "the key to the solution of the race problem in Dixie," because their "word is law and gospel to southern white men." As chair of NACW's Anti-Lynching Committee, charter member of the Anti-Lynching Crusaders, and member of CIC's Women's Division, Burroughs repeatedly denounced lynching, pointing to five major reasons "Why America Has Gone Lynch Mad":

1. National attitude of contempt for the Negro.
2. Nullification of the Fifteenth Amendment.
3. Emboldened by forty-five years of success of the lynching industry.
4. National silence.
5. In answer to the call of the blood bequeathed to their children, by two generations of lynchers.

The federal government must enforce the Fifteenth Amendment, she concluded, to prevent "bloodthirsty mobs" from wreaking "vengeance upon the defenseless."[10]

Impatient with acquiescent blacks, Burroughs told the CityWide Young People's Forum in Baltimore to "chloroform your 'Uncle Toms.' Negroes like that went out of style 70 years ago. They are relics and good for museums." She reiterated a consistent theme, urging her audience to "forget your color" and "stop apologizing for not being white and rank your race." Blacks must put aside individualism and materialism in order to participate in a great "crusade" for the African-American race. Another key theme was that black women, often treated as "slaves and servants" by Negro men, should be "glorified" because of their contributions to the "church, home, school, business."[11] But unlike white activists, Burroughs, who promoted the virtues of Victorian America, did not define feminism as a response to black male exploitation.

She was honored by an LL.D. degree in 1944 from Shaw University, in Raleigh, North Carolina, and by the Washington Chapter of the Lincoln University Alumni Association at its annual Founders Day Banquet in 1958. Burroughs, who had arthritis, diabetes, and heart disease, died of a stroke at Georgetown University Hospital in Washington, D.C., in 1961 and was interred in Lincoln Memorial Cemetery in Suitland, Maryland. In 1964, the school was renamed in her honor; and in 1971 a million-dollar administration-classroom building opened for elementary school-age pupils. In 1975, district mayor Walter E. Washington designated May 10 as Nannie Helen Burroughs Day. The Nannie Helen Burroughs School, Inc., offers an academic curriculum emphasizing basic skills and technology, "in a Christian atmosphere" to over 150 girls and boys in kindergarten through the sixth grade; it hopes to add seventh and eighth grades in the future. The Progressive National Baptist Convention, which broke away from the NBC, Inc., has moved its headquarters into the former Trades Building and appoints ten of the trustees, while the school appoints five. On the recommendation of the Women's History Landmark Project, the school was designated in 1991 as a National Historic Landmark.[12]

NOTES

1. "Nannie Helen Burroughs, Educator, Builder, Writer and Orator of National and International Renown," *National Baptist Voice* (March 19, 1927): 1, 12; Evelyn Brooks Barnett, "Nannie Helen Burroughs and the Education of Black Women," in Sharon Harley and Rosalyn Terborg-Penn, eds., *The Afro-American Woman* (Port Washington, NY: Kennikat Press, 1978), 107, 102; Casper LeRoy Jordan, "Nannie Helen Burroughs," in Jessie Carney Smith, ed., *Notable Black American Women* (Detroit, MI: Gale Research, 1992), 140, 138; Earl L. Harrison, *The Dream*

and the Dreamer (Washington, DC: Nannie H. Burroughs Literature Foundation, 1956), 77.

2. *Circular of Information for the Seventeenth Annual Session of the National Training School for Women and Girls Incorporated. 1925–1926*, 9, Nannie H. Burroughs Papers, Container #310 Miscellany, File National Trade and Professional School Brochures and Catalogs, Library of Congress; Harrison, 8–10, 15–26, 34, 36–37; Nannie H. Burroughs, "Who Started Woman's Day in Our Churches?" *Think on These Things* (Washington, DC: Nannie H. Burroughs Publications, 1982), 85–93.

3. Harrison, 15, 23.

4. Harrison, 13, 9; Nannie Helen Burroughs School, Inc. brochure, 1991.

5. Nannie H. Burroughs, "Negro Women and Their Homes," *Think on These Things*, 104–7; *Circular of the National Training School, 1925–1926*, 45, 41, 46.

6. *Circular of the National Training School. 1925–1926*, 13, 15.

7. Harrison, 56, 38–40, 48, 55–57; *Circular of the National Training School. 1925–1926*, 7, 9; "Nannie H. Burroughs Discusses the Training School Situation," *The New York Age* (January 14, 1928): 4, 9; Minutes of the Board of Trustees of the National Seminary and Trades School for Girls, June 2, 1927, Nannie Helen Burroughs Papers, Library of Congress, Container #310 National Trade and Professional School Controversy over the Status of the National Training School, file 1 of 4.

8. Quoted in Harrison, 62, 59, 64; "Baptist Convention Hardly Will Re-Open Nat'l Training School," *The St. Louis Argus*, August 5, 1938, 9; Statement made by Miss Burroughs at the close of her annual report to woman's convention at St. Louis, September 8, 1938; "Nannie Burroughs Answers Charges and Malicious Falsehoods Reported, Printed and Circulated About the National Training School," [third printing, 1938], 4–5, Burroughs Papers, Container #310, file 3 National Trade and Professional School Controversy over the Status of the National Training School.

9. Burroughs Papers: Minutes of the conference held November 16 and 17, 1938, at the National Training School for Women and Girls, Lincoln Heights, Washington, D.C.; "An Account of My Stewardship to the Trustees of the National Trade and Professional School, Inc.," file 3; "A Statement of Confidence in Nannie H. Burroughs," September 1, 1939, file 1, Container #310; "Nannie Burroughs to Be Last President of NBC's Women's Convention; Parent Body to Take Over," September 21, 1960, Container #308, file National Baptist Convention Miscellany; Harrison, 66–67, 92–93.

10. Nannie H. Burroughs, "The Dawn of a Day in Dixie," *Think on These Things*, 113, 112–18; "Nannie Burroughs Tells 'Why America Has Gone Lynch Mad,' " *Pittsburgh Courier*, December 23, 1933, 2d Section, 2.

11. " 'Unload Uncle Toms,' Says Nannie Burroughs," *Pittsburgh Courier*, December 23, 1933, 2d Section, 3.

12. Obituary, *Washington Post*, May 21, 1961, B6, and May 22, 1961, B8; Nannie Helen Burroughs School, Inc., brochure, 1991; Mrs. Mattie A. Robinson, president of the Burroughs School, interview, May 14, 1992.

WORKS BY NANNIE HELEN BURROUGHS

The papers of Nannie Helen Burroughs, consisting of correspondence, reports, student and financial records, newspaper clippings, and other memorabilia given to the

Library of Congress by Dr. Aurelia R. Downey and the Nannie Helen Burroughs School, Inc., in 1976 and 1977, are arranged in 354 containers, with a finding aid. They document her career and the history of the National Training School for Women and Girls, Inc., later the National Trade and Professional School for Women and Girls.

The Slabtown District Convention: A Comedy in One Act. 2d ed. Louisville, KY: s.n., n.d.; 7th ed. Washington, DC: s.n., [c. 1926]; 17th ed. Washington, DC: s.n., [1961]; Cover Title, 17th ed.: *The Slabtown District Convention: The Most Popular Church Play in the Country: A Comedy in One Act, Full of Wit, Good Sense, Practical Lessons.*

"Declaration of 1776 Is Cause of Harlem Riot," *The Afro-American* (Baltimore), April 13, 1935.

Words Of Life and Light. Washington, DC: Nannie H. Burroughs Publications, 1949.

Think on These Things. Washington, DC: Nannie H. Burroughs Publications, 1982.

WORKS ABOUT NANNIE HELEN BURROUGHS

Barnett (Higginbotham), Evelyn Brooks. "Nannie Burroughs and the Education of Black Women." In Sharon Harley and Rosalyn Terborg-Penn, eds., *The Afro-American Woman: Struggles and Images*, 97–108. Port Washington, NY: Kennikat Press, 1978.

Harrison, Earl L. *The Dream and the Dreamer*. Washington, DC: Nannie H. Burroughs Literature Foundation, 1956. Reprint ed., 1972.

Hine, Darlene Clark. *Black Women in America: An Historical Encyclopedia*. Vol. I, A-L. Brooklyn, NY: Carlson, 1993. S.v. "Nannie Helen Burroughs," by Evelyn Brooks Higginbotham.

Logan, Rayford W., and Michael R. Winston, eds. *Dictionary of American Negro Biography*. New York: W. W. Norton, 1982. S.v. "Nannie Burroughs," by Evelyn Brooks Higginbotham.

"Nannie Helen Burroughs Papers." *Quarterly Journal of the Library of Congress* 34 (October 1977): 356–60.

"The National Training School for Girls Appeals for Funds." In Gerda Lerner, ed., *Black Women in White America: A Documentary History*, 132–34. New York: Vintage Books, 1973.

Sicherman, Barbara, and Carol Hurd Green, eds. *Notable American Women: The Modern Period*. Cambridge: Belknap Press of Harvard University Press, 1980. S.v. "Nannie Helen Burroughs," by Juanita Fletcher.

Smith, Jessie Carney, ed. *Notable Black American Women*. Detroit: Gale Research, 1992. S.v. "Nannie Helen Burroughs," by Casper LeRoy Jordan.

Mother Joseph Butler

Tracy Mitrano

Mother Joseph Butler (1860–1940), founder of Marymount Colleges in New York and California, overseas programs in Paris and Rome, established more educational institutions in the United States and extension programs abroad than any other female educator. Superior general of her congregation, the Sisters of the Sacred Heart of Mary, Mother Butler also ranked among the highest reaches of the Roman Catholic church in the first half of the twentieth century. Religious leader, administrator, and institutional builder, Mother Joseph Butler stands as a cornerstone of American Catholic women's higher education in the first half of the twentieth century.

Mother Joseph Butler was born Johanna Butler in Kilkenny, Ireland, July 22, 1860. Raised in a happy family but in a country torn by political conquest and famine, Johanna left Ireland at age sixteen to become a postulant in a French order, the Congregation of the Sacred Heart of Mary. If Katherine Burton's hagiographic account of Mother Butler can be trusted for details, Johanna Butler braved homesickness and language barriers to become a favored postulant. She professed final vows after the customary five years and was sent to Portugal to teach. Political complications eventually forced a departure of her order there, and, after a brief stop in France, Mother Butler moved to America as a community superior for a new mission in Sag Harbor, Brooklyn.

A unique and bounteous financial gift from a rags-to-riches cousin, James Butler, complemented Mother Butler's personal courage and budding prowess for institutional development. Owner of a grocery store chain, James Butler brought Mother Butler to the attention of Archbishop Farley of New York in 1906. The cousin promised Mother Butler to establish a school for girls in memory of his recently deceased wife. In turn, Archbishop Farley promised his personal protection for Mother Butler on two conditions. First, he asked that she move her community out of the Brooklyn diocese and into his own. Second, he insisted that Mother Butler not relocate in Manhattan, at that time a beehive of competition among orders hoping to establish colleges for women. Agreeing to his conditions, Mother Butler transplanted her community in 1907 to the old Reynard Estate in Tarrytown-upon-the-Hudson. The academy that she opened a year later became the institutional base of the college. Mother Butler opened Marymount College in the fall of 1919.

Because Roman Catholic nuns self-consciously subsumed their individual identity into religion, Mother Butler's accomplishments can be understood only within the context of the institutional development of her order and of the college. Indeed, the order complemented the college. International in character (in contrast to diocesan orders), the Sisters of the Sacred Heart of Mary became an important cornerstone for innovative programs and growth of the college. In 1923 Mother Butler, with her assistant, Mother Gerard Phelan, established a Marymount overseas program in Paris; subsequent programs opened in Rome and London. Also in 1923, Mother Butler oversaw the establishment of a Manhattan extension of the Tarrytown campus, followed by the establishment of Marymount in Los Angeles in 1928 and in Santa Barbara in 1938.

Mother Butler's eye for progress encompassed micromanagement of her schools as well. In the year that Santa Barbara opened, Mother Butler initiated a campaign to improve the academic program at the Tarrytown campus. At its founding in 1919, the curriculum of Marymount College differed little from the academy, which closely resembled other elite female academies of its kind. The students, most of whom sported Irish surnames, wore the traditional plaid, jumper uniforms of Catholic schools and followed a curriculum for young women that dated back almost three centuries to the beginning of convent school education. Dominated by religious instruction, this curriculum included some literature, history, foreign language (French), arithmetic, penmanship, and refinements (choral singing and music lessons). Students wrote poetry and prose for a literary journal, sponsored an extra-curricular religious group (Children of Mary), and attended religious rituals and events such as daily prayers and the annual May Day festival. Religion, academics, and extracurricular activities blended into a seamless scholastic and social environment.

Over the course of the first twenty years of the college, little in the curriculum changed. In 1935 the course catalog reveals altogether only about fifty courses. Religion dominated the selections. Administrators required each student to take at least one course in religion every semester; the total amounted to a minor in religion no matter what any individual's major course of study. The Roman Catholic religious culture also influenced secular studies. For example, in both literature and history, course offerings clustered around the ancient and medieval eras. There was little recognition of the modern period and no mention of modern thinkers such as Voltaire, Kant, Hegel, Marx, Weber, or Freud.

Academic weaknesses measured by mainstream standards in the early curricula of Catholic women's colleges abounded. The humanities and foreign languages (Latin, Greek, French, and German, especially) greatly outnumbered all other categories of course work. Administrators grossly neglected the hard sciences. For example, Marymount offered only five chemistry courses: General, Quantitative, Qualitative, Organic, and Chemistry of Foods—the last more a cross between home economics and nutrition than chemistry. Four physics courses—Elemental, Mechanical, Electricity, and Acoustics—hardly represented contemporary academic physics. Chemistry and physics at least outnumbered the extremely meager selection in biology, which consisted of only General and Botany. The course guide did not recognize the social sciences as a curricular category. Only two courses in psychology existed, Lower, which, like Botany, focused on plants, and Higher, which concentrated on "the human soul, unity, spirituality, and immortality."[1]

By the end of the 1930s religion still dominated requirements and influenced course material. A literature course, for example, focused on The Greater Catholic Poets Since Chaucer; a Social Psychology course stressed "the class spirit, schools, parties, individual sets, social progress and decay, reform movements, moral and Catholic ideals."[2] A large number of courses in a broader historical scope complemented course work emphasizing Catholic culture, however. Modern history appeared for the first time, as well as a number of courses in American history in particular. English literature included course work on Shakespeare, The English Novel, and a course covering the literature of every century from the sixteenth through the nineteenth. Administrators updated classes in chemistry and physics, for example, by replacing Chemistry of Foods with Physical Chemistry. The selections in biology quadrupled, and the college even offered a special Pre-Medical course of study. Social sciences had their own category, and new disciplines included economics and sociology. In total, these reforms became the basis of Marymount's accreditation with Middle States Association and its curriculum for the subsequent three decades.[3]

From its very insulated origins in the academy, social life expanded tremendously. Religious societies, such as Sodality for the Children of Mary, communicated regularly with the National Federation of Catholic College Societies (NFCCS), a nationwide organization of religious groups on Catholic college campuses (both male and female). This organization sponsored a series of other clubs, such as the mission societies, and activities such as the annual Snow (Christmas) and May Queen festivals, the St. Joseph's Day Holiday, and St. Patrick's Day Parades. A debating club and sporting activities encouraged intermural relations with other Catholic women's colleges.

Academic clubs (one for almost every discipline) and traditional student societies (such as Glee Club or Drama) resembled those of mainstream schools. However, Marymount, as in Catholic women's colleges generally, allowed religiously oriented groups and activities to take precedence over secular activities. In no mainstream coeducational or women's college would a reader of the school newspaper find a photograph of a group of students kneeling in front of a statue with the caption, "Students kneel in prayer before a statue of Our Lady in preparation for the Rosary Procession in Honor of Our Lady of Fatima."[4] The campus community more highly revered the president of Sodality, for example, than the president of the student council. No one was more honored than the May Queen (frequently the president of Sodality) as the model of mid-twentieth-century American Catholic womanhood.

Socially, Marymount catered specifically to the upper-middle classes of the American Catholic community. Students from the general New York metropolitan area predominated, but in the heyday of Marymount roughly one-third of the student body hailed from a wide range of states around the country. Marymount even became the occasional choice of Catholic students from Europe and Latin America. A wave of Italian students, beginning in the 1930s, joined a predominantly Irish student body, reenergizing Marymount with the upwardly mobile spirit that had originally informed the college. Judging by the number of students with Italian surnames who participated in extracurricular clubs and events, these students contributed prodigiously to the aggrandizement of social activities.

A dynamic, upwardly mobile constituency also helped to create an exciting and urbane social life. In addition to the plethora of extracurricular activities generated by so many student organizations, the college itself sponsored many daily field trips and annual travel weekends. Once every year the entire population of the school descended on Manhattan for excursions everywhere from Radio City Music Hall to the Pakistan House. The student newspaper, *The Cormont*, frequently reported smaller groups of students visiting the Metropolitan Museum of Art, the New York Stock Exchange, or Lincoln Center for an opera.[5] A 1953 yearbook description of tea dances summed up the social, but specifically Catholic, character of this Marymount event. "Of a semi-formal nature, these gatherings provide an opportunity for students to entertain their friends on campus, and are also the starting point of new friendships—blind dates are invited from such colleges as Yale, Fordham, Princeton, and Holy Cross."[6] Like Barnard, Smith, or Vassar, Marymount held its formal balls at fashionable and expensive Manhattan hotels such as the Plaza and Waldorf-Astoria.[7]

A 1949 alumnae survey speaks to the success of a college that sought both to educate and to socialize young Catholic women into the mid-twentieth-century American Catholic community. Nine graduates held doctorates (four of whom were nonreligious), and there were four medical doctors, five lawyers, one doctorate in musicology (listed separately from the other nine), and fifty-seven masters' of arts and sciences (only eleven of whom were religious). Altogether, 26.4 percent of responding graduates had attended some form of graduate school, only 17.5 percent of which were in teaching. This figure falls far below that of most other Catholic women's colleges and probably reflects the social nature of the Marymount experience. Commensurably, the marriage rate to college-educated husbands was high. Of the 69.1 percent of respondents who were married, 65.4 percent married men with bachelor's, or better, degrees.[8] The survey neglected to ask the religious background of alumnae's spouses, because the assumption was that they were Catholic. For a Marymount girl to marry outside the faith would be not merely to abridge religious beliefs but to run counter to the vast web of personal associations she had created in her college years.

Although precise statistics are not currently available, an informal review of "Alumnae Notes" over the subsequent two decades suggests that both professional and marriage trends continued in much the same fashion. There was, however, an expansion of professional choices as graduates branched out from a singular focus on teaching in the early years of the college to encompass wider occupational fields such as social work and business in the post–World War II period and thereafter. With a premedical program, Marymount graduated a large number of students who went on to obtain medical degrees. A considerable number of graduates finished law degrees, including the 1984 vice presidential nominee for the Democratic party, Geraldine Ferraro. Notable graduates in addition to her include the stage and screen star Rosalind Russell and Barbara Smith Eagleton, wife of senator and onetime vice presidential nominee Thomas Eagleton.[9] Somewhat more typical of a high-achieving graduate would be Mary Galloway James, 1941 graduate who went on to marry, have children, and work as a lawyer. In 1982 the administration awarded James the degree Doctor of Laws, *honorius causa*, noting her work with "minorities and the public interest at large, recognizing that intellectual gifts and education are most fittingly employed in the service of others."[10] In this salutation lies a good summary of the highest aspirations Marymount instilled in its graduating seniors: marriage, motherhood, and service to the community.

In April 1940, three months shy of her eightieth birthday, Mother Butler passed away at home in her community on the Marymount campus. As was customary for the obituaries of female religious at that time, no cause was cited. Equally customary for a woman of her position was the couching of her personal accomplishments in the context of the burgeoning American Catholic community. Be the conventions of religious life what they may, a talent for development rooted in an era of extraordinary expansion for the Catholic church contributed toward Mother Butler's success. Elected superior general of the Sisters of the Sacred Heart of Mary in 1926, Mother Butler was the first American-based nun to head the French-based order.

She was also one of few American Catholics (male or female) to enjoy audiences with the pope. Indeed, in power and prestige within the community she ranked above other women religious and on par (excepting the obvious gender differences) with many of her male contemporaries in the New York diocese, including Archbishops Farley and Spelman. The founder of a series of colleges, she contributed early to a concept of centralized bureaucracy of individual institutions that would greatly influence higher education, particularly in the state university systems, in the latter half of the twentieth century. Mother Butler pioneered the overseas collegiate program. The reforms she engineered in curriculum and social life of Catholic women's higher education drove to the heart of twentieth-century Catholic Americanization.

Behind the veil of this cloistered nun, ambition burned brightly. Combining the financial gifts of her cousin with strong personal instincts, Mother Butler rose to the top of her world as a Roman Catholic religious leader and female educator. As a Roman Catholic nun, she implicitly accepted the notion of service to one's community; as an immigrant she expertly channeled the quintessential immigrant's drive for upward mobility into education for women and the betterment of her community. The fruits of her struggles keep her memory alive. Because of the cultural limits imposed on female religious in the Roman Catholic tradition prior to the Second Vatican Council, historians have few primary documents by which to trace the details of her movements or the interior of her mind. To dwell on the lack of such documents misses the point of Mother Butler's own aspirations and values, however. The college bureaucratic structure she built reflected the organic view of social relations in which she self-consciously placed herself. Hierarchical and by degrees increasingly centralized, each piece of this world was always and most importantly connected to all others. Her greatest accomplishment should therefore be viewed not as the achievement of one specific office or even a particular institution but as the extraordinary vigor with which she exemplified the Catholic ideal. Mother Butler seamlessly blended an individual identity into that of her religious community. Her accomplishments were *its* accomplishments, and she probably would not want to be remembered in any other way.

NOTES

1. Marymount College (MC), *Marymount College Catalogue*, 1935.
2. MC, *Marymount College Catalogue*, 1940.
3. Ibid.
4. MC, *The Cormont*, October 16, 1953, 23, no. 3.
5. MC, *The Cormont*, March 13, 1953.
6. MC, *The Elan*, 1953.
7. Helen Lefkowitz Horowitz, *Campus Life. Undergraduate Cultures from the End*

of the Eighteenth Century to the Present (New York: Knopf, 1987); Barbara Solomon, *In the Company of Educated Women: A History of Women and Higher Education in America* (New Haven, CT: Yale University Press, 1985).

8. MC, Box, Alumnae, "Alumnae Survey, 1949."
9. MC, Box, Alumnae, "Notable Alumnae."
10. MC, Program for the celebration of the Seventy-fifth Jubilee.

WORKS ABOUT MOTHER JOSEPH BUTLER

Burton, Katherine. *Mother Butler of Marymount*. New York: Longman, 1944.
Mitrano, Tracy. "The Rise and Fall of Catholic Women's Higher Education in New York State, 1890–1985" University Microfilms, 1989.
———. "A Century of Catholic Women's Higher Education, 1890–1990," rev. manuscript.

Mary Steichen Calderone

Natalie A. Naylor

Mary Steichen Calderone (b. 1904), a physician and public health educator, was a crusader for birth control and sex education. She edited the
first comprehensive textbook on contraception and was a pioneer in establishing the field of human sexuality in the mid-1960s.

Born on July 1, 1904, in New York City, Mary Steichen Calderone was the
older of two daughters of Clara E. Smith and Edward J. Steichen. Her
mother was from Springfield, Missouri, and her father, who had been born
in Luxembourg, immigrated with his family at an early age to Hancock,
Michigan, and later moved to Milwaukee, Wisconsin. Mary was always very
close to her father, who was a painter and later a famous photographer. Her
mother had aspirations to be a singer, and the Steichens' home in France,
where Mary spent the first ten years of her life, was a center for artists and
poets.[1]

Mary Steichen first attended a village school in France when she was nine
years old, but she had been "reading voraciously" for some time. With the
outbreak of war in 1914, the family left France, but the Steichens' marriage
was breaking up, and Mary was "farmed out" to relatives and friends. She
attended school in Connecticut for a year before entering the Brearley
School in New York City. She later recalled that Ann Dunn, a Brearley
teacher, had a major influence on her writing and life. Others were important
influences on her early life as well. She lived with Dr. and Mrs. Leopold
Stieglitz (he was the brother of photographer Alfred Stieglitz) while attending Brearley and first became interested in medicine during these years in
the Stieglitz home. She also continued to read extensively. She recalled years
later that Thomas Hardy, Scott, and Dickens were among the classics she
read from the Stieglitz's library. Her mother's sister, Aunt Charlotte, with
whom she stayed during the summers, taught her cooking and canning and
the "joy of physical work." Helen (Mrs. George) Pratt, a wealthy philan-

thropist and patron of Mary's father, befriended her, paying for piano lessons, taking her on trips, and being a model of altruism. Mary became estranged from her mother, whom she later regarded as a negative influence on her early life.[2]

As an adolescent, Mary Steichen was conscious that she was "the poor relation among girls who were exceedingly well-to-do, with fine clothes." She excelled in academics and was talented in music, acting, and writing. She left Brearley after her junior year, having decided she was "bored with high school," and entered Vassar College in 1921. By this time it was "taken for granted by everyone," including herself, that she would go to medical school. A half century later, she reflected, "Retrospectively, the most extraordinary factor I can now recognize is that never once while I was growing up do I remember anyone at any time ever suggesting that there was something I could not do simply because I was female. Everyone I knew or ever came in contact with simply took it for granted that whatever I wanted to do, I could do it."[3]

At Vassar she majored in chemistry and completed a premedical program. She found her science courses boring, however, and her grades in them were mediocre. She devoted her energies at Vassar to English, music, and drama productions and decided to become an actress. After graduating in 1925, she studied acting for three years under Maria Ouspenskaya and Richard Boleslavsky at their American Laboratory Theatre. She abandoned acting when she realized she "couldn't be first-rate," but her stage training, particularly diction, projection, and pacing, later proved valuable for her public speaking. She married a fellow actor, W. Lon Martin, in 1926, and they had two daughters, Nell and Linda, before divorcing in 1933. She collaborated with her father at this time on two "pioneering examples of the successful use of photographs in children's books" in *The First Picture Book* (1930) and *The Second Picture Book* (1931). These books illustrated objects familiar to very young children.[4]

This was a difficult period in her life. She worked as a salesperson, underwent Freudian analysis for two years, and took aptitude tests that steered her back to science and medicine. She began taking courses at Columbia University's Medical School. After the tragedy of her older daughter's death from pneumonia at the age of eight, she entered the University of Rochester. Originally she had intended to pursue a degree in nutrition, but friends convinced her to change to medicine. She received her M.D. in 1939 from the University of Rochester Medical School, had an internship in pediatrics at Bellevue Hospital in New York City, and received a fellowship for graduate studies at Columbia University's School of Public Health, where she completed her master's degree in public health in 1942.

During her fieldwork, she met Dr. Frank A. Calderone, a district health officer on the Lower East Side. (He later headed the World Health Organization and was medical director of the Health Service of the United Nations

Secretariat.) They married on November 27, 1941. Before the births of their two daughters, Francesca and Maria, Dr. Mary Calderone worked briefly for the American Public Health Association. While their children were young, she was employed part-time as a physician in the local public schools in Great Neck, New York.

In 1953, she became medical director of the Planned Parenthood Federation of America (PPFA). She later realized that she had been offered the position (which initially was half-time) because most male physicians regarded it as "a blind alley and professional suicide."[5] However, Planned Parenthood was on the verge of becoming not only an eminently respectable agency but also a leading organization for birth control. Under the leadership of Mary Calderone, new methods (including Emko Foam, the IUD, and the Pill) were tested in the PPFA centers.

Dr. Calderone suggested Planned Parenthood hold a conference on abortion to focus attention on the need for birth control. The conference volume that she edited, *Abortion in the United States* (1958), was a valuable source book that she felt highlighted the need for contraception.[6] *Manual of Contraceptive Practice* (1964), which she edited, was an important pioneering contribution to public health and medicine. The second edition was substantially revised and reprinted several times under the title *Manual of Family Planning and Contraceptive Practice* (1970). As a crusader for birth control, Calderone helped influence the adoption of positive policies on birth control and family planning by the American Public Health Association in 1959 and the American Medical Association (AMA) in 1964. She was a member of the AMA's Committee on Human Reproduction, which developed a position statement on these issues.

Her interests had been expanding beyond the techniques of birth control, and in 1960, she coauthored *Release from Sexual Tensions*. The reviewer in the *American Journal of Public Health* praised the frank discussion of sex and "relaxed personal tone" and concluded, "The book is preventive medicine by the written word at its best."[7] This book was favorably reviewed in religious, as well as medical and psychiatric, journals and was a selection of the Pastoral Society Book Club.

Religion had not been a significant part of Calderone's life until she began taking her younger daughters to First day [Sunday] school at a nearby Friends Meeting. She became involved herself and later recalled, "One day, I discovered I really was feeling the Quaker recognition of finding God in every person." Calderone became a Quaker in her fifties, and her religious faith is important to her. She has stated, "Everything I do, I do in the light of my faith. Absolutely."[8]

In 1961, Dr. Calderone was invited by the National Council of Churches to speak at its first North American Conference on Church and Family. Scheduled to speak on planned parenthood, Calderone focused instead on the importance of sex education. She and several other conference participants continued to meet as an informal group to discuss sex education, and Calderone proposed establishing a voluntary, nonprofit educational health organization. The Sex Information and Education Council of the United States (SIECUS) was incorporated in 1964, with its goals:

to establish man's sexuality as a health entity; to identify the special characteristics that distinguish it from, yet relate it to, human reproduction; to dignify it by openness of approach, study and scientific research designed to lead toward its understanding and its freedom from exploitation; to give leadership to professionals and to society, to the end that human beings may be aided toward responsible use of the sexual faculty and toward assimilation of sex into their individual life patterns as a creative and recreative force.[9]

Calderone had realized that "handing out contraceptives was not enough"[10] and, feeling she had accomplished what she could at Planned Parenthood, resigned her position with PPFA to become executive director of SIECUS. She borrowed money from her husband to start the organization. Initially, she received no salary from SIECUS, while the two male physicians who replaced her at PPFA were paid higher salaries than she had received. Thus, at the age of sixty, she had given up a secure, though underpaid, position to direct a new organization that had no funding and an uncertain future.

Human sexuality, she had realized, was not limited to reproduction, which had been the focus of her work at Planned Parenthood. Calderone had become committed to the importance of responsible sex education for a more enlightened understanding of sex and the role of sexuality in human lives. She embarked with missionary zeal: "I had to do it. Our whole society was ready and waiting for leadership." She later recalled, "I wanted to change the whole society—a modest goal!—and I knew I couldn't do it alone."[11]

The other cofounders of SIECUS were a lawyer, sociologist, clergyman, family life educator, and physician; the thirty members of the original Board of Directors reflected a similar diversity of occupations. Nearly half were college and university professors in the fields of sociology, medicine, and teacher education.

Mary Calderone was the driving force and preeminent figure in the early formative years of SIECUS. In her eleven years as executive director (1964–1975) and seven years as president (1975–1982), Calderone was its most effective spokesperson. She traveled thousands of miles every year, speaking to students, parents, educators, and physicians. She was a prolific author as well, writing articles for professional journals and popular magazines, contributing to encyclopedias and medical textbooks, and collaborating on several books. Sixty years old and a grandmother when she began what was to be her most significant work in sex education, Mary Calderone has been acknowledged as the "first lady of sex education."[12]

Under the leadership of Calderone, SIECUS began a newsletter (which expanded in 1972 to a journal, *SIECUS Report*); published discussion guides on sex education, homosexuality, masturbation, and other subjects; organized meetings and conferences; trained professionals, doctors, and teachers; provided consulting services; and generally acted as a clearinghouse. In the first months of 1965, SIECUS received nearly a thousand inquiries, more than one-third from educational institutions, one-quarter from physicians, and the rest from individuals and organizations. Its focus was on disseminating information and education. Sex education materials were reviewed, bibliographies developed, and an extensive library of resources on sex education established. Publications were sold at cost, and bibliographies were distributed on request. SIECUS raised money from memberships, subscriptions, contributions, and foundation grants. Calderone was an effective fund-raiser, and, within a few years, SIECUS had a staff of fifteen.

Other forces besides SIECUS were at work at this time that contributed to the interest in sex education. The United States Office of Education in 1966 announced that it supported "family life and sex education as an integral part of the curriculum" and that it would "support research and development in all aspects of family life and sex education." The federal government funded a SIECUS conference that year on "Sex, the Individual, and Society: Implications for Education."[13]

Calderone and SIECUS came under attack, beginning in the late 1960s, by the John Birch Society and the Christian Crusade. These groups attacked sex education as subversive and a communist plot and called Calderone an "aging sexual libertine." Calderone, as SIECUS's most visible spokesperson, bore the brunt of most of the attacks. Gordon Drake quoted her extensively (and inaccurately) in his Christian Crusade pamphlet, *Is the Schoolhouse the Proper Place to Teach Raw Sex?* (1968). A widely publicized battle over sex education occurred in the Anaheim, California, public schools in 1969. Though a Gallup Poll that year indicated that 71 percent of Americans supported sex education, some states prohibited teaching it, and California even specifically banned use of SIECUS materials. The controversies meant considerable publicity for SIECUS, but also a loss of some funding, which resulted in a cutback in staff. In the early 1980s, SIECUS came under attack from the Moral Majority and other conservative groups. In fact, Calderone was the subject of a segment of a "60 Minutes" program on CBS television misleadingly entitled, "Dirty Old Woman."[14]

In 1974, Dr. Calderone reflected on the accomplishments of SIECUS:

But SIECUS *has* accomplished something that is unique in society. We have succeeded in establishing in the minds of leaders in all professions and religions the concept that human sexuality is in and of itself, a healthy and vitally important part of man's life above and beyond the erotic acts that may or may not accompany it.[15]

Program innovations SIECUS initiated under Calderone's leadership included projects to assist community action (and help groups fight attacks on sex education), aid parents to teach their children, and generally to "assure that all people—including adolescents, the disabled, sexual minorities, and the elderly—have the right to affirm that sexuality is a natural and healthy part of their lives."[16]

Mary Calderone was effective as a sex educator because, as a colleague once observed, she is "one of those rare people" who "can talk about sex with ease and candor."[17] Moreover, Calderone was never afraid to speak frankly about controversial subjects. She held liberal views on homosexuality, masturbation, abortion, and sex education but was not an advocate of casual sex and, although she was hesitant to impose her views on others, did not believe teenagers were mature enough for sexual intercourse, urged responsible sex, and believed sex belongs primarily in marriage. In the midst of the sexual revolution, her personal views were highly moralistic (she called herself a puritan). Calderone was a popular speaker on college campuses and in her seventies was traveling 100,000 miles annually to give more than a hundred speeches a year. She wrote numerous articles and was frequently interviewed by the popular press; the SIECUS files are filled with clippings of newspaper articles on Calderone.

Calderone wrote her most important books on sex education in the early 1980s, and both were directed to parents. *The Family Book About Sex* (1981) was favorably reviewed and frequently reprinted in both hard cover and a paperback edition. It was acknowledged as "*the* significant book for the 80s; the most important source book for any professional working with parents. Also one of the best books for intellectually-minded parents."[18] *Talking with Your Children About Sex* (1982) discusses many of the questions children most frequently ask.

SIECUS continued to hold conferences, adopted position statements beginning in the early 1970s, and established education centers. It was affiliated with New York University's School of Education, Health, Nursing and Arts Professions from 1978 to 1990. When Mary Calderone stepped down as president of SIECUS in 1982 at the age of seventy-eight, she became an adjunct professor in the Program in Human Sexuality at New York University (NYU). She continued to teach at NYU until 1988.

Calderone was never active in political partisan politics and was not a member of the National Organization of Women (NOW). She considered herself a liberated woman and said she was "not a joiner, but a movement person." She once said she was "*not* a crusader for women's rights," but for "*human* rights."[19]

SIECUS was preeminently an educational organization, and Calderone, trained in medicine and public health, was a most effective educator. In an oral history interview, she said, "I don't look on myself as a teacher although people say I'm a teacher."[20] Calderone was a crusader and passionate about her work. Under her leadership, SIECUS became an important resource center and clearinghouse for sex education and information. Fittingly, SIECUS named its reference library the Mary S. Calderone Library in June 1984.

Mary Calderone has received many awards and honors. She is a fellow and life member of the American Public Health Association and a fellow of the Society for the Scientific Study of Sex. She is an honorary life member of the American Medical Association and the American Association of Sex Education, Counselors, and Therapists and a charter member of the American College of Sexologists. Dr. Calderone received a dozen honorary doctorates between 1967 and 1985, a Lifetime Achievement Award from the Schlesinger Library at Radcliffe in 1983, numerous other awards from colleges and health organizations, and in the 1970s, appeared on a number of polls as among the most influential women in the United States.[21]

Mary Calderone has played an important role in the humanization of sex, broadened the boundaries of public health in her work in birth control and sex education, and helped change attitudes toward birth control. She began her public career when she was almost fifty and was professionally active into her eighties. Although she often said she could not imagine retiring, she moved to a Quaker retirement community in Pennsylvania in the late 1980s.

An effective public speaker, persuasive writer, and controversial crusader, Calderone is strong-minded, forthright, dynamic, and charismatic—qualities that contributed to her success as an educator. She was officially a cofounder of SIECUS, but in actuality was the formative influence in creating it. SIECUS is still an important source of information on sex education and sexuality. Her college teaching was limited to a few years at the end of her career, but for three decades, she was an unusually effective educator through her work in voluntary health agencies and as a lecturer and author. Dr. Karl Menninger declared, "She's one of the great figures of our era who opened people's minds." She once avowed, "My mission as a scientist, as a human being, and as a woman [is to] press forward the boundaries of knowledge and understanding of human sexuality." Indeed, Calderone "more than any other single person, brought human sexuality out of the Victorian closet."[22]

NOTES

1. The Edward Steichen collection at the Museum of Modern Art includes some early photographs of Mary and her family; for reproductions, see, for example, Mary Steichen Calderone, *Edward Steichen* (Millerton, NY: Aperture, 1978). See also Mary Steichen Calderone, *Edward Steichen: The Early Years, 1900–1927* (Millerton, NY: Aperture, 1981).

2. Mary Brannum, "Mary S. Calderone, M.D.," in Mary Brannum, ed., *When I Was 16* (New York: Platt and Mink, 1967), 152–57; Mary S. Calderone, "Physician

and Public Health Educator," in Ruth B. Kundsin, ed., *Women and Success: The Anatomy of Achievement* (New York: Macmillan, 1974), 68–69.

3. Calderone, "Physician and Public Health Educator," 68–69.

4. Ibid., p. 69; Brannum, 163–64; *Current Biography* (New York: H. W. Wilson, 1967), 55.

5. Calderone, "Physician and Public Health Educator," 71.

6. James W. Reed, Interview with Mary Steichen Calderone, M.D., 1974, typescript in Mary S. Calderone papers, Schlesinger Library, Radcliffe College, 15–16.

7. Bruno Gebhard, Review of *Release from Sexual Tensions*, *American Journal of Public Health* 50 (1960): 1965.

8. Dan Gold, *Until the Singing Stops: A Celebration of Life and Old Age in America* (New York: N.P., 1979), 323; see also David Mace, "A Quaker Portrait: Mary Steichen Calderone," *Friends Journal* 17, no. 6 (March 15, 1971): 166–68.

9. Reprinted in Debra W. Haffner, "SIECUS: 25 Years of Commitment to Sexual Health and Education," *SIECUS Report*, 17 (March/April 1989): 1.

10. Dolores Alexander, "A Look at Mary Calderone: The Grandmother of Modern Sex Education," *Newsday*, February 22, 1966, 29; see also Thomas C. Hunter, *Beginnings* (New York: Thomas Y. Crowell, 1978), 63–64.

11. Lynn Gilbert and Gaylen Moore, "Mary Steichen Calderone," *Particular Passions: Talks with Women Who Have Shaped Our Times* (New York: Clarkson N. Potter, 1981), 258.

12. Nat Lehrman, "Playboy Interview: Dr. Mary Calderone," *Playboy* 14 (April 1970): 63.

13. SIECUS published the conference papers in a handbook for teacher training: Carlfred Broderick and Jessie Bernard, eds., *The Individual, Sex, and Society* (Baltimore: Johns Hopkins University Press, 1969); Haffner, 1, 2, 5.

14. Mary Breasted in *Oh! Sex Education!* (New York: Praeger, 1970) has documented how Drake quoted Calderone out of context (204–5), discusses the Anaheim controversy in some detail, and is rather critical of Calderone in her journalistic account of the sex education controversy. Drake was also the author of *SIECUS—Corrupter of Youth* (Tulsa: Christian Crusade Publications, 1960). The "60 Minutes" segment aired October 25, 1981; a transcript is in the SIECUS Library vertical files on Calderone in New York City. See also Gloria Lentz, *Raping Our Children: The Sex Education Scandal* (New Rochelle: Arlington House, 1979) for an example of the conservative criticism of Calderone, SIECUS, and sex education.

15. Lehrman, 240.

16. SIECUS, "Three Decades of Commitment to Sexual Health and Education," (1992).

17. Robert H. Laidlow, "Foreword" to Mary Calderone, Phyllis Goldman, and Robert P. Goldman, *Release from Sexual Tensions* (New York: Random House, 1960), vii.

18. Susan Snyder and Sol Gordon, eds., *Parents as Sexuality Educators: An Annotated Bibliography* (Phoenix: Oryx Press, 1984), 4.

19. Lehrman, 238; Gold, 324.

20. Reed, 36.

21. *Who's Who of American Women, 1991–1992* (Wilmette, IL: Macmillan Directory, 1991); 1984 résumé in SIECUS Library files.

22. Menninger quoted by Mary Vespa, "America's Biggest Problem? Fearless Dr.

Mary Calderone Says It's 'Fear of Sex,' " *People Weekly*, January 21, 1980, 77; Calderone quoted by Lehrman, 240; Arthur S. Freese, "Meet Mary Calderone," *Modern Maturity*, August-September 1978, 55.

WORKS BY MARY STEICHEN CALDERONE

First Picture Book. New York: Harcourt, Brace, 1930. Also *The Second Picture Book*. New York: Harcourt, Brace, 1931. Both by Mary [Steichen] Martin with photographs by Edward Steichen.

Abortion in the United States (ed.). New York: Hocker-Harper, 1958.

Release from Sexual Tensions (coauthor with Phyllis Goldman and Robert P. Goldman). New York: Random House, 1960.

Manual of Contraceptive Practice (ed.). Baltimore: Williams and Wilkins, 1964. Rev. 2d ed. entitled *Manual of Family Planning and Contraceptive Practice*. Baltimore: Williams and Wilkins, 1970.

"Physician and Public Health Educator." Autobiographical account in Ruth B. Kundsin, ed., *Women and Success: The Anatomy of Achievement*, 68–72. New York: William Morrow, 1974.

Sexuality and Human Values: Personal Dimensions of Sexual Experience (ed.). New York: Association Press/Follett, 1974.

Questions and Answers About Sex and Love (coauthor with Bride's Magazine). New York: St. Martin's Press, 1979.

Family Book About Sexuality (coauthor with Eric W. Johnson). New York: Harper and Row, 1981.

Talking with Your Child About Sex (coauthor with James W. Ramey). New York: Random House, 1982.

WORKS ABOUT MARY STEICHEN CALDERONE

Brannum, Mary. "Mary S. Calderone, M.D." in *When I Was 16*, 147–66. New York: Platt and Mink, 1967.

Breasted, Mary. *Oh! Sex Education!* New York: Praeger, 1970. See especially pp. 204–42.

"Calderone, Mary S(teichen)." *Current Biography*, 53–56. New York: H. W. Wilson, 1967.

Gilbert, Lynn, and Gaylen Moore. "Mary Steichen Calderone." Edited transcript of oral history interview in *Particular Passions: Talks with Women Who Have Shaped Our Times*, 255–63. New York: Clarkson N. Potter, 1981.

Gold, Don. "Dr. Mary Calderone." In *Until the Singing Stops: A Celebration of Life and Old Age in America*, 312–28. New York: Holt, Rinehart and Winston, 1979.

Lehrman, Nat. "Playboy Interview: Dr. Mary Calderone." *Playboy* 14, April 1970, 63ff. Reprinted in abridged form in Barbara Osborn Henkel, ed., *Foundations of Health Science*, 2d ed., 510–17. Boston: Allyn and Bacon, 1971.

Verpa, Mary. "America's Biggest Problem? Fearless Dr. Mary Calderone Says It's 'Fear of Sex.' " *People Weekly*, January 21, 1980, 77–82.

Mother Mary Regis Casserly

Mary J. Oates

Mother Mary Regis Casserly (1843–1917) founded in 1873 the Congregation of the Sisters of St. Joseph of Boston, a group that was to become the largest teaching sisterhood in New England. The phenomenal development of the Catholic parochial school system in America in the late nineteenth century represented a singular step by a church whose membership was predominantly poor and working-class. It was accomplished only because of the willingness of women to join the teaching sisterhoods that directed and staffed these schools. Nowhere was mainstream opposition to the parochial school stronger than it was in New England in the half century following 1870, and the sisters, under the leadership of Mother Mary Regis, met the challenges it presented creatively and confidently. By the time of her death, parochial schools and the sisters who staffed them were an integral and accepted part of the social fabric of the region.

Annie A. Casserly was born in Roscommon, Ireland, on January 1, 1843, the daughter of Thomas and Dora Kelly Casserly. When she was nine, the family emigrated to America, settling in Long Island, New York. In 1860, St. Joseph Female Academy opened in nearby Flushing, and the following year Annie enrolled. The school was conducted by Sisters of St. Joseph, a religious community founded in 1650 in Le Puy, France. The first sisters to come to America settled in St. Louis in 1836. From there, the community spread rapidly to other cities, developing, for the most part, as autonomous diocesan congregations. In 1856 Bishop John Loughlin of Brooklyn invited them to staff the parochial schools in his diocese.

Since in 1860 the community's motherhouse and novitiate were located near the academy, Annie Casserly had ample opportunity to observe the life and work of the sisters at close hand. In August 1863, two months after her graduation, she joined the community and received the habit six months later, taking Sister Mary Regis as her religious name. In March 1866, she professed her perpetual vows as a Sister of St. Joseph.

Our Lady of Mercy Elementary School in Brooklyn opened in 1867, and Sister Mary Regis was among its first teachers. There she confronted directly the economic and social plight of poor immigrants and their families. The experience buttressed her early conviction that educating the children of the poor and working class was the highest form of charity a congregation of women could undertake.

In 1873 Rev. Thomas Magennis, a thirty-five-year-old pastor from the Jamaica Plain section of Boston, visited the Brooklyn congregation to request faculty for a parochial school he hoped to inaugurate. Among the volunteers was Sister Mary Regis, who was appointed superior of the new mission. With three companions, the young superior arrived in Jamaica Plain on October 2, 1873, and immediately opened St. Thomas School. The 200 children who applied for admission represented 15 percent of the local school district enrollment.

A continuing challenge for teaching sisters of the 1870s was a dearth of economic resources. Parochial schools had to be "free," as parishioners, most of them poor, could not afford to pay tuitions. Pastors struggled, sometimes for years, to accumulate funds to construct and furnish schools. Rather than delay until a suitable building was available, Sister Mary Regis agreed that the sisters would use the church basement as a schoolhouse and accept only a small stipend to cover their living expenses. An 1874 account depicts the basement school as "bright and cheerful," with classrooms partitioned by movable walls. The Catholic press praised the new sisters as progressive and enthusiastic: "A more happy company of ladies cannot be found."[1]

Father Magennis, soon unable to pay the stipends he had promised the sisters, feared that they would have to return to New York. But Sister Mary Regis had no intention of giving up so easily. She assured him that the sisters would support themselves until his financial situation improved. For several years they accepted sewing contracts from local firms, covering baseballs with leather, making beanbags and shrouds, and embroidering religious vestments.

In 1876, encouraged by Archbishop John Williams and Father Magennis, Sister Mary Regis took the first step toward legal separation of the Boston congregation from the Brooklyn congregation by opening a Boston novitiate. She believed that more local women would join a sisterhood that focused on the needs of their home diocese. This step did not please all the sisters. Several, including two of the 1873 pioneers, departed for Brooklyn. But, in fact, her instincts were right. Only two Massachusetts women applied for admission to the congregation in 1877; three years later, ten received the religious habit.

As the first general superior of the autonomous Boston congregation, Sister Mary Regis became known as Mother Mary Regis, a title she retained for the rest of her life. Although in 1890 she declined reelection to this post, Mother Regis, as she was popularly addressed, remained the community's most influential member, revered by all the sisters as founder and spiritual guide.

In the mid-1870s the new congregation was unfamiliar to Massachusetts pastors proposing to open new schools. Even though Father Magennis, with whom Mother Regis worked in close collaboration, had for some years represented his district on the Massachusetts State Board of Education, his clerical confreres hesitated to follow his advice to engage Sisters of St. Joseph for their faculties. Finally, in 1879 Magennis solicited a testimonial letter from Bishop Bernard McQuaid of Rochester, New York, regarding the qualifications of the Sisters of St. Joseph *"as teachers"* in his diocese.[2] McQuaid's favorable reply had the desired results. Within a month, a South Boston pastor invited Mother Regis to conduct his large parochial school. The sister-annalist conveyed the delight of the sisters at the news: "Wonderful announcement today. Fr. Higgins has the approbation of the Archbishop to get us to teach his school, and no less than ten sisters are required to take charge. Poor Jamaica Plain will get a dreadful clear out."[3]

The enthusiasm of the sisters matched that of the Catholic laity. Poor and working-class parents, most of them Irish, expressed their appreciation for the efforts of the sisters on behalf of their children by contributions in kind and service. Typical was the generosity of Amesbury men and boys, who, after long days in local mills, turned out en masse in the evenings to dig the foundations for a parish convent and school. When the school opened in 1884, the 359 children enrolled represented nearly every child in the parish.

Although Mother Regis and Father Magennis generally concurred about educational policies, they disagreed about one critical matter. He believed that the best way for the congregation to become widely recognized was to accept as many schools as possible. He brushed aside her protests that the young sisters were neither properly introduced to the religious life nor trained in classroom management, noting that other sisterhoods were regularly placing novices in classrooms and that public school teachers were no better prepared. Like most clerics, he saw little need for preservice education since elementary school curricula required only brief review and since nature had equipped women with the necessary disposition and skills to manage young children. Mother Regis had little choice but to concede to his wishes since diocesan sisterhoods were juridically subordinate to the bishop and since Father Magennis was Archbishop Williams's appointed representative. The professional preparation of the young sisters became a matter of increasing concern to her as pressures for parochial school teachers heightened.

Under the leadership of Mother Regis, the community's reputation as the sisterhood that gladly accepted the most challenging schools in the archdiocese quickly grew. She rebutted every stereotype about the intellectual capacities and ambitions of the poor and insisted that the professional work of the sisters on their behalf be of high quality and publicly acknowledged. One strategy was to hold important school events in public halls. Another was to invite ecclesiastical dignitaries to preside. At the 1879 opening of the South Boston school, for example, the bishops of Peoria and St. Paul joined Archbishop Williams in an imposing and colorful inaugural rite.

Nineteenth-century Protestants continued to view the development of Catholic schools as a serious threat to social harmony, to developing public schools, and to the rapid assimilation of immigrants flooding Boston and its environs. The very hint that such a school was planned in a town unleashed a barrage of protracted criticism. Typical was an 1884 declaration of the Stoughton school committee that denounced St. Mary's School, enrolling 200 town children, as abhorrent to all true Americans.

Such pronouncements left Mother Regis unruffled. She simply worked harder to incorporate Catholic schools into local communities. Annual "open house days" allowed Stoughton residents, Protestant as well as Catholic, to observe the sisters at work. She invited the superintendent of the Stoughton public schools to award diplomas to the first graduates of St. Mary's School in 1884. Four years later the school became the first in the town to fly the American flag. Finally, in 1894, public acceptance of the school became official when its graduates were allowed to proceed to Stoughton High School without having to pass a special examination not required of public school children. This chronology of the advance to social acceptance was typical for most of the parochial schools Mother Regis opened.

Courses of study in Massachusetts parochial schools remained under the full control of the sisterhoods staffing them until 1913, when the archdiocese began to develop a central school bureau. From her arrival in Boston, Mother Regis determined that schools conducted under her direction would resemble local public schools in all essentials. In particular, she prohibited the practices reminiscent of European convent schools so favored by other sisterhoods.

Daily lessons in religion and moral values and a distinctly Catholic environment distinguished the schools, but in curriculum, textbooks, school calendars, and teaching methods her sisters resolutely followed local public school practice. This single step did much to deter charges that children attending parochial schools lagged behind their public school counterparts in academic progress and social integration. At the same time, she favored some innovative teaching practices not yet popular in public schools. Field trips to the Arnold Arboretum and major historic Boston sites were essential components of the educational program of the South Boston school in the early 1880s, and its freestanding theater attested to the prominence of music and drama in the curriculum.

The mandate of the American bishops at the Council of Baltimore in 1884 that every parish open a school had an untoward effect on the fledgling sisterhood. Pressures on Mother Regis for more teachers increased precipitously, since Sisters of St. Joseph, unlike most teaching sisterhoods of the era, were willing to teach boys. St. Thomas School in Jamaica Plain was the first parochial school in New England to be coeducational throughout the entire range of grades. However, before 1884, parishes in Massachusetts, unlike those in other dioceses, had opened schools casually, according to the enthusiasm and means of pastor and parishioners, with religious brothers teaching the boys and sisters, the girls. But since brothers were very scarce relative to sisters and since their stipends were approximately double those of the women, Boston parishes in 1872 had eleven schools for girls but only two for boys. The 1884 council demanded that this imbalance be rectified. Sisters of St. Joseph soon became the faculty of choice for pastors unable to find or afford brothers to teach the boys.

The most formidable problem facing Mother Mary Regis continued to be the professional training of the young women who were joining the community in increasing numbers by the mid-1880s. Educational qualifications for public school teachers were rising quickly and the sisters had to be prepared to meet them. But the low teaching stipends paid by the parishes and pressures from pastors for more teachers for the schools made progress in this area difficult to achieve.

As early as 1876, Mother Regis had engaged Larkin Dunton, the principal of the Boston Normal School, to instruct the seven novices in teaching techniques and classroom management. While at this time there were still few formal requirements for public school teaching, by the 1880s the normal school movement was well under way in Massachusetts. In this decade, Mother Regis commissioned experienced sister-teachers to travel to the various convents to instruct the other sisters. She hired lay professionals to give music and elocution lessons. In the summer, the sisters gathered at the motherhouse for lessons specific to the various grades and subjects. At the same time, she encouraged the sisters to educate themselves by taking advantage of local cultural resources.

Mother Regis saw in the opening of a female tuition academy in Cambridge in 1885 a critical way to advance the professional training of the sisters as well as the education of girls. She assigned to the new school her best-educated sisters. Although the corporate mission of her sisterhood was not the education of the wealthy, the school promised to provide a dependable income to supplement the small parochial school stipends, which barely covered the sisters' personal living expenses. Academy revenues would help to support central community needs, especially the education of the sisters.

St. Joseph's Academy and Boarding School, soon renamed Mount St. Joseph Academy, initially charged $270 annually for board, tuition, piano lessons, and laundry. Although its fees exceeded those of similar schools in Vermont and Connecticut, the school prospered, trebling in enrollment between 1887 and 1890. Under Mother Regis's direction, it offered girls a comprehensive curriculum resembling that of the best high schools of the day. The academy, according to a contemporary observer, aimed "to send forth to the world practical women imbued with a sense of the seriousness of life."[4]

By the 1890s, most applicants to the congregation were at least high school graduates, and a growing number, many of them former public school teachers, had normal school diplomas. By this decade, because of the foresight of Mother Regis, the community was able, albeit on a small scale, to undertake to educate sisters in specialized programs beyond convent doors. Those preparing to work with deaf children studied in Worcester and Buffalo institutions at this time, and a contingent of parochial school teachers enrolled in the Harvard University Summer School.

Mother Regis was convinced that public awareness was the best weapon to combat prejudice, not only against the parochial schools but also against their faculties. To confound sensational and prevalent stereotypes about nuns and convent life, she took the unconventional step of welcoming the public to the rites of reception of the religious habit and profession of vows. Although the first such ceremony in 1878 had been private, the second, held in October of the same year, took place in the parish church.

Contemporary newspaper accounts reveal that these impressive rituals aroused widespread interest. For example, the October 1888 reception and profession ceremonies attracted a large audience, which gathered in an outdoor pavilion at the community's Cambridge motherhouse. The nine young women who were to receive the habit dressed in white wedding gowns "with the customary bridal veil and flowers," each attended by an academy student, also in white, as bridesmaid. The six novices who were to profess their vows followed, "each bearing a lighted taper, attended by the Mother Superior and her assistant."[5]

During her seventeen years as superior general of the community, Mother Regis opened six parochial schools and an academy. By 1890, her sisterhood was well on its way to its position of leadership, in membership and number of schools, in the Catholic educational enterprise of New England. Despite a growing demand for more sisters for parochial schools, Mother Regis encouraged her successors to broaden their educational sphere to educate orphan and deaf children. Under her leadership, a Home for Deaf Mutes, which admitted children of all faiths, commenced in 1898 in Jamaica Plain with four children in attendance. As was her practice in parochial schools, she adopted proven teaching methods for the new school, in this case those of the Clarke Institution for the Deaf in Northampton, Massachusetts. Demand for admission rose so swiftly that in 1990 the state of Massachusetts agreed to provide public funding for the school. In 1904 Mother Regis oversaw its transfer to a 110-acre site in Randolph, where by 1910 fourteen sisters were instructing 120 children. The school continues today as the Boston School for the Deaf.

In 1899, the Sisters of St. Joseph answered an appeal from local clergy that they conduct an industrial school and home for orphan and poor girls over twelve years of age in the Dorchester section of the city. The Daly Industrial School accommodated one-hundred pupils and welcomed students of all faiths. At first its curriculum included only domestic and industrial subjects, a narrow focus that soon gave way to a more traditional curriculum. The school received no public support and was maintained by private donations, the contributed services of the sisters, and the sale of handicrafts.

In 1913, on her golden jubilee as a Sister of St. Joseph, Mother Regis retired to the community's motherhouse in the Brighton section of Boston. The sisterhood she had founded had expanded from four pioneers in one school to 211 members in 19 schools that enrolled more than 9,000 children. Women continued to join the community in increasing numbers, drawn by its distinctive vitality, its progressive character, and its single-minded commitment to the provision of quality Catholic education. By its seventy-fifth anniversary in 1948, 1,600 sisters were instructing about 35,000 students in 82 schools.

The 1909 annual report of the school for the deaf aptly captures Mother Regis's philosophy of education. At its core was the reverence for the individual that consistently marked her career as educator, administrator, and religious superior. Sister-teachers, the report declared, endeavored to make children

conversant with all that the world offers to those who speak and hear, to germinate in them the fruit of knowledge hitherto dormant; in a word, to make them glad to live, glad to know and practise virtue, always progressive, adding to the sense of living much of that which makes life worth the living.[6]

Mother Regis did far more than administer a large nonprofit corporation and supervise a network of schools in an era when few women held such posts. She also shaped public opinion by mobilizing women to join her in religious sisterhood to advance, through education, the integration of an outsider, working-class community into mainstream society. Her innovative spirit and enlightened leadership effectively enlarged the definition of free education to include not simply public schools but also parochial schools. The perennial designation of these institutions as "the sisters' schools" by citizens of all religious backgrounds bears witness to the critical role played by women in their development.

On October 16, 1917, Mother Mary Regis Casserly died at the Brighton motherhouse of her congregation, at the age of seventy-four, several days after suffering a stroke. She was buried in St. Paul Cemetery, Arlington. Her obituary describes her as light-hearted, energetic, and unwavering in her conviction that the education of the young was the preeminent way to manifest the social gospel.[7] The sisters of her congregation paid her enduring and fitting tribute by naming in her honor the Massachusetts women's college they founded in 1927.

NOTES

1. *Boston Pilot*, January 10, 1874.
2. Thomas Magennis to Bishop Bernard J. McQuaid, May 20, 1879, Archives, Archdiocese of Rochester, New York.
3. Motherhouse Annals, 1873–1921, June 26, 1879, Archives, Sisters of St. Joseph, Brighton, Massachusetts.
4. Mary Margaret Ryan, "The Sisters of St. Joseph, Brighton," in Henry Coyle, Theodore Mayhew, and Frank S. Hickey, eds., *Our Church, Her Children and Institutions*, vol. 2 (Boston: Angel Guardian Press, 1908), 216.
5. *Boston Pilot*, August 4, 1888.
6. Rev. Thomas Magennis, *Annual Report of the Boston School for the Deaf, 1909* (Randolph, MA: Archives, Boston School for the Deaf, 1909).
7. *The Pilot*, October 27, 1917.

WORKS ABOUT MOTHER MARY REGIS CASSERLY

Boleman, M. Magdalena. "Patterns in the Design." Unpublished ms., 1965. Archives, Sisters of St. Joseph, Brighton, MA.

Lee, M. Catherine. "Early History of the Sisters of St. Joseph, 1873–1916." Unpublished ms., 1916. Archives, Sisters of St. Joseph, Brighton, MA.

Meade, Agnes David. "Beginnings of the Sisters of St. Joseph in Boston." M.A. thesis, Boston College, 1941.

Oates, Mary J. "Organized Voluntarism: The Catholic Sisters in Massachusetts, 1870–1940." *American Quarterly* 30 (Winter 1978): 652–80.

———. "Professional Preparation of Parochial School Teachers, 1870–1940." *Historical Journal of Massachusetts* 12 (January 1984): 60–72.

———. " 'The Good Sisters': The Work and Position of Catholic Churchwomen in Boston, 1870–1940." In Robert E. Sullivan and James M. O'Toole, eds. *Catholic Boston: Studies in Religion and Community, 1870–1940*, 171–200. Boston: Archdiocese of Boston, 1985.

O'Hara, Juliana. "Educational Contribution of the Sisters of St. Joseph in the Archdiocese of Boston from 1873 to 1939." M.A. thesis, Catholic University of America, 1941.

A Sister of St. Joseph. *Just Passing Through, 1873–1943*. Boston: The Sisters of St. Joseph, 1943.

Sucheng Chan

Kofi Lomotey

Sucheng Chan (b. 1941), a political activist and scholar, is one of the most respected and influential figures in academe in general and in the field of ethnic studies in particular. The winner of a Distinguished Teaching Award from the University of California, Berkeley, in 1978, and the first Asian-American woman to become a provost in the University of California system, Chan has received half a dozen prizes for her scholarship and has held postdoctoral fellowships from the National Endowment for the Humanities (1973–1974 and 1992) and the John Simon Guggenheim Foundation (1988–1989). Most important, her career demonstrates that it is possible for a woman from an underrepresented group to fight for the civil and educational rights of members of oppressed groups while simultaneously maintaining the highest standards of excellence in teaching and research.

Sucheng Chan was born in China on April 16, 1941, to Kock K. Chan and Dora K. W. Chan. Her father was trained as an engineer in Germany, and her mother was one of the first women to receive a B.A. in sociology from the University of Shanghai. Her father's ancestors emigrated from Guangdong Province in southern China in the early decades of the nineteenth century to settle in Penang, Malaya (now called Malaysia), soon after the British colonized it.[1]

Working initially as common laborers in Malaya's developing tin mines and rubber plantations, the family attained middle-class status after several generations. Chan's paternal grandfather studied law in England and then returned to Malaya to practice.

Her maternal grandparents also traveled a great deal, but within the borders of China. Chan's maternal grandfather was a low-ranking official in the imperial bureaucracy in the last days of the Qing dynasty. Following the customary practice, he was rotated every three years to a different locality, usually in the interior of China. When his older children were in their early teens, his wife, an unschooled woman with bound feet, announced that she planned to take all their children to Shanghai, a big city with modern schools, so that they could receive the best education available. No one knows how she persuaded her husband to let her do this (such behavior was unheard of and quite unacceptable in old China), but the fact is that she did.

As a girl, Sucheng also heard stories about her paternal great grandmother, whose husband had died young, allowing her to become a matriarch in a patriarchal society. This woman, who had supported the 1911 Revolution in China, never hesitated to speak her mind, contrary to what was expected of "well-bred" Chinese women. When Sucheng was born, one of her aunts, who had produced a son, taunted Sucheng's mother with the question "What good does a university education do, when all you can produce is a girl?" Before Sucheng's mother could respond, the old matriarch, who obviously did not believe that only male children should be valued—as most Chinese did—declared loudly for all to hear: "Surely you must all know that the Chinese written character for 'good,' *hao*, is made of two components, one meaning son, the other, daughter. So, how can there be any good in the House of Chan without my great granddaughter?" Since Chinese were, and still are, very fond of good omens, this clever retort left everyone in the room speechless.

At the age of four, Sucheng was stricken at once with polio and pneumonia. All the doctors trained in Western medicine who examined her, as well as a Chinese fortune-teller, told her parents that she would not live for long. The next four years were extremely difficult ones, but she survived. Her lower body, where the muscles were atrophying, was constantly pierced with pain. In a China torn by war, no physical therapy was available, but Sucheng eventually learned to walk again by holding onto two parallel rows of chairs that she asked her mother to set up. Every time she fell, her mother gasped, whereupon she would tell her mother to leave the room, so she could try again without her mother's anxious gaze.

When Sucheng was nine, her family moved back to Malaya. There, she learned to swim in the warm waters of the tropics, while her general health improved. Her parents enrolled her and her younger sister in the Anglo-Chinese Girls' School in Penang and later in the Methodist Girls' School in Singapore, where English was the medium of instruction. Even though Chinese language schools also existed, her parents wanted her to learn English because they hoped eventually to send her to the United States for medical treatment and for higher education. Their wish came true in 1957, when the family was allowed to enter the United States under one of the Refugee Acts passed by the U.S. Congress in the 1950s.

Chan enrolled in William Cullen Bryant High School in Long Island City, New York. Although she was already quite fluent in English, she was not exempt from one of the major difficulties that immigrants experience. Her

English teacher repeatedly made fun of her "improper" American English (she had a British-Malaysian accent at the time) and forced her to imitate his New York Jewish accent. In her junior year, she took the College Entrance Examination Board's Scholastic Aptitude Test (SAT) on a trial basis and received a very high score in the quantitative test, but only a score in the range of 500 on the verbal one. She asked her English teacher for advice on how to do better on the verbal test when she was to take it again in her senior year. He told her that she should be satisfied with the score she got. "You're doing pretty well for an immigrant kid," he said condescendingly. Finding no help or encouragement from him, Chan bought several study guides and improved her vocabulary by teaching herself twenty words a day. Seven months later, she managed not only to increase her verbal score by over 200 points but also became the first student in the history of her high school to receive a "perfect" score of 800 in the English Achievement Test. To this day, that accomplishment gives her more satisfaction than anything else she has done. She graduated as the salutatorian in a class of over 1,000 students, winning the biology, chemistry, English, and several other awards.

Chan received dozens of letters from colleges and universities urging her to apply. She chose to attend Swarthmore College in Pennsylvania. Initially a premedical student, she changed her major to economics, with a minor in political science, at the beginning of her junior year because she believed that these subjects would help her to understand the contemporary social, political, and economic problems that concerned her.

Her extracurricular activities were just as instructive: during her freshman year, she joined a Marxist study group; in her sophomore year, she became involved in the emerging civil rights movement. She participated in many demonstrations and sit-ins but recalls seeing no other Asian Americans among the black and white faces. That did not deter her from developing a strong identification with the struggles of oppressed groups for justice and equality. Since at that time the members of her family had not yet become naturalized citizens, her parents forbade her to join her friends who went south on the Freedom Rides. Instead, she worked to raise thousands of dollars to bail her friends out of jail. When she approached her biology professor for a contribution, he admonished her that her biology skills could far surpass her fund-raising skills in time. Chan recalls with delight that, despite this admonition, she did manage to wrangle ten dollars out of him.

Chan received an M.A. in Asian studies from the University of Hawaii in 1965, after which she spent a year doing anthropological fieldwork in the Philippines and another year traveling in two dozen countries in Asia. She then went to the University of California, Berkeley, to study city and regional planning. She soon transferred into the Ph.D. program in political science, wrote a dissertation on the Long March, and received her degree in 1973.

Much of her time as a graduate student at Berkeley was spent in political activities. She worked in the anti-Vietnam War movement, where she met Asian-American activists for the first time. In 1969, she married a fellow graduate student, Mark Juergensmeyer, who was also working in the antiwar movement. The couple, who have no children, commute between Santa Barbara and Honolulu, where Juergensmeyer is the dean of the School of Hawaiian, Asian, and Pacific Studies.

In the late 1960s, Chan also became involved in the movement for ethnic studies. She participated in the 1969 student strike at Berkeley, which led to the establishment of an ethnic studies department on that campus. But unlike some of her fellow student radicals, who saw themselves mainly as revolutionaries, she was determined from the beginning to make Asian-American and ethnic studies into legitimate fields of academic inquiry. Before she completed her dissertation, she began teaching at Sonoma State University, where she served as an assistant professor for two years.

In 1974 she returned to Berkeley to join the faculty of the ethnic studies department. She remained there for ten years, during which time she did a great deal of research but did not publish much because her department was in a constant state of turmoil. Chan served on numerous departmental, faculty legislature, and campuswide administrative committees, all the while fighting a double battle. On one front, she fought against faculty in the traditional disciplines and administrators who seemed determined to shut down the radical ethnic studies department; on another front, she struggled against colleagues who felt that engaging in confrontational politics was more important than teaching and scholarship. Her battle to transform Asian-American studies from a social movement into an academic field of inquiry was often a lonely one. But in time, Chan became an effective power broker, often serving as the only channel of communication between her colleagues and other individuals on campus, whenever the two sides refused to talk directly to each other. She succeeded in this role because she understood the concerns of both sides and was therefore trusted by both.

Chan spent so much time adjudicating conflict and teaching an overload of courses that she found little time to write. So, one year after she received tenure, she decided she might as well get some formal credit for the administrative skills that she was displaying. In 1984, she left Berkeley to become provost of Oakes College, one of the eight colleges on the campus of the University of California (UC), Santa Cruz—the first Asian-American woman to be named a provost in the University of California system. Oakes College had been established as Santa Cruz's multicultural college. For complex reasons, by the time Chan arrived, the college had become a virtual outcast in the eyes of the rest of the campus. Its faculty and staff, on one hand, and the rest of UC, Santa Cruz, on the other hand, dealt with each other in the most antagonistic manner. During the search for a provost in the first year, the position was offered to three candidates, each of whom turned it down because they viewed the position as totally untenable. The following year, Chan took the job because, as a social scientist, she found the situation "sociologically fascinating." She had the unenviable and difficult task of bringing Oakes College back into the fold of the larger university and she succeeded in doing so.

While in theory UC, Santa Cruz's multicultural college was an unusually tolerant college with rare understanding, appreciation, and respect for different groups and individuals, in reality the mission was far from being fully realized. More specifically, many in the college (and the campus)—mostly European-American males—were not ready for an Asian-American woman provost. While Chan did an exceptional job as provost, it was not without numerous war scars.

During the 1987–1988 academic year, when Chan was planning to leave UC, Santa Cruz, many universities solicited her candidacy for a wide variety of high-ranking administrative positions. But Chan desired more time for writing. Instead of seeking to move up the administrative ladder, she accepted a low-key position as chair of the near-moribund Asian-American Studies Program at the University of California, Santa Barbara (UCSB). Within the short span of three years, despite budgetary stringencies, she completely rejuvenated the program by hiring some superb, young faculty and developing a major in the field.

Since 1986, Chan has produced ten books. She is at work on another half dozen. She hopes that her own writings, as well as the books in the Asian-American History and Culture series that she edits for Temple University Press, will help to secure an honored place for Asian-American studies in the structure of knowledge. Chan's work has done a great deal to demonstrate that scholarship in ethnic studies can be innovative yet solid. Her article "Chinese Livelihood in Rural California, 1860–1880: The Impact of Economic Change" received the Louis Knott Koontz Prize for the best article published in the *Pacific Historical Review* in 1984. Her first book, *This Bittersweet Soil: The Chinese in California Agriculture, 1860–1910*, won the 1986 Theodore Saloutos Memorial Book Award in Agricultural History, the 1987 American Historical Association Pacific Coast Branch Award for the best first monograph, and the 1988 Association for Asian American Studies Outstanding Book Award. A book she edited, *Quiet Odyssey: A Pioneer Korean Woman in America*, received the 1990 Association for Asian American Studies Outstanding Book Award. In 1991, the California Historical Society gave her its J. S. Holliday Award for her overall contributions to California history.

In recent years, Chan has devoted an increasing amount of time to research and writing, rather than to professional activities and administration, because she has been suffering from postpolio syndrome and various related degenerative neuromuscular conditions since 1987. Knowing that time is not on her side, she works as efficiently as her physical condition allows, accepting only a small fraction of the numerous invitations she receives to give lectures and keynote addresses around the country.

Despite her own difficulties, she continues to render assistance to dozens of graduate students and junior colleagues, some of whom she has not even met but who write her for advice and assistance. She has edited, line by line, most of the book manuscripts accepted in the Asian American History and Culture series that she initiated in 1990. This is the first series of scholarly books devoted to Asian-American studies, although two more have been established by other presses since then.

Though Chan has never shied away from confrontation—when it is needed—she prefers to deal with colleagues who routinely denigrate research by and about underrepresented groups by showing them that excellent work in ethnic studies does exist. She has spent so much time helping others advance their careers, she says, because she is fully aware of how pervasive racism still is in academe. She realizes that young scholars from underrepresented groups often have no one to turn to when they want an honest evaluation of their work—no one who will be tough as a critic but supportive as a mentor.

Chan believes that anger has been a great and positive motivating force in her life and career: often she has felt compelled to do something because she was angry about a certain situation. Rather than allow such anger to erupt in erratic ways, she has channeled it toward constructive ends. From the time she was very young, she has responded to condescension (toward her female or immigrant status) and pity (for her physical disability) by saying to herself, "You just wait—I'll show you what I can do!"

In retrospect, Chan thinks her physical handicap and her racial origins have affected her personality—and hence, her career—more than her gender has. Over the years, as she observed some of her extremely competent and smart women friends wither from the slightest criticism, it dawned upon her that being handicapped has, in fact, "saved" her from the normal socialization that most girls receive. Because her mother worried so much about simply keeping her alive, training her handicapped daughter to be a future wife and mother seemed quite unimportant, especially since physically handicapped persons are seldom expected to find mates in most Asian cultures. In any case, Chan never developed much of a gender consciousness. For that reason, even though she is a strong and tough woman, she does not identify strongly with feminists. She says that while she does not react to men the same way that many feminists do, neither does she feel completely comfortable in what is called women's culture. Because she was limited in her mobility, her closest companions have always been books—not children's, but adult books, even when she was very young—so she has always conversed in her head with the world's great writers and thinkers, rather than with playmates or girlfriends.

Neither has she ever felt insecure in public, her pronounced limp and shriveled leg notwithstanding. She is thankful that video cameras did not exist when she was young. When she was thirty-nine years old, she gave a keynote address that was videotaped. When she was shown the tape, she was shocked to see how badly she limped. But she immediately told herself that that was not the time to begin to feel self-conscious about how she looked.

Sucheng Chan is a personification of the belief that we can accomplish anything with will and dedication. This truism is reflected in her insistence upon learning to walk when crippled with polio at the age of four and in her determination to succeed on her own on the SAT and English Achievement Test. Her pioneering efforts in the area of Asian-American studies also stand as a testament to her sincere belief that we can accomplish what we seek to accomplish. Sucheng was perhaps the single most significant actor in the struggle to legitimate Asian-American studies in U.S. higher education.

Sucheng Chan is an academic's academic. She is an avid political activist while at the same time aggressively pursuing a rigorous agenda of scholarship. Sucheng Chan is among the leading scholars in the area of Asian-American studies.

Finally, Sucheng Chan is a mentor and critic to younger colleagues. As a member of an oppressed group, she has provided a unique contribution and perspective. Her guidance has reflected the conflicts and dilemmas faced by members of underrepresented groups, and she has been a role model for others who seek to be mentors and critics of younger colleagues. She has done much in the preparation and nurturing of a new generation of scholars from underrepresented groups who are committed to research and paradigms that provide new perspectives on these diverse population groups. She has also set the stage for colleagues to combine this scholarship with a political activism unparalleled in U.S. academic history.

NOTE

1. This information and much of the personal information in the text are from phone interviews with Sucheng Chan (March 18, 1992; May 22, 1992; July 22, 1992; August 1, 1992; September 5 and 22, 1992; October 5, 1992) as well as from letters and other documents received from her (August 14, 1992; September 22, 1992; October 13, 1992).

WORKS BY SUCHENG CHAN

"Chinese Livelihood in Rural California, 1860–1880: The Impact of Economic Change." *Pacific Historical Review* 53, no. 3 (1984): 273–307.
This Bittersweet Soil: The Chinese in California Agriculture, 1860–1910. Berkeley: University of California Press, 1986.
"European and Asian Immigration into the United States in Comparative Perspective, 1820's to 1920's." In Virginia Yans-McLaughlin, ed., *Immigration Reconsidered: History, Sociology, Politics,* 37–75. New York: Oxford University Press, 1990.

Quiet Odyssey: A Pioneer Korean Woman in America (ed.). Seattle: University of Washington Press, 1990.

Asian Americans: An Interpretive History. Boston: Twayne, 1991.

"The Exclusion of Chinese Women, 1870–1943." *Entry Denied: Exclusion and the Chinese Community in America, 1882–1943,* 94–146. Philadelphia: Temple University Press, 1991.

Entry Denied: Exclusion and the Chinese Community in America, 1882–1943 (ed.). Philadelphia: Temple University Press, 1991.

Peoples of Color in the American West (ed. with Douglas Daniels, Mario Garcia, and Terry P. Wilson). Lexington, MA: D. C. Heath, 1993.

WORKS ABOUT SUCHENG CHAN

"Asian Americans Rise to the Top Echelon in Higher Ed, But Advances Are Too Few." *East West* (October 30, 1985).

"Asian American Studies Scholar Appointed as Santa Cruz Provost." *Pacifica Tribune,* June 20, 1984.

"Burgeoning Asian Population in America Proves a Challenge and a Boon to Scholars Who Study Its History and Culture." *The Chronicle for Higher Education* (April 10, 1991): A5, A8–9.

"Exploring the Issue of Cultural Identity: Two Academics Give Their Views at a Conference on Chinese Migration." *The Straits Times* (Singapore), August 9, 1984.

"Historian Hopes to Help Erase Ethnic Stereotyping." *Santa Cruz Sentinel,* August 24, 1987.

"New Provost at Santa Cruz Eager to Make Changes." *Asian Week* (June 22, 1984).

"Prof Urges Colleagues to Do Committee Work: Involvement Leads to Better Chances for Advancement." *Asian Week* (February 10, 1989): 14.

"Sucheng Chan Wins April Student of the Month in Queens G.O. Council." *Bryant Clipper* (April 30, 1959).

Lydia Maria Francis Child

Ronald E. Butchart

Lydia Maria Francis Child (1802–1880), author and abolitionist, wrote in a wide variety of genres—novels, short fiction, scholarly historical treatises, political tracts, children's literature, and advice books. She launched the first children's magazine in the United States, was the first woman to edit a newspaper dedicated to public policy, published the first domestic advice books, and used the vehicle of sentimental literature to educate Americans about slavery. She was a leader among women of her era in the use of the written word to educate the public, exploring the limits of civic education through literature.

Child ranks among the nineteenth century's foremost women writers. With a greater breadth of interests and commitment than any female writer in the United States in her age, she set a lofty example of the civic educator. She mobilized logic, scholarship, and moral suasion, along with popular fiction, to educate and reform society; she used poetry, stories, and exemplary historical figures to inform and nurture children. She exploited an emerging medium—the magazine—an expanding book trade, and her era's passion for the didactic to become a pioneer among the "scribbling women" against whom Nathaniel Hawthorne grumped. Not content to limit her writing to domestic advice, sentimental literature, or religious meditations, the staples of her female peers, she entered the public arena, writing with force and conviction on controversial political issues. She spoke unflinchingly. For that she paid an enormous social and economic price.

Lydia Maria Francis Child, born Lydia Francis in Medford, Massachusetts, on February 11, 1802, to David C. Francis, (1766–1856) and Susannah (Rand) Francis (1766–1814), was the youngest of five children reared in the stern household of a baker. Her mother died when Child was twelve, an emotional blow that, paradoxically, may explain much about Child's later independence, social insights, and political activism; like Laura M. Towne,

Sallie Holley, Abby Kelley Foster, and other activist women in the nine-teenth century, she was not initiated by a strong mother into the conventions of "true womanhood."[1] Meanwhile, Child had the advantage not only of a good common school education but of the supportive intellectual mentor-ship of an older brother, Convers Francis, a Harvard graduate and Unitarian minister. The two carried on a lively, probing correspondence throughout Child's formative years. She added the name Maria when she was twenty and went by Maria for the rest of her life. Though nominally a Unitarian, she never embraced any creed.

At eighteen, Child began teaching school in Maine while living with a married sister. She returned to Massachusetts two years later to live with Convers Francis and his new wife and started a girls' school that featured active games and an emphasis on the students' independence. While teaching at that school, however, Child began work on a novel and thereby inaugu-rated a lifetime career as a literary educator.

Hobomok (1824), her first novel, foreshadowed some of the themes that would distinguish her writing throughout her life—interracialism, sympathy with Native Americans, and belief in women's independence. A second novel appeared in 1825. Shortly thereafter she established the nation's first monthly children's magazine, *Juvenile Miscellany*, serving as both its editor and primary contributor. It was an immediate success, and with it and a third novel, Child's reputation was established. Meanwhile, she married an ide-alistic young lawyer, David Lee Child, on October 19, 1828. Departing from the norm of nineteenth-century middle-class expectations, their relationship was marked by intellectual equality. It was also marked by extraordinary, but ultimately unavailing, economic sacrifice for David, extended separation and close friendship with young men for Lydia, and the separation of their fi-nancial affairs, yet withal a remarkable devotion to one another. They were childless.

After her success with novels and a children's magazine, Child pioneered a third genre, domestic advice books, including *The Frugal Housewife* (1829), *The Mother's Book* (1831), and *The Little Girl's Own Book* (also 1831). *The Frugal Housewife*, which went through a phenomenal thirty-three editions in the United States and multiple editions in Europe, included recipes and practical ideas on care of the household. As contrasted with Catharine Beecher's later *Treatise on Domestic Economy*, better remembered today, Child's advice books were not concerned with the rationalization of middle-class family life and female roles. Rather, they were intended both to assist those without luxuries to live within their means and to encourage greater female independence, intellectual cultivation, and realism.

An attentive reader of Child's work would have been aware of her emerg-ing political perspectives by the early 1830s—a budding feminism betrayed in the advice she gave women and in her fictional heroines, a nascent inter-racialism about to blossom into abolitionism foreshadowed in her novels and in some of her children's stories. Her foray into a fourth genre hard on the heels of her advice books revealed even more of her feminism. In the early 1830s she turned to historical scholarship, writing an ambitious five-volume study of women, the *Ladies' Family Library*. Under cover of that innocent title were biographies of female role models who were revolutionary thinkers and two volumes entitled *The History of the Condition of Women* (1835), whose anthropological data undermined her era's ideology of domesticity. Published between 1832 and 1835, the volumes were intended to expand women's thinking about their roles and their rights. Later feminist writers drew extensively from Child's work.

All of Child's expository writings were empirically grounded and reflected broad reading. Yet the volumes in the *Ladies' Family Library* and her three-volume study, *The Progress of Religious Ideas Through Successive Ages* (1855), were the most thoroughly researched and exhaustively written. The latter, which Child considered her best work, offended orthodoxy by evenhandedly comparing all the great religions.

By the early 1830s Child's career was virtually unparalleled among women writers in the United States. She was moving in Boston's intellectual circles, a friend of Harvard's George Ticknor, a frequent guest of the young transcendentalists, and an intimate of Margaret Fuller. Perhaps her crowning achievement in those heady years was her receipt of the privilege of using the Athenaeum, Boston's unrivaled private—and exclusively male—research library, only the second woman accorded the privilege. The *North American Review*, not given to hyperbole, remarked in 1833, "We are not sure that any woman of our country could outrank Mrs. Child."[2]

Few female writers have fallen from favor faster than Lydia Maria Child, however. Perhaps none have faced such a drumbeat of vilification or had a career so fully disrupted while continuing to write thoughtfully and competently. She was cast from the heights of intellectual respect and admiration upon her foray into a fifth genre, the expository political study. Her scholarly 1833 publication, *An Appeal in Favor of That Class of Americans Called Africans*, was the first book in the country to advocate immediate, rather than gradual, emancipation, to denounce racial discrimination, to oppose antimiscegenation laws, and to claim the intellectual equality of Africans and Europeans. While some of her earlier writings hinted at her antislavery sympathies, this work announced Child's allegiance to Garrisonian abolitionism.

Child wrote in *An Appeal*, "The only true courage is that which impels us to do right without regard to consequences."[3] The book was clearly an act of great courage, whose consequences included the virtual annihilation of her reputation. Angry parents canceled subscriptions to *Juvenile Miscellany*, forcing it to cease publication within a year. Sales of her remarkably popular domestic advice books plummeted. The Athenaeum canceled her privileges. Erstwhile friends snubbed her on the streets of Boston. The book indicated the price such courage exacted. Her loss coincided with her husband's declining fortunes, and the two lived out the following nearly half century in a not-always genteel poverty.

Yet *An Appeal* gave the struggling abolitionist movement a powerful weapon and swelled its ranks. Notable among those who credited Child with their conversion to abolitionism were Wendell Phillips, Charles Sumner, William Ellery Channing, and Thomas Wentworth Higginson. The book also gave Child "unprecedented political influence for a woman as one of the abolitionist movement's foremost propagandists."[4] In the latter role Child is perhaps best remembered, though her abolitionist activism falls far short of describing her importance as a nineteenth-century female civic educator.

Her new role included editing the *National Anti-Slavery Standard*, 1841 to 1843, making her the first woman in the United States to edit a paper devoted to public policy. She simultaneously became a columnist, inventing the journalistic sketch with her "Letters from New York," written for the *Boston Courier* and reprinted in the *Standard*. The "Letters" detailed her observations of New York City, particularly its poverty and suffering, and frequently conveyed abolitionist and other political themes. Through them Child sought to demonstrate to her readers that society "makes its own criminals, and then, at prodigious loss of time, money, and morals, punishes its own work."[5] The letters' lively, picturesque, and compelling stories recouped some of Child's earlier reputation. She republished "Letters from New York" in two volumes, many of them self-censored to make them more palatable to antiabolitionist and conservative readers. The volumes sold out eleven editions.

Child continued to educate the public about slavery for the next two decades through fiction and nonfiction. Her antislavery stories provided a vehicle for reaching readers who would not read abolitionist tracts. They were designed to arouse sympathy for slaves by detailing the inhuman conditions that slaves—particularly African-American females—were forced to endure. Several were fictional, sometimes carrying ironic titles such as her 1844 short story, "Slavery's Pleasant Homes," while others, such as those in *Authentic Narratives of American Slavery* (1835), reported actual events.

Child returned to the expository voice in 1860 with an extended abolitionist tract that attempted a new rhetorical strategy. In *The Right Way, the Safe Way, Proved by Emancipation in the British West Indies and Elsewhere* (1860), Child sought to develop a discourse with slaveholders, not to attack and alienate them. She couched her arguments for immediate emancipation in terms that would appeal to southern readers, rather than relying on absolute moral arguments, and buttressed her arguments with the testimony of prominent southerners. In addition, she addressed the problems of the social and economic conversion from slavery to free labor, expressing a sensitivity to southern realities unusual among abolitionist writers. The essay "was probably Mrs. Child's most logical and persuasive antislavery work since the publication of her influential *Appeal* twenty-seven years earlier."[6]

The issues about which Child was concerned to educate Americans went well beyond slavery and women's roles, however. Her concern for racial justice for Native Americans antedated her antislavery work. Her first novel, *Hobomok*, provided a highly sympathetic account of Native American life, while her third, *The First Settlers of New-England* (1828), revealed a maturing political consciousness and an effort to influence public opinion against government policy toward the Native Americans. She returned to those themes in her later short fiction and eloquently summarized her arguments against dispossession of the Native Americans in *An Appeal for the Indians* (1868), among her last major studies. If her vision was clouded by an unexamined allegiance to ideas of progress and individualism, she nonetheless advanced notable critiques of the contradictions between American beliefs and actions and contributed important themes to the antiracist tradition.

The collapse of *Juvenile Miscellany* and Child's absorption in reform reduced her contributions to children's literature to occasional pieces for magazines and newspapers. By the mid-1840s, however, she began writing again for children with collections of stories such as *Flowers for Children* (three series, 1844–1846), *Rainbows for Children* (1848), and *New Flowers for Children* (1855). Like her novels and short fiction, her children's literature educated while entertaining. She did not shield children from the social issues of the day, particularly slavery and racism, but wove those issues into stories and poems. Her stories also imparted "useful information" and sought to instill proper values for future citizens of a republic.

Only one of her books was expressly written for use in schools. Its specific audience and objective speak eloquently to Lydia Maria Child's vision and commitments. *The Freedmen's Book* (1865), published at Child's own expense, with all proceeds to be given to southern black education, was intended for use in freedmen's schools. It was not the first text aimed at the freed people, but it departed dramatically from competing curricular material. Its primary objective was to foster racial pride through biographical sketches of significant black figures, anticipating by a century a major concern of African-American educators inspired by the civil rights movement. Rather than the image of a docile black peasantry promoted by other textbooks, Child provided an image of strong, proactive, intellectual, and even (as in the biography of Toussaint L'Ouverture) revolutionary role models.[7]

As her own mortality began to weigh upon her, Child began to write for the elderly. She compiled two volumes intended to promote dignity and a positive view of aging and death. *Looking Toward Sunset* (1865) and *Aspirations of the World* (1878) were optimistic and upbeat. Like echoes of her advice books for the young written years before, these volumes gave hints on health and cleanliness and admonished older citizens to avoid stagnation through active participation in life.

Child relied almost exclusively on the written word to educate her era. Though she supported other women who broke with social convention to speak in public, she refused all offers to lecture. She was active in abolitionist organizations but was skeptical of much organizational effort.

Lydia Maria Child died on October 20, 1880, six years after her husband. Throughout her long career as an author, Child evinced an overarching sense of purpose or mission. Two years into the aftermath of *An Appeal in Favor of That Class of Americans Called Africans*, she expressed her educational vision to her brother:

Sometimes we may be tempted to think it would have been better for us not to have been cast on these evil times; but this is a selfish consideration; we ought rather to rejoice that we have much to do as mediums in the regeneration of the world . . . . You ask me to be prudent, and I will be so, as far as is consistent with a sense of duty; but this will not be what the world calls prudent. Firmness is the virtue most needed in times of excitement. What consequence is it if a few individuals do sink to untimely and dishonored graves, if the progress of great principles is still onward? Perchance for this cause came we into the world.[8]

Lydia Marie Child is not well known today, much to our own great loss. Others from her era are remembered—Louisa May Alcott, Harriet Beecher Stowe, Catharine Beecher, Mary Lyon, Lydia B. Sigourney. Of Child's prodigious output, most Americans know but one poem, and virtually none would identify her as the author: "The New-England Boy's Song About Thanksgiving" ("Over the river and through the wood to Grandfather's house we go . . . ") first appeared in her *Flowers for Children* (1845). It is ironic that only a children's verse would remain in the popular mind, for Child was one of our true pioneers in civic education, a woman who mastered nearly every genre of her age, inventing several herself, a woman who stepped onto the public stage when women were expected to retire to the nursery, a woman of great courage and integrity who paid dearly in fame and fortune for acting upon her convictions.

Through much of her writing, Child sought to teach by providing models for Americans to emulate. Her age and ours are diminished by having failed to hold her up as such a model. John Greenleaf Whittier said of Child, "No man or woman . . . rendered more substantial service to the cause of freedom, or made such a 'great renunciation' in doing it."[9] Likewise, few educators have shown us better how to live courageously despite the price.

NOTES

1. This interpretation was first advanced in Jane H. Pease and William H. Pease, "The Role of Women in the Antislavery Movement," *Canadian Historical Association Annual Report* (1967): 167–83.

2. Unsigned review [Grenville Mellen?], *North American Review* 37 (July 1833): 139.

3. Lydia Maria Child, *An Appeal in Favor of That Class of Americans Called Africans* (Boston: Allen and Ticknor, 1833, reprint, New York: Arno, 1968), 207.

4. Carolyn L. Karcher, ed., "Introduction," in Lydia Maria Child, *Hobomok and Other Writings on Indians* (New Brunswick, NJ: Rutgers University Press, 1986), xiii.

5. Milton Meltzer, *Tongue of Flame: The Life of Lydia Maria Child* (New York: Thomas Y. Crowell, 1965), 98.

6. Nancy Slocum Hornick, ed., "The Last Appeal: Lydia Maria Child's Antislavery Letters to John C. Underwood," *Virginia Magazine of History and Biography* 79 (1971): 48.

7. For a full discussion of *The Freedmen's Book* and other curricular material intended for the freedmen's schools, see Ronald E. Butchart, *Northern Schools, Southern Blacks, and Reconstruction: Freedmen's Education, 1862–1875* (Westport, CT: Greenwood Press, 1980), 135–55.

8. L. M. Child to Convers Francis, September 25, 1835, in Milton Meltzer and Patricia G. Holland, eds. *Lydia Maria Child: Selected Letters, 1817–1880* (Amherst: University of Massachusetts Press, 1982), 38.

9. John G. Whittier, *Letters of Lydia Maria Child, with a Biographical Introduction* (Boston: Houghton Mifflin, 1883), x.

WORKS BY LYDIA MARIA FRANCIS CHILD

Hobomok, A Tale of Early Times. Boston: Cummings, Hilliard, 1824.

The Frugal Housewife. Boston: Marsh and Capen and Carter and Hendee, 1829.

An Appeal in Favor of That Class of Americans Called Africans. Boston: Allen and Ticknor, 1833. Reprint, New York: Arno, 1968.

The History of the Condition of Women, in Various Ages and Nations. Boston: J. Allen, 1835. (Vols. 4 and 5 of *Ladies' Family Library*.)

Letters from New York, First Series. New York: Charles S. Francis, 1843. *Second Series*, 1845.

The Progress of Religious Ideas Through Successive Ages. 3 vols. New York: C. S. Francis, 1855.

The Freedmen's Book (ed.). Boston: Ticknor and Fields, 1865. Reprint, New York: Arno, 1968.

Aspirations of the World. A Chain of Opals (ed.). Boston: Roberts, 1878.

WORKS ABOUT LYDIA MARIA FRANCIS CHILD

Baer, Helene G. *The Heart Is Like Heaven: The Life of Lydia Maria Child*. Philadelphia: University of Pennsylvania Press, 1964.

Holland, Patricia G. "Lydia Maria Child as a Nineteenth-Century Author." In Joel Myerson, ed., *Studies in the American Renaissance*, 157–67. Charlottesville: University Press of Virginia, 1981.

Jeffrey, Kirk. "Marriage, Career, and Feminine Ideology in Nineteenth-Century America: Reconstructing the Marital Experience of Lydia Maria Child, 1828–1874." *Feminist Studies* 2, nos. 2–3, (1975): 113–30.

Karcher, Carolyn L. "Introduction." In Lydia Maria Child, *Hobomok and Other Writings on Indians*, ix-xxxviii. New Brunswick, NJ: Rutgers University Press, 1986a.

———. "Rape, Murder and Revenge in 'Slavery's Pleasant Homes': Lydia Maria Child's Antislavery Fiction and the Limits of Genre." *Women's Studies International Forum* 9, no. 4, (1986): 323–32.

Meltzer, Milton. *Tongue of Flame: The Life of Lydia Maria Child.* New York: Thomas Y. Crowell, 1965.

Meltzer, Milton, and Patricia G. Holland, eds. *Lydia Maria Child: Selected Letters, 1817–1880.* Amherst: University of Massachusetts Press, 1982.

Septima Poinsette Clark

Linda D. Addo

Septima Poinsette Clark's (1898–1987) involvement in American education began in 1916 on St. Johns Island, South Carolina, followed by
teaching positions in Charleston, South Carolina; McClellanville, South
Carolina; the mountains of North Carolina; Columbia, South Carolina;
and Monteagle, Tennessee. During the civil rights movement in the
1960s she organized Citizenship Schools for the Southern Christian
Leadership Conference. Clark's role as a teacher and political activist
spanned over forty years of momentous change in American educational,
social, and political life. Her background and role as a black educator
provide insight into American education as a whole as well as for a
specific group of citizens, black Americans. She made a significant contribution and difference in the lives of her students and the communities
where she taught because she was convinced that education without political power would not liberate blacks.

Septima Poinsette Clark was born on May 3, 1898, in Charleston, South
Carolina. Her father had been a slave and had also served in the Confederate
army as a water boy; he later became a caterer. Her mother was born into
a free family in Charleston but was reared in Haiti. Septima's father assumed
the surname of Joel Poinsette, who owned the plantation where he was a
slave. Joel Poinsette was a botanist who cultivated on his plantation a red
flower that later became known as the "poinsettia." Septima Clark was the
second child of eight (four boys and four girls) born to her parents. According to Clark, she was known as "Le Ma" in her neighborhood and had
decided by the age of ten that she wanted to be a teacher. Clark attended
the first public high school, Burke Vocational Institute, opened for African
Americans in Charleston in 1912. Although Burke Vocational Institute was
considered a high school, it offered only grades six through eight. Septima
spent only one year at Burke. She took an examination and was admitted to

a private black school, the Avery Normal Institute. The Avery Institute was established for blacks in 1865 with the help and financial support of the American Missionary Association.

At this time Avery Institute was known for preparing black teachers and for preparing students to enter college. The curriculum included Greek, Latin, philosophy, algebra, geometry, botany, English literature, and government. In his history of the school, Edmund Drago describes Avery Institute as the embodiment of the principles of W.E.B. Du Bois. Du Bois believed that the struggle for political equality for blacks would be led by the "Talented Tenth," an intelligent and politically active group of blacks. After graduating from Avery Institute, Septima Clark accepted a position in 1916 as a teacher-principal on one of the sea islands, Johns Island. Clark had completed the twelfth grade at Avery and was awarded a Licentiate of Instruction. This qualified her to teach in South Carolina.

Clark's school was a crude structure with an open fireplace and wooden benches without backs as seats for her students. An ax, a water bucket and dipper, a table and chair, and firewood were the only equipment provided for the school. Clark had to buy her own chalk and erasers. Black teachers were paid twenty-five dollars a month while white teachers with the same certificate as Clark's were paid eighty-five dollars. There were 132 students in the school and a staff of 2 teachers, who were also graduates of Avery Institute. Clark acquired her sense of mission in this first teaching position:

So, as I look back more than four decades to my experiences as a teen-age teacher, I realize that it was the Johns Island folk who, if they did not set me on my course, surely did confirm me in a course I had dreamed of taking even as a child, that of teaching and particularly teaching the poor and underprivileged of my own underprivileged race.[1]

After Clark left Johns Island to teach at the Avery Institute, another dimension was added to her mission as a teacher: political activist.

During her first year at Avery Institute, Clark participated in a petition drive organized by the National Association for the Advancement of Colored People (NAACP) in Charleston to pressure local authorities to hire black teachers for black public schools. It was the custom in Charleston to hire only white teachers to teach in black public schools. Clark responded to the appeal of her principal for volunteers to gather at least 10,000 signatures on petitions demanding that black teachers be hired in black public schools. Clark concentrated on what she called the "grass roots people." The petition drive was successful: "Soon we brought in a tow sack—we called it a croaker sack, I remember, back in those days—with more than 10,000 signatures to the petition."[2] By 1920, as a result of this campaign, black teachers were being hired to teach in the black public schools in Charleston. Not only was Clark now a dedicated teacher and political activist, but she also assumed another role. She met Nerie Clark, a sailor from Hickory, North Carolina, while teaching at Avery Institute, and they were married on May 23, 1920.

Until her husband was discharged from the navy, Septima Clark stayed with her in-laws and attended summer school at the then North Carolina Agricultural and Technical College in Greensboro, North Carolina. She taught in Mars Hill, North Carolina. After her husband was discharged from the navy, they moved to Dayton, Ohio. Nerie died there after an illness in 1925. Only one of the two children from the marriage survived, a son. A one-month-old daughter died as the result of a hernia operation. After her husband's death, Clark returned to Hickory, North Carolina, and her teaching position at the black public school in Mars Hill. In 1928 Clark left her son with his grandparents and returned to Charleston and her former teaching position on Johns Island. She stayed only one year and decided to take a teaching position in Columbia, South Carolina. She was attending summer school in Columbia when she was offered the new teaching position. She taught in Columbia from 1929 to 1947. She attributed her eighteen years in Columbia with providing her with the experiences that would equip her for her role as an educator and political activist during the civil rights movement of the 1960s.

Professionally, Clark considered her experiences in Columbia among the most satisfying, if not the most satisfying of her career as an educator, because she was able to pass the state teacher's examination, obtain undergraduate and graduate degrees, and continue to improve social and political conditions for blacks. She was an active member of the NAACP chapter in Columbia, and she enthusiastically involved herself in the NAACP campaign and court case to get a federal court to rule on the issue of equalizing the salaries of black and white teachers in South Carolina. In 1945 when the judge ruled that teachers with the same qualifications should be paid the same salary, Septima's salary was $62.50 a month.

After the court decision, the state of South Carolina began to require all teachers to take the National Teacher Examination. Clark passed the examination, and her monthly salary was increased to $117.00. Clark continued through night classes and summer school to pursue her dream to obtain an undergraduate degree. In 1942 she received a bachelor's degree from Benedict College in Columbia, South Carolina. Four years later she received a master of arts degree from Hampton Institute (now Hampton University) in Hampton, Virginia. Not only was Clark a dynamic and inspirational teacher and political activist, but she also taught adult literacy classes at night during the eighteen years she spent in Columbia. She left Columbia in 1947 to accept a teaching position in Charleston so that she could be near her elderly mother. Clark left Columbia convinced that she was prepared not only to continue teaching but also to continue as a community activist determined to improve life for her people.

But more important to me than the teacher-training programs and even the teaching itself, as far as my own development was concerned, I believe, were the opportunities

I had to participate in civic activities. My participation in the programs of the various civic groups not only strengthened my determination to make my own life count for something in the fight to aid the underprivileged toward the enjoyment of fuller lives, but also gave me excellent training in procedures that could be used effectively in the struggle.[3]

In Charleston, Clark's first assignment at the Henry P. Archer School was as a seventh grade teacher. The principal later discovered that she had taken courses in reading and gave her responsibility for "problem" students in grades four through seven who also needed remedial work in reading. Septima enjoyed this assignment and gained a reputation for being especially effective with remedial reading classes and with students who were considered "problems." However, her political activism made her the center of controversy. As chairperson of the black Young Women's Christian Association (YWCA) committee on administration, Clark challenged local social and racial taboos by inviting Elizabeth Waring, the wife of federal judge Julius Waites Waring, to speak at the black YWCA. Clark began to receive obscene phone calls after Elizabeth Waring's white neighbors saw Clark enter the Waring house to personally extend the invitation to speak. The Warings were not affected by the criticism because they were already unpopular in Charleston. Judge Waring was the judge who ruled in favor of equalizing the salaries of black and white teachers and also ruled that Democratic white primaries were illegal in South Carolina. The Warings and Septima Clark became friends and visited each other's homes. Clark was upset when she was criticized by blacks because she invited the Warings to her home. However, she discovered that blacks were afraid that the Ku Klux Klan would retaliate.

Even her principal criticized her on one occasion when he saw Clark leaving the Waring house. He told Clark that she was living dangerously. Clark did not let the criticism of whites and blacks interfere with her friendship with the Warings. The Warings were influenced by Clark and became interested in educational opportunities for blacks. After the death of the Warings in 1968 Clark discovered that they had left money in their will to provide a scholarship for a black student to attend the College of Charleston. Although the Warings had left Charleston to reside in New York City in 1950, Clark's friendship with them and her other political and civic activities resulted in her being perceived as a political radical by both blacks and whites in Charleston. She would eventually lose her job and the right to teach in South Carolina because of her reputation as a political radical and activist.

After the 1954 *Brown v. Board of Education* decision teachers in South Carolina were required to fill out a questionnaire. In South Carolina the NAACP was considered a subversive organization, and one of the questions on the questionnaire asked teachers to list organizations to which they belonged. Many black teachers who belonged to the NAACP did not list it on the questionnaire; of course, Septima Clark did. In 1955 the South Carolina legislature passed a law that made it illegal for any state or city employee to belong to the NAACP. Clark described her reaction to the letter informing her of her dismissal: "It wasn't long before I got my letter of dismissal. The Board of Education wrote me that it would not be renewing my contract to teach remedial reading at the Henry Archer School. My goodness, somehow or other, it really didn't bother me."[4] Clark attempted to organize a protest of the dismissals, but she discovered that most of her colleagues were afraid. Their refusal convinced her that blacks needed to be trained to understand their rights as citizens and the dimensions and impact of black citizens exercising political power. Thus, Clark accepted a position at the Highlander Folk School in Monteagle, Tennessee, in 1956.

The Highlander Folk School was organized in 1934 by two white Tennesseans, Myles Horton and Lilian Johnson. Horton and Johnson believed that all men and women are brothers and sisters and that people of different races and economic conditions should be able to live together in peace and harmony. The school conducted workshops and adult literacy programs. The major objective of the educational experiences at the school was to help farmers, miners, and ordinary laborers to develop self-esteem and awareness of their rights and roles as citizens. Clark was excited about her new position at Highlander Folk School as director and organizer of adult workshops at the school and throughout the South. Clark shared the philosophy of the founders of the school that education and especially the ability to read should be used to help miners, farmers, and workers in general to improve their lives politically, economically, and socially by utilizing the values of the democratic society in which they lived.

Clark was especially interested in getting one particular social activist, Esau Jenkins, from the Charleston and Johns Island area interested in adult literacy workshops. Clark had worked with Esau Jenkins when she taught in Charleston. Since 1948 Jenkins had been teaching adults how to read the Constitution and had also organized a self-help club, the Progressive Club. The members of the Progressive Club provided bail money for blacks arrested because of racism, organized a cooperative, and established their own grocery store. After the Brown decision Jenkins realized that blacks needed to be literate in order to exercise their right to vote. In 1957 Clark invited Jenkins to the Highlander Folk School to attend a workshop. Clark and Jenkins designed a vehicle to implement their idea of literacy as a means of political liberation for blacks on Johns Island and throughout the South. Myles Horton loaned money, without charging interest, to Jenkins and Clark to build a building for what they called "The Citizenship School" on Johns Island. It officially opened in January 1957.

After the Highlander Folk School was raided by the state police, Myles Horton met with Dr. Martin Luther King. In case his school was closed by the state of Tennessee, Horton wanted the citizenship program to be moved.

King suggested that Clark and the citizenship schools could be used to train civil rights workers. From 1961 until 1970 Clark worked for the Southern Christian Leadership Conference under the shield of the United Church of Christ. The association with the United Church of Christ was necessary because the Southern Christian Leadership Conference could not receive foundation grants. The citizenship schools were operated out of the Dorchester Cooperative Community Center in Liberty County, Georgia. The community center was owned by the United Church of Christ. Until the Voting Rights Act was passed by Congress in 1965, Clark and the teachers trained in the citizenship schools provided a valuable service. Blacks were taught how to answer the trivial and often ridiculous questions that registrars asked to prevent large numbers of blacks from registering to vote.

The teachers trained by the citizenship schools for this important task were local leaders in their communities who could read aloud and who could write their names in cursive. Between 1957 and 1970 there were 897 citizenship schools. These schools were held throughout the South in homes, beauty parlors, barber shops, churches, and even outdoors.[5] Clark describes what happened after the NAACP, the Congress of Racial Equality (CORE), the National Urban League, and the Student Non-Violent Coordinating Committee (SNCC) came together in 1962 to organize the Voter Education Project: "In the next four years all the groups together trained about 10,000 teachers for Citizenship Schools. During this period about 700,000 black voters registered across the South."[6] On January 19, 1970, Septima Clark retired to her home, purchased in 1927, at 17 Henrietta Street in Charleston. She looked forward to enjoying family, friends, and visits from her six grandchildren. In her autobiography and in interviews before her death in 1987 Clark indicated that she retired confident that her philosophy and methodology of education had made a difference.

Throughout her teaching career Clark always expressed a firm faith and belief in the American political system. She was the first to acknowledge that the system was not perfect and that blacks had been denied the rights and protection of a democratic system. She believed that education could be the vehicle of change for blacks and American society. Furthermore, she believed that a viable democratic society resulted from citizens who were active and full participants in their communities, states, and the nation. She stated this succinctly in her autobiography: "To me social justice is not a matter of money but of will, not a problem for the economist as much as a task for the patriot; to me its accomplishment requires leadership and community action rather than monetary investment."[7] Academic education and citizenship education had to take place simultaneously if blacks were to become first-class citizens. Clark's career as a teacher and social activist demonstrated that academic education and citizenship education can provide motivation for blacks and any oppressed people to change their lives and to develop self-esteem.

Clark demonstrated that illiterate adults were motivated to learn to read because they wanted to vote and learn other skills. Experienced educators were amazed at what she accomplished in the citizenship schools. Using the method that Clark had learned to teach reading at the Highlander School, she was able to do in 80 hours what it took the Adult Education Association, using the Laubach method, 150 hours to achieve. Septima Clark believed that her effectiveness as a teacher in the public schools and later in the citizenship schools could be measured by what her students did with what they had learned. Success was measured by her former students who not only voted but who were also participating citizens in their communities. Education should produce self-awareness and selfhood. Her motivation had come first from her parents and then her teachers; however, Clark as a teacher taught so that what happened in her classroom enabled the individual student to realize his or her own humanity.

Septima Clark's career as a teacher for fifty-four years demonstrated a belief in education and teaching as vehicles that enabled her students to realize that being in the world has possibilities. Her students were motivated to change their environments and to work as active participants in the development and achievement of a democratic society for all citizens. Her traditional students and later the adults in the citizenship schools began to realize their potential and what they could do to improve their lives. Finally, Clark knew what many contemporary sociologists and educators realize, that the disappearance of de jure segregation did not mean the end of hopelessness in black communities and that this hopelessness is often seen as apathy by outsiders. Students are motivated to learn when they realize that what they learn can help them understand the world in which they live. In the manual used in the Citizenship School on St. Johns Island was a map of the United States, with South Carolina and the Charleston area identified. The first lesson described the United States as a democratic nation, and the second lesson discussed the election laws in South Carolina. The essence of Septima Clark's philosophy appears in a statement describing the manual: "The booklet, therefore, is a very good example of the 'learning by doing' method of teaching. And, even more importantly, it helps the student learn by doing something of real practical value to him."[8]

NOTES

1. Septima Clark, *Echo in My Soul* (New York: E. P. Dutton, 1962), 52.
2. Ibid., 61.
3. Ibid., 76–77.
4. Ibid., 36.
5. Septima Clark and Cynthia S. Brown, eds., *Ready from Within: Septima Clark and the Civil Rights Movement* (Navarro, CA: Wild Trees Press, 1986), 69–70.
6. Ibid., 70.

7. Clark, 236.
8. Ibid., 201.

WORKS BY SEPTIMA POINSETTE CLARK

Echo in My Soul. New York: E. P. Dutton, 1962.

"Literacy and Liberation." *Freedomways* (1964): 113–24.

Interview with Septima Clark by Eugene Walker, July 30, 1976. Southern Oral History Collection, Southern Historical Collection, University of North Carolina at Chapel Hill.

Interview with Septima Clark by Jacquelyne Hall, July 25, 1981. Southern Oral History Collection, Southern Historical Collection, University of North Carolina at Chapel Hill.

Ready from Within: Septima Clark and the Civil Rights Movement (and Cynthia Brown, eds.). Navarro, CA: Wild Trees Press, 1986.

WORKS ABOUT SEPTIMA POINSETTE CLARK

Brown, Cynthia S. "Giving Aunt Donnie Her Due." *Social Policy* 21 (Winter 1991): 19–27.

Bullock, Henry A. *A History of Negro Education in the South from 1619 to the Present.* Cambridge: Harvard University Press, 1967.

Crawford, Vicki, Jacqueline A. Rouse, and Barbara Woods, eds. *Women in the Civil Rights Movement: Trailblazers and Torchbearers, 1941–1965.* Brooklyn, NY: Carlson, 1990.

Daise, Ronald. *Reminiscences of Sea Island Heritage: Legacy of Freedom on St. Helena Island.* Orangeburg, SC: Sandlapper, 1986.

Gallman, Vanessa. "Septima Clark: On Life, Courage, Dedication." *View South* 4 (July/August 1979): 13–16.

Fannia Mary Cohn

Ruth Jacknow Markowitz

Fannia Mary Cohn (1885–1962), a Russian Jewish immigrant of prosperous background, relinquished her privileged status for that of a factory worker and then a union activist. Her activities and experiences in
the labor movement, which she believed invested workers with power,
led to her interest and belief in workers' education, which Cohn insisted
would give workers the ability to use their power intelligently and
effectively.

Born April 5, 1885, in the town of Kletzk, near the city of Minsk, in the
Russian Pale of Settlement, Fannia Mary Cohn was the fourth of five children (four girls and a boy) of Hyman Cohn, the manager of a family-owned
flour mill, and Anna Rosofsky Cohn. Cohn and her siblings were privately
educated in direct contravention of *shtetl* tradition, which proscribed schooling for females, whose informal education was to be centered on their domestic duties. Formal education was reserved for males. Cohn's interest in
education was inspired by her mother, who encouraged her to read and to
prepare for a professional career. Despite their affluence, her parents sub-
scribed to radical political views, which perhaps induced Cohn to become a
socialist. However, unlike most other Jews who desired to change Russia,
Cohn eschewed the Socialist Bund and the Zionist movement. Instead, in
1901 she joined the outlawed Socialist Revolutionary Party, apparently seeing no contradiction in belonging to an anti-Semitic organization. Here she
was imbued with the revolutionary spirit that influenced her life and later
propelled her into the labor movement. After a brother was almost killed in
a pogrom, Cohn gave up all hope of a socialist transformation in Russia and
emigrated to America in 1904.

Cohn persuaded her parents to overcome their objection to her leaving
home by promising to continue her studies in New York. While Cohn was
part of the mass migration of Jews from Eastern Europe to the New World,

both her motivation and mode of travel differed greatly from those of the thousands of other young women who made the same journey. She came to America in search of freedom, not economic advantages like most; and she traveled second-class, not steerage like the majority of immigrants, courtesy of wealthy New York cousins. These relatives, with whom she lived, were pharmacists who owned a drug supply company and suggested that Cohn study pharmacology and then join their business. They also offered to finance her studies, but she rejected their offer since it conflicted with her sense of independence. She became the American Jewish Women's Committee's representative on Ellis Island, where she came into daily contact with the crowds of immigrants undergoing their chaotic arrival in America. Finding her work assisting immigrants too charitable in nature, she left after a short time to concentrate on preparing for the examination for pharmacy school.

In the middle of her studies, she changed her mind and decided to work in the labor movement, a move she attributed to her revolutionary background. As she explained, many years later: "If I wanted to really understand the mind, the aspirations of the workers, I should experience the life of a worker in a shop."[1] She chose to enter the labor movement as a sleeve maker in a garment factory and was soon involved in a torrent of strikes, initiated to alleviate the deplorable conditions under which workers toiled in the garment industry. In 1909, Cohn's life as a union official began with her election to the executive board of the newly created Local 41, which united the Wrapper, Kimono, and House Dress Makers into the fledgling International Ladies' Garment Workers' Union (ILGWU). She chaired the local's board from 1913 to 1914. During this time she wrote the first of many articles for the union newspapers, which were written in Yiddish, Italian, and English, stressing women's potential for unionization. Like several other immigrant women deeply involved in the labor movement, she made a conscious choice to remain single and dedicate herself to a career of leading workers within the labor movement.

At this time, Cohn realized that the press was an excellent vehicle for teaching the masses about socialism and trade unionism and that her writings would undoubtedly serve to advance her status within the union. Therefore, in 1914 she accepted a scholarship to attend the Women's Trade Union League School for Organizers in Chicago, where she hoped to improve her English. Cohn believed that a better knowledge of English not only would aid in her union work but would enable her to rise within the union. However, when she arrived in Chicago, she discovered that the league school had not been established yet. Arrangements were made for her to study economics and history at the University of Chicago, but she judged the course materially diametrical to her socialist orientation and she withdrew. Moreover, when the league provided English classes, she pronounced them inadequate and engaged a private tutor. Cohn remained in Chicago as a general organizer for the ILGWU, where she reached the pinnacle of her career as an organizer and where she firmly embedded her lifework within the matrix of the garment workers' union. In August 1915 she organized and led the first successful strike of the city's dress and white goods workers, which gained her unionwide recognition. Returning to New York the following year, Cohn was elected the first woman vice president of the ILGWU.

Cohn continued as a union officer until 1926, but her 1917 appointment to the ILGWU's General Educational Committee was her most significant assignment, which she deemed highly appropriate since she considered the education of the workers to be her calling. Cohn proudly noted that the union also believed education to be its most effective weapon in its struggle. This interest in workers' education can be traced to the traditional value placed on education by the Eastern European Jewish immigrants, who comprised the largest percentage of the union's membership, and these immigrant workers had been attending classes at the Workers School and the Rand School in New York City since 1900. The ILGWU's commitment to education was rooted as well in its philosophy of social unionism, which went beyond workers' concerns about wages and working conditions to encompass their need for recreation, education, health care, and housing. The underlying aim at all times was to build a stronger union, which was connected to the creation of a new and better social order.

Under the leadership of Juliet Stuart Poyntz, the union's educational director, the ILGWU initiated a series of innovative programs aimed to educate the individual worker, train new leaders, and foster class consciousness among workers, all of which were meant to strengthen the union. Poyntz established unity centers in the public schools that offered free classes in such subjects as the labor movement, economics, civics, and English instruction. Although courses in science, literature, art, and music were taught as well, the emphasis was on subjects that would enable workers to form sound judgments. Workers' universities for more advanced students were also formed, along with Unity House, a vacation home for young women garment workers, where they could learn about trade unionism in a friendly, social setting. However, Cohn and Poyntz did not get along well. Cohn was highly critical of Poyntz. She envied Poyntz's popularity and resented the fact that she did not come from an immigrant, working-class background. Despite their rivalry, when Poyntz resigned in 1918, Cohn devoted her life to promoting and expanding the programs originated by Poyntz.

Fully aware of women's issues and the problems confronting them in the male-dominated labor movement, where she was always viewed by male unionists as the token woman, Cohn tried to use the prestige and authority of her office to gain acceptance for women and to inspire other women to seek positions in the union. In an industry whose labor force was predominantly female, Cohn was convinced that unionism would fail unless women were organized. While she believed that education would equip women workers

with the means to emancipate themselves from traditional and social disa-
bilities, she argued that it would benefit the general membership, as well.
Cohn took great pains to construct educational programs that would attract
women, such as providing them with clean meeting rooms or classes that
would be of particular interest to women. Her intentions were always to
foster trade unionism. Although in later years, associates termed her an old-
fashioned feminist, Cohn never considered herself as such. Instead, she
claimed that she was merely a trade unionist and that her deep concern with
women workers arose from her commitment to trade unionism, rather than
to the women's movement.

By the 1920s, as one of the founders of the National Workers' Education
Bureau, a clearinghouse for workers' education programs meant to be the
centerpiece of the workers' education movement, Cohn had become an acknowledged leader in the burgeoning movement. She formulated an extensive new program for the union, based on her belief that education should
extend beyond the classroom, and sought to have the union's educational
department satisfy workers' intellectual, economic, and recreational needs.
She was instrumental in the establishment of Brookwood Labor College, the
first residential workers' college in the United States, persuading the
ILGWU to provide its members with scholarships to the college. Cohn also
helped organize both a camp and a residential school for workers' children.
Although the ILGWU also cooperated with the Bryn Mawr Summer School
for Women Workers, Cohn refused to serve on its organizing committee
because she was adamant that workers' education be directed by the trade
unions, not the universities. Throughout her career, Cohn was uncomfortable with middle- and upper-class women's involvement in labor causes, despite her own middle-class origins.

During the 1920s Cohn came to personify the workers' education movement through her numerous speeches and articles in the labor press. The
decade was a turbulent one for the ILGWU as it was wracked with a virulent
struggle between communist and socialist factions. Cohn's determination to
remain neutral and keep the Education Department above politics resulted
in both sides' distrusting her. In addition, by concentrating to such an extent
on workers' education, she became isolated from both the rank and file and
union leadership, all of which contributed to her losing the vice presidency
in 1925.

Recognizing that Fannia Cohn and workers' education were synonymous,
ILGWU leaders assured her that she would continue to head its Education
Department. But without the prestige and political authority conferred by
the office of vice president, the importance of both Cohn and the department
she headed diminished. Because of the highly charged political climate
within the union and Cohn's resolution to divorce workers' education from
politics, she found it necessary to modify her programs. To avoid eruptions
over ideology, she tended to avoid classes in such confrontational subjects

as political economy and to focus more on classes of a somewhat escapist nature like art and music. By the end of the 1920s, the workers' education movement was on the verge of collapse, and the Brookwood Labor College, which she had helped to found, almost disappeared. Although Cohn endeavored to divorce Brookwood from political controversy, it finally closed in 1937. Nevertheless, she single-handedly kept the union's Education Department alive during these years when the nearly bankrupt union lacked the money for supplies or even Cohn's salary.

By the time the Great Depression hit, the ILGWU was minus more than half its members and most of its financial resources and had lost its prominence in the trade union movement. Its Education Department was in disarray as well, having abandoned the philosophy and programs that had made it such a guiding force in workers' education. The New Deal and passage of the National Industrial Recovery Act, which recognized labor's right to organize, brought about a resurgence of the ILGWU. Its president, David Dubinsky, embarked upon a major organizing drive that quadrupled its membership. But its new members were American-born and unfamiliar with either the radical political views or the basics of trade unionism that had characterized their immigrant predecessors. The union's leadership was convinced that workers' education was the key to infusing new members with union solidarity and to reaping favorable publicity from the general public. Cohn was delighted and was prepared to throw herself into the revitalization of her department, proposing that its new motto be, "Enlighten new recruits."[2]

Although Dubinsky acknowledged that Cohn acted as "the mother of the Education Department,"[3] he refused to keep her in charge of the department she had come to regard as her private jurisdiction and to which she had consecrated her life. The ILGWU was making a concerted effort to appeal to younger, native-born members more interested in social activities and courses in managing union accounts than in classes in dialectical materialism. Because Fannia Cohn, with her Russian-Yiddish accent, embodied the older, foreign-born generation, she was replaced as educational director in 1935 by an Englishman, Mark Starr. The department's new direction concentrated on three divisions. A recreational and cultural branch sponsored a variety of activities aimed at individual enrichment combined with public relations programs designed to project a new image of American unionism. The traditional classwork section consisted of such traditional courses as union history and economics. The third segment, the Officers' Qualification Course, a prerequisite to union office, explained the mechanics of a modern union and the intricacies of the garment industry.

Although the work of the Education Department continued to expand and although she was allowed to retain the title of executive secretary, Cohn found herself relegated to the most marginal responsibilities until her only project was the Book Division. Frustrated and embittered, increasingly difficult and temperamental, she refused to consider retirement until the union forced the issue with a retirement luncheon in August 1962. Unable to accept retirement, she appeared at her old office daily, undeterred even by the removal of her desk. On December 24, 1962, she died of a stroke in New York City.

In part, Cohn's travails emanated from the prejudices of male unionists and from the changing visions of what workers' education ought to be. However, her own personality also contributed to her problems. Colleagues found her domineering and self-centered under the best of circumstances, but after repeated isolation and humiliations within the union, she grew ever more irascible and demanding. Because Cohn had invested her career with an almost-religious zeal, she came to regard the Education Department as her personal fiefdom, guarding it jealously and rebuffing attempts at collaboration. However, this same fervor is what enabled her to sustain the workers' education movement. Under her guidance, the movement acculturated immigrant workers, enlightened workers of all backgrounds, and provided the union with the means of developing qualified leaders from within its own ranks.

Cohn may have been powerless to stop her ideal of workers' education from mutating into a labor education that emphasized choral groups and picnics more than the study of Marxism, but her zeal sustained the idea of workers' education. Through her example, she inspired other women to strive for positions of authority in the unions and demonstrated that education need not be merely the means to escape the working class or a way to inculcate workers with middle-class values and beliefs. Instead, Cohn's programs offered a workers' education that would develop social consciousness, an understanding of economics and politics, and a determination to maintain workers' solidarity, all of which were meant to bring about a restructuring of American society.

NOTES

1. Fannia M. Cohn to Selig Perlman, December 26, 1951. Box 4, Fannia M. Cohn Papers, Rare Books and Manuscripts Division, The New York Public Library, Astor, Lenox and Tilden Foundations, New York.
2. Fannia M. Cohn, "Enlighten New Recruits," *Justice* 1 (December 1933): 24–25.
3. Interview with David Dubinsky, October 31, 1973, in Ricki Carole Myers Cohen, "Fannia Cohn and the International Ladies' Garment Workers' Union," Ph.D. diss., University of Southern California, 1976, 122.

WORKS BY FANNIA MARY COHN

Fannia Cohn Papers, Rare Books and Manuscripts Division, Boxes 1–18, New York Public Library, Astor, Lenox and Tilden Foundations, New York.

"What Workers' Education Really Is." *Life and Labor* 11 (October 1921): 228–34.
"Workingwomen and the Written Word." *Labor Age* 16 (May 1927): 18–19.
"Education Aids Workingwomen." *Labor Age* 17 (January 1928): 12–13.
"A New Era Opens for Labor Education." *Justice* (October 1, 1933): 9.

Articles by Cohn appeared in *American Federationist, Justice, Labor Age,* and *Workers' Education Bureau.*

WORKS ABOUT FANNIA MARY COHN

Cohen, Ricki Carole Myers. "Fannia Cohn and the International Ladies' Garment Workers Union." Ph.D. diss., University of Southern California, 1976.
Kessler-Harris, Alice. "Organizing the Unorganizable: Three Jewish Women and Their Union." *Labor History* 17 (1976): 5–23.
Schaefer, Robert. "Educational Activities of the Garment Unions." Ph.D. diss., Columbia University, Teachers College, 1951.
Wong, Susan Stone. "Fannia Cohn." In Barbara Sicherman and Carol Green Hurd, eds., *Notable American Women: The Modern Period,* 154–55. Cambridge, MA: Harvard University Press, 1980.
———. "From Soul to Strawberries: The International Ladies Garment Workers' Union and Workers' Education, 1914–1950." In Joyce L. Kornbluh and Mary Frederickson, eds., *Sisterhood and Solidarity,* 37–57, 69–74. Philadelphia: Temple University Press, 1984.

Johnnetta B. Cole

Kathleen A. Murphey

In July 1987 Johnnetta B. Cole (b. 1936) became the first black woman president of Spelman College in Atlanta, Georgia. Spelman, the oldest, largest, and most highly respected historically black, private liberal arts college for women in the United States, celebrated with jubilation Cole's acceptance of the position. The Spelman community could see in Cole a combination of strengths, some new to Spelman, that promised to reinvigorate their college and enrich its identity. Cole, an anthropologist with impressive academic credentials and an outstanding career in college teaching, could see in the Spelman students her own womanhood and African-American heritage. During her academic career Cole researched issues of race, gender, and class. Her progressive political views focused on social justice, including racial and gender equality. Spelman, committed to high-quality education for African-American women, became a place for Johnnetta Cole to act on these merged academic and political commitments.

Born Johnnetta Betsch, October 19, 1936, in Jacksonville, Florida, to Mary Frances Lewis Betsch and John Thomas Betsch, Sr., Cole enjoyed the privileges and respect accorded by both the black and white communities to a prominent African-American business family. Her maternal great-grandfather, Abraham Lincoln Lewis, had founded the Afro-American Life Insurance Company in 1901, the first insurance company, white or black, in Florida. It flourished, spreading to Georgia, Alabama, and Texas, until 1987, when it succumbed to bankruptcy, due to competition with white insurance companies that had opened their doors to blacks in the 1970s. During most of her life, however, the business prospered.

While Cole's self-described middle- or upper-middle-class family background did not spare her the pains of racism as a child growing up in the segregated Jim Crow South of the 1940s, it softened them. She remembers living well and eventually moving into the "enormously large" house of her great-grandfather.[1] She did not have to ride on the back of the bus, because she usually was driven to her destination. She attended a segregated Young Women's Christian Association (YWCA), which was, nonetheless, named after her great-grandfather; was the avid user of a segregated public library named after him; and swam at the only private beach for black Americans, which also bore his name. Because of the color of her skin, however, she could not swim in the swimming pool or play in the white park across the street from her home. Outside the protected circle where she was known, she suffered the stings of racism like other African Americans, such as the indelible experience of being called "nigger" and fears of encountering Ku Klux Klan violence.

Her father was born in Henderson, North Carolina, the son of an African-American woman and a German brick mason about whom the family knows little, other than that he was "six feet tall and had a strong presence." Her father attended Knox College in North Carolina but eventually graduated from Howard University. After marrying her mother, he worked in the family insurance company. Cole remembers a warm, loving, nurturing man who was also an active public servant, yet not averse to doing household chores. He died in 1953, while she was still a teenager.

Cole's mother, born and raised in Jacksonville, attended Wilberforce University in Ohio because of her family's intense involvement with the African Methodist Episcopal (AME) church, which supported the school. Cole's mother then taught college English and served as registrar for many years at Edward Waters College, a small black, AME-related school in Jacksonville. In later years she helped manage the family business. A talented musician, Cole's mother also directed all the choirs and played the organ and piano at the local AME church. Her death in 1975 affected Cole for years, so intimate was the relationship, so powerfully did her mother serve as a role model. Today Cole still experiences the relationship as one of the closest, most influential in her life.

Though barred from the cultural life of the segregated white world, Cole enjoyed a rich cultural life because of the experiences and expectations her parents brought into their home. They surrounded her with books and records, as well as the examples of their lives, actively engaged in professional work, the family business, the AME church, musical activities, and activist political organizations of the black community, such as the National Association for the Advancement of Colored People (NAACP) and the Urban League. The black women role models held up to her, such as Marian Anderson and Mary McLeod Bethune, inspired her.[2] Her family knew Bethune personally, though Cole remembers, with a smile, that as a child she was more impressed with Bethune's unusual hats, worn with dignity and style, than her accomplishments.

There was never any question as to whether Cole would attend college. Her "typically pushy," middle-class parents always sought the best education for her and her two siblings, Marvyne Betsch, her older sister by eighteen months, and John Thomas Betsch, Jr., her younger brother by nine years. Both siblings eventually followed professional careers in music. Their parents expected them all to do well in their schools, chosen to circumvent the weaknesses of the segregated school system.

During her years in Jacksonville, Cole's life revolved happily around family, schooling, lessons of all kinds, reading, scouts, YWCA activities, and her family's active involvement in the church and community. At the same time, however, she grew up extremely conscious of, and greatly angered by, the racist practices that pervaded daily life, especially the schooling of black children. She was appalled that black schools had no decent physical education, drama, or other special classes and that black children got hand-me-down books, while white children got new ones.

Johnnetta began her schooling in the Jacksonville public schools before she had reached the official school age. When she was eight, nine, and ten years old, she and her sister attended school in Washington, D.C., living with her paternal grandmother, Mattye Betsch, in order to avoid the half-day schooling Jacksonville then offered its black children. In Washington, Johnnetta first met her second husband, Arthur J. Robinson, Jr., who lived one door apart from them, where his family had moved so his father, previously a teacher, could attend medical school at Howard University. When she and her sister returned to Jacksonville, she attended a private school for African-American girls, Boylan-Haven, a Methodist-run school no longer in existence, staffed mainly by northern white teachers.

By the tenth grade Johnnetta convinced her reluctant parents to let her attend Jacksonville's one public black high school, Stanton. While she was there, her parents had her take a national test, which then allowed her, at age fifteen, early admittance to Fisk University. She entered Fisk after the eleventh grade without graduating. While at Fisk, she applied to Oberlin, where her sister already preceded her as a music major, and was admitted as a freshman at age sixteen. After graduating from Oberlin in 1957 with a B.A. in sociology, she went on to Northwestern University, where she completed an M.A. in 1959 and a Ph.D. in 1967, both in anthropology.

While Johnnetta Betsch studied at Northwestern under anthropologist Melville J. Herskovitz, she and Robert Cole, a student of economics, shared an intellectual world through their involvement in the African studies program. They came from very different backgrounds, he from a farming family in Iowa, she from a business family in Florida. He was white, she, African-American. Their marriage in 1960 upset both families, his more than hers, though over the years both families became reconciled to it.

To research their dissertations, Johnnetta and Robert Cole traveled to Liberia in 1962, where their first son, David, was born. Upon their return to the United States, they settled in the state of Washington, where Robert taught economics at Washington State University (WSU), while Johnnetta finished her dissertation. A second son, Aaron, was born in 1966. Johnnetta Cole became assistant professor of anthropology and director of a new black studies program at WSU in 1969. In 1970 she was recruited by the University of Massachusetts, Amherst, to be director of Afro-American studies and assistant professor of anthropology. In 1970 she also gave birth to a third son, Ethan Che. During her thirteen years in Amherst she progressed through the ranks to professor. From 1981 to 1983 she served, additionally, as associate provost for undergraduate education.

Personally and professionally Cole responded to, and was influenced by, the historical movements of the times throughout those years. She and Robert came back from Liberia into the middle of the civil rights and antiwar movements, both of which involved her profoundly. She explains:

I would describe my politics throughout that period and even now as Progressive, which is to say really insisting on questions of equality, *including* a far more equal distribution of the wealth of this nation, so [I have] a deep concern about issues of poverty, as well as those issues of war, civil rights.

Like other African-American women of her generation, she came more slowly to issues of gender, but the second wave of the women's movement in the 1970s also pulled her into its sway.

Cole's research interests have spanned the pan-African world, from her master's thesis on a black church on the south side of Chicago, to her doctoral research in West Africa, to her later work in Haiti, Grenada, Jamaica, and Cuba. In Cuba she looked especially at issues of race and gender in a socialist society. Her anthropological pursuits became housed academically in the newly developing areas of Afro-American studies, women's studies, and Latin American and Caribbean studies. Her edited anthologies, about anthropology and women, responded to needs she discovered by teaching in these fields.

The Coles divorced in 1982. Johnnetta Cole moved to New York City, taking a position as visiting professor in 1983–1984 and then professor of anthropology and director of the Latin American and Caribbean studies program at Hunter College of the City University of New York from 1984 to 1987. While she was there, friends submitted her name for the position of president at Spelman. Spelman's Board of Trustees, fully aware of her former activism, progressive politics, interracial marriage and divorce, and lack of traditional administrative experience, named Cole their president.

Spelman College, founded by two white, Baptist women from the North in 1881 to educate freed female slaves, expanded through the help of John D. Rockefeller and was named Spelman after his mother-in-law's family. The founders, each of whom served as president, were followed, consecutively, by two white women presidents and two black men. Now Johnnetta Cole "presidents" the college, as she likes to say, consciously turning her title into an action verb, where she is affectionately called "Sister President" by the students.

To some Cole was an unexpected choice by the trustees to lead what had often been perceived as an elite, coed, conservative institution. To others, however, as well as to herself, it soon became clear that this marriage of tradition to progressive political concerns and a sophisticated academic vision was a dynamic, surprisingly natural combination that immediately propelled both Spelman and Cole into the national spotlight. From her new position she gained a visibility and voice in higher education that have made her one of its leading, most sought-after spokespersons.

When Cole came to Spelman, she made it clear that she would respect its long-established traditions, as well as insist on change. In fact, continuity and change, a concept from anthropology, guide her tenure at Spelman as she seeks to build the college into a major center for research and study of and for women of color. During her first five years Cole succeeded in her initiatives of opening a Community Service Center through which 40 percent of the students engage in some form of community service, internationalizing the campus and curriculum through a Ford Foundation-supported International Affairs Center, and directing more students into academic careers through a Dana Foundation grant to finance mentored summer research experiences at Duke University. Under her administration Spelman has earned ever-higher accolades as a premier, historically black institution and top liberal arts college; its rankings, popularity, and selectivity have soared.

Cole's hope of building a $100 million endowment has been handsomely aided by two large gifts: on the day of her inauguration as Spelman's president in 1987 she announced a $20 million gift to the college from her good friends, comedian Dr. Bill Cosby and his wife Dr. Camille Cosby; in May of 1992 a gift of $37 million from a fund initiated by DeWitt Wallace, founder of *Reader's Digest*, again boosted the endowment. These major gifts, as well as Johnnetta Cole's highly visible leadership, have catapulted Spelman, the cause of predominantly black colleges, the issue of single-sex institutions, and the future of higher education into the national public spotlight, a spotlight that seems on its way to growing ever brighter as Cole's success at Spelman and her committed vision of the future of higher education become better known.

In accepting the presidency, Cole feared returning to the South, with its different environment of race relations, after many years in the North. Instead she discovered a new South, not devoid of racism, but without the rigid segregation she had known. She feared, too, the loneliness of the top, of being isolated in her presidential role. She found herself, however, warmly supported by staff, faculty, and students, as well as other women college presidents in the area. In 1988 she married Arthur Robinson, her childhood friend. Divorced and a father of two grown sons, he called her in 1987, after they had been out of contact for thirty-five years, to congratulate her on her appointment to Spelman, thus rekindling their friendship. At that time he served as assistant to the director of the library at the National Library of Medicine in Bethesda, Maryland. He now works in Atlanta at the Center for Disease Control as a public health educator.

Today Cole proudly proclaims herself first and foremost a teacher, even in her role as president of Spelman, where she defines most of her tasks as variations of teaching. Her appreciation of teachers goes back to her childhood, when several teachers, through their enthusiasm and use of interactive methods, opened new intellectual worlds to her:

These were people who were not necessarily acknowledged as brilliant intellectuals, because unfortunately our society fails to do that, that is, acknowledge almost any public school teacher, but these are people who really turned me on to ideas, and I would say were instrumental in giving me the impression that the world of ideas was a place that I might want to wallow around in.

To the charge that she has become more conservative, Cole replies that she has become more realistic. The term *conservative* connotes for her a commitment to the status quo. Instead, she sees herself responding realistically to a changed world; she views the lull in progressive politics as an opportunity to work through education. Her political and professional commitments have merged in a new way:

I would say that Spelman has given me the opportunity to put into real, genuine practice my beliefs on the race problem and the women question. How I look at education as a process, which is to say that it must involve a kind of activism, a form of social service, of community service, of volunteerism, is a way for me to express how I feel about the poverty question. And since a good deal of my own academic work is centered around issues of race and gender and class, yes, the life that I live now in some very definitive ways allows me to practice very deep beliefs and even, if you want to put it this way, to test theoretical positions.

"Presidenting" Spelman College requires long, overextended days. While being overextended has been the situation for most of Cole's adult life, her personality and talents appear to fit well to presidenting. Cole brings commitment, high energy, the ability to work well with diverse constituencies, and a relish for the teaching, speech-giving role that has been thrust upon her as she travels the country and the world, speaking for Spelman and about the challenges of educating women and all people of color:

If there is one message that I would want to communicate, it comes straight out of the middle of the Spelman reality. And that is not only the necessity but the possibility to educate well all women and all folk of color. We simply prove that every day at Spelman . . . . It's my hope that when increasing numbers of people use the term "American higher education," they see diversity within that includes a Spelman.

As Cole seeks to creatively solve problems, she strives for excellence, following not only her own standards and those of society, but also those of her own people, meaning "the Frederick Douglasses, the Sojourner Truths, the Marian Wright Edelmans, and the Martin Luther Kings," as well as many nameless people who represent "deep integrity, deep commitment."[3] Thus, for Cole a credible job is not good enough. She rejects living "in tones of the ordinary," actively seeking, instead, to live up to the "powerful language of one of the founders of this college who said Spelman women must have a loyal scorn for second best!"

In reflecting on what she hopes to have given her sons, of whom she is immensely proud, Cole includes the desire to live their lives not just for themselves, but for others as well; the disposition to question all aspects of their society; and "a mighty outrage against injustice, because I don't think people can live healthily if they've somehow made an accommodation to it." She also hopes that they truly accept "that women do hold up half the sky, to use the Chinese expression, and that one of their responsibilities in this world is to understand the fundamental equality of men and women."

To her "daughters" at Spelman, however, her gifts are both the same, yet different:

We don't live in a world of gender equality, and so to my 1800 plus daughters I hope I have given many of the same things, or given the same things including, though, a strong conviction that they have to demand that equality. And a willingness to work at having all of the things that are important in their lives, rather than concluding that I'm going to be this professional woman, so I can't have the marriage I want, or I'm going to have the marriage and family, forget being the research scientist. The willingness to struggle for all the things that they need for their own full development and joy, that's one of the things I hope I've given them by example.

Cole's résumé includes an extensive list of publications and a lengthy list of awards for outstanding accomplishment in the areas of teaching, research, and service. Nineteen institutions have awarded her honorary degrees. Cole serves on a diverse array of advisory boards, councils, and editorial boards, a diversity best epitomized by her board membership with Coca Cola Enterprises, as well as Sisterhood in Support of Sisters in South Africa (SISA), and her leadership role in one of the twenty community councils organized by former president Jimmy Carter in the Atlanta Project, a grass-roots organization fighting poverty and building community in Atlanta. While balancing these commitments with the daily tasks of presidenting, Cole also wrote *Conversations: Straight Talk with America's Sister President*. Further, following the U.S. presidential election of November 1992, she coordinated president-elect Bill Clinton's transition team "cluster-group" that coordinated assessment and appointments in education, labor, arts, and the humanities.

Johnnetta Cole speaks slowly with the clear, measured cadence of confidence and conviction. Her words, her deeds, her energy, her enthusiasm, her deeply held beliefs, and her openness inspire a new generation of Spelman students. By defining herself first and foremost as a teacher, she redefines the role of teacher to include the academic, the political, the spiritual, and the personal. By educating well the predominantly African-American women students at Spelman, she educates us all to the expanded possibilities of what an exceptional teacher can accomplish. By building on her deepest commitments, she brings renewed purpose and vision to the educational reality in which she works so well. A creative, progressive educator, Johnnetta Cole is helping lead Spelman, as well as U.S. higher education, forward, into the twenty-first century.

NOTES

1. This and all other quotes are from Johnnetta Cole, interview with author, Atlanta, Georgia, June 3, 1992.

2. Anderson, born in 1902, is the internationally known contralto. Bethune, 1875–1955, founded and served as president of Bethune-Cookman College at Daytona Beach, Florida. She was active in national black affairs and a special adviser to President Franklin D. Roosevelt on problems of minorities.

3. Douglass, 1817–1895, a former slave, was an abolitionist, writer, and orator. Truth, 1795–1883, a deeply religious freed slave, fought for abolition and women's causes. Edelman, born in 1939, an attorney and Spelman alumna who chaired Spelman's Board of Trustees from 1979 to 1988, founded and heads the Children's Defense Fund. Martin Luther King, Jr., 1929–1968, led the civil rights movement.

WORKS BY JOHNNETTA B. COLE

"Militant Black Women in Early U.S. History." *The Black Scholar* 9 (April 1978): 38–44.

Anthropology for the Eighties: Introductory Readings (ed.). New York: Free Press, 1982.

"The Making of the Cuban Nationality." In *Cuba: A View from Inside*, 3–9. New York: Center for Cuban Studies, 1985.

"On Racism and Ethnocentrism" (with Elizabeth H. Oakes). In Jo Sinclair, ed., "Afterward," *The Changelings*, 339–47. New York: Feminist Press, 1985.

All American Women: Lines That Divide, Ties That Bind (ed.). New York: Free Press, 1986.

"Women in Cuba: Old Problems and New Ideas" (with Gail A. Reed). *Urban Anthropology* 15 (Fall-Winter 1986): 321–53.

Anthropology for the Nineties: Introductory Readings (ed.). New York: Free Press, 1988.

Conversations: Straight Talk with America's Sister President. New York: Doubleday, 1993.

WORKS ABOUT JOHNNETTA B. COLE

Bateson, Mary Catherine. *Composing a Life*. New York: Atlantic Monthly Press, 1989.

Bernstein, Alison. "Johnnetta Cole: Serving by Example." *Change* 19 (September/ October 1987): 46–55.

Chrisman, Robert. "The Black Scholar Interviews: Dr. Johnnetta B. Cole." *The Black Scholar* 19 (November/December 1988): 60–64.

Edwards, Audrey. "The Inspiring Leader of Scholars (and Dollars)." *Working Woman* 14 (June 1989): 68–69, 72, 74.

McHenry, Susan. "Spelman College Gets Its First 'Sister President.'" *Ms.* 16 (October 1987): 58–61, 65, 99.

McKinney, Rhoda E. " 'Sister' President." *Ebony* 43 (February 1988): 82, 84, 86, 88.

Miriam Colón

Rosa Luisa Márquez and Barbara Shircliffe

Miriam Colón (b. 193?), Puerto Rican actress, producer, and director, has achieved distinction as a cultural educator. As founder and continuing leader of the bilingual Puerto Rican Traveling Theater (PRTT), which also operates as an innovative theater school in New York City, Colón has educated students in drama, playwriting, and poetry. The educational mission of PRTT has also strengthened the Puerto Rican artistic tradition on the mainland, energized the cultural life of the Puerto Rican and other Latino communities in New York, and elevated the awareness of the New York community as a whole to the Latin cultural tradition. Through the Traveling and Training Units of the PRTT, Colón has brought "relevant" theater of high quality to the working-class Hispanic neighborhoods of New York and has provided an educational environment for Puerto Rican (and other) aspiring artists, playwrights, and actors.

Juanita: Now we know the world don't change by itself. We're the ones who change the world. And we're gonna help change it. We're gonna go like people with dignity, like grandpa used to say. With our heads high. Knowin' there are things to fight for. Knowin' all God's children are equal. And my children will learn things I didn't learn, things they don't teach in school. That's how we'll go back home! You and I mamá, as firm as ausubo trees above our land. (Juanita's final speech in *La carreta* [The oxcart] by René Marqués)[1]

La carreta is a Puerto Rican theater classic that maps the trajectory of a humble family from the Island's countryside to the city of San Juan and from there to the barrio in New York. In New York in 1953 Miriam Colón first played, in Spanish, the character of Juanita, soon after the drama opened in her native Puerto Rico. She also starred in its English version at New York's Greenwich Mews Theater in 1966 and in 1967 played Juanita on tour. In August 1967 under the sponsorship of Mayor John Lindsay's Summer Task Force, Miriam Colón's newly created Puerto Rican Traveling Theater (PRTT) gave free outdoor performances of *The Oxcart* in parks and playgrounds throughout New York City. Since then Miriam Colón and her creation, the PRTT, have been inseparably linked to *La carreta* and to Juanita's aspirations for a better life. Colón produced the play at the Manhattan Center in 1977 to celebrate the tenth anniversary of the PRTT and again in 1992 to celebrate its twenty-fifth anniversary.

Colón chose to remain in New York City, defining her roles as theater person and cultural educator rather than, like Juanita, returning to her native Puerto Rico to grow "as firm as ausubo trees above the land that gives life." Colón's option constitutes a contemporary rewrite of the Puerto Rican saga—a saga of total dedication to her profession, theater, and her community, the New York Puerto Ricans in particular and the Latin American population in the city in general. Colón has become an important role model for this community.

Copper-skinned, tiny and intense, Miriam Colón was born in the city of Ponce in the southern part of Puerto Rico during the 1930s. She was the oldest daughter of Teodoro Colón, a dry goods salesman, and Josefa Quiles, both from a working-class sector of San Juan called Barrio Obrero, where Miriam spent her adolescent years. Her parents divorced while she was young, and subsequently her mother played a major role in supporting her career ambitions.

Miriam received a bilingual education in grade school. She first became involved in theater at age eleven, when she was a student at the Baldorioty de Castro Junior High School. At that time the University of Puerto Rico had an emerging theater program under the direction of Leopoldo Santiago Lavandero. The program's aim was to prepare native theater artists in all fields. In 1964 it acquired a traveling unit: el teatro Rodante Universitario, whose task was to take theater to hospitals, town squares, schools, jails— wherever the cart could be opened. The idea was fashioned in the spirit of Federico García Lorca's La Barraca, a university traveling theater that toured Spain in 1932. For Puerto Rican theater scholar Victoria Espinosa, the traveling unit "fulfills the purpose to the University by reaching the people, *educating and entertaining* the inhabitants of both town and country,"[2] objectives that would later guide the work of the PRTT in New York.

These two traveling theater projects inspired Miriam Colón to develop her own. She came upon the idea of theater while acting in school plays staged by university students and supervised by Santiago Lavandero at the Baldorioty de Castro Junior High School. She was so talented that Santiago Lavandero invited her to audit theater courses and participate in university productions. Colón trained and studied for five years, acting in major production, touring, and sharing the stage with older student-actors who later became professionals in both theater and theater education. Meanwhile, she graduated from high school, majoring in secretarial sciences.

After graduation Miriam Colón was ready for a more advanced career. Since she had already taken all the theater courses at the University of Puerto Rico, she was offered a scholarship through the auspices of then chancellor Jaime Banítez to study at Erwin Piscator's Dramatic Workshop and Technical Institute in New York. The scholarship afforded the young actress an opportunity available to few students entering the theater profession. Miriam and her mother migrated to New York, later to be followed by her younger brother and sister. Supporting her daughter's aspirations, Josefa Quiles took a job in a New York garment factory to help maintain their life in a single furnished room. Commenting on her mother's support, Colón recalled, "She never interfered, whether I wanted to be an actress or a nurse . . . what was important was that I was absolutely sure she loved me . . . she was so giving."[3] Throughout her life, Colón remained close not only to her mother but also to her siblings and her many nephews and nieces on the mainland and in Puerto Rico.

The young Colón spent her first two years in New York training and performing under the direction of the German director and his wife, María Ley. Then she auditioned for admission to Actor's Studio, the noted theater school directed by Lee Strassberg. Strassberg proposed an unofficial membership of one year during which time she would audit theater classes before preparing for a second audition. After the second audition she became the first Puerto Rican accepted to be a lifetime member. For fifteen years she remained active, and she continues to collaborate with the studio whenever asked.

After this intense training, Colón began her active and successful career as an actress by performing on Broadway in *In the Summer House*, opposite Dame Judith Anderson. Since then she has appeared frequently in Broadway plays, in off-Broadway plays, and in motion pictures, working nonstop in Hollywood for seven years. She has also appeared in television police series and soap operas, usually cast in complex ethnic roles representing Latinas and Philippinas. In 1989 she played Bernarda in Federico García Lorca's *The House of Bernarda Alba* at the Tyrone Guthrie Theater in Minneapolis. Despite the continuing demands of her career Colón's energies have been dedicated primarily to the development of the PRTT, and her commitment to that theater has always brought her back to New York City.

Miriam Colón's emergence as a Puerto Rican theater artist in the 1960s coincided with the emergence of the American civil rights movement and the cultural revitalization of ethnic communities that accompanied it. In 1965 Luis Valdéz (formerly with the San Francisco Mime Troupe) founded the Teatro Campesino to dramatize the grape picker's plight in California and to encourage pride in Mexican Americans. A vibrant black theater emerged as well, including groups such as the Black Arts Repertory, the Negro Ensemble Company, and the National Black Theater. Recognizing their immediate social, cultural, and educational value, art foundations began to sponsor these and other theatrical manifestations of the civil rights movement.

The awakening of ethnic consciousness also had its impact on more traditional theater. By the mid-1960s the New York Shakespeare Festival was taking Spanish-language productions on tour to reach Latino audiences in New York City, following a precedent set in the late 1930s by the Federal Theater Project's programs in black and Spanish-language theater. The New York Shakespeare Festival's 1964 production of Federico García Lorca's *La Zapatera Prodigiosa* (*The shoemaker's prodigious wife*) featured Miriam Colón in its leading role.

Aware of the impact of drama as a tool for instilling ethnic pride, Colón was determined to create a theater that would respond to the needs of the Puerto Rican community. In the 1950s she and playwright Roberto Rodriquez cofounded the first Spanish-language theater in New York City, Nuevo Circulo Dramatico. The company performed in Spanish, free, in the city's parks, streets, and jails until (like many other struggling small theaters) it was closed by the fire department.

The idea of a permanent traveling theater continued to guide Colón's work. In 1967, with the aid of an advisory board and her second husband, George P. Edgar (now deceased), whom she had married the previous year, Colón founded the Puerto Rican Traveling Theater (PRTT), a bilingual Latin American professional theater company. The PRTT was (and at this writing remains) a nonprofit, tax-exempt educational corporation, operating under Actor's Equity contract. The most prominent and consistent Puerto Rican theater in the United States, it has served as a model for others, such as the Pregones Group in the Bronx.

From its founding in 1967 into the early 1990s, the PRTT has been the vehicle for Colón's ideas and energies. She conceives the group's philosophy and constantly proposes new projects; chooses plays on account of quality, relevance, and message; selects directors, teachers, and administrators; leads fund-raising efforts, and acts and directs whenever necessary.

Juanita: Now we know the world don't change by itself. We're the ones who change the world.

When Colón founded the PRTT in 1967, her goal was to reach an audience of more than 2 million Puerto Rican migrants. By the early 1990s the immigration of other Spanish-speaking groups had increased her potential audience fivefold. The large Spanish-speaking migrant and immigrant community had an enormous impact on the culture of New York City, an impact reflected in Spanish street signs, Spanish television, Spanish curriculum in the public schools, Puerto Rican studies departments in the colleges and universities, and expanding activities of the PRTT. Colón's self-appointed task included not only the creation of a theater but also the creation of an audience. As most new members of the Spanish-speaking community had not been theatergoers before coming to New York, Colón had to educate each successive wave about the importance of theater and its potential for preserving cultural identity.

For Colón, the goal of the new theater was to reach out to sectors of the New York community that would not ordinarily come into contact with theater. The themes chosen for the productions were designed to reflect the experiences and concerns of the New York Latino community so that "they may be persuaded *to think, to compare, to react, to get either happy or very, very angry*; and this has happened."[4]

Although Puerto Ricans represent one of the largest ethnic minorities in New York City, they constitute the poorest segment of the total population.[5] The PRTT understood that physical poverty created by economic condition went hand-in-hand with spiritual poverty and sought to do something about it.

A principal problem of the alienated member of a minority group comes, not only from dissatisfaction with his material means, but also from a debilitating feeling of aloneness, of separation and confusion as to his sense of self worth. *We are able to confirm that projects in the arts play a key role in helping to establish bridges of communication with our undeveloped communities.* We further learned that the possibilities of successfully capturing their attention are greater when we *take into consideration their ethnic background, their interest, the subjects that are relevant to their reality and to their taste.*[6]

During its early years, the PRTT performed Puerto Rican plays written on the Island and in Spanish, plays that carried a strong social message, and adaptations of American dramas that could speak strongly to the Hispanic community. A particular form of bilingual theater was soon established. Each play was usually staged in both English and Spanish, with the same cast whenever possible. Audiences were asked which language they preferred, and their preferences were honored. Colón used "Spanglish," a mixture of Spanish and English, "only if it serves as a vehicle to dramatize the tragedy of transculturation." Celebrating bilingualism, she emphasized the preservation of Spanish because "identity and language are intertwined, and to allow the death of language and culture is to ultimately undo the core of a group's identity."[7]

Juanita: And we're gonna help change it.

In the 1970s Colón achieved three important objectives. She acquired a home for the heretofore itinerant PRTT, she established the Experimental Laboratory, which later became the Playwrights Unit, and she launched the Training Unit, a theater school for Hispanic youth.

In its early years, the PRTT operated as "a nomadic group," playing outdoors in the summer and using churches, homes, and other makeshift quarters the rest of the year. In 1972, however, the theater acquired its first "home" at 124 West 18th Street. Another more permanent move followed.

In 1974 Colón noticed a deserted firehouse at 304 West 47th Street. After pursuing city officials for several years, she got a long-term lease. "We finally had a theater dedicated to the work of Hispanic artists in New York City, in the heart of the theater district."

Permanent quarters for the PRTT enabled Colón to realize her goal of educating New York about the works of well-known Latin American dramatists such as Chilean Jorge Díaz, Brazilian Alfredo Días Gómez, Mexican Emilio Caballido, and Argentine Roberto Cassa, while continuing to stage the works of Puerto Rican authors such as Luis Rafael Sánchez, René Marqués, and Jaime Carrero. More than a hundred plays were produced in twenty-five years. The Traveling Unit also expanded its work, performing not only in the neighborhoods of New York but also, by invitation, in Spain, Colombia, Mexico, and Puerto Rico. An average audience of 10,000 people see the productions of the Traveling Unit every season in the five boroughs of New York and in Newark and Jersey City, New Jersey.

The Experimental Laboratory, established in 1972, paved the way for the Playwrights Unit, which offered aspiring playwrights an educational opportunity for the development of dramatic techniques through direct supervision and public readings. The Playwrights Unit became an important source of new works for the company's repertory. Plays relating to the Puerto Rican experience in New York, like Alloys Gallardoi's *Simson Street*, Toni Mullet's *The Magical Forest*, Alloys Iván López's *Lady with a View*, and Richard Irizarry's *Ariano*, are among the 8 or 9 plays staged by the company out of more than 125 created in this unique laboratory. Colón is proud that three of these plays have been published in an anthology, making them available to theater students across the country.[8]

Juanita: And my children will learn things I didn't learn, things they don't teach in school.

It has been Miriam Colón's desire to make her theater not only a bilingual performing group but also an educational institution "where we could train and experiment and share what we know with interested youngsters and adults; where students could be exposed to the theatre as an aesthetic and humanizing experience; *where youngsters could come in contact with disciplines not ordinarily offered in our present public educational system.*"[9]

Initiated by Colón, the Training Unit has been directed by educators such as Iris Martínez, Pepe Echegarary, Victor Fragoso, Manuel Yeskas, Vicente Castro, Alban Colón, and Gloria Zelaya. It offers free bilingual instruction to students fourteen and older in acting, dance, voice and diction, music (including jazz and Afro-Caribbean styles), and singing. It also offers special courses preparing students for auditions and teaching them how to assemble résumés.

The theater school is based on a three-year program with several objectives. The school's curriculum includes the study of "classic and contemporary world drama, as well as Latino theater," in order to simultaneously broaden students' "reading habits" and "cultural awareness." Theater is viewed as a means of developing students' ability to work as a team and share responsibilities. Studies in character and scene development are designed "to sharpen analytical skills." The school also sponsors student attendance of theater productions to "instill the desire for and habit of theater going."[10]

More than 4,000 students have participated in the special theater school, which has annual presentations of its achievements. Alumni have become resource people for theater production and educational projects such as teaching poetry and playwriting in community centers and schools, spreading and multiplying the theater school's impact. Since its inauguration, the company's operation has grown from $12,000 a year to $750,000, funds that have been raised by this strong-willed, enterprising woman and her collaborators. Economic support is derived from government as well as from private institutions.

In 1992, budget cuts from the various funding sources threatened the survival of the Training Unit. Colón was forced to charge a matriculation fee of ten dollars and to consider charging a modest tuition fee for classes in the future. Although Colón has been as successful at fund-raising as at all other aspects of managing the PRTT, she attributes difficulties with funding to ethnic prejudice rather than prejudice against her as a woman. According to Colón, "Minorities have been at the tail end of priorities and Latino cultural institutions have fared badly at the government, corporate, and foundational level."[11]

Seeing education as an important component of all PRTT activities, Colón is bewildered and indignant when funding agencies try to define education more narrowly:

There is no difference between theater and education because theater is education . . . . How could it not be education [when it teaches] our art, our literature, our poetry, our music . . . the talent of our scenic designers . . . the humanities, how each of us faces the dilemmas in life in a positive way. Education is more than learning the multiplication tables.[12]

For her achievements as a theater person, educator, and community leader Miriam Colón has received numerous distinctions that cross ethnic, as well as national, boundaries. In 1978 she was given the Extraordinary Woman of Achievement Award by the National Council of Christians and Jews. In 1981 the Puerto Rican Legal Defense and Education Fund honored her for Contributions to the Advancement and Enrichment of Human Potential. In 1986, she received the Maclovio Barraza Leadership Award from the National Council of La Raza, and in 1988 she received the Lifetime Achievement Award from the National Puerto Rican Coalition. In October 1992, she received the Premier Encuentro Award at the Kennedy Center in Washington, D.C. She has been awarded honorary doctoral degrees from St. Peter's College, Rutgers University, World University, Marymount Manhattan College, Inter-American University of Puerto Rico, State University of New York at Old Westbury, Montclair State College, and the City University of New York.

Yet, besides the titles and awards she has acquired, Miriam Colón's legacy has been her own life, a life of struggle, of shared self-pride, of dedication to her immediate Puerto Rican and Hispanic community and to the U.S. community in general.

Juanita: We're gonna go like people with dignity, like grandpa used to say. With our heads high. Knowin' there are things to fight for. Knowin' all God's children are equal.

Miriam Colón is an educator because she is a role model; she is an educator because the purpose of her life is guided by the generous sharing of experiences she cherished from her native Puerto Rico: a dream of change turned into theater, a theater turned into an option for many; a traveling oxcart theater that strengthens family, culture, and community values from Puerto Rico to New York and back; a theater school for others to follow. That continues to be her goal and pride. Juanita of *The Oxcart* still guides her thoughts and activities.

NOTES

1. Charles Pilditch, trans. *The Oxcart* by René Marqués (New York: Charles Scribner's Sons, 1969), 154.
2. Victoria Espinosa, *El teatro de René Marqués y la escenificación de su obra: Los soles truncos*, Ph.D. diss., Universidad Nacional Autonoma de Mexico, 1969, 81.
3. Miriam Colón, Interview with Maxine Seller, October 12, 1992.
4. Miriam Colón, Interviews with Luisa Márquez summers of 1976 and 1991.
5. Will Lessner, "U.S. Study Finds City's Poorest Are Puerto Ricans in the Slums," *New York Times*, November 17, 1969, 32: 1.
6. Miriam Colón, "Anatomy of a Summer Project," presentation for Vice President Hubert Humphrey's Conference, Mayor and City Coordinators: 1968 Summer Youth Opportunities Program, PRTT files, 1968, Washington, DC, 4.
7. Ibid.; twentieth anniversary program, PRTT files.
8. *Recent Puerto Rican Theater: Five Plays from New York* (Houston, TX: Arte Publico Press, 1991).
9. "Report 1972" (New York, 1991), PRTT files.
10. "The Training Unit" (New York, 1991), PRTT files.
11. Interview, October 12, 1992.
12. Ibid.

WORK BY MIRIAM COLÓN

Letters, interviews, proposals, and program notes are in the files of the Puerto Rican Traveling Theater company, New York, 1967 to present.

WORKS ABOUT MIRIAM COLÓN

Espinosa, Victoria. "El teatro de René Marqués y la escenificación de su obra: *Los soles truncos.*" Ph.D. diss., Universidad Nacional Autonoma de Mexico, 1969.

Kanellos, Nicolás. "Nuestro teatro." *Revista Chicano- Riqueña.* Vol. 1. Bloomington: Indiana University Research Center for Language and Semiotic Studies, 1973.

———. "Notes on Chicano Theatre." Bloomington: Indiana University Research Center for Language and Semiotic Studies, 1975.

Lahr, John. *Up Against the Fourth Wall.* New York: Grove Press, 1970.

Márquez, Rosa Luisa. "The Puerto Rican Traveling Theatre Company: The First Ten Years," Ph.D. diss., Michigan State University, 1977.

Márquez, Rosa Luisa, and Lowell Fiet. "Puerto Rican Theatre on the Mainland." In Maxine Seller, ed., *Ethnic Theatre in the U.S.*, 419–46. Westport, CT: Greenwood Press, 1983.

Phillips, Jordan. *Contemporary Puerto Rican Drama*, New York: Plaza Mayor Ediciones, 1972.

Waggenheim, Kal. *Puerto Rico: A Profile.* New York: Praeger, 1970.

Elizabeth Avery Colton

Amy Thompson McCandless

Elizabeth Avery Colton (1872–1924) was considered "the foremost authority in the nation on the standards of women's colleges in the South" in the first quarter of the twentieth century.[1] Her numerous publications helped high school students and their parents distinguish between "nominal and imitation" and "standard" and accredited colleges in seventeen southern states and provided an inestimable service to white, college-bound women in the early twentieth century. In addition to her regional efforts for educational standardization, Colton also encouraged her own institution, Meredith College in Raleigh, North Carolina, to adopt the matriculation and graduation requirements of the Association of Colleges and Secondary Schools of the Southern States.

Elizabeth Avery Colton was born on an outpost of the Choctaw Nation in Indian Territory on December 30, 1872, the first of eight children of James Hooper Colton, a Presbyterian minister and educator, and his wife, Harriet Eloise Avery Colton. Shortly before her birth, Colton's parents had left their home in Morganton, North Carolina, to serve as missionaries to the Choctaws in what is now Oklahoma. When James Colton became ill, the family returned to North Carolina, and Elizabeth and her younger siblings attended public schools in Jonesboro. Although she received an A.B. degree from Statesville Female College in Statesville, North Carolina, Colton discovered that Mount Holyoke College in Massachusetts, where she wished to continue her education, would not accept her as a freshman until she had completed an additional year of preparatory work. Her degree from a southern woman's college was not considered the equivalent of a high school diploma in the North.

Colton entered Mount Holyoke as a freshman in the fall of 1891, but she left the college the following year when her father died. As the oldest child, she felt compelled to find a job so that she could help support and educate the younger children. She subsequently taught for six years at Queens College, a woman's school in Charlotte, North Carolina, before returning north to earn a B.S. from Teachers College of Columbia University in 1903. She received her A.M. degree from Teachers College in 1905. After teaching English at Wellesley College in Massachusetts for three years, Colton accepted a position as head of the English department at the Baptist University for Women (later Meredith College) in Raleigh, North Carolina, in 1908. She remained at the college until illness forced her from the classroom in 1920.

From her own experience both as a student and as a teacher at women's colleges in North Carolina and Massachusetts, Colton was painfully aware of the inferior education provided women in southern institutions of higher education. "The typical college for women in the South," she wrote, "completes twelve or fourteen units of secondary work by the end of the sophomore year and devotes the junior and senior work largely to superficial courses."[2] Although some secondary schools deliberately misrepresented themselves as colleges, other institutions that tried to offer college-level courses found that they had to provide preparatory classes for students before they could matriculate. The sparsity of public high schools in the region meant that many young women did not have the background to do college work. Colton found that even her good students at Meredith took two years to complete the work in English composition that students at Wellesley, Vassar, and Mount Holyoke completed in one.

Similar problems existed in southern men's and coeducational colleges in the late nineteenth century. "The term 'college,'" Vanderbilt University's Chancellor James H. Kirkland noted, was "broad and vague" and like "charity . . . cover[ed] a multitude of sins."[3] There was virtually no regulation of degree-granting institutions in the region, and most state legislatures issued college charters to any individual or group willing to pay the requisite fee. Matriculation and graduation requirements varied tremendously from institution to institution. Because the public schools in the southern states did not offer the eight years of elementary training and four years of high school courses that were common in the schools of the Northeast and Midwest, the majority of southern colleges and universities "compensated" for regional educational deficiencies by organizing preparatory schools and/or by diluting the requirements for the baccalaureate degree. The South, Wake Forest College president William Louis Poteat bemoaned in 1916, was "recognizable by two unmistakable marks—the backwardness of its educational provision and its relative poverty."[4]

Concerned over the lack of consistent standards in southern schools, a group of university men created the Association of Colleges and Preparatory (later Secondary) Schools of the Southern States in 1895 in order to "elevate the standard of scholarship and to effect uniformity of entrance requirements." The organization sought to improve secondary education in the region so that preparatory work could be "cut off" from the colleges. The Association of Colleges developed a list of criteria to evaluate schools and colleges and admitted only approved institutions to membership.[5]

Both public and private women's colleges in the region found it difficult to meet the criteria for membership established by the association, however. Most lacked the faculties and facilities of their northern and male counterparts. Because of low endowments and/or meager appropriations, it was often impossible for women's schools to provide adequate libraries or scholarships for students. Many relied heavily on fees from their preparatory departments and from their special music and art courses for survival. Approximately half of the 400 students who attended Mississippi's Industrial Institute and College in the 1890s, for example, were preparatory students, while just ten students a year earned the bachelor's degree. Similar conditions existed in private denominational colleges. At the beginning of the twentieth century, more than half of the students at Agnes Scott, Hollins, Judson, and Salem were taking elementary or secondary courses.[6] Although only a fraction of the students at northeastern women's colleges were music or art students, the majority of students at many southern women's colleges were enrolled in special music or art programs. Colton considered this "predominance of preparatory and 'special-study' pupils" the "leading weakness of Southern colleges for women."[7]

Colton joined with other concerned women educators in the region to do something about these problems, becoming one of the seventeen charter members of the Southern Association of College Women (SACW). Organized during a summer school session for teachers held at the University of Tennessee in July 1903, SACW devised a program that paralleled that of the Association of Southern Colleges and Preparatory Schools. Whereas the latter talked of organizing southern institutions "for cooperation and mutual assistance," the former wished "to unite college women in the South for the higher education of women." The larger group focused on general standards at southern schools; the women's group, on "the standard of education for women." Both organizations wanted to improve secondary education and separate preparatory schools from the colleges.[8]

Colton played an important role in the Southern Association of College Women from its inception. In 1910 she was made chair of the Committee on College Standards of the SACW, and she set out to ascertain the true nature of the various institutions of higher education in the region that called themselves colleges for women. She read catalogs and promotional materials, toured campuses, studied financial reports, and then rated schools according to the criteria established by the Association of Colleges and Preparatory Schools of the Southern States. Between 1911 and 1918 Colton penned numerous pamphlets for both SACW and the Association of Colleges, describing the type and quality of education available at the various colleges throughout the South that accepted women. When SACW began to publish its *Proceedings* in 1912, the first volume included a paper by Colton on "Standards of Southern Colleges for Women," that had been presented at the annual meeting of the Association of Colleges and Secondary Schools of the Southern States in 1911.

Determined to help other southern women avoid her mistakes and acquire a "real" college education, Colton worked tirelessly to investigate the standards at colleges that admitted women and to make this information available to prospective college students. She hoped that the publication of her findings would not only encourage colleges "to improve their standards" but also "educate public opinion to such an extent that nominal colleges [would] be ridiculed out of existence."[9] Colton believed that the attempt by "Southern colleges for women to be everything combined—preparatory school, finishing school, and college"—hindered the development of academic standards in the region. It was impossible, she felt, for professors at institutions that enrolled students of all ages and abilities to offer college work. One so-called college Colton investigated had only three faculty members, who were responsible for all the school's preparatory and collegiate offerings. Such a task would have been overwhelming for even the best-trained professors, but these individuals possessed no degrees, only "a gracious personality, dignified bearing, and exquisite courtesy." In order to concentrate the region's resources where they would do the most good, Colton advocated reducing the total number of institutions of higher education and applying the name "college" only to four-year liberal arts institutions that met the standards of the Association of Colleges.[10]

The practice of calling "private secondary schools, 'special study' schools, and normal schools" colleges, Colton argued, led many students to "mistake nominal colleges for real colleges."[11] In a letter sent out to North Carolina secondary school students in 1915, Colton stressed the importance of attending a standard college and listed the approved institutions in the South that were open to women. North Carolina women who wanted to go to a standard college in the state had only one choice—Trinity (later Duke University)—since none of the women's colleges in North Carolina belonged to the Association of Colleges of the Southern States and the University of North Carolina did not accept women until their junior year. Goucher, Randolph-Macon Women's College, Agnes Scott, and Converse were the only standard women's colleges in the entire South in 1914; Sophie Newcomb and Westhampton were the only approved coordinate colleges. Students who wanted to go to a denominational college were even more restricted. The only Presbyterian college accredited was Agnes Scott. Methodists were limited to Randolph-Macon and Goucher; Baptists, to Westhampton or Baylor.

Colton served as secretary of the Southern Association of College Women from 1912 to 1914 and president from 1914 to 1919 and in 1915 was elected a member of the Executive Committee of the Association of Colleges and

Secondary Schools of the Southern States. During World War I she was appointed a member of the Advisory Council of the Woman's Liberty Loan Committee and of the Honorary Committee of the Woman's Committee of the Council of National Defense. She spoke regularly at the annual meetings of both the Association of Colleges and the Southern Association of College Women between 1911 and 1918, and her speeches were often reprinted and distributed to prospective students. Although Colton was too ill to participate in the first conference of the newly created American Association of University Women in 1921, the organization passed a resolution thanking her for her work in helping to bring about the merger of the SACW and its northern counterpart, the Association of College Alumnae.

Along with the Association of Colleges and Secondary Schools, the Southern Association of College Women lobbied state legislators throughout the region for legislation that would regulate the granting of charters with degree-conferring privileges. The two organizations issued a joint bulletin in 1918 containing a sample bill based on existing legislation in Pennsylvania and New York and a justification for such legislation written by Colton. The Raleigh branch of the SACW, to which Colton belonged, worked hard for the North Carolina bill, and Colton considered the 1919 passage of a "Bill to Restrict the Granting of Charters to Colleges" one of her greatest achievements in North Carolina.

In her quest for regional standards, Colton did not forget about her own institution. Many of her essays on colleges for women were republished in Meredith College's *Quarterly Bulletin*, and the college was treated no differently than the other schools whose programs she critiqued. Meredith, Colton knew, shared many of the same problems as other southern colleges for women. In 1909, for example, 117 regular college students were enrolled— and 167 special and preparatory students! Only 11.5 units were required for admission. Under these circumstances, there was no way professors could offer four years of college work. Colton's 1916 evaluation of "The Various Types of Southern Colleges for Women" classified Meredith as an "approximate," rather than a "standard," college.[12]

Fortunately for Colton, the administration of Meredith supported her efforts and shared her goal of membership in the Association of Colleges and Secondary Schools of the Southern States. In its April 1915 meeting the Board of Trustees congratulated the faculty for "the high standards attained by Meredith College" and declared its willingness "to comply, as soon as practicable, with the conditions necessary for entrance into the Association of Colleges of the Southern States."[13] Colton encouraged Meredith College officials to adopt the Carnegie unit for measuring high school courses and to raise entrance requirements to the fourteen units required by the Association of Colleges. Raising entrance requirements, in turn, permitted the faculty to teach more advanced courses. Colton estimated that Meredith increased its college offerings from 1.7 years in 1904 to 4 years in 1915. In the years after 1915 Meredith discontinued its academy, raised faculty salaries, increased its endowment, reformed its curriculum, and improved its college plant. The college was admitted to the Association of Colleges and Secondary Schools of the Southern States in 1921.

Not everyone welcomed Colton's frank evaluation of southern colleges for women. A poor rating in one of her pamphlets could ruin an institution. Although Colton encouraged every school "to try to become the best of its kind, whether that be a preparatory school, a finishing school, or a junior college," she bluntly stated that there was "no legitimate excuse for the prolonged existence of the majority of schools . . . doing mainly secondary work."[14] Included in this latter category was her own alma mater, Statesville Female College. Some administrators who felt themselves maligned by Colton's criticisms of their institutions promised lawsuits; one president threatened to shoot her. Colton asked Meredith's president what might happen to the college if the head of its English department were jailed for libel. Fortunately, President Vann supported Colton's efforts for educational reform, and no institutions or individuals followed through on their threats.

Colton, like most other southern progressives, found it hard to look beyond traditional confines of race and class. She was a middle-class, white woman educated at liberal arts institutions who wished to improve standards for other middle-class, white women attending liberal arts institutions. She was not concerned with the educational problems faced by poor whites or blacks in the region. She too often saw the slow student as lazy, unaware of the economic and social conditions that might hinder a young woman's intellectual potential. She worried little about the women who could not avail themselves of a good preparatory training. Although normal and industrial colleges were often the only public institutions of higher education open to women in many southern states, Colton urged students to attend private liberal arts colleges instead. But private colleges were too expensive for the majority of southern women, and Colton did nothing to encourage the liberal arts colleges or the state universities to open their doors to women. Colton, like the educational associations to which she belonged, ignored the institutions of higher education for African Americans in the region. She never rated a black college or discussed educational opportunities available to black women.

In the spring of 1919 Colton was hospitalized with an attack of "rheumatism," and in 1920–1921 she took a leave of absence from Meredith, hoping that a year of rest would improve her health. Her condition continued to worsen, however, and in the spring of 1921 she resigned her position as head of the English department. A spinal tumor made her a virtual invalid, and she spent her remaining days at a sanatorium in Clifton Springs, New York, where she died on August 26, 1924. She was buried in Forest Hill Cemetery in Morganton, North Carolina.

Colton did not live to see the improvements that occurred at southern colleges in the years before World War II. Private and public colleges for women abolished their preparatory departments, upgraded their curricula, and raised their endowments to meet the criteria of the Association of Colleges and Secondary Schools. Colton's classification of schools was adopted by the U.S. government, the General Education Board, and various church and state boards of education. As a consequence of Colton's efforts, opportunities for the higher education of white women in the South were considerably expanded.

NOTES

1. Mary Lynch Johnson, *A History of Meredith College* (Raleigh, NC: Meredith College, 1956), 118.

2. Elizabeth Avery Colton, "The Approximate Value of Recent Degrees of Southern Colleges," *Meredith College Quarterly Bulletin* 7, no. 2 (January 1914): 9.

3. James H. Kirkland, "College Standards—A Public Interest," reprinted from the *Proceedings of the Fourteenth Annual Meeting of the Southern Association of College Women*, in *Meredith College Quarterly Bulletin* 12, no. 1 (November 1918): 18.

4. William Louis Poteat, "Greetings," *Meredith College Quarterly Bulletin*, 9, no. 2 (January 1916): 48.

5. "Sketch of the Association of Colleges and Preparatory Schools of the Southern States," Association of Colleges and Preparatory Schools of the Southern States, *Proceedings of the Fourth Annual Meeting*, University of Georgia, November 1–2, 1898, vii.

6. Bridget Smith Piescal and Stephen Robert Piescal, *Loyal Daughters: One Hundred Years at Mississippi University for Women 1884–1984* (Jackson: University Press of Mississippi, 1984), 28; Elizabeth Barber Young, *A Study of the Curricula of Seven Selected Women's Colleges of the Southern States* (New York: Teachers College, Columbia University, 1932), 21, 37, 64–65, 96–99.

7. Elizabeth Avery Colton, "Southern Colleges for Women," *Meredith College Quarterly Bulletin* 5, no. 2 (January 1912): 9.

8. Marion Talbot and Lois Kimball Matthews Rosenberry, *The History of the American Association of University Women 1881–1931* (Boston: Houghton Mifflin, 1931), 46–48; Association of Colleges and Preparatory Schools of the Southern States, vii.

9. Colton, "Southern Colleges for Women," 19.

10. Elizabeth Avery Colton, "The Junior College Problem in the South," *Meredith College Quarterly Bulletin* 8, no. 2 (January 1915): 14, 9.

11. Elizabeth Avery Colton, "The Various Types of Southern Colleges for Women," *Meredith College Quarterly Bulletin* 9, no. 4 (May 1916): 3.

12. Colton, "The Various Types of Southern Colleges for Women," 8.

13. "Report of Committee on Admission of Meredith College to Southern Association of Colleges and Academies [*sic*]," Minutes of the Board of Trustees, Meredith College, April 13, 1915.

14. Colton, "Standards of Southern Colleges for Women," 475, 472.

WORKS BY ELIZABETH AVERY COLTON

Elizabeth Avery Colton Papers, North Carolina State Archives, Raleigh, North Carolina.

"Southern Colleges for Women." *Meredith College Quarterly Bulletin* 5, no. 2 (January 1912): 3–21. Reprinted from the *Proceedings of Association of Colleges and Preparatory Schools of the Southern States*, November 1911.

"Standards of Southern Colleges for Women." Report presented at the Ninth Annual Meeting of the Southern Association of College Women, April 1912. Reprinted for private circulation from *The School Review* 20, no. 7 (September 1912): 458–75.

Improvement in Standards of Southern Colleges Since 1900. Richmond, 1913. Reprinted from the *Proceedings of the Tenth Annual Meeting of the Southern Association of College Women*, Richmond, VA, April 15–18, 1913.

"Approximate Value of Recent Degrees of Southern Colleges." *Proceedings of the Nineteenth Annual Meeting of the Association of Colleges and Secondary Schools of the Southern States*, November 1913. Reprinted in *Meredith College Quarterly Bulletin* 7, no. 2 (January 1914): 3–18.

"The Junior College Problem in the South." *Proceedings of the Twentieth Annual Meeting, Association of Colleges and Secondary Schools of the Southern States*, October 1914. Reprinted in *Meredith College Quarterly Bulletin* 8, no. 2 (January 1915): 3–18.

"The Various Types of Southern Colleges for Women." Raleigh, NC: Edwards and Broughton, 1916. Bulletin 2 of 1916 Publications of the Southern Association of College Women. Reprinted in *Meredith College Quarterly Bulletin* 9, no. 4 (May 1916): 3–27.

"Junior College Requirements in the South." *Meredith College Quarterly Bulletin* 10, no. 2 (January 1917): 30–34.

The Distinctive Work of the Southern Association of College Women. Washington, DC: Southern Association of College Women Proceedings, 1917.

Bulletin for the Joint Committee of the Association of Colleges and Secondary Schools of the Southern States and the Southern Association of College Women to Secure Legislation Restricting the Granting of Charters with Degree-Conferring Privileges. Southern Association of College Women, December 1918.

WORKS ABOUT ELIZABETH AVERY COLTON

Dutton, Emily. *History of the Southern Association of College Women.* Washington, DC: American Association of University Women Archives, n.d.

Johnson, Mary Lynch. *Elizabeth Avery Colton: An Educational Pioneer in the South.*

N.p.: North Carolina Division and South Atlantic Section of American Association of University Women, n.d.

McCain, J. R. "Colleges for Women in the Southeast: A Hundred Years of Higher Education for Women—Progress and Problems." *Journal of the American Association of University Women* 30, no. 1 (October 1936): 7–10.

Talbot, Marion, and Lois Kimball Matthews Rosenberry. "The Southern Association of College Women." In *The History of the American Association of University Women 1881–1931*. Boston: Houghton Mifflin, 1931.

Anna Julia Cooper

Beverly Guy-Sheftall

Anna Julia Haywood Cooper (1860–1964), teacher, high school principal, historian, scholar, and college president, is one of the most
extraordinary African-American educators of the twentieth century. She
also has the distinction of being the first African-American woman to
write a book-length black feminist treatise, *A Voice of the South, by a
Black Woman of the South* (1892), a collection of loosely connected essays
that is a classic in African-American intellectual history. Cooper devoted
her entire life to the empowerment of African Americans and women.
She also sustained throughout her long life a passionate belief in the
power of education to liberate her people and women.

Anna Julia Cooper was born a slave during the Civil War in Raleigh, North
Carolina. Though there is some confusion about the precise date of her
birth, she indicated on a survey of racial attitudes of "Negro college grad-
uates" conducted in 1930 by Professor Charles S. Johnson of Fisk University
that her date of birth was August 10, 1860. Her enslaved mother was Hannah
Stanley Haywood (1817–1899), a domestic servant in the plantation household in Raleigh where the family lived; her father was probably George
Washington Haywood, her mother's white master, who never acknowledged
Anna as his daughter. In an autobiographical statement among the Anna J.
Cooper papers at Howard University's Moorland Spingarn Research Center,
she said this about her father and his relationship to her mother: "Presum-
ably my father was her [Hannah's] master, if so I owe him not a sou; she
was always too modest and shamefaced ever to mention him." There were
two elder brothers, Andrew J. and Rufus Haywood, and Anna was the youngest of the three children. Information about Cooper's early years in Raleigh
is scanty; in her statement on the racial attitudes survey, she reveals her
desire to be educated and become a teacher as far back as "kindergarten
age."

In 1868, when Anna was eight years old, she was awarded a scholarship to attend St. Augustine's Normal School and Collegiate Institute (previously the Normal School for the State of North Carolina), which was founded in 1867 by the Board of Missions of the Episcopal church for the purpose of training teachers for newly freed slaves. Becoming a "pupil-teacher" at eight, Anna stayed for fourteen years, completing her own course of study in 1877, and eventually became a tutor for other students enrolled there. An early manifestation of her sensitivity to sexism was her protesting female students' exclusion from Greek classes, which were only open to the male theology students. Her experiences with respect to the preferential treatment of males at St. Augustine's awakened in her a sensitivity to the urgent need for equality between the sexes in the educational arena. She also boldly appealed to the principal and was finally granted permission to enroll in George Christopher Cooper's class. A native of Nassau, British West Indies, he came to the United States in 1873 to study for the ministry at St. Augustine's; a year later he became a teacher, during which time he continued his studies. In 1876 he was ordained an Episcopalian minister. A romance developed between Rev. George Cooper and Anna Julia, and they were married on June 21, 1877. Two years later, when Anna was only nineteen, her husband died, ostensibly from hard work, and she became a widow, which she remained for the rest of her life. Following her death in 1964, Anna Julia was buried in Hargett Street Cemetery, Raleigh, North Carolina, beside the grave of her husband.

In the fall of 1881, Anna left St. Augustine's to attend Oberlin College in Oberlin, Ohio, famous for its Underground Railroad, so that she could continue her teacher preparation and gain a more solid education. She earned the A.B. in 1884 and the A.M. in 1887. Oberlin had opened its doors to women and blacks when other institutions of higher learning refused to do so. She had written to President Fairchild in July 1881 requesting a scholarship (which she was granted) and reasonable housing; arrangements were made for her to live with the family of Charles Henry Churchill, professor of mathematics and physics at Oberlin. Her relationship with the Churchill family lasted throughout her life. In the letter to Fairchild, she emphasized her financial predicament as well as her credentials from St. Augustine's, which were so impressive that she was admitted to the sophomore class:

Beside the English branches, Latin: Caesar, seven books; Virgil's Aeneid, six books; Sallust's Cataline and Jugurtha; and a few orations of Cicero . . . Greek: White's First Lessons; Goodwin's Greek Reader, containing selections from Xenophon, Plato, Herodotus and Thucydides; and five or six books of the Iliad . . . Mathematics: Algebra and Geometry entire.[1]

Her course of study included the classics, modern languages, mathematics, and science. She also took piano at the now famous Conservatory of Music, established in 1865, but lack of funds and time prohibited her from pursuing her love of music in as serious and sustained a manner as she would have liked. Her extracurricular activities at Oberlin included membership in the "LLS," a literary society for women, participation at "Thursday Lectures," and a series called "General X for Women." Her classmates were Mary Eliza Church (later Terrell) of Memphis, Tennessee, and Ida A. Gibbs. When the three of them graduated in 1884, they were among the first of a small group of African-American women to earn the B.A. degree. Mary Jane Patterson, also from North Carolina, graduated from Oberlin College in 1862 and is believed to have been the first African-American woman to earn a college degree in the United States. In 1880 she became the first principal of M Street High School for Colored Youth in Washington, D.C., a post Cooper would also assume twenty-one years later in 1901.

After completing the classical course, Anna had intended, upon graduation, to return to St. Augustine's to teach, but when she was offered a post consigning her to female students only, she refused, again objecting to sexism, and went instead in 1884 to Wilberforce College in Xenia, Ohio. Earning $1,000 a year, she headed the Department of Modern Languages and Literature. A year later, she returned to St. Augustine's in Raleigh for a smaller salary and taught Latin, mathematics, and Greek, having decided to settle in her hometown and build a house. During this time she joined the North Carolina Teachers' Association. She also became a surrogate parent to her brother Rufus's six children after his death in 1882. In 1887, Oberlin awarded her the M.A. degree in mathematics in recognition of her three years of teaching on the college level, and during the same year, she left Raleigh and began to teach mathematics and science (and later Latin) at the famous Washington Preparatory High School for Colored Youth (later M Street School and Dunbar High School). Also joining the faculty in 1887 was her classmate Mary Church, who taught Latin and German.

During this period a debate raged in the African-American community about the feasibility of vocational versus higher education, with Booker T. Washington of Tuskegee Institute most associated with the former argument and William E. B. Du Bois most associated with the latter. Cooper was clearly in the Du Bois camp and advanced her support of higher education for blacks and women in her major work, *A Voice of the South*, written before the Washington/Du Bois controversy over black education was in vogue. Following the resignation of Robert Terrell (Mary Church Terrell's husband) in 1901 as principal, Cooper succeeded him and remained principal until 1906. During her tenure the school soared, the curriculum was strengthened, and accreditation was attained for the first time. She also initiated a college preparatory track and helped to obtain admission for M Street graduates to prestigious colleges such as Harvard, Brown, and Yale. Despite the new directions in which she moved the school, her approach met with considerable resentment, especially among Booker T. Washington and his followers and the Washington, D.C., educational establishment. Following a nasty confrontation with the board, Cooper was fired, so she left Washington and joined the faculty at Lincoln Institute in Jefferson City, Missouri, where she taught foreign languages from 1906 to 1910. She was summoned back to M Street School (formerly the Preparatory High School for Colored Youth, founded in 1870) by the new school superintendent in 1910, where she joined the faculty and taught Latin for twenty years. This appointment came as a result of inquiries to Oberlin from Dr. John R. Francis, a black physician and a member of the D.C. Board of Education.

Following her retirement from the public schools after a distinguished career, Cooper became the second president in 1930 of the experimental Frelinghuysen University, a post she held for ten years; from 1940 to 1950 she was the registrar of the newly configured Frelinghuysen Group of Schools for Colored Working People. Frelinghuysen, founded by Jesse Lawson around 1906, was an evening school for working black adults who could not otherwise attend college.

Fulfilling a lifelong dream, Cooper began her doctoral studies in French literature and history at Columbia University in the summer of 1914. Three years later she satisfied the university's requirements for proficiency in French, Latin, and Greek and completed all of the course work. Previously, during the summers of 1911 through 1913, she studied and was awarded certificates in French literature, history, and phonetics at La Guilde Internationale in Paris, which enabled her to enter the doctoral program at Columbia. A significant accomplishment during this phase of her doctoral work was a translation of an Old French epic, "Le Pelerinage De Charlemagne," into modern French, which was published in Paris in 1925; she dedicated the publication to three outstanding teachers at Oberlin, James H. Fairchild, Charles H. Churchill, and Henry Churchill King. She had been influenced to pursue graduate study in France by the Abbe Klein of the Catholic Institute in Paris, who had visited M Street School in 1902 while Cooper was principal.

Cooper later decided to transfer her doctoral credits from Columbia to the University of Paris, Sorbonne, and completed a dissertation in 1925 at the age of sixty-five on "L'Attitude de la France dans la question de l'Esclavage entre 1789 et 1848" (The attitude of France on the question of slavery between 1789 and 1848). This memorable day on which the *soutenance* [doctoral examination] was conducted has been dramatically portrayed by one of her biographers:

Dressed in her academic gown with the crimson and gold master's hood of Oberlin College, Anna was escorted at the appointed hour into the Salle du Doctorat and to the front of the gallery with the audience seated behind her. The three judges entered through a door to the rear of the platform, and the signal was sounded for the formal academic inquiry to begin. Anna Cooper rose to her feet to await the beginning of

an experience that she later described as "significant and informative." . . . No osten-
tatious display was made when, with great dignity and at the end . . . one of the judges
delivered the verdict: "vous etes Docteur." In that instant, the dream became a
reality![2]

This ordeal, the details of which are carefully delineated in the Louise Daniel
Hutchinson biography, earned Dr. Cooper the distinction of being the first
African-American woman in Washington, D.C., to earn a Ph.D at the Sorbonne; she also became only the fourth African-American woman to earn a
doctorate, joining Drs. Georgiana Rose Simpson, Eva Beatrice Dykes, and
Sadie Tanner Mossell Alexander. The degree was actually awarded December 29, 1925, on the Howard University campus.

Dr. Cooper died in her sleep at her home in Washington, D.C., at the
age of 105 on February 27, 1964. In a poem, "No Flowers Please," written
in 1940 on her eighty-second birthday, she humbly states that she wants to
be remembered only as "somebody's teacher on vacation now, resting for
the fall opening."

Dr. Cooper experienced one of the most difficult yet stunning careers in
the history of the struggle for education among African-American women.
Never wavering from her philosophy of "education for service," she overcame every obstacle that the twin evils of racism and sexism put in her path.
Her awesome intellect, high standards, unequivocal positions, and tenacity
in the face of constant personal attacks both within the black community
and beyond make her one of the most memorable figures in the annals of
American education in the twentieth century. The educational reforms that
she initiated at M Street (now Dunbar High School) and Frelinghuysen were
pioneering. No less impressive was her persistent faith in the ability of African-American students to achieve excellence at their own institutions as
well as at the most prestigious universities throughout the country. Perhaps
Cooper's most significant legacy was her belief in the power of education to
liberate and empower women to participate in the transformation of a world
sorely in need of transformation.

NOTES

1. Letter to President Fairchild from Anna J. Cooper, July 27, 1881, Oberlin
College Archives, Fairchild Papers, box 4.
2. Louise Daniel Hutchinson, *Anna J. Cooper: A Voice from the South* (Washington,
D.C.: Smithsonian Institution Press, 1981), 140.

WORKS BY ANNA JULIA COOPER

"College Extension for Working People." *Journal of the (Oberlin) Alumnae Club.*
     Washington, DC, n.d., 34–38.

The Third Step (Autobiographical). Booklet. Washington, DC: Privately printed, n.d.

"The Higher Education of Woman." *The Southland* (April 1891): 186–202.

A Voice of the South by a Black Woman of the South. Xenia, OH: Aldire Printing House, 1892. Reprint, 1969.

"The Negro Exhibit at the Paris Exhibition." *National Capital Searchlight* (February 1901): 2–5. Anna Julia Cooper Papers, Moorland- Spingarn Research Center, Washington, DC, Howard University.

The Social Settlement: What It Is, and What It Does. Pamphlet. Washington, DC: Murray Brothers Press, 1913.

"*L'Attitude de la France a l'Eaard de l'Esclavaae pendant la Revolution.*" Ph.D. diss., University of Paris, Sorbonne, 1925.

"Souvenir: Xi Omega Chapter, Alpha Kappa Alpha Sorority." Washington, DC: N.p., December 29, 1925.

"The Humor of Teaching." *Crisis* (November 1930): 387.

Legislative Measures Concerning Slavery in the United States. Pamphlet. Washington, DC: Privately printed, 1942.

Equality of Races and the Democratic Movement. Pamphlet. Washington, DC: Privately printed, 1945.

Personal Recollections of the Grimke Family and the Life and Writings of Charlotte Forten Grimke. Washington, DC: Privately printed, 1951.

WORKS ABOUT ANNA JULIA COOPER

Carby, Hazel. " 'On the Threshold of Woman's Era': Lynching, Empire, and Sexuality in Black Feminist Theory." *Critical Inquiry* 12 (1985): 262–77.

———. *Reconstructing Womanhood: The Emergence of the Afro-American Woman Novelist.* New York: Oxford University Press, 1987.

Chamberlain, E. B. *The Churchills of Oberlin.* Oberlin, OH: Oberlin Improvement and Development Organization, 1965.

Culp, D. W., ed. *Twentieth-Century Negro Literature: or a Cyclopedia of Thought on the Vital Topics Relating to the American Negro, by One Hundred of America's Greatest Negroes.* Naperville, IL: J. L. Nichols and Co., 1902.

Gabel, Leona. "Anna Julia Haywood Cooper." In Edward T. James, ed., *Notable American Women, 1607–1950: A Biographical Dictionary.* Cambridge: Belknap Press of Harvard University Press, 1971.

———. *From Slavery to the Sorbonne and Beyond: The Life and Writings of Anna J. Cooper.* Northhampton, MA: Department of History of Smith College, 1982.

Giddings, Paula. *When and Where I Enter: The Impact of Black Women on Race and Sex in America.* New York: Morrow, 1984.

Green, Constance M. *Washington. Capital City. 1879–1950.* Princeton, NJ: Princeton University Press, 1963.

Halliburton, Cecil D. *A History of St. Augustine's College. 1867–1937,* Raleigh, NC: St. Augustine's College, 1937.

Harlan, L. R. *Booker T. Washington: The Making of a Black Leader. 1856–1901.* New York: Oxford University Press, 1972.

Harley, Sharon, and Rosalyn Terborg-Penn, eds. *The Afro-American Woman: Strug-*

gles and Images. Port Washington, NY: National University Publications, 1978.

Hundley, Mary G. The Dunbar Story, 1870–1955. New York: Vantage Press, 1965.

Hutchinson, Louise Daniel. Anna J. Cooper: A Voice from the South. Washington, DC: Smithsonian Institution Press, 1981.

Keller, Frances Richardson. "The Perspective of a Black American on Slavery and the French Revolution: Anna Julia Cooper." Proclamation of the Third Annual Meeting of the Western Society for French History, 165–76, 1976.

Klein, Abbe Felix. Au Pays de "La Vie Intense." Paris: Plan-Nourit, 1907.

Loewenberg, Bert, and Ruth Bogin, eds. Black Women in Nineteenth Century American Life. University Park: Pennsylvania State University Press, 1976.

Moss, Alfred A., Jr. The American Negro Academy: Voice of the Talented Tenth. Baton Rouge: Louisiana State University Press, 1981.

Sterling, Dorothy, ed. We Are Your Sisters: Black Women in the Nineteenth Century. New York: W. W. Norton, 1984.

Washington, Mary Helen. "Introduction." In Henry Louis Gates, Jr., ed., A Voice from the South, Schomburg Collection of 19th Century Black Women Writers. New York: Oxford University Press, 1988.

Who's Who in Colored America, 1930–32. New York: Who's Who in Colored America Corporation, 1927.

Woodson, Carter G., ed. The Works of Francis J. Grimke. Washington, DC: Associated, 1942.

Fanny Marion Jackson Coppin

Linda M. Perkins

Fanny Jackson Coppin (1837–1913) was one of the earliest African-American women college graduates. She was a prominent and influential educator of the nineteenth century. Coppin taught at, and headed, the prestigious Institute for Colored Youth in Philadelphia for thirty-seven years (1865–1902). Her role as principal was extremely significant in that women did not head coeducational secondary institutions with male faculty during this period. During her tenure at the Institute for Colored Youth, Coppin transformed the school and its curriculum, with students attending from throughout the nation and internationally. An outspoken feminist and community and religious leader, Coppin was involved in numerous women's and religious groups throughout her life.

Fanny Jackson Coppin was born a slave in 1837 in Washington, D.C. Little is known of her early childhood. Her maternal grandfather was John Orr, a prominent mulatto caterer and waiter with substantial property holdings in Washington. After he purchased his own freedom in 1825, Orr purchased in 1828 the freedom of his three sons but not his three daughters. He subsequently purchased his eldest daughter, Sarah, in 1840. She was then thirty years old and soon to be married. Upon his death in 1845, Orr freed his daughter Rebecca by will. However, in Jackson's words, he refused to free her mother, Lucy, "on account" of my birth."[1] In her autobiography published in 1913, Jackson mentions her mother only once and makes no mention of her father. However, in 1953, Alfred Vance Churchill, the son of Charles Henry Churchill, a professor at Oberlin College with whose family Jackson lived for six months while a student in 1865, suggested that Jackson was the daughter of a slave woman and a "Carolina Senator." This has never been substantiated, and no other reference has ever been made concerning her father. However, census records note Jackson as a "mulatto."

Despite her slave status, Fanny Jackson maintained a close relationship with the free members of her family. Her free Aunt Sarah Orr Clark earned only $6 per month yet saved enough to purchase Fanny's freedom by her early teenage years at the cost of $125. In 1850, due to the stringent resident requirements imposed after the Fugitive Slave Act of 1850 and better educational opportunities, Fanny moved to New Bedford, Massachusetts, to live with Elizabeth Orr, wife of Fanny's uncle John Orr. There she secured a job as a domestic. Due to her long work hours, she was unable to attend school regularly.

In 1851, she and her guardians moved to Newport, Rhode Island, again for better educational opportunities. To avoid becoming a financial burden to her relatives, she obtained a position as a servant in the home of the aristocratic author George Henry Calvert. The Calverts' household nurtured Fanny's love of the literary arts. With literary persons from Boston often visiting the Calverts, she described the home as one of "refinement and education."[2] In addition to the informal education she received from her contacts in the Calverts' home, she also hired a tutor one hour a day for three days a week from her earnings of seven dollars a month. Near the end of her six-year stay with the Calverts, she briefly attended the segregated public schools of Newport to prepare for the entrance examination for the Rhode Island State Normal School.

Jackson's life in Newport was active and pleasant. She learned to play the piano and guitar and was the organist for the Colored Union Church of Newport. The Calverts were childless, and Mrs. Calvert took a special interest in her and taught her sewing, darning, and needlepoint. Despite her seemingly uncomplicated life with the Calverts, Fanny's goals were "to get an education and to teach my people," goals that she described as being "deep in [her] soul."[3]

As planned, Jackson enrolled in the Rhode Island State Normal School, probably in 1859. In addition to taking the regular normal course, she studied French privately. Her desire to teach escalated, and upon finishing the normal school course, she stated that she still had much to learn. She wanted to attend Harvard; however, the institution did not admit women. Although disappointed that she could not attend Harvard, she heard that the curriculum of Oberlin College in Ohio was the same as that of Harvard and, more important, that African Americans and women were admitted.

In 1860 Jackson enrolled in the Ladies Department to prepare for the entrance examination of the Collegiate Department. In 1861, she entered the freshman class of the Collegiate Department, one of only 119 out of 1,311 students who were enrolled in that department. At that time, no African-American woman had graduated from that department. Nevertheless, Jackson, with tremendous self-confidence, was not discouraged from pursuing and obtaining a college degree. She was assisted financially at Oberlin by a variety of sources. Her Aunt Sarah Orr Clark provided some assistance, and Bishop Daniel A. Payne of the African Methodist Episcopal Church was so impressed by Jackson's determination and ambition that he provided her with a scholarship. In addition, she received a one hundred dollar grant from the Avery Fund of Oberlin College.

Jackson noted that although the Collegiate Department was opened to women in principle, "They [the administrators] did not advise it."[4] She recognized the challenge and the significance of her pursuit of a college degree and noted that when she recited in class, she "felt that I had the honor of the whole African race upon my shoulders."[5] She stated that if she had failed, it would have been attributed to her race. Jackson excelled at Oberlin and made an impressive academic record. She involved herself in nearly every aspect of life at Oberlin. In addition to her classes, she continued to take private French lessons. She sang in the First Church choir of Oberlin and in order to supplement her income taught piano to sixteen children of Oberlin's faculty.

Jackson was a noted scholar in all of her classes and in her second year at Oberlin was elected to the prestigious Young Ladies Literary Society. The society debated many questions that were foremost during the Civil War years. In addition to debates, it held programs that included the reading of poems, essays, and prepared orations. The largest of these programs took place during commencement week and was open to the public. Fanny Jackson appeared on these programs throughout her years at Oberlin. In 1862, she composed a poem, and in 1864 she gave an oration entitled "The Hero of Gettysburg" and appeared in a colloquy in which she depicted the continent of Africa. In addition to this experience, Jackson, as a member of Oberlin's Collegiate Department, was responsible for "compositions, declamations and extemporaneous discussions weekly; and public original declamations, monthly."[6] These activities provided her with a foundation in public speaking that enabled her to become an elocutionist of prominence.

During the Civil War years that Jackson attended Oberlin she was able to realize her goal of becoming a teacher of blacks. When freedmen began pouring into the city of Oberlin in 1863, she voluntarily established an evening class that met four nights a week. Most of the students were adults who came to class after working all day. Nearly all of the adults were illiterate, and Jackson taught them the basic rudiments of reading and writing. Despite her academic demands and the large number of music pupils she taught, she was extremely conscientious with her evening class and often conducted public exhibitions to display the work of her students. The evening school drew many visitors, and the local newspaper as well as abolitionist newspapers carried accounts of its progress. The class continued until Jackson graduated in 1865.

The success of Jackson's evening class resulted in her being chosen as the first African-American teacher in the preparatory department at Oberlin College. In 1865, she was elected class poet and graduated with a baccalaureate degree.

After graduating from Oberlin, Jackson was appointed principal of the female department of the Institute for Colored Youth in Philadelphia, a high school for African Americans founded by the Society of Friends in 1837. Because of the publicity she had received from her evening school at Oberlin, her outstanding academic accomplishments, and reputation as a gifted teacher, Jackson was well known to the Philadelphia black community.

The Institute for Colored Youth (ICY) was the most prestigious school for blacks in the nation. It included a preparatory department, girls and boys high school departments, and a teacher training course. The school's faculty included the most educated African Americans of the period. Jackson was a huge success at ICY. When the principal, Ebenezer Bassett, was appointed to the position of U.S. minister of Haiti in 1869, she was immediately promoted to principal of the entire school.

Jackson's promotion to principal of the institute was of great significance for a woman. Rarely, if ever, did women head a coeducation high school with male faculty members. Although one male member of the faculty protested the appointment, the all-white male Quaker Board of Managers stated that Jackson was even more qualified to lead the institute than the previous principal. In her four years at the institute prior to being appointed principal, Jackson had frequently been singled out for her outstanding teaching and leadership. Her ability to make learning easy and enjoyable became a trademark of her teaching style.

Immediately after Jackson became principal of the institute, she made many changes in the school that reflected her educational and personal philosophies. She believed strongly in giving respect to students. In her view, if students were treated with respect, they would likewise respect their teachers. Thus, she abolished corporal punishment at the institute in 1869, stating "The ability to discipline without force to back it up shows a much better prepared teacher, and speaks well for his influence over the school."[7] Although Jackson did not approve of corporal punishment, she was known as a strict disciplinarian. She did not hesitate to dismiss a student she thought was disrespectful or possessed improper character. She firmly believed that the character of a student reflected the character of the school. Always opposed to the tuition fees charged to the students due to the economic hardships of many African Americans, Jackson was able to have the fees abolished in 1877 by simply refusing to collect them. A strong advocate of her students, Jackson was also able to have public examinations abolished at the institute in 1881.

Jackson was a supporter of blacks of all socioeconomic levels and sought to keep the institute from being a haven just for the children of the Philadelphia black elite. As more southern African Americans migrated to Philadelphia, she attempted to make the institute available to as many of these newcomers as possible. Recognizing that requiring knowledge of reading, writing, spelling, arithmetic, and geography to enter the preparatory department was a barrier to many southern blacks with no prior education, Fanny Jackson persuaded the managers to abolish these prerequisites in 1884. The impact of the change in admissions policy was seen immediately in the preparatory school's enrollment. The number of students in that department increased from 255 in 1844 to 318 in 1885. Under Jackson's principalship, the institute began to attract a nationwide student body. Jackson was an extremely determined woman, particularly when it came to issues related to the education of the African-American race. When the Quaker managers refused to open a dormitory to accommodate the increasing numbers of students who were from outside Philadelphia, Jackson secured the house next door to the institute in 1884 and paid the rent for the students herself.

The institute was located within the heart of the Philadelphia African-American community and near the historic Mother Bethel African Methodist Episcopal (AME) church. *The Christian Recorder*, the national newspaper of the AME church, carried news of the institute and Jackson's activities, and she frequently wrote children's stories for the paper. In 1878, Jackson began a regular column entitled "Women's Department." Through this column, she was able to reach African Americans on a nationwide basis, particularly African-American women. Her column reported the achievements of women in education, employment, and other areas. She also reported cases of discrimination against black women. A staunch feminist, Jackson stressed in her column that women should pursue the same professions as men and not simply the traditionally female-dominated fields.

Jackson was active in many facets of the Philadelphia African-American community. She stressed self-determination and self-help. When the *Christian Recorder* was threatened with termination due to financial difficulty, she organized a community event to raise funds for the paper in 1879. Although Jackson was Episcopalian and the paper was a publication of the AME church, she stressed to the black community that the termination of the paper should be a concern of all blacks, not just those of the AME denomination, since the paper employed African Americans. The event that she organized cleared the debt of the paper.

Fanny Jackson met her husband, Levi Coppin, during the event that she organized in 1879 to save the *Christian Recorder*. Coppin, at least fifteen years Jackson's junior, was a native of Maryland and a licensed minister of the AME church. He was acting minister of the Mother Bethel AME when he met Jackson. Coppin and Jackson were married during the Christmas holidays of 1881 in Washington, D.C. At the time of their marriage, Rev. Levi Coppin had been transferred to Bethel AME Church in Baltimore. While it was the expectation that Fanny Jackson Coppin would resign her position at the institute and move to Baltimore at the end of the 1881–1882 school year, she remained at the institute until 1902.

At the time of her marriage, Fanny Jackson Coppin was in the midst of a campaign to establish an industrial department at the institute. As blacks were shut out of the growing technical and industrial jobs of Philadelphia, the new Mrs. Coppin stated that blacks should open their own industrial school. Coppin stated that her enthusiasm for the industrial school was spurred "as I saw building after building going up in the city, and not a single colored hand employed in the constructions."[8]

After a decade of speeches and fund-raising, the industrial department of the institute opened in January 1889. Far short of the advanced technical classes Coppin had hoped for, the industrial department offered courses in carpentry, bricklaying, shoemaking, printing, plastering, millinery, dress-making, and cooking. As the first trade school in Philadelphia for African Americans, the department was flooded with applications, and a waiting list of hundreds was maintained.

By 1884, Levi Coppin was able to transfer to the small Allen Chapel AME Church in Philadelphia. Although he wanted his wife to give up her position as principal after their marriage, he stated that she was devoted to her work and "had a fixed course in life, and stubbornly maintained it until it became a fixed habit."[9]

In addition to raising funds to establish an industrial department within the institute, Fanny Jackson Coppin was active in attempting to improve the employment situations of African-American women. With a committee of women from Mother Bethel Church, she opened a home for destitute young women in 1888. The three-story home included a matron and a visiting physician and offered nurses training. In 1894, Coppin opened a women's Exchange and Girls' Home. In addition to providing housing for students and working females, the home gave instruction in cooking, dressmaking, and domestic economy. Periodic exhibitions of the industrial work were given, and various articles made there were sold.

After her marriage, Fanny Jackson Coppin joined, and became active in, the AME church. She continued her interest in women's issues and was elected president of the local Women's Mite Missionary Society and sub-sequently became national president of the Women's Home and Foreign Missionary Society of the AME church. In 1888, she represented the organization at the Centenary of Missions Conference in London.

Fanny Jackson Coppin was politically active throughout her life. Although women could not vote, she viewed the franchise as important not only for men but for women as well. She frequently spoke at political rallies and most often was the only woman on the program. When the National Association of Colored Women (NACW) was established in 1897, she became one of the organization's vice presidents. In addition, she served on the Board of Managers of the Home for Aged and Infirmed Colored People in Philadelphia for over thirty years (1881–1913).

By the turn of the century, the years of activity began to take a toll on Fanny Jackson Coppin's health. She had spent endless hours working at the institute and had earnestly tried to find employment and housing for her students and other African Americans in Philadelphia. Her speaking engagements had been voluminous, and her involvement with civic and religious activities had been great. In 1897 she became ill with pleurisy. She never fully recovered, and in 1901 she announced her retirement as principal of the Institute for Colored Youth, effective June 1902.

Although Fanny Jackson Coppin made but one brief mention of her marriage in her autobiography, *Reminiscences of School Life, and Hints on Teaching*, from all indications, the Coppins' marriage was a close one. Levi Coppin appeared very proud to be the husband of such a distinguished woman. He often spoke and wrote of her with deep respect, admiration, and appreciation.

Although the school year was devoted to the institute, during the summers Coppin often traveled with her husband on behalf of the AME church. In 1900, Levi Coppin was elected bishop of the Fourteenth Episcopal District in South Africa. After her retirement from the institute in 1902, Coppin accompanied Bishop Coppin to Capetown, South Africa. Because of her poor health and her age, many in the black community feared that she would not survive the trip. Prior to the Coppins' departure, testimonials were given in Fanny Coppin's honor, and newspapers reported the audiences were overflowing at each occasion. Many turned out to pay tribute to her.

Gifts and money were given to Mrs. Coppin. A modest person, she was deeply touched by the outpouring of affection from the community and her former students. At a testimonial dinner given on her behalf, she stated that she had always had two schools—the institute and the Philadelphia black community. This statement summed up the educator's belief that her life's dream had been realized—"to get an education and to teach my people."[10] The many who had come under her influence responded gratefully. On the day of the Coppins' departure, scores of friends from throughout the nation traveled to New York to see the couple sail to South Africa. The press reported the scene as one of "deep interest and a degree of sadness."[11]

The Coppins arrived in Capetown, South Africa, in December 1902 and traveled into the interior of the country. As many had feared, the trip affected Coppin's health, causing fainting spells. She recovered and spent her time developing missions among the women of the country. At the AME school in Capetown, Wilberforce Institute, the African missions raised $10,000 to erect the Fanny Jackson Coppin Girls Hall as a symbol of their appreciation of the missionary-educator.

Spending only a year in South Africa, the Coppins departed the country in December 1903. After visiting several European countries, they arrived in the United States in the spring of 1904. Bishop Coppin was then appointed to the Seventh Episcopal District of the AME church, encompassing South Carolina and Alabama. Mrs. Coppin traveled to South Carolina with her husband; however, the South African trip had increased her health problems. By 1905, she was so weak that the remaining eight years of her life were spent primarily confined to her Philadelphia home on 19th and Bainbridge streets.

Despite Coppin's confinement, her mind and memory were intact. In her final years, she devoted her time to reading books and conversing with her many friends and former students. In the year of her death, 1913, she began writing her autobiography and book on pedagogy, *Reminiscences of School Life, and Hints on Teaching*. While she completed the major portion of the book, a former student, William C. Bolivar, compiled the section concerning the Institute for Colored Youth faculty and students, which was still in manuscript form at the time of her death.

On January 21, 1913, Fanny Jackson Coppin died at her Philadelphia home. Memorial services were conducted for the deceased educator in Washington, D.C., Baltimore, and Philadelphia. Known throughout her life as a champion of the poor, Fanny Jackson Coppin was modest and unassuming. A tall woman who dressed simply, she was a captivating speaker who never spoke with notes. Throughout her life she attempted to make education available to African Americans of all income levels. During her principalship at the Institute for Colored Youth she had tuition abolished so that the college prep school would be accessible to the children of the poor as well as the black middle class. Her concern for all blacks endeared her to the many poor blacks of Philadelphia. One observer of Coppin noted, "No so-called literary society or church festival was too humble to command her attendance."[12] A journalist in Philadelphia who had attended the institute commented that "even with her rare learning, she [Coppin] never made even the humblest appear uncomfortable."[13]

Coppin State College in Baltimore, Maryland, is named in honor of Fanny Jackson Coppin.

NOTES

1. Fanny Jackson Coppin, *Reminiscences of School Life, and Hints on Teaching* (Philadelphia: AME Book Concern, 1913).

2. Ibid., 16.

3. Ibid., 17.

4. Ibid.

5. Ibid.

6. *Catalogue of Oberlin College*, 1863–1864, 38.

7. *ICY Managers Minutes*, August 17, 1890.

8. Coppin, 24.

9. Levi Jenkins Coppin, *Unwritten History* (New York: Negro Universities Press, 1919; reprint edition, 1968), 356.

10. Coppin, 17.

11. *Christian Recorder*, October 22, 1902.

12. *New York Age*, November 8, 1890.

13. *Philadelphia Tribune*, February 1, 1913.

WORK BY FANNY MARION JACKSON COPPIN

Reminiscences of School Life, and Hints on Teaching. Philadelphia: AME Book Concern, 1913.

WORKS ABOUT FANNY MARION JACKSON COPPIN

Coppin, Levi Jenkins. *Unwritten History.* New York: Negro University Press, 1919. Reprint ed., 1968.

Drinkard-Hawskaw, Dorothy. "Fanny Jackson Coppin." In Rayford W. Logan and Michael Winston, eds., *Dictionary of American Negro Biography.* New York: Norton, 1982.

Fishel, Leslie H., Jr. "Fanny Jackson Coppin." *Notable American Women: 1607–1950. Vol. 1.* Cambridge: Belknap Press of Harvard University Press, 1971.

Perkins, Linda M. "Quaker Beneficence and Black Control: The Institute for Colored Youth, 1852–1903." In Vincent P. Franklin and James D. Anderson, eds., *New Perspectives on Black Educational History.* Boston: G. K. Hall, 1978.

———. "Heed Life's Demand: The Educational Philosophy of Fanny Jackson Coppin." *Journal of Negro Education,* (Summer, 1982): 181–90.

———. "The Institute for Colored Youth in Philadelphia, 1852–1902: An Argument for the Race." In David McBride, ed., *Blacks in Pennsylvania History: Research and Educational Perspectives.* Harrisburg: Commonwealth of Pennsylvania, Pennsylvania Historical and Museum Commission, 1983.

———. *Fanny Jackson Coppin and the Institute of Colored Youth, 1865–1902.* New York: Garland, 1987.

———. "Fanny Jackson Coppin and the African Methodist Episcopal Church: A Model of Nineteenth Century Feminist Leadership." In Dennis C. Dickerson, ed., *A Liberated Past: Essays in AME Church History.* Forthcoming.

Julia Etta Crane

Nancy L. Stewart

Julia Etta (Ettie)[1] Crane (1855–1923) was the founder of the first music supervisor training program in the United States connected to a state teacher training school. Although she spent almost all her life in the small town of Potsdam in upstate New York, her career affected the course of music education throughout the United States.

Julia Etta Crane was born in Hewittville, New York, on May 19, 1855, the oldest of six children of Samuel Coggeshall Crane (1822–1904) and Harriet Bissell Crane (1830–1893). Samuel Crane, a Maine native, traveled to California during the 1849 gold rush, then returned east to operate first a sawmill in Hewittville and later a chair factory in Potsdam. He was a justice of the peace, a member of the Potsdam Town Board, a thirty-second-degree Mason, and a Bible scholar and member of the Universalist church. He and Harriet Crane, his second wife, were married in 1854 in Brewer, Maine.

Growing up in Potsdam, Julia Crane attended the local public school and at age eleven began piano lessons. She sang in her church choir and by her early teens earned a reputation as a fine singer with a lovely voice and natural interpretive talent. She was often a featured soloist in the local singing schools. At fourteen, she entered the first class in the newly opened intermediate department of the Potsdam Normal and Training School, and upon her graduation in 1874, she began teaching in the Potsdam school system.

Crane benefited from Potsdam's rich tradition in both education and music. The town had been a site of teacher education since 1824, when the St. Lawrence Academy, predecessor of the Potsdam Normal and Training School, received its first state funding for teacher training, which soon became a regular part of the curriculum. As the move toward standardized education for teachers spread, New York State began granting statewide teaching certificates, and in 1844 the state established its first state normal school for teacher training in Albany. The Potsdam State Normal and Training School opened in 1869, in part because of the academy's previous reputation in teacher education. Music study and performance were part of the curriculum at both the academy and the normal school. At various times instruction included voice, piano, violin, and harmony lessons.

In addition, Potsdam had for many years been a center of musical activity in northern New York. One source of that activity was the singing schools. These short-term courses led by itinerant singing masters met in schools, churches, or homes for a few days or weeks at a time and provided some of Julia Crane's first musical experiences.

In 1861, charter members from twenty-seven different towns in the Potsdam area founded the Northern New York Musical Association to provide high-caliber musical experiences and performances to the upstate area. Between 1862 and 1891 the association sponsored twenty-six "conventions," each of which consisted of several days of rehearsal leading to a performance of a large work for chorus and orchestra. The first of these included four days of rehearsals and two concerts and involved 261 participants from Potsdam and the surrounding area. Over the years, many world-renowned soloists appeared in these events. Julia Crane undoubtedly sang in some of the concerts as a young woman, and later, after the association ended, she continued the tradition of large-scale musical performances in her own work.

Between 1874 and 1880 Crane's activities became more and more focused on music. In 1875 and 1876 she attended summer music institutes in Boston. In 1877 she moved to Shippensburg, Pennsylvania, where for three years she taught music, mathematics, and calisthenics in the normal school. When she returned to Potsdam in 1880 she opened her own voice studio and began accepting singing engagements in the area. The next year she accepted an invitation to accompany American counsul general Edwin Merritt and his wife to London, where she studied singing with Manuel Garcia, teacher of the famous singer Jenny Lind.

In 1882 Crane returned from London to Potsdam and reopened her successful voice studio. When Henry Watkins, president of the Local Board for the Potsdam Normal School, contacted her in 1884 and asked her to assume the recently vacated position of normal school music teacher, she was reluctant even to consider the offer. She protested that she enjoyed what she was doing and did not want to give it up. However, Watkins persisted. At that time the music teacher's duties including teaching one class per day, conducting the singing in daily chapel services, and preparing music for commencement and other special occasions. There would be plenty of time, Watkins promised, for private teaching and singing engagements.

Crane describes the historic negotiations:

I finally told Mr. Watkins that one class period per day was not sufficient time in which to do the work in music that ought to be done in a Normal School, that the only thing that would tempt me to take the position would be the privilege of working out a plan which had been in my mind from the time I completed my Normal course. My Normal School instructors had made me very enthusiastic over Methods of Teaching, and I had realized that it ought to be thought possible to give similar instruction in Normal music classes. The thought had often been in my mind that with proper training, Normal graduates might be as well fitted to teach the music of the grades as they were to teach reading or history.[2]

Watkins promised Crane he would do everything he could to support her plans, and she agreed to begin work in September 1884 at a salary of $300 per year. She immediately wrote the normal school authorities that neither the time nor the money allotted by the state for music teacher education was sufficient for its purpose:

I described the equipment necessary for a teacher to teach the music of the grades and the years of training necessary to acquire this preparation. Then I stated that I believed it was possible to so arrange a course of study in music that students entering with musical training might be fitted for teaching music, just as those who have studied reading and history learn in the Normal School the methods of teaching them. I then asked permission to do the work which I had outlined. The permission came and I started a piece of work, the results of which, as seen in the school today, I did not foresee even in my dreams.[3]

Before Crane's arrival, students at the normal school studied music for only one hour per day for one term. Crane revised the program to include daily singing and music reading sessions and made it possible for students who so desired to study music throughout their normal school course. At the same time, some of Crane's voice students joined the normal school classes in sight-singing and music methods to prepare to teach public school music.

As a result of the success of her innovations, two years later Julia Crane incorporated the Crane Normal Institute of Music and established the Special Music Teachers program. The year 1886 therefore marks the beginning of the first specialized music teacher training program in the United States connected with a normal school. The institute and the normal school jointly offered the public school music program, and for many years it was common for faculty to hold dual appointments.

At the time Julia Crane founded the Crane Normal Institute, music in the elementary school was usually taught by the classroom teacher. These teachers obtained their training from singing schools, private teachers, or conservatories, and the amount and quality of their experience varied widely. Music education focused on performance, with pedagogical subjects sometimes taught in special summer institutes like those Crane attended. Between 1850 and 1900 music became a common part of elementary and secondary education, music departments were incorporated into many colleges and universities, and the idea of special training for music teachers or supervisors gained wide acceptance. The founding of the Music Teachers National Association in 1876, the music section of the National Education Association in 1884, and the Music Supervisors National Conference, forerunner of today's Music Educators National Conference, around 1907, strengthened the teachers' increasing professionalism. In 1896 New York was one of the first states to establish special certification for music teachers. When Julia Crane established the Crane Normal Institute to train school music specialists, she responded to a need on the cutting edge of developments in education.

By 1896 Crane needed more space for her growing student body, so she bought a house in Potsdam to serve as the institute's teaching studios, practice rooms, and business office. Larger classes met in the normal school building. The house also provided living quarters for Crane and her sister, Harriet Crane Bryant, who taught at the institute from 1895 until 1931.

Crane made ensemble performance an important part of the institute's curriculum. As early as 1890 a small choral group with orchestra presented concerts, and by 1894 Crane had founded the Phoenix Club, a women's chorus still in existence at this writing. By 1905 the school regularly presented performances of large choral works with orchestra. Most of these concerts were conducted by Crane herself.

Enrollments continued to increase, and in 1909 Crane asked the board for additional space at the normal school. At that time she was negotiating with representatives of Syracuse University regarding the purchase of the institute. Although conflicts over budget control and the reluctance of some Syracuse officials to place a woman in such a prestigious position contributed to the eventual end of their discussions, Crane apparently used them for leverage with the normal school. The institute remained in Potsdam, and Crane was given a suite of several rooms in one of the normal school buildings, where her classes met for the next twenty years.

The curriculum in the institute and the normal school changed frequently in response to revisions in state certification requirements. By 1913 Crane coordinated two programs. The first was a course of study for classroom teachers in the normal school known as the Normal Course with Special Work in Music; the second was a course offered jointly by the Crane Normal Institute of Music and the Potsdam normal school called the Course for Supervisors of Music, for teachers certified to teach only music. Institute graduates by that time taught in public and normal schools in almost every state in the country, spreading the reputation of the program and sending students to study in Potsdam.

Crane believed that the goal of all education was to develop the potential of the individual and thereby contribute to a higher quality of citizenry based on good taste, high ideals, and a determination to do one's best. She said of music's place in education: "We believe that music has a power to reach the emotions which other branches of study do not possess, and that it is therefore not only a desirable factor in education, but an absolutely necessary element for fully rounded development."[4]

To Crane, the welfare of the individual child was of paramount importance. She said, "Unless music can be so taught as to serve as a valuable aid in the physical, mental, and moral culture of the pupil, it has no place in the common schools."[5] She knew that music teachers must understand not only music but also methods of teaching it. Thus, their training required study of music and of pedagogical theory, combined with the opportunity for supervised practice teaching like that provided for teachers of other subjects. She expected music teachers to sing well, play the piano, understand instrumental techniques, and know the history and theory of music as well as current educational philosophy and methods. In addition, the music teacher needed to be an excellent disciplinarian who was able to manage large classes, work in cooperation with other educators, and be an advocate for music instruction not just to students, but to teachers, parents, school boards, and the public. She stressed the importance of working with other teachers:

Until Music Supervisors realize that their work is an integral part of a great whole and that it has not served its purpose until it acts in harmony with the other parts of that whole, it is certain that music will never take its rightful place in the scheme of education.[6]

Crane constantly asserted the importance of music reading skills and believed they should be taught in the schools at the same time as other basic skills. She felt that the lack of such skills put children at a permanent disadvantage in any musical situation and made it difficult or impossible for them to develop an enjoyment or appreciation of music. She was a great believer in methodology and advocated a consistent sequence of instruction for every new aspect of musical training. This sequence progressed from imitation, recognition, and notation to study and recitation, oral tests of singing and music reading skills, written tests of notation skills, review, and, finally, appreciation.

In 1889, she completed the first edition of her *Music Teacher's Manual*, a carefully structured program of music study for students from kindergarten through grade school. The *Manual* included a complete step-by-step course of study for the primary and intermediate grades, many exercises to develop specific skills, lists of music and descriptions of music reading systems, and a discussion of the philosophical and psychological principles underlying her theories. She revised the book through seven subsequent editions; the last of these, in 1923, was completed after her death by her institute colleague Marie Schuette. The *Music Teacher's Manual* was the most extensive guide for public school music teachers available at that time. Later editions were adopted as texts by a number of music teacher training programs, and Crane received letters from all over the country praising it and requesting copies. Widely distributed and highly regarded, it helped to establish standards for music teacher training across the United States.

Crane's contributions to music education were not limited to the institute and the *Music Teacher's Manual.* She was also very active in professional organizations. She was a member of the National Education Association, the New York State Teachers Association, Music Teachers National Association, Music Supervisors National Conference, and the Eastern Music Supervisors Association. At a time when senior officers were nearly always men, she was at one time or another vice president of each of the national organizations—the music section of the National Education Association in 1896, the short-lived Society of American School Music Supervisors in 1899, and the Music Teachers National Association in 1900. In 1903 she conducted a music reading demonstration for the music section of the National Education Association in Boston and was one of a committee of ten appointed to formulate a statement of goals for each grade level. She was national secretary (1916–1917) and vice president (1921) of the Music Supervisors National Conference. From 1909 until 1918 she served on the Music Council of the New York State Education Department, where she helped formulate a high school music curriculum and revise the state public school music course, and she served on the State Examinations Board from 1909 until 1912. Through her work in national organizations she became acquainted with music teachers and supervisors from all over the country, and many of these contacts in turn sent students to the Crane Normal Institute.

Crane often appeared at conventions as a speaker, panel moderator, or discussion leader and regularly contributed articles to professional journals and publications such as *Etude* and *Musical America.* She taught summer courses at schools in California, Wisconsin, Maine, and Massachusetts and in 1901 served as the head of the public school music division of the Chautaugua Summer Institute. Her speeches and recitals were always enthusiastically received. One who heard her speak wrote:

You must get Miss Crane to talk to your teachers. My experience has been that among 1000 teachers about 800 know music but nothing of schools; 150 know about music and have had some successful experience in school work; 40 have added to these qualities the ability to sing or play; 9 are fine performers, good teachers, and understand fairly the pedagogy of their work, and one is a beautiful singer, plays the piano, understands music, is a born teacher, and so clear in her knowledge of the pedagogy of her work that she can impart her knowledge of the art of teaching to others. This one is Miss Crane.[7]

During the spring of 1923 Crane was troubled by fatigue and weakness, and the board of the normal school granted her a year's leave of absence from teaching. However, her condition was much more serious than anyone realized, and early in the morning of June 11, 1923, she died of a stroke at the Potsdam home of her sister, Jessie Crane Moore. According to her death certificate, she had suffered from arteriosclerosis for about five years. She lay in state in the auditorium of the normal school, which was filled to capacity for her funeral service, and she was buried in the Crane family plot in Bayside Cemetery in Potsdam.

Her contemporaries described Crane as a tiny woman, with high color, blue eyes, a kindly, gracious, dignified manner, and a musical speaking voice. She was generous with both her time and her finances and on more than one occasion provided needed funds for deserving students. Those who knew her spoke of her radiant spirit, her good humor, and her lack of ambition or pride. Her busy life was filled with training new generations of music teachers, developing the institute, leading professional organizations, writing, speaking, and active membership in the Potsdam Church of Christ, Scientist.

Financial problems plagued the institute at many points in its history, and on several occasions Crane investigated selling it to ensure its continuation. In early 1923 she tried to persuade the New York State legislature to purchase the institute and incorporate it with the normal school under state control. The measure failed to pass the legislature before her death. Her will stipulated that the school be offered to New York State first, then to any private purchasers who might be interested, with the proceeds of the sale going into a trust for the benefit of her three surviving sisters.

To ensure the school's survival, a group of concerned Potsdam businessmen bought it and operated it as a private corporation from 1924 to 1926. In 1926 the legislature finally passed a bill authorizing the state to purchase the school, which became the Crane Department of Music of the State Normal School at Potsdam. It is known today as the Crane School of Music at Potsdam College of the State University of New York.

Crane was a talented and dynamic woman who devoted her professional life to one cause: improving the quality of public school music teachers and public school music education. Through her institute, her *Music Teacher's Manual*, her lecturing, and her leadership in professional organizations, Julia Crane—educator, singer, conductor, and businesswoman—made an important contribution to the development of music education in the United States.

NOTES

1. The Crane School of Music Archives identifies Julia Crane's middle name as Etta. During her lifetime some sources cited her middle name as Etta; many others, including her institute letterhead from 1895 and her grave marker, used Ettie. She herself usually signed her name "Julia E. Crane."

2. Julia Crane, "History of the Institute," interview for the *Yearbook* (typescript, 1918), Crane School of Music Archives, Potsdam College of the State University of New York, 1.

3. Ibid.

4. Julia Crane, "A Talk," *Official Report of the Nineteenth Annual Meeting of the*

Music Teachers National Association (1897), 124. Quoted in William D. Claudson, "The Philosophy of Julia E. Crane and the Origin of Music Teacher Training," *Journal of Research in Music Education* 7 (1969): 402.

5. Julia Crane, *Outline of Work in Music in the State Normal and Training School, Potsdam, New York* (1885), 1. Quoted in Claudson, 400.

6. Julia Crane, "The Training of the Music Supervisor," *Journal of Proceedings of the Twelfth Annual Meeting of the Music Superintendents' National Conference* (1919): 84. Quoted in William D. Claudson, "The History of the Crane Department of Music, the State University of New York, College at Potsdam, 1884–1964," Ph.D. diss., Northwestern University, 1965, 147.

7. Marie A. Schuette, "Julia Ettie Crane" (typescript, n.d.), Crane School of Music Archives, Potsdam College of the State University of New York, 3.

WORKS BY JULIA ETTA CRANE

Julia Crane papers. Crane School of Music Archives, Potsdam College of the State University of New York.

Julia Crane papers. Potsdam Public Museum, Potsdam, New York.

Outline of Work in Music in the State Normal and Training School, Potsdam, New York. Potsdam, NY: Elliot Fay, 1885.

Music Teacher's Manual. Potsdam, NY: Elliot Fay, 1889; 2d ed., 1890; 3d ed., 1892; 4th ed., 1895; 5th ed., 1898; 6th ed., 1907; 7th ed., 1915; 8th ed., Potsdam, NY: Herald Recorder Presses, 1923 (posthumous, completed by Marie Schuette).

"A Talk." *Official Report of the Nineteenth Annual Meeting of the Music Teachers National Association* (1897): 117–24.

"History of the Institute." Interview for the *Yearbook.* Typescript, 1918, Crane School of Music Archives, Potsdam College of the State University of New York.

"The Training of the Music Supervisor." *Journal of Proceedings of the Twelfth Annual Meeting of the Music Supervisors' National Conference* (1919): 83–85.

WORKS ABOUT JULIA ETTA CRANE

Birge, Edward B. *History of Public School Music in the United States,* new and augmented ed. Bryn Mawr, PA: Oliver Ditson, 1937.

Claudson, William D. "The History of the Crane Department of Music, the State University of New York, College at Potsdam, 1884–1964." Ph.D. diss., Northwestern University, 1965.

———. "The Philosophy of Julia E. Crane and the Origin of Music Teacher Training." *Journal of Research in Music Education* 7 (1969): 399–404.

The New Grove Dictionary of American Music. New York: Grove's Dictionaries of Music, 1986. S.v. "Crane, Julia E(ttie)," by Margaret William McCarthy.

Schuette, Marie A. "Julia Ettie Crane." Typescript, n.d. Crane School of Music Archives, Potsdam College of the State University of New York.

Wakefield, Ralph. "A History of the Crane School of Music, Part 1." *The Quarterly* 31, Official Publication of the St. Lawrence County Historical Association

(January 1986): 3–14. Parts 2, 3, and 4 appeared in the April, July, and October issues, respectively. Potsdam College of the State University of New York reprinted the series in book form as *A Brief History of the Crane School of Music*, 1986.

Lucretia Crocker

Polly Welts Kaufman

Lucretia Crocker (1829–1886) was a pioneer woman school administrator and science educator. Crocker was closely associated with the liberal movements affecting education in her time. She demonstrated her commitment to equal rights for women by accepting the challenge to join Abby May and three other women in their successful drive for election to the Boston School Committee and, earlier, by joining the staff of Antioch College, under Horace Mann's presidency, to illustrate her pledge that women had a right to higher education. Her belief in the attainment of the full rights of African-American people was evident during her ten-year association with the Teachers' Committee of the Freedmen's Aid Society. During her decade-long tenure as the first woman supervisor in the Boston public schools, she also pioneered in the discovery method of teaching, particularly in mathematics and the natural sciences.

The daughter of Henry and Lydia E. (Farris) Crocker, Lucretia Crocker was born December 31, 1829, on Cape Cod in Barnstable, Massachusetts. She had a younger sister, Matilda. The family moved to Boston in 1848, where Henry Crocker worked in the insurance business and served as sheriff of Suffolk County in 1852. Crocker graduated from the State Normal School in West Newton, Massachusetts, in 1850 and continued there for four years as a teacher of mathematics, natural science, and geography.

Crocker gained the respect of naturalist Louis Agassiz, who lectured before the classes she taught at the normal school, and of educational reformer Horace Mann, who persuaded her to teach mathematics at Antioch College in 1857–1858. She supported Antioch's principles, particularly, she said, its "announce[ment] to the world, that the most liberal culture and scholarship are attainable by women without any sacrifice of true womanliness." Although she was successful, she refused Mann's request that she return for another year. She wrote him that the position "demands qualifications and preparations far beyond what I could bring."[1] Former students remembered their surprise at finding they were to have a woman teach them higher mathematics and cited her sympathy and clear explanations.

Crocker's methods of teaching closely approached Mann's and she was probably influenced by Johann Heinrich Pestalozzi's philosophy. She believed that a teacher must first excite the interest of students and allow them to discover as much as they could by themselves. Through questioning in the Socratic style, she believed, teachers should lead children "to think, to examine, and to express the results of their study." She printed her basic precept in italics in her *Methods of Teaching Geography: Notes on Lessons.* She wrote, "The teacher should *tell them nothing they can naturally find out for themselves.*" Once the interest of the students was aroused and their contributions made, the teacher, she said, should "supplement" with "bits of information" and illustrations. She emphasized observation and study of natural materials in the field when possible. Like Agassiz she preferred to teach with specimens. Textbooks were used for reference, not as guides. The purpose of review was not to cram for examinations but to demonstrate to students the dependence of "new steps . . . upon steps previously taken." Instead of "dull repetition," she said, "old facts or inferences" should be put "into new connections."[2]

Crocker was a devoted Unitarian, and her love of the study of natural history and geography both reflected and confirmed her deep religious feelings. The study of geography made one appreciate other countries and "ponder over the wisdom and power of God," she said. On the study of botany, she wrote an associate, "There are times in life when one wants and needs to get very close to nature, and when a little knowledge helps to unveil so much beauty that it fills the thought, as nothing else could, with a kind of sacred delight."[3]

From 1866 to 1875, Crocker worked with Ednah Dow Cheney and Abby May on the Teachers' Committee of the Freedmen's Aid Society, selecting and training teachers and making suggestions about the curriculum and the organization of the schools in the South. Conscious of the need of the teachers of the recently freed African Americans to learn from each other's experiences, she prepared a list of questions in order to have answers to circulate among the teachers. The few questions that survive showed that moral education was an intrinsic part of her teaching. First on her list was "means to . . . create a high moral tone in the school." Other questions show her views on student motivation: "methods of exciting enthusiasm for study" and "How often should the mental tension and physical weariness of pupils be relieved, and in what way?" Crocker's extensive visit to the schools in the South in 1869 became legendary for her successes in helping teachers and their pupils. Ednah Cheney accompanied her, noting that Crocker "was never more happy than among teachers."[4]

When the work with the Freedmen's Aid Society ended, Crocker's commitment to women's collegiate education led her in new directions. She joined the drive mounted in 1872 by the Education Committee of the New England Women's Club to elect women to the Boston School Committee, even though women had not yet attained school suffrage. A cornerstone of the Education Committee's plan to improve the schools was to upgrade the education of women teachers, a goal enthusiastically supported by Crocker. Although women had been permitted to enter the new Boston University since 1869, perhaps, the Education Committee suggested, women students would be allowed to enter Harvard if they could be well enough prepared. Because college preparation seemed to the women reformers to come down to a knowledge of Latin, Greek, and algebra, the conclusion they reached was that Boston Latin School should be opened to women. As bold a movement as it was, membership on the Boston School Committee appeared to be the only route to achieving the right of young women to attend public schools to prepare for entrance to college.

Crocker was reluctant to run for the office because she disliked being in the public view. When she was elected with four other women in 1875, she found it "hateful to be heralded," but she told her longtime associate in the Freedmen's Aid Society, William Lloyd Garrison, that she was willing to be "a pioneer in this new direction . . . as the representative of the cause of equal rights, irrespective of sex."[5]

Although Crocker, topping the ticket in her ward, was elected with Abby May and two other women to the Boston School Committee in December 1873, the successful women candidates were not seated until the next election a year later. Crocker and May were joined by Lucia Peabody, Kate Gannett Wells, Lucretia Hale, and Mary Safford Blake. In 1875 the School Committee was reduced from 114 members elected by wards to 24 members elected at-large. Under the new arrangement, Crocker, May, Peabody, and Hale were reelected and possessed a considerable increase in their power to make changes.

Crocker immediately concentrated her efforts on the upgrading of women teachers. Although May's proposal to extend the instruction at Girls' High to four years leading to a diploma failed, Crocker and Hale succeeded with a proposal to give Boston Normal School graduates preference in teaching positions. Their request to establish equal pay for women teachers, not actually fulfilled for one hundred years, was met with the logic of supply and demand and the explanation that women were paid their true market price.

Crocker's greatest challenge came during her second term on the Boston School Committee when her women associates decided to push for her appointment as one of six members of a new Board of Supervisors. At that time, Crocker was engaged in several educational projects. On the recommendation of Agassiz, she was chosen to organize the science department of Anna Eliot Ticknor's Society to Encourage Studies at Home in 1873. She also taught botany and mathematics at a private school for girls. In her mid-forties in 1876, Lucretia Crocker was ready to apply her past experiences, educational philosophy, and well-defined methods in a new direction.

Since only one woman had ever served as a Boston School administrator—Sarah J. Baker who came with the annexation of Roxbury to Boston in 1875—the women reformers' move to appoint a woman to the Board of Supervisors was nearly as bold as their efforts to gain seats on the School Committee. A petition of 162 names, headed by Garrison, supported Crocker's selection as a supervisor. Abby May led the campaign at School Committee meetings. Crocker was in an awkward position. If she resigned, she was in danger of alienating the men who voted for her. If she did not resign, she would be ineligible for the supervisory position. Finally she decided to submit a letter of resignation but carefully worded it, stating that she had decided to resign from the committee after "the advice and solicitation of several members of the Board, and of many earnestly interested citizens outside of it."[6]

Elected to the Board of Supervisors in 1876 with only one vote to spare, Crocker would not have been chosen without the women's votes and the women's drive. What is more, the *Woman's Journal*, the organ of the American Woman's Suffrage Association, pointed out, it "is a new point gained .... The women mean business and will prove their ability." The *Christian Register* also noted that Crocker "will not be insulted with half pay."[7]

Crocker became "the examiner of Oral Instruction, Geography, and Natural History." She tried to convince teachers to abandon "perpetual telling" and show students how "to earn their own facts" by observation, thought, and expression. In geography she placed a low emphasis on memorizing meaningless lists of place names and statistics and introduced map studies and activities.[8]

Crocker succeeded in her supervisory position, holding it for ten years until her death despite disagreements between the supervisors and Superintendent John Philbrick. Philbrick believed in using authoritarian methods, such as corporal punishment, as a substitute for what he perceived was a lack of support from families. Crocker, like the other school committeewomen, believed in the inherent goodness and future capabilities of children. The child's natural activity and physical needs were accepted and channeled into permissible behavior. Not only did Crocker and her women school board associates disapprove of corporal punishment, they also were opposed to "emulation," a method of inspiring good discipline through competition fostered by awards and elaborate annual exhibitions of pupils' work. Their ideas and policies represented a critique of male-dominated schooling and culture shared by women reformers of the time.

Crocker's influence on the other supervisors is evident in their reports. As a group, they worked to moderate authoritarian methods. The study of technical grammar, for example, was postponed until after language was used in oral lessons and daily written exercises. The spelling book was withdrawn from the schools, and spelling was taught in context. Writing with pencils on paper instead of with chalk on slates was introduced, and students copied words and sentences, not letters, as a method of learning to read. Overuse of textbooks was discouraged. Arithmetic was taught by applying numbers to real problems, using money and measurements.

On her own, Crocker introduced with great energy and persistence the study of natural science into the elementary schools and zoology and mineralogy into the high schools, organizing all the philanthropic resources she could find from her wide network for support. Upon Crocker's request, Ellen Swallow Richards, who, in 1873, became the first woman to receive a B.S. degree from the Institute of Technology (later, Massachusetts Institute of Technology [MIT]), joined her in giving lessons in mineralogy for two years in twelve schools.

As a way of providing her teachers with high-level training at virtually no cost to them, Crocker worked to expand the Saturday classes of the Teachers' School of Science, held in cooperation with the Society of Natural History and MIT. With the aid of friends, she raised money from such philanthropists as Mary Hemenway and Pauline Agassiz Shaw so teachers could obtain reference works and bring specimens into the public schools for their own classes. The parts of the flower, she believed, were best taught to students who each had a real flower in hand. In 1877, 616 teachers registered for the Teachers' School of Science, and 100,000 specimens were distributed throughout the schools. Louis Agassiz's son, Alexander, accepted four women teachers to study at his Newport Laboratory that summer. With the help of the Women's Education Association, the Society of Natural History later opened a summer laboratory for the study of sea life at Annisquam that was attended by many of the teachers who began their science studies at the Teachers' School. The Annisquam Laboratory later became the Marine Biology Laboratory at Woods Hole.

Although she was chosen a corporate member of the Association for the Advancement of Science, Lucretia Crocker never became a scientist in the sense of designing and carrying out her own scientific work. Rather, as Professor Alpheus Hyatt, who helped found the Teachers' School of Natural Science, said, she saw the natural sciences as an agency for "the reformation of the existing systems of education."[9] The remaining school committeewomen were eager to support her when they could in small ways as well as large. Abby May, for example, persuaded the School Committee to provide plants and flowers for high school botany classes.

That Crocker's leadership on the Board of Supervisors was indeed strong became evident in 1878 when Superintendent Philbrick lost his position to Samuel Eliot, the principal of Girls' High and a longtime supporter of women's education. Philbrick blamed his defeat on the committeewomen, denying that he was obstructing the work of the supervisors. He added, however, "If my successor is fully in accord with the lady member of the Board of Supervisors, I have no doubts that entire harmony will exist here-after."[10] When the *New England Journal of Education* supported Philbrick, saying he had been "dropped unceremoniously," Crocker withdrew her subscription, condemning the journal as "false to its opportunities—narrow—partisan." She discussed the possibility of starting another educational journal with Ednah Cheney because she wanted to be able to "recommend to teachers a really broad, high-toned educational journal."[11]

During this period, the school committeewomen, led by Abby May, Crocker's great supporter, succeeded in opening a Latin School for girls. Their achievement fell short of their original plan to make Boston Latin coeducational, a reform not actually achieved until 1972. The controversy over Superintendent Philbrick's reappointment and the unsuccessful efforts to make Boston Latin coeducational were probably behind Abby May's defeat for reelection in 1878. The public outcry following May's defeat, however, led to the awarding of school suffrage to all Massachusetts women the following year.

While serving as a Boston School supervisor, Crocker made her home in Rutland Square in Boston's South End, where she died at the age of fifty-six in 1886 of typhoid pneumonia. Memorial services were held at the Church of the Disciples (Unitarian), and she was buried in Mount Auburn Cemetery in Cambridge. A public school in the Jamaica Plain section of Boston named for her opened in 1885; it closed in 1950.

Lucretia Crocker is remembered as a pioneer woman educator to this day. In 1985 Massachusetts instituted the Lucretia Crocker Program, a statewide effort to improve schools by awarding fellowships to public school teachers to disseminate exemplary educational programs throughout public schools in the state.

Lucretia Crocker's career and particularly her ten years as a Boston school supervisor were among the great symbolic achievements for women active in the women's rights movement in her time. She represented the fulfillment of women's true abilities because she alone in the Boston schools held a high-level position with pay and authority equal to men's. Crocker's career represented real, as well as symbolic, achievement, because it allowed her to implement cultural and moral values shared by women educational reformers of her era throughout a major public school system over a period of time.

NOTES

1. Lucretia Crocker to Mr. Mann, August 4, 1858, Antiochiana, Antioch College.
2. Lucretia Crocker, *Methods of Teaching Geography* (Boston: Boston School Supply Co., 1884), 6–9.
3. Ednah Dow Cheney, *Memoirs of Lucretia Crocker and Abby W. May* (Boston: School Suffrage Association, 1893), 25, 30, 52.

4. Ibid., 26–38.

5. Lucretia Crocker to W. L. Garrison, May 21, no year, Garrison Family Papers, Sophia Smith Collection, Smith College.

6. *Boston School Committee Proceedings*, March 21, 1876, 47–49.

7. *Woman's Journal* (April 1, 1876): 105; (April 8, 1876): 115.

8. *Boston Public School Documents 1879*, no. 19, 3–18.

9. Cheney, 9–11.

10. *Boston Transcript*, January 23, 1878, 8.

11. Lucretia Crocker to Ednah Dow Cheney, July 16, no year, New England Hospital Papers, Sophia Smith Collection, Smith College.

WORKS BY LUCRETIA CROCKER

Lessons on Color in Primary Schools. Chicago: Interstate, 1883.

Methods of Teaching Geography: Notes on Lessons. Boston: Boston School Supply Co., 1884.

WORKS ABOUT LUCRETIA CROCKER

Blanc, Marie-Therese. *Femmes d'Amerique*, 223–40. Paris: A. Colin et cie., 1900.

Boston School Committee Proceedings and Documents, 1875–1886.

Cheney, Ednah Dow. *Memoirs of Lucretia Crocker and Abby W. May*. Boston: School Suffrage Association, 1893.

Green, Norma Kidd. "Lucretia Crocker." In Edward T. and Janet Wilson James, eds., *Notable American Women*, 407–9. Cambridge: Harvard University Press, 1971, vol. 1.

Kaufman, Polly Welts. "Boston Women and City School Politics, 1872–1905: Nurturers and Protectors in Public Education." Ed.D. diss., Boston University, 1978, 80–103. New York: Garland, forthcoming.

Sarah Ann Dickey

Clark Robenstine

Sarah Ann Dickey (1838–1904) began her career in education in the fall of 1857, teaching at a small school in Lewisburg, Ohio. Chosen by her church in 1863 for an expected missionary school, she arrived in Vicksburg, Mississippi, and began teaching in one of the first schools in the South for freed black slaves. Two years later, Dickey made her way to the Mount Holyoke Female Seminary, where she was graduated on July 15, 1869. Drawing upon her earlier experiences in Vicksburg, modeling the program at Mount Holyoke, and overcoming the intense hostility of the local white population, Sarah Dickey opened the Mount Hermon Female Seminary in Clinton, Mississippi, for the education of young freed black women on October 4, 1875. Referred to as "the Mary Lyon of the South" in the 1896 volume of *Woman's Voice*, Sarah Dickey's vision was to bring a version of Mount Holyoke to black women in post-Reconstruction Mississippi.

Sarah Ann Dickey was born April 25, 1838, near Dayton, Ohio, the fifth of the eight children of Isaac Dickey and his wife, whose maiden name was Tryon. Her father's ancestors were of Scottish stock and had come to America before the Revolution, finally settling in Ohio. Upon the death of her mother in 1846 her father, a poor farmer, had little alternative but to send most of the eight children to live with relatives. Consequently, Sarah spent much of her later childhood with an aunt living nearby, who was indifferent to Sarah's intense longing for an education. The aunt's pledge to send Sarah to school went unfulfilled. When her father returned at the time of the aunt's death in 1851, he found that his thirteen-year-old daughter could neither read nor write.

Subsequent arrangements were made, first with a widow, then with some cousins in the area, with the understanding that Sarah must go to school. The bargains were poorly kept, though she did manage to attend school sporadically and for very short periods of time, mostly in the winters. By the age of sixteen, she was barely literate. Even this most minimal exposure to formal learning must have acted as a spark, for to the great surprise of her relatives, Sarah announced that she wanted to be a teacher. Despite the admonishment that she lacked both the resources and the capacity to succeed, she persisted in following the promptings of what she would later describe as her inward guide. Sarah was finally able to attend school regularly by arranging on her own to work for a nearby family before and after school hours in return for room and board. To everyone's astonishment except her own, at the end of three years of intensive work, nineteen-year-old Sarah Dickey applied for, and received, a teacher's certificate. The first of many goals that she would set for herself had been met as she took her first teaching position at the school in Lewisburg, some twenty miles northwest of Dayton. Subsequently she taught in other rural schools in the area.

From her childhood, Sarah had had the idea of helping slave children learn to read, an idea probably influenced by her own lack of schooling as a young girl as well as by what she heard about slavery while growing up in largely pro-slavery southwestern Ohio. Her idea, however, was for the moment out of the question since laws in all southern states prohibited teaching slaves to read and write. Instead, she entered what would become a lifelong relationship when she became a member of the Church of the United Brethren in Christ (as the Evangelical United Brethren Church was then called) in Dayton on her twentieth birthday. She applied for an appointment to the church's foreign mission in Sierra Leone but was rejected by the Mission Board.

Sarah Dickey's first significant experience not only outside southwestern Ohio but with emancipated slaves came when her church's Mission Board, as the Emancipation Proclamation became effective January 1, 1863, quickly developed plans for establishing a school somewhere in the lower Mississippi to serve the newly freed slaves. Selecting a large, abandoned church in Vicksburg, the Mission Board opened the school on October 19, 1863, three and a half months after the city's surrender to Grant. Sarah Dickey was chosen as one of the first three teachers of the school and arrived in Vicksburg with the others on December 11, 1863. She was finally beginning what she considered her divinely inspired mission.

While both physical and social conditions were harsh, the May 1864 report of the school's progress sent north to the Mission Board remarked that in spite of the fifteen-cent enrollment fee and irregular attendance, some 300 newly freed slaves studied hard and learned rapidly. Some idea of the success of the school can be seen in the fact that the report to the Mission Board for May 1865 alludes to about 700 persons under instruction during the year. By early 1864 a United Brethren Church had been organized, and church services and a growing Sunday school also kept the Vicksburg mission busy. In the spring of 1865 the Mission Board located vacant land having what they thought to be a clear title and built their own building to use as church and school. But, with a change in military command and the resulting shift in policy after Lee's surrender in April 1865, military authorities returned the land to the original owners. Ordered to move their building as soon as possible but finding no site available, the Mission Board reluctantly closed the school a few months later. Even though the school closed, Dickey's year and a half at the Vicksburg mission proved to be one of the two significant influences on the later establishment of Mount Hermon.

Of great benefit for her work yet to come was the growth in knowledge and understanding that Sarah Dickey had gained of the people to whom she was dedicated. In her work at the Vicksburg school, she learned firsthand the difficulties the newly freed slaves faced in their rapidly changing environments. She learned something of their hopes for the future, their disappointments, and the ways slavery had conditioned them. She also became familiar with the southern scene and learned to live and work successfully with a variety of people. Although disappointed at the school's demise, Dickey saw an opportunity to do what she had increasingly felt the need to do—educate herself further.

The second significant preparatory period came when Dickey left Vicksburg and traveled back north, eventually to enter Mary Lyon's Mount Holyoke Female Seminary. Stopping first in Dayton to report directly to the Mission Board of her church and visit relatives, she was given the opportunity to serve in a Quaker mission in the South. Facing the dilemma of desiring more education yet being offered the opportunity for the very work to which she felt she had been called, Dickey struggled with the decision. Three and a half decades later she wrote of this time:

So one day when I was doing some work in a room alone and my heart was so burdened, I just stood up straight and said: "Lord, what shall I do?" And just as quickly as the words could be spoken, in the same decided tone, the answer came: "Go to Mt. Holyoke Seminary!" It seemed to me like an audible voice. Without another thought I just pressed my foot on the floor and said: "Go to Mt. Holyoke Seminary, that I will!" And when I said it I could command but ten dollars in the world.[1]

Though it was not an easy journey to South Hadley, Dickey arrived in the fall of 1865 with thirty-four cents to her name. By the final day of the allowed period of time she had passed all the required entrance examinations—Latin, English grammar, U.S. history, modern geography, and mathematics. Yet another obstacle remained. Since she had arrived after the beginning of the fall term, the few opportunities for a student to earn her way through the year had been taken. Luckily, one of the three students working her way through was called home, unable to return. Dickey was given that student's place. Not surprisingly, in addition to the obvious in-fluence of the academic program, equally influential was Mount Holyoke's domestic work system.

Instituted by Mary Lyon to reduce the cost of attendance, the domestic work system required that most of the necessary chores be performed by the students' working approximately an hour a day, with work assignments usu-ally made for a full term. Though encompassing a strict set of rules, which Dickey would ultimately incorporate into the work system at Mount Her-mon, the one feature that had the greatest impact on her was that most of the tasks were assigned not to individuals, but to groups called circles. Not only did work get done, but the group embodied a tightly knit sense of community and mutual support.

Sarah Dickey's four years at Mount Holyoke were difficult, both academ-ically and financially. But never losing faith in her mission, she graduated on Thursday, July 15, 1869. The three-day examination and graduation pe-riod for the thirty-eight graduates, reported in the July 16 edition of the Springfield *Republican*, marked not an end but a transition for Sarah Dickey. The further education she had so desperately sought was now hers, and, significantly, the seminary years had given her a sense of family and home that she had not enjoyed since her mother's death. Yet she remained unset-tled. Many years later, Sarah described what had happened to her early in her first year at the seminary:

When I had been at the Seminary about four weeks that same familiar voice said: "This is what the Lord wants you to do in the South: to build a Seminary like this for the colored girls." To that I answered, "No, that could not be the voice of God, for I certainly never could do such a work as that."[2]

But, by graduation in 1869 she was ready. She was sure that God, having guided her successfully through Mount Holyoke, would never ask her to do anything that she should fear to undertake. Her days of preparation were over.

Through the connections of two Mount Holyoke trustees who were also officers of the American Missionary Association (AMA), Sarah Dickey ar-rived in Raymond, Mississippi, in January 1870 to take a position at the AMA school there. Staying for one year, she left Raymond early in 1871 to become the head of a new, free public school for blacks in Clinton, Missis-sippi. Providing free schools for every child was a new idea in Mississippi, as well as an expensive one. But, to include black children was seen as a shocking waste and greeted generally with unmitigated outrage and hostility by the white population. Upon moving to Clinton to assume her new duties, Dickey found no white family willing to accept her as a boarder. Learning of her plight, black state senator Charles Caldwell offered her room and board, an offer she gladly accepted for three and a half years. Subject to constant social ostracism and frequent threats from the Ku Klux Klan, she went about her work unmoved in her determination to succeed. By the close of the school year in 1872 her work among the black students was being noticed favorably by some of the local white population. Even an article in the nearby *Hinds County Gazette* remarked on the progress made as evidenced by the thorough examination exercises.

But by the summer of 1872 Sarah Dickey returned to the idea of founding a seminary for black women. Leaving the Clinton free school, she wrote in a letter to a classmate:

I intend to establish a Mt. Holyoke Seminary for the colored girls. If my debts were paid at Mt. Holyoke I would begin my work next summer . . . . I have been here (in Mississippi) these two years for no other purpose than to investigate this matter and to ascertain as to whether it would be expedient to undertake such a measure; and also as to when it might be proper to do so. I am fully convinced that the people need just such an institution, and that they are ready for it now. I also fully anticipate the difficulties which I shall have to encounter, yet when God calls I have no right to plead difficulties as a reason why I should not cheerfully and heartily respond.[3]

Including in the letter a solicitation for aid, Sarah began working to accomplish her goal.

Locating 160 acres with buildings on the edge of Clinton for $6,000, Dickey obtained the property by the down payment of $10 with occupancy dependent on the payment of $3,000. Later, two promissory notes of $1,500 each were recorded to cover the balance. The initial name given to Sarah Dickey's projected school, listed in the April 1873 charter, was the Mississippi Female Seminary. Through a myriad of connections, including local influential blacks and sympathetic whites, friends and church in the North, and Mount Holyoke classmates, Dickey garnered support. Raising money first among blacks in Mississippi, then traveling north to Ohio and Mount Holyoke, she secured the first payment of $3,000 by the summer of 1875, and the name of the school was officially changed to, and recorded as, the Mount Hermon Female Seminary on the September 1875 Deed of Trust. With Charles Caldwell as the president of the biracial Board of Trustees, Mount Hermon opened on October 4, 1875. Sarah Dickey's dream was now reality.

As might be expected, life at Mount Hermon was never easy, and the first years were especially hard ones. Dickey explained the challenge of her work:

With never more than one or two helpers, I did a great deal of the teaching, about all of the preaching, managed everything, working a great deal with my own hands— in doors and out, and raised the other $3,000 on the purchase price of the property, and about $1,000 more for repairs, furnishings, etc., friends—Job's friends—on every hand awaiting the failure. But failure never came. God will never fail to take care of His own.[4]

When the Clinton free school closed, Mount Hermon was opened to the town's black children of both sexes as day students with their rudimentary learning left largely to older pupil-teachers.

Building upon the Mount Holyoke–instilled sense of family and home, Sarah Dickey set about providing her older female students with a thorough drill in every department of industry and household economy. Instituting a modified yet organized regimen, she modeled the daily schedule and family arrangements on the Mount Holyoke domestic work system. She regarded the necessary work as an integral part of her students' education, equally important as their literary training. Work was carefully supervised so that students held their assignments from four to six weeks and then moved on to another task. Punctuality, a new concept to most of the students, was insisted upon. Other parts of the weekly schedule included Sunday school, with students then free to attend the local church of their choice before returning for the afternoon service in the seminary's chapel; Tuesday evening vespers; and Friday literary programs, including recitations, readings, music, and singing.

Academically, Sarah Dickey attempted to develop a three-tiered course of studies based on the Mount Holyoke curriculum and leading to a diploma of graduation. The first tier was the necessary elementary work of the first four grades. Next, a three-year course beginning with a fifth reader led to the final third tier, called the higher English course, or advanced course. It was this last three-year sequence that was expected to develop into the Mississippi Mount Holyoke. The Mount Holyoke pattern, modified to meet local conditions, was still kept—a yearly requirement of Bible and English composition, the emphasis on science, and courses such as moral philosophy and the justification of Christianity.

The second course, called the Normal Course, was to provide students with a good understanding of all the subjects taught in the common schools of the state and prepare them to occupy positions as teachers in those schools. Among the subjects in this course were physiology, algebra, botany, hygiene, and theory and practice of teaching, with Bible and English composition in each of the three years. A report written in 1881 claimed that of the 400 students who had attended Mount Hermon in the first six years, at least 50 were teaching in the public schools of the state, though not all of them necessarily had completed the normal course.

The economic and social conditions in which the students found themselves served to exacerbate the enormous difficulty of the task that Sarah Dickey had undertaken. Emancipated blacks were subject to continuing segregation, and the constant intimidation by many whites often functioned to render the newly won black vote negligible. Economically, many still lived in extreme poverty as sharecroppers on plantations, owning little or nothing of their own and still at the mercy of the plantation owner. Unfamiliar with standard practices, they were often exploited by traders when they took their cotton to market.

In an attempt to alleviate the financial burden of tuition, raising money became a constant activity. One source of funds for Mount Hermon was the Slater Fund. Hearing of the establishment of this fund, Dickey made application, and Mount Hermon was first visited by Atticus Haygood, agent for the fund, in late September 1884. Citing the school as one of the best of its class, Haygood recommended, and the trustees of the fund provided, an initial grant of $1,000, an amount that came to be given yearly. In his 1887 report to the trustees, Haygood commented that the "Mt. Hermon Institute reports the opening as very good. Miss Dickey, 20 years in this service, is much encouraged. She could hardly go on without the help of the Slater Fund. Her work is admirable."[5] From all accounts, the last endowment from the Slater Fund was $1,000 for the year 1889–1890. With the continuing financial burden, Sarah embarked on an attempt to raise a permanent endowment, the failure of which signaled the beginning of the end for the fragile institution. Working tirelessly, she continued to solicit funds locally and make trips back north in an attempt to provide financial stability.

Sarah Dickey had always maintained a close relationship with her United Brethren Church in Dayton and worked closely during the 1880s with the Woman's Missionary Association of the church. She had even proposed that with the support of the association, Mount Hermon could train and prepare students for missionary work in Africa, a suggestion that was never implemented. So close was her relationship with her church throughout her adult life that she studied and became a licensed minister of the United Brethren Church in 1893, with ordination following in 1896. From this time she was permitted to administer the Sacrament of Holy Communion monthly at Mount Hermon, though there is no knowledge of her performing any other of the church's sacraments.

Becoming even more active locally, Dickey increasingly tried to protect the parents of her students, as well as other blacks, from continuing exploitation, often accompanying them to the local cotton market to ensure equitable compensation. In the mid-1890s, knowing that many still lived as tenants in former slave quarters, she borrowed money to purchase additional land near the school. This land she then subdivided and offered on credit to black families who wished to build their own homes on their own land. Meeting regularly with the residents of "Dickeyville," she discussed financial and employment problems, made interest-free loans when she could, and encouraged a sense of community.

The 1890s saw no abatement in the serious financial problems of Mount Hermon, and Sarah Dickey's constant laboring on all fronts finally took its toll. At the point of exhaustion, she fell ill late in the year 1903, and by the middle of January 1904 her illness had developed into acute pneumonia. She died in her room at Mount Hermon on January 23 and was buried in the spot on the school's grounds that she had selected. That she had made a deep impression on the entire local community was evidenced in the report of her death in the Jackson, Mississippi, *Clarion Ledger*: "She had a hard time for several years, but in due course of time the fame of her school went abroad, and pupils came from every direction. The result was that she died owner of one of the best private negro schools in the state."[6]

The school's reputation notwithstanding, the death of Sarah Dickey found Mount Hermon in a more precarious state than anyone had imagined, with various mortgages on the property, teachers' salaries overdue, and food and supplies running low. The trustees of the institution decided that the only hope was to find some organization interested in the work of the seminary and willing to take it over. With the incentive of an outside endowment from a private source for its work in the South, the AMA agreed to take over Mount Hermon within a few months after Sarah Dickey's death. But with the association's policy of divesting its more elementary schools and concentrating on its advanced schools and colleges, little interest was shown in the continuance of the seminary. Eventually, the normal course and boarding students were transferred to the AMA's nearby Tugaloo College, and the elementary school, in time, was dropped. The school lingered for another twenty years under the auspices of the AMA but was finally closed after commencement in May 1924. The property, with its dormitories, class-rooms, chapel, and farm, was sold to the Mississippi State Federation of Colored Women's Clubs, which opened a training school for delinquent black boys in April 1930. Seven months later most of the buildings burned down. The property was then split up and sold, the remaining buildings razed.

If "lasting contribution" is measured only in terms of tangible artifacts, then Sarah Dickey made little lasting contribution. Nothing of the Mount Hermon Female Seminary is still standing, and the name of Sarah Dickey has all but faded from a collective historical memory. However, since a lasting contribution surely can be something as modest as a reminder that not only "great men" ameliorate the lives of others, then Sarah Dickey's life—a study in ideals, conviction, and race relations—is noteworthy. Settling in Clinton, Mississippi, at the height of anti-North and antiblack feelings, she was able to establish an institution that came to earn the respect of the entire local population.

Influenced by the emphasis on family life and by the prominent role of religion at Mount Holyoke, Sarah Dickey devoutly believed in an ideal of Christian womanhood. Mary Lyon, like most other female educational leaders, had deeply held a belief that the crucial role of women was to bring about social salvation and regeneration. Lyon, Dickey, and many others believed that because women were more patient, understanding, nurturing, and moral than men, they would be the shapers of the Christian character and civic virtue necessary for republican citizenship. Regarding black girls as the native raw material of the South, Dickey applied this ideal at Mount Hermon and expected her students to become the regenerating mothers of their race, as well as teachers and missionaries for the battle of African Christian civilization in America.

The Mount Hermon Female Seminary never approximated the level of academic quality that Sarah Dickey experienced at her alma mater. It fell short in two crucial areas. First, in almost thirty years she was never able to develop a student body with the academic preparation proper for a seminary like Mount Holyoke, and apparently only one student ever completed the advanced course. Given their existence as slaves and the oppressive social and economic conditions imposed on blacks in the South after emancipation, this is hardly surprising. Second, she was never able to ensure permanence for Mount Hermon by raising an endowment for it.

Nevertheless, in the heart of post-Reconstruction Mississippi, Sarah Dickey provided elementary education to increasing numbers of black girls (and boys) and supplied teachers for the state's free black schools (such as they existed). She also exerted a positive effect on general race relations in her community. With little concern for her personal health and well-being, Sarah Dickey throughout her entire life exemplified the possibilities of human endeavor in the face of overwhelming odds.

NOTES

1. Sarah Dickey, *The Dew of Hermon*, no. 2 (July 1901).
2. Ibid.
3. Quoted in Helen Griffith, *Dauntless in Mississippi* (Northampton, MA: Metcalf Printing, 1965), 73.
4. Sarah Dickey, *The Dew of Hermon*, no. 1 (September 1900).
5. Atticus Haygood to Rutherford Hayes, November 21, 1887, in Louis Rubin, ed., *Teach the Freeman: The Correspondence of Rutherford B. Hayes and the Slater Fund for Negro Education, 1881–1893* (Baton Rouge, LA: Louisiana State University Press, 1959), vol. 1, 232.
6. Jackson, Mississippi, *Clarion Ledger*, January 26, 1904.

WORKS BY SARAH ANN DICKEY

The Dew of Hermon (ed. and publisher?), no. 1 (September 1900).
The Dew of Hermon (ed. and publisher?), no. 2 (July 1901).

There exist also a few personal letters of Sarah Dickey, held in the Mount Holyoke Alumnae archives.

WORKS ABOUT SARAH ANN DICKEY

Flagg, Elizabeth F. "The Mary Lyon of the South." *Woman's Voice* 7 (August 29, September 5, September 12, 1896).
Griffith, Helen. *Dauntless in Mississippi: The Life of Sarah Dickey, 1838–1904*. Northampton, MA: Metcalf Printing, 1965.
Woodworth, Frank J. "The Life and Work of Sarah A. Dickey." *Mount Holyoke Monthly* (January 1905).

Occasional references to Sarah Dickey and Mount Hermon are found also in the records of the Historical Society of the Evangelical United Brethren Church (Mission Board) Dayton, Ohio, depository.

Sarah Mapps Douglass

Linda D. Addo

Sarah Mapps Douglass (1806–1882) began her teaching career in 1828 in Philadelphia and taught black students for forty-nine years. Many of her students became teachers in black schools in Philadelphia and in the South after the Civil War. She opened a private female academy in 1820 and remained as a leader and teacher until 1853. In 1853 she became supervisor of the girls' department in the Philadelphia Institute for Colored Youth. She remained with the institute for the rest of her teaching career. She resigned her position when she married in 1855 but returned to the institute after her husband died in 1861. She was a charter member of the Philadelphia Female Anti-Slavery Society and secretary of the black Female Literary Association and a friend of noted abolitionists and feminists, Sarah and Angelina Grimke. Douglass's career as a black educator before the Civil War and after provides insight into the role that free blacks played in providing education for black youth in spite of opposition and meager financial resources. Furthermore, her career was significant because she was also an activist working to abolish the institution of slavery.

Sarah Mapps Douglass was born in Philadelphia in 1806 to Robert and Grace Bustill Douglass. Both of her parents were free blacks from families who were prominent leaders in the free black community in Philadelphia. Her maternal grandfather owned a bakeshop and was a member of the Free African Society. She had two brothers, Robert and James. Robert Douglass, Jr., was a portrait painter. Sarah's parents hired a private tutor for her, and in 1819 she began to attend a school for blacks organized by her parents and another prominent free black, James Forten, a maker of sails for boats. James Forten was the father of Charlotte Forten, who kept a journal of her role as a teacher in Port Royal, South Carolina, from 1862 to 1864. Charlotte and Sarah were friends. On July 23, 1855, Sarah Douglass married Reverend William Douglass, pastor of the St. Thomas Protestant Episcopal

Church. It was a short marriage because he died in 1861. They had no children.

Both of Douglass's parents became active in the abolition movement. Although Douglass and her mother were devout Quakers, they were often disturbed about the segregated schools supported by the Quakers and about the fact that blacks had to sit apart from the rest of the members at the Quaker meetinghouses. Gerda Lerner in her study of the Grimke sisters mentions an incident of Quaker discrimination that Douglass shared with the Grimke sisters (two Quaker abolitionists who had moved to Philadelphia from South Carolina).

Sarah Douglass told them of an incident that took place while she was visiting New York City. At a Quaker Meeting she attended no one spoke to her except one young woman, who addressed her with this question: "Doest thee go out a house-cleaning"? (When) Mrs. Douglass answered that she was a school teacher, the white lady expressed her astonishment and lost interest. Mrs. Douglass wept through the entire meeting.[1]

Although Douglass's mother continued to attend the Spruce Street Meeting House, Douglass did not attend as regularly as her mother because of the discrimination. She found it difficult to understand why the Quakers supported segregated schools and why most meetinghouses had "colored benches." It was difficult to understand, since the Quakers encouraged their members not to own slaves.

The Grimke sisters, influenced by black friends like Sarah Mapps Douglass, often defied custom and sat on the benches reserved for black Quakers. In spite of the discriminatory practices of the Quakers, they were the first in colonial Pennsylvania to establish schools for blacks. However, the free black community supplemented the Quaker schools in the nineteenth century with elementary schools staffed with black teachers. Sarah Mapps Douglass was an example of the many free black women who played an important role in these schools as teachers.

In 1828, after teaching briefly in New York City, Sarah Douglass returned to Philadelphia and established a female academy for black girls. Not only was she an inspiring teacher, but many of her students became teachers in black schools before the Civil War. After the Civil War she continued to train teachers, not only for black schools in the North but also for black schools in the South. In 1828 and continuing for several years Douglass was still supported by her parents. Douglass and her parents were determined to demonstrate that blacks could support their own schools. She received praise as an outstanding teacher from those who visited her academy. Alexander Crummell, a Quaker scholar and clergyman of Washington, D.C., described Sarah Douglass: "The first people of the city and their children in turn, sat at the feet of this refined and cultivated woman and received from her the ripe instructions of her well-cultivated mind."[2] Samuel Cornish, editor of the *Colored American*, described the academy in 1837:

The school numbers over 40, selected from our best families, where their morals and manners are equally subjects of care, and of deep interest. All of the branches of a good and solid female education are taught in Miss Douglass' school and together with many of the ornamental sciences, calculated to expand the youthful mind, refine the taste, and assist in purifying the heart.[3]

Not only was Douglass a teacher, but she also was noted for being an active member of the abolition movement. She was a charter member of the Philadelphia Female Anti-Slavery Society, organized on December 14, 1833. She served over the years as recording secretary, librarian, member of the Board of Directors, and member of the Education Committee. The major purpose of the Education Committee was to support the ten private schools for blacks in Philadelphia. Each member of the committee was responsible for a particular school. In 1838 Douglass allowed the Philadelphia Female Anti-Slavery Society to support her school financially. This arrangement lasted for only two years because other blacks criticized her for accepting help from the group. After all, she had been the one who had been proud of the fact that her school proved that blacks could support their own schools. The society had been paying her a salary of $300. Her letter stating that she would not like her school to continue under the supervision of the society was read at an April 1840 meeting of the group. However, the society decided to support Douglass's school with an annual donation of $125. She continued at her school until 1853.

In 1853 Sarah Douglass accepted a position as director of the girls' department at a new school called the Pennsylvania Institute for Colored Youth. In an agreement between Douglass and the Board of Directors of the institute, the directors agreed to provide "the Front Room for a school for girls, for one year, commencing 4th Month 4th, 1853—to provide desks and Seats, Stove & Coal for the said Room, to pay the said Sarah for the tuition of 25 scholars."[4] In the agreement she was to teach spelling, geography, reading, writing, and arithmetic. At a meeting of the Quakers, who were supporters of the preparatory school, on April 18, 1853, it was evident in the minutes that they were pleased with Douglass's work: "The School having been several times visited by members of the Committee was found in satisfactory order."[5]

Douglass added some nontraditional subjects to the curriculum, including physiology, and there is evidence that in the 1830s she taught physiology in her prior school. In a letter from a certain Samuel M. Janney to James and Lucretia Mott, Janney reported to the Motts that he was impressed when he visited Sarah's school to see that the children were studying physiology. He indicated that this was a subject that was not normally part of the school curriculum. After Douglass married in 1855, she took the medical course at the Ladies' Institute at the Pennsylvania Medical University. She was a student at the Pennsylvania Medical University until 1858.

Sarah Douglass remained at the Institute for Colored Youth until her retirement in 1877. After the Civil War the institute provided teachers for black schools that were established in the South. The institute later became a division of Cheyney State College. Robert C. Morris in his study of black schools established after the Civil War indicates that it was the opinion of many that the institute produced good teachers. After the Civil War Douglass joined the Pennsylvania Women's Branch of the American Freedmen's Aid Commission. She served as vice chairperson of the group. She was also a contributor to the black newspaper *The Anglo-African Weekly*, beginning in the 1850s. She wrote articles on education, hygiene, physiology, and abolition.

Sarah Douglass was an active member of the Pennsylvania Female Anti-Slavery Society. The society was established after the American Anti-Slavery Society encouraged women to organize auxiliaries. Douglass was one of the signers of the charter of the organization. There were three national meetings of the women's National Anti-Slavery Convention before women were allowed to join the male societies in 1839. Sarah Douglass served as treasurer. The only other black woman to hold an office was Grace Douglass, Sarah's mother, who was elected as a vice president. Sarah wrote articles for Garrison's periodical, *The Liberator*, using the pseudonym "Zillah."

In 1839, when the Massachusetts Anti-Slavery Society divided over the issue of whether William Lloyd Garrison should continue as president, Sarah Douglass and her mother wrote a letter supporting Garrison. They agreed with Garrison that churches and politicians were guilty of condoning slavery. They understood why Garrison advised abolitionists not to participate in the political process. Garrison's critics also were uncomfortable with his criticism of ministers and organized religion, but Douglass and her mother could identify with Garrison's criticisms of the churches. They were Quakers, and their church called for the abolition of slavery, but they had to sit on separate benches. Douglass agreed with Garrison that northerners could not say they were not guilty because they did not own slaves.

After the Civil War, Sarah Douglass discovered a new cause, becoming vice chairperson of the Women's Pennsylvania Branch of the American Freedmen's Aid Commission. Again, she was mainly interested in the educational endeavors on behalf of blacks. In addition to continuing to provide educational opportunities for blacks, she devoted her efforts to another cause, the black press. Douglass believed that the black community had to have a viable press. Her position was that the black press could be an independent voice only if it were supported solely by the black community; therefore she organized fund-raising fairs to support the black press. In the evenings she was involved in adult education at the Banneker Institute, where she taught reading, personal hygiene, and physiology.

Sarah Mapps Douglass is one of the unsung heroines and contributors to education for blacks in antebellum America and later in the Reconstruction era. Although she did not physically go to the South to teach freedmen, she continued to prepare students who became teachers in those schools. She believed that education would enable her students to assume their roles as active and responsible adults. Her approach as a teacher emphasized the transmission of values based on rational, ethical principles. Douglass's students were encouraged to see themselves as important and creative. As a devout Quaker, Douglass not only endeavored to get her students to acquire knowledge but also hoped that her students would realize that a dialectic existed within each of them. She emphasized to her students that knowledge was not enough and that students must also develop morally and, like Douglass, use their knowledge to help improve conditions for blacks. In an essay she wrote for *The Liberator* in the 1830s, she emphatically affirmed her belief that education and religion could be used as tools to help blacks and women achieve equality: "Yes, religion and education would raise us to an equality with the fairest in the land."[6] Sarah Mapps Douglass's career as a teacher for forty-nine years demonstrated that in spite of meager resources blacks could provide educational opportunities for themselves. Her career is also illustrative of the significant role and involvement of black women in antebellum and Reconstruction era education for blacks and of the importance of free black women in antebellum America.

NOTES

1. Gerda Lerner, *The Grimke Sisters from South Carolina: Rebels Against Slavery* (Boston: Houghton Mifflin, 1967), 133.
2. Anne Bustill Smith, "The Bustill Family," *Journal of Negro History* (October 1925): 644.
3. Sterling, Dorothy, ed., *We Are Your Sisters: Black Women in the Nineteenth Century* (New York: W. W. Norton, 1984), 128.
4. Minutes, Meeting of the Board of Managers of the Institute for Colored Youth, 1837–1855, Philadelphia Yearly Meeting of the Religious Society of Friends, Philadelphia. In Gerda Lerner, ed., *Black Women in White America: A Documentary History* (New York: Random House, 1974), 86.
5. Ibid., 87.
6. Sterling, 112.

WORKS BY SARAH MAPPS DOUGLASS

"Speech Delivered Before the Female Literary Society of Philadelphia," January 1837. In C. Peter Ripley, ed., *The Black Abolitionist Papers*, vol. 3, *The United States, 1830–1846*. Chapel Hill: University of North Carolina Press, 1991.
The Liberator, Boston, 1837–1840.
Friends' Association of Philadelphia and Its Vicinity for the Relief of Colored Freedmen, Papers, 1862–1865. Haverford College, Haverford, Pennsylvania.

Mother Mary Katharine Drexel

Mary J. Oates

Mother Mary Katharine Drexel (1859–1955) devoted her life and fortune to the education of African-American and Native American youth, without religious distinction. Despite an impressive history of educating thousands of children of poor and working-class immigrants in "free" parochial schools across the country, late nineteenth-century Catholics showed little interest in the education of America's least affluent members, blacks and Indians. Mother Drexel represents an outstanding exception. In collaboration with hundreds of women who, in time, joined the teaching sisterhood she founded, this trailblazing educator contributed uniquely and enduringly to the welfare of American society.

Katharine Mary Drexel, second child and second daughter of Francis Anthony Drexel (1824–1885) and Hannah Jane Langstroth (1826–1859), was born in Philadelphia on November 26, 1859. Both parents were native Philadelphians. Her father belonged to a prominent Roman Catholic family and headed the Drexel & Co. Banking Houses founded by his father, Austrian-born Francis Martin Drexel. Her mother, a Baptist Quaker, died five weeks after Katharine's birth. In 1860 Francis Drexel married Emma Bouvier (1834–1883) of Philadelphia, and in 1863, Louise, the only child of this union, was born.

Katharine was educated at home by private tutors and governesses. Annual family excursions throughout the United States and abroad, including extended "grand tours" of Europe in 1874–1875 and 1883–1884, supplemented lessons in English composition and literature, Latin, French, and piano. She attended weekly religion classes at the nearby convent of the Religious of the Sacred Heart. Her formal schooling ended in May 1878, and in January of the following year, she made her debut in society.

By word and example, Francis and Emma Drexel had nurtured their daughter's philanthropic instincts from early childhood. Emma was renowned throughout Philadelphia for her personal charity toward the poor, and Katharine participated actively in her mother's benevolent projects. As a teenager, travel deepened her vivid appreciation of the extremes of poverty and wealth her country encompassed. Rev. James O'Connor, pastor of the parish where the Drexel family summered, encouraged her interest in ameliorating the situation of the poor. Even after leaving Pennsylvania to serve as bishop in Nebraska territory in 1876, he remained her close friend and spiritual mentor until his death in 1890. In her twenties, through Bishop O'Connor, Dakota bishop Martin Marty, and Rev. Joseph Stephan, director of the Bureau of Catholic Indian Missions, Katharine became especially interested in the plight of Native Americans.

Upon the death of Francis Drexel in 1885, his daughters became immensely wealthy women. According to his will, they were to share equally during their lives in the income from a $14 million trust fund. If, at the death of the third daughter, there were no surviving offspring, the principal of the trust was to be distributed among approximately twenty charities in the Philadelphia area. Since Elizabeth Drexel Smith died in childbirth in 1890, leaving no children, Katharine and Louise Drexel Morrell shared the trust income until Louise's death in 1945. Louise was childless, so until her death a decade later, Katharine received the entire income from the trust.

By 1885, Katharine had already initiated a personal program of philanthropy on behalf of Indians. Convinced that education was the key to social and economic progress, she concentrated her efforts on the provision of high-quality free schools. After touring Europe to study educational practice and school construction, she launched in 1887 a Santa Fe boarding school for children of Pueblo Indians. Within a few years she was funding a dozen more Indian schools throughout the West. Her support encompassed not only the construction, furnishing, and maintenance of the schools but also the salaries, room, board, and clothing of religious sisters who staffed them. The most enduring and intractable problem she faced was how to find enough religious sisters to conduct the schools she was building.

At this time, the young philanthropist determined to act upon a long-felt call to the religious life. Initially, she considered joining an established sisterhood, but, given her interest in blacks and Indians and the fact that no sisterhood was exclusively devoted to their welfare, Bishop O'Connor, Philadelphia archbishop Patrick Ryan, and Pope Leo XIII proposed that she establish one that did. She accepted the challenge.

In May 1889, Katharine journeyed to Pittsburgh to prepare for the religious life by making a novitiate with the Sisters of Mercy. The news of her unorthodox life choice stunned Philadelphia society and disappointed some members of her family. She described the reaction of her uncle, Anthony Drexel: "Uncle Anthony dropped four or five tears; but he said he would not oppose anything which would contribute to my happiness. He thinks, however, that I am making the mistake of my life if I become a religious."[1]

Katharine Mary Drexel received the religious habit of her new order in November 1889 and took as her religious name Sister Mary Katharine. On February 12, 1891, she exchanged the novice's white veil for the black veil of the professed sister. As the founder of the Sisters of the Blessed Sacrament for Indians and Negroes, she added to the vows of poverty, chastity, and obedience, traditionally taken by sisters in all religious orders, a pledge "not to undertake any work which would lead to the neglect or abandonment of the Indian and Colored races."[2] Thenceforth, all her income, personal talent, and time would be devoted to their welfare. Over the course of her life, she was to give at least $40 million to the religious and educational progress of these groups.

By May 1891, the young mother superior, thirteen novices, and three postulants had settled into temporary quarters at the Drexel country estate in Torresdale, Pennsylvania. The cornerstone of the congregation's motherhouse in neighboring Cornwells Heights was laid a month later, and by the end of 1892 the fledgling community, now thirty in number, moved into its permanent home.

A boarding school for poor black children, erected on the motherhouse grounds, provided, in addition to an elementary school curriculum, training in domestic arts to prepare the children to support themselves in the future. There young sisters refined classroom techniques under the tutelage of experienced teachers, a practicum that supplemented formal course work at nearby Drexel Institute. In the summer of 1894, a vanguard of nine left the motherhouse for New Mexico to staff St. Catherine's Indian School in Santa Fe, the first of many Indian schools financed and conducted by Sisters of the Blessed Sacrament.

When Mother Mary Katharine Drexel pronounced her perpetual vows in the motherhouse chapel on January 9, 1895, her intense interest in the education of blacks and Indians was not widely shared by American Catholics, lay and clergy alike. "The South looks on with an angry eye. The North in many places is criticizing every act,"[3] reported Chicago pastor, Rev. John Tolton, the nation's first black priest. While some actively opposed her efforts, most remained dishearteningly indifferent. At the turn of the century, for example, while Mother Katharine was giving approximately $100,000 annually to support Catholic Indian schools and missions, annual donations for that cause from the nation's 12 million Catholics totaled under $75,000.[4] Although initially she had hoped to enlist wealthy lay Catholics to collaborate in the work of her new sisterhood, few showed sustained interest in it. A notable exception was her sister Louise, herself a generous supporter of black and Indian causes, who remained a faithful ally and trusted confidante.

In fact, Mother Katharine's strongest supporters always remained the growing number of women who joined her congregation. For more than four decades she served as their superior and spiritual guide, manifesting a unique leadership style, which melded justice, compassion, and respect for the individual. "Kindness is not kind unless it be special," she contended. "Special kindness is due everyone. It is in its fitness, seasonableness, and individual application that its charm consists." She set the highest standard for Sisters of the Blessed Sacrament in the matter of racial tolerance. "Have a cordial respect for others in heart and mind; if there is any prejudice in the mind we must uproot it, or it will pull us down."[5]

Largeness of mind joined boldness of vision to distinguish Mother Katharine Drexel among educational leaders. Although her schools were firmly rooted in the Catholic tradition, they welcomed students of all religious faiths and were conducted by racially integrated faculties. Nor was her share of the Drexel millions narrowly focused on schools conducted by her own sisterhood. Nearly all Catholic schools for Indians and blacks at some time benefited from her generosity.

Given her adamant views about the importance of education in the advance of the poor, Mother Katharine was doubly dismayed at the situation in the South in the early decades of the twentieth century. There the education provided blacks in public schools and the religious instruction provided them in most Catholic churches were equally deplorable. She decided that the most effective way to address both inequities was to open first-class Catholic schools for blacks throughout the region. The founding of Xavier University in New Orleans represented her most daring and innovative step toward this goal. As the nation's first black Catholic college, it directly challenged the racial divisions that pervaded ecclesial, as well as secular, society.

In 1915 she purchased the former campus of the Southern University for Negroes, a state college that had moved from New Orleans to Baton Rouge in 1912. Xavier University commenced as a high school, but by 1917 a two-year teacher training course, with a strong emphasis on English, had been added, reflecting its founder's eagerness to prepare well-qualified teachers for black schools, Catholic and public. Within eight years, Xavier University had received its charter as a liberal arts college. The teacher training program flourished, and in 1927 a college of pharmacy was added.

In order to provide a more spacious campus and to separate the college physically from the high school, Mother Katharine in 1929 purchased prime property in another section of the city. When its splendid Tudor Gothic campus and stadium were partially completed in the fall of 1932, Xavier University was formally dedicated, the thirty-eighth school for blacks conducted by the Sisters of the Blessed Sacrament in Louisiana. Its faculty of 20, including 8 sisters, instructed nearly 300 students in liberal arts, pharmacy, teaching, premedical studies, and home economics.

Protestant students, who consistently accounted for about one-third of the student body, took required courses in theology and philosophy but were not expected to attend Catholic religious services. Drexel money and the contributed services of the sisters kept tuition charges low, and by 1940, the university was drawing students from thirty-one states. By this time, it was fully accredited with a Class A rating by the Southern Association of Colleges. As soon as it became legally possible in 1954, its charter was amended to admit students of all races.

Not only was Xavier University the nation's first coeducational Catholic college, but it was also the only American coeducational college founded and governed by women. Church authorities heard from Mother Katharine a compelling case for coeducation and for women's legitimate place in the higher education of men. Since southern states mandated racially segregated schools and since male religious orders were not interested in opening a college for black men, an important student population was effectively excluded from Catholic higher education. To remedy so manifest an inequity, Mother Drexel and her council, according to the college annalist, "felt justified in undertaking the work that as a usual thing is carried on by men."[6]

While Xavier graduates in time entered a wide variety of fields, Mother Katharine's original interest in encouraging them to pursue careers in education bore remarkable fruit. She offered them good teaching positions in the rural schools she began to open in 1919. Soon twenty-four schools were flourishing throughout Louisiana, with young black lay teachers working as colleagues with Sisters of the Blessed Sacrament. Since some rural townships of the era provided teachers in black public schools for only four months annually, Mother Katharine kept a number of public schools open for the full academic year by paying the teachers herself for the additional months. In 1929, she employed eighty lay teachers in southern rural schools, Catholic and public. The long-term impact of Xavier graduates on Louisiana public schools has been notable. By 1966, 40 percent of the teachers and 73 percent of the principals in the black public schools of New Orleans alone held Xavier degrees, and hundreds more were teaching in similar schools throughout the state.

Throughout her long career, Mother Katharine Drexel met numerous racist challenges with invariable dignity and spirit. In these encounters, she made every effort to avoid publicity, convinced that it simply exacerbated social tensions. When, for example, a 1905 purchase of attractive Nashville property for a school for black children triggered widespread protest, she proceeded calmly with her plans, explaining her strategy to the local bishop: "It seems but prudent to protect our cause by being very quiet, since there seems to be a certain prejudice which I hope will blow over by quietly minding our preservation of the good we have undertaken without any aggressiveness."[7]

Even prolonged public pressure left her unmoved. The gentle courtesy with which she responded to harassing protests often left her opponents nonplussed. To the Nashville citizen who led the campaign against her school she wrote:

I think there is some misapprehension on the part of you and your neighbors which I should like to remove. The Sisters of the Blessed Sacrament, who have purchased the property, are religious, of the same race as yourself. We will always endeavor in every way to be neighborly to any white neighbors in the vicinity; we have every reason to hope we may receive from our white neighbors the cordial courtesy for which the Southern people are so justly noted.[8]

Southern pastors who discriminated by providing better accommodations for their white, than their black, congregants could expect no financial assistance from Mother Katharine. She funded church construction in the strictly segregated South only if she was guaranteed that an equal proportion of the church would be allocated to black worshipers. "She was not at all interested in a roped off back pew; she expected a definite promise that a whole aisle from transept to door would be reserved."[9] In general, all recipients of Drexel largess had to promise in writing that the money or property would be used only for approved purposes. Otherwise, it was to be returned to her or allocated by the local bishop to the needs of blacks or Indians.

Mother Katharine's legendary financial acumen was matched by an unerring instinct for when and where to buy real estate. Since her arrival in a town suggested that a black school might be about to open, she customarily used intermediaries in property purchases. She traveled extensively, painstakingly recording in a notebook particulars of the financial state and personnel needs of the schools, churches, and convents she was subsidizing. Potential sites for new establishments were investigated personally, and the hundreds of sisters she had assigned to remote schools in the West and South were visited faithfully and frequently. Mother Katharine's warm personality made a lasting impression on those she met in her travels. In 1966, George Hunton, an early Catholic champion of civil rights for blacks, recalled vividly his first encounter with her thirty-five years earlier: "She was an extremely vivacious person, always good-humored, a twinkle in her bright blue eyes. When she talked, her head seemed to dance, as she turned rapidly from one to another of the group she was addressing."[10]

Mother Katharine argued from religious faith as well as from justice that blacks and Indians deserved the same opportunities as those accorded whites. She explained to Bishop Thomas Byrne in 1904 why the Catholic church should repudiate a Nashville city council proposal to restrict the curriculum of the city's black public high school to industrial arts:

I must confess I cannot share these views with regard to the education of the Race. I feel that if amongst our Colored People, we find individuals gifted with capabilities, with those sterling qualities which constitute character, our Holy Mother the Church who fosters and develops the intellect only that it may give God more glory and be of benefit to others, should also concede this privilege to the Negro—this higher education.[11]

Consistent with these convictions, she took pains to ensure that all her schools were well built and well furnished, a policy that drew considerable criticism from white Americans of the era. The contemptuous tone of a *Time* magazine article reporting the 1932 dedication of Xavier University typified popular sentiment:

Many a white Southern college would look shabby beside Xavier, with its solid copper gutters, chromium equipment in the laboratory and home economics kitchen, auditorium with expensive indirect lighting and full stage, and half of the $3,000,000 Drexel library . . . . Resentful of such lavishness while so many Louisiana whites are hungry and jobless, Xavier's neighbors have suggested that the college motto be, "Is Yo' Did Yo' Greek Yit?"[12]

Mother Katharine's efforts to provide quality education for blacks and Indians extended well beyond brick and mortar to the heart of the schools, their faculties. Her sustained concern for the preparation of Sisters of the Blessed Sacrament as professional educators distinguished her from her counterparts in many other teaching sisterhoods, who before 1920 did little in this area. In the early 1890s Sisters of the Blessed Sacrament enrolled at the Drexel Institute of Technology and the University of Pennsylvania. Faculty from local colleges instructed novices and postulants at the motherhouse in child psychology and pedagogy. And when Catholic University in Washington, D.C., opened its summer school to members of sisterhoods in 1914, Mother Katharine's sisters were among the first to enroll. Later she established a house of studies near the university so that they could pursue graduate degrees during the academic year.

After serving as general superior of her congregation for forty-four years, Mother Katharine retired in 1937. She died at the Cornwells Heights motherhouse of a heart ailment on March 3, 1955, and was interred in a crypt below its chapel. She was ninety-six years old. At the time of her death, 501 Sisters of the Blessed Sacrament were conducting a university and 63 schools for blacks and Indians in 21 states.[13]

Numerous accolades came to this remarkable woman during her long life. In 1921, the U.S. Congress recognized her singular altruism on behalf of America's most neglected groups by amending the federal tax law to exempt from taxation those who contributed to charity more than 90 percent of their income in a given year. In 1939, she became the first woman to receive an honorary degree from Catholic University. Two years later, Emmanuel College in Massachusetts and Duquesne University and St. Joseph's College in Pennsylvania accorded her similar honors. Her highest tribute came posthumously, when in 1964, the Catholic church initiated the process to list her among its canonized saints. On November 20, 1989, this extraordinary educator of America's blacks and Indians was named "Blessed Katharine Drexel." Today approximately 350 Sisters of the Blessed Sacrament continue the work of their founder in 16 dioceses across America.

NOTES

1. Katharine Drexel to Bishop James O'Connor, April 6, 1889, Archives, Sisters of the Blessed Sacrament, Bensalem, PA.

2. Annals, Sisters of the Blessed Sacrament, 3–126, Archives, Sisters of the Blessed Sacrament.

3. Rev. John A. Tolton to Mother M. Katharine, June 5, 1891, Archives, Sisters of the Blessed Sacrament.

4. Rev. William A. Ketcham, director, Bureau of Catholic Indian Missions, "Editorial," *Indian Sentinel* (1904–1905): 31.

5. *Reflections on Religious Life Found in the Writings of Mother M. Katharine Drexel, Foundress of the Sisters of the Blessed Sacrament* (Cornwells Heights, PA: Sisters of the Blessed Sacrament, 1983), 15, 36.

6. Xavier University Annals, 22, 1925, 15–16, Archives, Xavier University, New Orleans, LA.

7. Mother M. Katharine to Bishop Thomas Byrne, July 14, 1905, Archives, Diocese of Nashville, TN.

8. M. M. Katharine (Drexel) to My dear Sir, n.d., Annals, Sisters of the Blessed Sacrament, 8–126, Archives, Sisters of the Blessed Sacrament.

9. Sister Consuela Marie Duffy, *Katharine Drexel: A Biography* (Cornwells Heights, PA: Sisters of the Blessed Sacrament, 1966), 244.

10. George K. Hunton, *All of Which I Saw, Part of Which I Was: The Autobiography of George K. Hunton, As Told to Gary MacEoin* (Garden City, NY: Doubleday, 1967), 51.

11. Mother M. Katharine to Bishop Thomas Byrne, December 7, 1904, Archives, Diocese of Nashville, TN.

12. "For the Tenth Man," *Time*, October 24, 1932.

13. *New York Times*, March 4, 1955.

WORKS BY MOTHER MARY KATHARINE DREXEL

Reflections on the Religious Life Found in the Writings of Mother M. Katharine Drexel, Foundress of the Sisters of the Blessed Sacrament. Cornwells Heights, PA: Sisters of the Blessed Sacrament, 1983.

The archives of Mother Katharine Drexel's congregation hold several thousand of her letters, her travel diaries, and many notebooks in which she recorded her spiritual reflections.

WORKS ABOUT MOTHER MARY KATHARINE DREXEL

Blatt, Genevieve. "Katharine Mary Drexel of Philadelphia." In Otto Reimherr, ed., *Quest for Faith, Quest for Freedom: Aspects of Pennsylvania's Religious Experience*, 180–94. Selinsgrove, PA: Susquehanna University Press, 1987.

Burton, Katherine. *The Golden Door: The Life of Katharine Drexel*. New York: P. J. Kenedy, 1957.

Duffy, Sister Consuela Marie. *Katharine Drexel: A Biography*. Cornwells Heights, PA: Sisters of the Blessed Sacrament, 1966.

Golden Jubilee, 1891–1941. Cornwells Heights, PA: Sisters of the Blessed Sacrament, 1941.

Hewitt, Nancy A. "Drexel, Mother Mary Katharine." In Barbara Sicherman and Carol Hurd Green, eds., *Notable American Women: The Modern Period. A Biographical Dictionary*, 206–8. Cambridge: Harvard University Press, 1980.

Kenny, Sister Mary Josephina. "Contributions of the Sisters of the Blessed Sacrament for Indians and Colored People to the Catholic Negro Education in the State of Louisiana." M.A. thesis, Catholic University of America, 1942.

Letterhouse, Sister Mary Dolores. *The Francis A. Drexel Family*. Cornwells Heights, PA: Sisters of the Blessed Sacrament, 1939.

Rockwell, Sister Mary Georgiana. "The Novitiate Training of Mother M. Katharine Drexel and the First Decades of the Sisters of the Blessed Sacrament, 1891–1910." Unpublished ms., n.d., Archives, Sisters of the Blessed Sacrament, Bensalem, PA.

Dolores "Lola" Gonzales

Bernardo P. Gallegos

Dolores Gonzales (1917–1975) profoundly affected the lives of many in New Mexico and Latin America as a curriculum writer, an elementary school teacher, a principal, a teacher educator, an author, a scholar, and an advocate for the interests of native peoples of New Mexico. She began her career in education in the public sphere as a catechism teacher and ended it as an associate professor of education at the University of New Mexico. A pioneer in bilingual and bicultural education, she was described in a memorial tribute in the University of New Mexico College of Education newsletter as a native New Mexican whose concern was to transmit the state's Hispanic heritage to Spanish-speaking children. This chapter reconstructs her life through what she wrote, biographical material, and oral interviews with her colleagues, students, and relatives.

Dolores Gonzales was born just seventy-one years after the invasion and occupation of her native homeland by U.S. military forces. The decades preceding her birth were characterized by a great deal of political struggle between the invading Americanos and the native New Mexicans who defended and promoted their interests consistently, oftentimes successfully. The conflict took on many forms, including the ballot box, armed rebellion, and political assassinations, such as the decapitation of the first appointed U.S. military governor. New Mexico, in fact, had changed from the status of a U.S. territory to a state only four years before Gonzales's birth.[1]

Her status as a native woman living under U.S. colonial rule was reflected through her writing and teaching. In 1974, for example, she raised the issue of Chicano resistance to United States cultural imperialism in the introduction to *Juegos y Canciones de Nuevo Mexico*, arguing that in addition to their pedagogical value, the songs and games served as "testimony that the Hispanic culture persists in the villages of New Mexico, in spite of the influence of a dominant culture."[2]

Dolores's childhood was spent in and around the village of Pecos. Her adolescence was tragically marked by the death of her mother, Pablita Herrera Gonzales. Being one of the oldest in a large family, she assumed the maternal role, along with related responsibilities for the family.[3] Her father, to whom she was very close, was an Hermano, a member of the local "brotherhood," a native, religious organization whose devout members wielded significant political and cultural influence in the villages of northern New Mexico. Referred to in the literature as "Penitentes," the members of this organization, once banned by the Catholic church, practice a form of spirituality and ritual that emerged from the sociocultural milieu of eighteenth-century New Mexico.[4] They are among the most ardent conservers of New Mexican Indo-Hispanic religious and cultural traditions.

As an educator in the public sphere, she began her career at an early age as a catechism teacher in Pecos.[5] In 1935, at the age of seventeen, Dolores began teaching in one-room schoolhouses in rural areas of San Miguel County in northern New Mexico, where she worked until 1941, when she began teaching in the village of Pecos, continuing until 1950. During this period she also worked on a bachelor's degree in elementary education and English at New Mexico Highlands University, which she completed in 1949. From 1950 to 1955 she served as a combination teacher-principal, while working during the summers on a master's in curriculum and teaching at Teachers College, Columbia University, which she completed in 1953.

Dolores's work began to take an international focus in 1955 as she became a demonstration teacher for the U.S. Agency for International Development (USAID) in Honduras, where she worked in the training of rural teachers as well as the preparation of instructional materials. Commenting on this period of her life, a friend and colleague stated: "In Honduras if you wanted to go out and supervise you had to get on horseback. Well, she learned how to horseback ride in the mountains, [in Pecos] and so she just fit perfectly in that situation."[6] In 1957 she accepted the position of elementary education adviser for the USAID program in Honduras with the responsibility of organizing and training a corps of supervisors and preparing a program for the training of about 700 teachers. Moreover, she acted as adviser to the government in the preparation of instructional materials. In 1963 she took over the same position in Costa Rica, serving until 1964, when she began work on a doctorate, which she finished at Pennsylvania State University in 1966.

Upon completion of the doctorate she took a position as textbook consultant for the University of New Mexico in Quito, Ecuador, which she held until 1969. At the time Ecuador was experiencing a great deal of civil strife. One colleague recalled that Dolores and he rode through countless tear gas attacks as well as demonstrations of workers and students. Moreover, being a native New Mexican posed other problems that European Americans in that context would not have encountered. A colleague reveals the complexities that Dolores was negotiating at this time.

We were a very closely knit group from New Mexico. She taught us that we [Chicanos] were perceived as second class citizens in Latin America because the Latin Americans read the paper and knew that we were perceived as second class here [United States]. She taught us that our form of speaking Spanish was okay. What it did for people like Eva, my wife, and myself is that we spoke more freely with the Ecuadorians. She taught us that our first duty was to the Ecuadorians who were our hosts; we were guests in their country. We made a lot of Ecuadorian friends through her because she said, "We don't need to hang around the American Embassy crowd all of the time because we can do that back home. It's a new experience; let's just learn everything we can about the Ecuadorians and that way we can do better and help them with the teacher training programs and the textbook programs."

This colleague related the following story, which reveals an emerging social consciousness and speaks in a powerful way about Dolores and her compassion for the socially and economically marginalized.

I also knew the private Dolores, and she was private, very kind. There was a street person, I think her name was Maria . . . really bad, filthy, carried everything she owned in a big blanket . . . Dolores supported her as long as she was there, with a little money and food . . . That's the way she was, the kind of person she was, very humane.[7]

In 1969 Dolores returned to New Mexico as an assistant professor at the University of New Mexico in the elementary education department. At this time her interest in writing stories for children and her feelings of allegiance toward the native children of her homeland coalesced in an institute that she created, with the goal of writing a set of culturally and linguistically relevant readers. The product of the institute was a bilingual reading series called the *Tierra del Encanto*.[8]

During this period Professor Gonzales also gained recognition as a pioneer and leader in the field of bilingual education. A colleague of hers recalled that after they returned to the University of New Mexico from Costa Rica, "she was a spearhead for bilingual education. . . . [She] started the whole bilingual program here . . . and got a group of people together to start writing."[9] Interviews with former students reveal that Dolores was the main professor in the area of bilingual education at the time and that most of the classes were offered by her.[10]

Also during this period, Professor Gonzales's role as change agent became more pronounced. One of the ways that this was manifested was in the formation of a group of bilingual professors. Recruited in 1970, a former student, who subsequently served as a professor at the University of New Mexico, described his experience as follows:

There were probably ten of us working in the institute. . . . To this day we're all very close. That program was a real pipeline, was one of the more important recruiting devices for Chicano students female and male. . . . Probably in 3 years . . . I suspect 15 or 20 students received their doctorates through that program. . . . So she was instrumental in supporting, encouraging, and helping those 15 students, at least 15 maybe more than that, to finish their doctorates and then [they] went on to create pretty impressive careers in other universities. If you subtract her program and her as a person that would be 15 less Chicano Ph.D. students working someplace in Bilingual Education in the country.[11]

Professor Gonzales's classes functioned as a space where the graduate students were able to feel comfortable with their voices and explore their own subjectivities. Speaking to this theme, this same student recounted the following:

I think she did a lot, not by preaching or not by talking verbally about things, but just by her own appreciation of the dialect and the folklore and traditions of New Mexico. She really taught us to be appreciative of that background. For a lot of us it was a real different kind of thing because we had been taught in a lot of ways that to speak Spanish was not the right thing to do and people had been punished in schools for doing that. She turned that around for a lot of us, not so much by telling us . . . but by having us create stories where we used the dialect. We used New Mexican culture as the basis for those materials. We spent a lot of time . . . introspecting in the sense of looking at ourselves, looking at our background, looking at our language, looking at all of what today would be called cultural capital. What made her so effective was giving Chicano students that sense of *orgullo* [pride] . . . in what they brought to the university.[12]

Professor Gonzales also encouraged her students to voice their opinions even if they were unpopular. An incident described by two former students speaks to this and reveals how she dealt with conflict, empowerment, and voice. Reflecting on a conflict in a department meeting in which she argued passionately for greater representation of people of color in the teacher candidate pool, one student recalled the following:

I said "You profess to be a bilingual/Multicultural department but you are not." I was somewhat angry and emotional about it and I went on and on. That night I called her and I said, "I may have gone overboard Dr. Gonzales, and I want to apologize if I embarrassed you." . . . And she didn't quite scold me but almost scolded me and said, "Luisa, don't you ever apologize for who you are and what you do. You did what you had to do and you said your important stuff and that was important to you and that's what counts." . . . Since then, . . . before I go into something that's kind of stressful and hard and complex I say, "Well how would she want me to do it and still be myself." I still hear her voice.[13]

Another interpretation of the incident comes from a male former student, who remembered:

A professor . . . said to Luisa, . . . "You have to learn not to be so assertive and not to be so strong about your ideas, you have to cool that." And I can remember Luisa telling Dolores about that and Dolores said, "Don't you ever put your ideas away and not let people know about them." . . . It was like, don't you ever not say what you think about critical issues . . . cause these were issues relating to the quality of education that minorities were receiving in the department. . . . I can remember that [other] professor told Luisa, "You're too emotional, you have to cool it, you have to calm down." And Dolores told her just the opposite, "You have to speak up, you have to be strong, you have to take your ideas and let people know what they're all about." . . . It was like from two Chicana professors . . . Luisa got two different messages; one was "Be quiet, conform, play the game, don't make too many waves," and from the other one saying, "You know you need to do what you need to do and when you've got ideas you better be strong about them."[14]

In attempting to reconstruct Dolores's life it would be shortsighted to overlook the social context of the times. The following recollection provides a glimpse of her views of the racial and ethnic conflict and the related violence that characterized the 1960s and 1970s in New Mexico as well as other parts of the United States. Recalling Dr. Gonzales's response to her question regarding minorities' using riots and violence in the context of social protest, Luisa, the same former student, stated:

She was very calm about it and she said, "Well, Luisa, the violence has already been done. This is a reaction to the violence." So she knew about cultural violence. . . . She knew the violence had already been done to a lot of oppressed groups. . . . So she didn't condone violence but she probably saw it as an inevitable state of affairs that had to happen before the bigger violators would shape up.[15]

Another former student stated:

The word empowerment is overused . . . but that word should have been around then because that was how she worked. . . . She had a way of making you face value issues, and creating situations where you have to . . . think about those real hard questions about ethnicity, about bilingualism, about culture, about a lot of things like that. . . . I can remember there were some real tear-filled sessions where people argued and debated . . . to the extent that people kind of broke down emotionally. . . . She didn't leave it there; she helped to bring it back more positively, so people were able to get over those kinds of things and get stronger . . . and learn from sharing experience, from sharing values, from not being ashamed of who we were and where we came from. It was a redoing of people's mental perspectives, of people's self perceptions, and of their ideas of who they were. . . . That's what Dolores was for a lot of students, a real role model . . . a real powerful person.[16]

In an article, published just one year before her death, Professor Gonzales expressed her views of the contemporary state of educational institutions and the power relations that characterized them. Today, these very issues continue to occupy a central place in the discourse surrounding education from primary schools to universities. Arguing for a school structure that was inclusive rather than exclusive in nature, Professor Gonzales critiqued traditional educational practice, based on "integration of students without acceptance of cultural contributions and without allowing minority groups to control their own destinies." Moreover, she characterized the lethargic pace of institutional change as a "frustrating response to the racial minorities' quest for dignity."[17]

In its place, she proposed a curriculum that was based on the lived realities of the students and that recognized as legitimate their cultural capital no matter what it may be. In the introduction to a collection of folk songs and games of New Mexico, she urged her readers to "value the children's linguistic diversity and their culture" and, moreover, to "use them as legitimate content material in the educational process."[18] Lamenting the institutional state of affairs in education, she wrote,

Unless we are able to cross a new threshold, the elementary school curriculum will remain an unsurmountable barrier to our nation's children. The exaggerated emphasis on conformity, on competition for its own sake, on constant evaluation unrelated to the curricular goals of a specific population, and on textbook bound curriculum practices, portray [*sic*] the weaknesses rather than the strengths of the elementary school curriculum.[19]

This article and her work as a teacher were based on a conceptualization of educational institutions as change agents for the empowerment of disfranchised and marginal groups in society. For example, when asked to recollect some of Professor Gonzales's social visions, one former student recalled:

You knew that in her behavior and in her lectures and in whatever she did, the book writing, the teacher training, that it was to change our world, to reconstruct a better world. She knew . . . things were bad in the world. Things were bad in education for a lot of people and she saw herself as a change agent. I think she was as progressive as people were in that time. . . . We're talking '71, '72. . . . She was right in the middle of all that innovation, change and reform, always talking about reformation. . . . Reform the schools to make sure, and it was always "minority kids need to succeed." She'd say, "We don't need to change the kids, we need to change the schools . . . the kids are ok.[20]

Ironically, while the theme of change permeated her work, Gonzales was in many ways very conservative, in particular, when it came to the preservation of the Indo-Hispanic culture of New Mexico. She seemed to have reconciled this contradiction, at least as it was manifested in the construction of gender roles, by supporting tradition within the context of the family, or the private sphere, while promoting change through her public self. During an interview one of her nieces, addressing gender roles, remembered her Aunt Lola being a "very traditional" woman in family affairs.[21] Her relationship with her father and her acceptance of the traditional responsibility within native New Mexican families that elder females should care for aging parents exemplify this. As a lifelong friend of hers recalled:

Her father went blind and got sick so Dolores had a home here in Albuquerque and she brought him there. She took care of him for quite a long time; he was an invalid, completely. Then she started getting sick; she suffered a lot with her cancer . . . she took care of him up to the point where she couldn't; she needed more help than he did by then.[22]

This tension between change and tradition as related to gender issues is further addressed in the following recollection by one of her students. Reflecting on his experience as a textbook writer under Dolores's supervision, he recounted the following:

She scolded us one time for putting girls in very passive positions, helping in the kitchen, or reading books, or sitting there doing sewing, doing things like that and we always had the boys out running around and climbing trees. She said, "You have to start paying attention to these little Chicanitas." I can remember that that was a very powerful statement to us. . . . And she said, "I don't want just the women in the kitchen in these stories, I went the little girls to be doing all the things that little boys do and I want little boys helping do the little things that we traditionally associate with girls." It was a real strong statement considering that it was 1970. She was tremendously traditional and at the same time very modern. It's like she could blend tradition and traditional Hispanic values and appreciate and reinforce those in our books and yet there was something very modern about her.[23]

Gonzales's personal life remains a mystery; in fact, her response in the personal information section of the several yearly biographical update forms at the university was a consistent "none."[24] She probably lived most of her adult life alone or with her father. She never married, and she had no children. Yet she participated in the birthing process in an intellectual sense. The safe space that she created and the gentle, yet powerful leadership that she exerted made it possible for her students to transform themselves. Even though she may not have been a prolific writer and researcher and thus was not well known in the larger academic community, in her native New Mexico her life had great meaning.

NOTES

1. Tobias Duran. "Francisco Chavez, Thomas B. Catron, and Organized Political Violence in Santa Fe," *New Mexico Historical Review* 59 (July 1984). See also

Tobias Duran, "We Come as Friends: The Social and Historical Context of Nineteenth Century New Mexico," Working Paper #106, Southwest Hispanic Research Institute, University of New Mexico, 1984.

2. Dolores Gonzales, "Introduction," *Canciones y Juegos de Nuevo Mexico* (Songs and games of New Mexico) (New York: A. S. Barnes, 1974), 14.

3. Interview, Frank Angel, Albuquerque, July 22, 1991.

4. Marta Weigle, *Brothers of Light, Brothers of Blood* (Albuquerque: University of New Mexico Press, 1976). See also Marta Weigle, *A Penitente Bibliography* (Albuquerque: University of New Mexico Press, 1976).

5. Interview, Phillip Gonzales, Albuquerque, August 1, 1991.

6. Interview, Frank Angel, Albuquerque, July 22, 1991.

7. Interview, Ambrosio Ortega, Albuquerque, July 12, 1991.

8. *Tierra Del Encanto Series* (Albuquerque: University of New Mexico/Albuquerque Public Schools, 1972 to 1977), Tireman Library, University of New Mexico.

9. Interview, Ambrosio Ortega, Albuquerque, July 12, 1991.

10. Interview, Luisa Duran, Albuquerque, July 19, 1991.

11. Interview, Leroy Ortiz, Albuquerque, July 19, 1991.

12. Ibid.

13. Interview, Luisa Duran, Albuquerque, July 19, 1991.

14. Interview, Leroy Ortiz, Albuquerque, July 19, 1991.

15. Interview, Luisa Duran, Albuquerque, July 19, 1991.

16. Interview, Leroy Ortiz, Albuquerque, July 19, 1991.

17. Dolores Gonzales, "The Elementary School Curriculum: Gateway or Barrier?" *Selected Readings in Multicultural Education*, (Las Vegas, NM: New Mexico Highlands University, March 1974), 20.

18. Gonzales, "Introduction," *Canciones y Juegos de Nuevo Mexico.*

19. Gonzales, "The Elementary School Curriculum," 20.

20. Interview, Luisa Duran, Albuquerque, July 19, 1991.

21. Interview, Sylvia Abeyta, Albuquerque, July 29, 1991.

22. Interview, Phillip Gonzales, Albuquerque, August 1, 1991.

23. Interview, Leroy Ortiz, Albuquerque, July 19, 1991.

24. Biographical Record, University of New Mexico, College of Education Archives.

WORKS BY DOLORES "LOLA" GONZALES

"La Ensenanza de las Artes del Lenguaje en la Escuela Primaria." Servicio Cooperativo Inter-Americano de Educacion, Ministerio de Educacion Publica, Tegueigalpa, Honduras, 1957.

"La ensenanza de las Matematicas en la Escuela Primaria." Servicio Cooperativo Inter-Americano de Educacion/Ministerio de Educacion Publica, Tegueigalpa, Honduras, 1957.

"Suplemento Para la Guia de las Matematicas." United States Agency for International Development, Ministry of Public Education, San Jose Costa Rica, 1964.

"La Ensenanza de las Ciencias in la Escuela Primaria." Latin American Project, Pennsylvania State University, 1965.

"A Study of Auditory Discrimination of Spanish Phonemes." Ph.D. diss., Pennsylvania State University, 1967.

"Bilingual Education for Multi-Cultural Sensitivity" (with Miles Zintz and Sabine Ulibarri). ERIC Clearinghouse on Teacher Education, 1971.

Tierra Del encanto Series. Albuquerque: University of New Mexico/Albuquerque Public Schools, 1972 to 1977. (Available in Tireman Library, University of New Mexico.)

Canciones y Juegos de Nuevo Mexico/Songs and Games of New Mexico (ed.). New York: A. S. Barnes, 1974.

"The Elementary School Curriculum: Gateway or Barrier?" *Selected Readings in Multicultural Education.* Las Vegas, NM: Highlands University, Department of Education, 1974.

Willystine Goodsell

Sari Knopp Biklen

Willystine Goodsell (1870–1962) was a scholar and teacher who devoted much of her adult life to the study of and advocacy for, the education of women. Some of this work developed an area of inquiry with particular parameters, such as the history of women's education in the nineteenth century. She also made a major contribution in her arguments against the work of G. Stanley Hall and Edward Thorndike on sex differences and gender expectations. Unfortunately, Goodsell's arguments had little impact at the time. Later in life she, like many progressives, became involved with eugenics groups. Because her papers have not been located, her life can be only sketchily portrayed.

Born in Wallingford, Connecticut, on January 8, 1870, to Willys Jacob and Jennie (Clark) Goodsell, Willystine Goodsell received all of her degrees and spent her career in higher education at Teachers College, Columbia University. She graduated from New Haven High School in 1888 and the Welch Normal Training School in 1892, where she also taught between 1890 and her graduation. She had several other teaching experiences before she went on for higher degrees. She taught at the Pennsylvania Charter School in Philadelphia between 1892 and 1898 and at the Springfield, Massachusetts, Grammar School between 1898 and 1902.

Aside from these teaching experiences, Dr. Goodsell taught for all of her academic career, thirty-one years, at Teachers College (TC), Columbia University. She received her bachelor of science in 1906, her master's in 1907, and her doctor of philosophy in 1910, all at TC. She stayed on at TC to work as an instructor from 1905 to 1910 while she was getting her degrees, as an assistant professor from 1910 until 1927, and as an associate professor until her retirement in 1936 at the age of sixty-six. She lectured on the family, the education of women, and the history of education.[1] In 1910 TC published her dissertation, written under John Dewey, *The Conflict of Nat-*

uralism and Humanism. In 1916, Columbia awarded her the Butler Medal in Silver for her book *A History of the Family as a Social and Educational Institution,* which had been published a year earlier.

While the central focus of Goodsell's work concerned issues of import to equality for women and women's education, she was also active in a number of societies and groups devoted to educational and social change, including the progressive education movement. She was elected in 1934[2] to the Board of Directors of *The Social Frontier,* an important progressive publication of the 1930s. As Patricia Graham has written, "*The Social Frontier* called itself 'a journal of educational criticism and reconstruction,' and throughout the thirties it presented the responsible radical positions of those educators who wanted the schools to lead in social rebuilding."[3] Goodsell was also a member of the American Civil Liberties Union and the Foreign Policy Association and directed the American Eugenics Society and the Euthanasia Society of America.[4] She founded, and was the first president of, the Women's Faculty Club at Columbia University.[5]

Except for the book that had been her doctoral dissertation, all of Willystine Goodsell's books engaged two subjects: the family and women's education. Perhaps because she was a historian, perhaps because she was interested in how institutions and people were shaped by their historical contexts, perhaps because she either challenged prominent scholars or pushed for such changes as equal rights for women, her books are characterized by a particular style of engagement. Before talking about the main psychological or sociological focus of her study, she historically traces the institution or activity from earliest times. *The Education of Women* (1923) and *Problems of the Family* (1928) trace the development of both topics from times of "ancient civilization." In her historical studies, for example, *A History of the Family as a Social and Educational Institution* (1915), she uses extensive anthropological and biblical material to conceptualize family types and changes in family life.

In *The Education of Women,* Goodsell argues for a quality and equitable education for women and challenges arguments brought by G. Stanley Hall and Edward Thorndike against girls' intellectual education as well as the "race suicide" arguments popular among some at the time who criticized the low birthrate among educated women. Her edited collection, *Pioneers of Women's Education in the United States* (1931), which presented selections from the writings of Emma Willard, Catharine Beecher, and Mary Lyon and contained an excellent introduction, discussing their contribution to the higher education of women in the United States, is perhaps most useful today because of the compilation of primary source material. However, her challenge to Hall, Thorndike, and others in *The Education of Women,* is perhaps her greatest intellectual contribution to the history of American education.

In the late nineteenth century there was a "remarkable unanimity of scientific opinion about women's limitations."[6] Dire warnings from Edward Clarke's *Sex in Education* in the 1870s about the dangers to women's health and reproductive systems from higher education gave way to similar pronouncements in "Sex in Education" in 1906 by Edward Thorndike, who argued that the abilities of women were not great enough to make them worth educating. James McKeen Cattell, chair of the psychology department at Columbia University, warned again of race suicide in 1909, as had G. Stanley Hall in 1903.[7] Their unanimity was broken as the twentieth century progressed not only because psychologists like Leta Hollingsworth did research that challenged these pronouncements but also because, as Rosalind Rosenberg points out, armchair theorists were pushed out by experimentalists.[8] It was the "heyday of empiricism."[9]

Goodsell marshaled wide-ranging empirical data in *The Education of Women* to take on Hall, Thorndike, and those who would limit women's access to education. This challenge is the main purpose of the book, which argues that education will not make women unfit for marriage and motherhood, but rather will increase their health. Goodsell asserts the centrality of evidence to her own arguments when she attacks the positions of Hall and others as "grounded far more upon opinion than upon experimental evidence."[10] The writer who could frame an argument served by experimental evidence should have an upper hand.

The Education of Women is indeed filled with statistics: about women's status, including marriage rates, exercise during the menstrual cycle, and medical measurements at birth, and about median school achievement rates of boys versus girls in various subjects. Today we would call much of these data descriptive statistics rather than experimental evidence, but the import is clear. Goodsell wanted to counter the claims of Hall, which she saw as representing "the social ideals and practices of the eighteenth century" but "garbed in a dubiously scientific dress of biology and psychology" on their own ground.[11] She also wanted to employ and reinforce the arguments of such researchers as Hollingsworth toward women's equality. Goodsell did not argue that women's intelligence and education should be sexless, but rather that women should not be measured only in terms of their marital and procreative abilities.

After an exploration of the history of women's education, the next several chapters explored questions about differential education for males and females. In "College Women and the Marriage Rate" Goodsell analyzed the statistics on the significantly lowered marriage rates of women attending higher education. Goodsell argued that college life influenced women in several ways. It heightened their sense of individuality, it raised their standard of marriage, and it made them desire to act on their skills to reaffirm their independence. Since so much of professional life was closed to women once they married, women would postpone marriage in order to partake in professional life.

What men wanted in wives and what women wanted for their own lives often did not correspond. "A certain group of unmarried men do show a marked desire to secure efficient home-keepers as wives." At the same time, the women that these men would meet in their social circles "have in many instances tasted the joys of economic independence and success in a chosen vocation and have little interest and less skill in domestic work." Goodsell called this situation an "impasse."[12] But she predicted that it would work out in the long run. Most women would not be able to resist nature's call and would become mothers as society adjusted to the importance of higher education for women. Others would remain single but would serve society anyway, either by tending the oppressed or by struggling for a better society. Goodsell's ideas suggest that women's differences should be honored.

Goodsell's next chapter examined sex differences in education, directly attacking Hall and Thorndike. In *Adolescence* Hall had glorified women's contribution to heredity and spirituality as wives and mothers as he critiqued their mental and competitive abilities.[13] Goodsell questioned his evidence as mere "masquerade," citing the medical research of Mary Putnam Jacobi on menstruation, the anatomical research on infants done by Hollingsworth and Helen Montagu, data on sex differences in mental abilities from Helen Thompson and others, and also the pronouncements of Edward Thorndike. Thorndike suggested that from the data he compiled on intellectual sex differences, the most striking characteristic he noticed was how slight were the differences. But Thorndike and Goodsell then went in different directions, Thorndike noting how the world's great achievements had been accomplished by men, a tendency he attributed to "the superior variability within the male sex." Gifted men were probably much more endowed than gifted women even if average men were not.[14] Goodsell attributed differences to the environment, that is, the social handicaps women faced.

How would higher education affect women's health? Goodsell cited studies by Hollingsworth and a Russian doctor named Voitsechovsky to show that women perform similarly to men whether they are menstruating or not. In the end Goodsell argued that scientific evidence "undermines," rather than supports, arguments against women's equality. Differences in education, Goodsell asserted, would arise from the fact that women are individuals with particular interests and skills.

These interests and skills, Goodsell noted, would not necessarily lead them to make good homemakers. In order to handle this problem Goodsell proposed that homemaking be"professionalized" and that cooperative work in preparing food and in cleaning be substituted for individual work. While reminiscent of the suggestions of Charlotte Perkins Gilman, whose work, interestingly, Goodsell does not cite, these ideas, for example, for public kitchens, are tremendously different from earlier ideas she expressed in *The Journal of Home Economics*. In 1912 she called for women to be taught about the family in an intellectual, rather than simply practical, manner so that they could make intelligent decisions about family life, hence increasing their connection to families rather than strengthening their alienation from them.[15]

In addition to challenging the arguments of psychologists such as Hall and Thorndike, Goodsell examined what the education of girls and women should promote. She saw the period when she wrote *The Education of Women* as a transition between women's former oppression and a greater emancipation to come. She argued against sororities but in favor of community life through such forms as Smith College's cottage system. She promoted greater physical education on behalf of women not only in college but in high school as well. Sex education should be taught to girls in school as well as by their families. Both technical and liberal studies contributed to a girl's education. She urged those interested in women's education to enhance its values in order to improve the lot of American women and to improve American life. What Goodsell promoted, in other words, was the kind of education that American girls generally receive today. In the end, Goodsell's views about women, education, and sex differences largely prevailed. We remember, however, Hall and Thorndike, not Goodsell.

In addition to writing about women's education, Goodsell was also active in it. She participated in the founding of Bennington College, an activity that brought together her interests in women's and progressive education. During the 1930s she started an archive in New York City for research materials on women. After Goodsell retired from Columbia University in 1936, she remained active until some time in the 1940s in community service and in writing. She died in May 1962 in Daytona Beach, Florida, at the age of ninety-two.

NOTES

1. *Who Was Who Among North American Authors*, vol. 1 (Detroit: Gale Research Co., 1976), 602.

2. Robert E. Engel, "Willystine Goodsell: Feminist and Reconstructionist Educator," *Vitae Scholasticae* 3 (Fall 1984): 355.

3. Patricia A. Graham, *Progressive Education: From Arcady to Academe* (New York: Teachers College Press, 1967), 71.

4. *Who Was Who in America*, vol. 5 (Chicago: Marquis Who's Who, 1969–1973).

5. Willystine Goodsell obituary, *New York Times*, June 1, 1962, 28.

6. Cynthia Eagle Russett, *Sexual Science* (Cambridge, MA: Harvard University Press, 1989), 189.

7. Edward Clarke, *Sex in Education*, (Boston: J. R. Osgood, 1873); Edward Thorndike, "Sex in Education," *Bookman* 23 (April 1906): 211–14; James McKeen Cattell, "The School and the Family," *Popular Science Monthly* 74 (January 1909): 84–95; G. Stanley Hall and Theodore Smith, "Marriage and Fecundity of College Men and Women," *Pedagogical Seminary* 10 (March 1903): 375–414.

8. Rosalind Rosenberg, *Beyond Separate Spheres* (New Haven, CT: Yale University Press, 1982), 91.

9. Quoted in Robert Bogdan and Sari Knopp Biklen, *Qualitative Research for Education*, 2d ed. (Boston: Allyn and Bacon, 1992), 13.

10. Willystine Goodsell, *The Education of Women* (New York: Macmillan, 1923), 97.

11. Ibid., 68.

12. Ibid., 53.

13. G. Stanley Hall, *Adolescence*, 2 vols. (New York: D. Appleton and Company, 1904).

14. Quoted in Goodsell, 72.

15. Willystine Goodsell, "A Plea for the Introduction of Historical Courses on Home into Higher Schools and Colleges for Young Women." *The Journal of Home Economics* 4 (April 1912): 111–25.

WORKS BY WILLYSTINE GOODSELL

A History of the Family as a Social and Educational Institution. New York: Macmillan, 1915.

The Education of Women: Its Social Background and Its Problems. New York: Macmillan, 1923.

Problems of the Family. New York: Century, 1928.

Pioneers of Women's Education in the United States. New York: McGraw-Hill, 1931.

WORK ABOUT WILLYSTINE GOODSELL

Engel, Robert. "Willystine Goodsell: Feminist and the Reconstructionist Educator." *Vitae Scholasticae: The Bulletin of Education Biography* 3, no. 2 (Fall 1984): 355–80.

Margaret Haley

Barbara Brenzel

Margaret Haley (1861–1939) was an elementary school teacher, a civic reformer, and a feminist. As president and then full-time business representative of the Chicago Teachers' Union (CTU), she forged a link between the Teachers' Federation and the Chicago Federation of Labor. Through teachers' organizations and through the National Education Association, she championed the rights of teachers and students.

Margaret Haley was born in 1861, the daughter of Michael Haley and Elizabeth (Tiernan) Haley. Michael Haley's family had emigrated from Ireland to Canada and finally settled in Joliet, Illinois. Michael and Elizabeth had eight children, of whom Margaret was the second child and the eldest of four sisters. Michael Haley was a farmer and later a stone quarry operator.

Margaret, or Maggie as she was often called, attended grade school in Channahon, Illinois, and completed high school in St. Angeles Convent, Morris, Illinois. Her father's business failures resulted in her leaving her studies early, and at age sixteen, in the fall of 1876, she began to teach at a country school near the village of Minooka in Dresden Heights, Illinois. In 1877, she moved to a grade school near Joliet. After attending a summer session at the State Normal University in Bloomington, Illinois, in 1881, she began teaching sixth grade at the Hendricks School, located in Lake, Illinois, near the stockyards just southwest of Chicago. In Lake, she was exposed to the hardships of the urban poor, especially their children. These years made her even more conscious of the harsh inequities that ran rampant through the lives of the poor.

Six years later, in 1889, Haley took a semester's leave to study with Colonel Francis Parker at the Cook County Normal School. Parker, who was famous for instituting a child-centered curriculum and new reading methods, was a central figure in the early progressive education movement. By studying with Parker and meeting with many of his colleagues and friends who believed that progressive education was the means by which to nurture a sensitive, thoughtful, creative, and socially responsible society, Haley became convinced that democracy, education, and labor had to go together. "There is no possible conflict between the good of society and the good of its members, of which the industrial workers are the vast majority."[1] She considered the public school to be the institution in "which the responsibility to be inspired by higher ideals . . . rests most heavily."[2] Haley felt increasingly compatible with those educators and social philosophers who were involved with progressive reform, particularly John Dewey at the Chicago Laboratory School and Ella Flagg Young, superintendent of schools in Chicago and the first woman president of the National Education Association (NEA).

Haley remained as an elementary school teacher at the Hendricks School until 1901. She continued to be frustrated with overcrowded classrooms, inadequate pay, and poor pensions. She was infuriated that the Board of Education promised a wage increase in three consecutive years beginning in 1888 and was not able to honor its pledge to increase the teachers' wages. Moreover, after the first year it had to cancel its pledge and even rescind the first raise. Convinced that there was deliberate wrongdoing behind the low pay for teachers, Haley uncovered many of the political machinations that were largely responsible. She was especially bothered by the fact that women teachers made an even smaller salary than their male counterparts. This meager pay was sanctioned by the Harper Commission in 1899, headed by William Rainey Harper, which included Charles W. Eliot, Nicholas Murray Butler, and Andrew Sloan Draper. These "administrative progressives," as David Tyack aptly called them, sought to centralize the operation of the schools.[3] Many of the men were businessmen or academic professionals in powerful universities.

This type of centralized planning offended Haley, who felt that teachers and local schools had to be in closer contact with the needs of the student and society. In her address to the NEA in 1904 she stated that "any attempt on the part of the public to evade or shift this responsibility must result in weakening the public sense of civic responsibility . . . besides further isolating the public school from the people to the detriment of both."[4] She went on to advocate that the power of the schools rightfully rests with the teachers and local organizations. She stated that the methods, as well as the objects of teachers' organizations, must be in harmony with the fundamental object of the public school in a democracy, to preserve and develop the democratic ideal.[5]

Haley became further embroiled with municipal politics as it bore directly on elementary teachers' pay and working conditions, especially with equitable pay for female teachers. In 1901, the year before she became the full-time business agent for the Chicago Teachers Federation (CTF), she and a colleague, Catherine Goggin, petitioned for a year's paid leave of absence. They were granted these leaves and worked full-time for the Chicago Teachers Federation. Haley then uncovered the fact that the Board of Equalization was in complicity with corporations and public utilities, which paid taxes only on tangible property, not their capital stock. Goggin and Haley realized that the shortage of public money for increasing the meager salary of elementary teachers, most of whom were women, was rooted in these tax exemptions. Angered by this rigging of taxable assets and rightfully linking this act of corruption to the low pay for teachers, she and Goggin were determined to continue the fight. They then understood why the city was unable to give the pay raises promised for the following year and had to take back the raises already meted out to the elementary school teachers. They were determined to fight the avarice of the municipal moguls and the corruption of the Board of Equalization. Encouraged by Judge John P. Altgeld and Mayor Edward F. Dunne, Haley and Goggin petitioned for, and won, a mandamus—a court writ—to prohibit this illegal tax exemption. They were overjoyed by their victory but soon realized that though they had won this battle, many more would follow.

As business agent for the CTF, Haley fought for tenure laws for the teachers and a decent pension plan. She also supported a system of teachers' councils, initially suggested by Ella Flagg Young. These councils were part of a progressive reform by which the teachers were to share authority with area superintendents in issues of curriculum and discipline.

Haley assumed that teachers were part of labor and that teachers and labor were working for a democratic society. She thus forged a link between the Chicago Teachers Federation and the Chicago Federation of Labor. Soon after, the CTF was disbanded and was replaced by a loosely organized National Federation of Teachers (NFT). Haley then became a member of the NEA and fought to have more active participation of teachers in this organization rather than only that of professors of education such as Butler and academicians such as Charles Eliot.

Ultimately, the NEA broke ties with labor, and it expected all teachers' groups to do likewise. This left Haley without the link in which she believed. However, she continued her fight for the goals she had always held—fair pay and decent working conditions.

Another problem was the lack of fair representation for teachers at NEA meetings. Halley worked to reverse this and was the first woman and elementary school teacher to speak from the floor of an NEA meeting. In 1903 she and the NFT defeated a motion made by President Eliot of Harvard and Nicholas Murray Butler of Columbia, thus establishing herself as an active member of the NEA.

The active fight for freedom and justice exhibited by progressive-era female domestic reformers, such as Jane Addams, Julia Lathrop, and Margaret Dreier, offered Haley a sense of being part of a circle of female reformers who, like her, sought fair representation and pay for all females. This sentiment was part of her impetus to urge Edward Dunne to place Jane Addams on the school board. Addams, although initially reluctant, agreed. Although Addams was sympathetic to the plight of female elementary school teachers, Haley became disappointed in Addams as she came to see her as a moral, not political, reformer and as one who sought compromise. Nevertheless, Haley and Addams continued to work together for better working conditions and decent pay for female teachers.

Although she was no longer formally working with the Chicago Federation of Labor, Haley championed many reform causes. She continued to work closely with the labor movement and helped organize the American Federation of Teachers. In addition, she continued to feel a deep allegiance for women in labor and worked with Agnes Nestor in the womens' Trade Union League.

Considered by many to be a nuisance and a scrapper, but by others a tireless crusader, she devoted her life to fighting for the rights of the underrepresented, whether because of gender, occupation, social class, or ethnicity. To this end she fought for the rights of children and championed womens' rights in all fields.

Haley continued her battle during her semiretirement. She died at age seventy-eight of pulmonary thrombosis and heart disease. A funeral service was conducted for her in St. Bernard's Catholic Church in Chicago, and she was then buried in Mt. Olivet Cemetery, Joliet, Illinois.

Margaret Haley summed up her life in her autobiography this way:

It is something, after all, to have lived for forty years upon a battleground, to have been even a small part in the gigantic struggle for justice: but as the plain grows dark I realize that I, like the land, have changed but little. Fighting Irish I was then, child of generations of men and women who had battled for something beyond immediate gain, beyond their own finite understanding. Fighting Irish I am yet . . . and fighting Irish I shall be if, God willing, I may be looking down from some high rampart of eternity when the last war for man's freedom has been won.[6]

NOTES

1. Nancy Hoffman, *Woman's "True" Profession* (Old Westbury, NY: Feminist Press, 1981), 291.

2. Ibid., 293.

3. David Tyack, *The One Best System* (Cambridge: Harvard University Press, 1974), 126–29.

4. Hoffman, 290.

5. Ibid., 291.

6. Robert L. Reid, ed. *Battleground: The Autobiography of Margaret A. Haley* (Urbana, IL: University of Illinois Press, 1982), 279.

WORK BY MARGARET HALEY

Battleground: The Autobiography of Margaret A. Haley. ed. Robert L. Reid. Urbana: University of Illinois Press, 1982.

WORKS ABOUT MARGARET HALEY

Cremin, Lawrence A. *The Transformation of the School: Progressivism in American Education, 1876–1957*. New York: Knopf, 1961.

Davis, Allen F. *American Heroine: The Life and Legend of Jane Addams*. New York: Oxford University Press, 1973.

Edwards, James, ed. *Notable American Women: A Bibliographical Dictionary*. Vol. 11. Cambridge: Belknap Press of Harvard University Press, 1971.

Hoffman, Nancy. *Woman's "True" Profession: Voices from the History of Teaching*. Old Westbury, NY: Feminist Press, 1981.

Murphy, Marjorie. *Blackboard Unions: The AFT and the NEA 1900–1980*. Ithaca, NY: Cornell University Press, 1990.

Tyack, David. *The One Best System: A History of American Urban Education*. Cambridge: Harvard University Press, 1974.

Zophy, Angela Howard, ed. *Handbook of American Women's History*. New York: Garland, 1990.

Helen Heffernan

Kathleen Weiler

Helen Heffernan (1896–1987) was commissioner of rural and elementary education in California from 1926 to 1965. A follower of the ideas of John Dewey, she was perhaps the most influential progressive educator at the state level in the United States in the 1930s and 1940s. Because of her progressive ideas, she became the focus of conservative attacks, but she continued to fight for a child-centered approach to education and for the rights of minority and poor children to an equal education. The center of a network of women educators and supervisors, she provided guidance and support to generations of teachers in California.

Helen Heffernan was born in Massachusetts in 1896, the youngest of nine children, and moved to Goldfield, Nevada, with her family by the time she was in the eighth grade. She attended high school in Goldfield and later the Nevada Normal School, from which she graduated in 1915. She then held a series of positions as teacher and principal in Nevada, Idaho, and Utah. From an early age, she was a supporter of women's rights and an advocate of women's suffrage. As a friend from her days at Goldfield later recounted:

During her first years of teaching in Goldfield, the campaign to give women the right of suffrage was underway, and Helen, as a young beginning teacher, went out on the streets to make speeches in support of it. . . . One day she was speaking on the street to a group of interested bystanders and a somewhat less than sympathetic man staggered up and demanded belligerently to know if the young suffragette knew what St. Paul had to say concerning women—Helen responded by saying, "Brother, it's been a long time since Paul said *anything* about women."[1]

In 1923, she received a B.A. from the University of California, and in 1925, she received her M.A., studying in the summers. From 1923 to 1926 she worked as a rural supervisor in Kings County, under county superintendent Miss M. L. Richmond, who had brought together an outstanding staff of women supervisors. She became active in the state Rural Supervisors Association and spoke frequently, describing her work in Kings County. In 1926, although she was only thirty and had been a rural supervisor for only three years, she was invited by the State Board of Education to apply for the vacant position of commissioner of elementary schools. Heffernan later claimed that the only reason she was appointed was that she had spent forty dollars (a large sum!) for a new hat to wear at the interview. But in fact, her abilities and her work in Kings County were well recognized, particularly among county superintendents and rural supervisors.

The early focus of Heffernan's work was on rural education, particularly after 1927, when the State Department of Education was reorganized and Heffernan became chief of the Division of Rural Education. Heffernan was concerned with supporting and strengthening the work of rural elementary school teachers, many of whom still worked in small one-, two-, and three-room schools. She became involved with rural education at a national level as well. In 1930 she was elected president of the Rural Supervisors Section of the National Education Association and, along with other women educators such as Mabel Carney, worked to encourage a Deweyan approach in rural schools. As she became increasingly involved with national organizations, her interest in progressive education and acquaintance with the ideas of the social reconstructionists also grew. In the winter of 1930, for example, she attended a conference of progressive educators funded by the Rosenwald Fund at Hot Springs, Virginia, which included state officials, heads of private progressive schools, and such national leaders as William Kilpatrick and Harold Rugg of Teachers College, Columbia.

Heffernan used a variety of methods to bring progressive educational approaches to rural schools: she was tireless in visiting schools and speaking at institutes and conferences; she created state demonstration schools; she encouraged and guided the work of rural school supervisors; and she organized the publication of state educational journals. One of her first actions upon being named commissioner was to begin the publication of the *California Exchange Bulletin in Rural Education*. The *Bulletin* was intended to foster an exchange among rural teachers and supervisors, but in essence it celebrated the progressive Deweyan approach to education that was increasingly shaping Heffernan's thought. Between 1928 and 1930 Heffernan edited a monthly section in *The Western Journal of Education* on rural education, which again gave her a forum to articulate and disseminate her ideas. She also reorganized the Rural Supervisors Association. Because of her own experience as a rural teacher and rural school supervisor, she was both sympathetic and respectful of the work of rural teachers, and she envisioned supervision as a democratic and collaborative process, modeled on her experience working under Superintendent Richmond of Kings County. The Rural Supervisors Association had an annual membership of between 120 and 150 during the late 1920s and 1930s. The group was thus small enough for personal friendships and alliances to be formed, and Heffernan was personally acquainted with most of the members. Heffernan envisioned an alliance between teachers and rural supervisors who would work together to introduce progressive and child-centered education.

Another major focus of Heffernan's work in rural education in the late 1920s and early 1930s was the organization of rural demonstration schools. These schools were established in the late 1920s and continued to exist through the 1930s. In 1930, there were twenty such schools, ranging from one- to five-room schools. Two of the most successful demonstration schools were the Woods School and the Escalon School in San Joaquin County. Heffernan described the significance of these schools in providing a model for progressive rural education:

These schools have been visited by nearly five hundred superintendents, supervisors, and teachers during the school year, and have provided an opportunity for showing a program of progressive education to many. One elementary school principal of many years' experience, when reporting at the state department after a visit to Woods and Escalon, said: "They are the nearest approximation of my ideal of what an elementary school should be of anything I have ever seen."[2]

These schools were organized on the Deweyan ideal of beginning education with the child and encouraging creative learning based on the child's social and natural environment. Heffernan saw the rural demonstration schools as providing a concrete example of the ways in which progressive educational ideals could be applied in a rural setting:

The rural environment is a fortunate situation for realistic educative experiences. The country around the school is rich in real things—animals, flowers, trees. . . . The trucks going by the door are the links between the life of the child and the great urban areas so dependent upon the toil of country folk. The rural school is close to basic human needs. All the institutions and occupations of society are to be found close enough to utilize and simple enough for children to understand.[3]

Throughout the 1930s, Heffernan continued to argue for progressive education, not only in rural settings but in urban schools as well, particularly after 1931, when the Division of Rural Education was reorganized to become the Division of Elementary and Rural Schools. In order to address the problems of elementary teachers in all settings, in 1931 she established the *California Journal of Elementary Education*, which was published through 1963. In this journal, she continued to present the ideas of Dewey, Kilpatrick, and other progressive educators. Typical of her approach is her article "A Statement of the Philosophy and the Purposes of the Elementary School," published in 1933, which began: "The philosophy of John Dewey is basic in the thought and practice of most advanced schools today. He maintains that education is life; education is growth; education is a social process; and education is a continuous reconstruction of experience."[4] Heffernan continued to publish several articles each year in the *California Journal of Elementary Education* on such topics as "The Reconstruction of the Elementary School Program" (November 1932), "Supervision Appropriate for Progressive Schools" (August 1937), and "How Can We Make a Rural School Democratic for Children, Teachers, and Parents?" (May 1940).

Heffernan's influence was felt by elementary teachers and supervisors throughout the state. With Corinne Seeds, the head of the University of California at Los Angeles (UCLA) laboratory school, she led a network of like-minded teachers and administrators, most of whom were women. She encouraged the formation of support groups among teachers and supervisors sympathetic to her ideals. In southern California in the 1940s, for example, a group of rural supervisors from eight counties met for several years. Each year they invited Helen Heffernan to meet with them. As a former member of the group recalled:

She was a tremendous leader who could always help us extend our vision and deepen our insights. One of her most amazing characteristics was that she could listen that first evening to those sixty persons introduce themselves and tell the school district in which they worked. From then on she could call each by name, and furthermore, talk in terms of what was going on in each of the districts![5]

Heffernan's collaborative and child-centered methods were enthusiastically endorsed by numerous supervisors, teachers, and State Teachers College instructors. During the 1930s she spoke frequently to prospective teachers on college campuses, including her frequent talks to the Rural Life Club at San Francisco State College, in which she encouraged student teachers to use progressive approaches in rural schools. A former San Francisco State student later recalled the impact of her presentation:

I wandered into the auditorium where a woman was speaking. . . . She talked that day about the challenge and significance of rural education. After she spoke, I vowed I would become a part of the most important of all professions. . . . She told me about an isolated one room school in Marin County. I went there to teach fifty Indian children and the children of Italian immigrants. She came so many times to visit us, and from her I came to understand that education is more—much more—than musty books which tell of a dead past. Surely she believed with John Dewey that "education is not a preparation for life. It is life itself."[6]

Heffernan clearly had a magnetic personality and inspired generations of teachers with her vision of democratic and progressive education. However, not everyone in California supported these ideas.

By the mid-1930s Heffernan's progressive vision increasingly came into conflict with conservative educators and local communities. This conflict first emerged around the issue of rural supervision. State superintendent Vierling Kersey recognized that rural supervisors controlled by Heffernan threatened the power of local county superintendents, and while he cautiously supported her progressive views, at the same time he was unwilling to enter into conflict with local superintendents or local interests. Heffernan estimated that approximately three-quarters of the rural supervisors were supportive of her progressive ideas. As she wrote, "Probably no professional group in the entire state is tied in its interests more closely to our program."[7] But local superintendents and conservative local communities were suspicious of what they saw as "liberal" ideas and outside control of their schools. Typical of letters complaining of Heffernan's influence and the power of local rural supervisors is a letter from the principal of the school at Farmersville to the state superintendent of education. The trustees in Farmersville, he wrote, "positively, do not like, nor will they tolerate being dictated to, nevertheless they are not hard to work with. . . . Two very good teachers which we had quit teaching several years ago and it is my firm belief because they thought they could not please the supervisors."[8] This kind of local opposition and the lack of support by the state superintendent led to the dissolution of the Rural Supervisors Organization in 1936. Although a statewide supervisors organization, including both rural and urban schools, was established in its place, Heffernan lost the close contact she had had with the smaller Rural Supervisors Organization. As a way of re-creating a network of educators, in 1940, Heffernan and Seeds instituted summer sessions for elementary school supervisors at UCLA in which they explored the implications of a progressive approach. These summer sessions were held annually through 1956.

The animosity of local communities to Heffernan's progressive ideas was heightened in the tense political climate of the 1930s. In rural California, Heffernan's attention in this period turned to a new problem—the influx of families of migrant farm workers and the need to provide schooling for their children. In the 1920s Mexican families had been recruited to work in expanding California agribusiness, replacing single, male migrant workers. In the 1930s the "dust bowl" migrants arrived from the southwestern United States. In response to this new population of migrant school-age children, migratory or emergency schools were supported by the state. Heffernan organized a number of conferences and published state pamphlets and articles on the education of migrant children and on the need to provide health and family services through the schools. She was one of the most outspoken state officials arguing for an equal and fair education for migrant children. As she argued in a 1938 conference on the education of migrant children:

If facts are to be faced realistically, we must admit that there is frequently discrimination against migratory children. Such children and their parents are wanted only as a solution to a labor problem. They are not considered an integral part of the community life; the children are not wanted in the regular schools because of considerations of cleanliness, health, or social status; and some socially myopic adults who would decry long hours of labor as barbarous for their own children, actually advocate labor rather than education for the migratory child.[9]

Speeches like this one doubtless contributed to the growing suspicion and animosity toward her by local politicians, business leaders, and conservative groups throughout the state.

With the outbreak of World War II, Heffernan became involved with the movement to provide day care and services to war workers and to provide adequate support for the rapidly expanding urban schools. She also faced the moral issue of the forced removal of Japanese-American families, including school-age children, to camps in 1942. Although the schools established in the camps were under the jurisdiction of the War Relocation Authority and not the state of California, Heffernan was concerned with the welfare of these children. She was not as public in her sympathy for the Japanese-American internees as was her friend Seeds, who received death threats after organizing a drive to bring food and blankets to the Japanese-Americans being held at the internment center at Santa Ana. But she did remain in contact with the superintendent of education at the Manzanar Camp, Dr. Genevieve Carter. In a letter to Dr. Carter on November 23, 1943, she raised the issue of trying to educate against prejudice and racial hatreds, citing favorably Carey McWilliams's talk on "the problem of education of minority groups," at a recent state education conference, which she felt would have been of value to the Manzanar teachers. In a pointed paragraph, she spoke of the dangers of discrimination to the social fabric of the country:

Because this feeling of discrimination lies so deeply entrenched in the cultural mores, I realize that education should attempt to formulate a longtime program designed to eliminate the dangerous bitterness and intolerance which exists. We still segregate the children of these minority groups by "gerrymandering," although our State law prohibits segregation for purposes of education. It will take years to break down this practice, but it is my belief that it must be broken down if any true acculturation of minority groups is to take place in this State.[10]

Throughout the 1940s, Heffernan was under attack from several conservative politicians and groups. As the progressive education movement became associated with more critical and politically radical ideas, all aspects of progressive education came under attack. Heffernan became a symbol of progressive and left-wing views, and even some of her supporters came to see her as a liability because of her strong public presence. Fred Trott, director of curriculum in Tulare County and a strong supporter of the state's education program, for example, wrote in a private letter to state superintendent Walter Dexter in 1943: "Miss Heffernan . . . often makes wild, unsubstantiated statements in public meetings and is not disposed to modify, or soften these statements. . . . When a community is defending its educational program, that is a good time to have Miss Heffernan stay in Sacramento."[11] Heffernan was also involved in defending curricular materials deemed unsuitable by conservative groups. In California, as was true elsewhere, social studies materials influenced by George Counts and Rugg from Teachers College, Columbia, were attacked as biased and "socialistic," and Heffernan came to their defense. In 1946 her pamphlet *Framework for Social Studies* was attacked by the California Society of the Sons of the American Revolution as injecting "political propaganda" and teaching "international socialism." This pamphlet remained in use, but the social studies series *Building of America*, a series of photographic texts on social problems in America, was not so fortunate. Although defended by Heffernan and other state officials and scholars, *Building of America* became the target of a number of right-wing groups in the 1940s, who eventually succeeded in having it removed from the schools.

Despite these attacks, Heffernan retained strong support from liberal groups and local educators and continued a wide range of activities in California, nationally, and internationally. For six months in 1942 she served with the U.S. Office of Education as field representative to the Inter-American Education project. After the war, from 1946 to 1948, she worked in Japan as elementary schools officer with the U.S. occupation government. In the early 1950s she advocated the right of special needs children in California to public education and was instrumental in the passage of legislation providing medical and educational support for these children. She held conferences promoting bilingual education and highlighting the needs of the large Mexican-American population in California. She wrote a number of children's books, textbooks, and numerous pamphlets issued by the California State Department of Education for teachers and supervisors on a wide variety of topics. She taught summer school courses at a number of universities, including San Francisco State, Berkeley, UCLA, Harvard, and Stanford. In the early 1960s she traveled widely, visiting schools throughout the world. In 1961, she conducted workshops in Kenya and Nigeria for African educators on the importance of providing equal educational opportunity for girls and women.

In the face of increasing criticism of progressive education in the McCarthy and cold war years, she remained steadfast in her commitment to child-centered and democratic education, arguing that attacks on progressive education were motivated by political, not educational, interests. As she wrote: "All of the research evidence of the 20th century vigorously opposes forcing formal instruction upon children at an early age. Public education which has contributed tremendously to the greatness of America has become the scapegoat for the fearful, the disgruntled and the disillusioned in the middle decades of the twentieth century."[12]

In the early 1950s, she opposed the use of A-B-C-D-F report cards as "an educational evil" used to blame children for the faults of an unresponsive school system. She continued to be attacked for this and other progressive beliefs by conservatives who accused her of abandoning academic standards. In an article in 1958 in *The Atlantic Monthly*, for example, she was used as an example of the decline of American education by Mortimer Smith, a founder of the conservative Council for Basic Education and author of right-wing popular attacks on progressive education. He denounced Heffernan as "a devote [*sic*] of Kilpatrickian progressivism who thinks schools exist for the purpose of social adjustment and the development of healthy personality and to whom all talk of academic standards and intellectual values is anti-diluvian."[13]

In 1962, she became the target of the conservative Max Rafferty in his successful campaign for state superintendent of public instruction. After Rafferty's election, Heffernan, protected by civil service regulations, remained in office, but with declining influence until 1965, when she retired without public announcement or ceremony at the age of sixty-nine. In 1966, her friends and supporters raised funds to dedicate a redwood grove on the Northern California coast in her honor. After her retirement she lived quietly in Sacramento until her death in 1987 at the age of ninety-one.

Helen Heffernan's accomplishments as an educator have been all but forgotten today. She was not a scholar or theorist, and, although she wrote widely, she was not an original thinker. Her interests were in shaping policy and inspiring teachers. The ideas she espoused derived from other thinkers, most significantly Dewey and Kilpatrick. She supported women's interests, labor, "minorities," and the poor, but she was not a political activist; instead she worked within the parameters of her position as a state official. In both her personal and professional life she surrounded herself with close women friends. She never married and lived alone, but she had a wide circle of acquaintances and carried on an extensive correspondence with friends throughout the world. As an articulate and dynamic woman in a position of authority and power, she seems to have evoked hostility and fear from some male educators, particularly in the 1940s and 1950s. As Seeds put it: "Helen's brilliant. The men all hate her. Oh, boy, they do! And they made her life miserable, but she's above it."[14] There are countless testimonies to her powerful personality and abilities as a public speaker. One women friend said later that Helen Heffernan was the only woman she could imagine as president of the United States. Her firm commitment to ideals of equality and social justice and her belief in the value of all children and the creative potential of teachers provide a model of what public education could be.

NOTES

1. *A Teacher Affects Eternity: Addresses at the Dedication of the Helen Heffernan Honor Grove at Prairie Creek State Park, October 1, 1966* (Privately printed), 6.

2. Helen Heffernan, "Rural School Supervision in Three California Counties," *The Western Journal of Education* (July 1929): 7.

3. Helen Heffernan, "Introduction," in *Organization of Learning Experiences in Small Rural Schools* (Sacramento: California School Supervisors Association, Northern Section, 1938), iii.

4. Helen Heffernan, "A Statement of the Philosophy and the Purposes of the Elementary School," *California Journal of Elementary Education* (February 1933): 109.

5. *A Teacher Affects Eternity*, 11.

6. Robert Treacy, "Progressivism and Corinne Seeds," Ph.D. diss., University of Wisconsin, Madison, 1971.

7. Helen Heffernan to Vierling Kersey, September 4, 1934, Vierling Kersey Papers, California State Archives, Sacramento.

8. George Snowden to Walter Dexter, June 7, 1944, Walter Dexter Papers, California State Archives, Sacramento.

9. Helen Heffernan, "Report of Conference on Education of Children of Seasonal Workers—Fresno State College, December 9-10, 1938," *California Journal of Elementary Education*, 7, no. 3 (February 1939): 185.

10. Helen Heffernan to Dr. Genevieve W. Carter, November 23, 1943, Bureau of Elementary Education Files, California State Archives, Sacramento.

11. Fred Trott to Walter Dexter, November 9, 1943, Walter Dexter Papers, California State Archives, Sacramento.

12. "Helen Heffernan Retires from Education Bureau," *The Sacramento Bee*, Thursday, September 2, 1965, D4.

13. Mortimer Smith, "How to Teach the California Child," *The Atlantic Monthly*, September 1958, 34.

14. Treacy.

WORKS BY HELEN HEFFERNAN

Newer Instructional Practices of Promise (ed.). Washington, DC: Association for Supervision and Curriculum Development, 1939.
Guiding the Young Child. Boston: Health, 1951.
The Kindergarten Teacher (coauthor with Vivian Edminston Todd). Boston: Heath, 1960.

See also the numerous short articles in *The California Journal of Elementary Education*, which Heffernan edited and to which she frequently contributed.

WORKS ABOUT HELEN HEFFERNAN

Hendrick, Irving. "California's Response to the New Education of the 1930s." *California Historical Quarterly* 53(1974): 25–40.
———. *California Education: A Brief History*, San Francisco: R. E. Research Associates, 1977.

Morpeth, Ruth. "Dynamic Leadership: Helen Heffernan and Progressivism Education in California." Ph.D. diss., University of California, Riverside, 1989.

Treacy, Robert. "Progressivism and Corinne Seeds." Ph.D. diss., University of Wisconsin, Madison, 1971.

Winifred Holt

Mary Tremblay

At the beginning of the twentieth century Winifred Holt (1870–1945) established one of the first education programs for blind adults in the United States.[1] She led the fight for the inclusion of blind children within the New York City public school system and pioneered in the establishment of kindergarten and nursery school classes for young blind children. Holt was one of the first people to work for the prevention of blindness through legislation and public education. In 1905, she founded the Lighthouse, the New York Association for the Blind, the first comprehensive program of services to the blind in the United States. During World War I, Holt traveled throughout France and Italy to develop education and job training programs for blind soldiers and later helped establish similar programs in thirty-four countries around the world. She believed that education could provide the blind with the means to secure "light through work."[2]

Winifred Holt was born on November 17, 1870, in New York City. She was the fourth of seven children of Henry Holt and his first wife, Mary Florence West. Her father had descended from seventeenth-century New England settlers. Her mother, who died when Winifred was eight years old, was the daughter of a wealthy New York City financier. Henry Holt remarried in 1886 and had four children from that marriage.

Henry Holt had graduated from Yale College in 1862 and received an LL.B. degree from the Law School of Columbia University in 1864. Following graduation he entered the publishing business in New York City and in 1873 founded Henry Holt & Co., which he headed until his death in 1926. His firm published many of the major literary works of the late nineteenth and early twentieth centuries.

Winifred Holt attended the Brearley School in New York City. This school had been established in 1884 to provide girls from upper-class families with a substantial college preparatory program that included a strong emphasis on music and the arts. Holt was brought up in an environment of wealth and culture and met many leading American and European literary and political figures. She attributed her real education to conversations with artists and writers who visited her family home. In 1886, at age sixteen, Holt worked as a volunteer teacher half a day a week at the newly established New York University Settlement house in the Bowery district of New York City. Here she encountered a family of German immigrants whose eldest son was losing his sight. Holt found medical treatment for the boy that saved his sight. This was her first experience with prevention of blindness, which became one of her major activities in work for the blind. Her father served as the first chairman of the Settlement House and encouraged his daughter in her charity work.

After graduation from Brearley School, Holt did not attend college but chose instead to pursue studies in art and music. Initially she studied in New York City, but when she contracted malaria in the 1890s she was advised to travel to Italy for her health. Accompanied by her younger sister Edith, she studied sculpture in the studio of the noted sculptor Augustus Saint-Gaudens in Florence. She returned to New York City during the mid-1890s and studied at the Art Students League of New York but again had to return to Italy due to ill health. In 1901, at age thirty-one, Holt and her sister Edith attended a concert in Italy and noticed a group of young blind boys who were offered unused tickets to attend the concert. Noticing the absorption of the young boys with the music, both sisters decided that the blind in New York City must also have an opportunity to attend concerts. Upon returning to New York in 1903, the two sisters established a ticket agency in the home they shared with their brother Roland to provide the blind with free, unused concert tickets that they collected from their friends.

From her interviews with the individuals who used the ticket agency Holt found that many of the blind in New York City were unemployed and un-educated and lived in poverty. With her sister she undertook a census to investigate the condition of the blind in New York State. The census soon outgrew their resources, and Winifred Holt successfully lobbied the New York legislature in 1903 to appoint the New York State Commission of the Blind to undertake the census activities. In this work she was assisted by Dr. F. Park Lewis, an ophthalmologist who had worked at the New York School for the Blind in Batavia, New York. Edith Holt acted as the volunteer secretary for the commission, which surveyed 9,585 individuals. The census attempted to identify the causes of blindness, the educational level of blind individuals, and their existing skills.

Along with their ticket agency and census work, the Holt sisters established a home teaching program with the help of two blind volunteer braille instructors, Louis Furman and Theresa de Frances. Furman and de Frances traveled throughout the city trying to locate other blind adults who could benefit from education.

The Holt sisters visited other educators working with the blind. They studied the methods of Edward E. Allen at the Overbrook School in Pennsylvania and met with Eben P. Morford, the blind director of the Industrial Home for the Blind in Brooklyn. In England, Winifred Holt met with Sir Francis Campbell, the blind expatriate American who had established the Normal School for the Blind and the Academy of Music for the Blind. Campbell's work particularly showed Holt the capacity of blind individuals as teachers and musicians, if they were given training and opportunity.

During this period the Holt sisters found that the American public, despite the work of Campbell in England and Allen and others in America, believed the blind to be objects of charity, "best taken care of in institutions and asylums," and that beggary was expected to be their occupation.[3] In 1905, along with her brother Roland, now a vice president in his father's firm, and her sister Edith, Holt established the Lighthouse, the New York Association for the Blind. It was the first agency in the United States to provide comprehensive services to the blind. Its goals were twofold: "(1) Educating the blind to the fact that they were capable of becoming happy and something close to self-sufficient; and (2) Educating the seeing public about the prevention of blindness and the capacity of the blind. These tasks all agreed, required preaching, teaching and object lessons."[4]

The house that was shared by Winifred, Edith, and Roland on East 78th Street in New York City was the first center for the New York Association for the Blind. Classes for learning job skills such as sewing, basket and broom making, rug weaving, piano tuning, and the operation of telephone switchboards were offered and often taught by the sisters. The operation of the New York Association for the Blind was financed with a loan of $400 and the sisters' dress allowances.

Holt lobbied for the establishment of a second New York State Commission for the Blind in 1906. This new commission, chaired by Dr. F. Park Lewis, was to "prepare a complete register of the blind in the state of New York and to investigate their condition and to report on the expediency of the establishment by the state of industrial training schools and other institutions."[5] Again Edith Holt volunteered as secretary, and the office was based in the Holts' home.

The work of the commission of 1906, reported in 1907, showed that 75 percent of the blind in New York state lost their sight after school age. State residential schools for the blind established in the nineteenth century provided some education for blind children, but there were no organizations in New York State to meet the needs of newly blind adults. The only provision for them was the poorhouse or a pension of fifty dollars given out in one lump sum each year. After they had used up their pension, there was no other financial support. Holt argued that these adults should have access to education that included vocational, academic, and athletic training and used the newly developing New York Association for the Blind programs to demonstrate the value of education for adults. The first public meeting of the association was held in March 1907. Holt used her family's connections to prominent business, literary, and political leaders to form the first Board of Directors and persuaded Joseph H. Choate, a successful businessman, to become the first president of the association. In addition she convinced Samuel Clemens (Mark Twain) and Helen Keller, recently graduated from Radcliffe College, to speak on behalf of the blind at the inaugural meeting.

In 1908 Edith Holt married Dr. Joseph Colt Bloodgood and moved to Baltimore, leaving Winifred Holt as the secretary and main fund-raiser for the New York association. Holt occupied both of these positions until the beginning of World War I in 1914. During this period Holt was able to gain the support of Louisa Lee Schuyler, a wealthy New York City woman from an old American family. Schuyler, who had never married, had been a leading figure in the development of social welfare work since the Civil War. She was appointed in 1907 as a trustee of the new Russell Sage Foundation and was able to secure funding for Holt from the foundation to rent space to move the New York Association for the Blind activities from the Holt home. By now the association offered a comprehensive program of services that included an information center, social settlement, music school, nursery school, and various job skills programs.

Holt argued that education, not charity, was important for both the blind adult and child to help them secure employment and live independently in society. She did not believe in segregation of the blind and argued successfully for the inclusion of blind students in classes with sighted students. These classes, the first in New York State, were modeled on the first public school classes for blind and sighted students, which had been started in Chicago by John B. Curtis, a blind teacher, in 1900. Holt was one of a small number of American educators who lobbied for the inclusion of blind students in public school classes, opposed by the educators who ran the state residential schools for the blind. They feared the loss of funding and public support if the new public school classes proved successful. The number of blind students in public school classes in 1910 in America was only 200, with over 4,600 students being educated in state residential schools. These proportions did not change until the 1950s. Why this early experiment in mainstream education for the blind was never fully accepted has not been studied. During this period Holt also established a model nursery school in the New York Association for the Blind program.

Like other progressive-era educators Holt believed that education for the blind would enable them to enter the work force and take their rightful place in society. She argued, along with others, for scholarships for the blind student in higher education in America "because the capacity of the blind for higher education has . . . been well shown by blind students who have taken honors at colleges here and abroad.[6] However, while some blind students continued to attend universities, university officials never recognized the blind student as anything other than an unusual student. Universities did not embark on any programs to help blind students on campus or encourage increases in enrollments of blind students. It remained the responsibility of the student to adapt to the university.

Another idea of Holt's gained more immediate recognition. In 1906, she had recognized that many blind adults had no hope of entering the work force, and the fifty-dollar a year pension ensured that they lived in poverty. To provide some employment for blind adults, she established employment workshops, first for blind men in 1908 and later in 1929 for blind women. Women were initially taught household skills and later domestic science in the Lighthouse education programs with the expectation that they could continue in their role as homemaker or seek employment in domestic service. Employment in other occupations for blind women was generally not considered until the late 1920s. In this approach the Lighthouse modeled the social ideas of the time about women's role in society. The early workshops provided employment for blind men in broom making and chair caning. The workshops were to be self-sufficient, provide salaries from the production of goods, and, ideally, lead to employment in the community. These workshops grew into the New York Association for the Blind Industries and were the precursors for the sheltered workshops that multiplied during the middle of the twentieth century. Rather than a temporary solution to unemployment, as Holt had intended, the workshops became a major long-term employment site for the blind in low-paying manual skill jobs.

In 1909, the New York Board of Education asked Holt to assess the value of various types of tactile print systems that were used in reading materials for the blind. In order to understand the issues, Holt learned to read and write braille. She conducted hearings and recommended that braille be the only tactile print used in the New York education system. In 1917 a national commission recognized braille as the universal American standard. Holt also established, in 1911, the first braille magazine for children, *Searchlight*, which was published until 1971.

A major finding of both the 1903 and 1906 New York Commissions for the Blind had been the large number of avoidable cases of blindness. The concept of prevention of blindness had not been widely recognized before the commissions' reports. One specific example was the finding that a large number of children were blind as a result of ophthalmia neonatorum, an infection of the eyes following birth due to venereal disease in the mother. This condition could be easily prevented if infants' eyes were treated with a solution of silver nitrate at birth. If not treated, the condition led to permanent blindness. The commission recommended standards for treatment of this infection by both midwives and physicians. Holt was successful in lobbying the governor of New York State and the legislature to pass a bill making the use of preventive treatment at birth mandatory. The legislation provided for punishment for neglect by either a fine or imprisonment. During its first year eighty midwives were arrested. Holt noted that after the first year there were fewer arrests as the treatment gained acceptance.⁷ This legislation was one of the first pieces of public health legislation in the world aimed at the prevention of blindness.

Holt introduced Louisa Schuyler to the field of prevention of blindness. They established the Special Committee for the Prevention of Blindness of the New York Association for the Blind. This committee, chaired by Schuyler, obtained a starting grant of $5,000 per year for five years from the Russell Sage Foundation. The committee's office was at Holt's home along with the already established Census Committee office. In 1915 the committee became the National Committee for the Prevention of Blindness and in 1928, the National Society for the Prevention of Blindness.

By 1911, the New York Association for the Blind had grown to include workshops for the blind, an employment agency, a residential club in New York City, and summer camp programs. Holt began to raise funds for a building to house these various activities. She organized a ten-day public exhibition at the Metropolitan Opera House, where over 300 blind persons showed their skill in manual, mechanical, musical, artistic, and athletic work. Holt used this exhibition to appeal to the public for funding and to provide an example of the potential skills of the blind worker. Again using her family contacts, she got President William Taft to officially open both the exhibit and, later, the building, which was completed in 1913.

Throughout her career Holt wrote articles and books to promote her ideas. Her 1914 biography of Henry Fawcett, a leading British politician, lecturer in political economy, and postmaster general of England, was written "to preserve . . . a great life, a life of deep significance not only to those who see, but especially to those who, like Fawcett, must depend for their vision on that inner eye which no calamity can darken."⁸ In 1922, Holt published *The Light Which Cannot Fail*, which contained stories of blind men and women with whom she had worked and summarized her philosophy and methods for educating and working with the blind.

Holt traveled throughout the United States and Europe to lecture on the education and employment needs of the blind and the value of public health prevention programs. She was a delegate to two major international conferences, in Edinburgh in 1908 and in London in 1914, that dealt with the new concept of prevention of blindness. In 1914, at forty-four years of age, she was awarded the gold-bronze medal of the National Institute of Social Sciences for her work on behalf of the blind.

With the beginning of World War I in Europe, Holt was invited by the French government to establish a Phare (Lighthouse) de France for those blinded in the war in France. She worked full-time to revise an existing program for the blind in Bordeaux into a new Phare de Bordeaux in 1914 and established a New Phare de Paris in 1915. In France, Holt worked with a number of leaders of the blind community and included them on her Board of Directors, as she had done previously in New York. At the Phare de Paris five of the professors were themselves blind, a fact that Holt was pleased to note. She described her educational philosophy: "It is our plan to give a soldier who has acquired 'ten eyes on his finger tips' and enough knowledge to make him reasonably independent, the necessary tools and materials to follow his calling at home or to send him into other centers of work where he, in turn, can teach his unfortunate comrades."[9] Holt not only established the Phare but continued to work as a teacher in the Phare and travel about wartime France to find blind soldiers who could benefit from her programs. Many of the blind soldiers also had other injuries, including amputations of hands or arms. This meant that the standard use of braille and tactile training had to be adapted. Throughout her work the overall goal remained the return of individuals to their community and family and, wherever possible, gainful employment.

Holt returned to America in 1916 and carried out a successful fund-raising lecture tour in North America, speaking to thirty-one groups and raising an average of $3,500 for each talk. When the United States entered World War I in 1917, she returned to France to work with the Red Cross and the American Medical Corps to develop services for men blinded in battle. She taught the first American men blinded in battle in local hospitals and later established a Lighthouse at Vichy, France, for the blinded American soldiers. By the end of the war she had opened two other Phares de France for the French, and in 1919 she also established the first Lighthouse in Italy. In 1920 Holt received the Italian gold medal for public health and, for her work in France, was made a Chevalier of the Legion of Honor in 1921.

In 1922, at the age of fifty-two, Holt married Rufus Graves Mather, an American art historian who was a member of the Italian Lighthouse board. Always a skilled fund-raiser, Holt used her wedding to launch a fund-raising campaign to purchase buildings for the French and Italian Lighthouses. Friends were asked to contribute money to the campaign instead of wedding gifts.

Rufus Mather joined actively in his wife's work, and between 1922 and 1937 they lectured and helped establish Lighthouses in thirty-four countries. They also continued to argue for legislation in these countries for prevention of blindness. In 1937, at the age of sixty-seven, Winifred Mather settled with her husband in Williamstown, Massachusetts. She continued in an advisory role with the New York Association for the Blind and helped in the expansion of other Lighthouses across the United States. Holt died on June 14, 1945, of congestive heart failure at the age of seventy-four.

Winifred Holt, the daughter of a wealthy and influential publisher, believed in the responsibility of the wealthy to provide welfare services through charitable agencies for the disadvantaged. Neither Winifred Holt nor her brother Roland married until late in their lives, and neither had any children. They shared a home on East 78th Street and shared a commitment to the development of services to the blind. This partnership enabled Winifred

Holt to work full-time first in New York City and later in Europe in establishing educational and social service programs for the blind. Three of her brothers, Roland, Henry, Jr., and Elliott, became vice presidents of their father's publishing firm. Winifred did not enter the business world as her brothers had done but chose the more accepted route for unmarried women of her social class—charity work.

Her family's wealth meant that Holt did not need to earn a salary for her work and gave her the opportunity to choose her own areas of charitable work. Indeed, she used wealth and social position to advance her vision of services for the blind. She never sought the chairmanship of the organizations she established, but behind the scenes in her role as secretary she was their guiding force. Recognizing the traditional leadership role of men within American society, she usually sought out prominent men from business or public affairs to head her organizations.

Holt was a pioneer in recognizing that education for newly blinded adults could fit them for employment in society. However, her expectation that education of the blind would remove barriers to employment were not fulfilled. During the middle of the twentieth century many of the workshops that had been set up for the blind, often called Lighthouses, did not become stepping-stones to employment and access to the community. Rather, they became permanent locations for the blind in low-paying jobs that offered no hope of entering the regular work force. Ironically, the Lighthouse of New York City was criticized by the National Federation for the Blind in the 1970s for using the blind in low-paying jobs while distributing state funding for the blind through an agency run by sighted individuals who themselves drew high salaries and used government funds to the detriment of the blind.

Today the work of Winifred Holt is generally unknown, and she has disappeared from the history of education for the blind. Because she chose to work behind the scenes, many of her contributions have been identified with the men she chose to lead her organizations. Helen Keller is the only woman who has been recognized as playing a role in the education of the blind at the beginning of the twentieth century, and her activities have received an undeserved mixed review from historians. The history of education for the blind is considered a history of both sighted and blind men who established schools, agencies, and national organizations to provide and promote education for the blind. The role of women in these organizations, as in other educational organizations, has largely been ignored.

Winifred Holt should be viewed as a pioneer educator. She took advantage of her upper-class background and wealth to work tirelessly, for over forty years, to develop a model of education and social service programs for blind adults. She was one of the first to recognize that blindness usually occurred after school age and that there were no programs in America to provide training and education to enable the blind adult to enter or return to the work force. Additionally, through her census work, she established that a large portion of blindness could be prevented, and she set the groundwork through the lay and medical committees to establish public health education programs for the prevention of blindness throughout the world.

NOTES

1. Throughout this chapter the terms *blind* and *blindness* have been used to reflect the language used during the period in which Winifred Holt worked. The term *blind* has in recent years been replaced by the term *visual impairment*.

2. "Light through work" was the motto of the Lighthouse. Winifred Holt, *The Light Which Cannot Fail* (New York: E. P. Dutton, 1922), viii.

3. Edith Holt Bloodgood and Rufus Graves Mather, eds., *First Lady of the Lighthouse* (New York: New York Association for the Blind, 1952), 31–32.

4. Ibid., 31.

5. *Report of the Commission of 1906 to Investigate the Condition of the Blind in the State of New York* (New York: N.p., 1907), 9.

6. Winifred Holt, "Typhlophiles or Friends of the Blind," *Charities and the Commons* (1906–1907): 415–17.

7. Holt Bloodgood and Mather, 33.

8. Winifred Holt, *A Beacon for the Blind Being a Life of Henry Fawcett the Blind Postmaster-General* (New York: Houghton Mifflin, 1914), xiv.

9. Winifred Holt, "The Lighthouse for Blinded Soldiers," *The Survey*, (October 14, 1916): 44.

WORKS BY WINIFRED HOLT

"Typhlophiles or Friends of the Blind." *Charities and the Commons*, (1906–1907): 405–17.
A Beacon for the Blind Being a Life of Henry Fawcett the Blind Postmaster-General. New York: Houghton Mifflin, 1914.
"The Lighthouse for Blinded Soldiers." *The Survey* (October 14, 1916): 43–44.
The Light Which Cannot Fail. New York: E. P. Dutton, 1922.

WORKS ABOUT WINIFRED HOLT

Allen, Edward E. "Pioneering of the Holt Sisters in the Prevention of Blindness." *Sight-Saving Review* (September 1934): 207–9.
Derby, George, and James Terry White. *National Cyclopaedia of American Biography*. New York: J. T. White, 1948.
Held, Marian. *My Fifty Years at the Lighthouse*. New York: Lighthouse, New York Association for the Blind, 1979.
Holt Bloodgood, Edith, and Rufus Graves Mather, eds. *First Lady of the Lighthouse*. New York: New York Association for the Blind, 1952.
James, Edward T., ed. *Notable American Women 1607–1950*, 209–10. Cambridge, MA: Belknap Press of Harvard University Press, 1971.

Koestler, Frances A. *The Unseen Minority*. New York: D. McKay, 1976.

Malone, Dumas, ed. *Dictionary of American Biography*, vol. 5, 364–65. New York: C. Scribner, 1964.

Matson, Floyd. *Walking Alone and Marching Together: A History of the Organized Blind Movement in the United States, 1940–1990*. Baltimore: National Federation of the Blind, 1990.

Report of the Commission of 1906 to Investigate the Condition of the Blind in the State of New York. New York: N.p., 1907.

Mari-Luci Jaramillo

Olga Vasquez

Mari-Luci Jaramillo (b. 1928), an early proponent of bilingual/bicultural education, is known for promoting quality education for Latinos throughout the educational spectrum.[1] She is a highly acclaimed spokesperson in the areas of multicultural education, teacher education, and Latina issues. Her extensive work as a speaker, consultant, and participant in many international educational exchanges in Latin America, Spain, and Germany was recognized with her appointment as U.S. ambassador to Honduras from 1977 to 1981 under the Carter administration.

Dr. Jaramillo was a member of the university academic community for more than twenty years. At the University of New Mexico, she worked as both professor and chair of the elementary education department, as well as special assistant to the university president. Before she left the university to join the Educational Testing Service as the assistant vice president of the northern California office, a position she still held in 1993, she served as the associate dean of the College of Education, responsible for curriculum, instruction, and student affairs. Throughout her career, she has shared her expertise through positions on boards of directors for such groups as the Children's Television Workshop, the American Association of Colleges for Teacher Education, the Tomás Rivera Policy Center, and the National Council of La Raza. She has participated on several national commissions studying issues in teacher education and Latino education. A recipient of many honors, one of her most valued awards remains that of Distinguished Citizen of New Mexico, which she received in 1977.

Mari-Luci Jaramillo's ability to maneuver in and out of multiple cultures with ease can be traced to her own family life in the little town of Las Vegas, New Mexico, where she was born on June 19, 1928. Her mother, Elvira Ruiz (1902–1988), and her father, Maurilio Antuna (1898–1976), raised their children in a context of language and customs that originated in two distinct Latino cultures. Mrs. Antuna identified with the Spanish Americans of northern New Mexico, who traced their roots to the *pobladores españoles* (Spanish settlers) of the late sixteenth century. By contrast, Mr. Antuna was a Mexican nationalist and was fleeing the Mexican revolution in the state of Durango when he arrived in Las Vegas, where he later met Jaramillo's mother. Many years later the multicultural world of Dr. Jaramillo's youth provided the necessary foundation for her to successfully interact within the cultures of Ecuador, Venezuela, Colombia, and Central America as promoter of the University of New Hampshire's Latin American program. She was at home in these cultures and readily acquired various dialects of Spanish. Jaramillo mused about being a citizen of the world, "earning a living, doing all those glorious things in Spanish, within my own culture, as well as doing them in English."

Although her family teetered on the verge of poverty, her humble beginnings were more of an impetus for hard work and dedication than a deterrent to success. Her parents provided an example of self-reliance, initiative, and tenacity that accompanied a push to "study, study, study." Her father was an accomplished musician and leather craftsman. He supported the family with the earnings of his shoe shop and the performances of orchestras and bands he organized. He was an avid reader and submitted numerous patents on electrical inventions. Jaramillo's mother recognized the value of education, though she herself had completed only seventh grade. Elvira Ruiz de Antuna did everything in her power so that her children would concentrate on their studies. She sewed clothes for them from the flour sacks she earned ironing for others and refused to assign chores around the house for fear that such tasks would distract them from their schoolwork. Jaramillo immersed herself in school activities, leaving very little time to learn to cook. She waited until after she was married to care about such matters.

Mari-Luci was the middle child, "the one who was supposed to have all the problems," yet in her family being the middle child allowed her to pursue a college degree. Immediately after graduating from high school, her older sister had to work to help the family. Her younger brother joined the navy at seventeen, during World War II, completing his general education at a later time. Raised in a home where studying was mandated by an autocratic father and supported by a devoted mother, Mari-Luci read voraciously and won the attention of her teachers early on. On many occasions her elementary school teachers invited her to read her stories or poetry to group meetings such as those of the Bridge Club. On one particular occasion, she received a brightly decorated cupcake for her reading of a Halloween poem. Thrilled with the offering, wrapped in a pretty orange napkin, the little eight-year-old ran home to share her prize with her mother, brother, and sister. It was one of the first of many honors and awards that Jaramillo would receive for her efforts in education.

On the night of her high school graduation Jaramillo won every award that was given. Her father, who by then had distanced himself from the family and lived in the spare room of his shoe shop, was so impressed that he agreed to help her with the first-quarter fees at the local university. She combined this support with money earned working at her father's shop after school and cleaning houses for fifty cents a house. Still dressed in the clothes her mother made from flour sacks, she enrolled at New Mexico Highlands University in 1945. Once in college, she "did what many other students from low-income backgrounds did"; she borrowed books from her classmates and in return outlined the readings and gave private tutoring on the material.

At the end of her first year of college she met Horacio Ulibarri; they were married the following fall. Nine years and three children later, she graduated magna cum laude from Highlands University. Jaramillo, like many women before and after, put aside her own career goals in order to follow her husband. However, she stayed true to her promise that she would continue her education and not let her marriage dissuade her from "serving her people," as a Chicano professor had admonished it might. When she found herself in a rural community where her husband had been assigned a teaching job, she read everything "she could get her hand on." In pursuit of knowledge and with plenty of free time, she made frequent trips to the library in Las Vegas and studied the flora and fauna of the local area, all the time missing "doing something with education."

By the time the couple moved back to Las Vegas, her first son, Ross, was two years old, and she was expecting her second son, Ricardo, who was born in 1950. Her daughter, Carla, was born a year after the family settled in with Jaramillo's mother and grandmother. Her new living arrangement provided live-in baby-sitters so that when the parachute factory, where she worked for four years, lost temporary funding, she was able to attend the university a semester at a time. She credits her ability to manage home and work, while pulling A's in school, "to the support she received from the women in her family."

Two incidents during her senior year in college were critical to her later success. The first one involved a threat to her continued education. When Jaramillo was not attending school because she could not afford tuition fees, her high school English teacher offered her a scholarship of one hundred dollars. Initially, Jaramillo refused, uncomfortable in accepting money and wanting to achieve her goals through her own efforts. She accepted on the condition that the money was a loan and only when the teacher, Miss Doherty, proposed that Jaramillo do the same for a deserving student in the future. She graduated in December 1955 and went straight to work in a remote mountain school. With the money she received from her first paycheck as a new teacher, she paid her debt to Miss Doherty. The second incident occurred in one of her courses when she gathered all her strength and resolve to speak out in class against a professor who blamed poverty on Latinos' own cultural deficit. She remembers her voice trembling as she countered that Latinos wanted screen doors in their houses like everybody else but lacked the funds to buy them. Instead of a reprimand, she received praise from the professor for her courage. She credits this speech with putting "the little risk taker from New Mexico" on the path to becoming one of the strongest advocates for Latinos.

In 1956, when her husband moved to Albuquerque to pursue a doctorate, she stayed with her children in Las Vegas and enrolled in a master's program at Highlands University. She attended classes at night and taught elementary school during the day. Her professors quickly recognized her teaching abilities and began placing student teachers under her supervision. The superintendent also recognized her abilities and pulled her out of the classroom to become a language arts consultant for the district. He had observed her work in a remedial reading class with many young boys who had come back from reform school, and he wanted her to help teachers learn how to work with reticent children. By the time she left the classroom, she had taught kindergarten and first and second grades.

Dr. Jaramillo called attention to the importance of native language and culture long before research substantiated their pedagogical validity and public funds supported such endeavors. She advocated currently accepted pedagogical strategies such as "collaborative learning," "whole language," and "bilingual/bicultural education" more from intuition than from established empirical guidelines. As she so aptly puts it, "Now they use technical language for things that I was talking about from the soul." She also instilled in teachers the philosophy of discovering each individual child rather than treating him or her as part of an anonymous mass. She spoke of developing in the child "a self-love for learning," because she feared that "if they only learned when a policeman was there, then we were in trouble." She had confidence that children seek to learn and advocated a curriculum that would foster human agency. She achieved recognition for this work, but as she later said, "It's not hard being a big fish in a small pond."

In the summer of 1964, she embarked on a path that catapulted her into the international arena and, subsequently, national service. It was a time when her personal life and professional goals coincided in her favor. Her move to Albuquerque, where her husband had been offered a position at the University of New Mexico, gave her the opportunity to test out her abilities as a "master teacher" at a local school. She requested to teach in one of the poorest schools in Albuquerque, where she tried out her newfound knowledge of English as a second language. Before she joined the district, she attended a summer institute on the subject at the University of California at Los Angeles with the leading linguists of the time. Her success with the new materials and techniques gained immediate attention, and her Albuquerque classroom became a demonstration site that attracted visitors from other parts of the country. Soon her reputation as master teacher spread into the university community.

In an effort to help foreign students from Latin America profit more fully from living in the United States, the University of New Mexico invited Jaramillo to teach a course in English as a second language. This experience led her to devote her life to saying, "Don't let anybody knock your language." Until then, she had felt personally insecure about her "New Mexican" Spanish but found that the only thing she lacked was technical vocabulary. Her intonation, structure, and breadth of vocabulary were all in place. Her knowledge of Spanish made it possible for her to accompany her students to their home countries, where she visited educational systems and taught courses on methods and curriculum development.

At the urging of her friends, Jaramillo enrolled in a doctoral program in 1968. She agreed to pursue a degree to regain her confidence and to deal with the losses she was experiencing as a result of both her recent divorce and her children's going off to college. Except for the drastic reduction in salary, graduate school was an easy undertaking for her: "There wasn't a book a professor assigned that I had not already read or translated into Spanish to use in my own courses." She continued to work full-time on half salary—the university did not allow her to work for a full-time salary—and she tied everything she studied to her work with her Latin American and Chicano students.

Her dissertation, "In-Service Teacher Education in a Tri-Ethnic Community: A Participant-Observer Study," proposed a model of social change that would diminish the disparity in educational achievement among Anglo, Native American, and Spanish-surnamed students. In essence, she advocated a cultural change in every level of the educational system that incorporated the knowledge and language of the three communities. Her "Esperanza model" called for changes in behavior, curriculum, and school-community relations—a notion of school reform revisited by scholars in the 1990s.

Although Dr. Jaramillo had many offers from other institutions, she continued in the Latin American Program as an assistant professor. By this time she had been teaching for over eight years and had become a migrant of sorts as she and others followed the social projects "that motivated people into getting an education." A lone female voice on behalf of Latino children, Dr. Jaramillo eventually joined the civil rights movement of the 1960s, traveling all over the Southwest, talking about the needs and contributions of Latinos. She spoke of a Third World not as a concept of deficit but as a reconstruction of multiple experiences, a place where differences are valid and exciting and represent resources—a new world created by the merging of two other worlds. Contrary to her critics, she was not "bottling poverty" but was proposing a philosophy of inclusion.

In 1972, she married Heriberto Jaramillo, who had come from Colombia to study educational administration at the University of New Mexico. In 1977 President Carter invited her to serve as ambassador to Honduras. This time Jaramillo's career came first, and her husband followed, fully supportive. He accompanied her to Honduras and engaged in varied public service projects while she carried out her diplomatic duties. Through his participation, Dr. Jaramillo was able to accomplish a great depth of involvement, reaching out to many groups. She opened the doors of the American embassy to previously excluded groups, such as *campesinos* (rural farmers), laborers, and rural women's groups. Recognizing the significance of this unprecedented gesture, the people of Honduras paid tribute to Jaramillo by awarding her Honorary Honduran Citizenship and the Order of Francisco Morazán, Order of the Great Silver Cross, Honduras. Many public functions were held in her honor when her term of office ended. In 1990, Dr. Jaramillo received the "PRIMERA" Award from the Mexican-American Women's National Association for being the first Latina to be appointed as U.S. ambassador, a fact that distressed her greatly because she felt that "we should be celebrating number 200th."

On her return to the United States in 1980, Jaramillo remained in Washington, D.C., as deputy assistant secretary for inter-American affairs for several months to help in the transition of political administrations. She found the policy-making process exciting but returned to New Mexico when the Republican party took office. She was ready to again pick up the agenda of social issues at the University of New Mexico. She continued to travel extensively, conducting workshops in Argentina, Colombia, Ecuador, Venezuela, and many parts of Central America. Throughout her career she has visited numerous regions in the Soviet Union, Africa, and the Mediterranean for extended periods, either teaching or visiting educational systems.

In 1987, Jaramillo joined the Educational Testing Service as vice president and director of the Bay Area offices headquartered in Emeryville, California. When questioned about the political implications of working for a company that has received a considerable amount of criticism from minority activists, she explained several folk misconceptions about the company. While it may seem that the company is exclusive and elitist, it is one of the few nonprofit organizations with Latino representation on the Board of Trustees, a level Jaramillo finds crucial for policymaking that affects minorities. Second, she explained that the ethnic composition of the specialists who construct and evaluate the measurement tools is diverse and includes African Americans and Latinos.

Jaramillo looks back on her life with tremendous satisfaction, which comes from doing what she has passionately believed in: to have helped individuals achieve their greatest potential and "to have always encouraged the young professionals to get out there and lead." Jaramillo looks toward the future when she will have the time to write about her experiences and Latina issues. Her activism and her public speaking has left little time to write academic manuscripts. Among other things, she looks forward to creating and testing theoretical propositions with young academics. However, it will be a long time before the "little shy risk taker from New Mexico" and grandmother of Kevin Potter, Geoffrey Smith, and Nícola Ulibarrí—her pride and joy—will leave her post as champion for Latinos.

NOTE

1. The quotes and personal information included in this chapter were taken from an interview with Dr. Jaramillo on August 5, 1991.

WORKS BY MARI-LUCI JARAMILLO

"In-Service Teacher Education in a Tri-Ethnic Community: A participant-observation Study." Ph.D. Diss., University of New Mexico, Albuquerque, New Mexico.
"Cultural Differences in the ESOL Classroom." *Tesol* 7, no. 1 (1973): 51–60.
"The Future of Bilingual-Bicultural Education." In R. Poblano, ed., *Ghosts in the Barrio: Issues in Bilingual-Bicultural Education*. San Rafael, CA: Leswing Press, 1973.
"Cultural Conflict Curriculum and the Exceptional Child." *Exceptional Children* 40, no. 8 (1974): 585–87.
"Cultural Pluralism: Implications for Curriculum." In Melvin M. Tumin, and Walter Plotch, eds., *Pluralism in a Democratic Society*, 248. New York: Praeger, 1977.
"Institutional Responsibility in the Provision of Educational Experiences to the Hispanic American Female Student." In Teresa McKenna and Flora-Ida Ortiz, eds. *The Broken Web: The Educational Experience of Hispanic American Women*, 262. Encino, CA: Floricanto Press, 1988.

WORKS ABOUT MARI-LUCI JARAMILLO

Delgado-Gaitlan, Concha. *Mujeres de La Raza: A Tribute to the Women of La Raza Who Have Contributed towards the Betterment of Humanity and Our Culture*. Berkeley: Babel Productions, 1971.
Press, Jacques Cattell, ed. *Leaders in Education: A Biographical Directory*. New York: R. R. Bowker Co., n.d.
Press, Jacques Cattell, ed. *Who's Who in American Politics*, 10th ed. New York: R. R. Bowker Co., 1985.

Katharine Kuh

Susan F. Rossen

Katharine Kuh (b. 1904) was an outstanding art educator and, as first curator of modern art at the Art Institute of Chicago, was one of a handful of women curators of her generation. Possessing a broad knowledge of the history of art, she was particularly responsive to the new artists of her time and eager to help the public understand and appreciate their work. Through a long career as a gallery dealer, as a writer on art, and, above all, as an innovative curator, she was a leader in visual education. Her exhibitions at the Gallery of Art Interpretation at the Art Institute of Chicago, the first permanent space in a museum devoted to the visual education of adults, guided viewers through such varied and unfamiliar visual areas as cubism, surrealism, and African art without becoming pedantic or intimidating. Preserved in the museum's archives are many letters of praise and gratitude from some of the thousands who saw her exhibitions. One visitor from Tennessee wrote to thank the Art Institute for his experience in the gallery, which "struck [him] as education in the very best sense of the word."[1]

Katharine Kuh's childhood and education equipped her well for trailblazing work in art education. The daughter of Olga Weiner and Morris Woolf, a silk importer, she was born in St. Louis on July 15, 1904, the youngest of three daughters in a family that appreciated art. When Kuh was a child, her family moved to Chicago, eventually settling in Highland Park, on the city's North Shore. While at Vassar College, where she majored in economics, she happened to enroll in a Renaissance art course taught by the young Alfred H. Barr, Jr. Just out of Princeton University, Barr, according to Kuh,

integrated art with history pretty much the way [he would later do] in installations at The Museum of Modern Art. He never isolated art. He tied it up to everything—movies, design, industry, life. Because he was so young, he talked our language, but he was light years ahead of us. . . . He made it easier for us to do what we [did], because he had the courage to do it first.[2]

Recognized today as one of the guiding spirits of modernism in America, Barr was named the first director of the Museum of Modern Art (MOMA), New York, in 1929. Though Kuh took only one course from Barr, it compelled her to pursue graduate studies in art history. She continued to look upon him as a mentor. In her subsequent museum career, Kuh aspired to many of the goals Barr had for MOMA: to focus on the art of the present and recent past and to relate it not just to the history of Western art but to that of other cultures (Asian, pre-Columbian, African, folk, and so on); to break down the barriers between "fine" and "applied" arts by fully integrating such media as film, photography, architectural and urban planning, and industrial and graphic design into the museum's daily life; and to use the museum and its collections, exhibitions, and publications as teaching tools designed to involve people meaningfully in the art of their own time.

Following the completion of her studies at Vassar in 1925, Kuh did graduate work in art history at the University of Chicago (A. M., 1929) and at New York University. After her marriage in 1930 to Chicago businessman George Kuh, she began her career as visual educator by teaching art history courses, in series of ten sessions each, to groups of around twenty in Chicago's northern suburbs. Some of these students, inspired by her talks and the discussions they prompted, went on to become serious and important art collectors. With the dissolution of her marriage, Kuh, increasingly frustrated by the conservatism of Chicagoans, which she attributed to a lack of meaningful exposure to modern art, opened a gallery in late 1935.

Kuh showed art so unconventional for Chicago that very little sold, and yet the gallery played a major role in educating the city toward an acceptance of modernism. It was the first Chicago gallery to exhibit photography and typographical design as art forms. Among the many painters, sculptors, and photographers whose work she displayed were Ansel Adams, Anni Albers, Alexander Archipenko, Alexander Calder, Stuart Davis, Alexej von Jawlensky, Wassily Kandinsky, Gyorgy Kepes, Andre Kertesz, Paul Klee, Gaston Lachaise, Le Corbusier, Fernard Leger, Man Ray, Marc Chagall, Joan Miro, Laszlo Moholy-Nagy, Isamu Noguchi, Emil Nolde, Pablo Picasso, Elliot Porter, and Brett Weston. Her interest in cultural pluralism also led her to exhibit various kinds of "primitive" art. Without adequate sales to support the gallery, Kuh conducted art history classes there, sometimes using her exhibitions as background for her lectures. These popular classes, held for women in the morning and couples in the evening, helped pay the Kuhs' bills.

The Katharine Kuh Gallery had an enormous educative impact on many aspiring Chicago art collectors, as well as on many young artists. The fact that, by the 1950s, important collections of modern art were being formed in Chicago is due in large part to Kuh's efforts first in her own gallery and then at the Art Institute. But it was not an easy road. In addition to her lack of commercial success, she and the gallery were the target of ferocious attacks from the Sanity in Art group (a reactionary organization that was founded in Chicago and grew nationwide in the late 1930s) and from local critics. Undeterred by such negative forces, she nonetheless was forced to close the gallery in 1942 because the war had interrupted the flow of art from Europe. Kuh, however, was not about to quit the fight: two years later, she took it with her into a new arena, the Gallery of Art Interpretation at the Art Institute of Chicago.

Historically, art education at the Art Institute had been the focus of three departments: Education, which handled tours and courses for both children and adults; Membership and Extension Lectures, which concentrated on adults; and the Children's Museum, a gallery space that had, since 1926, offered rotating exhibitions on subjects of interest to the young. In 1939, the Children's Museum changed its name to the Gallery of Art Interpretation, and its presentations were expanded to include shows related directly to the museum's collections and major loan exhibitions. Kuh attributed this new emphasis on adult educational programming—a major shift in the institute's policy—to Daniel Catton Rich. The Art Institute's dynamic director from 1938 to 1958, he would become Kuh's closest and most supportive colleague. Among Rich's many interests was finding new ways to explain art, including modern art. After Kuh joined the staff in 1943, Rich put her in charge of the Gallery of Art Interpretation, asking her to use the gallery, in part, to counteract the negative impact of such forces as Sanity in Art.

By the late 1930s and early 1940s, a few American museums had begun to experiment with visual education techniques. Leading the field was, not surprisingly, the Museum of Modern Art. In addition to its ambitious program of exhibitions on contemporary art and design circulated to museums and galleries throughout the United States, it had developed a pioneering educational project for primary and secondary school children. Under the direction of Victor D'Amico, this program organized exhibitions in which the main vehicles of communication consisted of striking juxtapositions of images and objects accompanied by short, evocative questions or statements.

But Kuh had an extraordinary model of art education at its most experimental right in Chicago: the New Bauhaus (which would later be called the Institute of Design). Originally conceived as an industrial arts school, it was opened in 1937 under the direction of Laszlo Moholy-Nagy. The dynamic Hungarian artist and educator had worked at the Bauhaus for some years before the Nazis closed the innovative German school at the outset of World War II. One year later, the architect Ludwig Mies van der Rohe, the last director of the German Bauhaus, arrived in Chicago to head the architecture program at the Armour Institute (which became the Illinois Institute of Technology), and an exciting period in the city's cultural history was inaugurated. As Kuh described it, "Mies with his extraordinary architecture and Moholy with his philosophy, energy, and excitement, they transformed the art life in Chicago. . . . It could never go back to what it had been before."[3] Kuh quickly became the close friend of both men, although the two were far from close themselves.

Among the number of European educators Moholy brought to Chicago was the Hungarian Gyorgy Kepes. Many of Kepes's and Moholy's principles and ideas had a strong impact on Kuh's experiments in the Gallery of Art Interpretation. To encourage their students' visual literacy, a major theme in Bauhaus teaching and writing, Moholy and Kepes insisted on an ahistorical approach to art. Their books, for example, include illustrations covering an encyclopedic range of periods, "high" and "low" art (a distinction they abhorred), anonymous and famous works, the documentary and the "artistic." They both investigated the nature of art as related to modern phenomena, including science and technology. Their school became a laboratory for broad education, encouraging the personal growth and the development of specific skills of each student. Kuh found Moholy's and Kepes's cross-cultural, antihieratic approach, which valued active, rather than passive, learning, very appealing.

The Bauhaus aesthetic played an integral role in the Gallery of Art Interpretation. Mies himself donated his time to designing what was his first museum space. The architect recast the old gallery on a shoestring budget, using strips of plywood that could be left bare or painted and carefully orchestrating the space for ultimate flexibility and simplicity. He was responsible as well for the dramatic installation of the inaugural exhibition in the remodeled space, "Who is Posada?" complementing a major display of the work of the famed Mexican printmaker organized for the Art Institute by another influential figure in Kuh's career, prints and drawings curator Carl A. Schniewind.

After the Posada show, Kuh began a series that rapidly set a standard for interpretive art exhibitions. Between 1944 and 1952, she assembled eleven such exhibits in the Gallery of Art Interpretation, each unique in its imaginative use of materials, installation, techniques, and succinct, engaging commentary. Subjects for shows varied; sometimes they related to Art Institute exhibitions, sometimes to its permanent collections. For the most part, they focused on artistic problems shared by artists working in every era and in every medium. Kuh borrowed pieces mainly from the Art Institute's collection, integrating works from a variety of periods and places and in a variety of media. In this way, she wrote, "rigid museum boundaries are broken down and art objects are seen more intimately in a new and fresh setting."[4]

In the process of organizing these shows, Kuh developed a set of exhibition principles that she found most effective in reaching her audience. First, she focused on the general public and not on the specialist or art world insider. To do this, she eliminated technical, subjective language and, indeed, as much as possible, labels themselves. (She complained mightily about an exhibition she had to install in the gallery before she had begun to generate her own shows there; "The People of Bali," organized by famed anthropologist Margaret Mead, had so much label copy, according to Kuh, that it took forty-five minutes just to read it all!) Perhaps even more important was her second goal: to explain visually, not verbally, how art works. Kuh's sensitivity to the importance of clear, simple language had been heightened after she conducted a class, early in her Art Institute tenure, for members of the International Ladies Garment Workers Union. After her first encounter with the group, she realized how distancing a standard art historical approach could be. As she later wrote, "The secret language of the art specialist is apt to antagonize the questioning layman. His ego is wounded and he retires, armed with deadly and familiar cliches: 'My little boy Johnny can do better than that.' "[5] Under her direction, the Gallery of Art Interpretation was dedicated to this kind of person. She kept her exhibition titles short and catchy, like "Close-Up of Tintoretto," avoiding the ponderous and pedantic. She used action words, such as "looking" and "seeing," as much as possible. Kuh's general rule was "to make only those statements on the wall which can be proven by visual examples, comparisons or contrasts."[6] To this end, she found that by posing questions, she could involve the viewer more effectively than by providing answers.

While photographs no longer exist of many of the installations, Kuh's 1951 book, *Art Has Many Faces, the Nature of Art Presented Visually*, which incorporates the concepts she used in her exhibitions and articles she published about the gallery, provides us with many illustrations of the techniques and devices she developed. The exhibitions themselves were designed to heighten curiosity and create a sense of the unexpected: asymmetrical installations were followed by rest spaces, objects placed above or below eye level, and materials arranged as units, instead of sequentially. Most intriguing was the use of nonart materials in order to relate art to other aspects of life. Driftwood from Lake Michigan and crudely fashioned ceramic toys proved just as effective in demystifying "high" art in these exhibitions as technological devices, such as color charts, X-rays of paintings, or a stereopticon. Kuh placed heavy emphasis on comparisons as a way of keeping audience participation high. Often two works, one the original and the other a replica, altered in some way, would be placed side by side, and the viewer asked to evaluate their relative effectiveness in communicating an idea. The products of very different civilizations and periods would be juxtaposed to demonstrate the universality of ideas or, on the other hand, the unending variety of individual and cultural expression. Kuh tested the success of these techniques by frequently visiting the gallery, watching the viewers' reactions, and listening to their comments.

Her exhibitions focused on single works of art ("Close-Up of Tintoretto"), on single artists ("Vincent Van Gogh, Artist"), on single themes

("Still Life Comes to Life"), on formal concerns ("Space and Distance"), and on a single medium ("Looking at Sculpture"). Kuh outlined her aims for the latter exhibition (1945–1946): "Most people know more about painting than sculpture. . . . [It is my desire] to eliminate . . . traditional pedestals and to show sculpture in all sorts of different ways with great variety and liveliness . . . [and to show] people that sculpture is not made only of bronze and marble and just for incidental decoration." She wished only to make "a few strong points so that the uninitiated go away without confusion. . . . Wherever possible we dramatize and make alluring." She called her approach "sugar-coated education."[7]

Kuh began the exhibition with a pile of what one critic described as "sizeable chunks" of aluminum, brass, bronze, copper, glass, iron, plastic, plaster, steel, stone, terra-cotta, wire, and wood to illustrate the variety of materials a sculptor might choose from. Using such examples as a naturalistic wooden head and a plastic-and-chrome, abstract construction by Moholy, Kuh demonstrated the suitability of material and technique to subject and expression. A mirror emphasized the many sides of a small bronze nude by Aristide Maillol. Light switches could be turned on and off to demonstrate how similar busts could be changed by different lighting.

Perhaps the most important contributions made by the Gallery of Art Interpretation were the exhibitions aimed specifically at helping audiences become more receptive to modern art. Kuh's goal in "From Nature to Art" (1944–1945) was to soften public resistance to the frequent distortions in modern art. Consciously avoiding the word "distortion," Kuh demonstrated the ways in which both the old masters and contemporary artists transform nature by using such devices as exaggeration, omission, and addition to convey their ideas. The emphasis Kuh placed on stylistic analysis illustrates the modernist approach to understanding works of art that underlay her work. While acknowledging that the period and personality of an artist exert profound influence on works of art, Kuh and other modernists believed that visual forms are universal, shared by artists across time and culture. To appreciate the formal artistic issues that had emerged as ends in themselves in the late nineteenth and twentieth centuries, people were urged to look again at older, "familiar" works. For example, if they were sensitized to the free brushwork, complex linear structure, spatial dynamism, and translucent color patterns in a painting by Tintoretto, they could become receptive to these qualities in the works of artists of all places and centuries, including our own.

"Explaining Abstract Art" (1947–1948) began with a panel that read, "The term 'abstract art' is new—but the idea is old." Kuh presented the viewer with examples of abstractions made by nature, using a seashell, and those made by modern technology, illustrated by machinery gears and industrial photographs. In a series of deft comparisons, using photographs, toys, and diagrams, as well as works of art, Kuh demonstrated how abstraction can be a rich and effective way to express such considerations as motion, space, light, feelings, and structure. "How Real Is Realism?" (1951) comprised mostly original works of art, spanning 500 years, juxtaposed in telling and provocative ways. Kuh attempted to question the concept, to make people consider whether realism actually exists in art or whether it is all illusion. At the entrance to the exhibit, the visitor confronted an assemblage of hands—sculpted, painted, drawn, and photographed—accompanied by this legend: "These hands look real, but none of them are real hands. Though they . . . seem natural they are not the work of nature, but of men. How realistic they seem depends not alone on the artist who made them, but also the person who looks at them." The text accompanying a group of children's drawings read: "The drawings of young children look real to them. Do they to you?"

These installations related to two pioneering special exhibitions in which Kuh played a central role: the 1947 biannual American Exhibition, devoted entirely to abstract and surrealist art, and the 1949 presentation of the Louise and Walter Arensberg Collection of twentieth-century art, which included in-depth representation of such artists as Marcel Duchamp and Constantin Brancusi. It is important to remember that during the cold war era in the United States, the avant-garde faced enormous opposition not only from the general public but also from some of the nation's leaders. Abstract art was attacked in Congress as subversive, its makers and supporters as communists out to destroy American art and traditions. Daniel Catton Rich was called a supporter of these "international art thugs."[8] Clearly, for Kuh and Rich, much more was at stake here than modernism. As they developed these two landmark exhibitions, Kuh prepared for the inevitable onslaught of derision and criticism. She organized installations in the Gallery of Art Interpretation that she hoped would build bridges for the museum goers to the difficult and demanding works that they would be confronting. She was successful. Not only did "Explaining Abstract Art" stay up for a record length of six months, but in 1952 she was asked to re-create it in Pittsburgh to accompany that year's Carnegie International, which, next to the Venice Biennale, was the most important showcase for contemporary art worldwide.

Two later educational exhibitions in the Gallery of Art Interpretation also traveled. Both "Vincent Van Gogh, Artist" (1950) and "Paul Cézanne" (1952) were developed in conjunction with major retrospectives that the Art Institute co-organized with the Metropolitan Museum of Art, and so they accompanied the installations in New York. Kuh's van Gogh show was adapted for circulation by the American Federation of Arts, visiting thirteen cities in nine states in 1951 and 1952. At least one Chicago critic expressed frustration that Kuh's exhibit on van Gogh was not made the first room of the large van Gogh retrospective, since it proved so critical to understanding the artist's oeuvre and so refreshing in its refusal to deal with any of the sensational biographical details that, for so many years, had obscured his true achievement.[9] So, two years later, when the Cézanne retrospective was installed in Chicago, the Gallery of Art Interpretation was moved from its first-floor location to a room within the exhibition on the second floor. *Newsweek* reported that shortly after the exhibit opened, the museum staff was forced to rethink the flow of visitors through Kuh's portion, so large were the crowds.

From the first years of her directorship of the museum gallery, Kuh received attention and praise from colleagues near and far. In an article on new trends in museum education, Grace L. McCann Morley, then director of the San Francisco Museum of Art, praised Kuh's effort as "the only case so far in which a major museum has set aside space for the regular presentation of teaching exhibitions of this general type," commenting on Kuh's exclusion of "the baffling medium of words" and on her encouragement of visitors to go at their own speed and to participate actively in the learning process.[10] Morley's interest in the project prompted her to ask Kuh to write about the gallery in *Museum*, journal of the United Nations Educational, Scientific, and Cultural Organization (*UNESCO*), published in English and French, in 1948 and again in 1950. These articles resulted in inquiries from as far away as Austria, Australia, and Brazil. In 1950, Kuh cooperated with the director of the Museuo de Arte Moderna in São Paulo in setting up an exhibit in Brazil based on devices and examples from several of her shows.

From the first, Kuh received requests for her ideas in published form. In 1951, Harper and Row published *Art Has Many Faces, the Nature of Art Presented Visually*. With 271 illustrations in 185 pages, it was more ambitious than the only other publication like it, Barr's brilliant, succinct, and influential *What Is Modern Painting?*, first published in 1943. Kuh's book is a skillfully organized and arranged assemblage of images drawn from many far-flung cultures and diverse periods and accompanied by words used sparingly "only as auxiliaries to point up and clarify the illustrations . . . aiding instead of directing the eye."[11] Elegantly designed by Gyorgy Kepes, the publication was praised by one reviewer as an "important milestone (still few in number) in the visual presentation of the visual arts."[12] *Art Has Many Faces*, in print for many years, served a generation of teachers and students of art appreciation in the 1950s and 1960s and fostered other influential texts, such as Joshua Taylor's *Learning to Look*.[13]

By 1954, receptivity to modern art in Chicago had grown so much, thanks in large part to Kuh's efforts, that she was named the Art Institute's first curator of modern painting and sculpture. With this appointment, Kuh changed the nature of Gallery of Art Interpretation, making it a showcase for important contemporary artists whose work had not been seen in-depth in the Midwest, such as Mark Rothko and Mark Tobey.

Kuh's involvement in visual education never ceased. In 1954, the Ford Foundation awarded the Art Institute what was then a very large grant,

$26,000, to develop an adult discussion program entitled "Looking at Modern Art." As chief consultant, Kuh prepared an illustrated manual and selected a group of leaders, art experts whom she trained in the techniques she had refined in her laboratory, the Gallery of Art Interpretation. Using slides, filmstrips, reproductions, and original works of art, participants were encouraged to compare and contrast works in various media and from various times and places so that they would understand that modern art is part of a continuous development and that, as Kuh put it in the manual, there "is no *one* way or necessarily *right* way to look at art." Kuh included in the manual excerpts from the writings of a number of authors and artists—from Clive Bell and Herbert Read to Pablo Picasso and William Carlos Williams—to demonstrate how many different points of view can coexist. Among the leaders, besides Kuh and Rich, were S. I. Hayakawa (then a professor of communications in Chicago, he later became a U.S. senator from California), Franz Schulze (critic and art history professor), and William E. Woolfenden, Jr. (then head of education at the Detroit Institute of Arts, he eventually became the first director of the Archives of American Art). They conducted a total of ten courses, with about twenty people each, in Chicago and its suburbs; Detroit, Michigan; and Akron, Ohio.

The group leaders were only to provide a starting point, channel discussion, and answer questions. The syllabus in the manual suggested four major themes around which to guide discussion. Under "Mobility and Multiplicity of Present Day Life," the group considered the impact of "primitive" art and of speed and resulting simultaneous experiences. In conjunction with "Effects of Science and Technology," they explored the impact of city life, new materials, psychoanalytic thought, and the machine. Three sessions were devoted to the "Break-Up and Reconstruction" of light and color, form, and design and content. The final meeting examined individualism and how freedom affects the artist. Kuh wrote, "If these ten meetings succeed even partially in opening the door to a difficult and new vision, then they will have accomplished their purpose." Kuh's program became a model for adult education classes that ask as much of the participants as of the leaders, a method that became a trend in American art museum education in the late 1950s and 1960s.

In 1967, the New York State Department of Education, with funds from the New York Council for the Arts, asked Kuh to create a visual education course for teachers. Called "Workshop in Looking," the twelve-session course was led by noted artist Hedda Sterne, assisted by Kuh, and included classroom discussions and activities as well as museum visits. She also conducted summer workshops at the University of Alaska at Anchorage for teachers, many of whom worked during the school year in one-room Alaskan schools. In addition to color reproductions, which she brought with her, she used indigenous art forms to enlarge the participants' perspective in the teaching of art.

In addition to resistance to modern art, Kuh encountered "extraordinary" sexism during her museum career, especially from all-male boards of trustees and other museum colleagues. "I was paid less and had to work harder," she remarked.[14] Nonetheless, by 1958, Kuh's achievements were so notable that following the resignation of Rich, who assumed the directorship of the Worcester Art Museum, rumors flew that she would be named the Art Institute's next director. Instead, the following year, she left for New York to write about art and artists for *Saturday Review*, a role she thought of as educational: "I tried to be . . . a bridge between our readers and the works of art that I enjoyed and that I wanted them to look at and understand."[15] In addition to her regular columns in the magazine, she authored several books and became a leader in yet another area: corporate collecting. Beginning in 1968, Kuh formed a collection for the First National Bank of Chicago, which had an impact on the subsequent collecting of other major American corporate organizations in the 1970s and 1980s.

In the years following the close of the Gallery of Art Interpretation, the innovative educational ideas and techniques central to it became a standard for many museums. While a number of Kuh's methods have been superseded by sophisticated, interactive technology and her modernist concepts by more pluralistic thinking, much of her approach and educational philosophy is clearly relevant over four decades later. The gallery's integration of mediums was an early manifestation of an approach that is currently being used in American art museums, which have become far less rigid and hierarchical in their installations. In our age, so glutted by information that much of it becomes meaningless, Kuh's goal—to eliminate in order to clarify—is a particularly meaningful challenge. The anxious political climate that fueled Kuh's crusade for modernism is not unfamiliar now, when in the 1980s and 1990s the rights of artists to freedom of expression have again been questioned. The legacy of Kuh's mission, which she carried out in all her activities with passion and perspective, is to involve the broadest possible public in the art of all periods, places, and times, but most especially our own.

NOTES

1. This chapter is adopted from Susan F. Rossen and Charlotte Moser, "Primer for Seeing: The Gallery for Art Interpretation and Katharine Kuh's Crusade for Modernism in Chicago," *The Art Institute of Chicago Museum Studies* 16, no. 1 (Spring 1990): 6–25, 88–90.

2. William McNaught, ed., "An Interview with Katharine Kuh," *Journal of the Archives of American Art* 27, no. 3 (1987): 3.

3. Rossen and Moser, 12–13.

4. Katharine Kuh, "Explaining Art Visually," *Museum* 1, nos. 3–4 (1948): 153.

5. Katharine Kuh, "Seeing Is Believing," *Bulletin of the Art Institute of Chicago* 39, no. 4 (April–May 1945): 53.

6. Ibid.

7. Letter from Katharine Kuh to Margit Varda, art editor, *Life*, May 9, 1946, the Art Institute of Chicago Archives.

8. Walter Trohan, "Reds Corrupt American Art, House Is Told: Chicago Director Hit by Dondero," *Chicago Tribune*, August 17, 1949.

9. The Chicago critic was Copeland C. Burg, "Kathryn (*sic*) Kuh Display Interprets Van Gogh," *Chicago Herald-American*, February 13, 1950; "Interpreter Kuh," *Newsweek*, February 25, 1952.

10. Grace L. McCann Morley, "Museum Trends: Exhibitions," *Art in America* 34, no. 4 (October 1946): 204.

11. Katharine Kuh, *Art Has Many Faces, the Nature of Art Presented Visually* (New York: Harper and Row, 1951), xi.

12. Churchill P. Lathrop, review of *Art Has Many Faces*, Archives of American Art, Kuh Papers, no. 2226, fr. 1319, without an identified source.

13. Joshua Taylor, *Learning to Look* (Chicago: University of Chicago Press, 1957; 2d ed., 1981). *What Is Modern Painting?* Introductory Series to Modern Arts 2 (New York: Museum of Modern Art, 1943) was reprinted eleven times over the next forty years and appeared as well in Japanese, Portuguese, and Spanish.

14. Interview with Kuh, New York, November 24, 1992. Kuh pointed out that she was never treated unfairly by artists or dealers, who welcomed her interest in them.

15. Avis Berman, interview with Kuh, *Archives of American Art*, November 10, 1982 (not publically available).

WORKS BY KATHARINE KUH

"Explaining Art Visually," *Museum* 1, nos. 3–4 (1948): 148–55.

"Vincent Van Gogh," *Museum* 3, no. 4 (1950): 272–74.

Art Has Many Faces, the Nature of Art Presented Visually. New York: Harper and Row, 1951.

Léger. Champaign-Urbana, IL: University of Illinois Press, 1953.

Columns in *Saturday Review*, 1959–early 1970s.

The Artist's Voice; Talks with Seventeen Artists. New York: Harper and Row, 1962.

Break Up: The Core of Modern Art. Greenwich, CT: New York Graphic Society, 1965.

The Open Eye: In Pursuit of Art. New York: Harper and Row, 1971.

WORKS ABOUT KATHARINE KUH

Berman, Avis. "The Katharine Kuh Gallery: An Informal Portrait." In Sue Ann Prince, ed., *The Old Guard and the Avant-Garde: Modernism in Chicago 1910–1940*, 155–69. Chicago: University of Chicago Press, 1990.

McNaught, William, ed. "An Interview with Katharine Kuh" (conducted by Avis Berman). *Journal of the Archives of American Art* 27, no. 3 (1987): 2–36.

Rossen, Susan F., and Charlotte Moser. "Primer for Seeing: The Gallery for Art Interpretation and Katharine Kuh's Crusade for Modernism in Chicago." *The Art Institute of Chicago Museum Studies* 16, no. 1 (Spring 1990): 6–25, 88–90.

Lucy Craft Laney

Jane Bernard-Powers

When Lucy Craft Laney (1854–1933) died, thousands attended her funeral, according to the *Augusta* (Georgia) *Chronicle*. Laney was an African American from Georgia who founded the Haines Normal and Industrial Institute in Augusta, Georgia, in 1896. The school was one of a handful of African-American institutions that developed national reputations in the progressive era. Her life spanned a remarkable period in American history—the Civil War through the early depression years. While a main focus of her life's work was formal education, her leadership extended into her local community, Augusta, Georgia, and into national circles of African- American women. Lucy Craft Laney's leadership in the African-American community grew out of the complex issues that faced African Americans in the years following the Civil War. Education, employment, health, institution building, and racism were among the challenges taken on by Laney in her career. Named by Georgia's governor Jimmy Carter as "one of the first three outstanding Georgia Negroes," she was a leader in interracial relations and a powerful role model for her contemporaries.

Lucy Craft Laney's life choices and opportunities were undoubtedly enhanced by her parents, who survived slavery to become leaders in their Macon, Georgia, community, where she was born in 1854. The advantages that her family afforded her, specifically, education and institutional support from the Presbyterian church, were mainstays and stepping-stones to her community work and career. Her mother, Louisa Laney, was taught to read by the Campbell family who had purchased her. When David Laney bought her freedom, she continued to work for the Campbell family, who helped Louisa to educate Lucy. They helped Lucy learn to read and write and were instrumental in sending her to secondary school and then to Atlanta University, where she proved to be an outstanding student. She graduated in 1873 and went on to do course work at the University of Chicago during summers. Education for a young black woman in the post–Civil War South provided a powerful advantage because it led to teaching, which was a high-status position for young women. In the case of Lucy Craft Laney it led not only to teaching, but to school administration and community leadership as well. Moreover, the value of education that her mother apparently taught her became the mainstay of her philosophy.

In addition to enjoying the advantages afforded by an education, Lucy Craft Laney had in her father a powerful role model. David Laney was a master carpenter who bought his own freedom and moved to Macon, Georgia, before the Civil War. He was characterized by A. C. Griggs, pastor of the Haines School, which Laney started, as a man who would not accept racial injustice, which suggests that he negotiated some difficult situations in the Reconstruction South. David Laney was also a prominent Presbyterian minister, "one of the most outstanding Negroes in Macon," and parenthetically the "one who rang the bell of the Washington Avenue Presbyterian Church" to announce emancipation.[1] He left Lucy with a source of spiritual strength and a significant source of institutional support. The Presbyterian church provided moral and financial support for Lucy Laney in the founding and maintenance of her school.

Lucy Laney's life blueprint included a close relationship with Christianity, an important dimension of her teaching and leadership in Augusta and elsewhere. She established a church on the Haines campus, employed a pastor for the church and the school, and included chapel in the daily life of Haines's students.

Absent specific reflections by Lucy Craft Laney, we can assume there were significant legacies from her parents. Laney benefited from her parents' resourcefulness, their stamina, their courage, their intellect, and their ability to negotiate issues of race. She was clearly privileged and part of an elite group of African-American women who were socially and economically able to concern themselves with a national agenda for African-American women in the progressive era, an agenda that focused on education as a critical means for "racial uplift."

Dorothy Sterling, editor of *We Are Your Sisters*, characterized Lucy Laney's school as a "beacon" for black southerners. In the founding of the school Laney was responding to the critical need for basic education in the Augusta community. In the school's growth and development she provided an academy of leadership for talented African-American youth, she nurtured organization, development, and other leadership skills among faculty such as Mary McCrorey Jackson and Mary McLeod Bethune, and she expanded the vocational curriculum to include nursing and kindergarten work.

Haines was started by Lucy Laney following her graduation from Atlanta University in 1873 and ten years of teaching in Macon, Milledgeville, Savannah, and Augusta. One account of the founding of the school says that she "was stirred by an editorial in the Savannah morning paper and decided to return to Augusta and yield to the request of her friends to open a mission school."[2] Another account written by A. C. Griggs, the Haines pastor and administrator, suggests that a representative of the Board of Freedmen, Reverend R. H. Allen, persuaded her to return to Augusta to do mission work for the church. She was, in any case, an educated and known member of the African-American community in Georgia who was urged to exercise some leadership in education and who felt the need to serve "her people." With the reputation and support of her family, a growing network of friends, and moral support from the Presbyterian Board of Missions, she started the Haines Normal and Industrial Institute. She began with five children in 1883 in the basement of Christ Presbyterian Church. By the second year the enrollment had grown to 234, and three years later the school was chartered as a normal and industrial school under the law of Georgia.

Laney originally intended the school to be for young women because she believed that women were the key to changing the quality of life for African Americans, but when her clients showed up at the door, they were both male and female. As the golden jubilee booklet characterized it, "She granted them [boys] permission to stay." The school took on boarders very early in its history and expanded the facilities, the faculty, the curriculum, and the reputation of the school over the years.

This somewhat courageous venture was successful for a number of reasons. First, the decline of public support for black education created a serious need for schools. Following the influx of American Missionary Association teachers in the post-war south and the expansion of education for African Americans (1866–1877), a reverse trend developed when state and local support for education was eroded, along with other protections provided by Reconstruction. African Americans were hungry for education, and schools in urban communities such as Augusta became "the beacons" that Sterling referred to.

A second factor in the success of the school was Lucy Laney's enterprising instincts and her ability to build a broad base of support. It is difficult to tell from the available sources where she learned to do fund-raising, yet it is clear that this was one of her strengths. In the third year of the school's existence, on the advice of a local Presbyterian pastor, she traveled to Minneapolis to the General Assembly of the Presbyterian church on a one-way ticket. This fund-raising trip did not yield much more than notes of appreciation and a ticket back home. However, she met Francine E. Haines of Milwaukee, the president of the Women's Executive Committee of Home Missions, who became a significant benefactor of the school. Haines donated the money to purchase land that led to the first permanent building of the school. Subsequently the Board of Missions granted money to the school when it became evident that it was going to succeed. Fund-raising was a challenge that Laney had to face for as long as she was alive, but it was evidently something that she became good at. An article in the *Augusta Chronicle* detailing her accomplishments on the event of her death mentioned the many trips that she made to northern cities to raise money. The campus was built on sizable endowments, including some made by alumni.

Accounts of the early days of Haines that serve as tributes to Lucy Laney's strength of character and resolve never fail to mention three catastrophic events in the school's history. There was a serious flood in the earliest days of the school, when "Miss Laney, Miss Freeman [her head teacher], and the children were marooned;" a typhoid fever epidemic that caused the death of Miss Freeman; and a fire.³ Laney's ability to overcome these major reversals, especially the loss of Freeman, who had been a major source of emotional support, contributed to her heroic stature in her community.

Lucy Craft Laney's philosophy of education was a delicate blend of African Americans' progressive feminism, W.E.B. Du Bois's academic vision, and Booker T. Washington's pragmatism. In a paper entitled "The Burden of the Educated Colored Woman," read at the Hampton Negro Conference in 1899, Laney outlined her central goals for women's education. She believed that women were the keystone to racial uplift and that education was the structure that would facilitate the uplifting. Well-educated women would help to eliminate the effects of ignorance and immorality in the African-American community by teaching children, young adults, and adults right living and specific habits of thrift, sanitation, and domestic skills. As she expressed it in her speech, "We would prescribe: homes—better homes, clean homes, pure homes; schools—better schools; more culture; more thrift; and work in large doses."⁴

In addition to teaching and modeling good Christian leadership and domestic skills, however, schooling was to challenge racism and to provide education for vocations. She differed with Booker T. Washington about which vocations African Americans should be trained for, arguing that they should be educated for teaching college students as well as elementary school children and that education for the professions was also within African Americans' grasp. Many of Haines's students went on to pursue college degrees and professional degrees, as is indicated in the golden jubilee listings of graduates and outstanding alumni.

The development of Haines's curriculum reflected Lucy Laney's pragmatic philosophy of tying the social and educational needs of African Americans in Augusta to the curriculum. She was a proponent of kindergarten education and thus established a kindergarten on the Haines campus in the late 1890s, along with a program to train kindergarten teachers. The consequences of increasing segregation in municipal facilities meant that the health needs of African Americans were being neglected in Augusta and elsewhere. Thus Laney set up a nursing education program at Haines by "pursuading a white graduate nurse from Canada" to join the Haines faculty.⁵ This program eventually was incorporated into Augusta's University Hospital. Laney's vision of African-American education that she translated into programs was fueled by her belief in continuing education—she both provided and took advantage of advanced work in education—and her ability to find resources to meet a need.

She was also a remarkable community education advocate. Given the lack of a community center for African Americans in Augusta, she opened the buildings and the grounds to social, cultural, and civic events. According to accounts provided by her niece, Margaret Laney, Lucy Laney invited nationally known artists such as Marion Anderson and Frederick Douglass's nephew, a violinist, to perform on the campus for students and the community in general.[6]

Lucy Laney's philosophy of racial uplift and service to the community extended to faculty relations as well. In particular, her assistant principal, Mary Jackson (later Mary Jackson-McCrorey), who worked with her for twenty years, became a colleague in national African-American feminist causes. Mary McLeod Bethune, future founder of Bethune College, taught at the Haines Institute early in her career, and she also joined the sisterhood of talented African-American women who were dedicated to "racial uplift," as they characterized it. Laney instilled in her students and her colleagues a sense of mission for "her people."

The vision and energy that Lucy Craft Laney brought to education and Haines were evident in her community activities as well. As a well-educated, articulate member of an elite group of African-American women, she was sought after as a speaker and organizer. For example, the health of southern African Americans was an issue that received considerable attention in the black community and in Atlanta and concerned Laney. She spoke to a conference sponsored by the Atlanta Neighborhood Union on "Mortality Among Negroes in Cities," citing the appalling conditions in which some blacks lived. Parenthetically, she also engaged in some finger pointing at the victims of the circumstances while she was decrying the circumstances. She was a firm believer in the tough-backbone approach to problems and believed that African Americans had to help themselves.

Lucy Laney's father had a reputation for standing up to racial injustice in Macon, and Lucy apparently followed in her father's footsteps. "Lucy Laney never toadies. She may have to hold her tongue, but she does not pretend to acquiescence in what she believes to be wrong," wrote a biographer in 1927.[7]

In a period that produced setbacks for African Americans, including the *Plessy v. Ferguson* Supreme Court case; lynchings; and federal, state, and local authorities who were reluctant to spend money on education for African Americans, the courage that women demonstrated in speaking out against racism seems remarkable. Nonetheless, Lucy Laney, together with Margaret McCrorey, Lugenia Burns Hope, and Charlotte Brown, took on the challenge of trying to change Young Women's Christian Association (YWCA) segregationist policies in the early 1920s. The event that precipitated overt challenges to racism in the YWCA was Lugenia Burns Hope's move to establish a branch in a black neighborhood of Atlanta, Georgia. The issue that was being challenged vis-à-vis the Phyllis Wheatley Branch of the YWCA was the authority of black women to make decisions apart from the white, southern, female leadership. According to national YWCA policy, decisions could not be made without the approval of the white leadership. Struggles between the local African-American leadership and the white field supervisor of "colored work" in the South led to the demise of the project and a public demand by Hope, McCrorey, and Laney for racial policy clarification and changes. This powerful group of black women drafted an appeal that Laney and Hope were to deliver to the national board. According to C. Neverdon-Morton's account of the issue, Laney and others met with the board on July 3, 1920, and presented a statement "on behalf of 30,000 Black women of the south," demanding the recognition of leadership for black women, the right to establish independent branches for blacks, and the appropriate employment of black secretaries from the National Office in the South.[8] The outcome of this action, according to Paula Giddings's historical account, was that the "efforts of Black women were ignored" and the minutes did not reflect the demands made. While an interracial conference held early in 1921 in Louisville addressed some of the concerns, it was not until 1946 that the organization took serious action to fully integrate African-American women into the association.[9]

What seems evident about Lucy Laney was not only that she was courageous, along with some of her prominent sisterhood, but that she was willing to work with organizations that discriminated against African Americans in the interest of changing policy and practice.

Lucy Craft Laney was a woman of remarkable stature in the African-American community. W. E. B. Du Bois described her as "the dark vestal virgin who kept the fires of Negro education fiercely flaming in the rich but mean-spirited city of Augusta, Georgia."[10] She has also been called the most important female black educator of the progressive era. In an era that celebrated African-American women's desire to serve and uplift their communities, Laney assumed heroic proportion. Her contributions to the education of African Americans; her ability to mentor women such as Mary McLeod Bethune, Janie Porter Barrett, and Charlotte Brown Hawkins, who went on to establish their own schools; and her willingness to build and sustain the network of African-American educators assure her a place among the most important women in education in the twentieth century.

NOTES

1. Augustus C. Griggs, "Lucy Craft Laney," *Journal of Negro History* 19 (1934): 97–102.

2. *Haines Golden Jubilee Booklet* (Augusta, GA: Historic Augusta, 1936), 36.

3. Ibid.

    4. Bert James Loewenberg and Ruth Bogin, *Black Women in Nineteenth-Century American Life: Their Worlds, Their Thoughts, Their Feelings* (University Park, PA: Pennsylvania State University Press, 1976).

    5. *The Augusta News-Review*, 1976, 8.

    6. Cynthia Neverdon-Morton, *Afro-American Women of the South and the Advancement of the Race, 1895–1925* (Knoxville: University of Tennessee Press, 1989), 229.

    7. Mary White Ovington, *Portraits of Color*, cited by Sadie Daniel St. Clair, "Lucy Craft Laney," in E. T. James, ed., *Notable American Women* (Cambridge: Harvard University Press, 1971), 366.

    8. Neverdon-Morton, 213–17.

    9. Paula Giddings, *When and Where I Enter* (New York: W. Morrow, 1985), 156–58.

    10. W.E.B. Du Bois, quoted in Beverly Guy-Sheftall, *Daughters of Sorrow, Attitudes Toward Black Women, 1880–1920* (Brooklyn: Carlson, 1990), 35.

WORKS BY LUCY CRAFT LANEY

"Mortality Among Negroes in Cities." Unpublished Remarks, 1896, Historic Augusta Incorporated, Augusta, GA.
"The Burden of the Educated Colored Woman." Paper read at the Hampton Negro Conference No. 3, July 1899.

WORKS ABOUT LUCY CRAFT LANEY

Griggs, Augustus C. "Lucy Craft Laney." *Journal of Negro History* 19 (1934): 97–102.
Guy-Sheftall, Beverly. *Daughters of Sorrow, Attitudes Toward Black Women, 1880–1920*. Brooklyn: Carlson, 1990.
Hine, Darlene Clark, ed. *Black Women in United States History*. Vols. 1-4. Brooklyn: Carlson, 1990.
James, Edward T., Janet Wilson James, and Paul Boyer, eds. *Notable American Women*. Cambridge, MA: Belknap Press of Harvard University Press, 1971.
Nobel, Jeanne. *Beautiful Also Are the Souls of My Black Sisters*. Englewood Cliffs, NJ: Prentice-Hall, 1978.
Smith, J. Carney. ed. *Notable Black American Women*. Detroit: Gold, 1990.

Mary Atkins Lynch

Rita S. Saslaw

Mary Atkins Lynch (1819–1882) has been called the Mary Lyon of the West and at the same time one of the most individual educators of women in western America. Atkins is often credited with the founding of the forerunner of Mills College for Women in California, Benicia Seminary, but her ideas on education are virtually unknown. Mary Atkins did indeed act as an eastern educational missionary to frontier California, where she promoted Protestant educational ideals born of her New England cultural heritage. She is best described by one of her former students: "Stern and unyielding when occasion required, at other times gentle and loving in the highest degree, sympathizing with us all in our personal sorrows, and inculcating a spirit of patriotism that nothing could alter."[1]

Mary Atkins Lynch was born in Jefferson, Ohio, on July 7, 1819. She was one of twelve children, ten of whom, one son and nine daughters, lived to maturity. The family home in Jefferson was described as one of culture and service. Her parents, Sarah Wright and Quintius Flaminious Atkins, were descended from early Connecticut settlers of some importance. Her father's paternal family owned the first mill in Wolcott, Connecticut, and his mother, Mary Gillett, was a well-educated woman who was the sister of the first minister of the town. Sarah Wright Atkins, Mary Atkins's mother, was also from a prominent family. Her father, Captain John Wright, was one of the first two settlers in Ashtabula County, Ohio, and he delivered the mail through the wilderness on the Cleveland to Detroit route.

Quintius Atkins was an adventurer both before and after 1804, when he married Sarah Wright. In 1798, when he was only seventeen years old, he enlisted in the war against the French and, in 1802, in the spirit of adventure, joined a group going to the wilderness in the Connecticut Western Reserve. Only two families predated his settlement on a farm site in Ashtabula

County, Ohio, and one was the family of his future wife. The life of adventure did not stop with marriage as the new family, Quintius, Sarah, and one daughter, set off to serve as missionaries to the Wyandotte Indians in Sandusky, Ohio. Forced to leave the mission in 1807 because of illness, Atkins continued a life of public service. He was in the infantry during the War of 1812 and was elected sheriff and later appointed judge in Ohio. His honor became well known when he was unsuccessful in an Ohio canal-building venture and forfeited his own property to cover the loss. Quintius Atkins was known to be a man of "honor and love" with "vigorous bodily and mental powers," often supporting causes, such as abolition, whether they were popular or not. Through Quintius Atkins's biographer, we know only that Sarah Atkins "was amiable and much respected."[2] Based upon this family history, Mary Atkins was indeed born into a cultured home that valued Presbyterian religious belief and education while encouraging the spirit of adventure and independence.

Atkins's early education took place at home. She went on to attend public schools in the Ohio Western Reserve and for one year the Huron Institute in Milan, Ohio. In 1836, because of her father's financial reverses, the family moved to New York, where he had a new position. Atkins continued her education and began a teaching career that lasted for forty-six years. Atkins, apparently not satisfied with her own level of education, returned to Ohio in 1844 and enrolled in the third year of the Ladies Course of Oberlin College. While at Oberlin, she was further embued with a religious missionary spirit and in 1844 formally became a Presbyterian. While a student at Oberlin, she was also a member of the Ladies Literary Society at the same time as the more famous Lucy Stone. She was a member of the Moral Reform Society. This spirit, which later took her first to Panama and then to California, began in the Atkins family and was further nurtured by her years at Oberlin and her friendship with the college president, Charles G. Finney. In a letter written years later, she reflected upon this exposure: "Every moment I am thankful for the visit at your house, and particularly for the privilege of hearing you read, talk, and pray."[3]

Atkins graduated from the Oberlin Ladies Course with distinction in 1845 at the age of twenty-six. Her commencement exercise was entitled "The Self- Mindful and Self-Forgettable Man." The college later gave her further recognition in 1877 with the award of an honorary master's degree. After leaving the college, she taught in Portville, Cuba, and Warsaw, New York. In just one year, she returned to Oberlin to become the assistant principal of the Ladies Literary Course. Atkins seriously considered foreign missionary work in Siam, but her father persuaded her to remain in Oberlin. She left this position in 1848 to become the principal of the Female Department of the high school in Columbus, and in 1849 she briefly worked as an assistant teacher in Dr. Lord's school in Columbus, Ohio. From 1850 to 1853 she moved to the position of principal of the Female Department of Hughes

High School in Cincinnati. In this position, Atkins was known to have received an unusually high salary for a woman.

Atkins was considered a woman of stature, as she was five feet seven inches tall. Her oval face was framed in straight brown hair, and her blue eyes were "level and direct."[4] While in Cincinnati, she became engaged to an engineer, who was sent to Panama and died there. Disturbed by poor health, the death of her fiancé, and a restlessness inherited from her father, Atkins corresponded with some businessmen in Benicia, California, about a school for girls that had just been founded in 1852. Atkins sailed from New York City to the Isthmus of Panama, hoping to see the grave of her fiancé. Here a radical change took place in her life when she decided to make the trip to the San Francisco area and the school in Benicia.

A letter written by Edwin A. Sherman to Susan Tolman Mills, the founder of Mills College, described California as Atkins found it. Sherman also described the trip that they both made from Panama to California. Sherman was returning to California from a visit to Boston, and Atkins was setting out on the first adventure of her lifetime. California, according to Sherman, was all young men, and, therefore, everyone laughed at the idea of founding a "female seminary." "Women," he said, "in those days in San Francisco and other places, were as scarce as doves' teeth."[5] Women indeed were less than 10 percent of the population of California, but this did not deter Atkins. The people of Benicia, California, where she was going, did not laugh at the idea of schools for girls. Atkins was fortunate to have a traveling companion, Sarah Pellet, another Oberlin student, who was headed to California to preach temperance.

The trip was not without travail, and Sherman described the problems and the two women in detail. They were dressed in "brown linen bloomers" for the trip by mule across the isthmus. They rode all night in the rain and arrived on the other side looking like "slim clothes pins in wet rags." He revived them both, Atkins and the temperance lecturer, with a drink of cognac. Sherman also remembered giving Atkins the sage advice to discard her unladylike bloomers when she arrived in California. In his letter, Sherman also recounted the counsel he gave that she would not succeed on her own in forming a school but that she should contact a man in Benicia who would help her. Sherman agreed to write to this gentleman on her behalf.[6] While this account differs from others stating that she had made contact before she left, both could be true, and Sherman could have helped her make contact.

Atkins's first impression of California also is preserved through a secondhand account, albeit a reliable one. "Benicia is all that I could wish . . . quiet almost to silence, beautiful as a picture, and healthy as the Garden of Eden."[7] Atkins's father repeated her description and also his advice that she not be discouraged with her low pay or the need to travel to the mining towns to recruit students to support the school and her educational ideas. He also encouraged her to continue to write, a career that Atkins must have abandoned, as there is no further evidence of her life as an author. "Write, my daughter, without fear! . . . How can you know your strength until you make trial of it?"[8] There is, however, a record of her long career as an educator and as a person who constantly tested her strength.

The town of Benicia was briefly the capital of California. The public schools came slowly to California, and Benicia Seminary, one of several schools in the town, was founded in 1852 to serve the small Protestant population. The trustees ran the school for the first two years, hiring Mary Atkins as principal in 1854. She remained there with the exception of one year, 1863, until 1865. The town and the school had easy access to the towns of San Francisco, Sacramento, and Stockton, but as noted in her father's letters, recruiting students from scattered areas and balancing a budget were tasks that called on her greatest abilities. So difficult was the task that her father begged her to return home after four years on the job. His fatherly concern dealt with many aspects of her life, even about her dress, asking if she wore crinoline, hoops, stays, and jewelry.[9] Fortunately she did not honor his request that she return home, and she stayed on in California to develop her school, which she bought outright in 1865 from the founders.

Atkins purchased a house that was remodeled for the school. She was totally responsible for all aspects of the management of Benicia Seminary, and she took this responsibility very seriously. Her objective was to take the relatively uncultured girls of California and "train healthy, companionable, self-reliant women, those prepared to be useful and acceptable in this school, in the family, and in society." It was most important that they meet the following standard: "All ladies should be able to spell correctly, to read naturally, to write legibly, and to converse intelligently; and therefore give unremitting attention to orthography, reading, writing, English grammar, geography, and the history of the United States."[10] Mary Atkins wished to build a school that would reflect her cultural background with a moral tone and intellectual level that would be superior to those of any other school on the West Coast. She also included daily gymnastics, facilities for bathing, beautiful grounds, and wholesome food because of her lifetime concern for the physical welfare of her students. She intended that the skills acquired would last for their lifetimes.

The central thesis of Mary Atkins's educational plan was self-discipline. She trained the young women in this self-discipline through multiple means, one of which was a daily fifteen-minute inspirational, character-building talk that contained words of praise, advice, and censure. In order to sing and pray, students also attended church each Sunday, sitting where they could not be seen by the young men. They also each observed a well-remembered "Sunday still hour," which was never to be violated; each young woman was to reflect upon her own behavior. "More than all, have the years shown me the wisdom of requiring us to observe a season of physical and mental retirement and quiet."[11]

An important part of the self-discipline was the keeping of a daily diary. Each student recorded her punctuality, deportment, lessons, and faithfulness. Here, Atkins showed concern for another educational principle, as this diary was occasionally sent home for the parents to read in order to create a "bond between principal, teachers, parents, and pupils." This activity emphasized self-discipline, and "all were proud to keep truthfully, for truth was her [Atkins's] watchword."[12] This education built character with great effort on the part of the teacher and student. Even Mary's father wrote that he thought the three-year program was very demanding.

Atkins early recruited the students and their parents to work together on the task of education. Student reminiscences and a letter written by Atkins to parents outlined the educational goals for each. To the parents she gave the task of choosing an appropriate school and the understanding that they had to allow teachers to do what they knew best, educate and discipline. While parents were invited to visit the classes, they were told to "wisely judge that those whose mind and heart were given to this one thing know best; and they have confidence in them, as Christian people, that what they know is best."[13]

Mary Atkins further cautioned parents to ignore frequent complaints from their children, who tended to exaggerate problems, and she further advised them not to indulge these young women with trips home or too much spending money. This advice might seem cruel in more permissive times, but Atkins felt that "teachers must feel, the child must know that the delegation, while it lasts, is unreserving."[14] Atkins's character, at times sympathetic and understanding, could also appear stern and cruel to her students: "To this day I can recall every lineament of her face, as well as her commanding figure and presence. But I was then altogether too young to appreciate this noble woman—nobly planned; nor did I ever outgrow my fear of her."[15] The personal and student control Atkins practiced assisted her in building a school that was held in esteem throughout the state of California.

School practice did not differ greatly from the activities that existed in eastern schools. The academic year consisted of two sessions of five months each with a brief Christmas holiday. The following costs were incurred by the students:

Tuition, lights, and washing	$340.00
Music	100.00
Ancient and modern language	40.00
Drawing and crayoning	60.00
Painting	80.00

Public examinations, lasting three days, were held twice a year and in culturally barren California were well attended. In this examination, each student stood and gave a lecture. The instructor interrupted to ask questions and correct misstatements or errors. A reporter viewing the examination noted that one of the teachers looked narrowly at the act of teaching but that in general, "they were sharp as needles, teacher and taught, as bright and as nimble."[16]

In their classes, students studied thoroughly until the material was absorbed. In a large classroom reserved for recitation, with teacher supervision, each student was required to recite complete lessons, "without questions, and/or suggestion, as to what came next."[17] The studies in the English course lasted three to five years and included the ornamental branches such as instrumental music, drawing, painting, and needlework. One difference from other schools was the heavy emphasis on gymnastics. The young women, dressed in bloomers, carried dumbbells and marched to music. This exercise lasted for forty-five minutes each weekday. The 900 books in the library included Dickens, Cooper, and Thackeray, as well as bound copies of student compositions, but former students commented that much of what they learned was not found in books but was learned from, and attributed to the personality of, Mary Atkins.

A student reminisced that from Atkins she had received "that which money could not buy, namely, inspiration, also a knowledge of what constitutes education."[18] This education included much more than current knowledge, moral development, and inspiration. As stated earlier, Atkins exhibited great concern for physical well-being and conducted health walks on the beautiful grounds of Benicia. Other physical activity took place in the music room at the school. A sewing hour was held there every Saturday morning, but more important, the room was used to learn and practice polite behavior and the "courtesies and formal etiquette of good society." One period at the end of each day was held in this room, where students were allowed to practice "music, dancing, and social intercourse. Here youth and exuberant life held sway."[19]

Atkins was known to laugh at herself and to be the author of many jokes; students often commented on the fun they had in the school. Atkins was also known for her bravery. One student remembered an evening when she turned away an intruder by shooting at him. She required all to eat every bite of the ample food served once it had been put on their plates. "Her manner was dignified, yes even stern, and one look from her keen gray eyes seemed to read me through and through."[20] She was known to confiscate sweets and then to warn parents about the evil of supplying this kind of food for their daughters. Though students remembered her stern rules, the most frequent comments always dealt with her understanding, concern, and fairness. None remembered her as a severe disciplinarian; rather, they recalled her "heart-to-heart talks" and the standard that she set as an ideal woman.

She had great personal charm, a clear vision, a broad outlook and lofty ideals. She had, in addition, that which gave her power, a sympathetic understanding of girl nature. This won for her immediately the love and cooperation of her students. She saw that the work she had undertaken was not one of mere educational supervision— that the call had come to her from the fathers and the mothers of the mining camps, the mountain hamlets, the arid desert towns, from every far-away settlement within the confines of this vast state. It was a call for help from the sturdy pioneers who were struggling with untold problems. It said, "Take our daughters, prepare them for the work awaiting them in the home, in the school room, in church affairs; make of them useful, progressive, intelligent women." She realized the responsibility and assumed it. "Character," she seemed to say, "must be the foundation of those who would build character before all else, and my girls are to be builders. With it must be intelligent growth that produces clear thinking. Experience and time will complete the structure." In this way, she reasoned, and once entered upon her task she never faltered.[21]

In 1863, Benicia Seminary was on sound financial footing and was well known throughout northern California. Mary Atkins decided to take a sabbatical trip to Hawaii, China, and Japan, leaving the school in the hands of Margaret Lamond. Perhaps the restlessness and missionary spirit of her youth had returned, and now a staunch Episcopalian, she set sail with a Baptist captain and his first mate. Her diary deals with her observations on geography, local customs, religious practice, and education. These accounts help to further confirm the image of a strong and opinionated woman. After attending a church service in Honolulu, she noted that these Episcopalians were barely reformed Catholics. To her they "seem more like Romanists than like Church people." Despite her concern for the Romish nature of the church, she felt that the missionaries had done well. "The natives are not as debased and degraded as I expected to see, and the community seems like an American people."[22] Atkins's teaching abilities were known in Hawaii, and she was asked to stay and teach at Punahou College. According to her own account, she resisted the temptation to stay and continued on her voyage.

The self-discipline exhibited by Atkins on her travels was typical of the manner in which she ran her school. She wrote that she read "a little poetry, a little French and have commenced the history of the Japanese."[23] Between bouts of seasickness she washed, starched, and ironed her handkerchiefs and collars. Always concerned about physical fitness, even at sea, she made certain that she slept for twelve hours each day.[24]

In many ways, the sailors became Mary Atkins's new students. She worried about the behavior of the first mate because he slept on his watch. This concern was undoubtedly tied to fear for her personal safety. The morals of the Baptist captain were also tested and after long discussions found to be satisfactory, and Atkins declared him to be a noble man. This was not true for the sailors, who swore too much, or Charlie Hare, a young fellow passenger, son of the ship's owner, who tried her patience sorely. Along with the above concerns, Atkins used her time at sea to study the work of the sailors. In her own words, "[The sailors] have helped make all the calculations from the observations, and am exceedingly anxious to know the reason of the work."[25]

Besides the adventure of travel on the high seas and seeing such exotic countries as Hawaii, Japan, and China, Atkins met the people who were to purchase Benicia Seminary and became the founders of Mills College. Cyrus and Susan Tolman Mills were missionaries on the island of Oahu and ran Punahou College in Honolulu. It was the Mills who requested that Mary Atkins remain in Hawaii. When she returned to Benicia, Atkins decided not to sell the school to Margaret Lamond, whom she had left in charge while she was on her sabbatical, and instead remained at Benicia to restore the school to the status that it held when she left. In 1865 she sold the school to the Mills, who had returned to the mainland for reasons of health. Mary Atkins realized $3,435 from this sale but left her school at a low point in its history. Many students and faculty had left with Lamond, and there were only ninety students and inexperienced teachers left in the once outstanding school. The Mills were able to return the school to a higher standard by increasing enrollment and bringing in three Mount Holyoke teachers. According to Atkins, Cyrus Mills was a "so-so" teacher, but he made all of his payments on time and moved her to tears "by his kindness when he came to San Francisco bringing her a present from her Benicia friends."[26] Mills sold Benicia Seminary in 1870 and founded the new school in Oakland that became the currently existing Mills College for Women. The story of Benicia Seminary continued, and in 1879 it was again purchased by Mary Atkins Lynch, but not until after she had returned to the East and married.

Atkins did not retire after selling Benicia but traveled to Europe, where her former teacher and friend, Charles Finney, arranged for her to meet his "Christian Friends." Finney described her successful teaching career and her visits to the Pacific missions, but the personal description is the most significant: "You will find her intelligent, frank, and trustworthy in all respects."[27] She then returned to Ohio, where she served as the principal of Central High School in Cleveland from September 1968 to March 1869. On March 29, 1869, she became the second wife of John Lynch, who was also a former Oberlin student. Her marriage ended her teaching career, but only temporarily.

John Lynch, a man of stature, was serving in the Ohio legislature as a state senator and was also a member of the Ohio Constitutional Convention. He was born a Roman Catholic in Ireland on February 1, 1825. He moved to Oberlin in 1846 and received his A.B. degree in 1851 and his M.A. degree in 1869. He, too, was greatly influenced by Finney, and renounced Catholicism in 1844, he said, after hearing Finney's powerful seminar: "It seems hard business for me to write. This is Easter Sunday. Oh, how I ought to rejoice for my deliverance from Roman superstition. My heart is cold. I feel wretched in view of my sins. I must try to be a more faithful servant."[28]

While a student at Oberlin, Lynch taught. He probably taught in the Prep School, where he taught girls, but was not pleased with the arrangements. He served in the Civil War and was an Ohio school supervisor. He also served in Louisiana in the Reconstruction government. After their marriage, the couple moved to New Orleans, where they lived for six years, and then moved to Philadelphia in 1876, where Lynch was the state commissioner to the Centennial Celebration. Their final move was to Santa Barbara, California, in 1877.

In 1879, Mary Atkins Lynch again bought Benicia Seminary and again became the principal. Calling on his teaching experience at Oberlin, John Lynch helped her with the teaching but in 1878 returned to the law and opened an office in Benicia. Under her direction, the school again experienced a rebirth, with increased enrollment and students coming from as far away as San Diego.

Both Mary and John Lynch worked until the time of their deaths, she on September 14, 1882, and he on June 14, 1900. She was buried in a pioneer cemetery, her gravestone marked with the following epitaph: "Solid blocks of pure marble best represent her."[29] In retrospect, a former student described her as a "sculptor chiseling the character of California womanhood from the primitive marble until then untouched."[30] There is no doubt that this little-known woman left a legacy in the West that could be compared with the work of Mary Lyon and Catharine Beecher in the East. It is most unfortunate that she is known mainly for the founding of the forerunner of Mills College for Women and not for her long career, shaped by her unusual personal strength and character.

NOTES

1. *Reminiscences of Young Ladies Seminary, Benicia* (Benicia students, typewritten), Mills College Library, 1920(?), 77.

2. Harvey R. Gaylord, *Biography of Quintus Flaminius Atkins*, (handwritten), 1876, Western Reserve Historical Society, MSS 2018.

3. Letter to C. G. Finney, June 20, 1867, Oberlin Archives, Finney Papers, Box 1, Folder 8.

4. Edward T. James, ed., *Notable American Women, 1607–1950*, Vol. I (Cambridge: Belknap Press of Harvard University Press, 1971), 66.

5. Letter from Edwin A. Sherman to Susan T. Mills, March 28, 1910, Oberlin Archives, Lynch Student File.

6. Ibid.

7. Mary Atkins, *The Diary of Mary Atkins, A Sabbatical in the Eighteen Sixties* (Oakland, CA: Eucalyptus Press, 1937), 2.

8. Ibid., 3.

9. Ibid.

10. Rosalind Keep, *Fourscore Years: A History of Mills College* (Oakland, CA: Mills College, 1931), 17.

11. *Reminiscences*, 56.

12. Ibid., 5.

13. *Catalogue, Young Ladies Seminary, Benicia College*, 1864, 21–23.

14. Ibid.

15. *Reminiscences*, 53.

16. Keep, 19–20.

17. *Reminiscences*, 54.

18. Ibid., 6.

19. Keep, 20.

20. Ibid., 31.

21. Ibid., 27–28.

22. Atkins, 13–14.

23. Ibid., 16.

24. Ibid., 30.

25. Ibid., 3.

26. Elias O. James, *The Story of Cyrus and Susan Mills* (Stanford, CA: Stanford University Press, 1953), 169–71.

27. Letter from C. G. Finney to friends in Europe, January 30, 1867, Bancroft Library Archives, University of California, Berkeley, Atkins Family Papers, Box 5.

28. John Lynch, handwritten diary, Oberlin College Archives, April 12, 1846.

29. James, 66.

30. "A Pioneer Daughter," *Oberlin Alumni Magazine* 28 (December 1931).

WORKS BY MARY ATKINS LYNCH

Catalogue, Young Ladies Seminary, Benicia, CA. Year ending June 1, 1864 (twelfth year).

The Diary of Mary Atkins: A Sabbatical in the Eighteen Sixties. Oakland, CA: Eucalyptus Press, 1987.

Atkins Family Papers, Bancroft Library, University of California, Berkeley.

WORKS ABOUT MARY ATKINS LYNCH

Gaylord, Harvey R. *Biography of Quintius Flaminious Atkins*. Q. F. Atkins Papers, Western Reserve Historical Society, MSS 2018.

Hosford, Frances. *Father Shiphard's Magna Carta: A Century of Coeducation in Oberlin College*. Boston: Marshall Jones, 1837.

James, Edward T., ed. *Notable American Women 1607–1950*. Vol. I. Cambridge: Belknap Press of Harvard University Press, 1971.

James, Elias Olan. *The Story of Cyrus and Susan Mills*. Stanford, CA: Stanford University Press, 1953.

Keep, Rosalind A. *Fourscore and Ten Years: A History of Mills College*. San Francisco: Taylor and Taylor, 1946.

"Notes of Scouting on Huron River and Sandusky Bay in the Autumn of 1812." Q. F. Atkins Papers, Western Reserve Historical Society, MSS 2018.

"A Pioneer Daughter." *Oberlin Alumni Magazine* 28 (December 1931).

"Recollections of the War of 1812–15." Q. F. Atkins Papers, Western Reserve Historical Society, MSS 2018.

"Reminiscences of Young Ladies Seminary, Benicia." Typewritten manuscript, Mills College Library Archives.

Student File, Mary Atkins Lynch. Oberlin College Library Archives.

Student File, John Lynch. Oberlin College Library Archives.

Mary Lyon

Susan McIntosh Lloyd

Mary Lyon (1797–1849) inherited one culture and ushered in another. Throughout her life, she held within her the joyous certainties and the terrifying questions that were her Puritan heritage. Yet she grew to womanhood in an age of experimentation: Americans were consciously seeking ways to build a virtuous and enduring republic, while new scientific knowledge was forcing the reformulation of human truths. Energized by her dual passion for saving souls and fitting young Americans for useful lives in a democratic society, Mary Lyon launched in 1837 the first fully endowed institution of higher education for young women: Mount Holyoke Seminary in South Hadley, Massachusetts. She raised funds from thousands of women and men, instead of relying on a few wealthy benefactors. During its twelve years under her leadership, Mount Holyoke offered to a skeptical public the best proof to date of women's ability to master college-level subjects. Its success inspired the founders of virtually every woman's college begun in the latter half of the nineteenth century.

Mary Lyon was born in 1797 and raised on a hill farm in Buckland, Massachusetts, between the Deerfield and Connecticut rivers. Some forty years earlier, her maternal great-grandfather, a disciple of Jonathan Edwards, had gathered his family to Buckland in a neighborhood of believers. Mary's father, Aaron Lyon, born in Sturbridge in 1757, joined this neighborhood as a boy. He married Jemima Shepard, seven years his junior, in 1784, soon after his long service in the revolutionary war and acquired his own farm, Mary's birthplace. As the fifth child in a family of six daughters and one son, Mary was early inducted into the daily routine of spinning, weaving, candle-making, and housework in which every farm girl was expected to share, but by her own account, she also lived a vigorous outdoor life. Her father's death when she was not quite six years old left her mother and elder brother to make the best of the one hundred rocky acres and the small herd of sheep and dairy cows. The Lyons continued to help needy neighbors, however, as well as tithing for their Baptist church, attending two Sabbath-day services every week.

Mary Lyon may have valued education in part because her own was hard to come by. Beginning at age four, she tagged along to a nearby school with her sisters. Her teachers could hardly keep up with her intense curiosity about the world, but when the school moved farther away, she could rarely attend. At home she shared all she had learned with anyone who would listen. This yen for warm, animated conversation was one aspect of Mary Lyon's gift for friendship, a gift that became crucial to her well-being as her family began to scatter. She was only thirteen when her mother remarried, leaving her as her brother's housekeeper on the farm. Nevertheless, she recalled later, "I would not let it make me unhappy."[1] She seems to have respected her mother's spiritual gifts and deeply to have loved and relied on her for thirty years more, just as she came to love her brother's wife and children. The farm was Mary's home base until she was twenty-two years old, when her brother packed his family into wagons and moved west to deeper soil.

When she was seventeen, Mary Lyon began her twenty-year career as a schoolteacher, earning the customary salary of 75 cents a week and "board round." Her first teaching was not altogether a success, for she often found herself too much amused by the antics of unruly pupils to maintain order in a roomful of thirty or forty children. She chided herself for her "mirthful tendencies" and her short supply of "natural dignity."[2] Yet these boisterous youngsters presented her a problem that would fascinate her throughout her career: how can young people be led to draw upon their inner sources of orderliness and energy? As she sought Christ's forgiveness for her own inner disorder and selfishness, her teaching was increasingly energized by her faith, until it became a ministry and a mission.

At age nineteen, Mary spent all her savings to pay for one term of education in "the higher branches" at the new Sanderson Academy in Ashfield and for board with an approved family nearby. Earnest academies such as Sanderson were nearly all begun by Calvinist-Evangelical Protestants bent on saving the souls of the young, but Mary was chiefly excited by Sanderson's intellectual challenge. Sleeping about four hours a night, rising in the dark to begin sixteen hours or more of studying and reciting by heart, she astonished her young teacher, Elijah Burritt, by her concentration and her keen grasp of geography, mathematics, and astronomy. Her classmates loved her for her frankness, her jollity, and her willingness to help others less able than she. When she ran out of money after one term, the Sanderson trustees voted to give her free tuition for a second. One of them, father of her classmate Amanda White, offered to board her among his eight children. She accepted this kindness, contributing to the family in return her entire store of homemade quilts and linens.

She also welcomed the tutelage provided by Amanda and her mother in fashionable ways of walking and dressing—even though the instruction could not entirely overcome the "defects in her manners" all too evident to her town-bred contemporaries, nor tame her energetic gait.[3] The White family was the first of several who became interested in Mary Lyon and counted it both a privilege and a Christian duty to help her. In 1818 she made a second crucial connection at the prestigious Amherst Academy, where she studied chemistry, rhetoric, and logic. Amherst's Female Department preceptress soon married the young geologist and botanist, Rev. Edward Hitchcock, later president of Amherst College. The couple became Mary Lyon's fast friends and tireless supporters.

Mary's brother moved away a few months later. It was a wrenching parting. Mary Lyon had no home of her own—nor even, very often, a room to herself—until she was nearly forty, when Mount Holyoke opened its doors. From 1819–1821, she taught school and "boarded round," gradually building the skills she would later pass on to hundreds of teachers and would-be teachers. Her developing pedagogy, innovative for its time, was importantly enriched in 1821 by her last long season of formal education: six months' attendance at Rev. Joseph Emerson's seminary for young women at Byfield in eastern Massachusetts.

Rev. Joseph Emerson offered Mary Lyon the confidence that young women could and should think logically, analyze, and dispute; should understand John Milton and Jonathan Edwards; should read Enlightenment authors such as Gibbon and Hume along with some of the precursors of Darwin (with fair warning that "these were the works of infidels"); should learn through questioning and discussion as well as by rote. She also absorbed Emerson's belief that the overriding purpose of education was spiritual, that knowledge should beget action, and that women as schoolteachers could carry out a special, holy mission to the young. For a while, book learning came first: friends saw Lyon "gaining knowledge by handfuls." But at Emerson's revival meetings, she also began to believe, as she put it to her students much later, that one should "study and teach nothing that cannot be made to help in the great work of converting the world to Christ."[4]

Through her late thirties, Mary Lyon was constantly assaulted by doubts of the worthiness of her own conversion: her passion for "human science" over "divine truth," her love of life and of all things living, seem to have convinced her that she was far too "earthly," possessed of a "strange, rebellious and wicked heart." Friends' accounts suggest nothing of this "rebellious, wicked heart," however, recording only that Lyon suffered a season of loneliness and depression at the time of her family's final dispersal in 1819. By her mid-twenties she had chosen her lifework, having refused at least one serious marriage proposal. From then on, she appeared only to grow in the sympathy and practicality that her way of teaching required of her.[5]

After Byfield, Mary Lyon spent three years as Sanderson Academy's first preceptress, taking time over holidays to study geology with Rev. Edward Hitchcock and attend Amos Eaton's lectures in chemistry and natural history at the new Amherst College. She kept in touch with Zilpah Polly Grant, a young teacher of awesome dignity and persuasiveness whom she had known as Rev. Joseph Emerson's chief assistant at Byfield. When Grant invited her in 1824 to become assistant principal at the newly endowed Adams Academy for young ladies in Derry, New Hampshire, she felt ready. She thus entered a ten-year partnership with this gifted, if hypochondriachal, woman.

At first, Mary Lyon's commitment to Grant's schools at Derry and (after 1828) at Ipswich, Massachusetts, involved only the thirty-week "summer" term. Back in Buckland, she began a ten-week winter school for older girls and young women. Through six years it prospered, its founding principal with it. She experimented with the Pestalozzi monitorial system she had helped to organize at Ipswich. She found herself fully able to urge her ninety students toward self-discipline through the Ipswich system of "self-reporting," a combination of daily or weekly public confession, imposed introspection and loving, shaming persuasion in the name of the Savior. She required students to pray or meditate for two "half-hours" each day. She conducted her first religious revivals in rhythm with the tumultuous public revival meetings held with increasing frequency in New England and New York State, but in her own self-effacing style: a "time for . . . mourning, solemnity and deep humiliation before God."[6]

Finally, a severe attack of typhoid fever made Mary Lyon realize how difficult it was to run the Buckland/Ashfield winter school without more financial support—help that an active group of local ministers had tried and failed to secure for her. Moving with her few personal effects to Ipswich in early 1830, she sent many a backward look at her beloved home region and the young women she had taught there—much more biddable, much surer of the true faith than the cosmopolitan daughters of eastern Massachusetts merchants or professionals. The four full Ipswich years proved, however, to be richly productive ones for Mary Lyon. They were also the final rehearsal for her establishment of Mount Holyoke Seminary.

Above all, she continued during these years her special mission to train young teachers. "How shall we lead children to think?" she asked them.

In a lesson make one or two points very luminous . . . . Trace cause and effect. The best thing for them [to] understand is mathematics . . . . Have comparisons and contrasts . . . . Have all scholars exert [equal] mental effort, but [the] younger should exert it less time . . . . Make their eyes sparkle once a day.

We must not try to appear learned and superior . . . . [Ask] what are the advantages of the monitorial [Pestalozzi] system? What are its evils? . . . Never introduce studies . . . merely for the sake of having the school appear well. Rise above such things.

Learn to sit with energy . . . . Fear not. Wear a cheerful face.[7]

When students' tuition money ran out, Lyon negotiated teaching positions for them with painstaking care.

As Zilpah Grant saw how competently Mary Lyon performed a multitude of administrative and pastoral tasks, she felt free to leave for several weeks at a time to improve her health, then, in 1831, for nearly a year and a half. Not only was Lyon responsible for each student's academic schedule but she supervised boardinghouse living for the out-of-town students. Rules were stringent, as they would be at Mount Holyoke. Loud laughing and frivolous visiting from room to room were strictly forbidden. Yet students recalled that she found hope in her heart for everyone in her charge. She became increasingly at ease with her ministerial duties. To modern observers it might seem harsh to separate the "professors" of the true faith from "those without hope" during revival prayers, but students seem to have taken her fervent wish for their salvation as yet one more aspect of her generosity. Nor did her antic sense of humor appear to contradict her care for young women's souls. "God . . . made you to be happy," she told them. The "Great Decision" for Christ is not "counter to the principles of nature."[8]

In Grant's mind, Ipswich Seminary's one weakness was its impermanent character. Supported by the trustees, Grant and Lyon began in 1830 a concerted drive for a classroom and laboratory building for 175 scholars, with a contiguous dormitory for 150 of them.

It soon became clear to the two women how difficult it was to persuade men to part with their money in support of women's education. Stuck halfway to their goal, with Grant away on one of her "cures," Mary set aside the "barrenness of soul" that may have been the consequence of their flagging campaign and made one last effort for Ipswich Seminary. She wrote her own new prospectus for a New England Seminary for Teachers, "strictly evangelical." She was certain that women's use of a $40,000 building and endowment fund would demonstrate to the nation that they deserved these resources fully as much as young men. "There is a great work to be performed before that time shall come which is foretold, and many hands are needed . . . not only those of ministers and missionaries, but also of females," she wrote her niece. This time, she would not leave the major work of fund-raising to the men, as she had in Buckland. With and without Grant's help, she contacted the merchants and clergymen who might support the project.[9]

The appeal failed. Yet the intense work of making it convinced Mary Lyon that a somewhat different approach could succeed. She had long been uncomfortable with the upper-middle-class Ipswich constituency and with the social distinctions most seminaries promoted. She had tried to persuade Grant to seek the support of less wealthy evangelicals, such as those who had founded Amherst College and Oberlin. The turning point in her own thinking came as she took the only long vacation of her life in the summer of 1833. On her 2,000-mile triangular trip west to Detroit, and southeast to

Philadelphia, she visited Emma Willard's school in Troy. She stopped at the female seminary at Clinton, New York, where young ladies did most of the domestic work of the boarding school in order to keep tuition low. She consulted with the trustees of struggling new schools, further enlarging the network of influential men who admired her own work. She talked with teachers everywhere.

The long journey clinched her decision to found and run a new kind of seminary. "During the past year," Mary Lyon wrote a close friend in the winter of 1834, "my heart has so yearned over the adult female youth in the common walks of life, that it has sometimes seemed as though a fire were shut up in my bones."[10] From 1834 on, the fire would flame in the open. She now thought of women's higher education not as a local pursuit but as a nationwide "cause" with consequences stretching forward to the Day of Judgment. Having assured her jealous friend Zilpah Grant of her gratitude and secured her permission to resign the following fall, Mary Lyon sat down to write a prospectus all her own.

Addressed to "the Friends and Patrons of Ipswich Female Seminary," Lyon's 1834 prospectus proposed a "separate and independent" seminary, supported by the broad "Christian public" and open to the "many promising young ladies" now denied an education at Ipswich because of its cost. The plan depended on:

1. Teachers possessing so much of a missionary spirit that they would labor faithfully and cheerfully, receiving only a moderate salary
2. Style of living *neat*, but very plain and simple
3. Domestic work of the family to be performed by the members of the school
4. Board and tuition to be placed at cost

Response was swift. The first donors were Ipswich students and their mothers, who knew Lyon's most recent work firsthand. But the net quickly widened to include hundreds of the "Christian yeomanry" in the Connecticut Valley, from common farmers to clergymen and manufacturers of modest wealth.

The "great work" of planning a permanent, accessible institution of higher education for women and, ultimately, raising over $60,000 (nearly $2 million in 1990s dollars) to build and support it, was Mary Lyon's unprecedented accomplishment. Her design became clearer over the next three years, as skeptics scoffed and the New England economy followed the rest of the nation into financial panic and depression. In the final circular before the 1837 opening, Mary Lyon told potential donors and applicants that Mount Holyoke would be "principally devoted to the preparing of female teachers"; unlike virtually all contemporary seminaries, it would accept no students under sixteen years of age, and all applicants for the three-year course must pass entrance examinations. "Look[ing] abroad on a world lying in wickedness," assuming the "work of renovating that world," Mount Holyoke—and schools modeled upon it—would redeem the long future "through the children of our country."

Objections immediately arose. Catharine Beecher and Zilpah Grant disputed the sacrificial teachers' salaries; in reply, Mary Lyon invoked the sacrifices of Saint Paul and the modern Christian missionaries. A skeptical editor criticized the "manual labor scheme"; Mary Lyon held her peace in public but continually asserted in private the democratic value and health benefits of the daily hour of domestic work she proposed, adding that "this simple feature (might) do away with much of the prejudice against female education among the common people" and make an impression on "the whole of New England." She shook her head over good men's fear of "greatness in women," when the two largest state organizations of Congregationalist ministers failed to endorse her project—after endorsing several new male colleges.[11]

But encouragement poured in from Connecticut Valley clergy. Further east, fifteen professors from the Andover Theological Seminary spoke up for "the cause" and tried in vain to persuade Lyon to site her school next to that citadel of orthodoxy. By the fall of 1834, Lyon had raised $1,000 and attracted a committee of men to help her. Over half of these were clergymen; others, like Professor Hitchcock, were men who had done their best for the failed Ipswich campaign. They hired Rev. Roswell Hawks to aid her as her agent. Now Lyon could decorously visit male donors as well as their wives; she could gain the courage to begin the constant round of travel and solicitation that she would later undertake alone.

Several times, as the economy flagged and the fund drive with it, male organizers or trustees came up with strategies that compromised the original plan. Could not the most generous donors help select the students who would attend? Should not Miss Zilpah Grant be invited to be coprincipal? In each case, however, Mary Lyon's polite objections—along with the extraordinary energy she was investing—were persuasive. Respectful of every child, youth, and adult she encountered, she nevertheless "made the impression on everyone . . . from the common day laborer to the president of a college, that if she had set herself to do anything, it was of no use to oppose her." In early 1835, she suggested "presuming on a few thousand dollars" to start construction on the five-story building she was designing, "lest friends may be discouraged" for lack of tangible progress. In July 1836, the trustees laid the cornerstone.[12]

Criticism continued to come from outsiders. The religious press refused to publish her articles, though its editors were more than willing to attack her. While she was insisting that Christian love was the "great motive," both for training as a teacher in her seminary and for contributing funds toward its establishment, her grand plan was being termed "unnatural, unphilosophical, unscriptural . . . impracticable, and anti-Christian," as a trustee would later recall. Most "unbecoming to her sex" was her willingness to ride all over the state addressing "promiscuous audiences" as well as ladies' church groups and sewing circles in sixty Connecticut Valley towns. Lyon responded only by making more speeches. Privately, however, she fought for self-control against "feelings discomposed by opposition," taking out her frustration in long letters to her women friends: "My heart is sick, my soul is pained with this empty gentility, this genteel nothingness. I am doing a great work. I cannot come down."[13]

In spite of dry times and setbacks, the funds came trickling in. The site was settled upon after South Hadley had offered $8,000 to host the new seminary. Mary Lyon was delighted with this central location and the views of nearby Mt. Tom and Mt. Holyoke. She lent $500 of her own to speed construction. She counted bricks at the building site and helped the trustees supervise the slating of the roof. Between fund-raising speeches, she served (unpaid) as major consultant to the family laboring to establish Wheaton Seminary in Norton, Massachusetts.

An undated campaign tally made after Lyon's second circular records $27,000 in pledges and receipts from 1,800 citizens of 91 towns or church groups, the two largest gifts being $1,000, the three smallest, six cents. As the fall 1837 opening date approached, and early pledgers reneged in the straitened economic climate, Mary Lyon decided that women should complete the building campaign, just as they had donated the initial $1,000. Handmade quilts and curtains came in by dozens to furnish the rooms. The pledges would not all be paid. The student rooms, planned for 120 enrollees, could not all be furnished for the November opening day. But it was enough to begin. Over 200 young women had applied to Mount Holyoke by late October 1837, most of them twenty years old or more; 80 of these arrived on opening day, to be warmly greeted by Mary Lyon before being swept into a group of seamstresses finishing the parlor curtains, a crew of pie bakers, or a clutch of younger students gathered on a pile of mattresses to review for the coming placement examinations. The pioneers thrived on the challenges of the first year.

Mary Lyon was always looking for better methods, always asking more of her students. Texts were rarely memorized in their entirety; rather, they were used as starting points. Lyon loved Milton, but Professor Hitchcock was most interested in her skillful approach to Butler's *Analogy of Natural and Revealed Religion*, a staple at men's colleges. Latin, still considered by most Americans too difficult for females to master, would be required at Mount Holyoke after 1846. While applications steadily increased to a high of 500 for 1847–1848, standards for admission were tightened to exclude those who could stay less than a full year. The first three-day oral examinations and "anniversary" exercises in June 1838 culminated in the graduation of just four seniors, all of whom became Mount Holyoke teachers the following fall. But forty-six graduated ten years later, and both graduates and nongraduates were in heavy demand as teachers. Probably over half of all students attending in Mary Lyon's day taught school for at least a short season, a preparation for marriage and motherhood that she warmly endorsed. A large fraction became career educators directly involved in the leadership of ten "daughter" schools and colleges—including Mills College—and seminaries in South Africa and Persia founded on Mount Holyoke principles.

The dozen Mount Holyoke years were on the whole richly happy ones for Mary Lyon. Her duties found her supervising the baking of bread while writing kindly letters of assistance to graduated or expelled students, at the same time keeping an eye on the work team in the ironing room adjoining the kitchen. It was her pride that no Mount Holyoke student or teacher had to depend on "the will of hired domestics" and that this "family" labor system based on "the principle of [student] equality" allowed the charge for a year's tuition and board to remain at $60.[14] Such a sum could be readily saved by any district schoolteacher in two years of work. It helped, of course, that no teacher, including Mary Lyon, took more than $200 a year in salary beyond room and board.

The principal performed intricate wonders of academic and social scheduling and regretfully dismissed those students who could not be cured of rule breaking by the relentless "self-reporting" sessions held daily in sections of twenty students and one teacher. She also organized the weekly Bible lessons, gave assembly talks three times a week, supervised the four to eight youngest teachers, held weekly faculty meetings, taught chemistry, and gave demonstration classes in algebra and botany. "Happiness is in activity," Lyon would say to her students. Alumnae of this era recalled being nearly as busy as their principal, with every moment of their fifteen-hour day planned out for them. But there was merriment as well. Calisthenics verged delightfully on dancing. On the mandatory outdoor walks or botanizing expeditions, students could at last talk well above the usual whisper. Friendships took root within the cooking or dishwashing crews and among students preparing together for examinations. "Miss Lyon's happiness was a living spring," wrote her first biographers; she wanted her "daughters" to take joy in life. On some Saturdays she organized berry-picking expeditions, sleigh rides, or shopping trips. As though in ignorance of gathering assumptions of "woman's delicacy," there were yearly climbs up Mt. Holyoke, even picnics atop Mt. Tom with a few select Amherst students. Thanksgiving was a joyous celebration of students' and teachers' culinary and decorating skills, a day of hospitality for crowds of South Hadley neighbors.[15]

"We can become almost anything we want to be," Lyon told her students. Her energetic example made a deep impression on them as she struggled to use for their benefit the "great power we have over ourselves." She would scold herself for nagging them about "mistakes . . . in little things. Be like

Christ—like *Christ*," she scribbled on a memorandum. She grew yearly in confidence as a spiritual guide, admonisher, and comforter. Death being an ever-present possibility within the seminary itself, her urgent sense of responsibility for her students' eternal life seemed logical enough to many. Hellfire was real to her. It would burn the "gospel-hardened" refuser "for ever and ever." Equally real was a beautiful heaven open to all who could "[find] the Savior precious." Every evening during a revival, Mary Lyon and her teachers conducted intense voluntary prayer meetings on the Ipswich pattern; then in recreation time, they visited quietly from room to room. "Many there are who cannot eat because of deep feeling," wrote one student in the journal kept for missionary alumnae; "the whole house is as still as on the Sabbath." An early assistant principal estimated that 1,000 of the 3,400 students who entered Mount Holyoke in its first twelve years did so "without hope" but that three-quarters of these resisters became professing Christians while attending. It was Lyon's proudest achievement.[16]

Missionary alumnae were Mount Holyoke's heroines, still more revered than the hundreds of schoolteachers who had attended the seminary. But even to those who would immediately marry, Lyon preached that "holiness leads us to the most vigorous action."[17] One could serve God richly as mother of an orderly family, baker of bread, and devoted helper in a local church. Whatever they did, she expected all her students to carry their faith into their adult activities, thus justifying the broad public support that had established and sustained Mount Holyoke.

Mary Lyon "was always experimenting," Hawks recalled; as president of the Board of Trustees, he "used to tiptoe past the door of her parlor lest, hearing his step, she call him in and propose something new." Yet, if her methods were original and her faith in women's abilities unusual, her goals were conservative. She knew, for example, how attractive some of her students found the feminist cause: "It is the mark of a weak mind," she told them, "to be continually comparing the sexes and disputing and making out the feminine sex as something great and superior." Mount Holyoke existed within—and to a large extent depended upon—a culture and legal system created by and for males. Male scholars frequently came to give lectures on scientific subjects. No woman ever gave the commencement address, though Mark Hopkins and other evangelical luminaries did. Every Sunday students and faculty went twice to hear the male preacher at the Congregational Church next door. Thus, male educators, donors, and divines continued to sustain and legitimate Mary Lyon's enterprise, as men's sanction would be invited by virtually every women's seminary or college until the 1880s. Given all she was trying to prove to a skeptical world, it may have been prudent for her to follow her own advice to teachers to "incite no needless opposition."[18]

Indeed, daily challenges within the seminary engaged all Lyon's attention through the 1840s. The most dramatic was the typhoid epidemic that opened the decade, against which the seminary's scrupulous sanitation measures seemed helpless. Nine students died. Yet enrollment soon rose again and remained at an average of 200 through the decade, filling a new wing of the building. Though increasing applications and requests for Mount Holyoke-trained teachers kept her constantly busy, her heavy responsibilities and her success in fulfilling them appeared only to deepen her serenity.

They did not improve her health. It is almost certain that she contracted tuberculosis soon after the student and Lyon family deaths of 1840, and she began to lose her hearing around 1846. Early in 1849, her sense of well-being and durability alternated with premonitions of death. In late February, a senior fell ill and died of erysipelas, an acute strep infection of the skin and subcutaneous tissue. Lyon had visited and prayed with her as was her custom, although she herself was ill with influenza. She contracted the young woman's disease. The sudden news of a beloved nephew's suicide seemed to halt her recovery. She died on March 5, 1849, at the age of fifty-two.

Mount Holyoke Seminary staggered but did not fall. Its reputation was strong, its large building nearly paid for, its Board of Trustees deeply committed. Certain that the school would endure for a thousand years, Mary Lyon had helped its alumnae organize themselves into a Memorandum Society. She had long chided students who referred to Mount Holyoke as "Miss Lyon's Seminary." The institution's greatest strength may have lain in its founder's willingness to share credit with, and delegate responsibility to, its trustees, her teaching colleagues, and student leaders. Their crusade to carry out her grand plans without her was one of the two richest tributes she could have earned. The other was the string of women's colleges that were established in the four decades following her death. Mary Lyon and Mount Holyoke Seminary had demonstrated both the need for, and the enduring possibilities of, higher education for American women.

NOTES

1. Quoted in Elizabeth Alden Green, *Mary Lyon and Mount Holyoke: Opening the Gates* (Hanover, NH: University Press of New England, 1979), 10.

2. Quoted in Beth Bradford Gilchrist, *The Life of Mary Lyon* (Cambridge: Riverside Press, 1910), 86; Edward Hitchcock, with Zilpah Grant Banister, Eunice Caldwell Cowles, M. C. Eddy, and Hannah White, *The Power of Christian Benevolence Illustrated in the Life and Labors of Mary Lyon* (Northampton, MA: Hopkins, Bridgman, 1851), 50–51.

3. Hitchcock et al., 91.

4. Hitchcock et al., 2d ed. (New York: American Tract Society, 1858), 211.

5. ML to Z. Grant 12/10/27, Hitchcock et al., 56; ML to ZG 12/30/23, Hitchcock et al., (1858), 41.

6. ML to ZG, 2/25/28, Hitchcock et al., 60.

7. Student notes, Gilchrist, 90, 92, 146–51.

8. Student notes, quoted in Gilchrist, 131, 130, 129.

9. ML to ZG, July 1832, Hitchcock et al. (1858), 102; ML to Abigail Moore, 1832, Hitchcock et al., 91.

10. ML to Hannah White, 2/26/34, Hitchcock et al., 126.

11. ML to ZG, 5/6/34, Hitchcock et al., 193; ML to HW, 8/1/34, Hitchcock et al.; ML to Catharine Beecher, 7/1/36, Green, 157; ML to ZG, quoted in Sydney R. McLean, "Mary Lyon," In *Notable American Women 1607–1950* (Cambridge: Belknap Press of Harvard University Press, 1971), 445.

12. Hitchcock et al., 279; ML to ZG, 4/8/35, Hitchcock et al., 209.

13. ML to CB, Hitchcock et al., 183; W. S. Tyler quoted in Gilchrist, 230; ML, quoted in Hitchcock et al. (1858), 345, 245.

14. ML, "Principles," in ibid., 297.

15. Gilchrist, 131; Hitchcock et al. (1858), 227, 224.

16. Student notes in Gilchrist, 372, 314; Gilchrist, 304; ML, *A Missionary Offering* quoted in Gilchrist, 279; ML to Mrs. Safford, Hitchcock et al., 331; ML in Hitchcock et al. (1858), 304; journal 12/46, Green, 247.

17. Student notes, Gilchrist, 131.

18. Roswell Hawks quoted in ibid., 289; ML to ZG, 12/23/35, Hitchcock et al., 219; student notes, Hitchcock et al. (1858), 155.

WORKS BY MARY LYON

Circulars and Prospectuses, 1833, 1834, 1836 and 1837. Mount Holyoke Archives, South Hadley, MA.
A Missionary Offering. New York: American Tract Society, 1843.

WORKS ABOUT MARY LYON

Gilchrist, Beth Bradford. *The Life of Mary Lyon.* Cambridge: Riverside Press, 1910.
Green, Elizabeth Alden. *Mary Lyon and Mount Holyoke: Opening the Gates.* Hanover, NH: University Press of New England, 1979.
Hitchcock, Edward, with Mrs. Zilpah Grant Banister, Mrs. Eunice Caldwell Cowles, Mrs. M. C. Eddy and Miss Hannah White. *The Power of Christian Benevolence Illustrated in the Life and Labors of Mary Lyon.* Northampton, MA: Hopkins, Bridgman, 1851; 2d ed., New York: American Tract Society, 1858.
Lansing, Marion, Ed. *Mary Lyon Through her Letters.* Boston: Books, Inc., 1937.
MacLean, Sydney R. "Mary Lyon." In *Notable American Women 1607–1950.* Cambridge: Belknap Press of Harvard University Press, 1971, 443–47.
Stow, Sarah D. Locke. *History of Mount Holyoke Seminary, South Hadley, Mass., during the First Half Century, 1837–1887.* South Hadley: Mount Holyoke Seminary, 1887.

Peggy McIntosh

Linda Eisenmann

Peggy (Margaret) Means McIntosh (b. 1934) is a self-described "teacher of teachers," best known for her phase theory of curriculum transformation regarding gender and race and for her faculty development work with school and college teachers. Beginning in the early 1970s, McIntosh examined how teachers and their students could jointly discover materials about people whose lives were seldom seen as a part of traditional history. These early efforts, undertaken as women's studies first emerged, began her twenty-year exploration of expanding the curriculum to include the words and lives of women. She also worked for the inclusion of under-studied aspects of men's experience as legitimate makers of knowledge. Currently, Dr. McIntosh pursues this work as associate director of the Center for Research on Women at Wellesley College and codirector of the National Educational Equity and Diversity (SEED) Project on Inclusive Curriculum. McIntosh holds honorary doctorates from Augustana College in Sioux Falls, South Dakota, and from the College of St. Catherine in St. Paul, Minnesota.

When asked about her family background, McIntosh prefers to reflect on her "family foreground," noting that "my family is very present to me, with what I call its 'ethno-specificity.' "[1] Peggy McIntosh was born November 7, 1934, in Brooklyn, New York. Her father, Winthrop Johnson Means, was born in 1899 in Windham, Connecticut, a descendant of New Englanders who included John Winthrop, first governor of Massachusetts Bay Colony. Means broke with family tradition by becoming an engineer rather than a Congregational minister. Orphaned in youth, he was educated at Phillips Exeter Academy, Harvard College, and the Harvard Engineering School, where he graduated in 1923. He worked for Bell Telephone Laboratories from his college graduation through his retirement.

However, Means's career progression was neither steady nor uneventful and affected his daughter Peggy. He began work as a mechanical engineer, but after seeing the devastation of the atomic bomb at the close of World War II, Means asked to be removed from any war work performed by Bell Labs. He ended work as an electrical and then electronic engineer, work which enabled him to participate in the computer revolution.

The realization by the Means parents that the "wide-eyed wonder of engineering" should give way to a "sober sense of its destructive capabilities" had a long-term effect. Winthrop and his wife, Margaret, became Quakers and members of the United World Federalists and eventually sent Peggy to a Quaker school. This shift in family views translated to Peggy as a belief that "winning, in the traditional sense, might not be an ethical priority in life." From the decisions of her parents and through the influences of other family members, McIntosh gained a sense of "permission to be independent" in her thoughts and actions.

McIntosh's mother, Margaret Vance Hoy Means, was born in 1901 in Easton, Pennsylvania, one of six children of a transplanted "Southern Virginia lady and a Pennsylvania Dutch father." Her grandmother refused to let her children attend school until after the age of eight, feeling that they could receive better training at home. McIntosh's mother was sent to Agnes Scott College in Georgia, her father's choice, to acquire a southern training lacking in Pennsylvania schools, but she eventually responded better to the opportunity to attend Vassar, the college her mother favored, where she had a far more cosmopolitan experience.

Both of McIntosh's parents, especially her mother, were accomplished and knowledgeable gardeners, instilling in Peggy a respect for natural growth and development that later became a useful metaphor for her view of educational growth. In considering the SEED Project, for example, McIntosh describes her sense of effectively "seeding" educational ideas through training groups of teachers and her recognition of the importance of creating the proper climate and habitat for each child and each teacher.

McIntosh's formal education took place in both public and private schools, beginning with the Kenilworth School in Ridgewood, New Jersey. She observed that her first grade teacher was the only one to have a very large desk: "All the rest of us had our own little ones, all arranged in rows in front of her large one." Something about this arrangement seemed peculiar and inequitable. As the morning of her first day in this class progressed, McIntosh made two more observations: first, the teacher was not doing a very good job at getting through to the children and second, she herself could do a better job. It seemed clear to her that there were better, easier, and more personal ways to reach her classmates. McIntosh's long commitment to teaching seems to have been sealed that day in her first grade classroom.

These initial concerns notwithstanding, McIntosh "loved school" and prospered academically and socially. However, she continued to observe that much of real interest to her and to others was ignored in the formal curriculum. Explaining her awareness decades later, she draws a pie chart with a wedge shaded in. That wedge, she explains, represents the small portion of children's lives and interests that is touched by formal schooling. The rest of the pie, in fact, contains most of what is interesting and vital to their knowledge of life. McIntosh conceptualized this notion decades later in her curriculum change work.

After Kenilworth School, McIntosh attended Summit Junior High and Summit High School in Summit, New Jersey. By the tenth grade, her parents opted for private schooling, first sending her to Kent Place School in Summit and later to the Quaker George School in Pennsylvania. McIntosh's decision to attend Radcliffe College was "a traditional choice"; her older brother Winthrop, now a professor of geology, was attending Harvard. McIntosh has a younger sister, Helen Means Armstrong, whose work with the United Nations International Children's Emergency Fund (UNICEF) Baby-Friendly Hospital Initiative and international breast-feeding networks prompts McIntosh to believe her sister is also committed to "working for change."

Following her graduation summa cum laude from Radcliffe in 1956 with a degree in English, McIntosh studied for a year at the University of London, then worked as an English teacher for three years in New York City. She returned to Radcliffe for an M.A. in English (1961) and earned her Ph.D. in English from Harvard in 1967. At the end of those graduate school years, she married Kenneth McIntosh, who graduated from Harvard College and Harvard Medical School and whom she had known for many years. He is now professor of pediatrics at Harvard Medical School and chief of infectious diseases at Children's Hospital in Boston. They married in Cambridge in March 1965. The couple has two daughters, Helen Carey McIntosh, born in Maryland in 1967, and Janet, born in 1969 in London, England.

A teaching position she assumed in 1970 at the University of Denver began McIntosh's involvement with curriculum change. Hired by the English department, she also directed the American studies program at a time when that new field was exploring the possibilities of interdisciplinary study. Working as a team, McIntosh and her colleagues began to ask questions of their students, themselves, and their curriculum. In faculty group sessions, they examined their definitions of "culture." They noticed that an element of exclusiveness appeared in all their definitions, as well as a sense that "the dailiness of life" was omitted from traditional course material. They decided to innovate the curriculum by dividing a team-taught course into two parts. For the first three weeks, they taught (albeit briskly) the traditional historical landmarks—"the regular story" of wars, presidents, elections, famous writers, and so forth. For the next eleven weeks, they decided to focus on "aspects of culture that had been left out."

Unaccustomed to such an approach, students first resisted any attention to women's lives, nonformal schooling, rural experience, children's history, racial concerns, autobiography, and other such elements. However, the experience was an awakening for McIntosh, who describes it as "the first time I crossed 'the fault line' " that separates traditional knowledge from all that lies underneath it in ordinary human lives. Although she did not theorize about this fault line until her 1983 landmark paper, "Interactive Phases of Curricular Re-Vision: A Feminist Perspective," in these courses McIntosh explored collaborative learning and pursued some of the first formal efforts at "balancing the curriculum."[2]

McIntosh left Denver in 1979 and in 1980 began a career at Wellesley College. She has taught in the undergraduate program, but most of her teaching has been through special programs of the Center for Research on Women. From 1979 through 1985, she directed the Andrew W. Mellon Faculty Development Program for college faculty, and from 1983 to 1987 she directed the Dodge Seminars in Women's Studies for Secondary School Teachers. Both projects included leading seminars of teachers who came together to consider how their disciplines "would need to change in order to reflect the fact that women are half of the world's population and have had half of the world's lived experience." Lists of the Mellon seminar participants include people who have made potent contributions to feminist knowledge, including Eve Sedgwick, Gloria Hull, Mary Roth Walsh, Mary Helen Washington, Anne Fausto-Sterling, Sandra Harding, Evelyn Fox Keller, and Jane Roland Martin.

In this heady atmosphere, McIntosh first presented her theory of the interactive phases of curricular "re-vision." Although other scholars, including Gerda Lerner, Marilyn Schuster, and Susan Van Dyne, have offered theories that describe the process of curricular change, Margaret Andersen notes that McIntosh's analysis "is unique in that it relates patterns of thought in the curriculum to human psyches and their relation to the dominant culture."[3]

McIntosh posits five phases—different from "stages" in that they are interactive and inclusive—of "personal and curriculum change that occur when new perspectives and new materials from Women's Studies are brought into a traditional curriculum or a traditional consciousness."[4] Using history as an example, McIntosh outlines the five phases: (1) the traditional "Womanless History"; (2) "Women in History" (only the notable few); (3) "Women as a Problem, Anomaly, Absence, or Victim in History"; (4) daily experience with "Women's Lives *As* History"; and (5) "History Redefined or Reconstructed to Include Us All."

Phase 1 represents the thoroughly traditional and too often familiar curriculum featuring the work of white men who constitute a "canon" in their field. As Andersen notes, we have "come to think of them as examples of the best of human life and thought."[5] However, McIntosh notes, this curriculum has been written by society's "winners," those who have made it to the top of the pyramid. The socially constructed pyramid represents the functions of competition that lead to a structure (social and psychic) that has room for only a few kinds of talent at the top and consigns most people and attributes to the wider base, where they are less visible and important.

Phase 2 appears to be a corrective to this exclusivity. It admits a "famous few" women who have managed to overcome odds and are seen to have approached a level of achievement near that of men. However, Phase 2 retains the exclusiveness of Phase 1: "It conveys to the student the impression that women don't really exist unless they are exceptional by men's standards."[6]

Phase 3 begins the movement off the pinnacles of power, looking instead to the wider group of women and functions of personality at the pyramid's base. This phase focuses on issues, especially issues of power, and "introduces us to the politics of the curriculum," noting both the deliberate and nondeliberate actions of those in the academy who have worked against women. Phase 3 thinking can produce anger as people realize that women have often been seen as a problem rather than a part of the norm. Disillusionment is another common feature, as scholars and students realize they have been vehicles for perpetuating this view. Phase 3 is partial, in focusing on victimization and inadvertently assigning women a "deficit identity." Nevertheless, it is useful in pointing to systemic, rather than individual, problems.

Phase 4 represents a radical shift in thinking: "Phase 4 vision construes the life below the break in the pyramid as the real though unacknowledged base of life and civilization." It focuses on lateral capacities and plural narratives. Now the curriculum becomes truly inclusive, "filled with rich variety," all of which is respected and validated as potential sources of reality and knowledge. This is the "culture" that McIntosh's Denver students at first resisted when it was included in their American studies courses. Phase 4 is marked by real collaboration among teachers, students, and nontraditional creators of knowledge.

Phase 5, still an ideal, will attempt to honor many kinds of knowing. The vertical and lateral understandings of knowledge will be balanced; a sphere or a globe may replace the imagery of pyramids and pinnacles. "Human collaborative potential is explored and competitive potential subjected to a sustained critique" in Phase 5. Patterns appear across cultures and systems. Understandings can develop that students and teachers can carry over into the public life of the world.

McIntosh's 1983 paper concludes with a thoughtful set of "theoretical narratives" that anchor the theory for many readers, as she describes the phases through the educational experiences of a fictitious group of "little women": Meg, Amy, and Jo, who attend college in different eras, experience curricula in Phases 1–3. Jo's twin daughters, Maya and Angela, use a Phase 4 curriculum that validates a wide spectrum of experience. Their younger sister Adrienne will help fashion a Phase 5 approach to knowledge.

Perhaps as a reaction to her own success with the curriculum work, Mc-

Intosh pursued another line of inquiry with two papers: "Feeling Like a Fraud" (1985) and "Feeling Like a Fraud: Part Two" (1989). Here McIntosh questions why so many women "experience feelings of fraudulence when singled out for praise, press, publicity, or promotion." Rather than stop with the popular answer that women have never been properly socialized to accept the trappings of traditional success, McIntosh urges women to heed the inner voice that makes them uncomfortable in such situations. That voice, in fact, may be raising a critique of the hierarchical structures that define "success" and "failure." In the 1989 paper, McIntosh explores "the feelings of *authenticity* which give us our ability to recognize our feelings of fraudulence." Honoring that feeling of public discomfort may actually lead women to political and social change; it may be telling them about a new way to lead, speak, and respond to others.[7]

In the last five years, McIntosh's work on curriculum change has evolved into a new era as she makes connections between the exclusions experienced by women and those that have racial, ethnic, and class bases. Beginning with "White Privilege and Male Privilege: A Personal Account of Coming to See Correspondences Through Work in Women's Studies" (1988), McIntosh gingerly entered this area, aware that her own position as an affluent white woman working at a prestigious, eastern women's college raised issues for her.[8] However, acknowledging the "ethno-specificity" of her situation has allowed McIntosh to address situations openly; as she explains, "My gender, age, and class have allowed me to say things that sound militant coming from people of color."[9] Her paper on white privilege lists forty-six ways in which she daily experiences privilege by contrast with her nonwhite colleagues in the same building.

McIntosh's 1990 paper, "Interactive Phases of Curricular and Personal Re-Vision with Regard to Race," extends her phase theory to race and multiculturalism. McIntosh opens with a twenty-year-old memory of an African-American colleague who told McIntosh, "I wouldn't want to be white if you paid me five million dollars." Remembering how the remark startled her at the time, McIntosh reflected a long while on the comment, eventually using it "to see my own culture as ethno-particular, ethno-specific, and in fact ethno-peculiar." Twenty years of studying the effects of women's exclusion have shown her that the "single-system seeing" often adopted by men in viewing women's "issues" is also used by many white members of the dominant culture—men and women alike. McIntosh reminds readers that such "monoculturalism, like all forms of single-system seeing, is blind to its own cultural specificity."[10]

Like her earlier work, the 1990 paper relates changes in thinking to transformations in the curriculum. McIntosh finds much of collegiate teaching mired in Phase 1:

With regard to race in the undergraduate curriculum, most of our universities still feature Phase One introductory courses in virtually all departments . . . . The courses feature winners in law, war, or trade; the getting and holding of literal or conceptual territory; the making of frameworks for understanding.[11]

The "deficit identities" of Phase 3 become even more problematic when applied to whole groups of people whose entire cultures are denied. Phase 4, which accepts plural narratives and leads to cultural pluralism, is still a long step away for most teachers, students, and institutions.

McIntosh is not without hope of a multicultural Phase 5 curriculum, however. Returning to her familiar topographical images, she envisions that in Phase 5 "my diagrammatic model of psychic and societal structures turns into a large, three-dimensional globe": "Each continent, each group of cultures, has its ranges, its 'peaks,' its dynasties, but mountain climbing is understood to be one particular human activity, not the only human activity."[12]

Most satisfying to McIntosh are sharing and developing her theory by working with teachers. Since 1987, she has codirected the SEED Project on Inclusive Curriculum with Emily Style, English teacher and diversity coordinator for the Madison, New Jersey, school district. With SEED, McIntosh facilitates teachers' own curriculum work by "putting teachers' discussion at the center, taking them seriously and giving them access to new resources." The project's aim is to "establish teacher-led faculty development seminars throughout the United States and the world," providing teachers with theoretical tools, physical resources, and intellectual support in fostering gender-fair and multicultural curricula.

The SEED Project and the similar earlier work in the Mellon faculty development seminars provide McIntosh her greatest rewards. In her theoretical work she tries for "coherence without coercion." However, she readily acknowledges that this type of thinking, with its focus on illuminating narrative rather than authority, may not, in fact, be a "lasting contribution," but "perhaps I'm not working for lastingness." She prefers the connectedness, the networking, and the "non-institutional" work that she and the SEED teachers perform together.

However, in speaking so vocally about reclaiming quiet voices, McIntosh has recently received sharp criticism from those who feel that such nontraditional sources weaken the curriculum by steering students away from the most recognized and "excellent" material of the past. In the first issue of *Heterodoxy*, McIntosh was named, along with Mary Daly, Sandra Harding, Donna Harraway, Carol Delaney, and Theresa deLauretis, as "one of the ten wackiest feminists on campus." McIntosh does not object to being compared with these other feminist thinkers, but she resents what she describes as a quite personal attack by far right-wing conservatives. The criticism has caused her to reflect on the development of feminist knowledge over the past twenty years, suggesting that it is "surprising that we went for twenty years without a major critique . . . given that we are calling into question the main assumptions about knowledge-making." Over those same twenty years,

McIntosh's faculty development work with teachers, her phase theory of curriculum transformation, her probing into privilege systems, and her creation of "theoretical narratives" have marked significant contributions to education.

NOTES

1. This quote and others from Peggy McIntosh, unless otherwise indicated, are from an interview with the author held at Wellesley College, Wellesley, Massachusetts, on August 28, 1992.
2. Peggy McIntosh, "Interactive Phases of Curricular and Personal Re-Vision: A Feminist Perspective," Working Paper #124, Wellesley College Center for Research on Women, October 1983.
3. Margaret Andersen, "Changing the Curriculum in Higher Education," in Elizabeth Minnich, Jean O'Barr, and Rachel Rosenfeld, eds., *Reconstructing the Academy: Women's Education and Women's Studies* (Chicago: University of Chicago Press, 1988), 49. This article is a good review of curriculum change theories.
4. McIntosh, 1.
5. Andersen, 49.
6. McIntosh, 8.
7. Peggy McIntosh, "Feeling Like a Fraud," Working Paper #18, Stone Center for Developmental Services and Studies, Wellesley College, 1985; Peggy McIntosh, "Feeling Like a Fraud: Part Two," Working Paper #37, Stone Center for Developmental Services and Studies, Wellesley College, 1989.
8. Peggy McIntosh, "White Privilege and Male Privilege: A Personal Account of Coming to See Correspondences Through Work in Women's Studies," Working Paper #189, Wellesley College Center for Research on Women, December 1988.
9. Interview with author, August 28, 1992.
10. Peggy McIntosh, "Interactive Phases of Curricular and Personal Re-Vision with Regard to Race," Working Paper #219, Wellesley College Center for Research on Women, 1990, 1.
11. Ibid., 8.
12. Ibid., 12.

WORKS BY PEGGY McINTOSH

"WARNING: The New Scholarship on Women May Be Hazardous to Your Ego." *Women's Studies Quarterly* 10 (Spring 1982): 29–31.
"Interactive Phases of Curricular Re-Vision: A Feminist Perspective." Working Paper #124, Wellesley College Center for Research on Women, Wellesley, MA, October 1983.
"Varieties of Women's Studies" (with Elizabeth Minnich). *Women's Studies International Forum* 7 (1984): 139–48.
"Feeling Like a Fraud." Working Paper #18, Stone Center for Developmental Services and Studies, Wellesley College, Wellesley, MA, 1985.
"White Privilege and Male Privilege: A Personal Account of Coming to See Correspondences Through Work in Women's Studies." Working Paper #189,

Wellesley College Center for Research on Women, Wellesley, MA, December 1988.

"Curricular Re-Vision: The New Knowledge for a New Age." In Carol S. Pearson, Donna L. Shavlik, and Judith G. Touchton, eds., *Educating the Majority: Women Challenge Tradition in Higher Education*, 400–12. New York: American Council on Education and Macmillan, 1989.

"Feeling Like a Fraud: Part Two." Working Paper #37, Stone Center for Developmental Services and Studies, Wellesley College, Wellesley, MA, 1989.

"Interactive Phases of Curricular and Personal Re-Vision with Regard to Race." Working Paper #219, Wellesley College Center for Research on Women, Wellesley, MA, 1990.

WORKS ABOUT PEGGY McINTOSH

Andersen, Margaret L. "Changing the Curriculum in Higher Education." In Elizabeth Minnich, Jean O'Barr, and Rachel Rosenfeld, eds., *Reconstructing the Academy: Women's Education and Women's Studies*, 36–68. Chicago: University of Chicago Press, 1988.

Lyons, Nona P. "Women's Education." In *Encyclopedia of Educational Research*, 6th ed., 1520–25. New York: Macmillan, 1992.

Minnich, Elizabeth Kamarck. "From the Circle of the Elite to the World of the Whole: Education, Equality, and Excellence." In Carol S. Pearson, Donna L. Shavlik, and Judith G. Touchton, eds., *Educating the Majority: Women Challenge Tradition in Higher Education*, 277–93. New York: American Council on Education and Macmillan, 1989.

Nelson, Cathy L. "The National SEED Project." *Educational Leadership* 49, no. 4 (December 1991/January 1992): 66–67.

Strang, Dorothy. "The National SEED Project: Including Us All." *Academic Forum* (Spring 1992): 1–3.

Deborah W. Meier

Susan McIntosh Lloyd

Deborah W. Meier (b.1931) is one of the most powerful advocates for public school reform in the nation. Her authority derives from her teaching experience, from her insight into the ways in which human beings learn and thrive, and from her success over twenty years in establishing inner-city schools that work. She has built a revolutionary vision of educational reform by focusing on the needs and drawing on the strengths of urban children and their families. Seeing classroom teachers as central to enduring change, she has brought them to the forefront of reform. She has founded two New York City public schools, has inspired several others, and as of 1993, is making plans to help begin ten more.

Deborah Meier was born in 1931 to Joseph and Pearl Larner Willen. The Willens lived in New Rochelle, near New York City and Joseph Willen's work with the Federation of Jewish Philanthropies, of which he eventually became executive director. Pearl Willen immersed herself in volunteer work for the American Labor Party. After the family moved to Manhattan, she helped to found the New York Liberal Party, the League for Industrial Democracy, and the Workers Defense League. Following World War II, she was president of the National Council of Jewish Women.

Deborah Willen admired her family and deeply loved her mother. She claims a happy childhood, infused with the expectation that she "would do something significant to change the world."[1] Both Deborah and her older brother, Paul, were sent for their precollege education to the Ethical Culture School, where, as in her home, children "were taken seriously and respectfully." For half a dozen years, no one called Deborah away from adventurous play with Paul and his friends, though she knew early that her daring set her apart from most girls (and she was glad of the distinction). She struggled to understand how this beloved and talented brother—not yet much of a reader, not a conventionally successful student—saw the world. As both children grew, they became, to Deborah's delight, their father's partners and antagonists in wide-ranging dinnertime discussions. In her time alone, Deborah Willen read and read and planned to be a novelist. "What is most unique about humans is that we can imagine what is not," she says. Children, no matter how poor, can imagine another world.

Deborah Willen chose Antioch College because it was one of the few good colleges whose rules were then identical for females and males. She thrived on its work-study program, but she soon gave up her hopes of becoming a novelist. After two years, however, her scholarly accomplishments earned her entry into the University of Chicago graduate school, where she began work on a master's degree in American history.

In 1952, one of the few places where Deborah, an avowed nonconformist with a passion for justice, could feel at home was a Trotskyist organization that resounded with talk and argument as stimulating as what she had known within her family. Fred Meier, a fellow socialist and university student, was an active and charismatic member of the organization. Deborah Willen had decided it was time to marry, and she was charmed by Fred Meier. The Meiers began their family life between street demonstrations of the Committee for a SANE Nuclear Policy and organizational meetings of the Congress of Racial Equality, many of these held in their home in a largely black Chicago neighborhood.

For some years, Deborah Meier had thought children uninteresting. But her heart changed as she bore her own three; her mind followed her children's intricate patterns of growth and found them all-absorbing. Still, she was Deborah Willen Meier, M.A., and she did not think of schoolteaching. "Women can do so much *more* than teach," she thought, following her parents' assumptions about her future.

She read John Holt and other prophets of neoprogressive school reform, however, and began to wonder. She started substitute teaching around the city of Chicago. At first her motive was to earn enough to pay for household help, but she soon grew fascinated with the work itself. Fred Meier saw how much it meant to her and cheered her on. Though the Meiers eventually separated, this support was crucial to her, especially at the beginning. "I thought I would be terrific," she recalls. "I was terrible. I left my raincoat in the first school I taught in and I didn't dare go back to get it." But she would not give up. She "had begun to see why teaching was so hard." She was especially interested in the "Freds" and the "Pauls"—children who, like her husband and brother, did not naturally engage with the world of school. (Her husband, whom she met at the university, had been a high school dropout and her brother, though now a young architect, had not been, as she put it, a conventionally successful student.)

Meier also became aware, however, of her humiliating status within the social system that is conventional public education. "I had never been treated with such little respect or common courtesy, even as a child . . . . It hit me like a ton of bricks."[2] As she settled on kindergarten teaching, one of her sons was struggling in a dismal first grade class. She was soon equally appalled by the disrespect often shown to schoolchildren. She wanted to walk out of her job, but she thought, "They're not going to get rid of me so easily." Schoolteaching raised questions for Meier that were not so different from those she had earlier asked as a socialist and civil rights activist: Why is inequality so entrenched in a society supposedly dedicated to equality? How can institutions change? How do individuals—especially growing children—come to terms with new ideas?

To get her teaching license, Meier finally took a clutch of the education courses she had been avoiding. She learned little from the courses but much from her fellow students at Chicago Teachers College, most of them from lower-income families. In 1964, she found a half-day job as a kindergarten teacher in the inner-city school her children attended. Meier discovered that year how much difference a supportive principal could make as she experimented with her own versions of the teaching philosophies of John Dewey and Sylvia Ashton-Warner. For one more year, in Philadelphia, Meier continued her part-time teaching in a Head Start program, while she took courses at the University of Pennsylvania and Temple University. Then in 1966, the Meiers moved to New York City's Upper West Side. The children entered the public schools, and their mother took up a kindergarten position at P.S. #144 in Harlem.

Though the Meier children's schools were as depressing for them and as patronizing to their parents as most of their Chicago schools had been, their mother was working under a woman principal who granted her freedom as well as intellectual respect. She had time for periodic study at City College and the Bank Street College of Education. Eventually she was running one wing of P.S. #144 as a four-room schoolhouse for children four to seven years old.

These were heady days for New York City educators hoping for change. Many elementary school teachers were deeply impressed by the British "open classroom" movement and its confident assumptions about children's need and right to choose their own best ways of learning within a rich, "prepared environment." Meanwhile, radical advocates of community control were getting ready to go to the barricades for poor parents' need and right to run their children's schools. City and union bureaucrats dug in. The stage was set for the bruising three-cornered New York school wars of 1967–1968. Meier continued on at P.S. #144, working for reconciliation. "All sides were right," she says.

In 1970, soon after the school wars subsided, Lillian Weber of City College asked Deborah Meier to work with her as one of several teacher trainers. Under contract both to the city and to participating schools, they "infiltrated" public schools to try radically to improve young teachers' efficacy.

"Weber was brilliant," says Meier, "a passionate woman with a strong social conscience." Meier thinks Weber may have been all the more important to her because her mother, warmly supportive of her in so many ways, had never quite understood her choice of career. But it was a terrible blow to the daughter when Pearl Willen was killed in an auto accident. The tragedy intensified Meier's desire to make her own way of teaching fulfill her family's broad humanitarian goals.

After two eventful years as "teacher trainer," however, Meier grew impatient. Only about half of her trainees seemed serious about teaching. She felt rootless without a classroom of her own, and she missed the partnerships with parents she had begun to build in her Harlem school. Teachers' fear of change sealed her conviction that whole schools must restructure themselves to give teachers far more responsibility, undercutting the need for them "to become lobbyists against change."[3]

Though the New York City "school wars" had sown cynicism among many educators, others were more determined than ever to make public schools work. The final compromise as to how schools should be controlled had divided the city into thirty-two districts, each with its own elected school board. One district had nowhere to go but up: district #4 in east Harlem, thirty-second in the city in standardized test scores, dismal in attendance, and high in teacher and student turnover. Its new superintendent was an experienced teacher and gifted administrator named Anthony Alvarado. Alvarado determined to break the cycle of low expectations and flaccid accomplishment that the district's largely black and Latino children had suffered for years. In 1972, he asked Deborah Meier, among others, if she would like to start an alternative primary school. Meier jumped at the chance, and the first Central Park East (CPE) school began.

In a nation whose public schools seemed to have lost their bearings, she set out to build a school that would foster children's intellectual growth, empower them as citizens, and welcome their parents' counsel and help in doing both. Central to the plan was management of the school by the classroom teachers who worked with the children every day. The faculty would first offer a primary school program; then, if parents and children kept signing up, they would add a grade each year up to sixth grade. In its small size, its close student-teacher bonds, its élan, it would be much like the fine private school Meier herself had attended.

During her six years of teaching and learning in New York, Meier had made friends all over the city, and several now came to work with her. Together they recruited other teachers, gathering colleagues rather than hiring subordinates; thus they broke all the conventions whereby principals and bureaucrats impose their decisions on teachers, absolving teachers of both responsibility and self-regard. Superintendent Alvarado and his assistant Seymour Fliegel supported her, and they left her alone. Meier and her colleagues had never worked so hard, nor so happily. They designed curriculum and ordered materials. They interviewed parents wishing to enroll their children to help the parents judge the fit between their child's needs and the school. They worked out strategies to fully challenge "retarded" and "gifted" children within heterogeneous classrooms. CPE school's cost per student had to approximate the city average, even though there would be more classroom teachers than was usual. To equip the classrooms, they searched the New York streets on garbage pickup day, scavenging chairs, sofas, secondhand tables, and orange crates. As they welcomed the first children and parents, says Meier, "we felt like the most powerful teachers in New York City."

Eliot Eisner of Stanford University summarized the sources of inertia in public education: parents' and educators' long-outdated images of impressive teachers from their own school days; teachers' attachments to familiar routines in a world of pedagogical fads and upsetting student behavior; a "rigid and enduring" tendency to define teaching as "telling" rather than intellectual empowerment; teachers' and departments' isolation from each other; and a nationwide reliance on "experts" whose place in academic hierarchies usually depends on their distance from low-status work with real children.[4] One might add to Eisner's list the systems of promotion and prestige within public schools, which award the highest salaries and the largest authority to those who leave classroom teaching to become principals or district officials. Deborah Meier set out to address each of these problems in Central Park East.

As the school year opened, Meier and the other Central Park East teachers hosted parents at school—or visited them at home if necessary—to talk over children's initial adjustment and future needs. Mistakes could be quickly corrected by a small faculty released from the traditional restrictions and excuses. The CPE children thrived. They worked daily with adults whom they saw as decision makers as well as friends, advocates, and sometimes judges; they went home to parents who, they knew, had importantly influenced their teachers' perceptions of them. Though all but powerless in the world's eyes and seen as congenitally "inferior" by racist Americans, they had a chance, now, of imagining a future as responsible, capable adults.

The bureaucracy kept hands off because CPE children's standardized test scores rose year by year, even though math/science projects, free reading, dramatizations, and creative writing had squeezed test preparation out of the school day. Meier, in turn, kept officialdom at arm's length. "It's better not to ask permission if you don't want 'no' for an answer," she says. Attendance was high and truancy rates were nil. More children enrolled, until CPE reached 270 students and 12 teachers, the maximum workable number, Meier now thinks, for a school whose faculty are broadly responsible for all its students. In the midst of high-rise housing projects, worn-out brownstones and glass-strewn vacant lots, Central Park East was a haven of safety, hard work, and fun.

Though Meier's original vision continued to guide the school, one organizational change seemed necessary. Following two years of seemingly interminable after-school meetings, the faculty collective began to sag with exhaustion. With her colleagues' agreement, Meier relinquished full-time classroom teaching to become CPE's director, while faculty continued to be the curriculum planners, recruiters of new teachers, and counselors of first resort for troubled students. By 1979, there were so many applicants for CPE's admissions lottery that Meier urged another group of teachers to open CPE II, a second district #4 alternative elementary school; Deborah Meier served as director of both schools for two years, until the teachers and parents of CPE II chose a director of their own. By 1982, a third school named River East opened.

Ninety-six percent of the sixth graders from the CPE schools led or inspired by Deborah Meier earned high school diplomas. Two-thirds went on to colleges, nearly twice the New York City average. "We were proud of them," says Meier.

But quite a few had come back to us and told us how horrible their high schools were. About 1984, we began to wonder—couldn't we do better? Several of us had read Ted Sizer's *Horace's Compromise*, and he had just started his Coalition of Essential Schools. We invited him down to talk with us about how you run a topnotch high school. He looked around the Central Park East schools, visited some classes, and said to us "Why don't you just keep this going through 12th grade?"

This was a daunting idea. A district #4 alternative high school would have to begin in seventh grade, and early adolescence is the "critical juncture" on the way to "the real world of adulthood," as Meier has said. "Every human characteristic . . . is heightened, sharpened, and more intensely experienced."[5] Educators' arguments intensify too, for example, over grouping and tracking and the balance between elective and required courses. In Meier's mind, however, these contentious issues are often false ones that barely conceal "time-honored educational malpractice." In spite of the student choices endorsed by progressives for half a century and embodied in huge "democratic," comprehensive high schools since the 1950s, Meier and Sizer believe that few genuine choices have been offered to urban minority students. Instead, most move anonymously through the grades, opting for, or being tracked into, one undemanding course after another.

School size is crucial. "Our kids are dying in these large high schools," says Meier. "Most human beings need to be known, and it is more critical when other things [in their lives] are also fragile."[6] "The real question is, what is special about every child? All the tracking that sorts the students and teachers who carry the highest status from the people and work which society . . . holds in contempt—it's *wrong*." Equally antidemocratic is the traditional high school's refusal to expect *all* future citizens to learn how to explore "the fundamental intellectual and social issues of their time."[7] Would it be possible for any public high school, large or small, to buck these pervasive, child-damaging expectations and assumptions?

"Try it," said John Falco, now assistant superintendent in district #4. So Meier and an adventurous group of teachers sat down to design Central Park East Secondary School (CPESS), which opened its doors in September 1985.

Again, the conventions had to be cracked, not least in order to secure a New York high school principal's license for a woman who had never taught any class beyond first grade, even a woman who had dutifully, impatiently taken the proper eighteen credits in "administration." But deciding on a size for CPESS (a maximum of 450) and a space within the same large building as the CPE I elementary school appeared easier, as did curriculum design. The pioneering faculty group included some teachers from the CPE schools, as well as experienced, dissatisfied high school teachers. "We realized that everything we knew about five-to-twelve-year olds was also true of adolescents," recalled Meier.[8] It is important—sometimes essential—to understand children's particular needs at particular ages, Meier knew, but 'developmentalist' clichés . . . can be misleading and dangerous" where they emphasize differences at the expense of our "common humanity."[9] Thus, as in the best kindergartens, most teaching would not be "telling" but "coaching." Teachers might introduce new questions or concepts; for the most part, however, the *students* would be the workers, seeking their own further information and meanings, their teachers their guides.

From its beginnings, Central Park East Secondary School has drawn richly on its membership in the new Essential Schools network, for Theodore Sizer's pedagogical philosophy aligned with Meier's own. "Less is more," Sizer maintains. Study of a few topics in depth makes it imperative to ask *why*? What is the evidence? How do we know what we know? If it matters, why does it matter? Furthermore, if academic offerings are organized around "essential questions" such as these—complex, never fully answerable questions that matter as much to adults as to children—then learning is inevitably *interdisciplinary*. It can be advanced by one versatile practitioner teaching both math and science (or combining the "humanities" such as writing, literature, history, geography, and civics) with 40 to 45 students in 2 cross-age sections—a far cry from the usual teaching assignment, which requires, for example, an English and a history/social studies teacher to teach 5 sections and 150 students each, then switch to a whole new group the next year.

At CPESS, math/science and humanities are each given daily two-hour time blocks. Such a schedule seems much more consistent with the way adult work is done than the traditional seven-period school day, in which students and teachers constantly "change the subject" after forty-five or fifty minutes. All teachers also lead an advisory group of twelve to fifteen drawn from their own students. These groups meet for an hour nearly every day and periodically for special celebrations, camping trips, or college visits. Credits and diplomas are earned not by time served in designated courses, but by *exhibition* of each student's mastery of knowledge and its uses.

Through nearly ten years, CPESS has largely followed its original design, adding a grade every year until, in 1991, the first students to arrive graduated. The citywide outlay per student, approximately $7,000 in 1992, did not pay for everything; a choice had to be made between art and music, two prominent CPE elementary subjects. Art won, though music remains an after-school option. A regular theater program is lacking. In spite of the performing arts' power to energize students as workers and exhibitors, Sizer and Meier are convinced that small schools must resist "add-ons" in order to win the advantages of their size. There is no football team. After-school sports are fervent, but the uniforms are T-shirts, and the sports director scrounges for supplies and volunteer help. Less is more.

As an elected faculty council—and later, a coprincipal—began helping with administrative decisions, Meier assumed ever more responsibility for writing about the schools she established and assisting others who want to invent their own versions of the Central Park East schools. Part of her work is to serve as president of the Center for Collaborative Education, a network of innovative schools that she and like-minded alternative school founders have set up to assist each other, link their schools with Sizer's nationwide Coalition for Essential Schools, and describe their reform strategies to the nation. The collaborative hosted 2,000 visitors in 1991–1992. Meier no longer teaches a humanities class of her own, though she meets almost daily with her advisory group.

"A first class academic education...doesn't preclude caring—it *requires* caring," says Meier. CPESS teacher-advisers and their advisees are free to explore all mutual concerns: drug use, violence outside the school (there is virtually none within it), plans for work or college, a boy's sorrow for a sick grandmother, a girl's celebration of a new sibling (or, on a few occasions, a baby of her own). Some concerns accumulate during students' weekly three-hour community service projects or (for older students) their career internships. Every student is known; everyone counts. A small school, writes Meier, is the best way to "learn the language of participation, that difficult public language necessary to becoming a member of a democratic society."[10] Learning at CPESS includes conversation and argument with well-known adults or conversation and argument *between* adults. In a faculty-managed school, the youngsters stretch to discern the adults' agendas, much as Deborah and Paul Willen had done at the family dinner table. Meier believes that "when you know your teachers are seriously arguing over . . . decisions that affect your school and your life," you come to realize that "it is good to be an adult," even in a neighborhood where many adults appear helpless to the young.[11]

Teachers can most clearly be seen as allies and advocates by the Senior Institute students working at the eleventh and twelfth grade levels. The older students spend one to three years assembling the cumulative portfolios and final exhibitions of their accomplishments in fourteen areas of understanding and skill. These will be judged not by the senior's own teacher but by other adults, including visiting experts in the area to be assessed—parents, career internship supervisors, or professors from nearby colleges. A younger student of the senior's choice also serves on this Graduation Committee. After an exhibition, quite often the student realizes he or she could do much better and insists on the chance to make a revised presentation, or portfolios are sent back by the committee for a reworking and a second (or third) try. It is a strenuous time for students and, ultimately, a proud one.

CPESS administers no admissions tests, selecting from applicants only to ensure priority to younger siblings and district #4 children and to see that diversity is maintained; for example, 20 percent of all enrollees must be in the "special needs" category. Students may come from outside the district if their enrollment contributes to ethnic and income-group diversity. As in other collaborative/coalition schools, children may choose CPESS only if their parents do too, agreeing to attend at least two parent-teacher-student conferences every year. For many parents or guardians, a collaborative school opens access to a dignified public role never before assumed. Numerous CPESS parents organize festivals, graduation activities, and fundraisers for special school projects or trips.

As of 1992, only 5 percent of CPESS students have failed to win a high school diploma, as against about 55 percent for comparable New York City students. Their families may move out of district #4, but nearly all the children keep coming, often traveling for an hour or more by bus and subway from the outer boroughs. Nearly all CPESS graduates go on to postsecondary education, most of them to four-year colleges. Nearly all others find useful work and come back to tell proud teachers about it.

Deborah Meier thinks she knows what makes the most difference. "Our kids *know* us." They have learned to connect with interesting, authoritative adults and "have come to understand that a responsible, rewarding adulthood is their birthright." The "exaggerated closeness" of the alternative schools helps young people deeply to understand that "we all belong to a common world."

Deborah Meier writes frequently about her own work and that of her colleagues and about the many problems in public education that remain to be addressed both within and outside the collaborative schools. She is a contributing or advisory editor of the *Nation*, the *Harvard Education Letter*, and *Dissent*. Her schools have gained welcome public notice each time she has received an honorary degree. In 1987, she became the first teacher to win a MacArthur Award; there was still more excitement in 1992, when she, with Theodore Sizer, raised $3 million from foundations to plan and launch ten new 270-student high schools in New York City, each of them to be paired with an existing coalition school during its first few years.

Active reform groups recruit Meier when they can. In 1970, she helped start the North Dakota Study Group, an informal klatch of progressive educators who will join her out on any limb. She is a founding member of the National Board for Professional Teaching Standards. She gives much time to the Holmes Group, which is struggling against odds to transform American schools of education, as well as to the Board of FairTest and other "assessment radicals," who question the use of all standardized tests. Yet none of these activities or distinctions would mean anything to Deborah Meier were they not based on her never-finished work of teaching herself, her colleagues, and above all, her students to "imagine the future." In this frame of mind, profound change is possible.

NOTES

I am indebted to Deborah Meier; Paul Schwarz, coprincipal of CPESS; Sonia Bailey, public relations coordinator at the Center for Collaborative Education; and CPESS students Alana, Jimmy, and Jacques.

1. Deborah W. Meier to author in interviews, June 1992. All quotations come from this source unless otherwise noted.

2. D. W. Meier, "Re-inventing Teaching," *Teachers College Record* 93, no. 4 (Summer 1992): 595; interview with author.

3. Meier, "Re-inventing," 599.

4. Eliot W. Eisner, "Educational Reform and the Ecology of Schooling," *Teachers College Record*, 93, no. 4 (Summer 1993), 610–18.

5. Susan Chira, "Harlem's Witness for the Chancellor," *New York Times*, August 10, 1992, 42.

6. D. W. Meier, in foreword to Anne C. Lewis, *Making It in the Middle* (New York: Edna McConnell Clark Foundations, 1990), 7.

7. Deborah Meier, "The Beautician Question: Can Secondary Education Be Progressive?" in K. Jervis and A. Tobler, eds., *Education for Democracy* (Weston, MA: Cambridge School, 1988), 71.

8. Lewis, 6.

9. D. W. Meier, "The Kindergarten Tradition in the High School," in Kathe Jervis and Carol Montag, eds., *Progressive Education for the 1990s* (New York: Teachers College Press, 1991), 135.

10. Mark F. Goldberg, "Portrait of Deborah Meier," *Educational Leadership* 48, no. 4 (December 1990/January 1991), 26–28.

11. Ibid.

WORKS BY DEBORAH W. MEIER

"The Beautician Question: Can Secondary Education Be Progressive," In K. Jervis and A. Tobler, eds., *Education for Democracy*. Weston, MA: Cambridge School, 1988.

"The Kindergarten Tradition in the High School." In Kathe Jervis and Carol Montag, eds., *Progressive Education for the 1990s* (New York: Teachers College Press, 1991).

"Re-inventing Teaching." *Teachers College Record* 93, no. 4 (Summer 1992): 594–609.
"School Days: A Journal." *Dissent* (Spring 1992): 213–220.

WORKS ABOUT DEBORAH W. MEIER

Bensman, David. "There Is a Rose in Spanish Harlem." Paper given at the AERA annual conference, April 24, 1992.
Goldberg, Mark F. "Portrait of Deborah Meier." *Educational Leadership* (December 1990/January 1991): 26–28.

Lucy Sprague Mitchell

Joyce Antler

Lucy Sprague Mitchell (1878–1967), writer, teacher, administrator, and social reformer, was a builder of experimental institutions and leading force in the education of young children in the early twentieth century. Founder and director of the Bureau of Educational Experiments which became the pioneering Bank Street College of Education, she helped link methods of progressive education to scientific research on child development. Her many books for adults and children and the innovative Writers' Laboratory and Public School Workshops she initiated brought her child-centered philosophy and practice to a wide public.

Lucy Sprague Mitchell was born in Chicago on July 2, 1878, the fourth of six children of Otho and Lucia Sprague. Otho Sprague had emigrated from Vermont to Chicago with his young bride shortly after the Civil War. With a combination of hard work, luck, and shrewdness, he and an older brother built a fledgling dry goods business into the largest wholesale grocery in the world, Sprague Warner & Co. The Sprague brothers became leading members of Chicago's merchant elite, active in the city's financial, cultural, and civic life. They helped establish the Chicago Orchestra, the University of Chicago, and the World's Fair held in the city in 1892.

In contrast to Otho's active world of business and philanthropy, Lucia Sprague's sphere was limited to the home, but it was not one she exercised with authority. A gifted musician, she lived under the pall of her husband's rigid rules for household order, suppressing her own gaiety and artistry. In temperament and instinct, Lucy Sprague Mitchell inherited much from each parent: from her father, her energy, confidence, and discipline; from her mother, a passionate and spontaneous love of color, art, and music. Entrepreneur and artist, rationalist and romantic, Mitchell blended these qualities into a unique combination of teaching, writing, and administration that shaped the philosophy and practice of the dynamic institution she created—

the Bureau of Educational Experiments (later known as Bank Street College of Education).

During her childhood and adolescence, the fortunate economic circumstances of her family seemed more of a burden than an opportunity. A lonely and repressed girl who chafed under her father's domestic discipline, Lucy did not attend school on a regular basis until she was sixteen: she broke down whenever she entered a classroom, twitching uncontrollably. But she read her way around her father's huge classical library, shelf by shelf, and wandered the neighborhoods of the city, learning by seeing. The programs in experimental education she developed in later years derived much inspiration from this self-guided instruction in history and geography.

After the Spragues moved to southern California in 1893, Lucy entered the Marlborough School, a girls' private preparatory academy in Los Angeles. Though the Marlborough School was primarily designed to give elite young women training in social deportment, for Lucy it provided the context for intellectual excellence and scholarly achievement. Headmistress Mary Caswell encouraged Lucy's plans for college and helped her with preparatory exams for Radcliffe College. Because of the intervention of Alice Freeman Palmer, former president of Wellesley College and a friend of the Sprague family since her appointment as part-time dean of women at the University of Chicago, Lucy was finally allowed to attend Radcliffe over the strong objections of her father. Alice Freeman Palmer and Jane Addams, Hull House's inspirational director whom Lucy had also met in Chicago, became lifelong mentors and dominant influences in her life.

Although deeply troubled by the subordinate status of Radcliffe women at Harvard, Lucy derived many benefits from her years at the college. Not the least of these were "getting free" from her family, as she wrote in one class reunion report, and gaining self-confidence as a leader of student organizations. Her intellectual growth was also stunning. Studying with the great men of Harvard's philosophy department—Josiah Royce, George Santayana, Hugo Munsterberg, George Herbert Palmer, and William James—during its so-called golden age, she sharpened her analytical skills, never fearing to challenge the masters when she held disparate views. Graduating in 1900, Lucy was the only Radcliffe student to receive honors in philosophy.

After college, Lucy spent a brief but unhappy time caring for her invalid father in California. Rescued again by Alice and George Herbert Palmer, she traveled abroad with them in Europe until Alice's sudden death in Paris. Lucy returned to Cambridge with the widower, helping with housekeeping, taking graduate courses at Harvard, and working for Radcliffe's dean. In 1903, recommended by Palmer, she accepted the offer of President Benjamin Wheeler of the University of California at Berkeley to assist the university's women students. Three years later, Sprague was officially appointed the University of California's first dean of women; serving as assistant professor of English as well, she was one of only two women on the faculty.

As dean, Lucy improved housing and social and curricular opportunities for women, abandoning the traditional "warden" function of the deanship to concentrate on educational issues. She started courses in sex education and introduced a "curriculum of experience," taking women students to explore social issues in the surrounding communities of Oakland and San Francisco. Lucy resigned her post in 1912, following her marriage to economist Wesley Clair Mitchell. After a wedding trip to Europe, the couple moved to New York, where Wesley Mitchell joined the faculty of Columbia University. Lucy began new work educating children, a career move she had decided on after a brief apprenticeship with Julia Richman, principal of a Manhattan high school, during a trip to the city in 1911. She took courses with John Dewey at Teachers College, Columbia, volunteered as a visiting teacher for Harriet Johnson at the Public Education Association, conducted psychological tests on city school children, and taught nursery school and kindergarten classes at Caroline Pratt's new Play School in Greenwich Village.

In 1916, after her cousin, Elizabeth Sprague Coolidge, offered to support an educational venture of Mitchell's choosing, Lucy established the Bureau of Educational Experiments (BEE), a cooperative association of some dozen members, dedicated to teaching and developing research on "progressive education and educational experiments." In its first years, it sponsored a variety of projects, including a farm labor camp, public school nutrition, educational testing, rural schools, play materials, day nurseries, sex and vocational education, and the Gary School idea. Its most important work came in 1919, when it launched a nursery school for children aged fifteen months to three years, which it joined to Caroline Pratt's Play School (later known as City and Country) for children aged three to seven. It also added an eight-year-old class taught by bureau staff. The school, directed by Harriet Johnson, launched a unique laboratory program that combined comprehensive research into the quantitative indexes of children's physical, social, and emotional growth with child-centered expressive curricula. As chairman of the BEE Working Council, which administered the nursery school, Mitchell helped coordinate the laboratory school program while providing overall direction to BEE projects.

A new phase of the BEE's growth came in 1931, when Mitchell, Harriet Johnson, and colleagues from seven experimental schools established the Cooperative School for Student Teachers to train teachers to work in experimental schools. The school's goal—to help students develop an "experimental, critical and ardent" approach to education that combined a "scientific attitude" with the "attitude of an artist"—was embodied in its innovative curriculum. From Monday through Thursday, students gained practical experience in placements at participating experimental schools. From Thursday afternoon to Saturday, they took an intensive series of seminars and workshops at "Bank Street," as the school and its parent-body, the BEE, were informally known after its move to larger quarters at 69 Bank

Street in 1931. These offerings consisted of "intake" courses, as Mitchell called them, which included her own core courses on language and the environment and courses taught by Barbara Biber, Jessie Stanton, Harriet Johnson (until her death in 1934), and others of the Bank Street cooperative body. The "outgo" portion of the curriculum consisted of courses in painting, dance, music, and dramatics, taught by outstanding artists, to help student teachers experience the world as openly and directly as did children. This curriculum was supplemented by the resources of the New School for Social Research and by a "curriculum of experience," similar to the one Lucy provided her students at the University of California; this time she took students to observe tenements, jails, courts, clinics, political rallies, and labor unions. Students also spent one morning a week doing fieldwork for social organizations.

In 1938, Lucy established a Writers' Laboratory at Bank Street to help potential writers of books for children to understand the dynamics of children's growth and to aid them in developing language, rhythms, and forms based on children's own speech. One of the first graduates of the laboratory was Margaret Wise Brown, author of *Good Night Moon* and hundreds of other popular children's stories, then a student teacher at Bank Street. Other writing students include Eve Merriam, Edith Thatcher Hurd, and Mary Phelps.

Another institutional milestone came in 1943, when Lucy convinced the New York City Board of Education to allow her to bring Bank Street's experimental teaching methods into the city's public schools. For three years, Lucy taught teachers and children at a Harlem elementary school. She relished a comment one young pupil made to his teacher to the effect that Lucy was a "genius . . . because she makes us know more than we thought we could."[1]

Mitchell continued at Bank Street, serving as chairperson of the board and as acting president, until 1956. The institution was chartered as the Bank Street College of Education in 1950. After retirement, she lived in Palo Alto, California, near one of her children, until her death from arteriosclerotic heart disease in 1967.

Lucy Mitchell's formative influence on progressive education stemmed from her multiple roles as teacher, administrator, and writer. Teaching was the work she considered primary. "If a big word [is] necessary [to describe her work]," she once wrote, "I'd rather [be] called an 'educator,' though to me the best title is 'teacher.'"[2] In her courses for Bank Street student teachers, Mitchell stressed her guiding belief in the unity of the arts and sciences and the need for firsthand experience. Her language courses aimed to reeducate students to regain the simple, direct approach characteristic of children's speech. Students did exercises to learn "to let things describe themselves directly" rather than in abstract, interpretive terms. Reviewing the language and imagery of Lucy's favorite poems or of children, they became sensitive to rhythms, sound quality, pitch, and structure.

In her course on environment (which one student called "ecology rediscovered"), Lucy stressed what she called "human geography." Using home-made "tool" maps, she showed students how to locate relationships between the earth's natural geographic features and patterns of food production, set-tlement, work, and politics. In her notable "five-finger exercises," students recorded everything they observed as they stood outside for fifteen minutes, keeping their eyes shut, but other senses open for the last five minutes. They then analyzed their notes, constructing social meanings according to the data collected. Lucy's students also prepared comprehensive studies of the com-munities in which they had been practice-teaching, comparing local work patterns with regional and national trends. In 1935, she inaugurated an an-nual "long trip," taking Bank Street students on an eight-day trip, usually to Appalachia and Washington, D.C., for an extended exploration of the social, economic, geographic, and political environment.

Many students in Bank Street's early classes found their lives totally changed by their classroom encounters with Mitchell. Mary Phelps and Mar-garet Wise Brown recalled that she could make any subject interesting, from "the habits of the octopus" to the "economic history of potatoes."[3] "She shook us out of our academic molds, quickened our sensibilities, and opened our eyes," recalled another student.[4] "To be a student was like being born again," commented Charlotte Winsor, a City and Country teacher who later joined Bank Street's faculty.[5]

Although Lucy liked administrative work least and always balked at being called Bank Street's "leader," she was, in fact, the institution's "prime mover," as Bank Street's distinguished research director, psychologist Bar-bara Biber, once put it.[6] Mitchell established a supportive and cooperative working environment at Bank Street that encouraged creativity and allowed staff to participate in institutional management. Although Mitchell chaired Bank Street's elected Working Council, she resisted all efforts to develop a more centralized administrative hierarchy. Under her chairmanship, Bank Street developed an alternative model of professionalism that provided status and esteem to women teachers, researchers, and writers.

Lucy Sprague Mitchell also wrote, coauthored, or edited six books for adults and over twenty books for children. Her first and most influential book was the *Here and Now Story Book*, published in 1921, a collection of forty-one stories or "jingles" for children, preceded by an introductory essay that announced a radically new departure in writing for children. Criticizing traditional stories for children, especially fairy tales but also tales of hunting and war and many ancient myths, Mitchell argued that children's stories should begin from their immediate, firsthand experiences—"the here-and-now"—and should be geared to their developmental interests. The form of the stories was as important as their content; Mitchell urged that they be constructed according to the patterns, rhythms, and sounds of children's natural speech. Though some critics attacked Lucy's theories for neglecting imagination, she and her supporters felt the charge was misguided. The *Here and Now Story Book*, translated into several languages, had widespread impact in the next decades. Other innovative works employed "here and now" principles, focusing on history and geography of interest to older children, for example, *Horses Now and Long Ago* (1926); *North America: The Land They Lived In for the Children Who Live There* (1931); and *Manhattan Now and Long Ago* (1934), with Clara Lambert. *Young Geographers* (1934) articulated Lucy's theory of "relationship thinking"—the importance of connecting earth forces, social groups, cultural traditions, and work habits—and provided a practical account of how teachers could assist children to construct geographic meanings through discovering these patterns. The book remains in use today.

Lucy was also responsible for *Our Children and Our Schools*, (1950), an account of Bank Street's Public School Workshops, and a number of Golden Books and other works for children. Her most unusual work was *Two Lives: The Story of Wesley Clair Mitchell and Myself* (1953), a literary tour de force that combined autobiography with a biography of her husband and the story of their marriage. One reviewer noted that it offered "a better look at changing human and sex relationships than Simone de Beauvoir gives."[7]

Mitchell's professional interests in education were deeply entwined with her personal life. The mother of four children, two biological and two adopted, she felt that her life was "highly focused . . . with everything concentrated on children, each aspect of my work illuminating the others."[8] Residing in a complex of buildings that Lucy owned on West 12th and West 13th Streets, which also housed the City and Country School and the Bureau of Educational Experiments (until its move to Bank Street), the Mitchell family—husband and children—were deeply involved in Lucy's educational ventures. At the same time, her educational theory and practice reflected the new life-styles that she, as a professional woman, had come to pioneer. The BEE's innovative nursery school and the many Bank Street projects in child development research and teaching that followed helped make it possible for generations of women to combine motherhood with full-time work.

Mitchell's work in early childhood education reflected the deep influence of Dewey-inspired goals of social reform. Believing that schooling was intimately related to community life at all levels, Mitchell expected that the development of intelligent, emotionally secure, and healthy children would inevitably lead to the creation of a more progressive and humanistic society. Her work thus sustained the activism of progressive-era women reformers at the same time that it used newer techniques of social science and professionalism to transform children's learning.

NOTES

1. Barbara Biber, *Lucy Sprague Mitchell, 1878–1967* (New York: Bank Street College of Education, 1967), 21.

2. LSM to Sally Kerlin, August 26, 1961, in Lucy Sprague Mitchell, *Two Lives* (New York: Simon and Schuster, 1953), 362.

3. Mary Phelps and Margaret Wise Brown, "Lucy Sprague Mitchell," *Horn Book Magazine* (May-June 1937), in Mitchell, 362.

4. Sally Morrison Kerlin, *Children and the Environment* (New York: Bank Street College of Education, 1971), 75, in Joyce Antler, *Lucy Sprague Mitchell* (New Haven, CT: Yale University Press, 1987), 319.

5. Biber, in Antler, 319.

6. Antler, 328–30, 363.

7. Ernestine Evans, "A Happy Family Album," *The New York Herald Tribune Book Review* (June 14, 1953), in Antler, xv.

8. Lucy Sprague Mitchell, Unpublished Autobiography, in Antler, 259.

WORKS BY LUCY SPRAGUE MITCHELL

For Adults

Young Geographers: How They Explore the World and How They Map the World. New York: John Day, 1934. Reprint, 1963.
My Country 'Tis of Thee: The Use and Abuse of Natural Resources (with Eleanor Bowman and Mary Phelps). New York: Macmillan, 1940.
Our Children and Our Schools. New York: Simon and Schuster, 1950.
Two Lives: The Story of Wesley Clair Mitchell and Myself. New York: Simon and Schuster, 1953.

For Children

Here and Now Story Book. New York: E. P. Dutton, 1921. Reprint, 1948.
Another Here and Now Story Book. New York: E. P. Dutton, 1924. Reprint, 1937.
Here and Now Primer: Home from the Country. New York: E. P. Dutton, 1924.
Horses Now and Long Ago. New York: Harcourt, Brace, 1926.
North America: The Land They Lived in for the Children Who Live There. New York: Macmillan, 1931. Reprint, 1940.
Manhattan Now and Long Ago (with Clara Lambert). New York: Macmillan, 1934.
Believe and Make-Believe (with Irma Simonton Black). New York: E. P. Dutton, 1956.

WORKS ABOUT LUCY SPRAGUE MITCHELL

Antler, Joyce. "Lucy Sprague Mitchell." In Barbara Sicherman and Carol Hurd Green, eds., *Notable American Women: The Modern Period*, 484–87. Cambridge: Belknap Press of Harvard University Press, 1980.
———. "Feminism as Life Process: The Life and Career of Lucy Sprague Mitchell." *Feminist Studies* 7 (Spring 1981): 134–55.
———. "Progressive Education and the Scientific Study of the Child: An Analysis of the Bureau of Educational Experiments, 1916–1940." *Teachers College Record* 83 (Summer 1982): 559–91.

———. "Was She a Good Mother? Some Thoughts on a New Issue for Feminist Biography." In Barbara J. Harris and JoAnn R. McNamara, eds., *Women and the Structure of Society: Selected Research from the Fifth Berkshire Conference on the History of Women*, 53–66. Durham, NC: Duke University Press, 1984.

———. *Lucy Sprague Mitchell: The Making of a Modern Woman*. New Haven, CT: Yale University Press, 1987.

———. "The Educational Biography of Lucy Sprague Mitchell: A Case Study in the History of Women's Higher Education." In John Mack Faragher and Florence Howe, eds., *Women and Higher Education in American History*, 43–63. New York: Norton, 1988.

———. "Having It All, Almost: Confronting the Legacy of Lucy Sprague Mitchell." In Sara Alpert et al., eds., *The Challenge of Feminist Biography: Writing the Lives of Modern American Women*, 97–115. Urbana: University of Illinois Press, 1992.

Phelps, Mary, and Margaret Wise Brown. "Lucy Sprague Mitchell." *Horn Book Magazine* (May-June 1937).

Raushenbush, Esther. "Three Women: Creators of Change." In Helen S. Astin and Werner Z. Hirsch, eds., *The Higher Education of Women: Essays in Honor of Rosemary Park*. New York: Praeger, 1978.

Mary Adelaide Nutting

Janice Cooke Feigenbaum

Mary Adelaide Nutting (1858–1948) was the first nurse to be granted the rank of professor in an institution of higher education. She was the director of the program in nursing at Teachers College, Columbia University, from 1906 to 1925. In this position, she worked to upgrade the programs of nursing education throughout the country.

Mary Adelaide Nutting, commonly referred to as Adelaide Nutting, was born on November 1, 1858, in Frost Village, Quebec. Her parents were Vespasion and Harriet Peasley Nutting. Both were United Empire Loyalists who had been born and raised in Quebec. Even though she had been raised in a family with very limited means, Harriet was devoted to books, poetry, and music. This was very unusual for her time, except for the upper class.

Adelaide was the fourth of five children. Charles was nine years older than Adelaide, while Arthur was four years older and James two. The family's first child, Ella Frances, had been extremely frail at birth and died in 1847. The youngest child, Harriette, was born in 1861. Since Adelaide was extremely small and frail when she was born, she reminded her parents of Ella Frances. Throughout her life, Adelaide was frequently ill.[1]

Even though the family had many financial problems, Harriet was adamant that all five of her children, not just her sons, be educated so that they could move up in society. Due to her mother's efforts, Adelaide had a varied educational background. After the family moved to Waterloo in 1861, she attended R. W. Laing's Academy there. Then, she studied French and music at a convent school in a neighboring town and spent a year at Bute House, a private school across the street from McGill College in Montreal. Then, at age sixteen, she went to Lowell to live with her father's relatives and continue her studies in music and art. As a result of all of this study, the young Adelaide Nutting was relatively well educated for a person of her era.

She aimed to have a professional music career, but this desire was never fulfilled.

In 1881, Nutting's mother moved with four of her children to Ottawa. Then, in 1882, Nutting joined her younger sister, who was teaching at the Church of England School for Girls in Saint John's, Newfoundland. Nutting tried to earn a living by teaching music to private students, but these efforts failed. She eventually returned to Ottawa in 1883.

During this year, her mother became very ill, and Nutting cared for her until her mother died on November 17, 1884. For entertainment, Nutting spent many evenings listening to debates at the House of Commons. Here, she saw government in action and learned the realities and intricacies of the political system.

As Harriet's condition worsened, Nutting realized how little she knew about how to help her mother most effectively. She became intrigued with the details of her care and had many questions for the physician. Following her mother's death, she was not sure what she should do to support herself. She eventually decided to move in with her brother Jim, a widower, and his family, so she could care for his children. She felt unfulfilled in this role, however, and very concerned that she was a burden to her brother and his family.

Adelaide began looking for some other work to pursue and ultimately decided to move to Baltimore in 1889 so she could attend the Johns Hopkins Training School for Nursing. She chose this program because three other Canadians had been appointed to the staff of the hospital: William Osler, a physician who was a graduate of McGill College; Henri Lafleur, a physician; and Isabel Hampton, who had been born in Welland, Ontario, and was now the superintendent of the hospital and school of nursing.

Nutting began her nursing career during a time when hospital training programs for nurses were proliferating. The first three American programs had opened in 1873. Philip and Beatrice Kalisch note that "by 1880 there were 15 schools, 323 students, and 157 graduates in the United States. Twenty years later these figures had soared to 432 schools, 11,164 students, and 3,546 graduates."[2] Throughout this period, the graduate nurses were employed primarily as private duty nurses who cared for patients in their homes. Meanwhile, the care of patients in the hospitals was provided by the student nurses supervised by the superintendent of nurses, who was usually the only trained nurse employed by the institution.

Students in these programs had extremely long work hours. They were responsible for caring for patients seven days a week, twenty-four hours a day. They typically received two weeks of vacation each year. Lectures were provided by physicians as time allowed.

However, as Hampton planned the program for the students in the Johns Hopkins Hospital Training School, she aimed to implement her own philosophy of nursing. The three goals of this philosophy were to establish nursing as a group of well-trained, elite women, to have nurses be given the control of nursing within all hospitals, and to establish a hierarchy of nursing within the hospitals.[3] Hampton believed this could be accomplished only by upgrading the educational component offered students in nursing programs and decreasing the number of hours that they had to work on the wards. Nutting quickly learned Hampton's beliefs and excelled as a student.

In 1890, the *Trained Nurse and Hospital Review* sponsored a contest for student nurses, who were asked to submit an article on a case study of caring for a patient with typhoid fever. Nutting won the prize of ten dollars, and her article was published in the March 1891 issue of the journal.

Nutting graduated from the program with a diploma in nursing in 1891. She then was appointed to be the head nurse on Dr. Osler's Men's Medical Unit. In 1893, she became Hampton's assistant and assumed some teaching assignments.

When Hampton married Hunter Robb in 1894, Nutting was named the superintendent of nurses and principal of the Training School. She assumed the position at Johns Hopkins in September 1895 and held it for thirteen years. In this role, she worked to implement the plans that Hampton had outlined for the school of nursing. These included establishing the standard of an eight-hour work day for students, implementing a six-month program of classes that students had before they were allowed to work on the wards, adding a third year to the length of the program, and ending the stipend that students received for working. She further wrote many articles and lobbied other programs to adopt these changes.

To prove the need for these changes during her initial year as superintendent, Nutting completed the first research project that studied the conditions of training schools in the United States. The results of this endeavor, "A Statistical Report of Working Hours in Training Schools," documented the overwhelming evidence of the long working hours and limited educational opportunities for students in training programs.

Beginning in 1898, Nutting and Hampton-Robb worked to establish the program in hospital economics for graduate nurses at Teachers College, Columbia University, which opened in 1899. Initially, the program was funded annually by $1,000, which was raised by donations from nurses to the Society for Superintendents and the Nurses Associated Alumnae.

From the inception of the program, James Earl Russell, president of Teachers College, encouraged Nutting to become the director of the program. He finally succeeded in this endeavor in 1906. Nutting was forty-nine years of age when she moved to New York City and became the administrator of the hospital economics program. The 1908–1909 Teachers College Bulletin lists her as professor of domestic administration within the department of domestic economy. Thus, she was the first nurse to be granted an appointment of professor within an institution of higher education. She served in this position until her retirement in 1925.

Throughout this time, Nutting wrote prolifically and made presentations at meetings of many organizations. Along with Lavinia Dock, she completed four volumes of the *History of Nursing*. She wrote two other books and published numerous articles in nursing journals. She further made frequent presentations to many nursing, medical, and social welfare organizations throughout the country.[4]

In her first years at Teachers College, Nutting refined the program further and sought financial backing to ensure the continuation of the curriculum. She accomplished this goal when Helen Hartley Jenkins, a member of the Board of Trustees of Teachers College, endowed the department with $200,000. This allowed the program to become the department of nursing and social hygiene in 1910.

While at Teachers College, Nutting attempted to improve the educational opportunities for nurses throughout the country. She believed this would occur if the public was confronted with the reality of the nursing programs, as medical education had in 1910 when the Flexner Report condemned many of its practices. Thus, she lobbied the Rockefeller Foundation, which funded the Committee on the Grading of Schools of Nursing in 1919, to identify the education required by public health nurses.

The results of this study were published in 1923 in *Nursing and Nursing Education in the United States* (commonly labeled the Goldmark Report), which highlighted the inadequacies of the majority of the hospital training programs throughout the nation. The study also recommended that graduate nurses should be hired and paid to do the work of the students. The report was greeted with much hostility by hospital administrators, the medical community, and even multitudes of nurses. The ultimate effect of the project was limited. It did, however, result in the Rockefeller Foundation's funding two university schools of nursing, one at Yale and the other at Western Reserve in Cleveland.

Throughout her time at Teachers College, due to her close friendships with two other nurses, Lavinia Dock, a militant feminist and pacifist, and Lillian Wald, a feminist and founder of the Henry Street Settlement House, Nutting was quietly, but extensively, involved in the suffrage movement.

Her primary political activity, however, focused on issues related to the advancement of nursing as a field for educated women. Her efforts resulted in the Maryland legislature's passing the bill that mandated the registration of nurses who were graduates of training schools and Congress's granting officer's rank to graduate nurses who had served in the Army Nurse Corp during World War I. As she pursued these endeavors, Nutting showed that she had acquired an accurate notion of how to influence the political system during her many evenings at the House of Commons in Ottawa.[5]

Nutting retired from Teachers College in 1925 due to her ill health. She continued to live in her apartment close to the campus. Her health was quite poor throughout her retirement, limiting the amount of traveling and speaking engagements that she could pursue. She did, however, devote much time and effort to writing letters and articles on issues related to nursing. She died on October 3, 1948, one month before her ninetieth birthday.

Adelaide Nutting held many offices in state, national, and international nursing organizations. She was the founding member and first president of the Maryland State Association of Graduate Nurses. She served as vice president of the Society of Superintendents in 1898 and was elected the first president of the American Federation of Nurses in 1905, serving in that position until 1913, when the group dissolved to form the American Nurses Association. She was president of the International Council of Nurses and was an official delegate to this organization's meeting in Cologne in 1912. She lobbied President Woodrow Wilson to organize the Committee on Nursing of the General Medical Board of the Council on National Defense in 1917. Wilson then appointed her chairman of this group. In 1917, she was elected to the Nursing Committee of the Henry Street Settlement. She also served as the honorary chairman of the Florence Nightingale International Foundation for approximately two decades until her death. She was an active member of the Committee on Devastated France following World War I and worked to establish a school of nursing in Paris.[6]

Nutting received a few prestigious awards in her life. In 1921, Yale University granted her an honorary degree of master of arts. During the same year, the Council of the National Institute of Social Science awarded her the Liberty Service Medal for her efforts in furthering the welfare of the nation through her war activities. As part of its celebration of its fiftieth anniversary, the National League for Nursing Education established the Mary Adelaide Nutting Award in 1944. The Award Committee granted the initial silver medal to Nutting herself.

Gender had a tremendous influence on Nutting's life. However, because of her mother's belief in the need for women to be educated as well as men, it may not have limited her opportunities as much as it did those of most other women of her social class. Nutting's dream of a career in the theater ended when her mother became ill, and as the older daughter in the family, she had to care for her. This activity of a "dutiful" daughter eventually led to her becoming a graduate nurse. Gender issues continued to affect her career as a nursing educator. Her efforts to improve the conditions confronting students of nursing in the hospital training schools were blocked by the patriarchal establishment of medicine. Ashley has documented how nursing's efforts to humanize health care and to improve the quality of professional nursing education have often been stifled by male physicians and hospital administrators, who continued to advocate the apprenticeship mode of training for nurses at the expense of the students' receiving an adequate education.[7]

Nutting's contributions to American education are primarily significant within the nursing field. She was able to partially fulfill one of Hampton's goals, to establish nursing as a profession of educated women. She accomplished this in two major ways. First, as director of the department of nursing and health at Teachers College, she guided her faculty as they developed and improved the types and scopes of programs available to nurses at the institution. The majority of the graduates of these programs then went on to teach in nursing programs across the country. They continued to spread Nutting's vision. Second, Nutting directed the work of the National League for Nursing's committees, which formulated the first two standard curricula in 1917 and 1927. These curricula became the guides for most nursing programs and definitely upgraded the standards of education.

Nutting's untiring dedication to the fight for officer's rank for graduate nurses who served in the armed forces in World War I also had a positive effect on education for women. As plans were made for the expansion of the nursing departments in the army, navy, and air force during World War II, they had to include the reality that the nurses had to have education credentials similar to those of the male officers in order to meet the requirements for an officer's rank. This meant that the basic educational requirement for nurses serving in the armed forces was the baccalaureate degree. To meet the numbers of nurses required to serve in World War II, the federal government funded the development of many new collegiate nursing programs throughout the country. Also, a scholarship program that pays the tuition and a stipend for students in baccalaureate and master's degree programs in nursing was established and continues today.

Meanwhile, Nutting's dedication to accomplishing a tremendous amount of work in the department may have limited the advancement of nursing as a profession. Throughout her career at Teachers College, she was quite aware of the educational credentials of the faculty teaching in the other departments. For example, the list of faculty in the 1910 *Teachers College Bulletin* included seven men with doctor of philosophy degrees, two with medical degrees, one woman with a doctor of philosophy in psychology, and one woman with a master of science degree. Isabel Stewart and Ella Crandall were teaching with Adelaide in the nursing program. All three of them had earned diplomas in nursing, but none had a college degree. Stewart observed that Nutting was frequently concerned that she did not belong in academe because she had not earned a college degree.[8]

To overcome this problem for her nursing faculty, Nutting constantly urged her students and staff to pursue their baccalaureate and master's degrees. Stewart was granted the bachelor of science degree in 1911 from Teachers College and was the first nurse to achieve a master of arts degree from Columbia University in 1913. She then completed all the course work needed for a doctor of education degree. Unfortunately, she never completed her dissertation due to the demands of her work load under Nutting.[9] Nutting seemed to believe that the master's level of education was adequate for nursing faculty. Thus, since Teachers College was the trendsetter for all programs of nursing education in the United States, because of this belief, the standard of education required for collegiate nursing educators was the master's degree. This has been one reason the nursing field continues to be viewed as less professional and less deserving of financial support than other areas of higher education.

During the past two decades, the standard for tenure in most collegiate nursing programs has been raised to the doctoral level. However, even now as the profession moves into the twenty-first century, most nursing educators begin their careers with only the master's in nursing degree. This is a significant contrast with the doctoral degree that is required to teach in most other academic areas. Nutting and Stewart were both conditioned by their gender to concentrate on the work at hand, which was caring for nursing education across the nation. Thus, the needs of this endeavor took precedence over their own personal growth and advancement and indirectly hindered the attainment of their goals for this profession.

Nutting's many accomplishments continue to have a positive influence on contemporary nurses and nursing education. Most nurses now receive their education in institutions of higher education, at least at the associate degree level. Faculty are expected to pursue advanced degrees and engage in research that improves patient care. Thus, nursing continues to advance. It does, however, have much work to accomplish.

NOTES

1. Helen Marshall, *Mary Adelaide Nutting* (Baltimore: Johns Hopkins University Press, 1972), 5.

2. Philip Kalisch and Beatrice Kalisch, *The Advance of American Nursing* (Boston: Little, Brown, 1986), 161.

3. Susan Armeny, "Organized Nurses, Women Philanthropists, and the Intellectual Bases for Cooperation Among Women, 1898–1920," in E. Lagemann, ed., *Nursing History, New Perspectives, New Possibilities* (New York: Teachers College Press, 1983), 13–45.

4. Janice Feigenbaum, "Historical Trends in the Role Expectations of Faculty in Collegiate Programs of Professional Nursing," Ph.D. diss., University of Buffalo, 1987, 304–6; Marshall, 371–75.

5. Janice Feigenbaum, "How Mary Adelaide Nutting Gained Control of the Army Nurse Corps for Nursing," unpublished manuscript, 1991.

6. Marshall, 289.

7. Joann Ashley, *Hospitals, Paternalism and the Role of the Nurse* (New York: Teachers College Press, 1976).

8. Isabel Stewart, "Oral History," in Archives at Teachers College Library, New York, undated.

9. Teresa Christy, "Portrait of a Leader—Isabel Maitland Stewart," *Nursing Outlook* 17 (October 1969): 45.

WORKS BY MARY ADELAIDE NUTTING

"Educational Status of Nursing" (Bulletin no. 7). Washington, DC: U.S. Bureau of Publications, 1912.

"The Nurse as an Educator." *American Journal of Nursing* 13 (September 1913): 927–37.

"Apprenticeship to Duty." *American Journal of Nursing* 21 (December 1920): 157–68.

"Thirty Years of Progress in Nursing." *American Journal of Nursing* 23 (September 1923): 1027–35.

A Sound Economic Basis for Nursing and Other Addresses. New York: G. P. Putnam's, 1926.

"Historical Summary of the Relation of Nursing Education to Universities." *American Journal of Nursing* 28 (June 1928): 588–90.

WORKS ABOUT MARY ADELAIDE NUTTING

Christy, Teresa. "Portrait of a Leader: M. Adelaide Nutting." *Nursing Outlook* 17 (January 1969): 20–24.

Feigenbaum, Janice. "Historical Trends in the Role Expectations of Faculty in Collegiate Programs of Professional Nursing." Ph.D. diss., University of Buffalo, 1987.

Marshall, Helen. *Mary Adelaide Nutting—Pioneer of Modern Nursing*. Baltimore: Johns Hopkins University Press, 1972.

Stewart, Isabel. "Mary Adelaide Nutting." *American Journal of Nursing* 25 (June 1925): 445–54.

Yost, Edna. "M. Adelaide Nutting." In *American Women of Nursing*, 3–21. Philadelphia: Lippincott, 1965.

Nina Otero-Warren

Lynne Marie Getz

Maria Adelina Emelia (Nina) Otero-Warren (1881–1965) was an educator, suffrage worker, author, and businesswoman of New Mexico. She served as superintendent of Santa Fe County schools from 1917 to 1929. She supervised adult education programs in New Mexico and Puerto Rico for the Works Progress Administration during the 1930s and 1940s and participated in efforts to preserve traditional arts and crafts of northern New Mexico. Active in the Republican party, she campaigned for women's suffrage and was the first woman to run for Congress in New Mexico in 1922.

Maria Adelina Emelia Otero-Warren, known as "Nina," was born on October 23, 1881, in Las Lunas, New Mexico, the daughter of Eloisa Luna and Manuel B. Otero, descendants of two of the most distinguished families of New Mexico. Her mother's family, the Lunas, dated their history in North America to the conquest of Mexico and two Luna brothers who served as captains in the army of Hernando Cortez. Later descendants settled in New Mexico in 1695, founding the village of Las Lunas. Nina's grandfather, uncle, and other members of the Luna family were active in territorial politics. On her paternal side the Oteros also traced their ancestry to an influential Spanish family that provided Mexico and New Mexico with prominent settlers, jurists, and political leaders, including Nina's uncle, Miguel A. Otero, territorial governor of New Mexico.

In 1883 Nina's father, Manuel B. Otero, was shot and killed in a dispute over a land grant. He was survived by his widow and three children: Eduardo Manuel, Manuel Basilio, and the youngest, Nina. In 1886 Nina's mother, Eloisa Luna, married A. M. Bergere, an English immigrant engaged in stock raising, insurance, and mercantile interests in Santa Fe. The couple had twelve children, of whom three died in infancy. Nina's half-siblings included Anita; Estella, who married conservationist Aldo Leopold; May, who married

Santa Fe attorney John J. Kenney; Antonio Jose; Consuelo, who married Herbert Mendenhall; Rosina, who married Leonard Smith; Isabel; Joseph Charles; and Dolores, who married Charles Carl Leopold.

Nina Otero was educated in private schools in New Mexico and attended college at the Academy of the Sacred Heart (later Maryville College) in St. Louis. In 1904 she married Captain Rawson Warren, an officer in the U.S. Army. They had no children. Following the death of her husband, Nina Otero-Warren left New Mexico in 1912 for New York City. There she joined the Vacation Committee, an organization that performed child welfare work among the city's poor. Called back to New Mexico in September 1914 by the death of her mother, she took charge of the household of her stepfather and the care of her six sisters and two brothers remaining in the family home at Santa Fe.

In 1915 the Congressional Union under the leadership of Alice Paul launched a suffrage campaign in New Mexico. Among the organizers sent to New Mexico by Paul was Ella St. Clair Thompson, who realized that the participation of prominent Hispanic women was crucial to reaching the state's Hispanic population. Thompson appealed to Nina Otero-Warren, whose uncle, father, and brothers were all influential members of the Republican party. Although too shy at first to speak in public, Otero-Warren went to work in the suffrage campaign. In 1917 Alice Paul persuaded her to assume the leadership of the Congressional Union in New Mexico, a role she performed until suffrage was attained in 1920. As a member of an important upper-class Hispanic family, able to speak in both Spanish and English, Otero-Warren appealed successfully to Hispanic politicians and voters of all classes.

Her experience with the suffrage campaign gave Nina Otero-Warren the confidence to pursue a public life. Her friends and relatives in the Republican party also saw her as a viable political figure, and in 1917 she was appointed as county school superintendent in Santa Fe by the Republicans. In the 1918 election she won this office in her own right and held it until 1929. She ran as the Republican candidate for Congress in 1922. Although she was defeated, she was the first woman in New Mexico to run for a national office. She remained active in Republican party politics, representing New Mexico as a national committee-woman. She took a political role in her club work as well, serving as chair of the legislative committee of the State Federation of Women's Clubs.

As Santa Fe County superintendent Nina Otero-Warren did much to upgrade a school system that had been plagued with indebtedness, poor facilities, and erratic schedules. She balanced the county school budgets, increased the salaries for teachers, and placed all the schools in the county on standard nine-month terms. Under her leadership two new four-year high schools for rural students were built, and the county's first school nurse was hired.

The majority of the schoolchildren of Santa Fe County came from Spanish-speaking homes and lived in small villages or farms. It was very important to Otero-Warren that such children receive a quality education and at the same time retain what was valuable of their own culture. She believed that the school should foster an appreciation of Hispanic culture by teaching Spanish folklore and the traditional arts and crafts. As school superintendent she wrote a new curriculum for the Santa Fe County elementary schools that included these modifications for the rural schools. She instructed teachers to incorporate traditional games, folk dances, weaving, pottery, tinwork, and woodcarving into the regular course of study if such activities were a part of the surrounding community. Each school was expected to emphasize activities that the student would meet in daily life. Thus the traditions of each community would be carried on to the next generation through the school.

The preservation of Hispanic culture was a lifelong concern to Otero-Warren, and through her writing, educational work, and personal influence she contributed to the movement to revive and sustain the traditions of northern New Mexico. She participated in the activities of the Spanish Colonial Arts Society, an organization founded by Mary Austin and Frank Applegate in the 1920s to preserve the traditional arts and crafts of New Mexico. As Santa Fe County school superintendent Otero-Warren arranged for the artwork of schoolchildren to be exhibited at society-sponsored events. Along with Austin and fellow educator Aurora Lucero, she collected old Spanish folk songs still being sung by Hispanic elders but soon to be lost. Otero-Warren also gathered stories, plays, superstitions, legends, and folk remedies. Much of this material was compiled in her book, *Old Spain in Our Southwest*, published in 1936. This book captures the charm of Hispanic culture in New Mexico, idealizing the simple way of life that Otero-Warren's people had followed for nearly 300 years and that she sincerely hoped to preserve.

Otero-Warren believed that the vitality of a culture depended not only upon the survival of time-honored customs and arts but also upon the continued use of the native language. She thought that the teaching of Spanish in the elementary schools was "not only desirable but necessary. Bilingualism will bring about a closer cooperation between the home and the school. The strongest tie between the two is language."[1] She encouraged students and teachers alike to think of bilingualism as a valuable tool, and she believed that the schools had a responsibility to help them to achieve fluency in both languages.

Otero-Warren recognized that Hispanics needed to learn many skills and values from the dominant society if they were to survive. The schools, in following a standard curriculum devised for mainstream children, made no accommodation for the special needs of Hispanic children. Poor instruction in English had held back many Spanish-speaking children in school and contributed to high drop-out rates as they grew older. To combat this problem, Otero-Warren proposed her own method of teaching English to non-English speakers. Otero-Warren stressed an empathic approach to teaching the non-English-speaking child, urging teachers to familiarize themselves with the experiences and home life of the student. She encouraged teachers to develop "a feeling of comradeship, friendliness, and mutual belief so that the child may be freed from embarrassment and self consciousness." The Hispanic child who knows no English "is extremely sensitive and timid, though he is actuated by the same impulses and craves the same attention as all children, and responds in the same way to right teaching procedures and treatment." A poorly trained or insensitive teacher only intensifies the difficulty of learning English.[2]

Otero-Warren thought that teachers working with Spanish-speaking children ought to be fluent in Spanish themselves and that students should not be punished for speaking Spanish in school. Few New Mexican educators believed that Spanish should be allowed in the classroom for any purpose, even though the state constitution allowed for the training of teachers in both English and Spanish to enable them to teach Spanish-speaking children. Educators were pressured to instruct students in English and to discourage or suppress the use of Spanish in the schools. Otero-Warren did not permit the use of Spanish in classroom instruction, but unlike many educators she urged teachers to employ the Spanish language in school in the form of songs, plays, and games.

In 1923 Nina Otero-Warren was appointed Indian inspector for New Mexico by the U.S. commissioner of Indian affairs. As Indian inspector she promoted ideas similar to those she advocated for the public schools. Indian culture must be preserved, she believed, and yet Indians must adjust to modern ways. The challenge of this dilemma had frustrated many previous reformers, but Otero-Warren thought the solution lay in educating mothers and children. The home life of Indians must be improved by teaching Indian women modern methods of hygiene and child care. She also believed that closer ties between the school and the home would give education a more central focus in Indian life. The present system of taking children out of the home environment and forcing them to reject their culture merely placed a wedge between the younger generation and their elders. Otero-Warren advocated a curriculum for Indians that taught them to appreciate their own culture and history and to practice the native arts of their people. Although Otero-Warren was unable to effect great changes in the policies governing Indian affairs in the 1920s, she did draw attention to poor living conditions in the Indian schools of New Mexico.

In her treatment of Indians Nina Otero-Warren was more sympathetic than some previous inspectors who despised all Indian culture. She was unable, however, to avoid the paternalism that had often characterized dealings between the Indians and the U.S. government. She supported the commissioner's prohibitions of certain Pueblo dances and the use of peyote, on the basis that these practices were financially, physically, or morally detrimental to the Indians. In disputes between Indians and Hispanics over title to land, she invariably defended the right of Hispanics to the land, claiming that these lands had been legitimately signed over to Hispanics by Indians in the earliest days of Spanish settlement.[3] Her own background as a product of an upper-class Hispanic family predisposed her views toward Indians.

With the onset of the Great Depression and the implementation of New Deal programs, Nina Otero-Warren had an opportunity for wider application of her ideas. In 1935 she was appointed as assistant regional director of women's activities for the Works Progress Administration (WPA). In this capacity she coordinated educational programs for "foreign-speaking groups," primarily Hispanic women, and helped to implement projects intended to improve the employment opportunities for women. She again became involved with efforts to encourage the practice of traditional arts and crafts and to create markets for such products. She hoped that these programs would create a permanent crafts industry for Hispanics of rural northern New Mexico, although these expectations were never fully realized.

In 1936 Otero-Warren became state supervisor for literacy, and in 1937 she was appointed state supervisor of education, both positions in the Education Division of the WPA. Otero-Warren conducted a survey of illiteracy in the state to determine the extent and nature of the problem. She set up literacy classes for workers in Civilian Conservation Camps and established adult education programs throughout the state. She stressed that teachers in these programs must make an effort to allow adult learners to preserve their self-respect by using appropriate materials and vocabulary from adult experiences. In keeping with her educational philosophy in general, she urged teachers to become involved with the community and to adapt the curriculum to the circumstances and needs of the people being taught. This direction extended to language instruction as well. Adults who did not speak English should be taught first in their native language, while they gradually learned English. Otero-Warren had to obtain special permission from WPA officials in Washington, D.C., to provide this bilingual instruction for adults.

Otero-Warren's experience with rural schools, bilingualism, and adult education led to her appointment in 1941 as special consultant on education for the WPA in Puerto Rico. She began her work by familiarizing herself with the history and conditions of Puerto Rico. She found that over half of the island's children did not attend schools due to a lack of facilities in the rural areas. Those children who did attend school were taught in Spanish until the fifth grade, while learning English as a second language. This educational system had resulted in a high rate of adult literacy. She also discovered that the existing WPA adult education program was not only impractical for the needs of adult students but humiliating to them as well. In her work Otero-Warren set up training sessions for teachers in which they received "the proper instruction on adult psychology, and training in the preparation of adult centered materials to meet the needs of the people."[4] Otero-Warren also introduced her bilingual method of instruction, which stressed the advantages of bilingualism rather than treating it as a handicap. Although she spent only five months in Puerto Rico, Otero-Warren was credited with reinvigorating a demoralized adult education program. Over a thousand teachers participated in her training sessions, many of them expressing deep gratitude for her fresh ideas and enthusiasm.

After her return to New Mexico Otero-Warren performed Red Cross work and served as chairperson of the women's auxiliary board of the State Council of Defense. She also worked as Santa Fe director of the Office of Price Administration. Following the war she set up her own real estate and insurance business in Santa Fe. She continued to live in her family home with her sisters, Anita and Isabel Bergere. Nina Otero-Warren died at her home on January 3, 1965, at the age of eighty-three. She had been a lifelong member of the Roman Catholic church.

Nina Otero-Warren is remembered as an effective champion of Hispanic culture, as well as a humane and dedicated educator. While she often assumed the role of "patron" in deciding what was best for Hispanics of the lower classes and Indians in general, she sincerely cared for the welfare of her people and did much to increase their educational opportunities. As an advocate of bilingual instruction and multicultural education, she was far ahead of her time.

NOTES

1. Nina Otero-Warren to Concha Ortiz y Pino, February 20, 1941, File #43, Bergere Family Collection, State Records Center and Archives, Santa Fe, New Mexico (hereafter NMSRCA).

2. Adelina Otero-Warren, *Curriculum for the Elementary Schools of Santa Fe County*, 1929, Folder #42, Bergere Family Collection, NMSRCA.

3. Nina Otero-Warren, untitled speech on Indians, ca. 1923, Folder #40, Bergere Family Collection, NMSRCA; "Mother and Babies First! Woman Indian Inspector Gives Warning to Save Red Race," June 11, 1923, clippings scrapbook, #105, Bergere Family Collection, NMSRCA.

4. Nina Otero-Warren, "My Work on the Island: An Account of the WPA Adult Education and Public School Projects in Puerto Rico," 1941, Folder #54, Bergere Family Collection, NMSRCA.

WORKS BY NINA OTERO-WARREN

"New Mexico Folk Song" (with Mary Austin and Aurora Lucero). *El Palacio* 7 (1919): 152–59.
"My People." *Survey* 66 (May 1931): 149–51.
Old Spain in Our Southwest. New York: Harcourt, Brace, 1936.

Nina Otero-Warren Papers, Bergere Family Collection, New Mexico State Records Center and Archives, Santa Fe.

WORKS ABOUT NINA OTERO-WARREN

Deutsch, Sarah. *No Separate Refuge: Culture, Class, and Gender on an Anglo-Hispanic Frontier in the American Southwest, 1880–1940.* New York: Oxford University Press, 1987.

Forrest, Susanne. *The Preservation of the Village: New Mexico's Hispanics and the New Deal.* Albuquerque: University of New Mexico Press, 1989.

Jensen, Joan M. " 'Disfranchisement Is a Disgrace': Women and Politics in New Mexico, 1920–1940." *New Mexico Historical Review* 56 (January 1981): 5–35.

———. "Pioneers in Politics." *El Palacio* 92 (1986): 12–19.

Reeves, Frank. *History of New Mexico: Vol. 3. Family and Personal History.* New York: Lewis Historical, 1961.

Whitney, Virginia K., and Josephine Koogler. *Women in Education: New Mexico.* Wichita Falls, TX: Nortex Press, 1977.

Alice Freeman Palmer

C. H. Edson and B. D. Saunders

Alice Elvira Freeman (1855–1902) served as the second president of Wellesley College from 1882 to 1887. A prominent leader in the world of higher education, she exhibited impressive competence in teaching and administration at a point in history when the capabilities and suitability of women to pursue higher education were under critical debate. After graduating from the University of Michigan in 1876, Freeman became head of the history department at Wellesley in 1879, was appointed acting president in 1881, and in 1882 began her illustrious— but foreshortened—career as president. At age thirty-two, facing the crossroads of career and marriage in circumstances that forced a choice, Freeman married Harvard philosophy professor George Herbert Palmer and resigned the presidency of Wellesley. After her marriage, she served as a trustee of Wellesley, as a member of the Massachusetts Board of Education, and as the first dean (of women) in the Graduate Colleges at the University of Chicago from 1892 to 1895 and was closely involved with the struggle of the Harvard Annex to achieve institutional identity as Radcliffe College. In 1902, Palmer died in Paris of heart failure following intestinal surgery.

Alice Elvira Freeman was born on February 21, 1855, in the farming village of Colesville in upstate New York. Her mother, seventeen-year-old Elizabeth Higley Freeman, had taught in a rural school before marrying James Warren Freeman, a hardworking Colesville farmer. The first of four children, Alice was raised in an atmosphere of poverty and hardship, later becoming the mainstay of her parents and three younger siblings as their family experienced lengthy separation, bankruptcy, illness, and death. Although James and Elizabeth Freeman struggled throughout their lives, the idealistic couple sacrificed comfort to follow avocational interests and to provide educational opportunities for their children. Recognizing unusual mental gifts in Alice, they began home tutoring of their first daughter at an early age.

A precocious child, Alice learned how to read by the age of three. She began her formal education in a rural school at five and enjoyed displaying her quick memory and pleasing voice when asked to stand and recite poems at village gatherings. When she was seven years old, James Freeman decided to leave the farm for two years of training at the Albany Medical College. He had earlier learned some medical skills by working with a local country doctor but desired the formal training needed to open his own practice. Believing in a social gospel that preached salvation through public service, Mrs. Freeman supported his decision and took on the responsibility of running the farm and the household in his absence. For her part, Alice was proud to be her mother's right hand: whether gathering eggs from the barn, combing her sister Ella's hair, bathing her other sister Stella, or dressing her brother Fred, Alice assumed numerous responsibilities that enabled the family to endure the two years of hardship.

When James Freeman returned home in 1864, he moved his family to Windsor, New York, to set up a small medical practice and to farm. At age ten, Alice entered the coeducational Windsor Academy, where she was introduced to such classical studies as Greek, Latin, French, and mathematics. These were happy years for Alice as she broadened her educational horizons, helped her father in his modest medical practice, joined the Presbyterian church, participated in numerous community affairs, and met Thomas D. Barclay. A young teacher with training from the Princeton Theological Seminary, Barclay had accepted a position at Windsor Academy in 1868 to earn money for further graduate studies. Recognizing great ability in Alice, Barclay devoted many hours to sharpening her mind, cultivating her tastes, broadening her knowledge of the world, informing her of new ideas about the higher education of women, and inspiring her ambition for high purpose in life. By 1869 he had fallen in love with his gifted pupil and offered his hand in marriage. Fourteen-year-old Alice consented to the engagement, but a pull toward higher education rather than marriage became stronger over the next two years. When Barclay left Windsor to begin graduate studies at Yale Divinity School in 1870, Alice realized that she no longer wanted to follow him; six months later the engagement was dissolved, and Alice turned her attention toward college.

Although strong believers in higher education and supportive of Alice's desire for self-improvement, the Freemans first objected to her yearning for further education. Unable to finance a college education for more than one child with the earnings of a country doctor and farmer, Dr. Freeman believed his meager resources should be saved for his son. Alice changed his mind by promising to finance not only Fred's college expenses but also the higher education of her sisters after her own graduation. Believing that a coeducational institution would offer more opportunity than a women's college, she fixed her sights on the University of Michigan. In June 1872, accompanied by her father, seventeen-year-old Alice traveled to Ann Arbor to see the university, attend commencement exercises, and take entrance examinations.

The beginning of Alice Freeman's career in higher education was not auspicious, for she failed the examinations. Following an interview with President James B. Angell, however, she was permitted to enroll on a provisional basis. Angell was impressed with her "high intelligence" and felt confident that she would succeed, particularly since her former teachers had described her as "a child of much promise, precocious, possessed of a bright, alert mind, of great industry, of quick sympathies, and of an instinctive desire to be helpful to others."[1] Freeman quickly justified the confidence others placed in her with hard work and swift absorption of her studies. Throughout her undergraduate years, she continued to receive attention and support from President Angell and other professors, who became her lifelong friends and mentors. In addition to excelling academically, Freeman was recognized as a prominent figure in several campus organizations and enjoyed an active social life of picnics, sleigh rides, and parties with other students.

Freeman's college years were not entirely blissful. Upon learning about her family's financial difficulties in the middle of her junior year, she dropped out of school for a term to earn tuition and help pay family debts. Without consulting her parents, she enlisted the aid of President Angell to secure a temporary position as principal of a small high school in Ottawa, Illinois. In January 1875, Freeman began the twenty-week school term and, by May, had so won the confidence of her pupils and the town that the board insisted that she remain. Declining the offer, she returned to Michigan, made up her lost credits, and graduated with her class in June 1876.

After her graduation, Freeman accepted a position to teach in a seminary for girls in Lake Geneva, Wisconsin. True to her promise to her father, she made arrangements to take part of her salary in tuition for her sister Ella, who was interested in attending the seminary. Freeman had reservations about her new position as she had to share a room with another teacher and accept a conditional salary, which depended on the success of the school. Intending to rest over the summer before starting her new job because of fatigue, she spent most of her time caring for her younger sister Stella who had become seriously ill with lung disease.

Several months after Freeman began her new position teaching Latin and Greek at Lake Geneva, she came down with a severe cold that weakened her lungs and intensified her chronic cough. Making matters more depressing, her family's financial difficulties grew steadily worse. To keep her spirits up, Freeman daydreamed about her future and set a long-term goal of pursuing doctoral studies in history. Although committed to earning money during the school year for herself and her family, she hoped to keep her summers free for study.

In June 1887, Freeman enrolled for summer courses at the University of Michigan. Through recommendations of President Angell, she was offered two positions for the 1877—1878 academic year: one as an instructor in mathematics at Wellesley College, the other as principal of a high school in Saginaw, Michigan. Freeman accepted the higher-paying position in Saginaw. A month after her arrival, she was joined by her sister Ella, who had accepted a teaching position in a local grammar school. In November, James Freeman fell into bankruptcy and had to sell the family home and property to pay creditors. Adding to the family distress, fifteen-year-old Stella was diagnosed as having tuberculosis. In response to the crisis, Alice and Ella joined their salaries, rented a large house, and moved the rest of the family to Saginaw.

A year later, in December 1878, Freeman received a second offer from Wellesley—this time to teach Greek. Again she declined, for not only was she bound to pay Fred's college expenses, but she was struck with grief over her sister's failing health. Both Freeman and her parents thought of Stella as the family star: gifted with shining beauty, brilliant wit, warm radiance, and remarkable intelligence. Freeman doted on Stella, almost as her own child, and had dreamed of giving her a superior education so that they would be joined in work one day. Watching her precious sister wither in pain was agony for Freeman. Stella died June 20, 1879.

Following her sister's death, Freeman received a third offer to teach at Wellesley. This time she accepted. Relieved of the responsibility of caring for her sister and buoyed by improved family circumstances (her father's medical practice was growing, and Ella had recently married), Freeman believed she could accept the position and still pay her brother's tuition. In July 1879, she became head of the history department at Wellesley, even though she understood that there would be long hours of work for low pay. Because Wellesley had few donors and low tuition, its founder, Henry F. Durant, had to stretch his fortune to pay the bills. No stranger to hard work, Freeman poured herself into all the responsibilities required of her position: teaching several courses in history, building a department organization, conducting a daily Bible class, supervising dormitories, and offering long hours of guidance in her dormitory room. Although impressed by the standards of scholarship Durant set at Wellesley, Freeman related to her family that his evangelical zeal most inspired her work:

Mr. Durant preached to-day. If only you could have heard him, all of you! . . . It is enough to break one's heart to see his grand white head among these hundreds of girls, and hear him plead with them for "noble, white, unselfish womanhood." . . . I never heard and never shall hear anything quite like it.[2]

By the beginning of her second term, the emotional strain of losing Stella, worries about the welfare of her family, and overwork took a toll on Freeman's health. Her chronic cough grew worse until she had a hemorrhage of the lungs in February 1880. Despite her condition, Freeman wanted to finish the term before resting; however, a physician warned that without immediate care she would die within six months. Burdened by her brother's expenses at the University of Michigan, she could not afford to go to a warm climate as prescribed. Instead, she rested with her family for several months and resumed her work at Wellesley in the spring term.

Freeman was not the only person to become seriously ill during her early years at Wellesley. Henry F. Durant and President Ada L. Howard both fell ill. Durant died in October 1881, and soon after, Howard's feeble health forced her to resign. On November 15, the trustees appointed Freeman, the youngest member of the faculty, to become acting president for the year. Years of facing adversity with courage and determination gave Freeman the confidence to assume the position, despite the obvious risks of failure. With characteristic inventiveness and confidence, Freeman devised a plan to involve the senior class in helping to maintain order by setting a high tone for younger students. Her strategy worked to reduce time spent on matters of discipline, allowing Freeman to turn to pressing administrative matters. Unlike Durant's autocratic leadership style, Freeman set up a systematic and collaborative administrative system with direct involvement of the faculty in decision making. Within a short period, she justified the confidence of her superiors and received the official title of president of Wellesley in 1882—the same year she was awarded an honorary doctorate from the University of Michigan.

During her years of leadership, Freeman built Wellesley into the modernized and respected institution that Durant had envisioned and, in the process, gained widespread recognition. She revised the curriculum, recruited talented teachers, connected the college to Boston academic circles, raised enrollment standards, promoted the establishment of preparatory schools, helped to found professional organizations for women, and continued to advance the leadership of other women at Wellesley by establishing consultative committees. Although strict about standards and behavior, Freeman radiated a warmth that gained the love of her students. Even as enrollments approached 600 toward the end of her tenure, she displayed her remarkable memory and sensitivity by remembering names and personal interests of the students.

Through her dedication to advancing higher educational opportunities for women, Freeman forged a path to eminence and national acclaim. In 1884 she was a delegate to the International Conference on Education in London and was elected to the first of two terms as president of the Association of Collegiate Alumnae in 1885. Using her renown to advantage, Freeman drew talented guest lecturers to Wellesley, including, in 1886, the widowed Harvard philosopher George Herbert Palmer. Studious and introverted, Palmer's temperament stood in stark contrast to Freeman's gregarious nature; however, Palmer perceived a potential for deep friendship between them and began a determined courtship. Meeting with Freeman on June 3, 1886, to discuss the learning problems of a student, Palmer commented on her apparent poor health and later that evening wrote to apologize for giving unsolicited advice:

I am afraid I was rude this afternoon in trying to steer you. I did not mean to be. What I was born for was to set the crooked straight, and sometimes I find myself attempting to straighten what is already much straighter than I could ever make of it. I know you care for your health. Your life is the life of so many. I was distressed to see you look so worn . . . when the world has so large a stake in you.[3]

In response, Freeman offered her own apology: "Yes, I do 'care for health,' and you were very good Friday, to assist me. If I did not respond to your wise counsels as gracefully as I should, it must be because I am used to giving advice rather than taking it."[4]

As their friendship progressed to mutual declarations of love, Freeman, forced to confront her mixed feelings about career and marriage, suggested they end the relationship. On September 1, she wrote: "I will never run the risk of spoiling your dear life and my work at the same time until both He and you and my own heart make it clear that taking that risk is greater service than anything else He has for you and me."[5]

Convinced of the rightness of his feelings above her misgivings, Palmer pressed his suit and on February 21, 1887—Freeman's thirty-second birthday—they became secretly engaged. By May, under pressure by her suitor to choose between her presidency and marriage, Freeman again grew ill, and Palmer took an even more insistent stand that she must leave Wellesley. After the public announcement of their engagement that summer, Freeman continued to vacillate about leaving her position, and Palmer continued to advance his vision of a conventional marriage. When they married in Boston on December 23, Freeman resigned as the president of Wellesley.

Following their marriage, the Palmers lived in Cambridge and soon built a large home with studies and visiting rooms so they could both work and entertain in comfort. Poems written by Alice Palmer indicate that she found great satisfaction in her marriage; nevertheless, certain verses suggest that she experienced ambivalence in reconciling her role as a wife with her own longings for greater professional challenges. In a verse to her husband, she expressed her frustrations:

> For the soft firelight
> And the home of your heart, my dear,
> They hurt, being always near.
> I want to stand upright
> And to cool my eyes in the air,
> And to see how my back can bear
> Burdens,—to try, to know,
> To learn, to grow.[6]

Despite lingering misgivings about missed opportunities, Alice Palmer succeeded in promoting important advancements for women, enhanced by the influence of a distinguished husband. From 1888 until her death, she served on the Wellesley Board of Trustees; in 1889 she was appointed to the Massachusetts State Board of Education and was elected to serve a second two- year term as president of the Association of Collegiate Alumnae; and in 1892–1893 she successfully helped to promote official recognition of Radcliffe College by Harvard. In 1887, Columbia College had recognized her outstanding service with an honorary L.H.D. degree, and, in 1895, Union College granted her an honorary LL.D. degree.

Perhaps one of her greatest challenges during her early years of marriage came when President William Rainey Harper invited her to serve as the first dean (of women) in the Graduate Colleges of the University of Chicago in 1892. With expectations of developing the new coeducational institution along egalitarian lines, Alice Palmer accepted the position—upon the conditions that she be in residence only three months of the year and that her friend Marion Talbot, then an instructor of sanitary science at Wellesley, be hired as resident dean. In addition to organizing programming and housing for female students, Palmer assisted Harper to hire faculty, set policy, gain support from the community, and influence trustees. Indeed, letters to her husband during this time indicate that she played a larger role than history records in the founding of the university. On October 9, 1892— eight days after the opening of the university—she wrote to her husband: "Dr. Harper is a great man but he needs some one to protect him against himself, all the time . . . . He trembled with excitement before going into chapel for the first exercise, and I had all I could do to brace him for it."[7] A day later Palmer wrote about her central involvement in the operations of the university: "I go from one interview to another . . . . If by rare chance I am left off a Committee by Dr. Harper, the men who are on it are sure to talk it all over with me, one by one."[8] Finally, Palmer wrote proudly about spoken praise from Harper: "Mr. Harper said yesterday, 'I could never have opened this university without you. I should have been *crushed*.' "[9]

Palmer was enthusiastic about her work in Chicago during the opening years of the university; however, by 1894 she began to sense disapproval from Harper regarding her advocacy for female students and her support of Robert Herrick and other eastern faculty members who were critical of the centralized structures of the university. By January 1895, problems between Palmer and Harper culminated in her resignation. On January 4, 1895, she reported Harper's negative response to her recommending a female faculty member for a higher position in another college. "As for Pres. H. he barely speaks," she wrote to her husband. "He is very much annoyed that I recommended Miss Wallace to Knox College, and thinks it very 'disloyal'!"[10] Five days later, Palmer again wrote to her husband about her further loss of esteem for Harper:

They finally voted yesterday to release Miss Wallace to go to Knox College. I will tell you when you come of her interview—and mine—with President Harper on that subject. I think we neither of us could ever quite respect him as a man again. He seemed off guard, a coarse, selfish person, without a fine touch in him any where.[11]

Later that year she terminated her official duties with the university.

After leaving the University of Chicago, Palmer continued her work advancing educational and social reforms. In addition to her continued involvement with Radcliffe, Wellesley, and the Massachusetts Board of Education, she was a member of the American Board of Commissioners for Foreign Missions, served as president of the Woman's Home Missionary Association of the Congregational Church, and was president of the Board of Directors of the International Institute for Girls in Spain. Although the Palmers were childless, they became surrogate parents and lifetime advisers for many young students—most notably, Lucy Sprague, who would later become an influential dean of women at the University of California. Having been an intimate member of the Palmer household during her student years at Radcliffe College, Sprague accompanied the Palmers on a European trip in the fall of 1902. Traveling across England, they visited the birthplace of George Herbert and other poets, sojourned with celebrated professors, and visited numerous museums. In France, they rented a spacious apartment at 67 Avenue Marceau and were settling in for the winter months when tragedy struck. Alice Palmer became acutely ill and on December 6, 1902, died of heart failure following surgery for a rare intestinal condition. She was forty-seven.

Six years after her death, her husband published *The Life of Alice Freeman Palmer*, a biography recording his perceptions of her personality, her achievements, and their marriage. According to Palmer, his wife had resigned her presidency, without regret, to join him in a partnership that had strengthened the couple for greater service to society. Alice Palmer left no public record of her thoughts and feelings about the significance of her life choice; however, her private letters and poems indicate that she experienced both joy and disquietude in her relationship with Palmer. During their courtship she expressed considerable anguish about resigning and, after their wedding, continued to feel torn between her devotion to a marriage ideal bound by established gender roles and a love of social and academic challenges that would further stimulate her exceptional talents in promoting educational opportunities for women. In a letter to her husband on April 30, 1892, she wrote:

"If I could once determine which is me!" I have been thinking a good deal about the year which is over . . . . I foresee, dear, that it will seem to you . . . [I am] very much the same dreary failure . . . . It is not what you want or like and I think sometimes we had better change it all. If only I could change myself! That is what is needed, I know, and I always fancy it will come—but it does not.[12]

Thus, although a forerunner in educational advancements for women, Palmer reflected conventional gender doctrines of her times, believing that women's character was "so delicately organized as to be fitted peculiarly for the graces and domesticities of life."[13] Beyond metaphors of domesticity, however, Palmer believed that women had to make their own way in the world and that they had the same rights as men to higher education. Throughout her career and married life, therefore, she interposed values from her traditional family and religious background with those of a liberal ideology in attempts to integrate Victorian conceptions of domestic and moral womanhood with progressive goals for female emancipation.

Palmer's early death ended opportunities for final reconciliation of her marital and professional aspirations; however, she left a legacy of impressive accomplishments, as well as timeless quandaries for successive generations to contemplate. Although memorialized by such educational leaders as President Charles W. Eliot of Harvard, President Caroline Hazard of Wellesley, President James B. Angell of Michigan, President William J. Tucker of Dartmouth, and President Mary E. Woolley, of Mt. Holyoke, perhaps it was Lucy Sprague, her "only daughter," who best captured her spirit. Writing of Palmer in her autobiography, Lucy Sprague Mitchell recalled:

She was an experience for anyone. To me, she seemed—and still seems—one of the great people in the world . . . . During the time she spent in Chicago, she lived with us. Her eager zest for life, her capacity to listen as wholeheartedly as she talked, her versatility, her light touch even in executive matters in which she was master, made her literally unique in my experience.[14]

NOTES

1. Quoted in George Herbert Palmer, *The Life of Alice Freeman Palmer* (Boston: Houghton Mifflin, 1908), 44.

2. Ibid., 110.

3. *An Academic Courtship: Letters of Alice Freeman and George Herbert Palmer, 1886–1887*, introduction by Caroline Hazard (Cambridge: Harvard University Press, 1940), 4.

4. Ibid., 6.

5. Ibid., 42–43.

6. Alice Freeman Palmer, *A Marriage Cycle* (Boston: Houghton Mifflin, 1915), 36.

7. Palmer to George Herbert Palmer, October 9, 1892, Alice Freeman Palmer Papers, Archives, Margaret Clapp Library, Wellesley College.

8. Ibid., October 10, 1892.

9. Ibid., October 12, 1892.

10. Ibid., January 4, 1895.

11. Ibid., January 9, 1895.

12. Ibid., April 30, 1892.

13. Alice Freeman Palmer, "A Review of the Higher Education of Women," in Anna C. Brackett, ed., *Woman and the Higher Education* (New York: Harper, 1893), 113.

14. Lucy Sprague Mitchell, *Two Lives* (New York: Simon and Schuster, 1953), 73.

WORKS BY ALICE FREEMAN PALMER

An Academic Courtship: Letters of Alice Freeman and George Herbert Palmer, 1886–87. Introduction by Caroline Hazard. Cambridge: Harvard University Press, 1940.

"A Review of the Higher Education of Women." In Anna C. Brackett, ed., *Woman and the Higher Education.* New York: Harper, 1893.

The Teacher: Essays and Addresses on Education (with George Herbert Palmer). Boston: Houghton Mifflin, 1908.

A Marriage Cycle. Boston: Houghton Mifflin, 1915.

WORKS ABOUT ALICE FREEMAN PALMER

Abbott, Lyman. *Silhouettes of My Contemporaries.* Garden City, NY: Doubleday, Page, 1922.

Association of Collegiate Alumnae. *Alice Freeman Palmer: In Memoriam, MDCCCLV–MCDII.* Boston: D. B. Updike, 1903.

Bordin, Ruth. *Alice Freeman Palmer: The Evolution of a New Woman.* Ann Arbor: University of Michigan, 1993.

Frankfort, Roberta. *Collegiate Women: Domesticity and Career in Turn-of-the-Century America.* New York: New York University Press, 1977.

Palmer, George Herbert, ed. *A Service in Memory of Alice Freeman Palmer Held by Her Friends and Associates in Appleton Chapel, Harvard University, January Thirty-First, MCDIII.* Boston: Houghton Mifflin, 1903.

———. *The Life of Alice Freeman Palmer.* Boston: Houghton Mifflin, 1908.

Solomon, Barbara. "Alice Elvira Freeman Palmer." In Edward T. James, ed., *Notable American Women.* Cambridge: Belknap Press of Harvard University Press, 1971.

Celestia Susannah Parrish

Marcia G. Synnott

Celestia Susannah Parrish (1853–1918) was a noted pioneer of progressive education in the South. Largely self-educated in her early years, she taught school and college to pay for her formal education, which culminated in a Ph.D. from Cornell University when she was forty-two years of age. As an educator, she successfully implemented John Dewey's educational theories and methods in the Muscogee Elementary School of the Georgia State Normal School in Athens. She also served as one of Georgia's first three state supervisors of public schools. Her 1914 survey of Atlanta's public schools for white pupils helped to promote progressive educational reforms. Finally, she worked to improve the academic standards of women's colleges and to open the doors of southern tax-supported universities to women students.

Celestia Susannah Parrish—Celeste Parrish as she was called—was born on September 12, 1853, on her father's Pittsylvania County plantation, near Swansonville, Virginia, the eldest of three children, two daughters and a son, of William Perkins Parrish and Lucinda Jane (Walker) Parrish, his second wife. Orphaned by their deaths when she was ten, she and her sister and brother went to live with two maiden and invalid aunts, under the guardianship of an uncle, William B. Walker. She continued the education begun at a private school on the plantation by reading books on her own, until she could attend another private school. After her uncle died in 1867, the aunts insisted that she support herself. In 1869, at fifteen years of age, she began teaching in the Swansonville public school and at other Virginia public and private schools. She experienced a "new 'birth' [as she] read 'Page's Theory and Practice of Teaching'" during one night. At dawn she "knelt over the book and promised the Lord to be a better teacher." It was, she recalled, "a baptism of the Holy Spirit, for from that time I devoted the best of my energies to my profession and lost no opportunity for professional as well as a personal culture." In 1874, she was offered forty dollars a month to teach in the Danville city schools, where she remained until 1883. At the same time, she earned a diploma, from 1874 to 1876, at the Roanoke Female Institute (later Averett College) in Danville, where her sister, whom she supported, was enrolled. In 1877, she experienced "another intellectual awakening," attending a six-week teachers' institute at the University of Virginia; she also studied elocution privately. Constantly striving for self-improvement, she walked six miles to take private calisthenics lessons and, on her own, read the great English authors and Greek and Latin authors in translation.[1]

Barred by gender from both regular admission and enrollment in a correspondence course at the University of Virginia, Parrish entered the State Normal School (later Longwood College) at Farmville in 1884 and graduated in 1886. She supported herself by teaching at Roanoke Female Institute in 1883–1884 and at the State Normal School in 1884–1886, before being appointed a mathematics teacher at the latter from 1886 to 1892. During a year's leave of absence in 1890–1891, she sought the greater opportunities for higher education available to women outside the South by studying mathematics and astronomy at the University of Michigan. In 1892, Parrish became professor of mathematics, philosophy, psychology, and pedagogy at the recently opened Randolph-Macon Women's College in Lynchburg. After persuading the president to give her twenty-five dollars to acquire equipment, she developed laboratory experiments for the required psychology course.

In 1896, Parrish earned a Ph.D. from Cornell University by transferring credits from previous studies, by passing examinations in subjects that she had studied on her own, and by attending summer sessions, beginning in 1893, where she encountered experimental psychologist Edward Bradford Titchener. Since she could not fulfill Cornell's one-year residency requirement and keep her position at Randolph-Macon, she pleaded for permission to substitute summer school study, first with President Jacob Gould Schurman and then with each of her professors. Her petition was granted. In January 1895, Parrish published "The Cutaneous Estimation of Open and Filled Spaces," based on her laboratory work at Cornell, in the *American Journal of Psychology*. Her struggle for the Cornell degree transformed her character, she wrote. "A very selfish, thoughtless, narrow-minded girl" became a religious woman for whom "the joy of the intellectual life" has dispelled "ignorance." During the summers of 1897, 1898, and 1899, she attended the University of Chicago, studying at John Dewey's Laboratory School in 1898 and 1899.[2]

Parrish had fulfilled her quest for "self-culture," despite personal and financial hardships, supporting not only herself but also her sister and brother and later contributing to the expenses of two nephews after her brother died. In the process, she had become a self-made woman—strong in character, resourceful, independent, and well educated. In three periodical articles published in 1901, she drew partly on her own experiences to challenge some of the prevailing stereotypes about "The Womanly Woman," "Women's Problems," and the extent to which gender should determine women's higher education. In the April 4, 1901, *Independent*, responding to a previously published article by a man, Parrish disagreed with the definition of a "womanly woman" as one who could not possess masculine virtues and hence needed male support. Because "true womanliness belongs, primarily, to the inner, not to the outer, life," she argued, "the womanly woman" may be "brave as well as gentle, firm as well as affectionate, undaunted in the defense of righteousness as well as modest in self assertion." Such a woman was "never" man's "dependent or his plaything."

In the October 31, 1901, *Independent*, Parrish pointed to the common failure "to discriminate between womanly strength and efficiency and 'mannishness,'" since women of intelligence and character have made far better mothers than those who were ignorant and timid. Rather than telling their daughters that certain activities either were forbidden by the Bible or would make them unmarriageable, mothers should teach "that nobility of soul is far more to be desired than 'winsomeness' of manner . . . that self-control needs to be cultivated more than 'emotionality;' that gentleness should be tempered by firmness . . . and sweetness by zeal for righteousness." By allowing women "to meet men on an intellectual basis," higher education freed them from reliance on their physical attractiveness. If they chose marriage, women should be prepared for its responsibilities, but they also could "live honorably and happily out of wedlock," as Parrish did. Men also needed, she believed, "a more general and better education" in order to appreciate women's full human capabilities.[3]

In the November 1901 *Educational Review*, Parrish rephrased the question that President M. Carey Thomas of Bryn Mawr College had asked in her address "Should the Higher Education of Women Differ from That of Men?" Believing that women should have the same higher educational opportunities, Thomas attacked male "professional sex jealousy." But Parrish contended that since the introduction of the elective system made it possible to accommodate the interests of both sexes, a somewhat different question should be asked: "Shall the Higher Education of Women Be the Same as That of Men?" Although thirty years of coeducation had not revealed significant differences between men and women, "prejudiced men" argued that women were not suited for advanced graduate and professional education and blocked their progress in universities toward professorships, department chairs, and administrative positions. As a result, Parrish argued, women continued to choose more extensive studies rather than the concentrated ones leading to professional advancement. While eventually they might make some progress, because, "given practical equivalence of natural endowment and scholarly equipment, women are, in nine cases out of ten, better teachers than men," they remained concentrated in the primary and secondary schools, where they had the most educational opportunities. Thus, their training would differ in some respects from that of men. Nevertheless, the greatest differences in the lives of educated men and women occurred not in the professions, but between wives who did not work after college and their husbands who had full-time careers.[4]

Parrish believed that while both husband and wife should have educational compatibility, their courses of study should prepare them for fulfilling different roles and jobs within marriage. But she urged both partners "to set on foot an immediate rebellion against two customs" that had deleterious effects:

The first is that of condemning the wife and mother to a tread-mill life of narrow duties and allowing the husband and father to monopolize the intellectual opportunities which ought to belong to them in common [and] the second is that of allowing the wife and mother to squander money in reckless self-indulgence, while the whole life of the husband and father is sacrificed to the money-making necessary to supply her wants.[5]

Propounding the views of progressive motherhood, Parrish contended that a wife and mother needed more than either "the old 'parlor boarding-school' regime" or a narrow academic specialization in college to prepare her to "assume the sanitary supervision of the home, the selection and preparation of the food, and the main social direction of the family." Parrish's social progressivism again revealed itself in her statement on parental responsibilities: "Society, I contend, has a right to demand that children born into it shall be sufficiently well born, well cared for, and trained to become contributors to the welfare of the social whole instead of dependents upon social bounty and blots upon our civilization." In rebuttal to President Thomas, she maintained that a Bryn Mawr Ph.D. degree would not prepare a woman "without further study to regulate her own life before and after marriage so as to secure the best results for her children." To run her household and family according to "scientific principles," she also should study physiology, hygiene, psychology, chemistry, bacteriology, and "social forces."[6]

While justifying as necessary some educational differences between husbands and wives, Parrish staunchly advocated both higher academic standards for women's colleges and seminaries and the admission of women to southern tax-supported colleges and universities. In 1903, she launched the Southern Association of College Women, together with Emilie Watts McVea, an English teacher, and Dr. Lilian Wycoff Johnson, an assistant professor of history, both at the University of Tennessee. Parrish served as the first president (1903–1905) of the association, whose two primary goals were to insist that college-level work be required for a college degree and to encourage the public to demand improved funding for both city and rural schools. Parrish also was vice president of the Association of Collegiate Alumnae, organizer of its first southern branch and president of the Virginia branch; and she helped establish an alumnae association at Randolph-Macon Woman's College. Active in the Young Women's Christian Association, she organized in Virginia and the Carolinas college associations and also branches for African Americans.

In the winter of 1902, Parrish moved to Athens, Georgia, as professor of pedagogic psychology and head of the department of pedagogy at the State Normal School (which became the State Teachers College and later a division of the University of Georgia). She persuaded philanthropist and University of Georgia trustee George Foster Peabody to donate $10,000 for an experimental classroom building, named Muscogee Elementary School, for his home county. It was the first practice school for southern white normal students that followed Dewey's principles. Peabody also donated $3,500 for laboratory equipment, so that Parrish could implement Titchener's methods in experimental psychology. She developed a *Course of Study* and wrote an instructional treatise, *The Lesson*, to show practice teachers that education should be an organically unified progression from kindergarten through high school and that children could be taught without traditional textbooks by introducing them to work units related to daily living. The majority of the eighty men and women in the 1905 senior class returned as teachers to the rural communities from which they came.

Recognizing the importance of reaching preschool children and involving parents in their children's education, Parrish founded Georgia's first Mothers and Teachers Cooperative Club and served as first state president of the Mothers and Teachers Association, which was later renamed the Parent Teachers Association. She was influential in the Georgia Educational Association and belonged to the National Education Association.

Her grasp of educational problems, her participation in General Education Board-sponsored conferences and her temporary fieldwork for that board in the area of school improvement prepared her for a new position as state supervisor of rural schools in the North Georgia District. Parrish was one of the first three state supervisors of schools and the only woman, selected by Governor Hoke Smith, a former member of the Atlanta School Board. She and Smith had spoken on occasion from the same platform during the campaign to obtain federal aid for vocational education.

Parrish's schedule as state supervisor would have daunted someone of less dedication and fortitude. By various horse-drawn vehicles, she visited annually each of Georgia's forty-eight mountainous counties, which collectively had over 2,400 rural schools, most of them dependent on sparse state funds, and some 3,800 teachers, four-fifths of whom lacked normal school education. To train these teachers, she led summer institutes in domestic science and agriculture, established combined summer normal schools at the district agricultural and mechanical schools, and lobbied for better financial support. She also worked to establish schools for illiterate adults. Mary E. Creswell, a State Normal School graduate who later became the first dean of the School of Home Economics at the University of Georgia, recalled Parrish's warning to parents at a night meeting in one mountain community. Unless they educated their children, she told them, the land that they had struggled to own would pass into the hands of outsiders who would "develop the resources which should be the heritage of Georgia children."[7]

In the spring of 1914, with the support of Marion L. Brittain, state superintendent of instruction, Parrish was appointed by Robert J. Guinn, president of the Atlanta School Board, to conduct a two-week survey of the city's schools for its 25,000 white pupils. She lived for a time in the home of Guinn, an educational and political ally of Hoke Smith, by then a U.S. senator. At a special meeting of the Board of Education on June 30, 1914, she presented for discussion the major ten points of her report. Her recommendation that a primary grade supervisor be hired was immediately approved, while the other points were adopted by the end of 1914. Guinn appointed Laura Smith, Parrish's former student, supervisor of primary education, and later he chose Joseph C. Wardlaw as superintendent of the school system. Parrish, Brittain, Wardlaw, and Smith all championed the progressive educational ideals of John Dewey. They also believed that students of divergent socioeconomic backgrounds needed different curricula. Guinn and Wardlaw campaigned to consolidate Atlanta's public schools in the name of "social-efficiency," until, in 1918, Guinn was forced to resign by mounting opposition both from teachers and parents, who objected to a number of his so-called reforms, and from political opponents.

For her report, Parrish had "tried to visit schools in different localities, serving different social classes, housed in different sorts of buildings, working under different community conditions, and having principals and teachers of different training and experience." She found severely overcrowded classrooms and some school buildings so physically deteriorated that they should be condemned. Equally critical, fifty to sixty pupils were taught together, rather than in smaller groups, by pedagogical methods that emphasized, especially in the elementary schools, repetitive drill and memorization at the expense of content and meaning. The grammar school curriculum needed to be completely reorganized to connect more closely "with the experience of the children, and with home and civic conditions." In addition, normal classes should be relocated, Parrish said, from the Girls' High School to an elementary school, staffed with skilled teachers, where students could have laboratory training. Then the Girls' High School should be combined with the English Commercial School, since its building was in bad condition and its college preparatory curriculum of little value to the 90 percent of the students destined for marriage and motherhood. Courses in art, science, literature, history, music, and household management would better prepare them for the economic and social realities of their later lives.[8]

To carry out these reforms, Parrish called for "the cooperation of parents, business men, organizations of women, city authorities, school officials, and teachers in a redirection of forces which will gradually vitalize the schools, help them to react upon the life of the city," and make them more useful. Since Atlanta spent twenty-two dollars per pupil, much less than either Richmond, Virginia (twenty-eight dollars), or Springfield, Massachusetts (thirty-four dollars), whose schools represented "the modern ideal," she recommended enactment of a local school tax.[9]

Because southern states segregated pupils by race, however, Parrish's recommendations did not benefit African-American pupils. Their inadequately funded schools lacked comparable educational resources. For example, by 1916, white pupils had 4 public high schools in Atlanta and 122 in the state, but African Americans, who were 46 percent of the secondary school-age pupils, had only 1 four-year public high school in Georgia. Moreover, neither the Atlanta school system nor the state of Georgia provided any training for African-American teachers, who had to obtain it at private black institutions.

Although Parrish did not play a direct role in the opening, in 1918, of the University of Georgia to white women, she was committed to the campaign to make it coeducational and influenced others through her educational and civic associations. For example, she belonged to the Georgia Federation of Women's Clubs, the Atlanta Woman's Club, and the Woman's Christian Temperance Union and served on the state board of the woman's committee of the National Council of Defense during World War I. In principle, the General Assembly had opened to women in 1889 all branches of the University of Georgia, except the School of Technology and the Medical College. But since officially the university remained closed to women, the Daughters of the American Revolution, the Colonial Dames, and the Georgia Federation of Women's Clubs joined forces to fight for coeducation. Women first began attending the university during the summer sessions instituted in 1903; they also were permitted to continue their studies between summer sessions and complete degrees. In 1911, four graduates of the State Normal School, among them Mary Creswell, took private study in bacteriology, which subsequently the University of Chicago accepted for credit. Finally, on September 18, 1918, the Board of Trustees voted to admit women to all schools of the University of Georgia.

Parrish planned to retire to her hilltop cottage in Clayton, where she spent summers. However, in 1918, just before her sixty-fifth birthday, she died of an illness at the Clayton home of her daughter, Mrs. James Stunt, whom she had adopted as a young girl around the time she moved to Athens. The Georgia General Assembly adjourned for her funeral. The Georgia Federation of Women's Clubs established in 1918 at the University of Georgia a Loan Scholarship Fund in her name to assist women students, the first of whom were officially registered in September 1919. At Randolph-Macon Woman's College, she was honored by the Celeste Parrish Experimental

Laboratory of Psychology. Her portrait was also hung in the Court House of Pittsylvania County, Chatham, Virginia. Georgia schoolchildren, her students, friends, the Federation of Women's Clubs, and the Parent Teacher Associations erected a stone at her grave in the Clayton Baptist Church cemetery. The inscription, from the funeral eulogy by M. L. Brittain, reads: "Georgia's Greatest Woman."

NOTES

1. Celeste Parrish, "Teacher Who Taught Herself," *Atlanta Journal* (April 17, 1932): 4, 27.

2. Ibid., 27.

3. C. S. Parrish, "The Womanly Woman," *Independent* 53 (April 4, 1901): 775, 777, 778; C. S. Parrish, "Women's Problems," *Independent* 53 (October 31, 1901): 2582, 2583, 2584, 2585.

4. Celestia S. Parrish, "Shall the Higher Education of Women Be the Same as That of Men?" *Educational Review* 22 (November 1901): 383, 386, 387–91. Thomas's address before the Association of Colleges and Preparatory Schools of the Middle States and Maryland was published in the *Educational Review* 21 (January 1901): 1–10.

5. Ibid., 392.

6. Ibid., 394, 395, 396.

7. Mary E. Creswell, "Personal Recollections of Celeste Parrish," 1952, Celeste Parrish Collection, Hargrett Rare Book and Manuscript Library, University of Georgia Libraries, Athens.

8. C. S. Parrish, *Survey of the Atlanta Public Schools* (Atlanta, GA: s.n., 1914; reprinted in 1973 by the Board of Education), 3–6, 13–19, 22, 23, 25, 30–33.

9. Ibid., 4, 28–29.

WORKS BY CELESTIA SUSANNAH PARRISH

A small collection of manuscripts and printed materials pertaining to Celeste Parrish is in the Hargrett Rare Book and Manuscript Library, University of Georgia Libraries, Athens.

"The Womanly Woman." *Independent* 53 (April 4, 1901): 775–78.
"Women's Problems." *Independent* 53 (October 31, 1901): 2582–85.
"Shall the Higher Education of Women Be the Same as That of Men?" *Educational Review* 22 (November 1901): 383–96.
"An Educational Development in Georgia." *Elementary School Teacher* 6 (November 1905): 134–45.
Course of Study: Muscogee Elementary School of the Georgia State Normal School, Athens (with Laura M. Smith and Mary E. Creswell). Athens, GA: McGregor, ca. 1908.
The Lesson [a treatise on conducting the recitation]. Athens, GA: McGregor, 1909.
Survey of the Atlanta Public Schools. Atlanta, GA: s.n., 1914. Reprinted in 1973 by the

Board of Education, with a preface and a biographical sketch of Celestia Susannah Parrish by Walter Bell.

My Experience in Self-Culture. Atlanta, GA: J. O. Martin, State School Supervisor, State Department of Education, 1925. Reprinted under the title of the "Teacher Who Taught Herself," *Atlanta Journal* (April 17, 1932).

WORKS ABOUT CELESTIA SUSANNAH PARRISH

Creswell, Mary E. "Personal Recollections of Celeste Parrish." Celeste Parrish Collection, Hargrett Rare Book and Manuscript Library, University of Georgia Libraries, Athens, 1952.

Ecke, Melvin W. *From Ivy Street to Kennedy Center; Centennial History of the Atlanta Public School System.* Atlanta, GA: Atlanta Board of Education, 1972.

Gibbs, Elise. "Celeste Parrish." In the Theodore Henley Jack Historical Association, ed., *Some Georgia Historical Sketches*, 69–71. Atlanta, GA: Hubard, ca. 1943.

James, Edward T., Janet Wilson James, and Paul S. Boyer, eds. *Notable American Women: A Biographical Dictionary.* Vol. 3. Cambridge, MA: Belknap Press of Harvard University Press, 1971. S.v. "Celestia Susannah Parrish," by Charles E. Strickland.

Malone, Dumas, ed. *Dictionary of American Biography.* Vol. 7. New York: Charles Scribner's Sons, 1934. S.v. "Celestia Susannah Parrish," by Lois K. M. Rosenberry.

Who Was Who in America. Vol. 1, 1897–1942. Chicago: A. N. Marquis, 1943.

Zeigler, May. "Growth and Development of Psychology at the University of Georgia." *Journal of Genetic Psychology* 75 (1949): 51–59.

Janine Pease-Windy Boy

Jon Reyhner

> Janine Pease-Windy Boy (b. 1949) is one of the most active living American Indian women educators. A member of the Crow tribe, she served as a delegate to the 1992 White House Conference on Indian Education and as a member of the U.S. secretary of education's Indian Nations at Risk Task Force from 1990 to 1991, where she was one of only two women on the twelve-member task force. Since 1982, she has been the first and only president of Little Big Horn College, one of the United States' twenty-seven tribally controlled community colleges. In 1990, under her leadership, Little Big Horn College earned full regional accreditation.

Janine Pease-Windy Boy was born September 17, 1949, on the Colville Indian Reservation in Washington state. Her own family background reflects a multigenerational, intercultural interest in American Indian education.[1] Her white great-grandmother, Sarah Walker Pease, met her Crow great-grandfather, George Pease, while working at the Unitarian Montana Industrial School for Indians, a mission school for Indians that lasted from 1886 to 1897. Founded only ten years after and a short distance away from Custer's Last Stand, this school was a pioneer effort to educate American Indians. However, it was not till about 1927 that the first Crow Indian graduated from high school.

Her paternal grandfather, Ben S. Pease, attended Sherman Institute in Riverside, California, which is still operated today as a Bureau of Indian Affairs Boarding School. He married Tillie Whiteman Runs Him. Her father, Ben Pease, Jr., was a master teacher, principal, and coach who also served as a Jobs Corps director. He married Margerie Jordan, daughter of Edwin and Florence Jordan Hocking, natives of Butte, Montana. Their daughter Janine is the oldest of four children: Joel Pease is currently a mathematics teacher on the Crow Reservation, Ben Pease is a medical doctor, and Linda Pease received her master's degree in education from Eastern Montana College and is working at Little Big Horn Community College. Janine spent her summers in the Crow Nation visiting relatives and received the traditional Crow name "One Who Prays." She has two children: Roses, born July 28, 1976, and Vernon, born May 2, 1979.

Janine Pease-Windy Boy is working to fulfill the promise of steps taken since the height of the civil rights movement in the early 1970s, including the passage of the Indian Education Act in 1972 and the Indian Self-Determination and Education Assistance Act of 1975. She is taking a lead in realizing the promise of the U.S. government's policy of Indian self-determination that was enunciated by Richard Nixon in his message to Congress on July 8, 1970, the same year she graduated from Central Washington University with a B.A. degree is anthropology and sociology:

The story of the Indian in America is something more than the record of the white man's frequent aggression, broken agreements, intermittent remorse and prolonged failure. It is a record also of endurance, of survival, of adaptation and creativity in the face of overwhelming obstacles. It is a record of enormous contributions to this country—to its art and culture, to its strength and spirit, to its sense of history and its sense of purpose.

It is long past time that the Indian policies of the Federal government began to recognize and build upon the capacities and insights of the Indian people. Both as a matter of justice and as a matter of enlightened social policy, we must begin to act on the basis of what the Indians themselves have long been telling us. The time has come to break decisively with the past and to create the contributions for a new era in which the Indian future is determined by Indian acts and Indian decisions.[2]

In 1971 Pease-Windy Boy served on the Washington governor's council for youth involvement. And in the mid-1970s, she worked as a counselor at the nation's first tribally controlled college, Navajo Community College, just a few years after it was founded, and then served as a director of the Upward Bound Program, a program to help prepare first-generation college students, at Big Bend Community College, Moses Lake, Washington. In 1977 she was appointed to the Montana state advisory committee on vocational education and became director of the Crow tribe's education program, where she did some of the initial work to establish Little Big Horn Community College. In 1981–1982 she directed the Eastern Montana College Indian Career Services, a program designed to support Indian students in their quest for a college degree.

Pease-Windy Boy sees education as part of a larger effort of American Indians to obtain civil rights. From 1983 to 1986 she was lead plaintiff in a voting rights case in Big Horn County. That case, which gained national attention, led to the first Crow Indian being elected to the Big Horn County Commission. She is still working to get schools on Crow Reservations to better reflect Crow values and culture, to give the Crow people more say in the education of their children, and to give Crow students a better chance for school success.

Pease-Windy Boy received her M.A. degree in education from Montana State University and the outstanding graduate achievement award in 1987 and in 1993 was working on a doctorate in higher education. She has honorary doctorates from Hood College and Gonzaga University. She has used her non-Indian education to help her Crow people shape a uniquely Crow educational institution at Crow Agency, Montana. The college she leads teaches approximately 25 percent of its courses in the Crow language, and the college emphasizes Crow and Indian studies. In keeping with the Crow value system, all faculty at the college, including the president, receive the same level of pay. The college's mission is

1. To intensify and expand the development of Indian human resources on the Crow Indian Reservation.

2. To promote and encourage community and reservation civil awareness of education and educational problems affecting Indians.

3. To establish and coordinate programs to train members of the Crow Indian community in the problems of Indian education in order that these persons may provide or administer programs or services.

4. To lower the college drop-out rate by providing a bridge between the reservation and the nonreservation institutions of higher learning; to increase the overall number of professionals, para-professionals, and skilled technicians in all of the disciplines; and to create a better match between the education and the manpower demand not only on, but also off, the Crow Indian Reservation.[3]

Most of the college's students are nontraditional. Many are mothers with children who are not able to leave home to further their education. The college emphasizes cooperative learning, peer tutoring, and other instructional methods that are compatible with traditional Crow culture. Students who are not successful are encouraged to retake courses with no penalty.

Besides her leadership of her tribe's community college, Pease-Windy Boy is active in the American Indian Higher Education Consortium (AIHEC), which represents the twenty-seven U.S. and Canadian tribal colleges. She served as president of AIHEC in 1983 to 1985 and treasurer from 1985 to 1990 and co-chaired their eleventh annual conference in 1992. She wrote about the theme of that conference, "From This Lodge, Pour Us a Dream to Become," which

is about our lodge, our home, the tribal college. Among our Indian people, the heart of our families, our clans and our tribes is always set in the lodge. Whether it is the sweat lodge, the Sundance lodge, the family lodge or the learning lodge, we find good things for life there. . . . Knowing the tribal colleges, you know that the learning place is anywhere in our homelands and knows no boundaries or limits.

The gift of life is carried in water, and with our lodges, the pouring of water is an essential moment in our traditional practices. Like water, our hopes and dreams pour from the knowledge and experiences we acquire through our tribal colleges. In the way of our visionary leaders, our tribal college students, faculty, administrators and trustees have dreams, that become the lives that we live and the communities that we build.[4]

Pease-Windy Boy is an advocate of Indian control of Indian education and sees tribal colleges as helping to preserve tribal culture while educating tribal members to take an equal place in the outside world. Her life's work as an educator has been to "Indianize" Indian education. This Indianization is not meant in a separatist sense, but in a pluralistic sense. Tribal colleges, despite inadequate funding, accept non-Indian as well as Indian students. American Indians have been part of the United States from the beginning. They have served as our nation's allies and later volunteered and served in the U.S. armed forces out of proportion to their numbers, and all Indians in the United States became citizens in 1924.

A frequent speaker at educational gatherings, Pease-Windy Boy spreads the message that Indian education does not have to mean cultural assimilation. Crow students can retain their native language and culture and be successful mathematicians, scientists, or whatever else they want to be. Previous educational efforts that attempted to eradicate tribal identities and Indian languages and cultures have helped make reservations pockets of poverty characterized by high unemployment and alcoholism. Her work at Little Big Horn Community College reflects her interest in giving Crow students back their Crow identity.

Over the last few years, the work of Janine Pease-Windy Boy has received increased recognition. Her work was recognized in the Carnegie Foundation for the Advancement of Teaching's 1989 special report on tribal colleges.[5] In 1990 she was named one of twenty-five trustees of the new Smithsonian National Museum of the American Indian, and in 1991 she was named the National Indian Education Association's National Indian Educator of the Year.

NOTES

1. Family information was provided directly to the author by Pease-Windy Boy.

2. Richard Nixon, "Special Message to the Congress on Indian Affairs," in *Public Papers of the Presidents of the United States, Richard Nixon: Containing the Public Messages, Speeches, and Statements of the President* (Washington, D.C.: U.S. Government Printing Office, 1971), 565.

3. *Little Big Horn College 1985–1987 Catalog* (Crow Agency, MT: Little Big Horn College, n.d.), 3.

4. Janine Pease-Windy Boy, Letter, in *From This Lodge, Pour Us a Dream to Become*

(Program for the eleventh annual American Indian Higher Education Consortium Conference, March 26–29, 1992, Billings, MT), 1.

5. The Carnegie Foundation for the Advancement of Teaching, *Tribal Colleges: Shaping the Future of Native America* (Princeton, NJ: Author, 1989).

WORK BY JANINE PEASE-WINDY BOY

Letter, in *From This Lodge, Pour Us a Dream to Become*. Program for the eleventh annual American Indian Higher Education Consortium Conference, March 26-29, 1992, Billings, MT, 1.

WORK ABOUT JANINE PEASE-WINDY BOY

Boyer, Paul. "We Just Can't Fail." *Tribal College* 2 (Spring 1991): 16–17.

Almira Hart Lincoln Phelps

Nancy G. Slack and Roger W. Armstrong

Almira Hart Lincoln Phelps (1793–1884) was a pioneer in the development of science education, especially hands-on education, in female institutes in the first half of the nineteenth century. She is well known for her best-selling secondary school science textbooks in botany, chemistry, geology, and physics, particularly her *Familiar Lectures on Botany*. Her teaching methods replaced rote learning of science, and her botanical books are credited with helping to develop the profession of botany in the United States.

Almira Hart was born on July 15, 1793, in Berlin, Connecticut, the youngest of seventeen children in the blended family of Samuel Hart and Lydia Hinsdale. Both ancestral families had come to America from England in the early seventeenth century, settling eventually in towns of the Connecticut River Valley. The Harts and the Hinsdales were both pioneering families whose members included many prominent settlers and leaders of communities ranging geographically from Dedham, Massachusetts, west to Hartford, Connecticut.

Almira's childhood was spent in a highly cultured, ascetic environment wherein the collected family read aloud the works of Shakespeare, Locke, and Milton and talked of current politics and of the exploits of their ancestors, especially those involved in the American Revolution. Her intellectual father, a soldier-politician and surveyor, was a political liberal and unorthodox in his religious beliefs. He loved controversy and opposed intolerance and bigotry at every turn. Her mother was a resourceful woman of great energy who displayed unusual skills as a manager of the large family unit. Too thrifty to hire help, she effectively distributed and supervised the multitude of tasks essential to the life of a large farm-based family at the end of the eighteenth century.

The young Almira was an avid reader of whatever books a farm girl could obtain. In her later years she recalled that her older sister (the ultimately more famous Emma Willard) had actively intervened to urge her to discontinue reading "worthless novels" and to undertake a program of serious self-education by reading works such as Hannah More's *Strictures on Female Education* and James Burgh's essays on *The Dignity of Human Nature*. Lydia Hart was perhaps the first to encourage interest in hands-on science in the family. Almira later pictured her mother dissecting the chicken and "forming a tolerably correct idea of human anatomy."[1]

Formal education for females was a newly emerging opportunity in 1800, and the Berlin district schools had begun to admit girls as full-time students. Almira's first formal teacher when she attended the Berlin summer school was none other than her sister, Emma. Soon after, Almira became a student in the newly established Berlin Academy, a significant improvement over the district schools.

In 1809, at the age of sixteen, Almira left the academy to accept a job as a teacher herself in a summer school in a rural district school near Hartford. At this time the winter school session was nearly always taught by men. There she boarded with a number of different families, some less genteel than others. It soon became obvious to her, however, that she would need more formal education. Formal secondary education was not open to girls at this time, with the exception of an early female seminary in Philadelphia.

By 1810, her sister Emma had married John Willard, a prominent politician and bank director in Middlebury, Vermont. Emma invited Almira to live with them and pursue her further education informally in the intellectual environment of Middlebury. John Willard, nephew of Emma's husband, attended Middlebury College and taught Almira mathematics. The following year John and three other Middlebury students boarded with the Willards. Women could not attend Middlebury at that time, of course, but there were often six "students," including Almira and Emma, and spirited discussions at the breakfast table. Thereafter the young men went off to their math and science studies at the college. Almira studied at home with Emma's help. Later, in 1815, the Middlebury branch of the Vermont State Bank, of which John Willard was a director, closed, and Emma Willard added to the family income by keeping a boarding school of seventy students at their home. Here she tried out new subjects and new methods, notably those for teaching geography.

Almira went off in 1812 to study at cousin Nancy Hinsdale's academy at Pittsfield, Pennsylvania. Here she studied more art than mathematics and no science. Nevertheless, her education was by this time considered sufficient for her to be elected as the regular teacher at Berlin Academy in Connecticut. This was the first time that a woman had kept a winter school in this town. She was elected over a male teacher, at least in part on the basis of an examination. She introduced map drawing in the geography class and had the older pupils teach the younger. The following year she ran her own boarding school in her mother's home in Berlin. At these schools she taught arithmetic and geography and even the analysis of Milton and Shakespeare— but no science.

In November 1815 Almira was hired to take charge of an academy at Sandy Hill, New York, on the Hudson River. Here she was lonely but wrote that she preferred "a life of usefulness to exercise the talents God had given her."[2] At this school for the first time she included natural science in her curriculum and used the new methods for teaching geography developed and subsequently published by her sister, Emma Willard.

Almira taught at this school for about two years, after which she, like her older sister, gave up teaching to marry an older and prominent man. In 1817 she married Simeon Lincoln, a printer and publisher and the editor of a conservative Federalist paper in Hartford, Connecticut. She wrote that when she married, she gave up poetry and literature for recipe books. Her life as a well-off Hartford matron included entertaining and good works through their church but ended abruptly with Simeon Lincoln's death in the yellow fever epidemic of 1823. Almira was left with two daughters ages one and two and many debts. She decided to go back to teaching for the financial support of the family. Ironically, she had more options as a widow than as a wife.

She taught at first in a district school in New Britain, Connecticut, but in 1824 she and her children moved to Troy, New York, to assist her sister. Emma Willard had petitioned the New York State legislature in 1819 for support of her proposed secondary school for girls. New York State chartered, but did not finance, her school, but the city of Troy did. By 1824 Emma Willard was the head of the Troy Female Seminary (later and currently, Emma Willard School), a ground-breaking institution that trained a large number of teachers and politically active women, including early feminist Elizabeth Cady Stanton.

Almira Lincoln not only taught at the Troy Female Seminary but she also continued her own studies. She learned Latin, Greek, French, Spanish, and higher mathematics and later taught these classes. At that time the second-year curriculum at the seminary included Logic, Rhetoric, Elements of Criticism, Euclid's Elements of Geometry, Day's Algebra, Natural Philosophy, and Paley's Evidence of Christianity. All this cost fourteen dollars a term in 1824. Students could also take drawing and painting, including velvet painting, French, Latin, and a choice of piano, harp, or guitar for extra fees. A course of Lectures on Natural Philosophy, Chemistry, or Botany was also available, at three dollars for each course.

There was special training for prospective teachers, and assistant teachers were selected from among the best students. The teaching staff had weekly meetings at which educational issues and practices were discussed. The two sisters apparently got along well, and when Emma Willard was ill in 1825, Almira took over the general educational administration. She was made vice-principal in 1829 and the following year was left in charge while her sister visited Europe. She did well. The *Troy Sentinel* of August 4, 1831, reported: "We are gratified that we can say that, for the year during which (in the absence of the Principal) Mrs. Lincoln has had the sole charge of the institution, it has maintained, in all its integrity, the high reputation which for several years it has enjoyed."[3]

It is not for her success as acting principal of Troy Female Seminary that Almira Lincoln (later Phelps) is most remembered. Her primary contribution to this fine school for young women, indeed, to female education in general, was her broad infusion into the curriculum of major new elements of science education. She did this both by her writings and by her own teaching methods. Her botany, geology, and chemistry classes did not use the unconnected rote learning methodology used in prior times. Almira Lincoln's science classes included both extensive demonstrations by the teacher and later, actual student manipulation of the objects of study (plants, minerals, chemicals), using apparatus such as microscopes, retorts, and pneumatic cisterns.

Almira Lincoln's nontraditional approach to teaching science—which over half a century later John Dewey would call "learning by doing"—was derived from the teachings of J. H. Pestalozzi, whose educational views represented the flowering of education reform begun a century earlier. Pestalozzi declared that all instruction should "start from simple beginning points," noting that "a total reliance on words (which are only sound and noise) is a hindrance to the real power of observation and to the firm conception of the objects that surround us."[4]

Almira Lincoln was undoubtedly introduced to Pestalozzi's teachings by her science mentor, Amos Eaton, who in 1825 founded in Troy, New York, what would become Rensselaer Polytechnic Institute (RPI). It is likely that Eaton had been exposed to Pestalozzi's methods by his own mentors, Benjamin Silliman of Yale and William Maclure of Philadelphia. The fact that Eaton opened a "Pestalozzian room" for children on his own RPI premises in 1829 suggests the fervor he felt for this new hands-on education.

Eaton's new methods of "communicating instruction by experiment and demonstration" would become the hallmark of his new Rensselaer school. In his book *Chemical Instructor* he states, "Let each student's own hands be applied to these operations." Nationwide, student involvement in laboratory work would not become widespread until after the Civil War. The importance of Amos Eaton's influence on Almira Lincoln's pedagogy was very great. To appreciate the impact of this colorful and ingenious man it is helpful to be aware of some of Eaton's own history.

After an early career as a lawyer and land agent, Eaton was convicted, perhaps on falsified evidence, of forgery in 1811 and sentenced to life imprisonment. He was pardoned by the governor four years later, a bitter period during which, however, he produced a popular botany manual. After his release he spent an intensive year at Yale (1916), where he studied chemistry and mineralogy under Benjamin Silliman and botany with Eli Ives. He then became a type of itinerant "preacher" of the wonders of botany, geology, and chemistry at lecture halls and lyceums throughout upstate New York, western Massachusetts, and Vermont. His lectures were immensely popular, due in large measure to his accompanying experiments, which utilized "about 50 dollars value of apparatus." Eaton rejected formal theoretical lectures, telling his confidant John Torrey: "I turn science into common talk. I illustrate the most abstruse parts by a dish kettle, a warming pan, a bread tray, a teapot, a soap bowl or a cheese press."[5] Torrey, later a famous botanist, was the son of Eaton's jailer. Eaton had given him his first botany lessons, using real flowers. In turn the young Torrey had brought botanical books to Eaton's jail cell.

Troy, New York, where Eaton had settled permanently in 1819, became the center stage of his zealous popularization of science. Female students became an additional target of his cause, and on the request of Emma Willard, science lectures by Eaton and his colleagues of the newly founded Rensselaer Institute became staples of the curriculum at the Troy Female Seminary. In the early years the young ladies traveled to Eaton's school to attend his "experimental lectures." Eaton, however, a leader among those of the time who believed in the equality of man and woman, invited a number of young women to apprentice with him, including Mary Lyon, who would found Mount Holyoke College; Laura Johnson, who would teach science for women at Rensselaer; and Emma Willard herself.

Soon after her arrival in Troy in 1924, Almira Lincoln went to, and was fascinated by, the courses in science given by Amos Eaton to the young women of Troy Female Seminary. It is likely that Emma Willard determined that her sister Almira would become the seminary's instructor of science and mathematics and encouraged her interaction with Eaton. Almira Lincoln found in Eaton a liberal, creative teacher with a very practical approach to teaching science. Seventy years prior to John Dewey's theory of "learning by doing," Almira Lincoln was becoming schooled in exactly that style—both as student and later, in Eaton's own words, as a "scientific associate."[6] Under his capable indulgence and enthusiasm she developed a deep love for the sciences and a desire to popularize botany, especially for women. Eaton's direct support included the provision of chemicals and apparatus to the new laboratory installed at Troy Female Seminary. In addition his young male students helped to make the preparations for the experiments that she used to illustrate her own lectures to her students.

Largely through Almira Lincoln's efforts science became a cornerstone of the Troy Female Seminary curriculum. "With the help of a Rensselaer student, she obtained the various gases, and made the preparations to illustrate by experiments her own lectures to the pupils. In due time she brought them into the laboratory, where they were trained to prepare experiments for the lectures, which they were appointed to give for the classroom, and for public examinations."[7]

As we have seen, the teaching of science to students of Troy Female Seminary preceded Almira Lincoln. But science courses at the girls' school itself became popular under Almira Lincoln. She later wrote about her botany classes at the Troy Seminary. It seems that the "chivalric" young men of Rensselaer School collected the plants for the girls. With this supply of fresh flowers, her students first classified them according to Linnaeus's sexual system (counting the number of stamens and pistils). This was the practical exercise. They then went on to more abstract principles, including the physiology of plants and natural relations between them. There was no suitable book available for instruction in botany at this level. In 1929 she published her own, using her lecture notes and the advice and help of Eaton. This book, *Familiar Lectures on Botany*, went through a great many editions, eventually selling, by the publisher's account, 375,000 copies.

Almira Phelps is probably best known as an author of this and other textbooks, but these books were originally intended and used for her own teaching. The botany one, in particular, was well reviewed and found its way all across the United States to the Arkansas Territory. It was used in colleges as well as secondary schools and even in Europe. Several well-known male botanists noted that they themselves began their studies with *Lincoln's Botany*, as it was popularly called.

In 1831, Almira Lincoln left Troy to marry the Honorable John Phelps. Phelps was a widower with six children, aged nine to twenty-six. Two of the Phelps's daughters attended Troy Female Seminary, as did Almira's daughter, Jane. Her younger daughter, Emma, and two of the Phelps children were at home with them when she, now Almira Lincoln Phelps, moved into her husband's home in Guilford, Vermont. Here and later in nearby Brattleboro, her life was similar to that of her first marriage. She appears to have accepted her place in the upper classes of that society, caring for husband, children and stepchildren, giving dinner parties and contributing to church activities. She wrote to her sister, "I find my present retirement sufficient and hope that I am enable [not only] to be useful in my domestic relation, but to be able to do some good in the society in which I am placed. I take great interest in the Sabbath School."[8] Soon there were again pregnancies and babies. A son, Charles, was born when she was almost forty and a daughter, Myra, when she was forty-two.

Her second marriage was different from her first, however. Almira Phelps was already a woman of accomplishments when John Phelps met her. She had already written her well-received botany book, and by all accounts he encouraged her to continue writing. He had become a member of the state legislature at thirty-four, and he held other offices, including that of state senator. He was absent for long periods during legislative sessions, living in Montpelier, the state capital. His absence may well have provided Almira with time for writing. She revised her botany text, *Familiar Lectures on Bot-*

any, reprinted in many editions up to 1869, and also wrote a second, more basic textbook, *Botany for Beginners*, reprinted up to 1891. She wrote her chemistry, geology and natural philosophy textbooks, all subsequently used in her own and other seminaries. *Geology for Beginners*, published in 1834, was described in 1868 as "a small volume which she never had the courage to revise, as the science has so shaken off its old distinctions, and become essentially changed by the force of new discoveries."[9] *The Female Student*, published in 1833 and in 1838 as *The Fireside Friend*, was published as volume 18 of the *School Library* issued by the Massachusetts Board of Education, in company with writings by well-known authors such as Washington Irving. She also edited her *Lectures to Young Ladies*, originally given while acting head of the Troy seminary, and contributed articles to *American Ladies Magazine* and *Godey's Lady's Book*. She wrote an address on "Female Education in Greece," an interest of hers and Emma Willard's, and wrote essays for the College of Professional Teachers.

John Phelps later wrote about his wife in the family Bible: "This lady was eminent as an authoress of various useful and popular works and general literature, science and education.... She also became distinguished as a practical Instructor of Youth."[10] A highly unusual husband for those times, John helped her immensely in her career as an educator. In 1838, he resigned as state senator. He was sixty; Almira was forty-four. She was offered a position to head a new seminary in West Chester, Pennsylvania. He encouraged her to accept, and together they moved from Vermont to Pennsylvania. Thereafter they moved to her schools in Rahway, New Jersey, and to the Patapsco Female Institute in Ellicott's Mills, Maryland. He helped her with the business aspects of these schools until his death.

Her impact on school curricula can be seen by examining the curriculum of the West Chester Young Ladies Seminary, a new school started at her arrival in 1838. She intended the school to provide young women with a liberal education equal to that provided at young men's schools. Her curriculum thus included ancient languages, higher mathematics, and particularly natural sciences. These were listed in the prospectus, together with their textbooks, four of which were by Phelps herself, those for natural philosophy (physics), chemistry, botany, and geology. Astronomy and mineralogy with texts by other authors were also included. Laboratory experiments were incorporated, and the prospectus also describes the chemical and philosophical (physics) apparatus, the mineral cabinet, and the library, open to all students at all times.

All studies were not intellectual, however; there were also music, drawing, and practical domestic skills. Tuition was $125 per term, quite an increase from that at Troy Female Seminary fifteen years before. This figure did not include lessons in music, languages, or drawing, all of which had small extra charges. The school was also involved in training teachers. Many of these young women already had some teaching experience.

Another feature of the school was the public examination, with which

Phelps was already familiar from her experience at the Troy Female Seminary. This examination took several days, and the students were examined orally in front of an audience. The first were reported fully and approvingly by the local newspapers. One male observer wrote, "The skills of the pupils in the important branches of Algebra and Geometry convinced me . . . that there exists an aptitude in the female and a capacity for mathematical learning equal to ours." He went on to describe their knowledge and ability in handling the apparatus in natural philosophy (physics), indicating that hands-on science teaching was part of the school curriculum at this time—1839. The same reporter was convinced that the girls' knowledge of science "was not gotten up for the occasion but existed in the mind."

The seminary in West Chester did not survive long in spite of all this publicity and commendation from the press. The Young Ladies' Seminary failed financially and closed, and its whole quite elaborate property was sold. Almira Phelps then moved, together with her obliging husband, to head the Female Institute at Rahway, New Jersey. Again there were complimentary editorials about her, this time in New York and Philadelphia. She was well known by this time as the writer of popular textbooks and as an educator. The publicity was good advertising for both this school and the education of daughters, as well as sons. The Rahway school had at the start sixty students and six teachers. There were day students as well as boarders, and Eunice Phelps, Almira's stepdaughter, was vice-principal.

Semiannual public examinations were the rule here also and were reported at length in the newspapers. The editor of the Philadelphia paper (the *U.S. Gazette*, April 28, 1841) wrote: "We find in Rahway . . . a school which is doing much for the character of the female mind . . . .The accomplished lady at the head of the institution, has an extensive fame as director of a good school, and it is gratifying to the friends of education to know that her abilities are appreciated, and her efforts and devotion rewarded."[11] That assessment followed a long and detailed description by the editor of the three-day public examination. Such great public interest in the education of young women seems surprising, but in April 1841 in Philadelphia it was apparently newsworthy.

In the fall of 1841, however, the Phelps family moved on once again, this time to Maryland. The Episcopal bishop offered her a large establishment, the Patapsco Female Institute in Ellicott's Mills, Maryland. Although Almira Phelps's biographer wrote that "Mr. and Mrs. Phelps commenced their work at Patapsco," it is clear that it was Almira's school. A letter from Almira's sister, Emma Willard, to a mutual friend, Lydia Sigourney, makes it clear that the offer was made to her: "My sister is about to remove her school from Rahway, a large and elegant establishment having been offered her by Bishop Wittingham . . . .I regret her greater distance from me but rejoice in her prosperity and opportunity of increased influence."[12]

In November 1841, Almira and John Phelps began their stay at the Patapsco Institute. It was to be her last and probably most important school. A special feature of this institution was that it trained teachers. Most of its student teachers came from New England and the Middle Atlantic states, but some from the South as well. They completed their own educations while serving as apprentice teachers.

Schools in the South were more likely at this time to teach young girls domestic and artistic accomplishments than trigonometry, but Almira Phelps raised the academic standards and the students' ambitions at Patapsco. She did this by a combination of a regular and quite rigorous course of study, scholastic incentives including the awarding of diplomas to those who finished the course, and considerable control of the lives of the young women who boarded at the institute. The latter even extended to the type of mail they could send and receive and what sort of visitors they were allowed to have—nonrelatives were discouraged, and even male cousins were suspect.

The curriculum was similar to those in her previous schools, including ancient and modern languages, considerable mathematics, the analysis of literature, and philosophy, as well as music and painting. Several natural science courses again used texts by Phelps herself. John Phelps helped with the administration and finances until he died in 1849. Almira Phelps remained in charge of the institute for another seven years. In 1854 she made an extended tour of Europe, together with her sister Emma and her children, Jane, Charles, and Myra. In 1855, however, Jane was killed in a railway accident in New Jersey. Almira was distraught and decided to retire from Patapsco Female Institute. She did this in 1856, moving to Baltimore for the rest of her life.

The theory underlying the methods that Almira Lincoln Phelps used in her teaching was not original with her but is traceable to Pestalozzi and to Amos Eaton, as described above. One basic idea was that the students should proceed from the known to the unknown, for example, making a map of their own village before confronting a map of the state or the United States. Rote memorization was to be discouraged. Pestalozzian ideas were discussed in *The American Journal of Education*. Both his ideas and those of Rousseau were known to Almira Lincoln when she wrote *Familiar Lectures on Botany*. By 1827 instruction by practical application and experiment was already going on at Rensselaer School, and as seen above, Troy Female Academy students were exposed to it there, too. Both knowledge of a subject and the development of intellectual faculties proceeded not from memorizing the book but from direct observation of nature. In the case of botany this meant to take apart live flowers and note the similarities and differences.

Familiar Lectures on Botany in the first and all subsequent editions utilized the Linnaean system, based largely on the numbers of stamens and pistils. By observing these the student could arrive at the Linnaean class and order and subsequently find the genus of her plant by comparing it with the descriptions of genera—all by the third lecture. Phelps realized that this was not a natural system of classification; in her later editions, for example, that of 1851, she included a whole chapter on the by then current "natural system." But she continued to use the Linnaean system for reasons of pedagogy; quite simply, it enabled a young student to identify her flower, exciting her interest in botany. Once her interest was aroused, she was ready for the more formal lectures on plant morphology and physiology. The 1851 edition even includes the "History of Botany from the Creation of the World to the Discovery of America" in the sixteenth lecture and covers the time to Linnaeus and "the present" in the following chapter.

To study botany, in Phelps's view, is to understand God's creation. There is a strong religious tone to the whole textbook; in fact, in her preface, "To Teachers," she recommends using this book to study plants "to illustrate the most logical divisions of Science, the deepest principles of Physiology, and the benevolence of God."[13]

Lincoln's Botany was thus a combination of an identification manual, originally of local plants but expanded in later editions to include plants of other parts of the country, and a botany text, used even in Europe. Phelps quoted a letter Madame Belloc wrote to her from France saying, "We are far behind your country in female improvement; we look to you for an example of what women can do. The books which are used in your female seminaries are above the capacities of our young women."[14]

Although her ultimate influence was probably most significant in botanical education, particularly if judged by her remarkably successful textbook, Almira Lincoln Phelps played a substantial role in chemical education. This was particularly true with regard to female education. It is noteworthy that over fifty years after her death, the prestigious *Journal of Chemical Education* saw fit to publish an article entitled "Mrs. A. H. Lincoln Phelps and Her Services to Chemical Education."[15]

Following the leads of Pestalozzi and Eaton, she introduced hands-on experimentation into the curricula of several female seminaries. It is likely that the first high school girls to handle and do experiments using retorts, syphons, pneumatic cisterns, and caustic potash at their own school did so at the Troy Female Seminary in its first laboratory room, added upon Almira Lincoln's initiative.

The students' experiments were incorporated into public examinations on a variety of chemical topics including "Application of Chemistry to Medicine," "Combustible Substances," and "Chemical Principles Involved in the Making of Bread."[16] In preparing for these exams, the students were also required to do extensive library research. Almira Lincoln Phelps's expectations for these projects bear a strong resemblance to those typically found for current independent study and research projects at the college level.

Although her college texts were not as influential as *Familiar Lectures on Botany*, the authors of the article in the *Journal of Chemical Education* acknowledge that she "presents chemistry as a living, growing subject, and

often compares opposing theories." Phelps's goal was to present an introduction to the language of chemistry, even to the neglect of profound ex-
plorations of chemical principles. Her pupils had complained to her about
the difficulty of chemical terms. Phelps had earlier translated a French chemical dictionary into English at Eaton's request. She "sought to present the
elements of the science in popular and attractive form."[17] Her chemistry
text, *Chemistry for Beginners*, was also used for a long time. An annotated
copy was recently found at Russell Sage College in Troy. It was probably
the secondary school text of a woman chemistry professor in the early days
of the college.

Almira Lincoln Phelps was not a research scientist, not even in botany,
for which she is best known. She did collect plants as early as her first days
in Troy with Amos Eaton and thirty years later on a trip to Switzerland.
She was the first woman member of the Maryland Academy of Science, to
which she donated her herbarium. She was the second woman, after astron-
omer Maria Mitchell, to be elected to the American Association for the
Advancement of Science (AAAS), to which she subsequently presented several papers. She was sixty-six at the time of her election in 1859. She herself
noted that she was elected by virtue of having "devoted the greater portion
of a long life to the study of science, and in seeking to render its elements
attractive to the young" but "with no pretensions to have been a
discoverer."[18]

Although Phelps was invited to join a prestigious scientific organization,
women, even of her accomplishments, could still be excluded from membership in teachers' organizations. She wrote in 1850 about the absurdity
that the new constitution of the Maryland College of Teachers forbade
membership to women teachers. A woman might be a principal of an institution and have made successful efforts to elevate the profession of teaching
and to secure competent teachers and indeed to train teachers. Nevertheless,
she was still not eligible for membership, "while any ignorant young man
in his teens, who is employed in teaching children, can become a member."[19]
Even the twenty-eight editions of her botany textbook, used all over the
country, could not achieve her election to this state teachers' organization.
Her interest in the improvement of education never flagged. In her old age
she was still corresponding with Henry Barnard and subscribing to his *American Journal of Education*.

Phelps's writings extended beyond education and science textbooks. She
wrote novels such as *Ida Norman* and *Caroline Westerley* for and about schoolgirls, all quite moralistic. They were well reviewed. After her retirement
from teaching she wrote about many subjects, from art to French literary
figures to "England under the Stuarts" and the "Life and Writings of Goethe." Some of these were published in the *National Quarterly Review* and
were themselves reviewed, not always favorably, in New York and Philadelphia newspapers.

Phelps's most interesting writing outside her science texts is her "Observations upon an Infant, During Its First Year, by a Mother," written about her own baby after her marriage to John Phelps. She wrote this journal five years before Darwin's own study of his infant. It was appended to Emma Willard's and Almira Phelps's translation of Necker's (i.e., Madame de Saussure's) *L'Education Progressive*. Phelps's "Mother's Journal" was later translated into French and Italian and published in Paris. It is truly an original piece of work, analyzing the baby's sensory perception and his physical and mental growth. Her emphasis was on curiosity, activity, and learning by doing in the baby's development, an emphasis in keeping both with her own views of education for older children and with later ideas about "progressive education," even for very small children.

Phelps was considerably involved in public affairs both at home and abroad. As early as 1828, she was caught up in the struggle of the Greeks for independence from the Turks. She and others in Troy collected funds and goods. After Greece's independence in 1829, she and Emma Willard were instrumental in setting up a school for girls in Greece. Phelps continued this work after her move to Vermont and later wrote about other oppressed people in Hungary and Cuba. She was also interested in cooperative societies in the United States and visited the Zoarites in Ohio and wrote an article about her visit. During the Civil War she addressed social problems at home.

Phelps, however, for all her fervor about women's education and the welfare of oppressed peoples, was a strong believer in the earlier view of woman's proper "sphere" or role. She was, after all, born in the eighteenth century, of an older generation. Elizabeth Cady Stanton was a student at Troy Female Academy when Almira Lincoln was vice-principal. Cady Stanton, Susan B. Anthony, and Lucy Stone were of the new generation who fought for women's suffrage, but Phelps and the other older generation women who had worked so hard for women's education were, for the most part, antisuffrage. Phelps, when nearly eighty years old, joined the Women's Anti-Suffrage Association. This group wrote an antisuffrage petition, which Phelps helped to circulate. It contained all the old arguments against women's suffrage. Phelps herself wrote:

If women vote . . . why should they not be compelled to bear arms . . . .Where is the sacred home, the nursery . . . at which woman is so often the ministering spirit? . . . There were certainly evils to be remedied in the condition of women—Legislatures have studied how to do this in regard to the rights of property, the guardianship of children, &e. Women have been appointed as post-mistresses . . . and members of scientific associations . . . .The writer and her sister, Mrs. Willard . . . ever maintained that in Education and Authorship they might be allowed to compete with men.

But equality did not extend to suffrage: "We do not ask for Women's Suffrage . . . .We ask to remain in the sphere in which God placed us."[20]

Phelps's circular was reviewed in the *Women's Journal*, apparently by a former student to whom many of these circulars were sent. The reviewer notes that her appeal is made especially to her former pupils and those of her "deceased sister, Mrs. Emma Willard," but they have "grown wiser than their teachers are and will not enlist under Mrs. Phelps leadership."[21]

There is no question that these were Phelps' real views. Many of her writings express them; to Phelps, woman's sphere literally went back to the Bible: "She [woman] was created to be the companion of man, to cheer his solitude and to assist him in his duties. This very relation implies a difference between them. A companion or assistant fills a secondary role."[22] Religion was central to her life. It was even reflected in her reasons for studying botany and other aspects of what were to her literally God's creation, as is very clear from her textbooks. Phelps's interests in writing and public policy continued into her last years. Her son Charles became a congressman, and she often visited Washington. In 1877, at the age of eighty-four, she visited President Rutherford Hayes and discussed South Carolina politics. She continued to take summer vacations in Saratoga Springs, New York, and in Gettysburg Springs, Pennsylvania, until she was eighty-eight. There were many distinguished guests at her Baltimore home, where she had both a library and a laboratory, including a telescope and laboratory apparatus. There she was said to try out new experiments and to teach her small grandsons. She continued the journal she had kept for seventy-five years until a week before she died, on July 15, 1884, her ninety-first birthday.

Almira Hart Lincoln Phelps spanned a very important period in American education, especially for female education. Her teaching career began in 1809 and continued through 1856. Her writing career went on much longer. She was important both in her development of a rigorous secondary school curriculum for girls, equivalent not only to better American high schools of today but even to the current curricula of the French *lycees* or German and Swiss *gymnasia*. In addition she developed new methods for teaching many subjects, methods involving the students' own experience rather than rote learning. Her methods were used for pupils of all ages and in many subjects, but especially in science. She herself developed many of the textbooks for these courses, particularly in botany, chemistry, and geology, and made it possible for other teachers, perhaps with less training in science than she had, to set up experiments and explain them to students. Thus, the use of laboratory equipment and actual hands-on instruction spread well beyond the schools at which Phelps herself taught, including other parts of the country. Although her botany book was written originally as a text for her own classes, it spread even more widely through its many editions to boys' secondary schools and even to colleges. It is difficult to determine the influence of this book. Books by Asa Gray and others gradually replaced it, as the natural system of classification eventually made the Linnaean system obsolete. Her chemistry and physics texts were more rapidly replaced, but hands-on science continued to expand.

Phelps's influence on education extended to other areas as well. She was a longtime advocate of physical education for girls, including outdoor education. While still at the Troy Seminary she was instrumental in acquiring additional land for this purpose. She tried to create in her various schools an atmosphere conducive to serious study, including a system of incentives and rewards—and undoubtedly stricter rules than we would today approve. She used her better students as student instructors even at Troy Female Seminary, and at Patapsco she instituted formal training for future teachers. In this respect her schools were the forerunners of the later state teachers' colleges. Normal schools were just starting in New England and were not established in Maryland until twenty-four years after the "normal" department, or teachers' class, was begun by Phelps at Patapsco. Her student teachers received both academic training and training in teaching, both theoretical and practical. Phelps published much of her advice to these student teachers; undoubtedly these ideas and methods also spread to other institutions.

Phelps's contemporaries, Emma Willard, the originator of Troy Female Seminary, and Mary Lyon, whose school became Mount Holyoke College, are both better known as educators than Almira Lincoln Phelps. The latter's contribution to women's education, particularly to science education, is probably equally great. She is a particularly interesting woman, in many aspects characteristic of the first half of the nineteenth century, but very much involved in post–Civil War issues as well. Through her writings she left us her views on marriage, religion, woman's roles in society, and child development and particularly on many aspects of education. Her views on some of these subjects were conservative, but her views on teaching methods and on child development were new, in some respects radical, to be taken up later by John Dewey, Jean Piaget, and others. A commentator of sixty years ago wrote this about Phelps: "During her lifetime the content of education changed from 'polite' folderol to a substantial mental discipline, based on the sciences, mathematics and ancient languages. Through her books and the institutions she served, she was an influential contributor to this change."[23]

It was a long and significant lifetime. When Almira Lincoln Phelps was born at the end of the eighteenth century, secondary education was not available for girls. By the time she died in 1884, women could graduate from colleges and state universities. They could even earn Ph.D. degrees at a few institutions in the United States. Phelps had a part in this revolution in female education, particularly in regard to science education.

NOTES

1. Emma L. Bolzau, *Almira Hart Lincoln Phelps: Her Life and Work* (Lancaster, PA: Science Press, 1936), 19.

2. Ibid., 38–40.

3. Ibid., 68–69, 83.

4. J. H. Pestalozzi, *How Gertrude Teaches Her Children* (5th ed., London: G. Allen & Unwin, 1915), 19.

5. E. M. McAllister, *Amos Eaton* (Philadelphia: University of Pennsylvania Press, 1941), 160–61.

6. Letter, Amos Eaton to W. Darlington, November 2, 1838, in McAllister.

7. Henry Barnard, "Mrs. Almira Lincoln Phelps," *American Journal of Education* 17 (September 1868): 615.

8. Letter, A.H.L. Phelps to Mrs. Samuel Hart, spring 1835, in Bolzau, 62.

9. Barnard, 615.

10. John Phelps in the Phelps family Bible, in Bolzau, 66.

11. Bolzau, 117.

12. Letter from Emma Willard to Lydia Sigourney, September 23, 1841, in Bolzau, 117–18.

13. Almira L. Phelps, *Familiar Lectures on Botany* (New York: Huntington and Savage, 1851), author's preface.

14. Emanuel D. Rudolph, "Almira Hart Lincoln Phelps (1793–1884) and the Spread of Botany in Nineteenth Century America," *American Journal of Botany* 71 (1984): 1161–67.

15. M. E. Weeks and F. B. Dains, "Mrs. A. H. Lincoln Phelps and Her Services to Chemical Education," *Journal of Chemical Education* 14 (February 1937): 53–57.

16. Almira L. Phelps, *Chemistry for Beginners* (New York: F. J. Huntington, 1834), 5.

17. Ibid., Preface.

18. Almira Phelps, in Bolzau, 447; Margaret Rossiter, *Women Scientists in America; Struggles and Strategies to 1940* (Baltimore: Johns Hopkins University Press, 1982), 7.

19. Bolzau, 382.

20. Ibid., 388–89.

21. Ibid., 390.

22. Almira L. Phelps, "Duties and Rights of Women," *National Quarterly Review* XXIX (June 1874), 29–54.

23. Thomas Woody, "Almira Hart Lincoln Phelps," in Dumas Malone, ed., *Dictionary of American Biography* (New York: Charles Scribners, 1934), 524–25.

WORKS BY ALMIRA HART LINCOLN PHELPS

Familiar Lectures on Botany. Hartford, CT: F. J. Huntington, 1829.

Dictionary of Chemistry, trans. of French work by L. N. Vauquelin. New York: G & C & H Carvill, 1830.

Botany for Beginners. Hartford, CT: F. J. Huntington, 1833.

Familiar Lectures on Natural Philosophy. New York: Huntington and Savage, 1833.

Lectures to Young Ladies. Boston: Carter, Hendee, 1833.

Chemistry for Beginners. New York: F. J. Huntington, 1834.

Geology for Beginners. Hartford, CT: F. J. Huntington, 1834.

"Observations upon an Infant, During Its First Year by a Mother." In Madame de

Saussure Necker, *Progressive Education*, appendix. Boston: W. D. Tickner, 1835.

The Female Student. London: Scott, Webster and Geary, 1837.

The Fireside Friend. Massachusetts School Library, Vol. 18, 1838, Reprint, Boston: Thomas H. Webb, 1942.

"Essay on Female Education." In J. R. Albach, ed., *Transactions of the 8th Annual Meeting of the Western Literary Institute.* Cincinnati, OH: Western Literary Institute and College of Professional Teachers, 1839.

Hours with My Pupils; or Educational Addresses, etc. New York: C. Scribner, 1859.

WORKS ABOUT ALMIRA HART LINCOLN PHELPS

Barnard, Henry. "Mrs. Almira Lincoln Phelps." *American Journal of Education* 17 (1868): 611–22.

Bolzau, Emma L. *Almira Hart Lincoln Phelps.* Lancaster, PA: Science Press, 1936.

McAllister, E. M. *Amos Eaton.* Philadelphia: University of Pennsylvania Press, 1941.

Rossiter, M. W. *Women Scientists in America: Struggles and Strategies to 1940.* Baltimore: Johns Hopkins University Press, 1982.

Rudolph, Emanuel D. "Almira Hart Lincoln Phelps." In E. T. James, ed., *Notable American Women.* Cambridge: Harvard University Press, 1971.

———. "Almira Hart Lincoln Phelps (1793–1884) and the Spread of Botany in Nineteenth Century America." *American Journal of Botany* 71 (August 1984): 1161–67.

Slack, Nancy G. "Nineteenth Century American Women Botanists: Wives, Widows and Work." In P. B. Abir-Am and D. Outram, eds., *Uneasy Careers and Intimate Lives.* New Brunswick, NJ: Rutgers University Press, 1987.

Weeks, M. E., and F. B. Dains. "Mrs. A. H. Lincoln Phelps and Her Services to Chemical Education." *Journal of Chemical Education* 14 (February 1937): 53–57.

Woody, T. "Almira Hart Lincoln Phelps." In Dumas Malone, ed., *Dictionary of American Biography.* New York: Charles Scribners' Sons, 1934.

Caroline F. Putnam

Ronald E. Butchart

Caroline F. Putnam (1826–1917), abolitionist and educator, spent the 1850s assisting her life companion, Sallie Holley, in the latter's speaking career in the service of abolitionism, and she spent much of the 1860s in relief efforts for the freed slaves. In 1868 she went into more direct work for the former slaves, founding the Holley School in Lottsburg, Virginia. She spent the next thirty-five years educating four generations of African Americans. She worked and lived among the freed people longer, and in some respects more successfully, than any of the first generation of female teachers of freedmen.

Of Caroline F. Putnam's early years we know little. She was born somewhere in Massachusetts on July 29, 1826. Her father, a physician, died while she was young, probably before her tenth year; his name, the town of her birth, and her middle name remain mysteries. Her mother, Eliza (Carpenter) Putnam, an abolitionist and staunch Calvinist, remarried to Levi Peet, a farmer of modest means from southwestern New York State, when Caroline was fourteen. Nothing is known of Caroline's schooling or work before she achieved her majority. We can only speculate whether she, like many young women of her era and circumstances, taught in her neighborhood common schools. Her education was apparently solid, however, for when she entered Oberlin College in 1848, she was admitted to the second year of the Ladies' Course.

For a woman to enter college in 1848 was unusual. The notion of higher education for women was still novel and would continue to call down derision for years to come. For Putnam to attend college appears even more unusual. Domestic and retiring, the stepdaughter of a back-country farmer who some considered crude and uncultured, she seems an unlikely candidate for the intellectual, religious, and social agitation of Oberlin College. The influences that led her to Oberlin at twenty-two years of age remain, unfortunately, part of the impenetrable riddle of her childhood and youth.

True to its reputation for activism and change, Oberlin College had a profound impact on Putnam. The impact on her was, however, one that the college neither intended nor endorsed. Despite its theological radicalism, Oberlin was socially conservative. In its programs, policies, and pronouncement, the college strove to reinforce women's subordination to men and their subservience in church and society. The Ladies' Course was intentionally inferior to the course of studies intended for men; the college prohibited women from speaking in "promiscuous" or mixed company; a strict gender division of student labor, along with sermons on women's sphere, provided precept and preaching on women's place in the college's evangelical vision of the good society. Similarly, Oberlin espoused a conservative form of abolitionism, one firmly opposed to the immediatism, radicalism, and moral critique of abolitionists aligned with William Lloyd Garrison. More than all other goals, Oberlin intended to build evangelical Christianity.

Under the influence of Oberlin's rich student culture, intellectual ferment, revivals, and social activism, Putnam flourished. Yet the spirit she nurtured, the intellect she honed, the commitments she fostered were not those sanctioned by Oberlin College. Along with her classmate Sallie Holley, Putnam moved from subservience to independence and eventually to the women's rights movement, from evangelical antislavery to Garrisonian abolitionism, and from Presbyterianism to Unitarianism. She sharpened her critical intellectual skills against the whetstone of conflicting values and ideas.

Putnam and Holley left Oberlin together in 1850 when Holley graduated; Putnam did not complete her degree. They were seldom apart for more than a few months at a time for the rest of Holley's life. For the next decade Putnam sought a sphere of usefulness in abolitionism. She traveled with Holley, promoting and assisting as the older woman established a reputation as an effective public lecturer on abolitionism. Putnam's letters to the *National Anti-Slavery Standard* reported on their work and Holley's lectures, while her own official duties for the National Anti-Slavery Society took her door-to-door, speaking to strangers about Garrisonianism, offering tracts, and soliciting donations.

Those were years of torment and struggle for Putnam. Her work as colporteur called for an assertiveness, tenacity, emotional toughness, and self-confidence she felt she lacked. Craving domestic security, a sense of place, and a circle of friends, she dreaded the often hostile confrontations with strangers, the rootlessness, and the travel.

Her respite came in 1861, when the Civil War shifted abolitionism from moral suasion to frenetic efforts to provide immediate relief and education for the freed slaves and to mobilize government action on their behalf. For two years she relished her reprieve from the spotlight, visiting her mother, recently widowed for a second time, and working to refurbish a house she had bought with Holley in Buffalo. By 1864, however, the two reentered the lecture field, bending their energies toward freedmen's aid, resuming the old roles.

Throughout their early years together, Putnam took her cues from Holley. Eclipsed by Holley's fame, she subordinated her own yearnings, content to serve in small ways in the struggle against slavery. As Holley's career began to falter in the later 1860s, however, Putnam seized the initiative. She defined her own trajectory, one more congenial with her sense of self. She established her career for the next three and a half decades and her central passion for the next half century. In November 1868, Putnam moved to Lottsburg, Virginia, to launch a school for the freed slaves of the area.

Seven years earlier, within months of the opening of the Civil War, an unprecedented, spontaneous educational movement had begun. It had first appeared in Virginia, not far from Lottsburg, and in the Sea Islands of South Carolina. It had spread rapidly throughout the South, wherever African Americans seized their freedom. It had come from them, from their insistent demand for knowledge and literacy. It was met by their own teachers where they could find them. It was answered as well by the rapid proliferation in the North of voluntary organizations and by the redirected work of several churches and missionary organizations, all mobilized toward the aid and education of the freed people.

By 1868 the effort was no longer novel. Indeed, by then northern interest had begun to wane. Caroline Putnam, then, was not among the earliest pioneers in freedmen's education. While still an act of enormous courage, her effort may have lacked the drama of the first southern black schools, held on the verandas of abandoned plantation mansions, in shell-shattered buildings, or beside infamous slave pens. Yet Putnam founded what would become one of the most unique and independent of the thousands of freedmen's schools taught by white northern women.

Although named after Sallie Holley, the Holley School was always Putnam's school. She sustained it throughout her lifetime, developing singular means of financing it. She taught in it daily for thirty-five years and then remained beside it to support and encourage it for the remainder of her life. She understood the unique needs of rural black southerners and adapted the school, the pedagogy, and the curriculum to those needs.

The two greatest problems facing all the freedmen's schools were finding the means to sustain the work financially and negotiating the often implacable hostility of southern whites. For funding, most of the freedmen's schools established by northerners (the freed people launched hundreds of schools on their own initiative) looked to three sources: sponsoring organizations such as established missionary societies and secular aid societies; the Bureau of Refugees, Freedmen, and Abandoned Lands, the government's inadequate response to the social problems created by the war and emancipation; and the freed people themselves, in the form of tuition or subscriptions. However, sponsoring organizations left the teachers dependent upon distant organizations' success at raising funds among a northern population quickly losing interest in the racial problems of southern society. The Freedmen's Bureau could aid education only indirectly and withdrew that aid in

1870. The freed people—landless, penniless, surrounded by hostile white neighbors, dependent upon a devastated agricultural economy—could contribute but little, though they consistently supported the schools financially despite their poverty. Meanwhile, the most common response of northern female teachers to southern white hostility toward them and their work was to endure social ostracism and isolation.

Putnam addressed the funding problem by establishing the Holley School on an independent financial foundation. She received partial funding from the American Missionary Association for a portion of one year only and minimal assistance from the Freedmen's Bureau. Tuition was nominal, depending upon ability to pay, and never covered expenses. Putnam relied instead on private donations from northern friends, on her own savings, and on contributions of labor and fuel from the freedmen.

The most innovative and important source of support, however, derived from her position as postmistress for Lottsburg, an appointment she gained in 1869. The post proved to be beneficial not so much because it generated income, which was paltry, but, more important, because it altered the perceptions and softened the opposition of local whites toward black education, thereby addressing the problem of southern hostility. Putnam housed the post office in a corner of her schoolhouse, which obliged all its patrons to come into school, where they observed the reality of black intellectual progress and became acquainted with the school and its teachers. Her actions lent status to the school and undercut the social isolation that left many other freedmen's teachers open to attack. As she remarked many years later, "There is *respect* for our school—if not honor!—by these white *ladies*! who call for mail & see us at work."[1] Although she was never accepted by the white community, her actions defused much potential antagonism and fostered more formal intercourse with white southerners than was known by virtually any of her counterparts.

Putnam's hold on the position of postmistress was never fully secure. It was a political appointment, so every Democratic victory in presidential politics brought the specter of dismissal and possibly the risk of closing the Holley School. Yet she persevered, retaining her appointment through the political influence of northern friends until she voluntarily relinquished it in 1903 as she prepared for retirement.

The post office appointment was a means to an end, however. The central purpose of Putnam's life was her work for, and solidarity with, African Americans. The Holley School was her expression of a commitment that stretched back to her days at Oberlin. At the Holley School she could live that commitment in harmony with her own self-perception, happily at work that was settled and rooted, surrounded with familiar faces, building a domestic circle for herself and Holley.

Putnam was committed to expanding black freedom through education. She understood better than many of the freedmen's teachers that education was inevitably political—that it would either contribute to greater power and autonomy or prepare for new forms of domination. The curriculum and pedagogy of her school did not flinch from that understanding. Her lessons were infused with political content intended to provide freed people of color with examples of moral courage drawn from the abolitionist struggles and with heroes, black and white, to whom they could turn for inspiration in their struggle for broader freedoms. The students spent portions of every year preparing for particularly important celebrations in the Holley School calendar: December 2, John Brown's Day, with recitations from his last speech, readings from biographies, his portrait wreathed in holly leaves; Washington's Birthday, "always the best prepared for—as the 3 months of winter brings the fullest school,"[2] though devoted not to the slaveholder Washington but to Wendell Phillips, firebrand abolitionist; July 18, Fort Wagoner Day, in memory of Robert Gould Shaw and the African-American soldiers of the Fifty-Fourth Massachusetts Infantry, observed by the students relating "the eloquent story of their martyrdom, in choice extracts, poems, & tributes of grateful remembrance."[3] The entire community was invited to those celebrations, providing a curriculum of memory and pride to Lottsburg's freed people.

The materials used in the classrooms, too, were chosen for their potential to provide social visions that transcended the limitations imposed by black southern rural poverty and racist oppression. U.S. history was studied from a history text by abolitionist and Civil War hero Colonel Thomas W. Higginson, anathema to the South. Newspapers, current magazines, historical artifacts, and biography enriched daily lessons, bringing into the classroom political and social views unpopular among white Virginians. Maps, picture books, photographs, and illustrations filled the school, providing "texts—for the little lessons—I endeavor to plant in these dear 'dark' minds."[4] The songs chosen to conclude one memorial celebration were all written by women, and the struggle for women's rights found its place in discussions and lessons. As in any nineteenth-century school, the Scripture had its place in her classroom, though with a decidedly Unitarian slant.

The lessons were frequently dialogical rather than didactic, with teacher and students reading and talking about subjects and learning flowing in both directions. Above all, the lessons were participatory and active. Classes frequently abandoned the schoolroom to study elementary botany in the nearby fields, to obtain material to study under the school's microscope, or to observe the transit of Venus through a bit of stained glass after studying the phenomenon in a science text. Photographs of the Holley School, dating from the 1890s, reveal a classroom dense with visual stimuli, much of them self-consciously political, some—such as a wall covered with circus posters— more generally educational and whimsically aesthetic.

Had the early progressive educators cared about black education, they could hardly have found a better model for the rural progressive school than the Holley School, despite its isolation from, and indifference to, pedagogical fashion. From its beginning it took the child and the community as the central issue, adjusting its calendar, its class periods, its curriculum and teaching, and its classroom resources to their needs. Given the poverty of Lottsburg's black community and the consequent need for its children's labor, school was held year-round. Putnam did not attempt to impose strict attendance on children whose labor was needed in the field and the household, discovering early that southern black children learned from one another when they could not attend class. Children came and went as the cycles of agricultural labor required, the older children out much of the year, the younger finding more time for school. In some families, only one child could attend at a time, and the children alternated weeks or months when they could seek to further their schooling. Understanding that poor agricultural communities could not afford, and had no use for, clocks, Putnam made no effort to impose northern industrial notions of punctuality on southern rural life and work cycles. She engaged learners at times appropriate to them.

Formal education did not define the limits of Putnam's work. Well aware that economic change and attendant political action were as vital for the future of the freed people as literacy and numeracy, Putnam encouraged land reform and served as financial adviser to many African Americans. Sallie Holley, who joined Putnam in Lottsburg in 1870, involved herself in the campaign to ratify the new constitution and constitute a new government, organizing the freedmen and attempting to protect their rights. Both women used the school as a depot for used clothing from the North, bartering clothing and many other staples for services or produce, serving both poor whites and blacks. A few young freed people used Putnam and Holley as a placement agency to link with sympathetic northern families in whose homes they could work in order to study or serve apprenticeships. The two women practiced the racial equality they preached, dining at the homes of their students and in other ways meeting the freed people on terms of equality, at least at the level of interpersonal contact.

Ironically, Sallie Holley, after whom the Holley School was named, was of much less consequence to the school than Caroline Putnam. She never accommodated herself to the isolation and obscurity of teaching in a black school. She apparently taught only intermittently, spending months out of every year traveling in the North. While she invested her own savings in the school and was influential in gaining some financial support for the school from northern donors, she became increasingly embittered, estranging herself from her abolitionist friends and finally from Putnam herself. Putnam was unwavering in her devotion to Holley, though they finally lived in separate houses on the Lottsburg compound. Sallie Holley died while visiting New York City, on January 12, 1893.

Caroline F. Putnam taught in the Holley School virtually daily, six days a week, for thirty-five years, taking only infrequent, short vacations. She had occasional assistants, northern white women who taught with her for short periods, particularly during the winter months when attendance often rose to seventy or more students. She employed her own more advanced students as assistants as well. Her assistants recorded the pleasures of working and living with Putnam—her intellectual energy and curiosity, her delight in her students and her garden, her bustling good nature as she managed school, post office, and household.

Her own letters, filled with loving descriptions of the native flora and her happiness in work fitted to her sense of self, reveal a quick, penetrating mind linked to an unswerving commitment to the ideals that had animated her since her Oberlin days. She penned letters blasting the perfidy of Booker T. Washington at Atlanta, understanding as early as any of his critics the social and political dangers of his position. She condemned the accommodations of Hampton Institute and its principal, S. C. Armstrong, the darling of northern philanthropy. She railed against the *"savagery"* of southern lynchings. Yet her spirit remained cheerful. She closed one letter in 1895, "What a dear, charming world it is, with its stars, & flowers, & angelic & demi-angel people!"[5]

In 1903, at seventy-seven years of age, Putnam retired as postmistress and scaled back her work in the classroom. She continued to live at the Holley School, however, and to oversee its affairs until her death. She did not retire from active service in behalf of her abolitionist and reform commitments. Rather, she expanded her reform interests, supporting peace and anti-imperialist movements, temperance, and the protection of animals. Yet race relations continued to occupy the center of her attention. She became an uncompromising opponent of Booker T. Washington and other accommodationist leaders in black education, a supporter of the Niagara Movement, and a harsh critic of national race policies.

Caroline F. Putnam died in Lottsburg on January 14, 1917, after over forty-eight years in the South, thirty-five of them devoted to teaching the freed slaves and their children and grandchildren. Only Laura M. Towne, who died in 1901, taught among the freed people for more years; none of the first generation of freedmen's women teachers spent longer among them.[6] Putnam's ashes lie in the black cemetery across the road from the school she founded and nurtured for most of her life.

The Holley School occupied a building that Putnam and the freed people of Lottsburg built themselves. It was filled with books and materials beyond the dreams of most children in the segregated and increasingly desperate black schools of the South. Its teachers were well educated and committed to their tasks. Like the school Laura Towne founded in South Carolina, the Holley School was an oasis in the desert that Jim Crow had blasted in the old Confederacy. Ironically, neither school had any measurable impact beyond the local community. Neither was known beyond small circles of northern supporters. Both were led by women who were uncompromising in their demand for racial justice. Their gender and their commitments may explain much about their not being known then and now.

NOTES

1. Caroline F. Putnam to Elizabeth Goddard May, March 29[?], 1895, Samuel May Papers, Massachusetts Historical Society (hereafter, May Papers); Putnam to May, January 20, 1889, May Papers.
2. Ibid., March 9, 1884, May Papers.
3. Ibid., November 25, 1883, May Papers.
4. Ibid., May 11, 1894, May Papers.
5. Ibid., April 16, 1895, May Papers.
6. Laura M. Towne was among the first teachers to arrive on the Sea Island of South Carolina in April 1862. She opened what came to be known as the Penn School in September 1862 and served from then until her death in 1901.

WORKS BY CAROLINE F. PUTNAM

Putnam wrote synopses of many of Holley's speeches for the *National Anti-Slavery Standard* while traveling with Holley.

Letters by Putnam are scattered across many collections, particularly the Elizur Wright Papers, Library of Congress; the Samuel May Papers, Massachusetts Historical Society; the Emily Howland Papers, Cornell University; and the Alcott Family Papers, Harvard University. Many of Holley's letters were compiled by Putnam after the older woman's death and published in John White Chadwick, ed., *A Life for Liberty: Antislavery and Other Letters of Sallie Holley* (New York: G. P. Putnam's Sons, 1899; reprint, New York: Negro Universities Press, 1969).

WORKS ABOUT CAROLINE F. PUTNAM

Herbig, Katherine Lydigsen, "Friends for Freedom: The Lives and Careers of Sallie Holley and Caroline Putnam." Ph.D. diss., Claremont Graduate School, 1977.
New York Evening Post, January 27, 1917 (obituary).

Polingaysi Qöyawayma

Jon Reyhner

Polingaysi Qöyawayma (1892–1990) was an innovator in shaping Hopi education in the United States and preserving Hopi cultural traditions. Her English name was Elizabeth White. Born one of nine children in a traditional Hopi family, she was educated by missionaries, taught thirty years in the U.S. Department of Interior's Bureau of Indian Affairs (BIA) schools, and then helped revive traditional Hopi ceramics. The first two periods of her life, bridging two cultures, are recounted in her autobiography, *No Turning Back*, which is now being used in college classrooms to help sensitize non-Indian teachers to the need for cultural understanding.

As a child in the pueblo of Oraibi, one of the oldest continuously inhabited villages on earth, Polingaysi Qöyawayma remembered good times and bad times, feast and famine, bountiful rains and searing droughts. There were times "people clawed through refuse piles looking for kernels of corn they had discarded in more prosperous times."[1] From birth, her extended family taught her "to pray. Getting up at dawn and going to the mesa's edge to voice one's thankfulness for life and all good was part of the established Hopi pattern."[2]

While the Hopi pueblos had their first contact with European immigrants in the sixteenth century, their isolation and lack of anything those immigrants wanted kept them relatively free from interference in their way of life until the end of the nineteenth century. All this changed around the time of Polingaysi's birth. The Indian agent called out the Tenth Cavalry during the winter of 1890–1891 and again in the summer of 1891 to force Hopis to send their children to school. In 1894 troops were called out again, and nineteen Hopi men were sent to the federal maximum security prison on Alcatraz Island in San Francisco Bay for one year for resisting cultural assimilation to white America. Polingaysi's mother hid her from Navajo policemen "carrying guns and clubs" who gathered up children to enroll in school.[3]

Some time after her sister was caught and enrolled in a BIA day school below the mesa, Polingaysi became curious and followed her sister to school. At the school her teacher gave her a new name, "Bessie," and did not allow her to speak the only language she knew, Hopi. In her autobiography Polingaysi describes students being booted and slapped and one having an eraser shoved in her mouth for not behaving the way the teachers wanted. Polingaysi, reflecting the even-tempered nature of her people, became very cautious and seems to have avoided such punishments. In 1906, the pressures exerted on her village led to a split in which the progressive faction literally pushed the conservative antischool faction out of town. Her grandfather proposed this less violent solution to the bitter dispute: for safety reasons, on the day of the shoving match, Polingaysi's parents sent her to stay for the day with the Mennonite missionary H. R. Voth, who employed her father as a laborer.

That same year she met a wagonload of students going to "the land of oranges." Desiring to go, she learned that her parents must first give written permission. Denied permission by her parents, she hid in the wagon, was caught, but then managed to convince her parents to let her go. She rode by wagon to Winslow, Arizona, and then boarded a train to Sherman Institute in Riverside, California, where she spent four years without returning home. There, "little ones and teenagers attended the classes and worked wherever they were assigned."[4] The school had a farm, and food was plentiful.

When she returned home, the poverty of the Hopi land made her heartsick, and she could not return to the old life. She criticized her parents for not buying a white man's bed and table and was unwilling to get married. She tried to turn her parents into white people, and the Hopi elders laughed at her. She quotes her mother as saying, "What shall I do with my daughter, who is now my mother."[5] Only later did she come to realize that her white teachers "had no conception of the true needs of Indian people."[6] Her father went forty miles to speak to the new Mennonite missionary, Jacob Frey, about his daughter's problems, and the missionary took her in and gave her a new name, "Elizabeth Ruth." Missionaries saw traditional Hopi beliefs as "utter folly and abysmal sinfulness."[7]

Unable to fit in as a missionary, she took advantage of an opportunity to live with a missionary in Newton, Kansas, and to further her education at Bethel Academy from 1912 to 1914. In Kansas she was refused service in a restaurant for being "colored," and again on a rail trip to Pennsylvania she was discriminated against. When she returned home again in the summer of 1913, she was criticized by her relatives for acting "white," found her parents "unkempt," and saw "women stripped and marched through a dipping vat like so many cattle."[8] Again, unable to adjust, she returned to Kansas to further her missionary education.

When she again returned to Hopiland, she did not find either success or fulfillment as a missionary. Like many new converts to a religion, she was overzealous. An influenza epidemic in the spring of 1919 gave her the opportunity to substitute-teach Navajo students at Tuba City, Arizona. "From the first she saw the need of relating their schoolwork to their everyday experiences."[9]

In the fall she attended the Los Angeles Bible Institute. On her return home she started building a house below the mesa near her parents but again found missionary work unsatisfying. In 1924 she was offered a position of housekeeper at the Hotevilla Day School and was then asked to teach beginners and first graders. Some Hopis accused her of "ungrateful backsliding" for giving up missionary work.

As a new first grade teacher, she was nervous, but she felt that she at least knew the language her students spoke. However, her supervisors soon reminded her she was forbidden to speak Hopi to her students. In her mind she questioned her supervisors' directives and the English curriculum she was required to teach: "What do these white-man stories mean to a Hopi child? What is a "choo-choo" to these little ones who have never seen a train? No! I will not begin with the outside world of which they have no knowledge. I shall begin with the familiar. The everyday things. The things of home and family."[10] She wrote a friend that teaching materials for Indian children did not exist and that the basal readers had only skyscrapers and white children, both of which were useless for teaching Indian students. Instead of using the materials purchased by the BIA, she took her students into the desert and taught them using their natural surroundings, which was a revolutionary idea in that time. In defiance of her supervisors she continued to substitute familiar Hopi legends, songs, and stories for Little Red Riding Hood. She found her students loved these stories translated into English, but parents questioned what she was teaching, saying, "We send them [our children] to school to learn the white man's way, not Hopi. They can learn the Hopi way at home."[11]

Despite these complaints she persevered in trying to help her children "blend the best of the Hopi tradition with the best of the white culture, retaining the essence of good, whatever its source."[12] In 1927, Henry Roe Cloud observed her teaching while he was working on a study of the BIA for the U.S. government. He supported her teaching efforts, as had some of her other supervisors. Soon after, she was transferred to teach on the Navajo Reservation, where she met and married Lloyd White, a part-Cherokee teacher, in 1931. However, the marriage did not work out, and she never had any children of her own.

Upon the appointment by Franklin D. Roosevelt of John Collier, a long-time critic of the BIA, as commissioner of Indian affairs in 1934, Qöyawayma found "overnight" her teaching methods supported, to the "consternation" of the older teachers. She met the wife of secretary of interior Harold Ickes and through her influence was able to get a transfer back to a Hopi school.

But her new colleagues, who resented her use of influence, did not welcome her. She became depressed, but falling back on the core values of her Hopi and Christian upbringing, she practiced acceptance of her situation and non-resistance. She continued to fight "parrot learning," a common Indian school practice where students memorized English with little or no comprehension of what they were learning.

Collier was aware of other countries' educational approaches to aboriginal education, especially Mexico's, and foreign criticism of the United States' treatment of its native population. The BIA held summer institutes to give teachers special training in teaching Indian students. In 1941 Qöyawayma was chosen to demonstrate her teaching methods to other BIA educators at one of these summer training institutes in Chemawa, Oregon. She had found that her method of educating children, starting "from what they already know, not from a totally new, strange field of experience," reduced the chance her students would withdraw into a shell.[13] She wrote a friend in 1941: "If the teachers to the Hopi or other tribes would come to them with human interest and love and take them for what they are and where they are and begin from their world with them results would be success. There should be less teacher dominance and theories. . . . Teacher and child should meet on mutual ground."[14]

Owning one of the few large houses in an area with no public lodging available, Qöyawayma fell into operating informally what would now be called a bed-and-breakfast inn. Her house, built by a cottonwood tree planted by her father, hosted many travelers, including Margaret Mead and Ernest Hemingway. Upon her retirement from the BIA in 1954, she received the Department of Interior's Distinguished Service Award.

Besides teaching, Qöyawayma worked to revive the tradition of Hopi pottery, traveling to the Rio Grande pueblos in an attempt to relearn lost skills. She became an accomplished potter, and the Phoenix's Heard Museum had a special exhibition of her pottery in 1945. In the 1960s, many hippies, having rejected their own materialistic culture, came to the Indians to find meaning in their lives. Qöyawayma was understanding and compassionate with the ones who made it to her doorstep.

She also cofounded the Hopi Scholarship Foundation to "teach Hopis to teach." She felt a scholarship fund was "vital because we Indians have become so dependent upon Bureau of Indian Affairs and the government that we have no sense of money. Too much has been given us. That weakens the people."[15]

Her nephew Al Qöyawayma, also an accomplished potter, paid tribute to his aunt in the catalog for his own 1984 showing:

With regard to the clay, I have a beautiful and patient teacher, my aunt, Polingaysi Qöyawayma. . . . It is through her hand and encouragement, under grandfather's cottonwood tree in Oraibi, that I have learned. More than teaching me specific skills, she shared with me the greater gift of self-discovery and experimentation in the clay. . . . She has let me turn back, she has led me beyond the threshold of this modern world to see the way of our ancient Hopi people and to see the Truth written in their hearts.[16]

He also continues her work in education, helping start the American Indian Science and Engineering Society, based on talks with his aunt, and serving on the board of the Institute for American Indian Art.

In 1971, while walking, she was hit by a car and suffered serious injuries from which she never fully recovered, and in 1984 she suffered a stroke. In her autobiography she summed up her philosophy:

[Indians] should be regarded as valuable assets to the nation and to the world, for that is what they can be, once their talents and special abilities are recognized and encouraged.

But don't ask them to peel off their brown skins and become white men. Peel though they might, there'd always be another layer of brown underneath. No. Rather, ask them to be themselves, help them to realize the value of their own heritage. Too much time has been spent in trying to teach them to cast aside the Indian in them, which is equivalent to asking them to cease being. An Indian can no more be a white man than a white man can be an Indian. And why try? There is infinite good in the Indian culture pattern. Let's look at this thing objectively, understanding each other with charity; not disparaging the differences between us, but being gratefully aware of the good qualities we may adopt, one from the other.[17]

In contrast, as a child, "she and her companions had been treated like dumb little animals because they did not speak the language of the school authorities."[18]

Polingaysi Qöyawayma paid a price for her independence, her success as a teacher pioneering culturally appropriate teaching methods, and her achievements restoring and extending the art of Hopi pottery making. Her marriage failed, and she suffered criticism from both her own people for being "white" and white educators who saw no need to adapt education to Hopi ways. Her uncle scolded her in 1913, saying:

You proud and stubborn girl! Why are you straying from the Hopi way of life? Don't you know it is not good for a Hopi to be proud? Haven't I told you a Hopi must not pretend to hold himself above his people? Why do you keep trying to be a white man? You are a Hopi. Go Home. Marry in the Hopi way. Have children. . . . Leave these white people who are leading you away from your own beliefs.[19]

However, she was able to learn to meet criticism with serenity and to appreciate the good in both Hopi and non-Hopi ways of life. Her contributions to both Hopi education and Hopi art have justified the sacrifices she made to travel her own road. In recognition of her achievements she received the

Arizona Indian Living Treasure Award, the Heard Museum's Gold Medal, and the Arizona Author Award.

NOTES

1. Polingaysi Qöyawayma (Elizabeth Q. White), *No Turning Back: A Hopi Indian Woman's Struggle to Live in Two Worlds* (Albuquerque: University of New Mexico Press, 1964), 8.
2. Ibid., 15.
3. Ibid., 19.
4. Ibid., 63.
5. Ibid., 69.
6. Ibid., 73.
7. Ibid., 30.
8. Ibid., 106.
9. Ibid., 115.
10. Ibid., 125.
11. Ibid., 126.
12. Ibid., 127.
13. Ibid., 174.
14. Letter from Polingaysi Qöyawayma to Jean Glasser, June 3, 1941, in Jo Linder, ed., *When I Met Polingaysi Underneath the Cottonwood Tree* (Mesa, AZ: Discount Printer, 1983), 51.
15. "Mrs. Elizabeth White Remembered." *Hopi Tutu-veh-ni*, January 25, 1991, 4.
16. Al Qöyawayma, "Artist's Foreword," in *Al Qöyawayma: Hopi Potter* (Santa Fe, NM: Santa Fe East Gallery, 1984), 7.
17. Qöyawayma, *No Turning Back*, 174.
18. Ibid., 174.
19. Ibid., 90.

WORKS BY POLINGAYSI QÖYAWAYMA

The Sun Girl: A True Story About Dawamana, the Little Hopi Indian Maid of Old Oraibi in Arizona—and of How She Learned to Dance the Butterfly Dance at Moencopi— As Told by Her Lifelong Friend Po-lin-gay-wi (Mrs. Elizabeth White). Berkeley, CA: Gillick Press, 1941.

No Turning Back: A Hopi Indian Woman's Struggle to Live in Two Worlds (as told to Vada F. Carlson). Albuquerque: University of New Mexico Press, 1964.

Broken Pattern: Sunlight & Shadows of Hopi History (with Vada Carlson). Happy Camp, CA: Naturegraph, 1985.

WORK ABOUT POLINGAYSI QÖYAWAYMA

Jo Linder, ed. *When I Met Polingaysi Underneath the Cottonwood Tree*. Mesa, AZ: Discount Printer, 1983.

Jesse Bushyhead, in the fall of 1838, led one group of tribal members as the Cherokee tribe made a march enforced by the U.S. Army to a new territory west of the Mississippi. Bushyhead followed the route of another group whose company included Evan Jones, one of the Baptist Foreign Board missionaries who had begun his work with the tribe in 1821. Through Tennessee, Kentucky, a portion of Illinois, and Missouri the contingents traveled, finally crossing the western border of Arkansas Territory and reaching their destination in February 1839. The deaths as a result of the Cherokee Trail of Tears did not touch the Bushyhead family, although the estimates are that one-fourth of the Cherokee tribe died before and during removal. Births as well as deaths occurred. One of these births was Carrie's sister, Eliza Missouri, who was born at Cape Girardeau, Missouri, in January.

The Bushyhead family settled at a site about six miles from the Arkansas border in a place first named Bread Town and later simply identified as Baptist Mission, located in what was to become known as Indian Territory before becoming the state of Oklahoma. The family consisted of Jesse and Eliza Bushyhead, Jesse's mother, three sons, and four daughters. Later two other children, a son and a daughter, were born. Although they lived for "nine months and one day" in a tent, the family soon had a comfortable home in the midst of a developing settlement.[1] Described as "a public place," various structures included a store, a saddlery, and a blacksmith shop; with such evidence of the formation of a community, the settlement was selected as a post office location.[2] Most of the Cherokee people scattered about, locating in sites adequate for raising crops and maintaining livestock; but within the settlement proper of Baptist Mission was a cluster of houses. In addition to the Bushyhead home, a former student who boarded with the Bushyhead family related that "the neighborhood consisted of Mr. Evan Jones' home, the schoolhouse, which was near by, and then came Granny Bushyhead's house, and Mr. Upham's."[3] Willard Upham was a teacher and Baptist missionary sent by the Baptist board to assist in teaching and mission activities. Before Willard Upham's arrival, Baptist board missionaries Thomas Frye and Sarah Hibbard also lived at Baptist Mission for a short period.

By far, the most important component of the settlement became the Baptist Mission School, which Carrie, along with her brothers and sisters, attended. At first, two schools were established: a mission school supported by the Baptist board and a Cherokee Nation–supported school. In 1841, the Cherokee Nation had authorized funding for the establishment of eleven public schools, to be located throughout the districts of Cherokee territory. Sarah Hibbard taught at the mission school, and Thomas Frye received an appointment to teach at the Cherokee Nation school in 1842. In 1846, the mission school closed, leaving the Nation's school the only school for the area. Most of the early schools were staffed, as was the Baptist Mission School, with missionaries; and Willard Upham succeeded Frye as the teacher of the Cherokee Nation school in 1847. As the Cherokee Nation negotiated its claims with the U.S. government, money was available to increase, almost annually, the number of Cherokee Nation–supported schools. Due to the sparsity of early schools, some children were sent to board at Baptist Mission, often lodging with the Bushyhead family.

Surrounding Carrie from the time of her childhood were the influences of the Baptist church, the schooling process, and her father's activities with the Cherokee Nation government. Jesse Bushyhead quite early had taken advantage of the schools established in the Southeast before removal and had taught at a school in the old Cherokee Nation. After the family's settlement at Baptist Mission, Bushyhead, in 1840, became one of the chief justices for the Cherokee Supreme Court and frequently traveled between Baptist Mission and Tahlequah, the capital of the Cherokee Nation, located some twenty-five miles westward. Bushyhead's activities as a Baptist preacher also continued, as did his Bible translation work with Evan Jones, making his life one of continual service to the church and the Cherokee Nation and making his home a busy one of activity and visitors. When he was about forty, Bushyhead's life was cut short by a fever; he died in 1844. Bushyhead's legacy to his children of a service-oriented life undoubtedly had an influence on young Carrie's attempts to gain as much education as possible and her subsequent decision to become a teacher. Perhaps due to her completion of curriculum offered at Baptist Mission, she apparently went to board at another mission school located some fifteen miles south of Baptist Mission, where she was taught by a female missionary.

By 1851 an opportunity for more advanced education was available for Carrie. The Cherokee Nation opened its highly lauded high schools, the Male and Female seminaries at Park Hill, near Tahlequah; and Carrie was among the inaugural class of the Female Seminary. Her sister, Eliza, entered the seminary the following year. The curriculum offered at the Female Seminary was comparable to that of the eastern preparatory schools of the same time period; this was not surprising since the seminary teachers had been recruited from eastern colleges. In addition to the conventional curriculum, including grammar, mathematics, history, and geography, students were expected to master Latin as well as study modern languages and to become familiar with such literary figures as Molière and Goethe. In February 1855, Carrie completed her courses of study at the Female Seminary, ranking first in her class of twelve students, ready to begin her teaching career.[4]

A gap, however, existed between teacher preparation and teaching application. Carrie's study at the Baptist Mission was conducted in English as was the case at other missionary schools. That English was the language of instruction excluded the majority of Cherokee children from gaining much education in the early schools situated in the rural areas, an exclusion that certainly persisted at the level of instruction offered by the male and female seminaries. The exclusion was due not only to language but also to the seminaries' tuition costs, so students were primarily from the wealthier and more privileged families. The complaint of elitism was offered to the Cherokee Nation Board of Education, and some redress was made by scholarships offered to indigent students. Since Sequoyah had developed the Cherokee syllabary of eighty-five characters by the 1820s and had demonstrated the effectiveness of reaching Cherokee people through Cherokee language materials, alternative educational methods were available. It can be assumed that the Cherokee Nation's Board of Education lacked the resources, teacher training, or materials to provide for instruction in Cherokee. To this can be added the early decision to pattern schools in the traditional mold of white schools, since the use of English as a medium of instruction was considered by whites and most Cherokee mixed-bloods a marker of "being civilized." Only the white missionaries and the Cherokee clergy appeared to work actively to produce Cherokee-language materials in order to provide religious instruction in both languages.

With the approval of the Cherokee Nation's examining board for teachers, Carrie's first teaching assignment was in Tahlequah, reportedly assisting at the Female Seminary. In 1858 and 1859, she was assigned a teaching position at Muddy Springs School in Flint District, located south and west of her home in Goingsnake District. A rural school, Muddy Springs had an enrollment of fifty students. Her responsibilities as a teacher included finding a place to board within the community and instructing classes of students who had varying levels of ability in the English language. The Board of Education had established a standard curriculum for all Cherokee Nation-supported schools, and the disciplines of study provided perhaps insurmountable challenges for the Cherokee-speaking children. In 1859, a report on Cherokee education contained the observation that the "mass of real Cherokees remain supine, if not opposed to a civilized education."[5]

The Civil War interrupted the progress of the Cherokee Nation. A people factionalized even before removal mostly along lines of mixed white-Cherokee ancestry and ensuing economic divisions, the Cherokee Nation had adherents for both the North and the South. The issue of slavery penetrated the Cherokee Council meetings, with wealthy slave owners demanding a pro-South declaration, although Chief John Ross continually advocated a neutral position for the Cherokee tribe. The moral question of slavery also became an issue for the different mission denominations in service to the tribe, and the Baptist board even inquired whether Evan Jones could take action, by "receiving to membership no slaveholders."[6] In 1850, Jones could identify only four church members who owned slaves; one of the members was Eliza Bushyhead, Carrie's mother, whose household had long included a slave woman. With so few people involved, the issue was not pressed; but Evan Jones and the Baptist church became identified with the antislavery forces. Tensions mounted as the factions grew stronger and the pro-South voices swayed the Cherokee Council to support the Confederacy. Tribal operation funds were affected since honoring the removal treaty's funding stipulations was a congressional prerogative, and the Cherokee Nation's schools were closed after 1859.

Civil War conflicts in the Cherokee Nation were particularly devastating as hostilities were between Cherokee factions in addition to the Union and Confederate militaries. Seeking safety, some Union sympathizers moved to Kansas, where John Ross ostensibly had been escorted under guard by the Union army, while others moved to be within the protection of the nearest Union garrisons. Carrie stayed at Fort Gibson, at the western fringe of the Cherokee Nation, during the war years and taught at a school that included not only Cherokee students but also Union supporters from other tribes. Among her students was Alice Brown Davis, a notable woman who became a twentieth-century leader of the Seminole tribe.

After the Civil War, the Cherokee Nation again faced the task of rebuilding. The educational system was put back in place, but not without some difficulty. Some schools needed new construction, and the communities again had to assume the responsibility for providing school structures. Some school locations changed, as the Civil War conflicts had brought about shifts in the population. In 1867, the Cherokee Nation reopened thirty-two schools, and Carrie Bushyhead received the Baptist Mission school assignment. Willard Upham, shortly after the closure of the schools in 1859, had left the area, making it possible for Carrie to teach where she had begun her own education.

Teaching for the Cherokee Nation schools in the latter 1800s was in many ways similar to teaching in any public school system; yet, the differences were marked. A centralized authority consisting of the Nation's Board of Education and a superintendent of education made the decisions concerning the educational system. Its duties included establishing the length of the school terms, approving examination procedures for both teachers and students, selecting the textbooks, making teacher assignments, and submitting the budget for the education system. For instance, an account of the 1875–1876 school year in part contains Board of Education decisions to continue the two annual school terms of twenty weeks each, to relocate certain schools to areas of greater population, and to authorize textbook purchase from a company in St. Louis, Missouri. However well structured the system appeared, the language difficulties of English instruction to Cherokee speakers continued. John Jones, the son of Evan Jones, as the United States' agent for the Cherokees, reported in 1872:

The schools attended by half-breeds speaking English are doing well, and are of great benefit to the children. But those attended by full-bloods, speaking only the Cherokee language, are accomplishing but little good. The children learn to read, spell, and write the English language, but do not understand the meaning of words . . . .The great desideratum for this class of children is a system of education which shall take their own language and make it the medium of conveying to them a knowledge of the English language, and also make it a medium of conveying to them the rudiments of a common education. Then, by the time they would have learned the English language so as to use it with facility, they would have acquired a considerable knowledge of arithmetic, geography, and history, and the structure of both languages.[7]

To this end, Jones, a speaker and writer of the Cherokee language since his childhood at Baptist Mission, recommended textbooks that would be simplified and practical and provide instruction in both English and Cherokee.

In recognition of the language problem, the Cherokee Nation acted on Jones's recommendation and authorized him to produce bilingual textbooks. The Board of Education also paid care to the selection of teachers and revised instructional methods used in the schools. Teachers whom the Cherokee Nation designated as native increased, as well as the number of teachers who spoke Cherokee and English. Although additional study is required, enough evidence is available to suggest that the Cherokee Nation educational system had advanced to a point at which teachers were receiving their teacher preparation within the nation. In 1886, of 103 teachers employed, those who were designated "native" teachers totaled 89, of whom 33 were bilingual, with the remainder of the teachers classified as either "noncitizens" or "adopted citizens."[8] By the late 1870s, the Nation also distinguished between Cherokee-speaking schools and English-instructed schools. School regulations also reflected the need for language transition by requiring at least one morning and one evening of English instruction in the Cherokee-speaking schools. Later, the regulations included a daily minimum of two hours of English instruction.

Likely, the regulations had little effect on Carrie Bushyhead's instructional methods since she was one of the bilingual teachers enumerated by the Cherokee Nation. Her teaching assignment continued to be renewed at the Baptist Mission School, amid some amount of change that had been occurring in her home community and in the student population. The original Baptist Mission inhabitants dwindled. Evan Jones, after living in Kansas during the Civil War, returned to the area but lived at first with his son John in Tahlequah and later returned to Kansas. After fifty years of ministry to the Cherokee tribe, he died in 1872 while on a visit to Tahlequah. Carrie's mother also died in 1872, leaving Carrie to head the Bushyhead house at Baptist Mission since her surviving brothers and sisters had established their homes elsewhere. The outlying community, disrupted and somewhat scattered by the war years, moved back, and Carrie's pupil population increased from fifty-nine students in 1871 to seventy-five students in 1877.

While Carrie's life assumed a quiet but busy existence, other members of her family gained distinction in the affairs of the Cherokee Nation. Her sister, Eliza Missouri, who was described as "Tahlequah's most distinguished citizen," had married Bluford West Alberty in 1871, and the couple became the stewards of the Male Seminary, responsible for the nonacademic management of the seminary.[9] In 1885 the Albertys bought and managed the noted National Hotel in Tahlequah, which Eliza maintained alone after her husband's death in 1889. Dennis Wolfe Bushyhead, Carrie's brother, became active in the political affairs of the Nation and was elected to the office of treasurer in 1871 and 1875. Dennis Bushyhead added to the prominence of the Bushyhead family when he was elected principal chief of the Cherokee Nation for two consecutive terms, in 1879 and in 1883.

In 1876, Carrie married William R. Quarles, a noncitizen from Cobb County, Georgia. Quarles was the postmaster at Baptist Mission, the post office having been reopened after the Civil War. Carrie continued teaching at the school, and she and her husband were active in the Baptist church. Although Carrie and William had no children, they reared several orphaned children, as well as some of Carrie's nieces and nephews. In 1882, the wife of Dennis Bushyhead died; and his three youngest children, Sarah, Lizzie, and Dennis, came to live with Carrie and William while the oldest child stayed in Tahlequah with Eliza. Altogether, the number of children reared by Carrie and William Quarles is estimated to be between twelve and fourteen.

With the exception of a few intermittent terms, Carrie remained the teacher at Baptist Mission until 1893. Baptist Mission was no longer the only school in the area. The number of Cherokee Nation schools increased as communities undertook to petition the Board of Education for a school assignment and to construct a building suitable for a school. In the area once served exclusively by Baptist Mission, other schools with names of Devine, Shiloh, and Piney were established. Some of the schools were located within a few miles of the Bushyhead home, and Carrie's niece, Sarah, could ride on horseback to teach at the schools assigned to her.

In addition to the children cared for by Carrie and William, their home was filled with frequent visitors. The rural area along the Arkansas state boundary had none of the amenities associated with larger places in the Cherokee Nation like Tahlequah or Fort Gibson. As a consequence, Carrie's home became almost like a hotel, for visitors to the area who had no other place to stay. During the intermittent times when she was not teaching at the Baptist Mission School, other teachers assigned to the school also boarded at her house. Her great-niece remembers a large dining table, which would seat perhaps twenty people and which was needed to accommodate the many visitors to her home. Carrie's interest and support of the nearby Baptist church also brought visitors to her home. In keeping with the Bushyhead tradition of service to the Baptist church, Carrie and William Quarles in 1895 gave the church some land adjoining the church grounds to be used "for a Parsonage and for church purposes."[10]

In the last years of her life, Carrie was witness to events leading to the breakup of the Cherokee Nation and to the fusion of Indian Territory with

Oklahoma Territory to form the state of Oklahoma in 1907. Strongly opposed by the Cherokee Nation and the other tribes comprising Indian Territory, the issue of statehood had arisen in the post–Civil War years; but the tribes were unable to withstand the forces aligned in favor of statehood. After the decades of building, rebuilding, and shaping institutions to fit the needs of its citizens, the Cherokee Nation closed its schools and other tribal operations in 1906 and turned them over to the control of a state government.

The life of Carrie Bushyhead Quarles ended on February 23, 1909, at the old Bushyhead home. The tributes that were paid her speak of her kindness and service to community members and of her lifelong commitment to teaching and to the church. In an age of Cherokee history when women's names are not reflected in leadership positions, Carrie Bushyhead Quarles carved a niche for herself in what was perhaps the only accepted outlet for female leadership, teaching. To have been a Cherokee teacher to Cherokee students, to have lived through the Cherokee tribe's most trying times, and to have contributed to an exemplary tribal educational system are more than adequate legacies.

Four miles north of Westville, Oklahoma, is a small white church with a sign reading "Old Baptist Church Moved over trail of tears from Georgia 1838."[11] The church with its sign are all that call attention to a place once known as Baptist Mission. The schoolhouse is gone; and the old Bushyhead home, now transformed both outwardly and inwardly by a series of owners, would not be recognizable. Across the road from the church is a cemetery where the grave of Carrie Bushyhead Quarles can be found.

NOTES

1. Letter written by Jesse Bushyhead, 1839, in Grant Foreman Collection, Box 3, Oklahoma Historical Society, Oklahoma City.

2. Quoted in William G. McLoughlin, *Champions of the Cherokees Evan and John B. Jones* (Princeton, NJ: Princeton University Press, 1990), 204.

3. Narcissa Owen, *Memoirs of Narcissa Owen, 1831–1907* (Washington, DC: s.n., 1907; reprint, Siloam Springs, AR: Siloam Springs Museum, 1980 and Owensboro, KY: McDowell, 1980), 20.

4. No class rankings are documented. Information is from the great-niece of Carrie Bushyhead, Mrs. Ruth Self of Westville, Oklahoma, and a letter written by Mrs. Fite in 1909, printed in *Goingsnake Messenger* 8 (February 1991): 13.

5. *Report of the Commissioner of Indian Affairs*, 1857, 216.

6. "Minutes of Board of Education, Cherokee Nation, December 15, 1895–February 8, 1878," Oklahoma Historical Society, Oklahoma City.

7. *Annual Report to the Commissioner of Indian Affairs*, 1872, 236.

8. The designations are common throughout the Cherokee Nation's nineteenth-century history to distinguish between Cherokee citizens, white noncitizens, and adopted citizens who were officially regarded as Cherokee citizens.

9. Carolyn Thomas Foreman, "Aunt Eliza of Tahlequah," *Chronicles of Oklahoma* 9 (March 1931): 54.

10. "Bill of Sale," in A. D. Lester, "History of Cherokee Baptist Mission," *The Cherokee Nation News*, September 14, 1971.

11. The inaccuracies concerning the origins of the church are noted: Baptist Mission was established in 1839 by Cherokee contingents from Tennessee.

WORKS ABOUT CAROLINE ELIZABETH BUSHYHEAD QUARLES

Keith, Harold. "Memories of George W. Mayes." *Chronicles of Oklahoma* 24 (Spring 1946): 40–54.

Meserve, John B. "Chief Dennis Wolfe Bushyhead." *Chronicles of Oklahoma* 14 (September 1936): 349–59.

Owen, Narcissa. *Memoirs of Narcissa Owen. 1831–1907.* Washington, DC: s.n. 1907. Reprint, Owensboro, KY: McDowell, 1980 [and Siloam Springs, AR: Siloam Springs Museum, 1980.

Self, Ruth (great-niece of Carrie B. Quarles). Interviews, 1990–1992, Westville, OK.

Ellen Swallow Richards

John L. Rury

Ellen Swallow Richards (1842–1911) was a pioneer woman scientist and the guiding spirit of the home economics movement in the United States. Raised as an only child by parents who were dedicated to education, Richards became a lifelong devotee of science and its practical use for social betterment. She was the first woman to receive a degree from the Massachusetts Institute of Technology and was for most of her life its only woman faculty member. Richards was a founder of the modern science of sanitation, and it was largely through her vision that the field of home economics took shape after 1900. Never a radical, she was a champion of women's education who believed that women had a major role to play in American civilization through their work in the home. In the end, however, Richards's commitment to science guided her convictions, and the emerging sciences of sanitation and home economics were her greatest legacy.

Ellen Henrietta Swallow was born in 1842 in Dunstable, Massachusetts, a somewhat remote town near the New Hampshire border. Her father, Peter, was a farmer and schoolteacher, an unusual male occupation in Massachusetts, even in the 1840s. Her mother, Fanny, also had been a schoolteacher. An only child, Ellen lived in relative isolation and was educated largely at home. She assisted her father with work on the farm and, under the direction of her mother, gained something of a reputation for her sewing and baking skills. There can be little doubt that Ellen's childhood experiences on the farm, taught by both her parents but particularly her father, exerted an important influence on her later career. She later recalled her father's determination in a saying of his that she was particularly fond of : "Where anyone else has been, there I can go." Ellen noted that it was "not a bad motto, but adventurous spirits go beyond this and do what has never been done before."[1] With this outlook she went out into a world with few career options for women.

Ellen does not appear to have received much formal education before the age of seventeen, when her family moved to Westford so that she could attend the local academy. For the next eight years she studied on her own, attended lectures, and taught school, all in hopes of eventually going on to college, an atypical aspiration for young women at this time. Because her mother was often ill, it was difficult for Ellen to concentrate on her studies, and she experienced considerable frustration during these years. Like other young women of this era who were devoted to their parents, Ellen had to weigh her commitment to her family against her compelling desire to learn. Both of her parents, however, were highly supportive of her aspirations for higher education.

Ellen Swallow also expressed misgivings about marriage in these years and viewed with some distress the experiences of her female friends who had married. She apparently did not want to compromise her own commitments to learning and personal growth and wrote of never binding herself with the "chains of matrimony." Although she eventually did marry, these concerns reflect the depth of her commitment to learning at this stage of her life, a time when many of her friends were starting their own families.

Not until 1868, at age twenty-five, did Swallow finally go off to college. There were few options for young women wishing to attend a college in the East at this time. Swallow chose Vassar, then a newly established women's college with a substantial endowment, dedicated to the principle of high-quality liberal arts education for young women. Her years of study at home and at Westford evidently had served her well, for she was classified a special student with advanced standing upon her arrival, and in her second year she was designated a senior. Vassar was becoming an important center for women's education in the sciences in these years, and Swallow eagerly gravitated to these courses. She was such a good student and had learned so much prior to coming to the college that she earned money throughout her stay there tutoring other students in Latin and mathematics. Her science teachers made the greatest impression on her, however, and when she graduated in 1870, Swallow was determined to continue her pursuit of scientific inquiry. All told, the two years she spent at Vassar were a turning point in her life. She had discovered how exciting the formal study of science could be, and she was determined to continue with it.

There were virtually no clear avenues for women interested in scientific careers in the latter nineteenth century, but Swallow was undaunted. Following graduation she hoped to continue her study of chemistry. First she planned to teach science abroad, and when that plan failed, she wrote to commercial chemists in Philadelphia and Boston, hoping to secure an apprenticeship. In the fall, however, at the suggestion of one of the chemists, she applied and was admitted as a special student to the fledgling Massachusetts Institute of Technology (MIT), then only five years old. She thus became the first woman to study at MIT, perhaps the first admitted to any scientific institution of higher learning in the United States. She was admitted without any fee, not because of financial need (as she supposed at the time), but rather because the administration wanted to keep her status uncertain should any protest develop over her enrollment there. The idea of women's engaging in scientific research was most unusual at this time, and both Swallow and her mentors at MIT were constantly aware of the possibility of controversy (even though she later said that had she known of her status at the time, she would not have studied there). Although she eventually played a variety of roles at MIT and spent the rest of her life there, Swallow was always careful to conduct herself in a manner commensurate with the norms and expectations of the institute and the larger, largely male scientific community.

In 1873 Swallow received a bachelor of science degree from MIT, again the first woman so honored in the history of the institution, and also a master's degree in chemistry from Vassar. She continued her graduate studies at MIT in chemistry for an additional two years but was never awarded a doctorate, again at least partly because of the institution's desire to avoid controversy (in 1875 she would have received one of the first doctoral degrees in chemistry in the United States).

Conscious of her position at MIT, Swallow wrote while she was a student that she believed her moderate views on women's rights issues and her willingness to do "womanly duties . . . to clean up and sort of supervise the room and sew things, etc." accounted for her being accepted by the men at MIT. "Even Professor A. accords me his sanction when I sew his papers or tie up a sore finger, adjust the table, etc.," she later wrote. "Last night Prof. B. found me useful to mend *his suspenders* which had come to grief."[2] Swallow believed that if women were to make advances in science at this time, they could not be perceived as posing a threat to men or using science to alter their status as women. This was a perspective that came to characterize her later career, as she sought to employ science to augment and professionalize existing female roles. Although she was committed to advancing the cause of women in science and society, Ellen Swallow's first allegiance was to science and to determining ways in which its practical application could improve life for everyone.

While a student at MIT, Swallow met Robert Hallowell Richards, then a young member of the faculty. He proposed, and they were married in 1875, taking up residence in a Boston suburb. For the next decade Swallow, now Richards, assisted her husband in his work as a metallurgical engineer and researcher, sharing his enthusiasm for scientific inquiry and academic discourse. On field trips during the summers, she often served as his chemist, experimenting with various ways to transform metal compounds. This work resulted in her election to the American Institute of Mining and Metallurgical Engineers as its first woman member.

During these years Richards also became increasingly interested in popular education, particularly as it concerned science and scientific issues. She had taught science briefly in Boston while a student at MIT. Later she organized a science section of the Society to Encourage Studies at Home, corresponding personally with women interested in scientific issues. She wrote an educational booklet on health issues for women that was circulated widely by the society. At the same time she helped to organize the Association of Collegiate Alumnae, which later became known as the American Association of University Women.

As the above activities might suggest, the scientific education of women was a major interest for Richards at this time. Through the Woman's Education Association of Boston, she arranged to establish a Woman's Laboratory at MIT. The laboratory remained open for seven years with donated faculty time (including Richards's as an assistant) and cash donations from a number of benefactors (including Richards herself). Ellen Swallow Richards devoted long hours to working with the students at this facility, supporting their efforts and encouraging them to pursue careers in science. This was the point where her interests in women's rights and science converged. Through this work Richards finally felt she could advance both the cause of women and the spirit of scientific inquiry.

Eventually the young women under her supervision were admitted as regular students to MIT, and by the early 1880s a number had graduated. In 1883 the Woman's Laboratory closed, as MIT had established new facilities for its female students. While Richards had long campaigned to accomplish this end, its achievement left her a little dejected (she also reported having reservations about women being trained alongside men in the first two years of work at the institute). Complaining that she felt like a "woman whose children are all about to . . . leave her alone," she reported that "everything seems to fall flat and I have a sense of impending fate which is paralyzing."[3] She would not be happy until she found a new avenue of work to sustain her abiding interest in science and the lives of American women.

The answer to her dilemma came just two years later, when MIT established a chemical laboratory to study problems in sanitation, with Richards as an assistant. Richards had undertaken a wide range of practical sanitation problems in the Women's Laboratory, ranging from the testing of building materials and cloth to analysis of foods and groceries. She had published a manual on the chemistry of cooking and cleaning in 1882. With the arrival of the sanitation laboratory she also received a faculty appointment, as instructor in sanitary science (again, a first for a woman at MIT), a post she held until her death in 1912.

Richards worked on a wide range of projects in the sanitation lab, including a major multiyear survey of the Massachusetts water supply, which received national attention. Out of this project the first normal chlorine map was drawn up, a standard tool in subsequent water supply studies. When MIT established the nation's first program in sanitation engineering, Richards taught courses in analysis of environmental problems to an entire generation of students who went on to careers in public sanitation. With her work in the sanitary engineering program at MIT, she became a vital member of the scientific community and a productive faculty member of one of the nation's leading scientific institutions of higher learning.

All of this was only a prelude, however, to what became Ellen Richards's principal contribution to American life: the home economics movement. Like other middle-class Americans of her generation, Richards was concerned about the apparent decline of living conditions in the nation's cities, particularly in the rapidly growing immigrant communities. She was in a position to observe these problems firsthand in nearby Boston and became involved in a series of efforts to introduce instruction in domestic science in the public schools there. The development of squalid urban slums, she reasoned, called for improved training in the principles of sanitation and other household arts. In the latter 1890s she supported a proposal to establish a special girls' high school for science and the arts in Boston, in hopes that advanced training in domestic science could be made a part of the curriculum. (Not until 1907 was such a school, the High School of Practical Arts, established.) Richards did help establish a series of classes in housekeeping at the Women's Educational and Industrial Union in Boston, a local reform organization. In general, support for many of her ideas was slow to develop, but this did little to diminish her enthusiasm. Although classes that were offered were generally limited to instruction in cooking in the years prior to 1900 and did not become widespread, they marked a beginning of a sustained interest in popular education for Richards.

In the early 1890s Richards was also involved in a series of abortive attempts to promote better eating habits and higher standards of nutrition in the nation's major cities. Although the kitchens that she and other women reformers of the time helped to open did not succeed, they did represent an ambitious attempt at popular education. In 1893 Richards ran a kitchen as a part of the Massachusetts exhibit at the Chicago World's Fair, with a detailed exhibit about the nutritional values of different foods. Following this she became a widely consulted expert on nutritional questions and contributed to federal bulletins on the subject.

Beginning in 1899 Ellen Swallow Richards, with the assistance of Melvil and Annie Godfrey Dewey (Melvil Dewey was director of libraries for the state of New York), organized a series of annual summer conferences in Lake Placid, New York, aimed at discussing ways of improving home life in modern society. Although the first conference was small (participants numbered only ten), a wide variety of leading figures in American letters and science and education attended each year. At these meetings the term *home economics* was coined, and the essential ideas of the home economics movement were developed. Eventually, the conference appointed special subcommittees to draw up curricula and to represent the new field of home economics at the meeting of the National Education Association and other professional groups. In the space of a decade, Ellen Richards's career interests went from scientific research and education to curriculum development and educational policy formation on a national scale.

In 1908, in Washington, D.C., a meeting of prominent educators formed the American Home Economics Association (AHEA), and a new discipline was formed. By acclamation, Richards was elected the association's first president. Like other progressive reformers of the day, early AHEA members worried that the growth of big cities, with their crowded immigrant slums, threatened the stability of the social order. Home economics was seen as an answer to these problems. Sounding an alarm that resonated with these concerns, Richards declared that the home economics movement was "nothing less than an effort to save our social fabric from what seems inevitable disintegration."[4] With her election to this position of leadership in a national educational organization, Richards had become an important progressive authority on the use of education to resolve some of the period's most pressing social problems.

Perhaps the best expression of Richards's ideas about the use of home economics and sanitary science to resolve social problems appeared in her book *Euthenics*, published in 1910. *Euthenics* was a term she coined as a counterpart to the more widely known word *eugenics*, or "race betterment." While eugenics was concerned with the use of genetic research to control a wide range of perceived social problems (and eventually led to abuses, such as sterilization campaigns), euthenics aimed at "the betterment of living conditions, for the purpose of securing efficient human beings." In Richards's mind, better sanitation, improved nutrition, and better education were the essential elements to "developing better men now," rather than in the future. The key to this was "right living conditions," which included "pure food and a safe water supply, a clean and disease free atmosphere in which to live and work, proper shelter, and the adjustment of work, rest and amusement."[5] In short, through a systematic and rational program of scientific inquiry and education, the home economics movement could address both physical (sanitary and nutritional) and psychological (work, rest, and amusement) needs of American families. This, Richards believed, was vital to the future of the nation.

The home economics movement enjoyed a great deal of success, and within a few years home economics courses were being offered in high schools across the country. By 1920 nearly a third of all women in high schools across the country had enrolled in these courses, and the Smith Hughes Act—passed by Congress in 1917—had designated home economics a branch of vocational education eligible for federal support. Before long, home economics also became a popular course of study at many colleges and universities, providing women with a field of study that focused on problems related to gender issues, as well as traditional themes of sanitation, nutrition, and family life. Given these developments, home economics proved to be one of the most rapidly adopted curricular innovations in the history of American education. Ellen Richards had a vision that was eagerly embraced by educators across the nation.

Home economics was not without its critics, of course, and it continues to be a source of considerable controversy in education. Perhaps the biggest problem it entailed was gender segregation in the curriculum. Since virtually all home economics students were women (while shop or industrial education students were male), there developed considerably more segregation of males and females in high schools and colleges with the adaptation of these curricula. Home economics often became a haven for capable women scholars who were unable to secure appointments in their own fields because of discrimination, but its existence may have deflected criticism of institutions for not hiring women for positions in other academic fields. Finally, the development of home economics, and its strong identification with women probably served to reinforce the notion that a woman's place was in the home and in this way inhibited the advance of women in the prestigious male-dominated professions. In this way, the development of home economics may have made it even more difficult for other women to follow the paths that pioneers such as Ellen Richards herself had followed.

Unfortunately, Richards did not live to witness the success that her ideas enjoyed in the second decade of the twentieth century and beyond. She died of heart disease in 1911 at the age of sixty-eight, at her home in Boston. Friends and colleagues hailed her many accomplishments, as well as her compassion and wide-ranging intellect. Although she had earned a substantial income from her many activities, she left virtually no estate because she had given so generously to the various causes she was involved with and had traveled so extensively. As a progressive scientist, Richards was a firm believer in the proposition that the world could be improved through the rational use of existing resources and through education. In her vision of improved living conditions she anticipated many of the ideas of the environmentalist movement of the late twentieth century, but most of her prescriptions for change focused on individuals and families, not government agencies or corporations. In Richards's view, everyone needed to become something of a sanitation engineer if society were to successfully contend with its mounting problems of waste and unhealthful living. The home economics movement, even with its flaws, was a material embodiment of this vision. In this respect, Ellen Swallow Richards was the household engineer to an entire nation and one of the foremost popular science educators of the twentieth century.

NOTES

1. Caroline L. Hunt, *The Life of Ellen H. Richards* (Boston: Whitcomb and Barrows, 1912), 9.

2. Ibid., 91.

3. Ibid., 149.

4. Ellen Richards, "The Social Significance of the Home Economics Movement," *Journal of Home Economics* 3, no. 2 (April 1911): 117.

5. Ellen S. Richards, *Euthenics: The Science of Controllable Environment* (Boston: Whitcomb and Barrows, 1910), x.

WORKS BY ELLEN SWALLOW RICHARDS

The Chemistry of Cooking and Cleaning. Boston: Whitcomb and Barrows, 1886. Reprint, 1910.

Home Sanitation: A Manual for Housekeepers. Boston: Ticknor, 1887.

Domestic Economy as a Factor in Public Education. New York: New York College, 1889. Reprint, 1989.

Food Materials and Their Adulterations. Boston: Home Science, 1889.

Sanitation in Daily Life. Boston: Whitcomb and Barrows, 1907.

Air, Water and Food for Colleges (with A. G. Woodman). New York: John Wiley, 1908.

Euthenics: The Science of Controllable Environment. Boston: Whitcomb and Barrows, 1910.

Conservation by Sanitation. New York: John Wiley, 1911.

A bibliography of her works can be found in the *Journal of Home Economics*, October 1911, a special memorial issue dedicated to her life.

WORKS ABOUT ELLEN SWALLOW RICHARDS

Hunt, Caroline. *The Life of Ellen H. Richards.* Boston: Whitcomb and Barrows, 1912.

James, Janet Wilson. "Ellen Swallow Richards." In Edward T. James, ed., *Notable American Women 1607–1950: A Biographical Dictionary.* Cambridge: Belknap Press of Harvard University Press, 1971.

Solomon, Barbara Miller. *In the Company of Educated Women: A History of Women and Higher Education in America.* New Haven, CT: Yale University Press, 1985.

Tyack, David, and Elisabeth Hansot. *Learning Together: A History of Coeducation in American Schools.* New Haven, CT: Yale University Press, 1990.

Julia Richman

Selma Berrol

Julia Richman (1855–1912) was the first Jewish principal in the New York City public schools and the first woman and the first Jew to become a New York City school superintendent. Richman was widely known and respected as an innovator in the education of immigrant children in the public schools. She was also an important figure in the German-Jewish community. Her work at the Educational Alliance, the most prominent settlement house for New York's Jewish immigrant population, and as a religious school educator was highly valued by her contemporaries and helped to make her a notable woman.

Born in the Chelsea district of New York City in 1855, Julia Richman, with the exception of six childhood years spent in Huntington, Long Island, lived in the city all her life. Her parents, Moses and Theresa Melis Richman, were Jewish immigrants from Bohemia, then part of the sprawling Austro-Hungarian Empire. German in both language and culture, like many others in the heterogeneous Hapsburg dominions, the Richmans soon found a place in the growing German-Jewish community of New York City. As was true for many of his peers, Moses Richman, an artisan, used his skill as glazier to become a small entrepreneur. His five children, therefore, were born into a petit-bourgeois family and grew up in an upwardly mobile, middle-class environment.

Julia's one older and two younger sisters elevated their status through marriage to well-to-do members of the German-Jewish community, and her brother, Daniel, prospered as his father's business associate and later as a successful merchant in his own right. Julia's life, however, was very different from the ones led by her siblings and most of her contemporaries. She never married, and she pursued a career and achieved distinction, even renown, as an educator and community activist. Richman accomplished this success while remaining very much a part of the middle-class German-Jewish milieu in which her family moved and in spite of the fact that her peer group had little regard for an unmarried woman. As Rosa Sonnenschein, the editor of the *American Jewess*, a magazine targeted at German-Jewish women, said in 1989, "Marriage is the foremost aim of the American Jewess as it was for her mother and grandmother."[1] It was not, however, Julia Richman's aim.

Denied the automatic status that came with marriage and anxious to avoid the derogation and pity that were the usual lot of a spinster, Julia Richman used her successful career in the school system and her activities in the Jewish community to become the equal of women who had fulfilled the more traditional roles of wife and mother. She did this by adapting to the values of her circle that said that women were best suited to care for children and do good works for the community. Staying within these prescribed fields, she operated creatively and energetically as an educational reformer and in this way found a meaningful place in the society of her day.

While still in her teens Julia Richman chose to follow a course that would set her apart from most of the women she knew. As a young adult, she took advantage of every opportunity to be a leader. In maturity, she built on her earlier activities and established herself as a truly important figure in the public schools and the Jewish community. The focus of both aspects of her dual career was the same: the education of Jewish immigrants from Eastern Europe and their children. Using public and private funds, Julia Richman intended to turn all the "little aliens" from Russia and Poland into productive and patriotic Americans in the shortest time possible. The public sector would provide a basic education; a host of organizations outside the schoolhouse would do the rest.

Growing immigration, including large numbers of Eastern European Jewish immigrants, during the four decades that preceded World War I coincided with Julia Richman's rise in the public school system and the Jewish community. Richman completed her formal education at the Female Normal School (later Hunter College of the City University of New York) in 1872 and became an elementary school teacher shortly thereafter. After a few years as vice-principal, she was promoted to principal in 1884 and appointed district superintendent of schools in the heartland of New York City's Eastern European Jewish immigrant community, the Lower East Side, in 1889. There she remained until her death in 1912. During the same years she began a parallel career within the private sector. She moved from Sabbath school teacher at her family's synagogue, Ahawath Cheses (later the Central Synagogue), to the leadership of the Young Ladies Charitable Union (forerunner of the Young Women's Hebrew Association) and board member of the Hebrew Free School Association, which later became a part of the Educational Alliance, the most important settlement house serving New York City's immigrant Jews. Along the way she found time to lecture at the Jewish Chatauqua Assemblies and the National Education Association as well as to be a charter member of the National Council of Jewish Women.

With the exception of her early years as a teacher in the Yorkville district of New York City (then home to second-generation Germans and Hungarians, only a handful of whom were Jewish) and her first foray into religious school education, Richman was primarily concerned with the education of immigrant children. Given her energetic personality and strong ambition, it is likely that Richman would have had considerable impact on whatever field she chose. Richman reached maturity at a time of deep concern for a multitude of urban problems, including troubled schools, and a time when the established Jewish community was undergoing rapid change. She made her work in these areas.

As a principal and later as a district superintendent, Julia Richman was an innovator. Much of what she initiated in the schools was applicable to all children, including immigrants. One example of this was a scheme for continuous promotion she began when she was the principal of Grammar School 77. Under this arrangement, a child who completed the work of his or her grade could move up to the next without waiting for the end of the school year. Julia Richman argued that this would prevent a bright child from becoming bored while at the same time allowing the teacher to spend more time on the "dullards" in the class. She gave a similar reason for grouping children by ability, a procedure that was later adopted by all New York City schools. Another of her innovations, one that was specific to immigrant children, was classification based on knowledge of English at the time of arrival in New York. Additional initiatives were targeted at poor children, immigrant or native-born. In common with other educators of her time she was concerned with the "white plague" (tuberculosis) and instituted open-air classes on rooftops and a modified curriculum to improve the health of tubercular children. Richman introduced special classes aimed at making poor boys and girls into productive adults. One way to achieve this, she thought, was to teach domestic science and manual training, both of which she introduced into the schools of her district.

Worried that the parents of her charges might not understand the importance of education and might withdraw children from school too soon, Richman encouraged the organization of parents' associations at her school while at the same time urging the authorities to be less lenient when issuing working papers. Many of the foreign-born children did not have birth certificates, and officials at the Board of Education often accepted parental statements as to the child's age if the son or daughter was tall enough. Reluctant to allow even one child to go without at least six years of schooling, Richman objected strenuously to this practice. She wanted even the most difficult of the early dropouts, often troublesome students, to be educated. Saying that there were no bad boys, only bad schools, she pressured the Board of Education to establish a special school for truants and incorrigible boys and raised funds to pay a counselor to work there.[2]

In common with other progressive reformers, Julia Richman believed that personal counseling, along with other kinds of social work, was essential in poor neighborhoods. A school-and-home visitor was based in her district headquarters, and another such social worker was used in the settlement, Teachers House, which she established on the Lower East Side in 1906. She was also concerned with health habits and nutrition, saying that sick and hungry children could not learn. As a result of her efforts, both as an individual and in cooperation with other reformers, school nurses and nutritious "penny lunches" came to the Lower East Side schools.

Like many other progressive educators of her day, Richman wanted schools to educate the "whole child." This perspective however, did not dilute her interest in teaching basic skills. In the course of her manifold activities, she found time to coauthor a mathematics textbook series, a book on teaching civics, and a host of articles on topics such as phonics and simplified spelling. Most of what she wrote stressed methodology. How to teach arithmetic, civics, and other subjects, rather than what to teach, seemed to be the purpose of her books and articles. This impression, however, was misleading. Her writings illustrated the central themes in her philosophy of education: children must know their duties, not just their rights; teachers must be respected, if not loved; and loyalty and patriotism were the hallmarks of good citizenship—hard work, thrift, and discipline were essential to a long and happy life.

Julia Richman's career coincided with the start of a period of great change in the New York City schools. By the 1890s there was widespread dissatisfaction with the locally controlled ward school system that had been established fifty years earlier. Although intended to give parents a greater voice in school affairs, the ward schools had fallen into the hands of political machines whose interest in graft and patronage had resulted in a corrupt, inefficient, and inadequate educational system. Muckraking journalist Joseph Mayer Rice exposed these conditions in his articles on New York City, later published as the *Public School System of the United States*, which appeared in *Forum* magazine in 1892. Rice's articles touched off a reform movement that four years later ended the ward system in Manhattan and the Bronx (Brooklyn, Queens, and Richmond were not yet part of New York City) and substituted a citywide Board of Education. A Board of Examiners was created in order to assure that teachers would be appointed on merit alone.

The reformers' victory opened a window of opportunity for Julia Richman. District superintendents were now to be appointed by the central Board of Education and that made it possible for her to achieve a promotion for which she had striven, without success, for several years. Aware of Julia Richman's dedication to the cause of Americanizing the Eastern European Jews, the newly appointed superintendent of schools, William H. Maxwell, appointed her superintendent for the Lower East Side, and she more than lived up to his expectations.

Not content with educating and Americanizing immigrant children in the schools, Julia Richman tried to influence their parents and the Eastern European Jewish community as a whole. At one point her passionate attack on the street peddlers of the Lower East Side almost cost her the superintendency. In June 1908, for example, she criticized the police for not issuing summonses to the pushcart peddlers who turned many East Side streets into noisy, dirty bazaars. The Jewish community, still reeling from the blows inflicted by the depression of the previous year, was outraged. Led by labor leader Joseph Barondess, they petitioned the Board of Education to remove Richman, arguing that she was manifestly unfit to direct the education of their children.

One of the reasons she was able to keep her position was the valuable role she played as liaison between the Board of Education and her colleagues on the Board of Directors of the Educational Alliance. The lines between Julia Richman, private citizen, and Julia Richman, educator, were frequently blurred. She used her work in the Jewish community to help with school projects and vice versa. The English-to-Foreigner classes developed at the Educational Alliance, for example, became the "vestibule classes" for newly arrived children in the public schools. When the alliance had extra space and the schools were overcrowded, Richman negotiated a lease between the alliance and the Board of Education for an annex to an existing school, and she had no hesitation in using the "clout" of the prominent men who were fellow directors at the Educational Alliance to refurbish and maintain Seward Park, one of the few public recreational areas available to Lower East Side residents.

By 1908 Julia Richman was a nationally known expert on Americanization, consulted by officials of other big city school systems who were also feeling the pressure to change immigrants into Americans in the shortest possible time. Her views, however, were not universally shared. Unlike Richman, Jane Addams, among others working with the new arrivals, believed that immigrants brought cultural gifts as well as problems, and Hull House celebrated ethnic holidays not observed by Americans as a whole. Generally, the reputation of Richman's work, if not her angry words, was accepted by most of her coreligionists, and her reputation was high within the established Jewish community. As teacher, coauthor of a morality text named *Jewish Ethics*, and coeditor of a widely used weekly Sabbath school magazine, *Helpful Thoughts*, she added to her already prominent position as an educator in the Jewish community.

How much prominence did Julia Richman finally achieve? She achieved enough to have the flags on all the school buildings of New York fly at half-mast when she died and enough to have eulogies from Superintendent Maxwell, individual members of the Board of Education, and officers of the Educational Alliance and the National Council of Jewish Women, eulogies that filled many columns in the leading New York City newspapers. A final and permanent tribute was the erection of a new high school to bear her name.

Eulogies, of course, must be read with the proverbial grain of salt, but in Julia Richman's case there was a basis in fact. She had some important firsts to her credit: she was in the first graduating class of what became Hunter College, she was the first Jewish principal in the New York City public schools, and she was the first woman and first Jew to be a New York City school superintendent. In addition, while she was the principal at Grammar School 77, she created a showplace for immigrant education to which visitors came from all over the world, eager to see the innovations she had begun. Promotion did not dull her desire for reform; she continued to innovate as district superintendent. The National Education Association rarely invited women to speak, but for Julia Richman, they made an exception. Organizations as disparate as the Young Women's Hebrew Association and the Public Schools Athletic League owed their beginning to her. Clearly, she made her mark on the schools and society of her native city.

Had she lived longer, Richman's mark might have been even greater. Unfortunately, when she died in a Paris hospital, she was only fifty-seven years old. A neglected attack of appendicitis while on board a ship taking her to a vacation in France led to peritonitis and death. In terms of worldly goods, Julia Richman had achieved very little. Her estate came to only $3,000. The number and prominence of the people who came to her funeral, however, make it clear that she had accumulated considerable prestige and respect. A memorial meeting held at her beloved Public School 62 on what would have been her fifty-eighth birthday was additional evidence of the stature she had achieved.

The chairman of the Board of Education, Egerton L. Winthrop, gave the opening address at her funeral, and her friend and collaborator Richard Gottheil, professor of philosophy at Columbia University, spoke at the end. The organizations that sent representatives to the services testified to the breadth of her interests. On the program were representatives of the Alumnae of the Normal College, New York Council of Jewish Women, Educational Alliance, Public Schools Athletic League, Jewish Chatauqua Society, Jewish Protectory, National Education Society, North American Civic League for Immigrants, Public Educational Association, and the School Citizenship Committee. Except for the absence of an organization that would indicate the extent of her religious commitment, the list represents her life's work.

When she was ten years old, in the course of a quarrel with a friend, Julia Richman had said that she expected "all New York to know my name."[3] Her remark was prophetic. In 1916, when the new woman's high school that was named for her opened its doors, the ceremonies were widely reported, and Superintendent Maxwell expanded on the remarks he had made at her funeral:

She had the welfare of every . . . pupil at heart. . . . Her chief . . . care was to facilitate and encourage individual abilities . . . .The . . . New York schools are indebted [to

Richman] for many excellent features of their work. . . . Her untimely death deprives the city of the services of one of its valuable superintendents and citizens.[4]

His statement was an appropriate evaluation of a notable woman educator.

NOTES

1. *American Jewess* (January 1989): 208.
2. Julia Richman, "Incorrigible Child," *Education Review* 31 (January-May 1906): 485.
3. Addie R. Altman and Bertha R. Proskauer, *Julia Richman* (New York: Julia Richman High School Association, 1916), 5.
4. New York City Board of Education, *Journal* (June 26, 1912): 1219.

WORKS BY JULIA RICHMAN

"Women Wage Workers with Reference to Directing Immigrants." *Papers of the Jewish Women's Congress*. Philadelphia: Jewish Publication Society for America, 1894, 1107.
"A Successful Experience in Promoting Pupils." *Educational Review* 18 (June 1899): 23–29.
Methods of Teaching Jewish Ethics (with Eugene Lehman). Philadelphia: s.n., ca. 1904.
"The Incorrigible Child." *Educational Review* 31 (January-May 1906): 484–506.
Good Citizenship (with Isabel Richman Wallach). Cincinnati: American Book Company, 1908.
"Seward Park." *Charities and Commons* 20 (April-September 1908): 295–98.
"What Share of the Blame for the Increase in the Number of Truants and Incorrigibles Belongs to the School?" *Proceedings and Addresses of the National Education Association* (1909): 222–32.
"A Social Need of the Public School." *Forum* 52 (January-June 1910): 161–69.
Helpful Thoughts: A Weekly Magazine for Sabbath Schools (ed., with Rebecca Kohut and Richard Gottheil).

WORKS ABOUT JULIA RICHMAN

Altman, Addie R., and Bertha R. Proskauer. *Julia Richman, An Appreciation of the Great Educator*. New York: Julia Richman High School Association, 1916.
Berrol, Selma. "Agent of Change in the Urban School." *Urban Education* (January 1977): 361–81.
———. "When Uptown Met Downtown." *American Jewish History* 60 (September 1980): 139–50.
———. "Julia Richman and the German Jewish Establishment." *American Jewish Archives* 38 (November 1986): 137–77.
———. *A Notable Woman*. Forthcoming.
Brickman, William, and Paul Boyer. "Julia Richman." *Notable American Women*,

1607–1950: A Biographical Dictionary. Cambridge: Belknap Press of Harvard University Press, 1971.

Kransdorf, Martha. "Forty Years in the New York Public Schools." Ph.D. diss., University of Michigan, 1979.

Helen Mansfield Robinson

Sam Weintraub

Helen Mansfield Robinson (1906–1988) was a nationally recognized teacher and researcher in the field of reading education. She served as a member of the faculty at the University of Chicago from 1944 until her retirement in 1968. In 1961, she was appointed to the William S. Gray Research Professorship in Reading. She was the first person to hold the chair, the fifth woman to hold a named chair in the history of the university, and the thirty-sixth member of the university faculty to do so. She was appointed director of the Reading Clinic in 1944 and later initiated the establishment of the Reading Research Center. In 1973, Robinson was invited to be one of the four founding members of the Reading Hall of Fame and served as its first president/secretary. She was professor emeritus in the department of education at the University of Chicago at the time of her death.

Born to George Merwin Mansfield (1876–1960) and Mabel Lynn Butts Mansfield (1881–1962) on May 28, 1906, Helen Mansfield Robinson was the eldest of four children. Both parents were born near Athens, Ohio, and grew up not far from each other. Merwin Mansfield eventually took over his father's farm. Mabel Butts was a self-made teacher before she married. She passed an exam permitting her to teach and taught in a one-room schoolhouse for several years. Included among her pupils were her younger brother and a cousin. After marriage she lived on the family farm as a homemaker.

Robinson's formal schooling began in a one-room country school outside Athens. She learned to read sitting on her grandfather's lap before she went to school. There was only one teacher throughout her elementary schooling, an understanding man, Carl Love. On the first day of her first year of school, Love put her in first grade; on the second day, he moved her into the second grade; on the third day, she was placed in the third grade. Under Love's guidance, she completed her elementary schooling in four years, when she was ten years old. Because of her age and because she lived in the country, she did not begin high school the following year. Love gave her his college algebra and psychology books, which she studied that year. In addition, she took violin with a musician from nearby Athens. She assumed considerable responsibility, too, for the care of her younger twin brother and sister.[1]

After a year at home, she went on to high school in what was then the University Training School at Ohio University. She received her A.B. from Ohio University in 1926 with a major in mathematics. Upon graduation, she was offered a position as critic teacher of mathematics in the Training School but refused it in order to accept a fellowship in psychology from Ohio State University. Her M.A. degree was awarded in 1927. In 1928, she was named an instructor and acting director of the Bureau of Special Education at Miami University in Oxford, Ohio. The following year at the age of twenty-three, she was appointed an assistant professor and director of the bureau and served there for another two years.

In her capacity as director of the Bureau of Special Education, Robinson was called upon by schools to test youngsters whom they labeled as retarded learners or mentally deficient. Upon examining these children, she noted that many were average or superior in intelligence, but they were having problems with reading. Her investigations into the problem of reading disability led her to decide to study with William S. Gray, one of the preeminent scholars in the field. Gray was at the University of Chicago, and in 1931, Robinson accepted the position of superintendent of the Orthogenic School at the university and also began her doctoral studies there. From 1936 to 1943 she also served as the psychologist for the Orthogenic School. In Chicago she met and married Daniel W. Robinson in 1933 (he died in 1963).

During her doctoral program, Robinson studied not only with Gray, who served as her major adviser, but also with Guy Buswell, Charles Hubbard Judd, and L. L. Thurstone, all leaders in the field of education. Upon completion of her Ph.D. in 1944, she was appointed an instructor in the department of education at the University of Chicago and directed and reorganized the reading clinics there. The several reading clinics, then operating independently, were centralized into one administrative group. Under her direction, research was conducted by faculty and graduate students in the clinic. At this time, too, several books that she edited were published. These were based on the research done with disabled readers in the clinic; some of Robinson's own research appeared in these volumes, as well as that of students whose research she had directed. The clinic quickly gained worldwide recognition.

Robinson was promoted to assistant professor in 1948 and to associate professor in 1952. She was made a full professor in 1960. In 1953, Robinson took over as the chair of the annual Reading Conference from Gray, who had first organized it in 1937. She remained director of the conference through 1961, editing the proceedings from 1953 to 1961. Well over 100,000 copies were sold through the University of Chicago Press.

In 1946, *Why Pupils Fail in Reading*, a book based on her dissertation, was published by the University of Chicago Press. The book remained in press for some twenty-five years and through at least nine reprintings. It is recognized as a classic in the field. In her doctoral seminars, Robinson would often tell students that the study was a failure and ask why; she referred to the fact that the question implied in the title had never been answered satisfactorily. In actuality, the book is a major contribution and has influenced thinking about causal factors related to reading difficulties since its publication.

Robinson's findings pointed to a multicausal theory of reading problems as opposed to a single-factor theory. Although the single-factor theory is still espoused by various individuals, each promoting a specific cure, the preponderance of professionals deem reading problems to be multicausal. In the book, the research literature on each factor investigated as a possible cause of reading difficulty is reviewed in depth. Even more important, the study serves as a model for interdisciplinary research. In conducting the research, Robinson headed an interdisciplinary team consisting of three ophthalmologists, a pediatrician, an endocrinologist, a speech specialist, a psychiatrist, a social worker, a neurologist, and an otolaryngologist. The team worked together for five years, studying thirty poor readers ranging in age from six to fifteen years. In addition to heading the team, Robinson acted as psychologist and reading technician. The team members worked together not only in identifying problems in their individual area but also in interpreting the findings on each child. When pathological conditions or physical defects were discovered, efforts were taken to correct or eliminate them if possible. Corrections were made prior to any remedial work, in an effort to determine if the condition had any effect on the subject's reading. Where several corrective measures were involved, they were administered in a controlled sequence in an effort to determine the effect of each. This study was the first comprehensive survey and attempt to appraise the significance of various possible causal factors in the case of each of several severely disabled readers. Although the study is now almost half a century old, some of the findings, verified by subsequent research, have significance today and still form what Gray referred to as "a broad conceptual framework both for future research concerning reading retardation and for the guidance of teachers."[2]

The care with which the study was undertaken, the depth with which the prior research was reviewed, the fact that the study was long-term, as opposed to the all too frequent one-shot type of research for which educational research is often criticized, are all typical of the individual who conducted the research. Throughout her professional career, Robinson displayed great care and thoroughness in planning, in writing, and in thinking. Indeed, among her greatest strengths was her ability to plan and to organize. Among her strengths, too, were her seemingly limitless graciousness and her willingness to spend many hours helping students and even total strangers. Students and colleagues found her to be not only intelligent but also wise.

As her career progressed at Chicago, so did the demands on her professionally. National and international recognition followed. In 1957, the Illinois College of Optometry awarded her an honorary doctor of optometric science degree. This was the result of her interest in, and work with, visual problems and their relation to reading. Several of her research reports on vision and reading appear in the two *Clinical Studies in Reading* monographs that she edited, as well as in a third one that she coedited. In 1963, she was given the Apollo Award by the American Optometric Association, again in recognition of her efforts to understand the role of visual defects in reading problems. The award is the highest honor given by that national association in recognition of advancement of knowledge concerned with vision.

In 1953, Robinson established a four-week intensive summer program for teachers of reading. The workshop attracted participants from all the states as well as from several foreign countries. Outstanding educators from around the country were featured as part of the workshop. As the workshop format was adopted in a number of other universities around the country, attendance at the one in Chicago began to dwindle, and the summer workshop was eventually abandoned in 1965. In the summer of 1967, Robinson received a grant to direct a National Defense Education Act Institute held for reading consultants and coordinators, professors of reading, and reading clinic directors. The institute was attended by forty individuals, selected from among several hundred applicants. The participants melded into a closely knit group who maintained contact with one another and with Robinson through a newsletter published for a number of years by two of the institute participants.

In the mid-1960s, through the efforts of Robinson, the university received a grant from the Carnegie Foundation to develop a two-year master's program for students wishing to become reading consultants and coordinators. The program was unique, involving a year of course work followed by a year of internship experiences as reading consultants/coordinators. Graduates were placed in a geographical area some one hundred miles surrounding Chicago. The new reading consultants and coordinators were used to work with new interns in the program. It was hoped that their school district would pay for the internship experience, thereby making the program a self-continuing one. Applicants were carefully screened and accepted into the program only after having been observed in their own classrooms and undergoing a series of interviews and written examinations. The two-year program required full-time residency at the university. Over the three-year period in which the program operated, some sixteen students received their master's degrees. At least four of them later went on to complete doctorates at other institutions.

In addition to her work at the university, Robinson continued to be active in the broader professional arena. In 1960–1961, she served as president of the National Conference on Research in English (NCRE). NCRE at that time was a group limited to one hundred individuals, with membership by invitation only. All were interested or actively engaged in research in aspects of literacy. Selected members of this group met for a several-day planning session at the university to consider and outline a proposal for what was to become the U.S. Office of Education First Grade Studies. Robinson organized and chaired the sessions at Chicago. From 1958 to 1961, she held office as a member of the Board of Directors of the International Reading Association (IRA). Earlier, in 1951–1952, she had served as president of the National Association of Remedial Teachers, one of the parent organizations of IRA. On several occasions, she was asked to have her name submitted as a candidate for the presidency of IRA but repeatedly refused to do so, although she served on a number of committees for that organization.

The beginnings of the 1960s dealt several severe personal blows to Robinson. Both her father and William S. Gray died, the latter in an untimely accident. She referred to Gray as her professional father. Gray, a consummate professional, had requested that Robinson fulfill his speaking obligations should he be unable to carry them out. Thus, she assumed both her own and Gray's commitments for the year following his death. Inasmuch as both were in great demand as speakers, the engagements undertaken that year left little opportunity for much else.

Robinson never felt completely comfortable speaking before an audience. At times, she voiced the thought that speaking did not come easily to her and openly expressed a desire to be a more charismatic speaker. Once, upon reflecting about a well-known speaker who could charm his audience but had little to say, she decided that she would rather be able to make people think than to mesmerize and charm them.[3]

She was a remarkable teacher. One student commented that being in her class was like watching someone paint a beautiful picture. She would fill in the broad outline first, then complete small segments, and finally go back to the total picture again, brushing in the final touches. In doctoral seminars her skill and knowledge as a teacher and scholar really shone. A young man working on his doctorate with her once drew the analogy of a mother dog's shaking her puppy by the scruff of the neck to teach it something. He commented that Robinson had done the same things with his mind—she shook it up to get him to think.[4] Robinson's doctoral students were her particular joy. She gave freely and willingly of her time in guiding them through a rigorous program. In the first six years of the IRA's Outstanding Dissertation Award, three of her students were recipients of the award, and others were among the top five.

In 1925, Gray published the first summary of the research in reading that had been done prior to that time. He continued the publication on an annual basis. At his death, Robinson took over what had become the Annual Summary of Investigations Relating to Reading. It involved identifying, abstracting, and categorizing all published research relating to reading on a yearly basis. Her major contribution to the summaries was her categorization schema. She built upon what Gray had done but made the categories much more precise. As noted earlier, one of her major strengths was her ability to organize almost anything. Those organizational skills were put to excellent use in developing the categories for the summary, in running the summer workshops, and in establishing one centralized reading clinic on the campus.

In 1960, Robinson was promoted to full professor in the department of education, the first woman to achieve such status in that department. Arguably her greatest honor was bestowed in 1961, when she received the first appointment to the William Scott Gray Professorship in Reading. She was the first woman in the department and the fifth woman in the history of the university to hold a named chair; she was the thirty-sixth member of the faculty to be so honored.

In addition to being the Gray professor, she also chaired the Reading Program and established and headed the Reading Research Center at the university. Her teaching responsibilities now involved primarily a yearlong series of doctoral research seminars in reading. First established by Gray, the three series seminar dealt with research in each of three major areas of reading: sociology, psychology, and pedagogy. In addition, Robinson chaired a seminar for students and faculty interested in presenting and discussing research in reading. The seminar met in the evenings biweekly and was by invitation only. In it, students and faculty presented proposals for research, discussed their current research, or brought a study to the attention of others for discussion and critical analysis. The discussions, under Robinson's guidance, were lively and insightful.

In the mid-1960s, Robinson was asked to produce and edit a new book on reading for the National Society for the Study of Education (NSSE). She called together a group of leaders in the field to help plan the book. In 1968, *Innovation and Change in Reading Instruction* appeared as Part II of the Society's sixty-seventh Yearbook Series. Because of numerous and rapidly developing changes in the field of reading, the focus of the book was on the innovations and changes that had occurred since the appearance of the 1961 NSSE yearbook on reading as well as on those in the process of occurring. Robinson wrote the final chapter of the book, "The Next Decade," and in it offered criteria for evaluating research, suggested problems in need of immediate investigation, and pointed to future trends. In the chapter Robinson called attention to the wealth of information about the processes of learning to read that could be secured from carefully planned continuous or periodic examination of children's reading behavior. Robinson's plea for the investigation into higher-level comprehension processes is one that is being heeded even today. The recognition that basic-level reading skills are being well taught is documented in the research. It is at the level of higher thought processes that students fall down, as do efforts at teaching. Her call for a focus on the need for programs for illiterates is still timely. She asked, too, for an increased use of books, magazines, newspapers, and pamphlets and other reading materials in schools. She ends her chapter by writing, "If segments of or all of society expect excellence in reading instruction, society's members need to accept their responsibilities for providing support for teachers—not just financial support but the support of all correlated agencies of the society."[5] Her admonition is as relevant in the 1990s as it was a quarter century ago.

William S. Gray was often referred to both as the father of reading and as the father of Sally, Dick, and Jane, the characters appearing in the primary levels of the Scott, Foresman reading series for which he was major author. Robinson took over that task also and remained the major author on the Scott, Foresman series from 1960 through the late 1970s. She oversaw the development of a program that ended the reign of those three happy children and incorporated much good children's literature. She attempted to incorporate the findings of research into the new materials. Under her guidance the company developed and brought out special program materials to aid the teacher in instructing the corrective reader, who was somewhat disabled in reading but not severely so; additionally, separate materials designed to enhance reading for the gifted were introduced. The new programs were unique. Even so, she considered them as less important than her professional writings and her research. Indeed, she tried to keep this aspect of her work separate from her other professional contributions.

It has been noted that Robinson was the first woman to hold a position as full professor in the department of education at the University of Chicago. Her advancement to that position would undoubtedly have been faster had she been a male. Her salary was not commensurate with that of the male members of the faculty. She received less because she was a female and because she was committed to remain in Chicago. For Robinson, in an era before the women's movement came to the forefront, the pay differential was assumed to be normal. She felt that she was where she wanted to be, doing what she wanted to do, and the money did not matter. Had she not been married, it is possible that her salary would have been better. Even then it is doubtful that she would have received a salary commensurate with that of male faculty members or commensurate with her worth, given the tenor of the times. Her promotion through the academic ranks was slower, too, than it might have been for a male faculty member. She was an instructor for four years following the granting of her degree before being promoted to assistant professor. She had to request promotion to that level before it was granted.[6]

In 1963, her husband died, adding another blow to what had already been a disastrous decade. Not long after the death of her father and of Gray in 1960, her mother had passed away (1962). Robinson dealt with grief and personal problems in the same manner that she handled her professional life. She did not show outward signs of grieving to others but kept her feelings locked within. She was stoic in reacting to various tribulations. Perhaps this was due to the independence built into her by her parents. As the eldest of four children, she was expected to do more in helping with farm chores, in taking care of her younger siblings, and in many other ways. In addition to being the first-born, the fact that she was exceptionally bright reinforced her parents' tendency to expect more of her, an expectation that she invariably fulfilled.

Fred Jobe, a friend of long standing, asked her to marry him when his first wife died. In August 1965, they were married in a small chapel on the University of Chicago campus in a private ceremony attended by immediate members of the family only. Jobe had a rare sense of humor, along with a keen intellect, and knew how to use them to lighten her load. He could make her laugh at herself and enjoy things that she had not taken the time to appreciate before. Jobe delighted in her prominence and supported her professional achievements. He was retired as director of ophthalmic research for Bausch and Lomb in Rochester, New York. They had met through a shared interest in visual problems and their impact on reading. After they originally met in the late 1930s, he had become increasingly interested in visual factors impeding reading achievement and had spent a summer studying and reading at one of the summer workshops directed by Robinson.

In 1968, desiring to spend more time with her husband, Robinson took an early retirement from the university (she was sixty-two), and they moved to a home they purchased on Canandaigua Lake in New York. The warm months were spent there, while winters were spent in a mobile home on Longboat Key near Sarasota, Florida. In 1969, she received the William S. Gray Citation of Merit Award from IRA, the highest honor given by the organization.

Increasingly, she withdrew from active involvement in professional activities. She continued abstracting research studies for the annual summaries until 1975 but then withdrew because of a stroke suffered by her husband. She wanted to spend as much time as possible with him and devoted her life to that end. Jobe died in the fall of 1980. They had been married for fifteen years. She missed him greatly. Her professional activities virtually stopped, and she felt herself lacking in current information in the field. She came out of retirement to do one final paper on the contributions of Gray. The paper was presented at IRA in a special celebration on the one hundredth anniversary of his birth. Thus her last publication, entitled "William S. Gray: The Scholar" (1985), appeared over fifty years after her first publication in 1929.

In her lifetime, Helen Mansfield Robinson was a recognized leader in the field of reading. Her study, *Why Pupils Fail in Reading*, remains a classic of its kind, a model for interdisciplinary research. It is also a model for its rigor and depth. Her contributions to the understanding of disabled readers remain relevant in the 1990s. Her multicausal factor theory in reading disability is not only still relevant today but dominant. She was a leader in teacher education in reading, designing the program for reading consultants as well as guiding the development of a unique reading series. She headed the reading program at Chicago after the death of William S. Gray, continuing it as one of the most visible, respected, and prominent in the world. Her contributions were recognized through the many honors conferred upon her by various professional organizations as well as by the named chair the University of Chicago bestowed upon her. She was a leader in her field, always on the forefront of knowledge. Her commitment to research as a basis for the improvement of instruction in reading and the development of a sound knowledge base was unwavering.

NOTES

1. Donna Mansfield Kowanda, personal communication, August 1992.
2. William S. Gray, "Preface," in Helen M. Robinson, *Why Pupils Fail in Reading* (Chicago: University of Chicago Press, 1946), vii.
3. Helen M. Robinson, personal communication, October 1965.
4. Oliver Andresen, personal communication, May 1962.
5. Helen M. Robinson, "The Next Decade," in Helen M. Robinson, ed., *Innovation and Change in Reading Instruction* (Chicago: University of Chicago Press, 1968), 430.
6. Helen M. Robinson, personal communication, September 1968.

WORKS BY HELEN MANSFIELD ROBINSON

Why Pupils Fail in Reading. Chicago: University of Chicago Press, 1946.
"Diagnosis and Treatment of Poor Readers with Vision Problems." In Helen M. Robinson, ed., *Clinical Studies in Reading II*, 9–28. Chicago: University of Chicago Press, 1953.
"Corrective and Remedial Instruction." In Nelson B. Henry, ed., *Development in and through Reading. The Sixtieth Yearbook of the National Society for the Study of Education.* Part I, 357–75. Chicago: University of Chicago Press, 1961.
"Promising Solutions." In Helen M. Robinson, ed., *Controversial Issues in Reading and Promising Solutions. Supplementary Educational Monographs Number 91*, 170–73. Chicago: University of Chicago Press, 1961.
"The Next Decade." In Helen M. Robinson, ed., *Innovation and Change in Reading Instruction. The Sixty-Seventh Yearbook of the National Society for the Study of Education. Part II*, 397–430. Chicago: University of Chicago Press, 1968.
"Visual and Auditory Modalities Related to Methods for Beginning Reading." *Reading Research Quarterly* 8 (Fall 1972): 7–39.
"William S. Gray: The Scholar." In Jennifer A. Stevenson, ed., *William S. Gray: Teacher. Scholar. Leader*, 24–36. Newark, DE: International Reading Association, 1985.

WORKS ABOUT HELEN MANSFIELD ROBINSON

"News of the Quadrangles." *The University of Chicago Magazine* (May 1961): 13.

"Reavis and Gray Professors Appointed." *Newsletter*, University of Chicago: Graduate School and the Department of Education (May 1961): 1–2.

Weintraub, Sam. "Dr. Helen M. Robinson: A Dedication." In Sam Weintraub, ed., *Summary of Investigations Relating to Reading*, v–vii. Newark, DE: International Reading Association, 1989.

Sister Blandina Segale

F. Michael Perko, S.J.

The saga of women educators in America has recently been illuminated by the study of those who taught under religious auspices. One of the most impressive of these was a Sister of Charity named Blandina Segale (1850–1941). Her career, which spanned nearly seventy years of active service, involved the foundation, administration, and teaching in a series of schools across the American Southwest during the years after the Civil War. Perhaps her most innovative work was the formation of the Santa Maria Institute in Cincinnati, one of the first Italian Catholic settlement houses in the United States.

An examination of Sister Blandina's life not only provides a portrait of one of America's most impressive Catholic religious women but also serves as a prism through which to view the experience of immigrants and of a cohort of heretofore rarely studied American women.

Rose Marie Segale was born on May 23, 1850, near Genoa, Italy, in the village of Cicagna, the fifth child of Francesco and Giovanna Malatesta Segale. Unlike many who emigrated to America, the Segales were relatively prosperous, with Giovanna having roots in the nobility and Francesco being the owner and overseer of several orchards.[1] Thus, the reason for their decision to emigrate is unclear. However, they left Genoa in May 1854, and, after difficult overland travel and a long voyage, they arrived in New Orleans in August.[2]

Their first years in the United States were lived in poverty. Hard work, however, resulted in growing prosperity for the family. The years also brought three new births, the death of one daughter, and moves to successively larger apartments until, by the 1860s, they had their own house. Francesco began with a fruit stand and ended up a prosperous middle-class merchant.

The children, too, proved to have both drive and native intelligence. Two of them discovered an aptitude for painting signs and sold these to other merchants. Blandina's own shrewdness is shown by an event that occurred during these early years. Her brother, Andrea, had opened a dry goods store in Lexington, Kentucky, in 1862, and her parents had gone south to help their son, leaving the daughter home to mind the younger children. After reading a report of unusually cold weather in Lexington, she went to the bank and withdrew $150, bought a wholesale consignment of men's gloves, and shipped them to Lexington. The twelve-year-old's initiative resulted, according to her own account, in a $325 profit for her brother.

Her mother was bitter in her opposition to her talented daughter's entering a religious community. Nonetheless, on September 13, 1846, Blandina entered the Sisters of Charity, a branch of the community of women founded by the American Episcopalian convert Elizabeth Bayley Seton.

In many respects, the young woman's career from this juncture onward might well have resembled that of so many religious women who gave their lives to the foundation and growth of Catholic schooling in America. After her initial years of religious formation, her first assignments were in parish schools in Dayton and Steubenville, Ohio. Fate—or providence—intervened, however, to provide her with a context well suited to her entrepreneurial abilities, the American frontier.

Her community had taken on assignments in the Southwest in the mid-1860s, and in 1872 Blandina was sent to Trinidad, Colorado. Her own account of traveling there is characteristically witty. Refusing her now-reconciled mother's offer of $1,000 emergency money, she boarded a train and headed west. Although she expected hospitality at the Kansas City convent where she decided to break her journey, she found herself instead a virtual prisoner. The community there, which had experienced problems with fake sisters' imposing on their hospitality, would take no chances with this stranger.

Traveling first by construction train and then by stage-coach, she arrived in Trinidad on December 10. The public school in which she was to teach was built of adobe and measured forty by fourteen by eight feet. The sisters also ran a private academy next door for daughters of wealthier citizens. Over the following five years, Blandina furnished and expanded both schools, relying on her charm to convince local citizens to donate materials and labor.

At the same time, her interests in the broader community came to the fore. Of the sisters in Trinidad, she was the only one to learn Spanish, which gave her access to a far wider range of people. By the time of her departure, she was engaged in informal social work with Mexican families, a self-defined chaplaincy at the local jail, and the burial of homeless drifters.[3] She had become a woman of the frontier.

Her 1877 transfer to Sante Fe opened new arenas of activity. In 1878, she built an industrial school for girls, causing a local scandal by pounding nails and acting as a hod carrier. Subsequently, she founded St. Vincent's Hospital, which became one of the region's major social welfare institutions.

She also began what would become a characteristic endeavor, political activism. She was successful in lobbying the president of the local school board to publicly fund the sister teachers' salaries. She achieved territorial subsidies for St. Vincent's Hospital, which allowed it to receive destitute patients. When the county cut its subsidy for the burial of unclaimed bodies, Blandina publicly threatened to pile the corpses at the coroner's door, with the result that funding was restored.

These administrative activities, however, were only part of her ministry. An intense interest in people brought her into contact with gunfighters, socialites, and prostitutes. She became an informal ethnographer, studying Mexican-American folk religion. Unlike many "do-gooders" from Anglo missionary organizations, she became a valued part of the local culture.

In 1881, Blandina was transferred again, this time to Albuquerque. During her eight years there, she once again proved herself the entrepreneur and builder. Recognizing that the town's expansion would necessitate a new school, she begged for funding in mining camps. Despite the hostility engendered by a series of anticlerical governments, she and another sister traveled to Mexico, venturing as far south as Chihuahua. Local inhabitants were so amazed by her daring that they offered her $1.4 million in confiscated church property, which she piously refused. The ability this excursion manifested to shatter the confined activity sphere of Victorian American women also made her a local legend. Her concern with schools made her determined to get financing to back school warrants that previously had been used to pay teachers but had never been funded. Success in lobbying the legislature to achieve this added to mounting respect for her as a formidable figure in territorial politics.

Concerns with broader social welfare issues again brought her skills to bear on a variety of projects. She became intensely interested in the situation of Native Americans. While superiors refused her request to teach on a local Apache reservation, she was able to use her entrepreneurial skills to found two schools for Catholic Indians in the city itself and to provide the beginnings of education at several local pueblos. She also helped to found the Wanderers' Home for homeless men and began efforts to rehabilitate alcoholics. Administratively adept though she was, her dominant interest continued to be in people rather than institutions.

The year 1889 witnessed her return to Trinidad. Tension had been developing between the sisters there and the local school board over the wearing of religious garb by those who taught in the public school. The decision of superiors to send Blandina to deal with the situation is a testimony to the regard those in charge of the community had for her considerable political talents.

Here, however, she suffered her first defeat in the political arena. The tide of nativism had reached the Southwest, and there was little possibility of swimming against it. In 1892, she and another sister were presented with an ultimatum: wear secular garb or resign as public school teachers. In what seemed an impossible situation, she saw her only choice as asking her superiors for reassignment.

She was sent to Pueblo, Colorado, as principal, for the first time in her career, of a Catholic school. Her ministry stretched well beyond schooling to include visitation at the jail and insane asylum, as well as an unsuccessful attempt to achieve free textbooks and lunches for the city's Catholic schools. After a brief time here, however, she was recalled by her superiors. The last line of her western journal, "*Adios,* Trinidad, of heart-pains and consolations," is an eloquent epitaph not only for her time there but for all the years of her ministry on the frontier.[4]

Blandina's next four years were spent in the tame environment of southern Ohio, as Catholic school teacher and principal. Changing population demographics shortly provided a new scope for her considerable talents and resulted in the crowning achievement of an already productive life.

The last decades of the nineteenth century witnessed a change in the ethnic makeup of Catholic immigration to Cincinnati. Where previously the Irish and Germans had dominated the city's Catholic life, Italians were diversifying the community to a considerable degree. While the 1890 U.S. census lists 431 Cincinnati children with parents born in Italy, the one taken ten years later puts the number at 1,741.[5] The ecclesiastical effect was enhanced by the radical difference of Italian church culture from the cultures of previous Catholic immigrants. Italians were used to a church that had been financed largely through the beneficence of the nobility. Thus, they were unused to a situation in which popular support determined the number and quality of church institutions. Moreover, the cultural supports that had kept Italians Catholic in the old country generally were lacking in America.

The problem was made more urgent by the willingness of evangelical pastors to fish in troubled waters. In Cincinnati, Methodist clergy had been successful in starting missionary activity among the Italians, anchored in a settlement sponsored by wealthy soap manufacturer James Gamble. Part of their efforts involved the establishment of a school, as well as religious services.[6]

Alarmed by these events, a priest suggested to the superior general of the Sisters of Charity that they might broaden their work to include Italian immigrants. Logical candidates to staff it were close at hand. The Segales, Blandina and her blood sister Justina, who had entered the community after her, were among its few Italian members. Blandina's entrepreneurial skills would be put to good use once again. In 1897, the community agreed to take on this new ministry.

Blandina soon found out that the task was considerable. While the archbishop of Cincinnati supported the project, he offered little but good wishes. Similarly, the Sisters of Charity were able to provide the two sisters as personnel, but no financial support. Finally, a change in superiors general from

Mother Blanche, who had encouraged the project in its founding stages, to the headstrong Mother Sebastian, who had little use for it, created problems with the equally impetuous Blandina. Beginning with religion classes in the basement of a local church, the sisters had expanded to a variety of other activities. In 1899, however, Mother Sebastian forbade Blandina to open a night school and, two years later, ordered her transferred to an orphan asylum. Blandina's political acumen, however, came to the fore once again, with the result that she was reassigned to settlement work within six months and, within a few years, had her night school.[7] Used to having her own way, Blandina had once again gotten what she wanted.

Her efforts came together in the Santa Maria Institute, a Catholic settlement designed initially to serve Italians but also meeting the needs of Syrians and other later immigrants. Besides daytime education and the famous night school for working boys, there was a residence for working girls and a clothing distribution center. Social work activities included hospital visitation and the outplacement of children, indigents, and those needing medical care.[8]

Within the following years, the threat of Protestant proselytization subsided. Spurred on by the success of the institute's activities, however, Blandina was quick to begin new ones. By the early 1930s, the institute had become a full-service institution. Day and night schools taught the traditional curriculum, while special classes in Italian, English, and speech were taught, as well as religious instruction for children in public schools. Like many settlements, Santa Maria Institute provided basic citizenship classes. Organizations like the Boy and Girl Scouts and Red Cross met within the institute's confines. There were also social clubs for particular groups like young men and married women. Both men and women could take part in the choir, join the orchestra, or act in dramatic productions.

Blandina's tenuous project had become a well-established institution. It began to sponsor new agencies to meet particular needs. Santa Maria Institute served as a focal point for the formation of parochial schools for several Italian parishes. These later were also sites for the religious education of public school students. A free kindergarten and a school for the blind were begun under the institute's auspices. There was steady growth in a day nursery that had been founded in 1918, culminating in its inclusion in a citywide "milk station" and clinic program established in 1921. By the mid-1920s, there were two branch settlements operating as well. What had begun in a series of religious education classes for Italians offered in church basements had grown, in the space of twenty-five years, to a complex network of institutions serving a diverse clientele.

As usual, the scope of Blandina's concern went well beyond even the broad programs of the Santa Maria Institute. In her efforts to help the young, she became a juvenile court probation officer. Political causes included efforts to end the sexual exploitation of young women in Cincinnati and the regulation of child labor. In 1910, she traveled to New York to study new techniques in the education of the deaf. Internal conflict in Memphis's Italian community found her there attempting to mediate. Even a 1932 trip to Italy, the first since her immigration seventy-eight years earlier, was more than a vacation. While there, she lobbied Vatican officials for clergy to serve immigrant Italians and studied new social work and teaching methods. The only bounds for Blandina's interests, even at this advanced age, were those set by her curiosity.

Blandina's vitality had long belied her chronological age. Much of her most important work had taken place after her sixtieth birthday. However, by the 1920s, her age was becoming evident in several respects. The death of her sister, Justina, in 1929 was a severe blow. Besides their family ties, Justina had been her closest collaborator in the formation of the Santa Maria Institute.

In 1933, she was transferred from the Santa Maria Institute to the infirmary at the community's motherhouse. She remained active until 1938, when a broken hip resulted in a hospital stay of several months and the necessity of using a wheelchair. In September 1940, she fell again. While there was no physical damage, the psychological shock was intense. She remained confined to her room until her death on February 23, 1941, at the age of eighty-nine.

Even before her death, Blandina's saga captivated many, especially those fascinated by the romantic lore of the American frontier. Her sanitized diary, *At the End of the Santa Fe Trail*, went through several printings by a major Catholic publisher. Subsequently, the producer Samuel J. Engel bought the film rights to her life story.[9] Although a movie was never made, the early television series, "Death Valley Days," cast one of its episodes around the legend of her meeting with Billy the Kid. The combination of religious sister and pioneer builder fascinated many.

The same qualities that made Sister Blandina a successful politician and entrepreneur, however, created friction with some. One person's frontier adventurer was another's pushy nun. Thus, the evaluation of one of the candidates for editor of *Veritas*, the Santa Maria Institute's periodical, in the late 1920s: "I cannot accept your offer because, frankly speaking, I believe that it is impossible to work along with you. This frank language may seem rude, but as you always praise yourself in your frank and, some times, bold manner of talking, I am just answering you in your own way."[10] It is not hard to see how someone could have come to this assessment. Blandina was far more interested in goals than in means and could run roughshod over those who opposed her. While her blunt and aggressive style may have appealed to some, especially on the frontier, it offended others both there and in Ohio.

The blame for conflicts with her religious superiors, too, cannot always be laid on them. Especially in the rigidly hierarchical system of management that characterized Roman Catholicism in the nineteenth century, her penchant for acting first and obtaining approval later could easily have been seen as thinly disguised disobedience. Jealousy may well have motivated some of those in authority who opposed her. However, her high profile left her vulnerable to the charge of egotism. There can be little doubt that, especially by her later years, she had come to relish her place in the limelight.

However, the same traits seen as vices by those dedicated to maintaining structures were, for the most part, virtues in one whose goal was to create new ones. Ultimately, too, one has to take into account that her activities were overwhelmingly directed not to self-aggrandizement but to the welfare of those people in society least able to take care of themselves. Shortly after her death, a Cincinnati gossip columnist offered this tribute:

Sr. Blandina is in her grave these two days but Mr. Dan Aieto thinks it is never too late to remember people like Sister Blandina. . . . Mr. Aieto tells Cincinnatus that when they were still new immigrants Sister Blandina came along to them just to be friendly. New immigrants feel forlorn in a strange, new world and she took them by the hand. She taught them to sew and to keep house in an American fashion, taught them what it meant to be a worthy American. Sister Blandina went on to other work but it wasn't as if she had really gone: She remained bright in all the lives.[11]

It was a fitting epitaph.

Besides providing insight into an extraordinary American educator, Sister Blandina Segale's life offers a prism for examining a critical time in American life. The expansion of the frontier, immigrant explosion, and establishment of Catholicism as a national force were all shifts with which she was intimately involved. In a wider sense, she also stands as an icon of all those women educators who both symbolized and shaped life in immigrant America by their energy, piety, and clarity of vision.

NOTES

1. Blandina biographical file, Archives of the Sisters of Charity of Cincinnati— hereafter cited as ASCC.

2. Sr. Therese Martin manuscript, Blandina File, ASCC.

3. Blandina's slightly edited western diary was published as *At the End of the Santa Fe Trail* (Milwaukee: Bruce, 1948). For accounts of the Trinidad period, see 25–80.

4. Ibid., 283.

5. *Report on the Population of the U.S. at the Eleventh Census, 1890*, vol. 1, part 1 (Washington, DC: U.S. Census Office, 1895), 670–73; *Census Reports, Twelfth Census of the U.S. Taken in the Year 1900*, vol. 1 (Washington: U.S. Census Office, 1901), 796–99.

6. An example of this is found in an undated clipping describing Gamble's donation of the old Wesleyan Female Seminary as a deaconess home to be used for an Italian kindergarten and mission. Sr. Blandina's blood sister, Sr. Justina Segale, con-

firms these activities in her diary entry for January 25, 1898. Both items are found in the Santa Maria File, ASCC.

7. Mother Sebastian to Blandina, October 13, 1899, Blandina File, ASCC; Sr. Justina's diary entries for September 12, 1901, and March 2, 1902, Justina File, ASCC.

8. The story of the foundation of the Santa Maria Institute is found in Sr. Blandina's notes, "Santa Maria," January 31, 1938, 1–2. Early services are indicated in the *Second Annual Report, the Santa Maria Educational and Industrial Institute* (Cincinnati: Santa Maria Educational and Industrial Institute, 1899), 1; and the *Third Annual Report of the Santa Maria Institute for the Year 1900* (Cincinnati: Santa Maria Educational and Industrial Institute, 1900), 4, as well as the manuscript, "Santa Maria Institute" (1916), 2. All of the above are found in the Santa Maria File, ASCC.

9. Samuel J. Engel to Sr. Mary Noreen, March 28, 1958, Blandina File, ASCC.

10. Rev. G. Allais to Blandina, March 8, 1928, Blandina File, ASCC.

11. Cincinnati *Enquirer*, February 27, 1941.

WORKS BY SISTER BLANDINA SEGALE

Blandina biographical file, Archives of the Sisters of Charity of Cincinnati.
At the End of the Sante Fe Trail. Milwaukee: Bruce, 1948.

WORKS ABOUT SISTER BLANDINA SEGALE

Minogue, Anna C. *The Story of the Santa Maria Institute*. Cincinnati: Santa Maria Institute, 1922.
Perko, F. Michael. "The Founding Mother: Sister Blandina Segale, Schooling, and Social Welfare, 1872–1933." *Review Journal of Philosophy and Social Science* 12 (1987): 111–28.

Lucy Diggs Slowe

Elizabeth L. Ihle

Lucy Diggs Slowe (1883–1937) served as dean of women at Howard University from 1922 until her death and developed a student life program for women that was ahead of its time. In an era when upper-middle-class black women were urged to play the role of traditional homemakers, Slowe emphasized the need for women to be prepared for the job market and for responsibilities of active citizenship. While still an undergraduate at Howard in 1908, Slowe helped charter Alpha Kappa Alpha sorority and served as its vice president. In later life she helped begin the National Association of College Women and founded the Conference of Deans and Advisors of Women in Colored Schools. As any member of Alpha Kappa Alpha sorority can attest, Lucy Diggs Slowe is best known today as one of the founders of the first sorority for black college women. However, she deserves to be better known for her other accomplishments. Largely through her position of dean of women at Howard University from 1923 to her death in 1937, Slowe was a leader in formulating a vision of the role of black college women that went far beyond the heavy gender stereotyping of her day.

Lucy Diggs Slowe was born in 1883 in Berryville, Virginia, the heart of the apple orchard country. Her father, Henry Slowe, died while she was still an infant, and the death of her mother, Fannie Potter Slowe, four years later forced her to move with her six siblings to Lexington, Virginia, to the home of Martha Slowe Price, her paternal aunt. When Slowe was nine, her family moved to Baltimore in order to take advantage of better educational opportunities, a move not uncommon among aspiring black families of the late nineteenth century.

Slowe graduated as salutatorian from Baltimore High School in 1904 and achieved the first of her many firsts: in this case, she was the first female graduate of the high school to receive a scholarship from Howard University in Washington, D.C. During her subsequent four years at Howard she was active in numerous literary, social, musical, and athletic activities. In her senior year, 1908, she served as president of the tennis club, was a charter member of Alpha Kappa Alpha, the first Greek letter sorority for black women, and served as its vice president.

For the next seven years Slowe taught English at Douglass High School in Baltimore and worked toward a master's degree in student personnel work during summers at Teachers College, Columbia. She received her degree in 1916 but returned periodically to Teachers College afterward for further education. In 1916 Slowe moved back to Washington to teach English at Armstrong High School. In 1919 the city selected her to organize Shaw Junior High School, the city's first junior high for blacks. In doing so, she called upon a faculty member from Teachers College to teach an extension course on the junior high school for teachers of both races. This action was the first of many that demonstrated her high regard for the Teachers College faculty and also gave evidence of her efforts to foster integration. She served as Shaw's principal for the next three years.

During her career in public education, Slowe was also active as an organizer in her private life. She was a charter member of the District of Columbia College Alumnae Club, founded in 1910 at the home of Mary Church Terrell. This organization was in many ways a black counterpart of the white Association of Collegiate Alumnae, the forerunner of the American Association of University Women. The Alumnae Club was open to women holding bachelor's degrees and concerned itself with improving women's education. The club funded girls' scholarships at the city's two black high schools, gave receptions for female high school graduates, and talked to girls' mothers about the importance of higher education. The club was incorporated in 1920, and three years later it launched the National Association of College Women, which is still active today. Slowe served as the first national president from 1923 to 1929 and continued to lead the organization in encouraging women to pursue higher education. The association published an annual proceedings and a journal, to which Slowe occasionally contributed. Slowe's earliest publication for the association, in the 1923 *Proceedings*, was an article urging members to encourage young women to consider social work as a vocation, and throughout her career she consistently encouraged women to consider nontraditional careers.

In 1922 Slowe was approached by Howard's president J. Stanley Durkee about becoming Howard's first dean of women, a position that female students had been requesting since 1913. Durkee, the last of a long line of white Congregationalist ministers who led Howard, was supportive of student activities and recognized their educational value; in this respect he and Howard were far in advance of the repressive student policies at other leading black institutions, such as Fisk and Hampton. In Slowe, Durkee recognized someone who shared his philosophy. She did not accept Durkee's offer of employment immediately but negotiated for a higher salary and permission to live off-campus. Although she did not receive the salary she wanted, she did receive leave to live away from campus. This provision was important for it demonstrated that already Slowe had decided that a dean of women should be an educational leader rather than a student watchdog, and it also proved to be a major source of irritation to Mordecai Johnson, Durkee's successor. Slowe purchased a house twenty minutes away by foot and five by car.

Slowe's first few years at Howard witnessed a number of apparently well received but predictable innovations in women students' life. Most of these were activities already established at many white coeducational and women's schools but relatively new in black higher education: a Christmas Vespers service, a concert-lecture series, teas, coffee hours, current events discussions, volunteer activities in the community, and book clubs. She also encouraged an annual gift service as a way of raising funds to establish a loan program for needy women students.

One of her first actions as dean of women, however, was more extraordinary. She formed a Women Students' League, a kind of student government association of which every female student was automatically a member. Few black colleges at the time had any form of student government, and so establishing such an activity for black women was almost unheard of. But Slowe's philosophy of student life had not been shaped by black colleges. Because of her continuing contact with Teachers College after the completion of her degree and other professional activities, Slowe absorbed much of the philosophy of faculty women leaders in student personnel work such as Esther Lloyd-Jones, Sarah Sturtevant, and Harriet Hayes, all of Columbia, and Thyrsa Amos of the University of Pittsburgh. She applied her growing insights to Howard. Reasoning that women needed to get experience in working together for the common good, in decision making, and in citizenship, Slowe thought that such a league was an appropriate place to begin. The league immediately began sponsoring an annual Women's Dinner, which grew in size until it became one of the major social functions of the year, attracting not only a sizable portion of the student body but also numerous alumnae. She also hired women to live in the residence halls who were fully qualified to be faculty members and who were charged with making residence hall living as educational as possible.

Slowe's actions were a result of her perception of black college women. She thought that they needed special urging to take an active part in their education and community because of their previous training in passivity. It can be hypothesized that in some cases black, middle-class parents went to extremes to ensure that their daughters did not suffer from stereotypes of sexual promiscuity and consequently overemphasized the ideal of the pure lady with its concomitant passivity. Slowe alluded to the adverse impact of religion in suppressing women's natural activism and girls' adoption of a psychology of acceptance and inaction. She observed that sex was a barrier to achievement within the black community itself and that such a secondary role for women was neither desirable nor realistic:

Frequently, Negro college women come from homes where conservatism in reference to women's place in the world of the most extreme sort exists. . . . Many parents still believe that the definition of women found in an eighteenth century dictionary is true today: "Woman, the female of the man. See man." Regardless of the wish of many parents that their daughters become adjuncts of "man," modern life forces them to be individuals in much the same sense as men are individuals.[1]

Because of students' previous training in passivity, Slowe thought that the extracurricular college environment at Howard should develop students' powers of initiative and self-direction and provide worthwhile experiences in group living, group cooperation, and group welfare. She worried that if students did not receive guidance in choosing their extracurricular activities, then students would choose only what they had previously been exposed to and remain as uneducated when they left college as when they entered. Instead of controlling students in their leisure time by useless rules and regulations, college administrations should encourage students to form committees and arrange activities. "If faculties of our institutions realized how much the students gain from a well-diversified and properly guided series of extracurricular activities," Slowe concluded, "they would not dismiss this phase of the student's life as being unworthy of their attention and support."[2]

Despite Slowe's philosophy and early successes, not all was well at Howard. President Durkee, who was generally flexible and conciliatory, finally faced a well-publicized student strike opposing compulsory Reserve Officers' Training Corps (ROTC) training and discontent from alumni. He resigned in the spring of 1926 and was replaced by the university's first black president, Mordecai W. Johnson, a former Baptist minister with degrees from Moreland, Chicago, and Harvard. During the first few years of Johnson's tenure, no evidence indicates any serious difficulties between him and Slowe, although Johnson obviously tangled with other faculty and administrators and won in nearly every case.

The necessity of black women's preparation for a career continued to be one of Slowe's keen academic interests. In a 1934 speech at the annual meeting of the National Association of College Women, Slowe pointed out that black women, even if they married, needed to be able to earn money. "There is no guarantee that they will not be called upon to earn their own living," she warned, because she recognized that in the black community a woman's employment was often more stable and reliable than a man's.[3]

Slowe was also very much aware of the double discrimination faced by black women on the grounds of both race and gender, and because of that she maintained that guidance was more critical for them than for white women. Her concern prompted her to study women students' future plans.

A study of Howard freshmen indicated that 92 percent of 153 freshmen women planned to teach, while only 5 had chosen social service.[4] The remainder were divided among library science, business, law, and medicine. Slowe reasoned that teaching was popular because it had the fewest obstacles. On the other hand, she wrote:

Very few Negro college women enter business because of two reasons: first, lack of capital; second, because the great commercial world is closed to them. A few go into medicine and law but nor [sic] nearly enough to meet our needs, for tradition is strong in many places against women in these professions, and getting established in them quite difficult. Social work and library science are beginning to attract them in larger numbers, but not many openings are to be had in these fields. For the majority of the large libraries of the South Negroes cannot even draw books from them to say nothing whatever of entering them as trained librarians. In view of the restricted opportunities for earning a living it is not surprising to discover in my own institution that 90% of the women are preparing for careers in teaching.[5]

In 1936 Slowe reported also on a survey of the entire female student body at Howard, but it is unclear if this survey was a separate one or simply a more encompassing version of the other. In the larger survey nearly half, or 44 percent, planned to teach; 16 percent were undecided; 6 percent planned to be nurses; 3 percent were going to enter medicine; another 3 percent into dietetics; and 2 percent into administration; the rest were unaccounted for.[6] What makes these figures particularly interesting is the significant decrease in numbers planning to teach, and perhaps this decline is attributable to the success of two other innovations of Slowe's at Howard.

Slowe initiated a Women's Vocational Seminar, which was mandatory to freshmen but open to other students, in 1929 and began a mentoring program in the following year. The former consisted of a number of speakers representing a variety of professions; the latter matched carefully selected seniors with freshmen. It is possible that the information made available in the seminars plus the exposure to the thinking of more mature students stimulated such a sizable reordering of students' vocational plans that the number of students planning to teach declined significantly.

Slowe was concerned with college women's preparation for life beyond career choice, however. She maintained that women college graduates needed to know how the government worked and how to use their leisure time in a worthwhile manner. She shared with many other educators the assumption that black college women had special obligations because of their privileged education. "College women," she wrote, "should be prepared to go into their own communities and enrich the life of their communities through their knowledge of proper recreational and cultural activities."[7]

Slowe thought also that black colleges were not preparing women sufficiently to fulfill these postcollege obligations. They did not provide sufficient role models of women with authority; observing that nearly all of college faculties, Boards of Trustees, and presidents were male, she complained that women employed by colleges were almost always relegated to supervising dormitories or residence halls. Classrooms were not much better. In 1933 she surveyed 44 black colleges, inquiring what courses women were taking, and learned that only 41 percent took political science, 37 percent economics, and 62 percent sociology. She concluded that these percentages indicated poor advising and a consequent deficiency in college women's education since these subjects were critical to an understanding of, and full participation in, American life.[8]

Slowe's insistence that black college women understand American governance and be prepared to assist their communities reflected her larger concern with social justice. Although not so much a radical in her racial views as in her feminist views, Slowe did work for social justice and integration. In a speech to the Club of Prospective Deans of Women at Columbia University in January 1926, for instance, Slowe noted that college is a place where all races should come together. She worked with whites in her private volunteer activities and thought that communication between racial groups was very important, both on and off the campus. When Boston College consulted her about the propriety of housing black women students on its previously all-white campus, she advised the college not to create a separate residence hall for black students but to put two black students in each of the existing residence halls.

Slowe's activities away from campus continued throughout her career at Howard. In 1935 she helped found the National Council of Negro Women and served as its first secretary; she also founded the Conference of Deans and Advisors of Women in Colored Schools. She served on boards of various welfare agencies in the Washington area and worked with the National Young Women's Christian Association and the Women's International League for Peace and Freedom. She also kept up her tennis game, winning a number of trophies, and sang contralto in her church choir.

Simultaneously, Slowe increased her influence at Howard. She was successful in having a portion of the Howard campus set aside exclusively for women and was instrumental in the construction of a special women's residence hall. She developed a Panhellenic council to coordinate women's Greek activities and initiated an annual weekend conference to promote women's student leadership; her mentor, Thyrsa Amos of the University of Pittsburgh, was the guest leader at the first of these conferences. She is also credited with being a major influence on Howard's assistant dean of men, Thomas E. Hawkins, who later became dean of men at Hampton. Her staff of assistants were loyal.

Despite these achievements, or perhaps because of them, Slowe eventually fell out of grace with President Johnson. He removed her from the Council of Deans, froze her salary, and in 1934 tried to force her to move back to campus housing.[9] Their struggle was long and bitter. Although she finally agreed to move to campus, she and Johnson could never agree on a suitable location, and she never actually made the move. She maintained that having to move was a violation of her initial agreement with Durkee, which she had in writing, that the move would cause considerable financial hardship. A number of letters about housing passed between her and Abraham Flexner, the chair of the Board of Trustees. In the meantime, Johnson sought to cut her staff and budget, even though the depression did not apparently cause a crisis with Howard's enrollment or federal appropriation. Johnson refused her request to add a dietician to her staff and insisted that her staff take over housekeeping supervision of the women's areas. Over breaks in the academic year, he allowed the women's residence areas to be used by other groups, who, Slowe charged, damaged them.

In the fall of 1937, at age fifty-three, in the midst of her struggle with Johnson, Slowe became seriously ill with influenza and kidney disease and missed a number of weeks at work. At one point, Johnson reportedly sent a message to her that he was going to replace her if she were not back at work within twenty-four hours. When Slowe died on October 21, 1937, her family requested that Johnson take no part in the funeral service nor sit on the platform. Later that fall the Howard Alumni Association mentioned Johnson's "hate, ill will, and malice" toward Slowe in an enumeration of reasons that Johnson was an unsatisfactory president.[10] Johnson survived this attack as well as many others, remaining president of Howard until 1960.

The Washington public schools named a school after Slowe, and a window in the Howard University Chapel honors her. Hundreds of new pledges of Alpha Kappa Alpha annually memorize her name as one of their sorority's founders. Beyond these tributes to a life productively lived, Slowe deserves scholarly recognition from professionals in student personnel work, feminists, and historians of education. Her enlightened practices in student personnel work and her forward-looking attitudes about women and their place in both the university and society mark her as an activist and a thinker well ahead of her time.

NOTES

1. Lucy D. Slowe, "The Colored Girl Enters College," *Opportunity: The Journal of Negro Life* (September 1937): 276.

2. Ibid., 279.

3. Lucy D. Slowe, "The College Woman and Her Community," speech at the National Association of Colored Women, 1934, Atlanta University, Lucy D. Slowe Collection, Moorland-Spingarn Research Center, Howard University, 90-6, folder 120.

4. Lucy D. Slowe, "Education of Negroes," manuscript in the Moorland-Spingarn Research Center, Howard University, 90-6, folder 129.

5. Ibid.
6. Slowe, "Colored Girl," 278.
7. Slowe, "The College Woman and Her Community."
8. Slowe, "Colored Girl," 277.
9. Rayford W. Logan, *Howard University: The First Hundred Years* (New York: New York University Press, 1969), 292.
10. Ibid., 336.

WORKS BY LUCY DIGGS SLOWE

"The College Woman and Our Public Life." *Journal of the National Association of College Women* (April 21–23, 1927): 26–28.
"The Dean's Conference at Fisk." *Journal of the National Association of College Women* (April 5–6, 1929): 14–15.
"The Dormitory: A Cultural Influence." *Journal of the National Association of College Women* (1931–1932): 11–14.
"What Contributions Social Activities Fostered by the Institutions Make to the Moral and Social Development of Students in Negro Colleges." *Quarterly Review of Higher Education Among Negroes* 1, no. 2 (April 1933): 11–15.
"Higher Education for Negro Women." *Journal of Negro Education* 2 (July 1933): 352.
"Some Impressions from Two Conferences of Deans of Women." *Journal of the National Association of College Women* (1934–35): 38–41.
"The Colored Girl Enters College—What Shall She Expect?" *Opportunity: The Journal of Negro Life* 15 (September 1937): 276–79.

WORKS ABOUT LUCY DIGGS SLOWE

The Moorland-Spingarn Research Center at Howard University houses the papers of Lucy Diggs Slowe.

Ransom, Joanna Houston. "Innovations Introduced into the Women's Program at Howard University by the Late Dean Lucy D. Slowe." *Journal of the National Association of College Women* 14 (1937): 51–52.
Turner, Geneva C. "Slowe School." *Negro History Bulletin* (January 1955): 90–91.
Wright, Marion Thompson. "Lucy Diggs Slowe." In Edward T. James, ed., *Notable American Women, 1607–1950*, 299–300. Cambridge: Belknap Press of Harvard University Press, 1971.

Hilda Worthington Smith

Emily C. Jones

Hilda "Jane" Worthington Smith (1888–1984) was a pioneer in the workers' education movement of the 1920s and 1930s, a movement dedicated to offering educational opportunities uniquely relevant to the lives of industrial workers of that period. Smith's particular interest was in the education of women workers, an area to which she made important contributions for many years.

Hilda Worthington Smith, born in New York City on June 19, 1888, was the first of three children of Mary Helen Hall and John Jewell Smith. Mary Helen Hall was the daughter of Charles Mason Hall, a New York attorney, and Elizabeth Peaslee Hall. John Jewell Smith was a prosperous businessman and a widower with a grown daughter when he and Mary Hall married in 1884.

Smith and his brother-in-law, William C. Baker, had formed a steam heating company in New York City in 1859. Baker, Smith & Company grew rapidly, installing steam heat in many New York City office buildings. John Smith became president of the company and remained in that position until his death in 1901.

Hilda's brother, Jewell Kellogg Smith, was born two years after her, and her sister, Helen Hall Smith, was born in 1892. The family lived in New York City near Central Park and spent the summers at their home in West Park, New York. Helen, like her sister Hilda, developed an interest in social work, particularly the needs of neglected children, which led to her work in various social programs and settlement houses. While the sisters' interests coincided in many respects, Helen did not follow in her sister's educational footsteps but rather pursued her career in social work without benefit of a college degree.

Hilda's mother was personally supportive of her daughters but did not share their views of a woman's role in the world. Still, despite some disagreements on women's rights and Hilda's own career, Hilda and her mother remained very close. Perhaps Mrs. Smith could have convinced her dutiful daughter to abandon, or at least defer, education and career for a more conventional life. However, to her credit, she respected Hilda's aspirations, even if she did not fully support them.

Hilda Smith received an education reserved to the affluent of her time. She completed her secondary education at the Veltin School in 1906 and was graduated from Bryn Mawr College in 1910. Her own positive educational experiences and the influence of the women she came to know at Bryn Mawr cemented Smith's lifelong belief in the value of a broad, liberal education for industrial workers as well as the members of her own middle class. During her first years at Bryn Mawr, Smith became interested in suffrage and social work through her association with the college's president, M. Carey Thomas, and faculty members such as Susan Kingsbury. The network of socially and politically active women friends and colleagues that Smith acquired during her years at Bryn Mawr sustained and supported her throughout her life.

Although middle-class women of that era were expected to remain at home, Smith received her mother's consent to return to Bryn Mawr for a year of graduate work. There Smith gained her first experience with adult working students in the Bible classes she taught for black women service workers. In 1911, she earned an M.A. in ethics and psychology from Bryn Mawr and returned home to become her mother's companion as societal expectations dictated. During her stay at the family's home in upstate New York, Smith, never inclined to idleness, volunteered in a variety of community projects.

In 1912, again with her mother's acquiescence, Smith returned to graduate school, enrolling in a two-year program at the New York School of Philanthropy. Smith interrupted her studies in 1913 to accept a position supervising a dormitory at Bryn Mawr. A year later, she returned to her studies at the New York School of Philanthropy and, in 1915, received a degree in social work. At a time when few women received any higher education, Smith's professional degree was exceptional.

Smith returned in 1916 for what would be a long tenure at Bryn Mawr, to establish and direct the Bryn Mawr Community Center, one of the first of its kind in the country. The center provided the town's residents with a variety of activities and services, including after-school boys' and girls' clubs, a women's club, a library, hot lunches for children, a kindergarten, evening lectures and entertainment, and space for night classes for immigrants to study English. Smith's mother and aunt moved to Bryn Mawr and lived with her for a year, in which time they volunteered at the center. Her mother died in 1917, and Smith suffered depression over the loss for a number of years. Smith served as director of the community center until 1919, when she accepted a position as acting dean, then dean, of Bryn Mawr College, a position she held until 1921.

During Smith's tenure as dean, Bryn Mawr's president, M. Carey Thomas, proposed that the college establish an on-campus summer school for industrial women workers, patterned on the workers' education movement in England, which served as her inspiration. Such a school seemed the perfect project for Smith, who worked on the planning and, in 1921, became the first director of the Bryn Mawr Summer School for Women Workers in Industry.

The workers' education movement was rapidly taking hold in the United States in the early 1920s, with Brookwood Labor College opening the same year as Bryn Mawr's summer school. Within a few years, a richly diverse assortment of experiments in workers' education exploded across the country, and Hilda Smith's summer school at Bryn Mawr became the model for many other workers' education projects.

Some within the movement who viewed class-conscious workers' education as a necessary component of radical social and political change criticized Smith and her colleagues as do-gooders because of their liberal ideology, which emphasized the education of each individual as the best path to social progress. Indeed, middle-class educators like Smith sometimes seemed unclear as to how their particular brand of workers' education would lead to social change for the working class as a whole. Too, Smith and her associates seemed naively unprepared for the conflict that resulted when radical leftist summer school students, as some were, clashed with the affluent Bryn Mawr alumnae who financed the program. Still, all those engaged in the workers' education movement agreed that the intent was not to raise individual workers from their class but to improve the condition of the entire class, even if they disagreed on how to accomplish that goal.

Smith, like other educators in the movement, was convinced that workers needed classes and schools specifically structured to their lives. Regular adult education simply did not serve their needs, as evidenced by the low numbers of working-class people enrolled in conventional adult education courses. Industrial workers of that age began working so early in their lives that few had the opportunity to attend high school, and many did not finish grammar school, rendering traditional adult education courses incomprehensible. Additionally, schools staffed by middle-class teachers were often perceived by the children of the working-class as inhospitable places, leaving them with little affection for the traditional classroom. When asked why workers needed special classes, Smith explained another reason frequently cited by worker-students and their teachers:

These workers have a special interest in industry. They do not find that industrial interest featured in the usual night school class or the university extension course. Usually, they find the group in these classes very mixed, and their own experience in industry is not used as part of the teaching method as it is in a workers' education class. They have something to contribute. They have their very vital and practical experience and they want to contribute that, and they want to discuss with the teacher their own industrial problems.[1]

Women industrial workers came to Bryn Mawr's summer school from diverse backgrounds and with a wide variety of academic skills. Entrance requirements were a sixth grade education, or its equivalent, loosely interpreted, and experience in industrial work in a nonsupervisory position. The students attended the school on scholarship but still suffered financial hardship due to time lost from jobs. Many of the women worker-students were foreign-born, especially in the early years of the school, with limited English skills but possessed of a political sophistication lacking in many of the young workers born in the United States. The women differed in culture, ethnicity, language, religion, politics, and race (after 1926, when black women were admitted as a result of a student vote). Some were experienced activists in the labor movement; others came from backgrounds steeped in antiunionism. From such disparity, Smith and her colleagues attempted to reach across the chasm of class differences separating them from these women workers in order to engender the cohesiveness necessary for the school's success.

Smith and the faculty were not uniformly successful in bridging class differences, but most of the worker-students seemed to accept the relationship with Smith and her counterparts as more than simply noblesse oblige. Both faculty and students learned a new appreciation for the dissimilar experiences of others, and for many years Smith received letters from former students who referred positively to their experiences at Bryn Mawr. The success of the school was difficult, if not impossible, to measure quantitatively since no degrees were conferred, and the school's goals were quite general. Some women did become more active in the labor movement and in workers' education, but a causal link between that activity and the school would be speculative. Still, many of the women experienced increased self-confidence, and student evaluations were usually very positive.

To the extent that such cross-class endeavors worked at this time in the nation's history, much of the success was attributable to Smith's commitment to self-government for the students and to their active participation in the development of the school's curriculum. The defining rule of workers' education, to which Smith steadfastly adhered, was that any educational activity must be based on the real life experiences of the students and must build upon those experiences so that the learning had relevance to the students' lives.

As Smith knew, educators within the movement ignored this reality at their peril. Worker-students sacrificed a great deal to attend any type of class or school and, usually fighting fatigue and poverty, had little tolerance for a lecture on economic theory unrelated to their daily lives. However, teachers who made the effort and had the experience to make their classes speak to these students' lives found no more eager or dedicated students in any college classroom. The classes that students and teachers deemed successful relied primarily on group discussion in which the teacher served as a source of specialized information, as a guide, and as a participant, recognizing that teacher and student roles were frequently reversed. The enthusiastic response from the students was a major factor that kept Smith serving as director of the summer school for the next twelve years.

Smith was a leader in developing teaching methods and materials that incorporated the lived experiences of industrial workers. The Bryn Mawr summer school under Smith's direction was one of the pioneers in such innovative methods as dividing the curriculum into fields of human experience rather than formal subjects; involving students in course planning; and utilizing discussion in small, informal classes. The curricula, methods and materials developed during Smith's years at Bryn Mawr were used widely throughout the workers' education movement.

As other summer schools patterned after Bryn Mawr came into being, the need for coordination to avoid duplication of effort became paramount. In 1927, Smith helped to found the Affiliated Schools for Workers, a clearinghouse for workers' education that involved a broad spectrum of residential and nonresidential workers' schools. Smith served as the first director and chair of the board. By 1939, the organization had expanded far beyond its original goal and was serving the wider workers' education movement. The group changed its name to the American Labor Education Service to more accurately reflect its work.

As the workers' education movement grew, Smith saw a need for a year-round residential school for women workers. With her sister, Helen, Smith purchased property near the family's summer home on the Hudson in West Park, New York, in 1928. The following year she established the Vineyard Shore Labor School on the property she donated to the school. Vineyard Shore was one of many workers' education programs victimized by the financial devastation of the depression, and the school ultimately closed. The campus later housed the coeducational Hudson Shore Labor School, of which Smith was a founder and member of the Board of Directors. When Hudson Shore closed as a residential school in 1951, it was incorporated into Rutgers University's labor education program. Smith served on the program's advisory committee for two years.

In 1933, in the midst of the depression, Smith traveled to Washington, D.C., in search of increasingly scarce funds for workers' education. Instead, she found a job in President Roosevelt's Federal Emergency Relief Administration (FERA) and later the Works Progress Administration (WPA). Smith was hired as a specialist in workers' education within the Emergency Education Project (EEP). Her primary task was to set up a program to train unemployed teachers for a massive workers' education program. Although she had not sought the position, Smith was excited by the possibilities for expanding workers' education. Not everyone shared her enthusiasm. She was criticized by some who feared that the workers' education movement would be undermined by governmental control and that the government would support only superficial educational efforts.

Smith knew the challenge she faced in wresting a meaningful educational experience for workers from the bureaucratic tangle of a program intended primarily to provide relief to the unemployed. Still, the EEP's workers' education program seemed to Smith an innovation capable of giving workers' education a permanent place in the nation's educational fabric. The nationwide demand for both teachers' training and workers' classes proved to be enormous.

By the summer of 1934, Smith and her associates established training centers for unemployed teachers throughout the nation. In the course of her work, Smith labored to mollify state administrators reluctant to cooperate with a federally funded program, red-baiting conservatives who objected to any educational endeavor with even a hint of class consciousness, and teacher-trainees uncomfortable with the controversial economic and political topics commonly discussed in workers' education. The centers struggled to transform, in a mere six-week summer course, hundreds of unemployed teachers with no knowledge of, or interest in, workers' education into sympathetic and moderately skilled labor educators.

The results were varied but impressive, given the limitations inherent in developing an educational component in a relief program. Many thousands of workers attended classes taught by the newly trained teachers during the 1930s, and the demand never abated. Indeed, the New Deal workers' education program has proved to be the largest and most comprehensive endeavor in workers' education yet undertaken.

As another part of her work for the New Deal administration, in 1934 Smith organized and directed the Camps and Schools for Unemployed Women, a program championed by Eleanor Roosevelt. Nicknamed "She-She-She camps," the residential programs for unemployed women were compared, unfavorably by their opponents, with the Civilian Conservation Corps (CCC) public service work camps for unemployed men. In addition to providing the mostly young, often malnourished women with basic nutritional needs, the camps offered education in health and homemaking skills and some workers' education. Many of the women took advantage of their first opportunities to participate in sports and recreation. However, the women were not allowed to participate in work projects similar to those that made the CCC camps so successful.

Ignoring the recommendations of Smith and her advisory committee that the women be involved, like the men, in public work projects, New Deal administrators prohibited any work outside the camps by the women residents. Despite the project's apparent recognition of traditional women's roles, evidenced by the focus on homemaking skills and the limitations on other job training, the idea of young women's leaving their homes and living in the camps was considered by many to be dangerously permissive. The camps were controversial from the beginning and were even considered radical by many conservatives. Never as widespread, well funded, or accepted as the men's camps, the women's camps closed in 1937.

In the women's camps, as in the workers' education program, Smith's commitment to a long-term program of education conflicted with the New Deal's short-term goals of relief and economic recovery. The programs should be understood in terms of the obstacles they overcame as well as the admittedly limited results.

After the WPA ended, Smith briefly remained in Washington as a consultant in labor education. From 1943 to 1945, Smith served the Federal Public Housing Authority as chief of the Project Services Section. She directed the management of housing for war workers, continuing her interest in workers and in education by coordinating tenant organizations and educational and health services.

In 1945, Smith accepted the position as chair of the National Committee for the Extension of Labor Education, a coalition of university and labor groups seeking to establish a federal program similar to the already successful agricultural extension service. Smith coordinated the broad coalition's efforts to lobby Congress for the passage of the Labor Extension Bill, which provided for federal funding of workers' education classes. For a time, the coalition seemed likely to succeed. Workers' education had become more acceptable, perhaps because few of the class-conscious experiments dedicated to restructuring society had survived the depression. Also, the newer university extension programs that replaced them seemed, like the labor movement, to accept the capitalist economic system and emphasized labor- management relations.

Like workers' education efforts throughout the history of the movement, the fight for a governmental labor extension program was beset by conflicts between some in the labor movement who opposed what they perceived as interference by "outside intellectuals" and educators who believed the interests of workers could be served by universities with some input from labor. Generally, however, the extension bill received broad support from both the labor movement and the universities. The defeat of the Labor Extension Bill seemed to result from a concerted McCarthyesque attack by some sectors of business and industry on the idea of government funding for workers' classes they labeled as "communistic." The effort for labor extension ended unsuccessfully in 1951, after a bitter congressional battle. Nevertheless, a number of university labor extension programs were created as a result of both the workers' education program of the New Deal era and the fight for a governmental labor extension service. Indeed, current union-sponsored labor education and university labor studies programs owe a debt to the methods developed by Smith and others in the early years of the workers' education movement.

In 1952, Smith received a grant from the Ford Foundation to write a history of workers' education in the United States and spent two years gathering materials and writing. Over the next decade, Smith worked as a consultant for a variety of programs involving education, housing, and services for the elderly. Her last governmental appointment in Washington was as a consultant in the Community Action Program of the Office of Economic Opportunity (OEO) in 1965. Smith welcomed the opportunity to direct staff training for community centers, utilizing, once again, her experience in teacher training.

In 1972, after seven years with the OEO, Smith, then eighty-three years old, retired from her long and distinguished career in education and public service. Even then, she continued to write and remain active, publishing her autobiography in 1978. She died on March 3, 1984, ending a long, productive, and creative life.

NOTE

1. Digest of the Proceedings of the Third Annual Meeting, American Association for Adult Education, May 14–16, 1928, Swarthmore College, Swarthmore, PA.

WORKS BY HILDA WORTHINGTON SMITH

Women Workers at the Bryn Mawr Summer School. New York: Affiliated Summer Schools for Women Workers in Industry and American Association for Adult Education (jointly), 1929.

Education and the Worker-Student (with Jean Carter). New York: Affiliated Schools for Workers, 1934.

"New Plans for Adult Education." *American Federationist* 41 (March 1934): 261–67.

"Federal Cooperation in the Education of Workers." *Journal of Adult Education* 6 (October 1934): 499–505.

"The Student and Teacher in Workers' Education." In Theodore Brameld, ed., *Workers' Education in the United States*, 181–202. New York: Harper, 1941.

People Come First: A Report on Workers' Education in the Federal Emergency Relief Administration, the Civil Works Administration and the Works Progress Administration, 1933–1942. New York: Adult Education Fund, Ford Foundation, 1952.

Opening Vistas in Workers' Education: An Autobiography. Washington, D.C.: Author, 1978.

Hilda Worthington Smith Papers. Archival Collection, Schlesinger Library, Radcliffe College, Cambridge, MA.

WORKS ABOUT HILDA WORTHINGTON SMITH

Heller, Rita. "Blue Collars and Bluestockings: The Bryn Mawr Summer School for Women Workers." In Joyce Kornbluh and Mary Frederickson, eds., *Sisterhood and Solidarity*, 107–45. Philadelphia: Temple University Press, 1984.

Kornbluh, Joyce. "The She-She-She Camps: An Experiment in Living and Learning,

Emily Eliza Ingham Staunton

Richard L. Wing

Emily Eliza Ingham Staunton (1811–1889) was cofounder (with her sister Marietta Ingham) of what is recognized by many as the first university for women in the United States, the Ingham University of Le Roy, New York. Though herself the beneficiary of less than a complete seminary education, she established the first female seminary in western New York and enlarged its scope and services until the New York legislature granted it a charter in 1857 as a university for women and the U.S. commissioner on education recognized it in 1887 as one of the top colleges for women.

From the opening of the Inghams' Attica Female Seminary in 1835 until Emily severed ties with Ingham University in 1883, she educated her students to serve well within their allotted sphere of the home, the church, and the classroom. A number of her students—not all of whom had graduated—and some of her faculty associates were instrumental in establishing daughter schools in the upper Midwest and in such distant places as California, Hawaii, and the Middle East. However, her great dream of establishing a permanent collegiate institution for women was thwarted by a host of factors, including inadequate funding, competition from New York normal schools, the coeducational explosion, and loss of community support.

Emily Eliza Ingham and her twin sister, Julia Ann, were born on March 5, 1811, in Saybrook, Connecticut, the tenth and eleventh children of Amasa (1768–1845) and Mary Chapman Ingham (1773?–1820). Her father operated a farm and engaged in other enterprises in this community at the mouth of the Connecticut River.

Throughout her life, Emily had a special relationship with sister Marietta, fourteen years her elder. The close tie between these two began shortly after Emily and Julia Ann were born. Their mother feared that she was then on her deathbed and formally gave baby Emily directly into the care of Marietta;

Julia Ann in like manner was given to another older daughter, Anna. Though Mary Ingham eventually regained her health and bore three more children, she did not take back her gift, and Emily continued to be both sister and ward of Marietta. The arrangement later proved fortuitous for women's education: of the pair, Marietta was the entrepreneur who built the initial capital and who served as agent and business manager for the Ingham schools, while Emily was the educator and the guiding spirit of the three Ingham institutions.

Marietta was born in Saybrook on November 25, 1797, the third child and first daughter of Amasa and Mary. Practically nothing is known of Marietta's education. It most likely took place either at home or in the schools of Saybrook before she and Emily moved up the Connecticut River to Middletown, but no records or narrative has been located.

For Marietta, the years between leaving Saybrook in 1820 and reaching Attica in 1835 were devoted to the millinery business. Though depicted as tiny in stature and never particularly robust, Marietta was able by 1835 to earn and save what was then a large sum (reportedly $5,000) for a missions project.

According to longtime family friend Lucy Seymour Parsons, Marietta and Emily Ingham moved north around 1820 to Middletown, Connecticut, where they lived for about seven years. Emily, then about nine, probably had begun her schooling in Saybrook and continued in Middletown. Then, likely in 1827, Marietta and Emily relocated to Pittsfield, Massachusetts, where sisters Anna and Julia Ann lived and where Emily embarked on her "advanced" education at the Pittsfield Female Seminary, followed by at least part of a year at Ipswich Female Seminary, north of Boston.

Emily Ingham's educational genealogy extends back to the Reverend Joseph Emerson's pioneering girls' school, the Seminary for Teachers, begun at Byfield, Massachusetts, in 1818. Unlike other educators of his day, Emerson advocated the vocation of teaching as commendable for women. Speaking at Saugus in 1822, Emerson stated:

Next to the domestic circle, the school room is unquestionably the most important sphere of female activity. . . . It seems desirable that females should have a much greater share in literary instruction than is now assigned them. . . . Surely no one can doubt that every intellectual power and faculty of the female, should be unfolded and improved to the greatest possible degree.[1]

His school quickly gained recognition for high-quality instruction in academic basics, focusing on the careful study of a few subjects at a time rather than superficial exploration of myriad fields. His ideas were reflected in the lifework of Zilpah Grant, Mary Lyon, and Emily Ingham, and the impact of his philosophy on their schools and in the schools founded by their academic "daughters" has been noted by the biographers of each of the three as being significant.

At Byfield Zilpah Grant, under whom Emily was to study at Ipswich, began her own seminary education in 1820 and met fellow student Mary Lyon in 1821. From Byfield Grant moved to Ipswich to become principal of the Ipswich Female Seminary in 1828, with Mary Lyon as assistant principal, and for the next eleven years the Ipswich school pioneered in training women teachers.

Under Zilpah Grant, Ipswich was a strongly Christian school, and Emily Ingham likely felt right at home there. In Saybrook, she and her family had been active in the Saybrook Congregational Church, which held to a strong evangelistic interest in missions. Then, according to Lucy Seymour Parsons, seminary and university teacher and Emily's longtime friend, at Ipswich Emily became "imbued with a Missionary spirit and it was her ardent wish to go on a mission to Greece; but her sister, Marietta, proposed to her that they should both become Missionaries to what was then known as 'the far west.' "[2]

The sisters headed west in early 1835, bound for the educational and religious wilderness of the Chicago region via New York's Erie Canal. For a Sabbath's rest, they disembarked about 250 miles west of Albany in the village of Brockport and rode the stage south to Attica, a community whose "Greek" name fascinated them. During the sisters' brief stay in the village, the Reverend James Boylan Shaw, pastor of the local Presbyterian church, and other citizens persuaded them to establish their new school in Attica. Marietta and Emily used their capital to erect a brick structure to house their Attica Female Seminary, which opened in the summer of 1835. One of the earliest surviving documents in the Ingham collection is an Attica Female Seminary handbill dated July 29, 1835, which outlines a course of studies very similar to that at Ipswich.

While theirs was not the first academy in the Genesee country to admit girls (coeducational Middlebury Academy, chartered in 1819 to serve boys in the village of Wyoming some nine miles southeast, claims that honor), Attica Female Seminary was the first school for young ladies only.

After two years, the sisters were persuaded to move fourteen miles east to Le Roy by the appeal of a citizen's group from that village and the offer of a newly vacant mansion in which to house the school. Into this facility, eventually the core structure of the university, the Inghams promptly admitted seventy-six women to their nongraded, secondary-level seminary and forty-one pupils to the primary (preparatory) department. Many of the students were drawn from middle-class farm homes and parsonages. This was the clientele Emily sought: religious young ladies needing an inexpensive education and desiring to teach or to serve Christendom in other ways. In recognition of this growth, the school was renamed, becoming Ingham Collegiate Institute in 1852. In 1857 further educational progress was reflected in yet another name change—Ingham Collegiate Institute became Ingham University. The Le Roy seminary's curriculum also resembled that at Ipswich and had some common features with Mount Holyoke's. Over the next dozen years, it gained academic strength as it grew in scope.

Some members of the Le Roy faculty deserve mention for their roles in American education: Diantha E. Gray, listed in 1838–1839 as coprincipal with Emily Ingham, and her husband, Rev. Harvey A. Sackett, helped organize Elmira College in 1855; later she was a member and president of the Board of Trustees of the New York Medical College for Women. Teacher and 1841 alumna Julia A. Lake Warner founded the Lake Geneva (Wisconsin) Seminary in 1869, where she served as principal for 18 years. Mary J. Mortimer accompanied Catharine Beecher from Le Roy to Milwaukee in 1850, where she taught for seven years in the Milwaukee Normal Institute and High School, and in the Milwaukee Female College and at Baraboo Female Seminary in Wisconsin, then returned to Milwaukee as principal of Milwaukee Female College (later Milwaukee-Downer College). Lucy Ann Seymour, after five years of teaching at Le Roy, relocated to Michigan as the wife of the Rev. William L. Parsons, who in 1853 was named as secretary of Catharine Beecher's American Women's Education Association; Lucy Seymour Parsons operated the school which Miss Beecher recast as her Milwaukee Normal Institute and High School and later led a similar institution in Dubuque, Iowa.

During the seminary years, some degree of contact was maintained with Emily Ingham's mentors from New England. In 1850, Catharine Beecher took Ingham teacher Mary Mortimer west to work with Lucy Seymour Parsons. In 1856, Zilpah Grant visited with Marietta Ingham and the Stauntons at Le Roy as she rested from a tiring trip west, and the group "took tea" one afternoon there with Emma Willard, the highly regarded founder of Troy Seminary and author in 1819 of a widely acclaimed plan for the improvement of female education.

A decade after moving to Le Roy, Emily Ingham married Phineas Staunton on June 3, 1847. Phineas was born September 23, 1817, near the village of Middlebury (now Wyoming) in the town of Middlebury, New York, the sixth of ten children of Major General Phineas and Mary ("Polly") Thomas Staunton, seven of whom were girls. As a youth, Phineas taught himself to be an artist. He left home at age eighteen to study art in Philadelphia and to paint (portraits, especially) in New Orleans, Savannah, New York City, and Buffalo.

Following their wedding, the Stauntons took an extended honeymoon trip to Europe, where Phineas painted copies of major works by "some of the most famous of the old masters," such as Rubens, Titian, Raphael, and Rembrandt, while Emily Staunton examined European education. Phineas's European copies were later listed in an inventory of the art college; however, the seminary's catalogs before and after Emily's trip show little discernible impact of her studies on the institution's curriculum or programs.

Over the next twenty years, Phineas assisted the schools in many ways. Without doubt, he and the Ingham sisters made an interesting threesome: Marietta, the shrewd business manager; Emily, the pious teacher with her dream for educated women; and Phineas, the noted artist, member of a leading local family, and avid adventurer.

Phineas served in 1861–1862 with the One-Hundredth New York Volunteer Infantry Regiment in the Civil War as executive officer and acting commander. Replaced by a politically appointed colonel, he resigned and returned to Ingham. Then, in 1867, he was chosen as staff artist for a joint Williams College–Smithsonian Institution exploration across South America from Equador to the mouth of the Amazon. He sickened in Quito, probably from yellow fever, and died there on September 5, 1867.

One of the truly large questions in women's higher education at the century's midpoint was, What is a fitting college curriculum for women? Emily Ingham Staunton and her faculty faced two obvious alternatives: create a special curriculum just for females or use the same curriculum as in men's colleges. Among the faculty were several who knew the Mount Holyoke concepts of Mary Lyon: Emily Staunton herself, who had studied under Mary Lyon; Mary Ann Wright Dunlap, who later helped shape Elmira College's curriculum; and Marilla Houghton, an 1846 graduate of Mount Holyoke. Others there had experienced the traditional men's college approach: Rev. Charles Mattoon, A.B. from Middlebury; Phineas Staunton, whose alma mater is unknown (although Hamilton College awarded him an M.A.); and Dr. Samuel Hanson Cox, who helped found New York University, in addition to teaching at Auburn and Union. But their curricular choice was less philosophical than pragmatic: all seemed to agree that if women were to prove that they could handle college as well as men could, they must follow the men's curriculum.

In 1852 through 1857, in a major attempt to provide a college-level education for western New York's women, the Ingham sisters upgraded their female seminary to a quasi-college known as the Ingham Collegiate Institute. Chartered by the New York State legislature on April 6, 1852, the new collegiate institute was empowered to create a normal, a seminary, and a collegiate department, to appoint professors and teachers, and to award diplomas.

The *Catalogue* of the Le Roy Female Seminary for 1851–1852, published in late spring, shows the seminary was ready to be a full college: the document contains a full listing of offerings for all three collegiate years, identified as the junior, middle, and senior classes. The junior class was to study arithmetic, grammar, and rhetoric during the first term; algebra, history, and physiology the second; and algebra, botany, and natural philosophy (science) the third. The middle class schedule included algebra, geometry, and astronomy in the first term; algebra, geometry, bookkeeping, chemistry, and electricity in the second; and geology, mineralogy, botany, and evidences of Christianity in the third. Seniors were slated for moral science, trigonometry, and government in their first term; technology, mental philosophy, and history of civilization in their second; and elements of criticism, Upham on the Will, and Allison on Taste in their third. In addition, a knowledge of one of the languages (Latin, Greek, French, or German) was required for the collegiate course.

The 1851–1852 *Catalogue* also explains briefly the program for the preparatory department and the normal department, and it outlines a fourth division: the department of literature, art, and general reading. Annual enrollments in all collegiate institute departments (including preparatory) averaged roughly 215, with about 17 graduates in a typical year.

In 1857, the New York legislature finally recognized what Emily Ingham Staunton and her associates had accomplished by creating the Ingham University of Le Roy and authorizing it to grant degrees. (In the language of its charter, this university for women was an "amendment" of the collegiate institute.) As a university, Ingham was organized into six departments. The elementary department included courses taught in the common school branches, while the academic department offered two years of study at the academy level, in preparation for college work.

At the college level, Ingham's classical department offered the collegiate course of four years' work, and its literary department, with the same faculty, offered the literary course, involving three years of study. The music department was "quite distinct" and had its own faculty, as did the art department. Eventually, these two latter departments welcomed a few men as students, probably in the hope that doing so might increase revenues without compromising the classical and literary education offered to females.

Emily Ingham Staunton's central philosophy for the institution was to provide a school that would educate a woman—*within her allotted sphere*—to her highest and best ability and thus enhance her capabilities to serve well and in ladylike, Christian manner her earthly family and her civic family at school and church. This position, proclaimed in the seminary's *Catalogues*, was formally stated for the university by Chancellor Samuel Hanson Cox in 1857, affirmed by Professor Henry J. Van Lennep in 1876, and reiterated by ex-chancellor William W. Totheroh in 1890. Several graduates did achieve national prominence in music, physics, art, and physical education, and there is evidence that some of Ingham's later alumnae became active feminists. But the Ingham institution's influence appears to have been strongest in the relatively safe middle ground of preparation for schoolteaching and enlightened motherhood. Statements by alumnae affirm that an Ingham education did allow women to reach their greatest potential, though they almost always exercised this realized potential within what was then seen as women's providential arena of serving the extended family.

In this context, it is notable that Ingham University was not only an institution for women but an institution by women. While the controlling boards were always male (save for continuing board memberships for Emily and Marietta Ingham, both of whom were reported in board minutes as active participants), the Ingham faculty was predominantly female.

The testimony of materials in the Ingham Collection is that Ingham University, like its founders, was essentially a product of the religious milieu of the era, but not narrowly so. While Emily and Marietta grew up in the Congregational church and felt a call to missionary service, neither they nor their institutions were bound into sectarianism. Unfortunately, this cannot be established directly from the words of the sisters; beyond statements in early *Catalogues* that most likely came from Emily's hand, there exist few other writings by her and none by her sister Marietta. Instead, the prime clues come through the surviving words of trustees, chancellors, students, and bystanders. They tell us, without question, that Ingham was an institution devoted to life, to service, and to women's education within a Christian frame of reference as commonly found in the nineteenth century.

As the embodiment of Emily Ingham Staunton's vision for educating young women, Ingham University achieved more than token significance. There is good evidence that Ingham University was a reasonably equivalent institution to Elmira Female College and Vassar College, both of which were then (and are now) recognized as significant institutions of higher education for women. The reference to Ingham in the following passage from Thomas Woody's text on women's education provides some measure of the quality of Ingham's educational program.

In the *Report* [*of the Commissioner of Education of the United States*] for 1886–7, the Commissioner called attention to . . . those colleges which "as is well known are organized and conducted in strict accordance with the plan of the arts college." . . . The latter, forming "Division A," included seven institutions—Bryn Mawr, Vassar, Ingham University, Wells College, Wellesley, Smith, and the Society for Collegiate Education of Women, at Cambridge.[3]

The effect of Emily Ingham Staunton's university on the students' lives is difficult to measure, for so few personal statements survive. But those that do—from student Anner Peck's journal of 1862 and 1863 through 1864 to alumna Sarah Whiting's 1911 reminiscences of Emily Ingham Staunton and her school—hint strongly that Ingham University was successful in preparing its young women for life in a larger world, even if it remained essentially the world of academe plus the domestic sphere. The Ingham Alumnae Association members showed their great institutional loyalty through a series of innovative, though futile, last-ditch plans to raise money, and later they held regular commemorative convocations. Alumnae appear to have been deeply and truly saddened by their alma mater's demise.

Under Marietta's hand, the Ingham schools achieved a reasonable measure of financial stability. Had Emily Ingham's university been sustained financially, it seems reasonable to believe that today it would still be a well-known and respected institution. However, Emily and her educational vision received a major setback when Marietta died on June 5, 1867, a brief ten years after the university was chartered. Subsequently, as adequate money slowly became the prime criterion of survival, the university—despite its apparently high-quality educational offerings, its strong faculty, and its devoted student body—was not able to complete its fourth decade.

Beyond cash shortages exacerbated by declining enrollments and the lack of a substantial endowment, other facts aided the demise of Emily's university. Besides the death of Marietta (the same year that Emily lost her husband, Phineas), statements in the Ingham papers indicate that the men who attempted to pick up Marietta's fiscal tasks probably were not as well qualified, skillful, or dedicated to women's higher education as she had been. Another factor was the dominant role played in the university by Emily Ingham Staunton herself (reverentially known as "Madame Staunton"); it remains difficult to separate the life of Emily Staunton from the life of the university. Her resources and talents were entirely dedicated to her vision of fine education for women. When her failing health prevented her from providing the strong guidance needed after the mid-1870s, the institution quickly felt the loss and did not long survive her own death.

Emily Ingham Staunton died on November 1, 1889, in Oil City, Pennsylvania. Her remains were transported back to Le Roy, and she was laid to rest beside her sister Marietta on the Ingham grounds. Later, when the Ingham University property was about to be sold, the caskets of the sisters were reinterred in Le Roy's Machpelah Cemetery.

In exploring the life and work of Emily Ingham Staunton, an entity laced with the influence and assistance of sister Marietta, one is struck with a feeling of admiration at what she and her sister were able to do. The integrity and strength of her character illuminate the limited number of Ingham-related materials extant. Anna Peck, a new Ingham University student in 1862, spoke almost reverently of engaging Mrs. Staunton in a brief conversation and being chided gently by her for the occasional use of slightly imprecise or inelegant words. An anonymous essay, attributed to alumna Agnes McGiffert Bailey, mentioned that Emily Staunton "sometimes met and rebuked me over some apparently trifling matter. But those slight admonitions sank deep, because of her personality, her intense earnestness under the calm exterior, her great love, and her yearning to eliminate from us every least thing that was crude or unseemly."[4]

Sarah F. Whiting, an 1864 Ingham graduate and later professor of physics at Wellesley, wrote in 1911:

All the elements which the most philosophical thinkers now believe should enter into the wisest training of women, which were possible to the times, Emily Ingham Staunton implanted at Le Roy—graces of womanhood, advanced learning, consecrated Christianity . . . .That "those who had received should freely give to the world" was the teaching of Ingham. . . . [Women's educational opportunities] will go on to a higher development for women and the world . . . [and] all who study the history of the movement will accord to Emily Ingham Staunton the place of Pioneer in the Higher Education of Women.[5]

NOTES

1. Joseph Emerson, *Female Education—A Discourse Delivered at the Dedication of the Seminary Hall in Saugus, Jan. 15, 1822* (Boston: Samuel T. Armstrong and Crocker & Brewster, 1822), 9, 15.
2. Ingham University Alumnae Association, *1890 Alumnae Catalogue of Ingham University (Memorial Number)* (Le Roy, NY: The Le Roy Gazette, 1890), 63.
3. Thomas Woody, *A History of Women's Education in the United States* Vol. 2 (New York: The Science Press, 1929), 185.
4. "The Stones in Ingham's Buildings," manuscript attributed to Agnes McGiffert Bailey, presented at alumnae gathering in 1911.
5. Sarah F. Whiting, "Mrs. Emily Ingham Staunton," manuscript of presentation at memorial for Emily Ingham Staunton, 1890.

WORKS ABOUT EMILY ELIZA INGHAM STAUNTON

Most Ingham materials are in the recently microfilmed Ingham Collection of the Le Roy Historical Society, Le Roy House, Le Roy, New York.

Ingham University Alumnae Association. *1890 Alumnae Catalogue of Ingham University (Memorial Number).* Le Roy, NY: The Le Roy Gazette, 1890.

Russell, Marian A. "Ingham University." In *The Annual Report of the Le Roy Historical Society.* Le Roy, NY: Le Roy Historical Society, 1969, 3–9.

Strobel, Jean D. "Ingham University." Undated (but post-1965) manuscript.

Van Lennep, Henry J. *Ingham University: Historical Sketch and Description.* Buffalo, NY: Haas, Nauert, 1876.

Wing, Richard L. "Ingham University, 1857–1892: An Exploration of the Life and Death of an Early Institution of Higher Education for Women." Ph.D. diss., State University of New York at Buffalo, 1990.

Lois Meek Stolz

Julia Grant

Lois Meek Stolz (1891–1984) was a trailblazer in the fields of child development and early childhood education who skillfully intertwined teaching, research, and social activism in all of her work. According to renowned child psychologist Robert R. Sears, "Usually people have the mentality of hard scientists or they have the desire to change the world through social programs. She had both."[1] A child psychologist by training, Stolz spent a long and vigorous life as an advocate for quality daycare services, a researcher in the service of parents and children, and an educator in child development.

Lois Meek was the second child of Alexander Kennedy Meek and Fannie Virginia Brice, born on October 19, 1891, in Washington, D.C. Her parents were separated while she was a young child, and she and her brother were raised by her father and paternal grandparents, who were natives of Tennessee, in Washington, D.C. Her father was a lawyer for the U.S. Senate.

In later life Stolz described herself as a frivolous adolescent uninterested in the benefits of higher education. She was a tall and handsome young woman who belonged to a high school sorority and hosted many parties. Her future as a society woman was undercut, however, by her father, who demanded that she pursue an education that would enable her to earn her own living.

At her father's insistence, Lois Meek attended the Washington Normal School and surprised herself and her family by graduating at the top of her class. After graduation she taught in the Washington public schools for four years and became a "model" teacher, whose classroom was observed by teachers in training. Her teaching was influenced by her membership in the Progressive Education Association, which taught her to inquire into the motivations behind children's behavior and to develop innovative, activity-oriented approaches to elementary education. She simultaneously pursued a

B.A. degree from George Washington University, where she became intrigued by John B. Watson's *Behaviorism* and decided to pursue a degree in educational sociology.

In 1921 Meek enrolled at Teachers College, Columbia, to study for the master's degree. Because her adviser looked askance at female graduate students, he permitted her to choose her own course of study. Meek eagerly signed up with professors whose books had inspired her, bringing her into contact with such luminaries as educational theorists John Dewey and William Heard Kilpatrick; psychologists R. S. Woodworth and Edward Thorndike; and early childhood educator Patty Smith Hill.

Meek attributed John Dewey with inspiring her with a concern for education as a tool for social justice. Dewey and Meek shared political values as well. While Meek was a graduate student, both she and Dewey registered as socialists, but when they attempted to vote at the New York City polling place, which was controlled by the Democratic party, they were told that they must either produce their high school diplomas or take literacy tests at another location if they wanted to vote. The two resolutely boarded the subway and traveled to an old public school building where they took the tests and returned to the polling place to vote socialist.

Meek also found an ally in Patty Smith Hill, who assisted her with obtaining scholarship money so that she could enroll in the doctoral program at Teachers. She decided to specialize in child psychology, a newly emerging field of study perceived as being hospitable to female social scientists. Meek's dissertation, a study of the emotional factors in children's learning, was published in 1925 by Teachers College.

The course of study Meek chose was timely. A public impressed with the ways in which modern medicine had helped to reduce infant and maternal mortality hoped that the science of child development would provide them with the tools to raise physically and mentally healthy children. One of only a few individuals with training in child psychology in 1924 and with formidable intellectual and organizational skills, Lois Meek was well placed to play a pivotal role in the burgeoning child development movement.

The young Ph.D. was faced with two intriguing job offers. She could remain at Teachers College as an assistant professor or she could enlist as educational secretary for the American Association of University Women (AAUW), where she would direct an ambitious program of child development and parent education for college women. Meek's advisers, including Edward Thorndike, suggested that she accept the AAUW's offer, warning her that she might be patronized at Columbia as a recent graduate student and that she would be smart to return as an experienced professional, advice that would stand her in good stead.

Meek's position with the AAUW was controversial. The organization sought to foster the study of child development among college-educated women, a direction perceived by some influential AAUW members as a backward step for college women. Members such as Virginia Gildersleeve, president of Barnard, and Ellen Pendleton, president of Wellesley, were fearful that the diversion of women's talents and energies from traditional scholarly pursuits would endanger the AAUW's attempt to integrate the academy and further ghettoize female scholars. However, equally influential members, including Ada Comstock, president of Radcliffe, and Aurelia Henry Reinhardt, president of Mills College and the AAUW, applauded the new direction, claiming that higher numbers of educated women were choosing marriage and motherhood and that their college training had done little to prepare them to raise physically and mentally healthy children.

In 1922, Helen Thompson Woolley, the well-known child psychologist and chair of the AAUW's Educational Policy Committee, delivered what Meek deemed a "shocking" speech to the national convention, urging the assembly to conduct a campaign for parent education.[2] Woolley's speech was followed by a sizable grant from the Laura Spelman Rockefeller Memorial that was to be used to develop a program in parent education for college-educated women. Although the program was primarily geared to homebound women, officers of the organization garnered additional support from members by arguing that the fields of child psychology and preschool and parental education would provide socially validated career opportunities for educated women.

At the AAUW Meek inaugurated an ambitious, well-publicized campaign to enjoin college women to study children. She published articles about children in popular and professional journals, traveled to AAUW branches throughout the country, and occupied leadership positions in numerous organizations dedicated to parents and children. Thousands of AAUW members were induced to participate in child study clubs, where mothers read about, and discussed problems in, child development. The groups allowed educated mothers to integrate personal and academic interests and often inspired members to launch community child welfare efforts.

While at the AAUW, Meek developed a commitment to early childhood education that would shape the rest of her career. In 1926, under the tutelage of Patty Smith Hill, she chaired, and subsequently was elected the first president of, the National Committee on Nursery Schools, which exists today as the National Association for the Education of Young Children. Meek also edited *Preschool and Parental Education: Twenty-eighth Yearbook of the National Society for the Study of Education* (1929), a landmark volume that documented the advent of a new field of endeavor. In 1929 she traveled to Russia in order to survey the services offered women and children; there she witnessed excellent on-site infant day care for working mothers, and her experience in Russia infused her thinking about day care in the years to come.

With an impressive résumé as an expert in child development, Meek was asked in 1929 to return to Teachers College to assist Helen Thompson Woolley in directing the Institute of Child Development; a year later she was appointed director of the institute. The institute was one of several organizations devoted to interdisciplinary research on children established during the 1920s. The institute closed due to the withdrawal of funds from the Laura Spelman Rockefeller Memorial in the 1930s and lack of support from Columbia, but Meek remained at Teachers as director of the department of child development and guidance through 1939.

At Teachers College Meek remained committed to early childhood education, instituting a nursery school for working mothers that included a half-day Saturday session. As a board member of the Child Welfare League she lobbied to raise the minimum standards of day nurseries. She also helped to initiate the Works Projects Administration (WPA) Nursery School Program and remained on its Advisory Board throughout the span of its existence. She marshaled the talents of numerous Teachers College faculty and students on behalf of the project, sending them to locations throughout the United States to set up government-sponsored nursery schools where children whose parents were on relief received physical examinations and nutritious meals. The nursery schools were organized primarily to provide work for unemployed teachers and other personnel, but they were pivotal in disseminating the concept of early childhood education to the American public. Meek worked relentlessly to ensure that nursery schools and day nurseries were truly educational rather than merely custodial.

Travel to the Institute of Child Welfare in California had introduced Meek to Herbert Rowell Stolz, a physician and onetime director of the institute, and in 1938 the two married. Meek had briefly married in 1924, but she rarely spoke of her failed marriage or her parents' divorce. As a spokesperson for children and families, Stolz appears to have had difficulty acknowledging her own family's departures from convention. Her second marriage, however, was marked by rewarding professional collaboration and companionship.

Following her marriage, Lois Meek Stolz resigned from Teachers College and settled down in California with her husband for a short period of research and writing. She finished writing a picture book for parents in 1940 entitled *Your Child's Development and Guidance*, which won the *Parents Magazine* award for that year. The book charted the physical and mental progress of children from birth to six years of age, focusing on the process of development and attempting to reverse the behaviorist dictates of child training that had dominated the field in the 1920s and 1930s.

An active member of the Progressive Education Association, Stolz also participated in a project designed to structure a secondary school curriculum in accord with the principles of adolescent development. The findings of that project were published in a volume entitled *The Personal-Social Development of Boys and Girls with Implications for Secondary Education* (1940). She simultaneously assisted Herbert in analyzing data on the somatic development of young boys, resulting in their joint monograph, *Somatic Development of Adolescent Boys* (1951), which is considered a classic work. Between 1937 and 1945, she wrote a series of articles on parents and children for *Woman's Home Companion*, one of which addressed the special problems of working mothers.

But Stolz's period of quiet research did not last for long. Later she remarked that governmental concern for children surfaces only during periods of crisis, and the crisis of World War II provided her with the opportunity to establish the kind of quality day care that she had long envisioned. The Lanham Act supplied states with federal funds for day-care centers as part of the war effort, and California's governor Culbert Olsen invited Stolz to coordinate emergency day-care services for California. Stolz agreed to take the job but soon became frustrated with the political and administrative obstacles to establishing day-care centers in California. Thus she was receptive when Edgar Kaiser called her in 1943 and asked for her assistance in orchestrating a massive system of on-site day care for women working in the Oregon shipyards.

Kaiser's Portland shipyards employed approximately 25,000 women during World War II, many of whom had left farms and small towns for blue-collar jobs. Portland had few public or private day-care centers that catered to the needs of women workers, so the shipyard had to contend with chronic lateness and absenteeism. Conversations between Kaiser and Eleanor Roosevelt eventuated in a decision to erect two day-care centers at the plants. The centers would be partially funded by the federal government, since Kaiser planned to charge the overhead to the War Department. Kaiser spoke with the heads of several governmental agencies, and all agreed that the ideal person to implement the project was Lois Meek Stolz.

Stolz was astounded at the scope of the endeavor. Kaiser planned to administer two centers, each capable of caring for up to 1,125 children. Kaiser and Stolz agreed that their services should be based on the needs of women workers, which resulted in a number of radical innovations. Architects were already busy constructing two large buildings, each composed of fifteen rooms that emerged as spokes from a central playground. There would be round-the-clock care to accommodate the women's staggered working hours. Unlike most day-care centers of the period, the centers would accept children as young as eighteen months old. At Stolz's suggestion, an infirmary was instituted for the care of children who were mildly ill. Emergency care, including baby-sitting for mothers who needed to run errands or perform housework, was available, as well as routine care. An additional service was proposed by Eleanor Roosevelt, who had witnessed prepackaged food programs in England. Thus the center furnished precooked, nutritious dinners to mothers who were too tired to produce a wholesome evening meal for their families.

Stolz enlisted her former student James Hymes to direct the daily operations of the centers, and together they recruited highly educated personnel from throughout the country to work at the pioneering centers. Unlike the typical day-care teacher of today, these men and women were well paid and received excellent benefits. At their height the centers serviced a total of 1,005 children in one week. Paradoxically, a wartime emergency had helped to create services for women and children unparalleled before or since. Sadly, the centers closed abruptly as the war came to an end.

Discouraged by the closing of the centers, Stolz soon found new enterprises to engage her interest. She had been away from academe since 1939 when she was recruited by Stanford in 1945 to fill a last-minute vacancy in their psychology department. In 1947 she was appointed professor of psychology and soon was developing a doctoral program in child development and guidance. Stolz always considered herself a teacher first and foremost, and she enjoyed her contacts with graduate students at Teachers and Stanford, many of whom went on to become noted figures in child psychology and early childhood education.

Her ability as an undergraduate teacher was soon rewarded by a standing-room-only course in child psychology, which was crammed with veterans studying on the GI bill. She found herself besieged with GIs during office hours, but instead of discussing class work, they spoke of their frustration with their own children. This experience motivated Stolz to compose a study investigating the effects of war service on veterans and their children. She received a grant from the National Institute of Mental Health to conduct the study, and her book *Father Relations of War-Born Children* was published in 1954. The study stressed the difficulties to be overcome by families when fathers are separated from their children at birth and the dangers of the application to children of military techniques of discipline and punishment. Stolz's relationship with her own father had been close, and the study reinforced her belief in the centrality of the father-child bond.

In Stolz's work, *Influences on Parent Behavior*, published in 1967, she continued to explore the nature of the parent-child relationship. This study examined the impact of parents' values and beliefs on their childrearing strategies. Warning against the danger of oversimplifying motivations for parental behaviors, Stolz argued that such behaviors are the product of a dense weave of social and personal factors. The study took seriously the impact of class and gender on childrearing practices, emphasizing particularly the distinctions between the value systems of mothers and fathers.

Stolz also continued her efforts on behalf of the problems of working mothers, believing that many of the public criticisms of them were unfounded. She chaired an AAUW committee that conducted an investigation of the effects of maternal employment on children in 1959. That study resulted in a widely reprinted article by Stolz that argued that there was little merit to traditional criticisms of working mothers. The findings would be pleasing to contemporary feminists; Stolz contended that working parents were more likely to share household tasks and that working mothers were less likely to endorse traditional sex roles. Stolz's conclusion that the kind of substitute care that a child receives is the crucial determinant in his or her adjustment is widely held today.

Although Stolz officially retired from Stanford in 1957, she continued to remain at the forefront of efforts to assist parents and children until her death in 1984. She was awarded the Distinguished Contribution to Psychology Award in 1967 from the American Psychological Association (APA), and in 1968 she received the G. Stanley Hall Award from the Division of Developmental Psychology of the APA. Toward the end of her life her reminiscences proved invaluable to historians interested in the history of early childhood education and child development. In 1983, just a year before her death, she delivered the keynote address to the fiftieth anniversary session of the National Association for the Education of Young Children. Her research on parental behavior was also resurrected in 1983 at the fiftieth anniversary meeting of the Society for Research in Child Development. A charter member of the organization, Stolz provided commentary on her own work at the convention.

An unusually self-reliant individual, Stolz continued to read widely, attend conferences, and grant interviews to researchers even while she coped with cancer during the last decade of her life. She is remembered for her critical role in the dissemination of childrearing information to parents in the 1920s and 1930s, her unceasing championship of early childhood education, and her ability to tailor research and practice to the real needs of parents. A charming and gregarious woman, she insisted on remaining in her Palo Alto home, surrounded by friends, former students, and relatives until her death on October 24, 1984.

NOTES

1. Millicent Dillon, "The Influence of Lois Stolz on her Students and on National Attitudes to Child Development Research," *Stanford Campus Report* (April 12, 1983): 1.

2. Ruby Takanishi, "Lois Hayden Meek Stolz: An American Child Development Pioneer," oral history (1978), 14.

WORKS BY LOIS MEEK STOLZ

A Study of Learning and Retention in Young Children. New York: Teachers College, Columbia University, Bureau of Publications, 1925.

Preschool and Parental Education: Twenty-eighth Yearbook of the National Society for the Study of Education. Bloomington, IL: Public School Publishing, 1928.

Personal-Social Development of Boys and Girls (with Judith Chaffey and Harriet Cramer). New York: Progressive Education Association, 1940.

Your Child's Development and Guidance. Philadelphia: Lippincott, 1940. Rev., 1950.

Somatic Development of Adolescent Boys (with Herbert Rowell Stolz). New York: Macmillan, 1951.

Father Relations of War-Born Children. Stanford, CA: Stanford University Press, 1954. Reprint, New York: Greenwood Press, 1968.

"Effects of Maternal Employment on Children." *Child Development* 31 (1960): 749–82.

Influences on Parent Behavior. Stanford, CA: Stanford University Press, 1967.

WORKS ABOUT LOIS MEEK STOLZ

Dillon, Millicent. "Stolz, 91, Sees Children as Our Prime Resource." *Stanford Campus Report*, March 30, 1983.

Horn, Margo. *An Interview with Lois Meek Stolz*. Oral history at Stanford University Archives, Stanford, CA, 1984.

Hymes, James L. "The Kaiser Child Service Centers." In *Early Childhood Education: Living History Interviews, vol. 2*, 27–55. Carmel, CA: Hacienda Press, 1978.

Senn, Milton J. E. "Oral History of Lois Meek Stolz." *Child Development Oral History Interviews*. Bethesda, MD: National Library of Medicine, 1968.

Takanishi, Ruby. *An American Child Development Pioneer*. Oral history of Lois Meek Stolz at the Schlesinger Library on the History of Women, Radcliffe College, Cambridge, MA, 1978.

Marion Talbot

C. H. Edson and B. D. Saunders

Marion Talbot (1858–1948) served as dean of women at the University of Chicago from 1899 to 1925. An influential university administrator, indefatigable advocate of coeducation, and indomitable defender of women's academic abilities, Talbot strove to mitigate the barriers that constrained higher educational opportunities for women during the progressive era. In addition to her pioneering administrative achievements on behalf of women scholars, Talbot left a lasting imprint on the field of home economics and was instrumental in founding the Association of Collegiate Alumnae. Following her retirement from the University of Chicago in 1925, she served two terms as the acting president of the Constantinople Women's College in Turkey. Talbot died in Chicago at the age of ninety, leaving a legacy for future generations of women through both her own pioneering achievements and her persistent advocacy for coeducational opportunities.

On July 31, 1858, in Thun, Switzerland, Boston travelers Emily Fairbanks Talbot and Dr. Israel Tisdale Talbot greeted the arrival of their first child, Marion. As reform-minded humanitarians imbued with antebellum hopes for the creation of a just society through collaboration of the sexes, both parents welcomed the birth of a daughter. While raising Marion and succeeding children Edith, Winthrop, and Russell, the Talbots won prominence in the social, intellectual, and medical life in Boston through personal achievements and dedication to numerous reform causes. The endeavors of the couple to manifest their reform ideals in daily life not only brought great benefit to the community of Boston but provided both their sons and daughters with richer educational, cultural, and vocational opportunities than those present in their own youth.

Although both parents had been reared within inclusive Yankee traditions as descendants of Massachusetts colonists, neither had experienced a background of privileged circumstances. Born in Sharon, Massachusetts, on October 29, 1829, Israel attended a rural school and, subsequently, earned his tuition for medical training by teaching in a small private school established by his aunt in Baltimore, Maryland. Before Israel wed Emily Fairbanks on October 29, 1856, he had completed all his formal medical training, including credentials from the Homeopathic Medical College of Pennsylvania in 1853 and an M.D. from Harvard Medical School in 1854. Skilled in both surgery and homeopathy, Dr. Talbot had risen to prominence by 1855 as a result of performing the first successful tracheotomy in the United States. Determined to expand homeopathic medical training in Boston, he played a leading role in uniting the New England Female College and the Massachusetts Homeopathic Hospital to form the Boston University School of Medicine, one of the first medical colleges to accept students of both sexes on equal terms. When the coeducational school opened in 1873, Talbot served as dean and professor of surgery, positions he held until his death in 1899.

Several years younger than her husband, Emily Fairbanks was born February 22, 1834, on a farm in Winthrop, Maine. Raised in a locale with limited schooling opportunities, she received home tutoring from a mother reputed to possess exceptional intelligence. As a teenager in Augusta, Maine, Emily demonstrated her own extraordinary talents by successfully teaching in an unruly school that had discouraged others from completing their terms. In 1854 she accepted a teaching position in Baltimore, where she and Dr. Talbot met for the first time. An individual of exceptional force and commitment, Emily Talbot played important roles in social and medical reform organizations, gave birth to six children, nurtured the four who lived, and actively campaigned for equal educational opportunities for women. Recognizing impediments to the higher education of her daughters and other women, Emily was instrumental in the founding of the Massachusetts Society for the University Education of Women and is credited with the idea for forming the Association of Collegiate Alumnae. Emily also gained support for the opening of the Boston Girl's Latin High School in 1877, helped to pilot kindergarten programs, and served as secretary to the Department of Education of the American Social Science Association in the 1880s.

Raised in Boston during the twilight of its golden era as a cultural center, Marion Talbot acquired many of the humanitarian and intellectual credos that inspired her parents toward social activism. As a child, Marion experienced a milieu of progressive optimism and social responsibility as her parents strove to give life to their ardent faith in the ameliorative powers of educational and institutional reform. Intent on creating a more humane civilization while restoring an ascribed social order, the Talbots were avant-garde in feminism and health reform but were not egalitarians or revolutionaries. Consequently, Marion's parents grounded the education of their children on a liberal social vision based on conventional assumptions that individuals schooled in accepted intellectual traditions and manners of the dominant culture would be natural guardians for progressive institutions.

Reflecting both liberal and conservative beliefs, the Talbots devoted steadfast attention to home tutelage of their children and extended to their daughters a form of mental training traditionally reserved for sons. Within the rituals of domestic relationships and social gatherings, they endeavored to refine the abilities of their children by encouraging the arts of literacy, conversation, and written discourse. By age twelve, Marion had sufficient confidence in exposition to write letters to the editor of the *Women's Journal*. Determined to augment higher educational opportunities for their daughters, the Talbots not only secured home tutoring in Greek and Latin but campaigned for access to the best preparatory schools in Boston. Unable to enroll fifteen-year-old Marion in the Boston Latin School in 1873, they helped her gain entry to the Chauncey Hall School—an academy in Boston that accepted a few female students each year for limited course work.

By 1876, through a combination of parental tutelage, private instruction, and formal schooling, eighteen-year-old Marion gained conditional admission to Boston University. Along with many college women of her generation, Talbot crammed laboriously to meet entrance conditions and keep pace with male students drilled for college by Boston Latin School, Roxbury Latin School, or Cambridge High School. Inspired by the presence of Helen McGill, Anna Howard Shaw, Anna Oliver, and other notable women who composed the first wave of female scholars to receive undergraduate and graduate degrees from Boston University, Talbot persisted against the odds to earn her bachelor of arts in 1880 and her master of arts in 1882.

According to Lois Rosenberry, her friend and later coauthor of *The History of the American Association of University Women*, Talbot had an "absorbing desire to make herself and her education useful" following graduation; however, she found barren prospects for positions considered suitable by individuals of her educational and cultural background.[1] Like other young women who had been willing to undergo any hardship for the sake of education but who were met with the "cold shoulders of society," Talbot's "eyes were now opened to the unreasonable and manifold obstacles to women's education and later use of that education as the foundation for a career."[2] Seeking to broaden vocational prospects for herself and others, Talbot began her lifelong commitment to promote the newly formed Association of Collegiate Alumnae (ACA). Undertaking to fulfill the original visions that her mother had for the organization, Talbot served as secretary of the ACA for its first thirteen years, was president from 1895 to 1897, and was an influential force in its expansion into the nationwide American Association of University Women in 1921. Her dedication to advancing opportunities for women through mutual support and cooperative promotion of common interests became one of the memorable achievements of her lifetime. In addition, through her early affiliation with the ACA she formed lifetime friendships with her two most influential mentors: Professor Ellen

H. Richards of the Massachusetts Institute of Technology (MIT) and Alice Elvira Freeman, president of Wellesley College.

In 1884, under the guidance of Richards, Talbot began a new program of studies at MIT to prepare herself for professional work in the emerging fields of public health and social sciences—subjects that not only occupied the attention of her parents but became the focus of her long academic career. After earning a specialized degree in sanitary science in 1888, Talbot spent the next two years teaching sanitary and domestic science at Lasell Seminary in Auburndale. In 1890, on the recommendation of her other professional mentor, Alice Freeman Palmer, Talbot accepted a position to teach at Wellesley. Alice Freeman had resigned the presidency of Wellesley upon her marriage to Harvard philosopher George Herbert Palmer in 1887; however, she remained an influential trustee of the college and helped to advance Talbot's career. Two years after Talbot began teaching sanitary science at Wellesley, Palmer opened another professional door, which led Talbot to a distinguished administrative career and a place in history.

In 1892, President William Rainey Harper of the University of Chicago attracted the eminent Palmer to come to Chicago with promises of developing the institution as a coeducational and egalitarian prototype for modernized higher education in the twentieth century. Palmer accepted the position of dean (of women) in the Graduate Colleges, with the conditions that she be in residence only three months of the year and that Marion Talbot would be hired as resident dean. Harper agreed. Expressing confidence in the organizational skills Talbot displayed during their mutual work with the American Association of Collegiate Alumnae, Palmer wrote to Talbot, "I made my going conditioned on yours."[3]

Intrigued by the "novel" features and "excitement of a new undertaking," yet hesitant about leaving family, friends, and professional commitments, Talbot experienced "mingled feelings" about moving to Chicago.[4] Her mother urged her to consider the offer because of greater opportunities for women in the experimental climate of the West; however, before reaching a final decision, Talbot wrote Harper about her interest in establishing a department of public health, with courses in sanitary science and jurisprudence. In the same letter, she expressed her willingness to assume a role supervising the care of female students but sought assurance that she and other women would be entering an atmosphere of intellectual cooperation. In lieu of acceding to her academic proposals, Harper offered Talbot the alternative of working in her field as assistant professor of sanitary science within the newly formed department of social science and extended the title of dean (of women) in the University Colleges for her work with female students. Persuaded by her own visions and entreatments of associates to "turn a kind ear toward Mr. Harper's propositions" for the university and by opportunities to "help shape its policy at the outset in some very important lines," Talbot accepted both appointments.[5]

On September 19, 1892, surrounded by a crowd of well-wishers, Talbot and Palmer boarded the train to Chicago. Possibly as symbolic protection against the perceived crudities of Chicago and the perceived folly of what some called "Harper's Bazaar," Florence M. Cushing pressed into Talbot's glove a tiny box containing a piece of the Plymouth Rock. With a symbol of her heritage clasped in her hand, with the best wishes of her family and friends in her heart, and with hopes of molding strong coeducational foundations in a new university in her mind, Talbot began her fateful trek to Chicago, where she would spend the remainder of her long and celebrated career.

Heartened by expectations of engendering coeducational liberty, equality, and unity, Talbot and Palmer teetered on planks laid over mud to attend the first faculty meeting at Chicago on October 1, 1892. In a room overlooking the swamp on which the rest of the campus was to be built, Talbot and Palmer listened as President Harper intoned his desires that the university would become "one in spirit, if not necessarily in opinion."[6] Despite inauspicious surroundings, months of residing and working in makeshift structures, and "scrambling over piles of lumber and shavings and nearly falling thro [sic] the holes in the landings where loose boards served as treads," Talbot and Palmer persisted toward their goals.[7] Cognizant of skepticism about coeducation by many influential academicians and leading citizens, the vigilant partners trod on the conservative planks of society with equal caution.

From the outset, Talbot and Palmer were determined to prove to critics that "the presence of women should never mean the lowering of any standards, intellectual or social."[8] Correctly assuming that their fledgling innovations were under nationwide and local scrutiny, they were on guard to monitor behavior of female students "lest some slight misstep might harm the whole undertaking."[9] As resident dean responsible for upholding refined behavior in an experimental setting, Talbot walked a fine line between cultivation and imposition of standards. In cases of uncertainty, she inquired into local customs for comparison with eastern proprieties but was not always satisfied that undiscriminating conventions of the surrounding "nascent culture" would preclude censorious review from connoisseurs.[10] "The free and easy Western standards on the one side and the conspicuousness of our position on the other," Talbot complained to her sister Edith, "make the social situation rather complex."[11]

Beyond energies spent in social vigilance within campus walls, Talbot and Palmer devoted considerable attention to community obligations expected of upper-class women. Mindful of the importance of public patronage and support, they attended social gatherings, participated in local events, and helped Harper in gaining large donations for campus dormitories, organizations, and scholarships. Despite gratifying successes (the Chicago Women's Club raised $1 million for the university between 1892 and 1893), Talbot wrote that the strain of performing social and other nonacademic duties consumed "nervous strength," cost them bouts of "cold and fatigue," and detracted from their academic pursuits.[12]

Notwithstanding entailed sacrifices, Talbot and Palmer focused considerable attention on administrative groundwork to institute their conceptions of an ideal organizational structure. Perceiving residential arrangements as central components in promoting the intellectual and social development of female students, they expended considerable energy overseeing the construction of student housing. Adapting from traditions of parental tutelage and a British dormitory prototype designed to further the education and leadership training of upper-class males, they envisioned a residential system of houses in which deans and other models would exemplify principles of cooperative living, refined tastes, artful discourse, and skilled leadership. To supplement their systematic design for cultivation of female potential through residential housing, Talbot and Palmer hoped to join female undergraduates, graduates, faculty, community activists, and Chicago socialites through a network of women's organizations.

In the opening year of the university, prospects for creating an outstanding coeducational campus appeared promising; however, during the second academic year, Palmer began to distrust Harper upon sensing his resentment of her advocacy for female faculty. Within another year, further deterioration of mutual esteem culminated in her resignation. Feeling bitter contempt for Harper as a "coarse, selfish person, without a fine touch in him anywhere," she left the university in 1895, leaving her hopes for developing a strong community of female scholars to her colleague and successor, Marion Talbot.[13]

Upon departure of her mentor, Talbot assumed Palmer's leading position of dean (of women) in the Graduate Colleges and was promoted to associate professor. Remaining hopeful that females could circumvent obstacles to win full recognition for their scholarship, Talbot assumed conciliatory but insistent postures in "standing as both sympathetic critic and loyal supporter of the men and institutions whose efforts in behalf of women [were] one of the wonders in a century of wonders."[14] In later years, Talbot grieved that institutional promises to extend opportunities to "both sexes on equal terms" were "somewhat of a mirage," but she remained proud of her pioneering achievements.[15]

Throughout her tenure as dean, professor, and self-appointed advocate for female faculty, Talbot labored ardently to build institutional structures that would advance educational opportunities for female students and win full recognition of the scholarly accomplishments of female faculty members. Instrumental in the formation of a women's community that attracted outstanding female scholars and increasingly well known for both her intellectual integrity and social consciousness, Talbot earned institutional and nationwide acclaim for her accomplishments. In 1899, President Harper recognized her leadership by originating the title of dean of women for her position as the highest female administrator in the university. Interpreting her role as the overseer of all campus matters involving women, Talbot promoted further development of women's groups and campaigned for a central organization "to unite the women of the university for the promotion of common interests."[16] In 1901, she gained approval to form the Women's Union, a club that served to link female students, faculty, and civic reformers. Fifteen years later, through the donation of La Verne W. Noyes in memory of his deceased wife, the Ida Noyes Hall, considered as "the finest building for women in the country," was opened to house the Women's Union.[17] By this time, Talbot had also organized a central administrative council and advisory committees to assist her in the direction of campus organizations and programs for women.

Although effective in promoting concepts of a campus community of female scholars, Talbot met with disappointment in gaining institutional acknowledgment of their scholarship. However principled her stances, tenacious her persistence, and refined her diplomacy, Talbot failed to secure full coeducational equality. Contrary to the commitment shown by university women in "upholding and advancing the intellectual and social standards of the university," the institution failed to fulfill its promise to give full recognition to women for their "intellectual and administrative gifts."[18] Despite impressive academic achievements, women received only nominal increments in appointments, fellowships, or promotions during Talbot's years at Chicago. She was also unable to oblige the university to redress disproportionate allocation of institutional resources. Before her retirement, however, Talbot joined with Elizabeth Wallace and Edith Foster Flint (the only three women out of 150 to hold full professorships) to present to the president and the Board of Trustees a formal document delineating concrete evidence of institutional discrimination against female students and faculty. After submitting the document in December 1924, the three waited with "trepidation for the repercussions from this bolt," and although they were relieved when the board verified their allegations, they were later disheartened that "on the whole no great progress was made."[19]

Commensurate to trials she experienced in promoting the careers of female colleagues during the thirty-three years of her deanship, unexpected challenges faced Talbot in advancing her own professional interests. Possibilities for Talbot to pursue the applied and interdisciplinary approaches of sanitary science through the department of social science looked promising in the early years. Initially, Chairman Albion Small promoted faculty involvement in urban reform. With institutional approval, Talbot delivered lectures in the community and formalized reciprocal agreements with progressive social activists Jane Addams, Florence Kelly, and Julia Lathrop to secure student apprenticeships in organizations involved with public health, sanitation, labor legislation, and reform of prisons and criminal courts. Over time, however, institutional trends toward theoretical specialization convinced Small to direct the department toward abstract research, thus diminishing Talbot's opportunities to realize her visions of coordinating applied public health programs.

In 1902, Talbot began to reformulate her academic objectives by proposing her own specialized department within the domain of household technology—an emerging discipline that acquiesced to conventional conceptions of women's proper sphere but circumvented constraints of established departments and offered a base for further extensions of social feminism. Following two years of exploratory designs, Talbot gained approval to establish the department of household administration in 1904. Along with her associates Sophonisba Breckinridge and Alice Peloubet Norton, she designed a broad curriculum: Talbot providing courses in chemistry, physiology, and bacteriology as foundations for her specialty in sanitary science; Breckinridge offering instruction in Legal and Economic Position of Women, Consumption of Wealth, and The State in Relation to the Household; and Norton teaching about the practical aspects of home finances and dietetics. Conceiving the departmental curriculum as a step forward toward rational and scientific training of women for enlarged roles in society, Talbot saw household administration as expanding the executive abilities of women in community affairs and strengthening their position as administrators of family income. Ever mindful of her dual roles as critic and supporter of society and its institutions, Talbot's academic vision remained consistent: to instill students with the "vigor and breadth of view, discipline of character and freedom of mind" to discard outgrown customs but at the same time to preserve the timeless family traditions to outlast any industrial, educational, or social system.[20]

Talbot did not fully realize her high expectations for complete coeducational equality in either her administrative or academic careers at the University of Chicago; nevertheless, she found satisfaction and hope in the "whole-hearted devotion" of her female colleagues to carry forth the spirit of their mutual cause.[21] Upon her retirement in 1925, Talbot continued to lend her notable talents in the service of women's education. In addition to serving two terms as acting president of Constantinople Women's College in Turkey, she continued her involvement with the American Association of University Women and was still offering advice in meetings at the age of eighty-nine. Having outlived her closest relatives, friends, and colleagues, however, Talbot spent her last days frail and lonely, dying in Chicago of chronic myocarditis on October 24, 1948.

As one of the first women within university walls to earn an advanced degree, gain a faculty position, head her own department, and hold high administrative office, Marion Talbot stood as an inspiration to female students. Although unmarried and childless, Talbot gave life to an extended family of female scholars and passed on hopes that victories of her generation would hearten future women toward claiming "the right to use their powers" and take their "place among the great universities of the world."[22] Despite continuing barriers, her hopes remain timeless.

NOTES

1. Marion Talbot and Lois Rosenberry, *The History of the American Association of University Women, 1881–1931* (Boston: Houghton Mifflin, 1931), 5.

2. Marion Talbot, "Debate at the Saturday Morning Club," February 11, 1882, handwritten manuscript of speech in Talbot Family Papers, Special Collections, Boston University (quoted passage is lined out, suggesting it was not verbally delivered); Talbot and Rosenberry, 6–7.

3. Marion Talbot, *More Than Lore* (Chicago: University of Chicago Press, 1936), 4.

4. Ibid., 2–5.

5. W. G. Hale to Talbot, no date, reproduced in University Publications Office, *One in Spirit: A Retrospective View of the University of Chicago on the Occasion of Its Centennial* (Chicago: University of Chicago Press, 1991), 17.

6. Harper's statement, a hallmark of the university, was recorded in notes Talbot made of the meeting. As the university recorder failed to take minutes, the official minutes were later compiled from Talbot's notes. The first page of her notes is reproduced in ibid., ix.

7. Talbot to Israel and Emily Talbot, September 20, 1892, reproduced in ibid., 19.

8. Talbot, *More Than Lore*, 64.

9. Ibid., 71.

10. Ibid., 58.

11. Talbot to Edith Jackson, February 13, 1893, in Marion Talbot Papers, Special Collections, Joseph Regenstein Library, University of Chicago Archives.

12. Ibid.

13. Palmer to George Herbert Palmer, January 9, 1895, Alice Freeman Palmer Papers, Archives, Margaret Clapp Library, Wellesley College.

14. Marion Talbot, "Present-Day Problems in the Education of Women," in Geraldine Jonçich Clifford, ed., *Lone Voyagers* (New York: Feminist Press, 1989), 109–10.

15. Talbot, *More Than Lore*, 14, 131.

16. Ibid., 75.

17. Ibid., 200.

18. Ibid., 141, 142.

19. Ibid., 140.

20. Marion Talbot, *The Education of Women* (Chicago: University of Chicago Press, 1910), 31.

21. Talbot, *More Than Lore*, 141.

22. Ibid., 142, 143.

WORKS BY MARION TALBOT

The Education of Women. Chicago: University of Chicago Press, 1910.

The Modern Household (with Sophonisba Breckinridge). Boston: Whitcomb and Barrows, 1912.

The History of the American Association of University Women, 1881–1931 (with Lois
     Rosenberry). Boston: Houghton Mifflin, 1931.
More Than Lore. Chicago: University of Chicago Press, 1936.

WORKS ABOUT MARION TALBOT

Fitzpatrick, Ellen. "Marion Talbot." In Geraldine Jonçich Clifford, ed., *Lone Voy-
     agers.* New York: Feminist Press, 1989.
———. *Endless Crusade.* New York: Oxford University Press, 1990.
Gordon, Lynn D. *Gender and Higher Education in the Progressive Era.* New Haven,
     CT: Yale University Press, 1990.
Rosenberg, Rosalind. *Beyond Separate Spheres.* New Haven, CT: Yale University
     Press, 1982.
Storr, Richard J. "Marion Talbot." In Edward T. James, ed., *Notable American
     Women*, vol. 3. Cambridge: Belknap Press of Harvard University Press, 1971.

Mary Church Terrell

Doris Marguerite Meadows

Mary Church Terrell (1863–1954) was a teacher, writer, school board member, international lecturer, political advocate, and founder of a wide variety of educational institutions. Born in the year of the Emancipation Proclamation and dying just after the desegregation Supreme Court decision *Brown v. the Board of Education of Topeka Kansas*, Terrell confronted the dual realities of racial segregation and gender subordination with a variety of educational strategies. She became a national and international leader of social and educational activism and reform.

Mary Eliza Church (called Mollie) was born on September 23, 1863, in Memphis, Tennessee. Her parents, Louisa and Robert Reed Church, were newly emancipated slaves who were already relatively prosperous. Her father, who could pass for white, was the son of a plantation owner and a slave. Even though her parents experienced little physical brutality in slavery, Mary always remembered the heartrending fact that her mother, as well as her paternal grandmother, had been sold away from their mothers when they were very young children.

By the time Mary was born, her father was the proprietor of his own business, and her mother owned and operated a beauty salon. Her parents taught Mary race pride and courage in the face of prejudice. Shortly after the Civil War her father was shot in the head during a race riot when he ignored warnings to abandon his business. Although left for dead, Robert Church survived the wound and continued to demonstrate fearless opposition to any abridgment of his rights in the violent age of Jim Crow.

When Mary Church was five years old, her parents divorced, and she and her younger brother went to live with her mother. A year later, Louisa Church decided to send Mary to school in the North. In the interest of a better educational opportunity, Mary boarded with a family in Ohio and attended the "Model School" connected with Antioch College. After two years she transferred to the public schools in Yellow Springs, Ohio. In order to prepare her for matriculation at Oberlin College, Mary's mother moved her to Oberlin, Ohio, where she again lived with another family. Although Mary lived away from home for most of her childhood and only visited her parents, she was steadfast in her gratitude for her educational opportunities. Church also gained an early sense of independence and an understanding of the importance of educational opportunities for African Americans.

A critical turning point at Oberlin occurred when Church elected to take the four-year classical course, or "the gentlemen's course," rather than the usual two-year literary course designated for women, even after warnings that her choice would spoil her chances of getting a husband. At college Mary Church experienced little direct prejudice, though there was one occasion when she was discriminated against for an award. Overall, she worked hard in a demanding program that provided seven hours of required study periods each day. She became an editor of the *Oberlin Review* and excelled at her studies. Despite her success in college Church was unable to get summer work in New York City, but her family was able to support her.

Robert Church had become very wealthy when Memphis experienced yellow fever epidemics in 1878 and 1879 and people fled the city. He stayed and purchased real estate with all of his savings. When the city returned to prosperity, his fortune was made. Therefore, after her graduation in 1884, Mary Church was expected to adopt the life of a "southern belle" (a "real" woman) and not engage in any kind of work. Her father argued that Church's employment would deprive a needy person of an income.

Mary Church chafed under these sexist expectations, especially since her college dream was to "promote the welfare" of her race.[1] Nationwide she was one of only five African-American women graduates from the Oberlin College program. Like many women of her generation, Mary wanted a useful, productive life. After a year she secretly applied for jobs while staying with her mother. She secured a position at Wilberforce University, where she taught five classes in a variety of subjects ranging from mineralogy to French and was assigned the tedious job of secretary of the faculty. When Mary notified her father of this position, he became furious and refused to communicate with her for a year. The following summer Mary returned to Memphis and convinced her father that she was following her own sense of duty and won his support. At the end of her second year at Wilberforce, she received an appointment to teach at the segregated "M Street" School for African-American students in Washington, D.C. There she became the assistant to Robert H. Terrell, a Harvard graduate and the man she would later marry.

At the end of her first year in Washington, Mary Church took two years' leave of absence to fulfill her dream to study in Europe. She traveled with members of her family in the summers and lived with French, German, and Swiss families and later in a pension in Italy while she pursued her studies and perfected her language skills. Although these years fulfilled her intellectual goals, Church felt that her efforts were needed in America. In spite of marriage proposals and educational opportunities in Europe, Mary decided to return to her job in Washington, D.C., where she confronted the rapid spread of race prejudice, growing segregation, and hostility to public social activism by women.

In spite of her extraordinary education, Mary Church was again the assistant to Robert Terrell, even though there was a critical demand for educated people in colleges. In her autobiography Church expressed no disappointment. Her work teaching language engaged her talents and provided an opportunity to use her skills to educate African-American students.

Since married women were not allowed to teach, Mary Church had to resign her position when she married Robert Terrell in 1891. Nevertheless, with her husband's encouragement and support she continued her educational career. She turned to the women's club movement. Black women formed clubs partly because they were excluded by white clubs but also because of their shared desire to "elevate the race" and to come together "to do good." Mary Church Terrell was elected the first president of the National Association of Colored Women (NACW) and transformed its social clubs to educational and political vehicles for the elevation of black women and the race.[2]

The NACW club work of Mary Church Terrell is probably among her best-known achievements. This original and unique national organization was controlled by African-American women and became the basis of a national network, the vehicle for the creation of social reforms, and a training ground for leadership. As in much progressive reform, local groups were directed by educated, Protestant, middle-class women who hoped to "uplift" many of the less fortunate members of the race. The movement was essentially conservative in many ways since it preserved women's place in its efforts to "purify" the home and failed to critique the restrictions of the "women's sphere." In 1900 Terrell wrote that the NACW's most important and effective work was in the home: "The purification of the home must be our first consideration and care."[3] In 1899 Terrell wrote that "in the mind and heart of every good and conscientious woman, the first place is occupied by home."[4] This focus not only constrained the role of women but also seemed to acknowledge racist charges about the "problem" of morality in home training. While Terrell herself moved away from the racial and class implications of this narrow focus, the selection and language used in the definition of some of these issues testify to the strength of the constraints of the contemporary discourse and the power of racial and gender castes.

In her first presidential address to the National Association of Colored Women, Terrell acknowledged problems of segregation, vice, poverty, and ignorance but stressed the environmental sources of these difficulties and their susceptibility to change. She also suggested that the substantial progress already achieved by the race as a whole was a source of racial pride and the basis of the solidarity, volunteerism, and grass-roots organization required for reform. Terrell's reform agenda consisted of the establishment and extension of preschool education at home and in school through the establishment of mothers' clubs and free kindergartens for every community. The NACW became a powerful force for preschool education and the establishment of institutions to provide it. Even though the organization's motto, "Lifting As We Climb," reflected the class and status concerns of middle-class African-American women, the organization focused on common concerns and efforts rather than on distinctions engendered in wealth and education. The kindergartens, clinics, schools, Mother's Clubs, homes for girls, homes for the aged, and day nurseries founded and supported by these groups addressed the needs of all classes of women.

In the 1890s Mary Church Terrell experienced the caste nature of her own social place and the double bind of race and gender despite her own established respectability. In five years she lost three children shortly after birth. Terrell strongly suspected that the inferior conditions and inadequate equipment of the segregated hospital in Washington, D.C., had critical roles in the deaths. When she became pregnant for the fourth time, she went to stay with her mother in New York, and her daughter, Phyllis, survived.

Terrell exerted substantial educational policy power after she was appointed to the Board of Education of Washington, D.C., in 1898. As the first African-American woman to serve in that capacity, Terrell used her position to effect personnel changes and to advocate curriculum reform. Politically Terrell remained loyal to Booker T. Washington and his followers. She prevented W.E.B. Du Bois's appointment in the system and supported Washington's choice. Yet, Terrell's own opinions were changing to more radical beliefs. In her twelve years as a board member she was an especially vigorous advocate for justice for African-American students and stressed the need for the study of the African-American heritage.

These concerns led her to several other educational careers. At the turn of the century popular magazines and invited lectures were two critical educational forums. In spite of serious difficulties in getting her work considered, Terrell was able to publish in popular magazines and specialized publications major articles on lynching, the convict lease system, discrimination, black life and history, and women's rights.

Like many progressives, Terrell believed in the educational power of mass media magazines, popular lectures and the critical role of publicity in shaping opinions of voters as well as policymakers. She began her journalistic efforts to inform and educate readers about the role and duties of educated African-American women and proceeded to demonstrate that role with her own journalistic instruction. Her 1904 article in the *North American Review* entitled "Lynching from a Negro's Point of View" used statistics and examples of lynching to demonstrate that racism and ignorance, rather than rape, caused lynchings.[5] Given the temper of the times, Terrell's article, which explicitly named and described many heinous crimes, was an important dissent and required great courage. Less inflammatory journal articles had resulted in firings, harassment, and forced migration of writers. Terrell also wrote a later exposé of peonage in the United States. The fact that her explicit description of "What It Means to Be Colored in the Capital of the United States" was published anonymously reflects the fact that the difficulties and dangers of exposing racism increased during the first decade of the twentieth century. Terrell's journalistic career reflected the growing institutionalization of segregation, so that her later articles appeared primarily in specialized African-American publications.

Another important source of popular education was the lecture circuit tour, which proved to be more accessible, though Terrell disliked leaving her family for weeks at a time. Nevertheless, she decided that these lectures on the race issue to white audiences were critical to the education and reform of society. Mary Church Terrell signed a contract for a series of lectures on contemporary topics about African-Americans with an "upbeat" message. Yet, the vicious racism of the period pressed her to take ever more radical positions. Her husband, Robert H. Terrell, was a federal judge appointed by the Republicans and supported by Booker T. Washington, but Mary Church Terrell found herself in disagreement with Washington's ideas on many issues, especially his emphasis on vocational education rather than civil rights.

These different priorities were apparent in the Brownsville controversy. After several hostile incidents aimed at African-American troops stationed at Brownsville, gunfire erupted at midnight on August 13, 1906, and the soldiers were accused. However, when no evidence was found and no soldier confessed, Theodore Roosevelt discharged all three companies without a court-martial. Terrell appealed directly to the secretary of war, William Howard Taft, and obtained a temporary stay of Roosevelt's order, so that she could get an investigator to interview the accused men before they were sent home. Although this effort proved futile, the experience converted her to a more radical position. Mary Church Terrell later became one of the founding members of the National Association for the Advancement of Colored People (NAACP), despite Booker T. Washington's objections expressed to her husband.

Terrell also became a pioneer in the fight for women's suffrage. Her experience as the daughter of a working mother, her association with Frederick Douglass, her marriage to Robert Terrell (a strong suffragist), and her friendship with Susan B. Anthony convinced Terrell of the importance of the vote for women. She used her international experience and linguistic facility to join international suffrage networks, even though her role was constrained by her race. She gave an important address in German to the International Council of Women when they met in Berlin in 1904. Although there was opposition, Terrell insisted on linking the issues of gender and race. At home she was active in the National American Woman Suffrage Association and encouraged African-American women to become suffrage activists, even though racial tensions existed in the organization. Terrell also routinely picketed the White House in the cause of women's suffrage.

After the franchise was obtained, Terrell became increasingly active in the Republican party and helped organize African-American voters. During the next two decades she combined her political work with a focus on interracial understanding. However, her life changed dramatically during this time. Robert Terrell suffered a debilitating stroke in 1920 and died in 1925. In spite of her extraordinary education and valuable language skills, Mary Church Terrell found regular employment elusive. Exceptional grades on civil service tests and political service were not guarantees of a government career. At one point she did hold a clerk position, but when it was discovered that she was black, she was fired.

The pressure of the depression, family financial obligations, and poor health made this discrimination even more difficult. However, Terrell refused to become embittered and instead devoted her energies to a wide variety of causes, especially those related to discrimination. During this period she published her voluminous autobiography entitled *A Colored Woman in a White World*. In over 400 pages Terrell explicitly describes the growing racism of the period 1890 to 1930 and details her achievements despite the obstacles, frustrations, and difficulties of race and gender. In the preface of the book H. G. Wells praised its quality, and the work received good reviews.

Terrell's political activities took on a more militant tone and focus. She waged a successful fight on behalf of minority membership in the District of Columbia branch of the American Association of University Women. Always aware of her own privilege, she used her fame and influence to force the issue of prejudice. "I thought I would be an arrant coward," she noted, "unless I opened the way for other colored women."[6]

In the 1950s Terrell began local radical antisegregation tactics in Washington, D.C. These efforts developed a model of a series of strategies that extended resistance to segregation to the streets, strategies that became commonplace in the civil rights movement. As a pioneer for civil rights she led picketing, boycotting, and lawsuits to end segregation of public facilities in Washington, D.C., until victory was finally won in the Supreme Court. This issue was only one of many that Terrell participated in through her membership in many general and specialized organizations, committees, panels, and lobbying groups. By the 1950s Terrell was a familiar figure at the forefront of more radical strategies. She maintained that rights practiced in the 1890s needed to be restored in the 1950s. She also began to support Democrats who spoke for equal rights.

Terrell's educational activism was exemplified by her efforts to educate the public, especially young people, about the contributions of African Americans. She wrote magazine articles about important achievers such as Samuel Taylor Coleridge, Paul Lawrence Dunbar, Phillis Wheatley, George Washington Carver, and Frederick Douglass. As a member of the District of Columbia Board of Education she sponsored a resolution that made February 14 "Frederick Douglass Day" in all public schools attended by African-American students. She maintained a constant crusade to educate the public about the contributions of African Americans and to establish landmarks and memorials recognizing their accomplishments.

In spite of her own success, Terrell always remembered the less fortunate. Her work demonstrated the transcendence of self-interest in the efforts made by middle-class activists. In her eighties she mounted an exhausting campaign on behalf of Rosa Ingram, a Georgian sharecropper accused of murdering a landlord as he attacked her. Even after Ingram was convicted, Terrell continued her advocacy and led a delegation to Georgia to seek Ingram's parole. The year was 1953, and Terrell was ninety years old.

Mary Church Terrell died in 1954, leaving a substantial legacy as an educator and activist. Her demonstration of courage, persistence, creativity, and resourcefulness defined an educational mission of social activism and resistance in the face of overwhelming adversity.

NOTES

1. Mary Church Terrell, *A Colored Woman in a White World* (Washington, DC: Randsdell, 1940), 60.

2. Beverly W. Jones, "Mary Church Terrell and the National Association of Colored Women," *Journal of Negro History* 67 (Spring 1982): 20–33.

3. Mary Church Terrell, "The Duty of the National Association of Colored Women to the Race," *AME Church Review* (January 1900): 350.

4. Wilma Peebles-Wilkins, "Black Women and American Social Welfare," in Darlene Clark Hine, ed., *Black Women in United States History*, vol. 4 (New York: Carlson, 1990), 41.

5. Mary Church Terrell, "Lynching from a Negro's Point of View," *North American Review* 178 (June 1904): 853–68.

6. Janice Leone, "Integrating the American Association of University Women, 1946–1949," *Historian* 51 (Winter 1989): 428.

WORKS BY MARY CHURCH TERRELL

The Papers of Mary Church Terrell, 1863–1954 (microform). Library of Congress, Washington, DC.

"Duty of the National Association of Colored Women to the Race." *AME Church Review* (January 1900): 340–54.

"Club Work of Colored Women." *Southern Workman* (August 8, 1901): 435–38.

"Lynching from a Negro's Point of View." *North American Review* 178 (June 1904): 853–68.

"A Plea for the White South by a Coloured Woman." *Nineteenth Century* (July 1906): 70–84.

"The Disbanding of the Colored Soldiers." *Voice of the Negro* (December 1906): 554–58.

"What It Means to Be Colored in the Capital of the United States." *Independent* (January 24, 1907): 181–86.

"Peonage in the United States: The Convict Lease System and the Chain Gangs." *Nineteenth Century* 62 (August 1907): 306–22.

A Colored Woman in a White World. Washington, DC: Randsdell, 1940.

"I Remember Frederick Douglass." *Ebony* (1953): 73–80.

WORKS ABOUT MARY CHURCH TERRELL

Giddings, Paula. *When and Where I Enter.* New York: William Morrow, 1984.

Harley, Sharon. "For the Good of Family and Race: Gender, Work and Domestic Roles in the Black Community, 1880–1930." *Signs* 15 (Winter 1990): 336–50.

Harley, Sharon, and Terborg-Penn, *Afro-American Woman: Struggles and Images.* New York: Kennikat Press, 1978.

Hine, Darlene Clark, ed. *Black Women in American History.* New York: Carlson, 1990.

Jones, Beverly W. *Quest for Equality: The Life and Writings of Mary Eliza Church Terrell, 1863–1954.* New York: Carlson, 1990.

Leone, Janice. "Integrating the American Association of American Women, 1946–1949." *Historian* 51 (Winter 1989): 423–45.

Scott, Anne Firor. "Most Invisible of All: Black Women's Voluntary Associations." *Journal of Southern History* 56 (February 1990): 3–20.

Shepard, Gladys. *Mary Church Terrell—Respectable Person.* Baltimore, MD: Human Relations Press, 1959.

Sterling, Dorothy. *Black Foremothers: Three Lives.* New York: Feminist Press, 1988.

Martha Carey Thomas

Theodora Penny Martin

Martha Carey Thomas (1857–1935), more than any other woman of her generation, was responsible for dispelling doubts about women's intellectual capacity and for bringing about the social acceptance of the college-educated woman. Emancipated herself by higher education, she devoted her life to that cause, believing that only through equal education would women achieve political, economic, and social equality with men.

For most Americans in the decades following the Civil War, girls' education beyond grammar school was still a much debated topic. A girl's future role as wife and mother, opponents believed, demanded only the rudiments of literacy; in addition, rigorous intellectual training strained a girl's mental capacity, had deleterious effects upon her physical and emotional health, and conflicted with her innate femininity. Consequently, public high schools for girls were few, most private girls' academies emphasized feminine accomplishments, college opportunities were rare, and graduate training for women was virtually nonexistent. The few women who were college graduates were open to ridicule and social scorn. Through the force of her own example and through the intellectual life she offered women at Bryn Mawr College, Carey Thomas undercut the prevailing narrow and negative assumptions about women and education. In doing so, she widened and enhanced educational opportunities for girls and women at all levels of the educational system.

The roots of Martha Carey Thomas's character, interests, feminist philosophy, aspirations, and achievements lie deeply embedded in her family background and childhood environment. Born January 2, 1857, and reared in Baltimore, Maryland, she was the eldest child in the union of two prominent Quaker families. Her Thomas ancestors, emigrants in 1651 from Wales to Maryland, engaged in commerce, through marriage acquired land, and eventually entered the professions. James Carey Thomas, her father, was a respected physician, active, in addition, as a Quaker preacher and a trustee of three Quaker-founded institutions of higher education. A nineteenth-century gentleman scholar, Dr. Thomas encouraged his daughter's passion for broad liberal learning—up to a point.

The English Whitalls settled in New Jersey in the 1680s but eventually joined the active Quaker community in Philadelphia, where Mary Whitall, Carey Thomas's mother, was born and educated. Prosperous farmers and small merchants, the Whitalls were more devout, philanthropic, and indi-vidualistic than the publicly active Thomas clan. Never averse to the public spotlight and with a strong, at times willful, sense of self, Carey Thomas clearly inherited from both families. A long line of dynamic Whitall women preceded Carey Thomas. Denied a college education, Hannah Whitall Smith, Thomas's aunt, a dedicated feminist, iconoclastic orator, and author of evangelical Quaker tracts, strongly encouraged her niece's educational ambitions, as did Thomas's more conventional mother, who always regretted that no women's college had existed in which to continue her own studies. Although the mother of ten children (four boys and four girls survived in-fancy), Mary Whitall Thomas was active in charitable Quaker undertakings. In later life she became a trustee of two Quaker schools and an officer in the Women's Christian Temperance Union.

Although Carey Thomas subsequently rebelled against what she termed "narrow Quaker horizons" and strict dogma, she grew up in a world where the Friends' "inner light" was not denied to women. Quaker women were considered the mental and spiritual equals of men and encouraged to speak publicly at Quaker meeting. The doctrine of equality, however, gradually eroded as Quakers entered secular community life and assimilated prevailing views on the primacy of women's domestic role. Thus, although Mary Whi-tall's money eased the financial burdens of the large Thomas family, Carey Thomas early observed that her father, as male, wielded the final authority in all matters of importance, such as her education. Nevertheless, Quaker history, with its roll call of intrepid individuals, and Quaker regard for ed-ucation made an impact on the young "Minnie," as the family called their precocious daughter.

Young Minnie's naturally executive and exuberant temperament was stim-ulated by her place in the family: not only was she the cherished first child, but she was soon given responsibilities for supervising her siblings. A kitchen accident at age seven resulted in near fatal burns and a year's convalescence, during which she became the universal center of attention, a position she never willingly relinquished—in or outside the family—until the end of her life. Undaunted by the slight limp that remained with her, Minnie thrived on physical activity—rock climbing, skating, roof scaling—especially if it involved risk, competition, and an opportunity to prove herself and, in so doing, to prove the equal abilities of females and males. As an adult, although outwardly more conventional, Thomas brought that same venturesome spirit to the academic arena. She was never afraid of failure—and seldom admitted it.

Just as strong as her impulse to action was Minnie's early self-conscious feminism; at thirteen she noted with pride that a teacher had called her "a woman's righter." In the same year, determined to follow her father into medicine and spurred on by *Boys Play Book of Science*, she decided to study the anatomy of a mouse. She caught and drowned the mouse with some aplomb, but skinning it was another matter. At length dismissing her trembling hands as "*feminine* nonsense," she completed her experiment and wrote in her journal: "I greatly prefer cutting up mice to sewing worsted."[1] Throughout her life, Thomas fought to change the role into which girls were socialized: "sewing, cooking, taking care of children, dressing, and flirting" was her accurate adolescent catalog.[2] Quaker principles and Whitall examples provided a positive foundation for Minnie's feminist outlook, but the circumscription of her mother's life by domestic duties seems to have strengthened her resolve for an independent life. Marriage, she believed at that time, doomed women to lives of domestic stultification, relieved only by philanthropic efforts. Independence was necessary for creative achievement and could be gained only through higher education, which would give a woman a profession of her own. For Minnie, feminism and education were inextricably linked. That belief determined the medium and the message of the rest of her life.

Even though her family held knowledge and culture in high regard and had economic means sufficient to support schooling for their children, Carey Thomas struggled for her education. The heat of that struggle eventually became the life breath of Bryn Mawr College. Mary Thomas taught her daughter to read at an early age, but it was not until Minnie was eight and her younger brother John was old enough for school that she was finally sent along with him. Several years at a newly founded Friends' school in Baltimore demonstrated Minnie's aptitude and passion for study, and in 1872 her parents agreed to send her to Howland Institute, a Quaker girls' school near Ithaca, New York. Enrolled in the classical course, Minnie initially viewed Howland as a stepping-stone to newly opened Vassar College and a medical career. She was persuaded otherwise by a perceptive woman teacher who believed the most pressing need in the cause of women was for scholars and who challenged Minnie to become a great one. "I will devote my life to study," Minnie wrote home, "and will try to work some good from it."[3] For the rest of her life, learning delighted Carey Thomas, but after Howland her scholarship became primarily a tool in the cause of women's education: by her example she would prove that women were capable of, and would benefit from, the highest education.

Convinced that Cornell would challenge her more than Vassar and that its coeducational degree would carry more weight, Minnie chose to continue her studies there. Although her father had delivered an address at Minnie's Howland commencement extolling advanced intellectual training for women, Dr. Thomas denied his own daughter's request, believing that her already faltering faith would be undermined and that her study would unfit her for future domestic happiness. Her mother's ardent support and the single-mindedness that characterized Thomas throughout her life, as both blessing and bane, won the day. A year later, in 1875, she enrolled in Cornell, passing examinations that earned her junior standing.

At Cornell Carey Thomas assumed her androgynous middle name, continued her work in classics, and was elected to Phi Beta Kappa. Cornell exposed her to a wider world, and she believed she profited from her study there; nevertheless, she felt coeducation to be a "fiery ordeal." The men resented the women's presence, and it took great determination for a woman to claim an equal share of the instruction.

After graduation in 1877, Thomas returned to Baltimore intent on graduate study at newly opened Johns Hopkins University, of which her father was a trustee. As one of three women, she was admitted to study Greek "on certain conditions": namely, that she not attend classes. After a year of frustrating solitary study, she learned that even upon successful completion of examinations, women might be awarded a certificate instead of a degree, and she withdrew from the university. Describing the year that followed as "a horrible blank," Thomas wrote in her journal, "I am lost."[4] Despite her social and intellectual advantages, like most young American women for whom few outlets existed save domesticity, she saw nothing ahead for her, nothing "to do." The graduate school she built later at Bryn Mawr, which would enable women to train for the professoriat, was one response to that problem.

Before long she turned her sights on German universities, which then represented the highest academic rigor and excellence. Sustaining her in another protracted battle with her father was a group of five young women, dedicated feminists, who met regularly for informal discussion. Although not a scholarly community, the group nevertheless made clear to Thomas the importance of the support of women in academic endeavors; at Bryn Mawr she later created and zealously guarded from outside distractions a close and elite community of women scholars. At twenty-two, with the financial help of her mother at home and family connections abroad and accompanied by her close friend Mamie Gwinn, Thomas began attending lectures in philology at the University of Leipzig. Eight other women were enrolled, but none had applied for a degree. Thomas often complained of the drudgery of study and the German emphasis on science rather than "spirit," but she was fueled by a dual sense of purpose: her own exceptional progression through scholarly ranks and the symbolic importance for women of her achievements. In 1882, after three years of arduous and promising study, her sex once again became a barrier as German authorities refused to allow women to register for doctoral examinations. Disregarding, as always, the obstacles in her way,

Thomas, in an amazing tour de force, transferred her work to the University of Zurich and within six months earned her Ph.D. summa cum laude. The unparalleled distinction—she was the first foreigner and first woman to be so honored—gave her the public recognition and the self-assurance she needed to apply, at age twenty-six, for the presidency of Bryn Mawr College, scheduled to open in three years. "Study . . . and influence," she had written two years earlier, "are the two things I care about."[5]

But it was not as president that Carey Thomas made her first influence felt at Bryn Mawr. Even though her father and three other relatives were on the all-male Board of Trustees, her sex, her lack of experience, and the trustees' doubts about her loyalty to Quaker principles outweighed her flawless academic credentials. Instead, she was appointed dean and professor of English. Bryn Mawr had been founded in 1880 by Joseph W. Taylor, a trustee of Haverford, a Quaker college for men, in order to provide women, under Quaker auspices, a similar college experience. The expansion of mental faculties, Taylor believed, would strengthen the character of the young upper-class women for whom he envisioned the college and would produce much needed "teachers of a higher order."

James E. Rhoads, a physician and Bryn Mawr trustee, was appointed the first president of the college. Thirty years Thomas's senior and temperamentally her opposite, he nevertheless created an administrative environment in which her energies, enthusiasms, ideas, and goals flourished to such an extent that Dean Virginia Gildersleeve, a contemporary at Barnard College, observed that Thomas "had practically created Bryn Mawr College."[6] In essence what Thomas did was to change Taylor's ideal from the development of unassailed character to the development of unquestioned intellect.

The keystone and distinguishing mark of Carey Thomas's vision for Bryn Mawr was its graduate school. While the few women's colleges worthy of the name still maintained a preparatory department for underqualified students, Thomas looked to the other end of the spectrum. She believed that if women were to compete in the same arena with men, to be judged as always by male standards, women must be offered an education absolutely equal to men's, including university-level work. Although she realized that the majority of women would not become professional scholars, Thomas believed that a demanding undergraduate curriculum designed to pave the way for graduate work was also the best course of study for any serious college woman. In addition, the graduate school would serve as a drawing card for young, ambitious faculty to offset the then dubious task of teaching young women, something few had experienced. As her drive and imagination entered into decisions about students, faculty, curriculum, buildings, and cultural and social life, Bryn Mawr opened with an atmosphere most conducive to the development of Thomas's highest ideal for women: an independent life of "intellectual renunciation," which abjured personal pleasures for dedication to a life of the mind.

Throughout her thirty-seven years at Bryn Mawr as dean and later as president, Carey Thomas's actions were guided by one overriding concern: the creation and preservation of Bryn Mawr standards. The college must equal or surpass the best men's institutions in order to prove without a doubt women's intellectual equality. Her first act as dean was to rewrite the trustee's original entrance examinations, setting more rigorous requirements and establishing standards as demanding as Harvard's, the premier men's institution (Haverford was never her measure of comparison). Simultaneously, she spearheaded the founding of the preparatory Bryn Mawr School in Baltimore, designed expressly to assure a flow of well-qualified girls into the college. Selection of college faculty, upon whom Thomas believed lay the entire future of the institution, came next. Although Smith College had just opened its doors to women with a curriculum imitative of Harvard's, Thomas found the scholarship of its faculty, especially women's, unequal to the task—some presenting only a precollegiate education. Only ten women in the United States in 1885 held Ph.D.s, and without hesitation, Thomas chose a predominantly male faculty, most with German training, to staff the college, hoping that Bryn Mawr's own graduate school would soon reverse the situation. Taught and tested to the most demanding standards, Bryn Mawr women themselves, she rightly reasoned, would recognize their own excellence and further the cause of women's education with assertive confidence.

Any suggestion that women be offered a course of study different from men's was anathema to Thomas's educational philosophy; a mind was gender-neutral. Bryn Mawr's conservative curriculum was firmly grounded in the classics, and although there were some electives, most courses were required subjects chosen for the "mental discipline" they imposed. Like most educators of her day, Thomas believed that not all subjects trained the mind equally well; Greek, Latin, and mathematics were thought especially to sharpen the intellect. For years Bryn Mawr women culminated their studies with a dreaded oral examination, in Thomas's office, in sight translation. Difficulty was stimulating, Thomas said, if the stakes were worth it. Art and music were not initially included in the curriculum, a decision influenced by Quaker stricture and Thomas's determination to bar anything that betokened "women's sphere." "Practical courses" were exiled as well. Child study, domestic science, and teaching would dilute the quality of the curriculum; she believed it was Bryn Mawr's duty to transmit unimpaired "the precious intellectual heritage" she herself had won with such difficulty. In the cause of women, Thomas's initial efforts began with the individual, not with institutions, except insofar as Bryn Mawr might serve as a model. Well-educated, exceptional women (Bryn Mawr women) would break down barriers and inspire others to follow. In time her narrow, gradual approach to reform broadened to include suffrage and women workers' rights.

Thomas's decisions about student life were also predicated upon the elevation and protection of Bryn Mawr standards. The women were to be treated and to comport themselves like scholars, not schoolgirls. Unlike students at other women's colleges, they were excused from domestic chores. The life of the mind came first. Living in many other ways an ascetic campus life, the women were encouraged to exuberance in celebration of scholarship. They wore academic robes to class, designated intellectual topics for conversation at meals, and reveled in Lantern Night, when the light of learning was passed from sophomores to freshmen. They were free to come and go at will, and neither classes nor chapel was compulsory. The student Self-Government Association was the first in the country; it made and enforced the few rules necessary for community life. On the surface contradictory, Thomas's refusal to adopt an honor code was based not on suspicion of students but on an unwillingness to risk any question about the integrity of the women's work. As her administrative duties burgeoned, Thomas had scant time for personal relationships with students, and she led them, as she had done throughout her life, as a symbol of what a woman with brains and determination could achieve. In her chapel talks, replete with florid rhetoric, and in the Oxford-inspired campus she built, she enthusiastically conveyed the joy and beauty of the scholarly life.

Despite Thomas's clear vision, breaking new ground was not easy. University men like Harvard's president Charles Eliot believed the roles of men and women to be complementary, not equal, and he publicly predicted Bryn Mawr's failure. Although a few professional women colleagues, like Alice Freeman Palmer, president of Wellesley College, were her allies in the cause of women's higher education, few shared Thomas's approach (Freeman, for example, championed the educated wife and mother as woman's ideal); and Thomas, as always, was more then willing to go it alone. The measure of her struggle is reflected in her rhetoric, which often employed images of conflict. "As I watch [women students'] gallant struggles I sometimes think that the very stars in their courses are conspiring against them." "Pitfalls lie on all sides of us; controversies past and present darken the air; our path leads us thru hard-won battles." But Thomas gloried in combat, and her sharp tongue gave as good as she got. "Goldilocks," she announced in 1913, "has gone forever."[7]

In 1894, only after her longtime companion Mary Garrett offered Bryn Mawr $10,000 a year on the condition of Thomas's presidency, did the trustees elect Thomas as Rhoads's successor by a margin of one vote. It took eight more years before she was also elected a trustee, a post Rhoads had held concurrently without question. That little changed in college policy when she moved into the president's office attests to Thomas's original shaping force as dean. Recognized now as a national figure, she spent more time off campus successfully soliciting funds for the college endowment (by 1898 Bryn Mawr was one of only twenty-nine American colleges with an endowment of more than $1 million), building a powerful alumnae association, serving as the first woman trustee of Cornell, speaking for the cause of women's higher education (she was instrumental in opening up Johns Hopkins Medical School to women), and stumping for suffrage (the first women's college president to do so), but never keeping less than an eagle eye on every facet of Bryn Mawr.

Although she was accused by some of becoming more autocratic as time went by, Thomas could not be accused of ossification. After 1910 she loosened her grip on Bryn Mawr's scholarly isolation from the workaday world (and conceded that it was possible to combine a career with marriage) and introduced several socially relevant, even "practical" programs. The educationally progressive Thorne Model School, which offered graduate training in teaching; the graduate department of social economy and social research, which tied theory to social work practice; and the Summer School for Women Workers in Industry, a model liberal arts program for unschooled blue-collar workers, were Thomas's initiatives, often achieved over faculty objection that such programs would lessen Bryn Mawr's scholarly reputation. However, only twenty- five years after Bryn Mawr's founding, there was no longer any question about women's intellectual capacity. Now the focus could be shifted to the use they would make of their education.

Thomas retired from the presidency of Bryn Mawr in 1922. Always an inveterate traveler, an Anglophile with a passion for high nineteenth-century culture, she spent long periods in Europe, attempting along the way to write her memoirs, but the contemplative life had never engaged her passion. She was a competitor with a flair for the dramatic, a politician with the gift of inspiring others, an idealist with a broad pragmatic streak—above all, an active leader of women. Thomas died of heart failure December 2, 1935, a month after her final speech at Bryn Mawr celebrating the fiftieth anniversary of the college. At her request, her ashes were buried in the cloisters of the college library.

Thomas is criticized by some today for her elitism, separatism, and gradualism in the cause of women. Such views demand too much of her and judge her out of historical context. Thomas saw education as the fulcrum in women's lives; change in the fulcrum would affect all else. If women proved themselves men's intellectual equals, they were then deserving of equality in all arenas. If her educational philosophy, like that of W.E.B. Du Bois's "talented tenth," holds little currency in the late twentieth century, it is because extraordinary women and people of color, like Thomas and Du Bois themselves and the students they educated, opened the gates.

In 1991 the U.S. National Park Service designated the M. Carey Thomas Library at Bryn Mawr a national historic landmark. While the building is a fine example of the "collegiate Gothic" architectural style Thomas pioneered at Bryn Mawr, the official citation focuses on the library, with its aloof, cloistered, and soaring beauty, as a symbol of Thomas's achievements: opening up the highest reaches of scholarship to women, providing them with a respected and supportive avenue of approach, and heralding their cause along the way.

NOTES

1. Marjorie E. Dobkin, ed., *The Making of a Feminist: Early Journals and Letters of M. Carey Thomas* (Kent, OH: Kent State University Press, 1979), 44–45.
2. Ibid., 50.
3. Ibid., 93.
4. Ibid., 151.
5. Ibid., 209.
6. Virginia Gildersleeve, *Many a Good Crusade* (New York: Macmillan, 1954), 131.
7. M. Carey Thomas, "Present Tendencies in Women's College and University Education," *Educational Review* 35 (January 1908): 83; M. Carey Thomas, "Should the Higher Education of Women Differ from That of Men?" *Educational Review* 21 (January 1901): 1; Patricia H. Labalme, ed., *A Century Recalled: Essays in Honor of Bryn Mawr College* (Bryn Mawr, PA: Bryn Mawr College Library, 1987), 125.

WORKS BY MARTHA CAREY THOMAS

"The Bryn Mawr Woman: Notes for the Opening Address, 1899." In Barbara M. Cross, ed., *The Educated Woman: Selected Writings of Catharine Beecher, Margaret Fuller, and M. Carey Thomas.* New York: Teachers College Press, 1965.
"Education of Women." In Nicholas M. Butler, ed., *Education in the United States.* Albany, NY: J. B. Lyon, 1900.
"Should the Higher Education of Women Differ from That of Men?" *Educational Review* 21 (January 1901): 1–10.
"The College." *Educational Review* 29 (January 1905): 62–84.
"Present Tendencies in Women's College and University Education." *Educational Review* 35 (January 1908): 64–85.
"The Future of Woman's Higher Education." In *Mount Holyoke College: The Seventy-Fifth Anniversary.* Springfield, MA: Springfield Printing and Binding, 1913.

WORKS ABOUT MARTHA CAREY THOMAS

Dobkin, Marjorie H., ed. *The Making of a Feminist: Early Journals and Letters of M. Carey Thomas.* Kent, OH: Kent State University Press, 1979.
Finch, Edith. *Carey Thomas of Bryn Mawr.* New York: Harper, 1947.
Flexner, Helen T. *A Quaker Childhood.* New Haven, CT: Yale University Press, 1940.
Frankfort, Roberta. *Collegiate Women: Domesticity and Career in Turn-of-the-Century America.* New York: New York University Press, 1977.
Horowitz, Helen L. *Alma Mater: Design and Experience in the Women's Colleges from Their Nineteenth-Century Beginnings to the 1930s.* New York: Knopf, 1984.
Labalme, Patricia H., ed. *A Century Recalled: Essays in Honor of Bryn Mawr College.* Bryn Mawr, PA: Bryn Mawr College Library, 1987.

Meigs, Cornelia. *What Makes a College? A History of Bryn Mawr.* New York: Macmillan, 1956.

Veysey, Laurence R. "Thomas, Martha Carey." In Edward T. James, Janet W. James, and Paul S. Boyer, eds., *Notable American Women.* Vol. 3. Cambridge: Belknap Press of Harvard University Press, 1971.

Joyce Sachiko Tsunoda

Sucheng Chan

Joyce Sachiko Tsunoda (b. 1938) is a pioneer in higher education in the state of Hawaii as well as in the nation. As the first woman to become chancellor of community colleges in the University of Hawaii System, she is now the highest-ranking Asian-American woman administrator in institutions of higher learning in the United States. Even though Asian Americans are well known for their academic achievements at all levels of education—especially as research scientists and engineers—relatively few Asian Americans, men or women, have reached the higher echelons of college and university administration. A large majority of those who have become deans, provosts, chancellors, or presidents are serving in Hawaii and California. Among this handful of Asian-American top-level administrators, Tsunoda has had the second longest tenure, next only to Bob Suzuki, president of California Polytechnic University at Pomona.

Joyce Tsunoda was born on January 1, 1938, in Osaka, Japan. Her father, Yukio Nishimura (1910–1945), was a baseball player who twice visited Hawaii with his college baseball team to play exhibition matches. Tsunoda's mother, Edith Sueko Higashi (b. 1911), is a nisei (a second-generation Japanese American), who met her future husband while serving on Hawaii's local welcoming and hospitality committee for those exhibition matches. When Yukio Nishimura proposed to her during his second visit, she said yes. She left Hawaii to be married in Japan, where her husband had already become a popular star athlete. He was the ace pitcher for the Hanshin Tigers, Japan's equivalent of the Dodgers.

Four children were born of this union, all girls. Joyce, whose Japanese middle name, Sachiko, means "child of happiness," was the oldest. In the early 1930s, when Japan's armies marched into Manchuria—a region rich in natural resources located in northeastern China—and occupied it, many Japanese civilians followed in the army's wake. They set up businesses and built roads, bridges, railroads, and telephone and telegraph lines, in order to better exploit the region's resources and to control the Chinese and Manchu populations living there. Tsunoda's father, who by then was employed by the Japanese Telephone and Telegraph Company, was one of the civilians sent to work in Japan's new informal empire on the Chinese mainland. His two younger children were born there. He was declared missing in action and presumed dead during World War II.

When Joyce was ten years old, her widowed mother decided to move the family back to her native Hawaii. Given her father's fame, the family's return was noted in two newspapers—the *Hawaii Herald* and the *Honolulu Star Bulletin* on May 7, 1948. The latter carried a front-page article on the event: "Home again after 11 years: Mrs. Sueko Nishimura and her four daughters among 1,443 on *General Gordon* inbound from Orient trip." They settled on the island of Oahu, where Joyce attended Haleiwa Elementary School. She does not recall any difficulties in adjusting to life in Hawaii, as her mother had all along raised her children according to American values and norms. Joyce did so well in school that she was allowed to skip the eighth grade. To earn pocket money for herself as well as to help her mother support the family, she took baby-sitting and housekeeping jobs throughout her junior high and high school years.

In her senior year at Leilehua High School, she won a prestigious Bausch and Lomb National Science Award and the graduating class's Physics and Activities awards. Her achievements were noted in the local press when she graduated from high school in June 1956. The *Hawaii Hochi* carried a story, "Overcoming Difficulties: Immigrant Girl Graduates as High School Valedictorian," while the *Honolulu Advertiser* had one entitled "Joyce Nishimura Finds That Dreams Come True." She received the Leilehua Alumni Scholarship, which, along with an Elks National Scholarship, helped finance her freshman year at the University of Hawaii, where she enrolled in the Teachers' College of Education with the aim of becoming a mathematics and science teacher.

In her sophomore year in college, due to a schedule conflict, Joyce sought permission to delay taking a required education course in order to enroll in an organic chemistry course. Her adviser denied her request. When she started arguing with him, he told her she should leave the College of Education if she preferred chemistry to education. Unintimidated, Joyce promptly transferred to the College of Letters and Science. This, as she recalls today with a chuckle, was her "first rebellion." Her three uncles, who felt an obligation to keep an eye on their four fatherless nieces, lectured her sternly about her "foolish decision." They told her there were no jobs for women in chemistry. But Joyce was not to be deterred.

Tsunoda's chemistry professor, who strongly supported her decision, recommended her for the Rama Watumull Memorial Scholarship, which she held from 1957 to 1959. Her senior year in college was supported by a

Scholarship for the Outstanding Senior in Chemistry, a Sigma Xi Undergraduate Research Award, and a National Science Foundation Undergraduate Research Fellowship. She graduated Phi Beta Kappa and cum laude in 1960, winning the O. C. Magistad Award of the American Chemical Society for Outstanding Chemistry Graduate.

Her graduate studies were supported by a four-year predoctoral fellowship from the National Science Foundation. Her first research publication appeared during her second year in graduate school. She received her Ph.D. in biochemistry in 1966 from the University of Hawaii. She then worked as a research associate in the department of biochemistry and biophysics in the School of Medicine at the University of Hawaii for two years with postdoctoral fellowships from the National Science Foundation and the National Institute of Health. Her research resulted in publications in *Biochemistry and Biophysics Research Communications*, *Archives of Biochemistry and Biophysics*, and *Journal of Biological Chemistry*.

A member of her dissertation committee, Leonard Tuthill, called her one day to ask her to help him start a chemistry program at the newly founded Leeward Community College. After mulling the offer over, Tsunoda accepted it. She taught at that institution for four years. As she recalls, that job was a "real challenge," because, as "open-door" campuses, Hawaii's community colleges, like those in other states, draw students with widely divergent levels of academic preparation.[1] The students in her freshman chemistry classes ranged from those who did not know the difference between a numerator and a denominator to those who had taken excellent high school chemistry courses.

At Leeward Community College, Tsunoda first discovered her penchant for administrative work and for campus politics. She served as cochair and chair of the Faculty Senate (1969–1970 and 1970–1972, respectively) and acted as convenor of the Community Colleges Faculty Senate from 1970 to 1972. In those years, she realized that "who you know matters as much as what you know."

Others, too, noticed her political skills. In 1973, the provost of Leeward Community College and the president of the University of Hawaii jointly nominated her for an American Council on Education Administrative Internship, which offers training to faculty who evince a potential for filling administrative positions. Tsunoda became the first individual from Hawaii to hold such an internship. She served this apprenticeship primarily in the office of the president at the University of Hawaii, but she also had an opportunity to spend time at universities in different parts of the U.S. mainland, stretching from Cornell University in the East to the University of Oregon in the West. One of the projects she worked on during this year was a proposal that eventually helped establish the 1202 Postsecondary Education Commission for Hawaii.

At this juncture, Tsunoda realized she had come to a fork in the road in her career development. Did she want to continue as a faculty and research scientist, or did she want to become an administrator? She chose the latter and accepted an offer as associate dean of community services and special programs at Leeward Community College. She served in this capacity for two years, raising more than $2 million from both state and federal sources to start a brand new theater, among other things. In this job, she paid particular attention to continuing education and off-campus programs and set up guidelines for the use of the college's facilities by the public.

In April 1976, Tsunoda became provost of Kapiolani Community College—only the second woman to head a community college in the history of the state. At that time, Kapiolani Community College was housed in two locations five miles apart in downtown Honolulu. One of her main tasks was to plan for the development of a new campus. This project proved far more challenging than expected. People who lived in the neighborhood of the fifty-two-acre site at the foot of Diamond Head (Honolulu's much photographed landmark) chosen for the new campus began objecting strenuously to the potential increase in human and automobile traffic.

It took all of Tsunoda's public relations skills over a period of seven years to persuade the public to accept the campus's existence. She skillfully used the community's concerns to advantage: she won approval for an architectural design that created what is probably the most environmentally tasteful and lovely campus in Hawaii's system of public higher education. Tsunoda credits Patricia Saiki, the most influential Republican, Asian-American woman politician in Hawaii, with helping her to win legislative approval for the more expensive design. Today, those who had opposed the project most fiercely are among the institution's staunchest supporters. During this period, Tsunoda also served for seven months in 1982 as acting assistant vice president for academic affairs in the University of Hawaii System and from time to time as acting chancellor for community colleges whenever the incumbent was out of town.

On January 14, 1983, the same day that she turned the first shovel of dirt for the construction of the new buildings on the Kapiolani Community College campus, Tsunoda was named chancellor of the entire community college system in the state of Hawaii—seven campuses enrolling over 20,000 regular, credit students and some 50,000 noncredit students a year.

In her years as an administrator, five ideas have served as Tsunoda's guiding philosophy. First, she says, "We should never forget we are here to serve the community, but we are not simply the public's servants but also its educators." As such, faculty, administrators, and staff members in colleges and universities bear a responsibility for presenting the pros and cons of various proposals, so that the public can make informed choices. This belief apparently rose out of her experiences in winning public approval for the Kapiolani campus.

Second, Tsunoda is completely "dedicated to the open-door philosophy of education." She thinks of the community colleges as "quintessentially American" institutions. She frequently quotes John F. Kennedy, who said that even though not everyone has equal talents, each individual in American society has the right to develop his or her talents to the fullest. The community colleges are one of the main vehicles available for people from all kinds of backgrounds to gain the skills to realize their potentials, Tsunoda declares.

Third, she believes it is important to spread this philosophy of education beyond the borders of the United States—particularly to nations in Asia and the Pacific Basin, with which the United States is interacting with increasing frequency and in ever more complex ways in the realms of trade, culture, politics, and trans-Pacific migrations. When she retires, Tsunoda hopes to become "an education ambassador," traveling to as many countries as possible to spread the community college model and particularly its spirit.

Fourth, she thinks that some of the difficulties that many women professionals experience are, at least in part, of their own making. What she means is that too many women think they have to be superwomen: they feel compelled to perform well both in their traditional roles as "good" daughters, wives, and mothers, and in their careers. She herself has survived because she learned long ago to say to herself, "I can't do everything—something has to go." In retrospect, she says, this private "fight with herself" has been far more difficult than any public battles in which she has been engaged.

When Tsunoda says "something has to go," she does not mean that she has given up any particular set of activities in its entirety. Rather, within each sphere of her life, she has learned not to worry about all the details all of the time. At home, she had to force herself to stop feeling guilty about not keeping her house "spic and span," even though as a Japanese-American woman, she was brought up to be a meticulous homemaker and had earned her way through school partly by cleaning other people's houses. She says she is still a neat person, but whenever she feels like going shopping instead of cleaning her house, she can now do so without feeling bad at all. That, she admits, took years to learn, given her socialization.

Her ability not to worry about all the details at work, in comparison, came more easily. Quite early in her career, she learned to delegate responsibility—"to let other people take care of such details as giving out the keys," as she puts it. Until she became an associate dean, however, there were not too many people to whom she could delegate responsibility. But as she rose in the ranks, delegating became a real necessity. Nowadays, as chancellor, she fully trusts the provost of each community college to run his or her own campus. Even in those instances when she thinks her direct participation or personal intervention might solve a problem more quickly, she resists the temptation to micromanage the affairs of the colleges within the system. What has given her enormous satisfaction is that in each position she has held, she has built an administrative team whose members share the common goal of serving the community as effectively as possible. She is also known for her excellent relations with the faculty. The ability to communicate clearly about goals and procedures, she observes—whether to fellow administrators, staff, faculty, students, or the public—is a critical aspect of teamwork.

Finally, Tsunoda says that individuals in positions of responsibility must have a sense of humor. In particular, they should be able to laugh at themselves. Those who are too serious become vulnerable to "burnout," feeling upset at every criticism or failure. As a corollary, she also thinks it is important for busy women to be "good to themselves." She believes that women tend to "punish themselves too much." Compared with men, they do not seem to pat themselves or other women on the back often enough. Women who aspire to climb up the career ladder should not be surprised that they will have to work harder than their male peers—all the more reason they must treat themselves well. Tsunoda does not consider herself a feminist per se, in the sense of marching in demonstrations in support of various women's issues, but she does try her best to support other women in various ways.

As for discrimination, Tsunoda has encountered relatively little, operating as she has done in Hawaii—a state where Asian Americans are in the majority. Once in a while, though, men have said to her, "You're a machine." She reports that they always say this jokingly, but their sarcasm is not lost on her. As she becomes more active and visible in the national and international arenas, however, she has begun to notice some "differential treatment" of her as an Asian American and as a woman.

Tsunoda's busy life is indeed a phenomenon to behold, for, in addition to her "regular" administrative duties, she has taken on an enormous range of public responsibilities. At the national level, she is currently a member of the Northwest Association of Schools and Colleges Accrediting Commission, the Commission on the Future of Community Colleges of the American Association of Community and Junior Colleges, the American Council on Education's Advisory Committee on Undergraduate Education in Foreign Languages and International Studies, the Pacific Postsecondary Education Commission, the Western Association of Schools and Colleges' Appeals Hearing Board Panel, and the Pacific Regional Education Program's Policy Advisory Council. At present, she is also chair of the American Council on International and Intercultural Education.

Tsunoda's past involvements in national educational organizations include service on the boards of directors of the American Council on Education (1982–1986), the National Center for Higher Education Management Systems (NCHEMS) and its subsidiary, NCHEMS Management Services, Inc. (1979–1986), the National Council of Community Services and Continuing Education's executive committee (1979–1980), and the Advisory Council on Developing Institutions of the U.S. Office of Education.

Tsunoda's public service in Hawaii include past and present membership on the boards of directors of more than two dozen groups that range from schools to civic clubs to community theaters to "cultural garden parks" to professional organizations. Many of these associations, such as the Honolulu Manpower Planning Council, the Year 2000 Task Force on [Hawaii's] Economic Futures, the Pearl City [the town where Tsunoda lives] Community Association, the Momilani Community Association, the Waianae-Nanakuli Model Cities Education Task Force, and the Waipahu Advocates for the Elderly Advisory Committee, are dedicated to promoting the economic and social well-being of local citizens. At present, she is involved with Historic Hawaii, a group dedicated to preserving Hawaii's multiethnic and multicultural heritage, the Hawaii Tourism Council, devoted to promoting Hawaii's number one income earner, the Honolulu Committee on Foreign Relations, which educates its members and the public on contemporary foreign affairs, the International Women's Forum, the Rotary Club, the Young Women's Christian Association (YWCA), and the Kaimuki Businessmen and Professional Association, among others.

These contributions to higher education and to the commonweal have been recognized. In 1983, the *Honolulu Star Bulletin* selected her as one of nine individuals dubbed "Stars for the '80s in Education." The following year, she was one of four women chosen as "1984 Hawaii Headliners" by Women in Communications, Inc. Two honors were bestowed on her in 1988: the Outstanding Award in Public/Private Partnership, given by the Organization of Women Leaders, and the Person of the Year Award, given by the Western Region of the National Council of Community Service Directors. The University of Hawaii Alumni Association honored her with its 1990 Outstanding Community Service Award, while the YWCA of Oahu gave her its 1990 Outstanding Individual Achievement Award in Education.

How does Tsunoda manage her time and juggle her myriad responsibilities so that she not only does so many things but does each of them well? Quite apart from her philosophy—that she cannot do everything and that some things "have to go"—she gives most of the credit to her family. Through the years, her mother has lived with Tsunoda's family and helped to raise her children and take care of housework. Her husband, Peter T. Tsunoda, a public accountant whom Joyce married six weeks after graduating from college, has likewise shared in all aspects of parenting. Enormously proud of her achievements, he long ago learned to adapt their family's schedule to her busy calendar. The *Hawaii Hochi*, in a front page story on February 10, 1983, noted the contributions of her mother and her husband in a story entitled, "Joyce Tsunoda Reaches Her Success Today—with Help from Husband and Mother."

Tsunoda's two daughters, Sharon Sayuri and Brenda Yukari, grew up as active, well-adjusted, high-achieving youngsters. Sharon went to Japan to study the Japanese language at Waseda University and remained there when she married an orthopedic surgeon. She gave Tsunoda her first set of grandchildren, a boy, followed two years later by a girl. Brenda studied biological anthropology at Harvard University on a scholarship, received a master's degree in public health from Yale University, and now does research at a cancer research center. From a subjective perspective, in summing up her life up to this point, Tsunoda states unequivocally, "I am more proud of having raised two girls to be independent, self-sufficient women who also happen to be happily married than of anything else I've done."

Objectively, Tsunoda's greatest achievement has been her ability to work with many different kinds of people to overcome problems, meet challenges, and get things done in a highly politicized setting. Like any other system of public higher education, that in Hawaii is dependent on state funding. The community colleges in Hawaii are part of the University of Hawaii System, whose headquarters are located only several miles from the state capital in Honolulu. This physical proximity, as well as the fact that Hawaii is a relatively small state, where the leaders in various walks of life have many opportunities to interact socially, allows the state's politicians to be more aware of, and more involved in, the affairs of the university than their counterparts elsewhere can be. Furthermore, unlike the situation in most states, where usually only the president and chancellors and their staff deal with the legislators, in Hawaii deans and even individual department chairs are often called upon to appear in person on short notice at legislative hearings to explain and justify their budgetary requests and academic programs. In such an environment, only those administrators who understand the subtle nuances of power—how it is distributed, exercised, challenged, compromised, and counterbalanced—manage to survive and succeed. Joyce Tsunoda has not only survived but risen steadily in the ranks, in the process winning an increasing number of friends and admirers.

NOTE

1. Personal information and quotations by Joyce Tsunoda are from two interviews with Tsunoda, August 22, 1991, and September 12, 1992.

WORKS BY JOYCE SACHIKO TSUNODA

"Effect of Diisoprophylfluorophosphonate of Papain, Chymopapain and Bromelain" (with M. Ebata and K. T. Yasunobu). *Biochemistry and Biophysics Research Communications* 9 (1962): 1973.
"Amino Acid Sequence Around the Reactive Thiol Group of Chymopapain" (with K. T. Yasunobu). *Journal of Biological Chemistry* 241 (1966): 4610–15.
"Changes in the Conformation of Chymopapain During Activation" (with M. Ebata and K. T. Yasunobu). *Biochemistry and Biophysics Research Communications* 22 (1966): 455.
"The Amino Acid Sequence of Ferredoxin from *Micrococcus Aerogenes*" (with K. T.

Yasunobu and H. R. Whiteley). *Journal of Biological Chemistry* 243 (1968): 6362.

"Mammalian Lipic Acid Activating Enzyme" (with K. T. Yasunobu). *Archives of Biochemistry and Biophysics* 118 (1969): 395.

"Conducting Community Needs Assessments" (with G. Warfel). Working Paper for the National Council on Community Services and Continuing Education, 1978.

"Hawaii's Community College, Hui Kukakuka." In Richard J. Brass, ed., *Community Colleges: The Future and Staff, Program, and Organizational Development.* Stillwater, OK: New Forums Press, 1984.

"International Education Is Not a Luxury." Guest editorial, *Journal of Community, Technical and Junior Colleges* 59, no. 3 (December–January 1988–1989): 63.

WORKS ABOUT JOYCE SACHIKO TSUNODA

"Chancellor Named for College System." *Honolulu Star Bulletin*, July 20, 1983.

"Distinguished Alumna: Joyce Tsunoda." *Manoa*, Fall 1991.

"Dr. Joyce Tsunoda: Can a Chemist Find Happiness as an Educator?" *Hawaii Herald*, May 1, 1987.

"Joyce Tsunoda: From Hard Times to Chancellor." *Honolulu Advertiser*, July 24, 1983.

"New Provost Is a 'Down to Earth' Person." *Kapi'o* (Kapiolani Community College Newspaper), May 11, 1976.

"The Role of Community Colleges." *Honolulu Star Bulletin*, May 7, 1987.

"Stars of the '80s—Education." *Honolulu Star Bulletin*, February 22, 1983.

"Woman Proposed as New Provost." *Honolulu Star Bulletin*, March 19, 1976.

Julia Strudwick Tutwiler

Marcia G. Synnott

Julia Strudwick Tutwiler (1841–1916), educator, college president, prison reformer, and writer, challenged the conventional behavior prescribed for southern women. A skillful lobbyist for her causes, she made public speeches, met with boards of trustees, visited jails and prisons, traveled alone, and acted independently without incurring social criticism. Tutwiler "did much to free other women from the prejudices of the day," wrote Clara L. Pitts, an early biographer, and, "by being an 'old maid' without seeming to feel the disgrace, she made life much easier for other unmarried women."[1] Instead of being pitied as a spinster, she was admired as an educational pioneer who taught young white women to become economically independent. On the other hand, she did not campaign for the educational and economic advancement of African Americans. As a paternalist, she deplored their mistreatment but believed that racial segregation was an educational and social necessity. Thus, her class and race, like her gender, circumscribed the role she could play as an educator and social reformer in the post-Reconstruction South.

Born August 15, 1841, in Tuscaloosa, Alabama, Julia Tutwiler was the third daughter and third of eleven children of Henry and Julia (Ashe) Tutwiler. Her father, whose ancestors emigrated from German-speaking Switzerland to Pennsylvania and then settled in Virginia, entered the first class of the University of Virginia in 1825, where he studied mathematics and classics for four years and then law for a fifth year; he received the university's first master of arts degree. In 1831, Tutwiler moved to the newly opened University of Alabama, where he was chair of ancient languages. On December 24, 1835, he married Julia Ashe, whose father, Pascal Paoli Ashe, had moved from North Carolina to become steward of the University of Alabama. Tutwiler resigned in 1837 with the rest of the dissatisfied faculty and taught at several small Alabama colleges before establishing in 1847 the Greene

Springs School for Boys near Havana, Alabama, where he remained until his death in 1884. The school, once called the "Rugby of the South," maintained high academic standards in classics, mathematics, and the sciences and respected students as individuals, placing them in classes according to their preparation. Dr. Tutwiler also believed in equal educational opportunities for girls.

From an early age, Julia Tutwiler learned to act as an intellectual equal with males. She first applied what she had learned by teaching some of the twenty slaves owned by her father. At sixteen, having received the approximate equivalent of two years of college work, she was sent to Philadelphia, where she attended Madame Maroteau's French boarding school. She spent the Civil War years teaching at the Greene Springs School, since her father, an antisecessionist Whig, would not allow her to be a nurse. Afterward, she returned to Philadelphia to sell the property that her father owned and used the proceeds to attend the newly opened Vassar College in January 1866. Although she taught some French and German classes that spring, her funds were insufficient to enable her to return the following fall. In 1866–1867, she taught and served as assistant principal at Greensboro Academy in Alabama; appointed principal in 1867, she was joined by another woman as coprincipal in 1868. Because of the school's run-down condition, both women resigned in 1869. Tutwiler again assisted her father at Greene Springs. In 1872–1873, she studied Latin and Greek privately with a professor at Washington and Lee College in Lexington, Virginia, where one of her brothers was then enrolled; she also obtained a teaching certificate.

In the summer of 1873, she and her brother went on a European tour, during which she sought admission to the Deaconesses' Institute at Kaisersworth, located on the Rhine River near Düsseldorf, Germany, where Lutheran sisters operated a hospital and a normal school. The curriculum emphasized the German language, literature, hymnology, geography, basic arithmetic, pedagogy, and sewing and housewifery. During the next two years, she lived in Berlin and attended lectures; and, after passing two examinations, she received the normal school teacher's certificate from the Prussian Board of Education. To help support herself, she taught in a small German boarding school and wrote three children's stories and articles for *St. Nicholas Magazine* (1875–1876) and two articles for *Appleton's Journal* (1876). After returning to Alabama, she taught modern languages and English literature from 1876 to 1881 at the Methodist-affiliated Tuscaloosa Female College, whose president, Dr. Alonzo Hill, had worked with Dr. Tutwiler at Greene Springs. In 1878, she took a leave of absence to report for the *National Journal of Education* on the Paris Exposition. She also wrote on French trade schools for women.

In 1879–1880, Tutwiler launched her great crusade, which she called "her vocation," for jail and prison reform by organizing the Tuscaloosa Benevolent Association. The questionnaires it distributed to all county jails led to an 1880 act to correct their unheated and unsanitary conditions. Buoyed by "faith in the old-time Whig vision of politics" that change could be effected by educated men and women appealing to decency and reason, she and some of her students visited prisons on weekends, conducting religious services and providing Bibles for inmates. She developed strong ties with Alabama clubwomen, among them the Woman's Christian Temperance Union, which she joined in 1884. Appointed its superintendent of prison work, she campaigned, assisted by a free railroad pass, for the following reforms: state funding for night school and Sunday school teachers in prisons at the coal mines (1887); the assignment of women to separate prisons (1888–1889); the classification of prisoners by age, which resulted in establishing the Alabama Boys' Industrial School, the South's first juvenile reform school for white boys (1890); a law appointing a state prison inspector; and abolition of the system of leasing convicts, most of whom were black. Called "the Angel of the Stockade," she achieved all of these reforms except ending the convict lease system, which continued until 1928. Since black and white inmates were taught separately, she offered to assist Booker T. Washington in establishing a reform school for black boys; but not until 1911 did Alabama open the Reform and Industrial School for Negro Boys. The Julia Tutwiler Prison for Women at Wetumpka acknowledged her work.[2]

In the fall of 1881, she was appointed coprincipal with Dr. Carlos G. Smith, her maternal uncle and former president of the University of Alabama, of the Livingston, Alabama, Female Academy (incorporated January 15, 1840). In 1883, as a result of her advocacy, among that of others, the Alabama legislature established the Alabama Normal College for Girls (incorporated February 22, 1883) at the Livingston Female Academy. The two schools subsequently were consolidated into the Livingston Normal College (now Livingston State University). In exchange for free tuition, normal students agreed to teach for two years in the state's public schools. This was the first appropriation—$2,000 for tuition for fifty pupils and $500 for school appliances—given by Alabama only to women.

In 1890, Tutwiler was elected president of Livingston Normal College. Assisted by eight teachers, all of whom were women, "Miss Jule," as students called her in affectionate respect, taught literature, German, mental and moral philosophy, and normal methods, usually without a textbook. Students remembered her well-modulated voice and piercing gray eyes and the way she maintained a quiet, but absolute authority, while holding their interest by dramatizing lessons. Because Tutwiler thought that it would be deceiving the students and the public for the Normal College to offer a degree, students could earn either teacher certification after a two-year course or a diploma after four years of study. She taught them German pedagogical methods in a kindergarten department that she established for the town's preschool children. Students were also required to take physiology and were taught secretarial skills and sewing, dress cutting, and fitting, so that they could live on a teacher's salary. The uniformed students regularly received Bible instruction, attended morning and evening religious exercises, and, on Sunday, were escorted to a church of their parents' or their own choice. Between 1883 and 1904, 210 students graduated from the normal school and 73 from the literary department.[3]

Before the establishment of a State Board of Examiners in 1899–1900, Tutwiler had proposed uniform teacher certification standards but warned in a paper, "Defects of the State Examination Law and the Remedy Proposed," that teachers needed to know more for a first grade certificate than just the necessary texts to pass examinations in twelve subjects; they also needed "that indefinable essence called 'culture,' which should vivify all they have learned." To obtain a professional certificate for life, the teacher would prepare, through correspondence schools at state colleges and universities, for an additional examination in each of eight subjects. Those holding life certificates should be qualified to enter, without examination, the senior class of Alabama Polytechnic Institute at Auburn. Yet because of weak preparatory education, most normal students were taught on the secondary level. In 1908, Livingston Normal College joined two other normal schools and five colleges in founding the Association of Alabama Colleges, which pledged to adopt college admission requirements based on the fourteen Carnegie units of secondary school work, a move Tutwiler favored.[4]

Tutwiler's progressive educational theories guided instruction at Livingston Normal College: every student was treated as an individual and encouraged to seek knowledge for its own sake; a broad experience was educationally valuable (classroom lessons were supplemented by visual aids and field trips); lessons should be organized and connected systematically to show the unity of knowledge; children and teachers needed to develop broad, cultural knowledge; each individual should be economically independent and trained to help others; and educating character was of crucial importance. In recognition of her work, the National Education Association elected her in 1884 to a two-year term as a national "counsellor" or member of the Board of Directors; in 1891, she was elected president of its department of elementary education and a member of the Board of Directors.

Influenced by her experiences at Kaisersworth and her visits to the *Ecoles Professionelles* of Paris, Tutwiler consistently argued that the surplus of women caused by the Civil War and westward expansion necessitated that southern women become self-supporting. In the 1882 *National Journal of Education*, she published her paper on "The Technical Education of Women," which, in 1880, for decorum's sake, the superintendent of education had presented on her behalf to the Alabama Education Association. While acknowledging that a woman's true sphere and vocation were in her home, she urged the establishment of federally and state-funded schools, modeled on the French trade school program, in which women could learn one or more of ten handicrafts and receive a general literary and cultural education. She also suggested both apprenticeships in handicrafts for young women and institutes for adult women.

In 1888, three years after Mississippi established an Industrial Institute and College for Girls, Tutwiler again advocated industrial education for white girls when she herself presented a paper to the Alabama Education Association. Supported by women's clubs and agricultural groups, she wrote letters and lobbied and was influential in persuading some legislators to support the 1893 bill that Sol D. Block independently sponsored authorizing a grant for the Alabama Girls Industrial School, which opened at Montevallo in October 1896. She was offered the presidency of the school, which later evolved into Alabama College (now the University of Montevallo), at $1,200 per year salary. Preferring to continue as president of the Alabama Normal College, she declined; the man accepting the offer received $2,000 per year.

Tutwiler's next educational campaign opened to qualified white women the University of Alabama, an institution whose presidency her father had twice declined. After reading the university's original grant from the U.S. government, which specified that it was for the education of the state's "youth," she carefully prepared the groundwork by writing numerous letters and meeting with influential people, including a governor. When she appeared in person before the University of Alabama's trustees on June 28, 1892, the men were initially amused by the presence of the first woman before the board. But, impressed by her "strong and eloquent appeal," they took seriously her petition "that the doors of the University be thrown open to Females." The committee on instruction, rules, and regulations, to which it was referred, decided unanimously in her favor. However, she protected the girls' colleges from competition for their freshmen by persuading the trustees to restrict admission to the sophomore and higher classes to "young women of not less than eighteen years of age of good character and antecedents who are able to stand the necessary examinations . . . provided that suitable homes and protection have been provided for them."[5]

The first two women that the university admitted had studied at the Alabama Normal College; they enrolled as special students seeking a certificate of proficiency. Between 1896 and 1899, the number of women enrolled in the academic department, including freshmen admitted in 1897, rose from five among 131 students to twenty-six among 180. To accommodate female students, the Board of Trustees established in 1898 the Julia S. Tutwiler Annex, a cooperative dormitory on campus. Tutwiler's students soon won honors: in 1900, one of her graduates earned the A.B. degree, with the only honor awarded to the senior class; another was chosen to read a thesis at commencement; and two were the first women to receive fellowships and earn master's degrees, an A.M. in 1901 and an M.S. in 1904. In 1899, the University of Alabama added Livingston Normal College to its list of University Auxiliary Schools, whose graduates could be admitted by certificate and without examination. The University of Alabama honored Tutwiler by an LL.D. in 1907, by a plaque and the Julia Strudwick Tutwiler Scholarships, and, in 1915, by Julia Tutwiler Hall, its first large, women's dormitory.

For years, Livingston Normal College operated quite efficiently because of a strong faculty and an efficient secretary and business manager, while Tutwiler, who was often "so utterly oblivious" of time and "the practical side of life," pursued her various campaigns. However, after the Normal College came under complete state control in 1907, Tutwiler found her sometimes casual business practices of putting her own money into the college account to pay for its expenses criticized by the trustees appointed by the governor. In 1907, George W. Brock was appointed business manager and chair of ancient languages and mathematics. On April 18, 1907, Tutwiler wrote Governor B. B. Comer that her brother-in-law had predicted that her efforts "created here something far too good for a woman, and that some man will now kick me out." She asked permission to finish her plans "to make of every student who leaves the school a missionary of Christianity and culture." But Tutwiler's impulsiveness, strong moral convictions, and inexperience working with nonfamily members made it difficult for her to become part of the educational system mandated by the Alabama constitution of 1901. Her personal style had come into conflict with the realities of the South's gender and political conventions.[6]

In 1910, Tutwiler was retired and designated Alabama's first president emeritus, promised a salary of $100 a month, and honored by a portrait. Brock, who was then appointed president, soon made enemies among Miss Jule's devoted supporters. He criticized not only what he saw as Tutwiler's uncomplimentary traits—lack of forgiveness, desire to dominate others, carelessness in keeping records, and untidiness in personal appearance—but also the college's lack of an administration classroom building and comfortable and sanitary student housing. On the other hand, Tutwiler had spent her own money on the residential cottages, whose limited conveniences paralleled those of most of the local homes, and had generously loaned money to students unable to pay the annual charges ($108 in 1903–1904). Brock also was blamed for approving the termination of Miss Jule's salary after one year, the disappearance of her portrait (replaced by another one in 1937), and the deletion of any reference to her work in his reports. Tutwiler was unable to secure a retirement allowance from the Carnegie Foundation. However, Alabama clubwomen and several prominent men rallied behind her, honoring her by portraits, plaques, endowed scholarships, markers, and newspaper and magazine articles. On September 14, 1915, the state legislature approved a joint resolution expressing sympathy for her illness from cancer and recognizing her as a teacher and a humanitarian.

Tutwiler also actively participated in religious organizations, attended cultural congresses, and wrote poetry. Brought up a Presbyterian, she preferred the Episcopalian liturgy but joined local churches while president of Livingston. One of the first members of the Chautauqua Assembly, she became a faculty member in 1885 of this adult educational movement at Monteagle, Tennessee, where she built a house and several cottages. In the summer of 1893, she attended three cultural congresses at the Columbian World's Fair in Chicago: Congress of Representative Women of the World, the International Historical Congress of Charities and Corrections (secretary for Alabama), and the International Congress of Education (an honorary vice president). She also read an article at an assembly in the Women's Building and was appointed a judge for the World's Fair Department of Liberal Arts. Her poetry and songs celebrated anniversaries, organizations, and festivals. For example, she wrote "The Star-Spangled Banner of Peace" for the International Peace Association. Other poems included "Dixie Now," "The Southern Yankee Doodle," "When Laurels Bloom," in honor of Commodore Matthew Fontaine Maury, and "Duty," written for the Robert E. Lee Centennial. Her poem "Alabama," which was adopted as the state song in 1931, had been written in Germany in 1873 and celebrated her state's landscape, natural resources, and people.

On March 24, 1916, Tutwiler died of cancer in Birmingham. Her ashes were buried in the family plot in the Greene Springs Cemetery. Her property, worth some $15,000 by 1926, was left to the "Girls of Alabama" through a scholarship loan fund. In recognition of her thirty-two years of service, the Woman's Christian Temperance Union donated to each prison a shelf of textbooks and the administration and classroom building at Livingston Normal College was renamed Julia Tutwiler Hall. Called "Alabama's First Citizen," she was one of the first eleven inductees into the Alabama Hall of Fame in 1953; and in 1970 she was one of the first three inducted into the Women's Hall of Fame at Judson College.

NOTES

1. Clara L. Pitts, "Julia Strudwick Tutwiler," Ed.D. diss., George Washington University, 1942, 241–44.

2. Paul M. Pruitt, Jr., "Julia S. Tutwiler: Years of Experience," Part Two, *Alabama Heritage*, no. 23 (Winter 1992): 35, 33, 38–39; Pitts, 223.

3. Lucille Skinner Powell, quoted in Pitts, 112–13; Tutwiler, quoted in Pitts, 111.

4. [Julia S. Tutwiler], "Defects of the State Examination Law and the Remedy Proposed," undated, *Notes and Papers*, Tutwiler Collection, W. Stanley Hoole Special Collections Library, University of Alabama, Tuscaloosa.

5. Julia S. Tutwiler, "How the Girls of Alabama Pushed Open the Doors of the State University, *Some Ancient History*," Tutwiler Collection, Hoole Special Collections Library; Minutes of the Board of Trustees of the University of Alabama, June 28, 29, 30, 1892, University Archives.

6. Lucille Skinner Powell, quoted in Pitts, 114; Pitts, 248–50; Tutwiler, quoted in Anne Gary Pannell and Dorothea E. Wyatt, *Julia S. Tutwiler and Social Progress in Alabama* (University: University of Alabama Press, 1961), 90.

WORKS BY JULIA STRUDWICK TUTWILER

The Henry and Julia Strudwick Tutwiler Collection of manuscript and printed materials is in the William Stanley Hoole Special Collections Library at the University of Alabama in Tuscaloosa. There also is a Tutwiler Collection in the Alabama Department of Archives and History in Montgomery.

"The Charities of Paris: What One Woman Can Do." *The Churchman* 39 (1879): 240–41.

"The Technical Education of Women." *National Journal of Education* 3 (November 1882): 201–7.

"Our Brothers in Stripes." *National Educational Association Journal of Proceedings and Addresses, 1890.* Topeka, 1890.

"Coeducation and Character." *Papers and Proceedings,* Tenth Annual Session of the Alabama Education Association, July 1–3, 1891, privately printed; Washington, DC: Library of the U.S. Office of Education, Federal Security Administration.

"A Year in a German Model School." *National Educational Association Journal of Proceedings and Addresses, 1891.* New York, 1891. (Also read at the 1891 annual meeting of the NEA in Toronto.)

"Individualization by Grouping." *National Educational Association Journal of Proceedings and Addresses, 1892.* New York: National Education Association, 1893.

WORKS ABOUT JULIA STRUDWICK TUTWILER

James, Edward T., Janet Wilson James, and Paul S. Boyer, eds. *Notable American Women: A Biographical Dictionary.* Vol. 3. Cambridge: Belknap Press of Harvard University Press, 1971. S.v. "Julia Strudwick Tutwiler," by Dorothea E. Wyatt.

Malone, Dumas, ed. *Dictionary of American Biography.* Vol. 10. New York: Charles Scribner's Sons, 1936. S.v. "Julia Strudwick Tutwiler," by Hallie Farmer, "Henry Tutwiler," by Hallie Farmer.

Moore, Eoline Wallace. "Julia Tutwiler: Teacher." *Birmingham-Southern College Bulletin* 27 (January 1934): 3–35.

Owen, Marie Bankhead. *Our State—Alabama.* Compiled by Marie Bankhead Owen from the four-volume historical work written by her husband, Thomas M. Owen, *History of Alabama and Dictionary of Alabama Biography.* Montgomery, AL: Birmingham Printing Company, 1927.

Pannell, Anne Gary, and Dorothea E. Wyatt. *Julia S. Tutwiler and Social Progress in Alabama.* University: University of Alabama Press, 1961.

Pitts, Clara L. "Julia Strudwick Tutwiler." Ed.D. diss., George Washington University, 1942.

Pruitt, Paul M., Jr. "Julia S. Tutwiler: Years of Innocence." *Alabama Heritage,* no. 22 (Fall 1991): 37–44, 50.

———. "Julia S. Tutwiler: Years of Experience." Part Two. *Alabama Heritage,* no. 23 (Winter 1992): 31–39, 44.

Who Was Who in America. Vol. 1, 1897–1942. Chicago: A. N. Marquis, 1943.

Emma Hart Willard

Natalie A. Naylor

Emma Hart Willard (1787–1870) was one of the preeminent educators in antebellum America. She was the author of *A Plan for Improving Female Education* (1819) and founder of the Troy Female Seminary (1821), which provided advanced education for young women. Willard was an excellent teacher, the author of popular geography and history textbooks, an advocate of common schools, and a pioneer in teacher education.

Emma Hart Willard was born February 23, 1787, in Berlin, Connecticut, her ancestry including such prominent first settlers of New England as Thomas Hooker, Richard Hinsdale, and Steven Hart. Her father, Samuel Hart, was a farmer who also had been a militia captain in the revolutionary war and a member of the Connecticut General Assembly and held other public positions. Emma was the sixteenth of his seventeen children. His first wife, Rebecca Norton, bore him seven children before she died; he later married Lydia Hinsdale, Emma's mother.

Emma attended the local district school, but much of her early education was in the Hart home. Her parents read aloud to her, which inspired her interest in books, and she became a "voracious reader" of history, travel, and poetry books from the village library.[1] Her father was an independent thinker and held liberal political and religious views; he discussed Locke and other authors with her. When she was fifteen, Thomas Miner, a 1796 graduate of Yale, opened an academy in Berlin, which she attended for two years. This opportunity of studying with a teacher who inspired and stimulated her was a turning point in her life. Years later she asserted, "No better instruction was given to girls in any school, at that time, in our country."[2]

Emma Hart began teaching in the village school in 1804, at the age of seventeen. On the first day she reluctantly used corporal punishment to bring order and establish her authority over the undisciplined children. Thereafter, her students made good progress; she had begun what was to be her lifelong profession. Like many others at that time, she initially alternated periods of teaching and furthering her own studies. She especially wanted to improve her skills in drawing and painting and studied in Hartford, first at the Misses Pattens' school (with financial assistance from one of her brothers) and the following year at Mrs. Lydia Royse's school. Meanwhile, she opened a select school in her father's house during the summer of 1805 and, in the winter of 1806, was invited to take charge of the Berlin Academy. Since women at that time usually did not have an opportunity to teach in the winter sessions when older boys attended, she clearly had established a good reputation as a teacher. Soon she had offers to teach in schools in three different states. Deciding to accept the situation closest to home, she became the female assistant at an academy in Westfield, Massachusetts, in the spring of 1807. After one term, she left for Middlebury, where she was in full charge as preceptress of the female academy.

While teaching in Middlebury, Hart met John Willard, a native of East Guilford, Connecticut, who had given up the practice of medicine for politics and public office. Dr. Willard was twenty-eight years older than she and twice widowed, with four children. They married on August 10, 1809, and their one son, John Hart Willard, was born in September 1810. It was a very happy marriage, though she initially faced resentment from his children, three of whom were living at home.

For the first five years of her marriage, Emma Willard focused on running the household, but she continued her self-education. She read medical books from her husband's library, and he encouraged her study of physiology and other subjects. Their house faced Middlebury College, and when one of her husband's nephews lived with them while a student there, she had an opportunity to study his textbooks, learning geometry, science, and moral philosophy. These were subjects then generally thought to be beyond the purview of women.

Emma Willard returned to teaching in 1814, when she opened a boarding school in her home, her husband having suffered financial reverses. Tuition and boarding fees from students enabled her to help support the family while working in her home. (Their son was now four and a half years old.) As she later wrote a friend, "My leading motive was to relieve my husband from financial difficulties. I had also the further object of keeping a better school than those about me."[3] Initially, the curriculum was similar to that in other schools for young ladies of the time, with needlework, music, dance, and other "ornamental," as well as literary, subjects, but Willard soon was gradually introducing more advanced studies such as history, mathematics, and language. The school prospered, and within a few years, she had seventy girls enrolled, forty of whom boarded with the Willards. She was aided by an "excellent housekeeper and a very good assistant" teacher in the school.[4] Assistance from Middlebury College was more elusive. Emma Willard wanted to attend the examinations to become more familiar with college standards, but her request was denied and her students not permitted to audit any of the college classes. Well aware by now of the more advanced studies available to young men, she studied new subjects herself and taught them to her students.

Willard was a very effective teacher, and her pedagogy was enlightened. In an era when great stress was put on rote memorization, she wanted her students to understand the subjects. She used recitation to ensure that her students would remember, but her goal was to "make the pupil capable of *communicating*." After such thorough teaching, not only were her students well prepared for the public examinations she conducted, but they themselves were "soon capable of teaching."[5] Thus Emma Willard began preparing her own assistants and future teachers.

During these years Emma Willard also developed her "plan for Improving Female Education." She wrote, revised, and perfected her proposal but initially discussed it only with her husband. Willard was astute enough to realize the temper of the times and to realize that she would be "regarded as a visionary, almost to insanity" to try to promote her ideas herself. She waited until her reputation as a teacher increased and, as she later recalled, she "might be sought for in other places, where influential men would carry my project before some legislature."[6] In 1819, Willard shared her ideas with the father of one of her students. He was sufficiently impressed to bring her plan to the attention of a friend, who in turn presented it to New York governor De Witt Clinton.

Willard was bold enough to seek state funds to endow an educational institution for women, but she knew that suggesting a college for women would be thought absurd; therefore she coined the name "female seminary." Furthermore, consistent with the prevalent idea of "separate spheres," she hastened to assure her readers that "the seminary here recommended, will be as different from those appropriated to the other sex, as the female character and duties are from the male."[7] As Anne Firor Scott has pointed out, however, this was a tactical decision, for the institution Willard envisioned and the Troy Female Seminary she established were very similar to the men's colleges of the day.[8]

It took nearly a year before Governor Clinton responded. He wrote Willard that he would be "gratified to see this work in print, and still more pleased to see you at the head of the proposed institution."[9] More significantly, in his next message to the legislature, he urged action to improve women's education. Emma and John Willard went to Albany to lobby for the proposal, discussing her plan in person with the governor and legislators. The Willards printed at their own expense 1,000 copies of *An Address to the Public; Particularly to the Members of the Legislature of New-York, Proposing a Plan for Improving Female Education.*

This was not the first essay on women's education in America. Benjamin Rush, a physician, signer of the Declaration of Independence, and college professor, had addressed his fellow visitors of the Young Ladies Academy at Philadelphia on "Thoughts upon Female Education" in 1787, and Judith Sargent Murray's writings also had articulated the importance of women's education. Indeed, in the late eighteenth century, an ideology of "republican motherhood" developed the idea that women needed to be educated so they could be better mothers and instruct their sons for responsible citizenship.

Emma Willard now embarked on a crusade for women's education. She publicized her ideas, sending her *Plan* to prominent citizens for endorsements and copies to bookstores on consignment. Willard asserted that reform was necessary and believed it could not be achieved by individuals but required state support. She stressed the role of women as wives and mothers and argued that improving women's education would "elevate the whole character of the community." She couched her arguments deferentially and appealed to men's self-interest. She noted that "were the interests of male education alone to be consulted, that of females becomes of sufficient importance to engage the public attention."

Willard's basic assumptions were that "feminine delicacy" required that "girls should be educated chiefly by their own sex" and that boarding schools were "the best mode of education" for young women. Most existing institutions, however, were private ventures dependent on tuition and fees. This limited equipment and accommodations and promoted stress on "showy accomplishments, rather than those, which are solid and useful." Too often, education for daughters was only for amusement or to prepare them to please men. The schools lacked accountability, permanence, and uniform standards.

The *Plan* described Willard's ideal female seminary as one with an endowment, Board of Trustees, "suitable instruction," and a building with "commodious rooms," equipped with a library, musical instruments, paintings, and apparatus. As in most schools of the time, Christianity and moral character were the preeminent goals, and teachers were expected to be examples to their students. Although Willard did not list all the standard literary branches to be taught (since that would depend on the length of the program and entrance requirements), she did specifically urge the importance of "philosophy of the mind" (psychology) and natural philosophy (science). Domestic instruction was important, and she felt a "systematic treatise on housewifery" was needed. The "ornamental branches" would be optional, but she recommended "drawing and painting, elegant penmanship, music, and the grace of motion" through dancing (which also provided exercise). Willard specifically excluded ornamental needlework—a very popular activity in schools for young ladies—as a "waste of time." "Useful needle-work" could be either an admission requirement or taught in the domestic department.[10]

Willard envisioned a three-year program with a minimum entrance age of fourteen. Clearly she intended this to be more advanced education than was available in the common schools. A particular benefit she cited was that these seminaries could furnish teachers and thus improve the common schools. She felt women were generally better teachers and less expensive than men, who would be freed for other occupations.

Alma Lutz, Willard's biographer, notes that the *Plan* has been called the "Magna Charta of the rights of women in matters of education" and describes it as reading "like a lawyer's brief." Frederick Rudolph has called her *Plan* "a model propaganda document." Moreover, Anne Firor Scott points out that Willard's *Plan* was "one of those formative documents . . . that laid out a set of ideals and expectations so persuasively that it set the terms of discussion for half a century."[11]

Yet Willard was not successful in achieving her immediate goal of state financial support. Governor Clinton urged her to move her school to New York, and citizens of Waterford offered to provide a building. New York granted a charter to the "Waterford Academy for Young Ladies" and included it on the list of institutions to share in the Literature Fund, but the legislature defeated a proposal to provide a $5,000 endowment. Still hopeful that New York would provide financial aid, in the spring of 1819 Emma Willard moved her school to Waterford, New York. In 1820, despite Governor Clinton's recommendation for an appropriation, the assembly rejected the proposal, and the regents determined that the Waterford Academy could no longer receive money from the state literature fund. Clinton had alluded to the difficulties when he told the legislature, "I trust that you will not be deterred by common-place ridicule."[12]

After the Waterford trustees petitioned the state for financial support unsuccessfully again in 1821, Willard realized she needed to look elsewhere for assistance. Some citizens across the river in the manufacturing city of Troy, New York, invited her to move her school there. Local support proved decisive. By a combination of a special tax and private subscription, a building was purchased and renovated for her school. Troy Female Seminary was not incorporated until 1837 and did not obtain any money from the state until 1838, when it was accepted by the regents.[13] But Emma Willard's school had found its permanent home.

Willard was an excellent teacher and administrator. Her school had a fine reputation, and the number of students increased. Ninety were enrolled at the opening session in September 1821, including twenty-nine young women from Troy. The seminary was very much Emma Willard's creation, and within a decade, she almost single-handedly achieved an institution that approached the ideal she had set forth in her 1819 *Plan*. She specified plans for the building, organized the curriculum, and selected the textbooks, although there was a Board of Trustees and an advisory committee of local women. Her husband was the school doctor and business manager. Most of the teachers had been her students, whom she had trained in her methods. Over the years, she added advanced subjects, including higher mathematics, history, physiology, and natural philosophy. In most cases, she taught these subjects first to herself and then to her students. She proved that girls could learn these "masculine" subjects without jeopardizing their femininity and marriageability, though some of the upper-middle-class parents initially were apprehensive about these subjects as well as her domestic instruction, which they felt was too vulgar for their daughters. Willard always insisted on ladylike behavior, and a course in aesthetics was part of the curriculum. Daughters of ministers received special consideration on tuition, no doubt a means of encouraging their fathers to recommend her school. By 1831, the school enrolled more than 300 students, one-third of whom were boarders.

When teaching, Willard sought to integrate the history, geography, and literature of a period. She devised new methods, using classification and maps to teach geography, and wrote *Ancient Geography* (1822). Willard collaborated with William Channing Woodbridge and published later editions as the ancient geography portion of *A System of Universal Geography* (1824). This book soon became the standard geography text and was reprinted numerous times. Willard prepared a number of other geographies and atlases, often using original and sometimes domestic images. She also wrote U.S. histories, which were very popular. These textbooks increased her fame as an educator. The royalties helped subsidize Troy Seminary and not only relieved her of financial anxieties but brought her wealth.

After her husband's death in 1825, Emma Willard assumed responsibility for the financial affairs of the school. Public examinations in February and July modeled on those in colleges demonstrated the quality of her instruction. In 1824, Willard had invited her widowed younger sister, Almira Hart Lincoln, to assist her in teaching in the seminary. Lincoln, who had been Emma's student in Berlin and at Middlebury, had taught in various schools before her marriage.

Emma Willard, accompanied by her son, John, spent seven months in Europe in 1830–1831, leaving her sister as head of the seminary. Willard wanted to become familiar with schools in Europe and to have a much-needed rest. She visited schools for young women in France and England, virtually none of which she felt were up to the standards she had achieved at Troy. Willard had met General Lafayette when he visited her seminary on his 1825 tour of the United States and corresponded with him; he invited her to visit, and she was introduced at the French court. Willard recruited a French and music teacher for her seminary and perfected her own French. Willard enjoyed writing verse and before she embarked, at the request of her students, had left a book of her poems to be published, entitled *Fulfillment of a Promise*. On the return voyage, she wrote "Rocked in the Cradle of the Deep," her one poem that achieved some popularity as a hymn.

Emma Willard was interested in the struggles for independence in Greece and sought to help establish a women's school in Athens to train teachers. To support this cause, Willard wrote a number of essays, published under the title *Advancement of Female Education* (1833), organized a Troy Society for the Advancement of Female Education in Greece, and donated the profits from her *Journal and Letters from France and Great Britain* (1833). This financial support resulted in adding a normal department to a school operated by the Episcopal Missionary Board in Athens, and a total of $2,500 was sent to Greece to support students until the board consolidated its fundraising efforts.

Willard's practice from her days in Middlebury was to train some of her most able students to be her assistants; later they became teachers in the seminary or were placed by Willard in other schools. Indeed, she considered Middlebury the first normal school. At Troy, Willard prepared 200 teachers before the first state normal school opened in Massachusetts in 1839.[14] From 1839 to 1863, 597 Troy students were sent out to teach. Moreover, Willard waived tuition charges for deserving students who wanted to teach; she expected them to repay her from their earnings. Willard loaned a total of $75,000, and she was frequently asked to send or recommend teachers. More than 700 students received instruction on credit from 1839 to 1863.[15]

Many of the seminary graduates founded schools modeled on Troy, and Willard kept in contact with them by correspondence and circular letters. In 1837, she organized the Willard Association for the Mutual Improvement of Female Teachers, which formalized the network she had created. By these means, her influence spread throughout the country.

After a dozen years at Troy, Willard began to get restless. She continued to train teachers but was not regularly teaching any of the classes herself. She did preside at the examinations and was a "regal" presence at the seminary. She selected her successor, Sarah Lucretia Hudson, who had first been her student in Waterford at age eleven and whom she later adopted. Sarah was a beneficiary of Willard's personal revolving scholarship fund, began teaching in the seminary at age sixteen, and became a vice-principal at twenty-one. Moreover, in 1834, Sarah Hudson married Emma's son, John Hart Willard, who took over the business arrangements for the seminary. After Troy finally received sufficient assets from the city to receive a charter from the state and became eligible for state funds, Emma Willard turned over the seminary to Sarah and John Willard in 1838.

Emma Willard had met Christopher Yates, a physician from Albany and New York who courted her and whom she married on September 17, 1838. They moved to Boston in January 1839, but the marriage was disastrous. After nine months, she left him, citing "difference of opinion and uncongenialities of mind" in the separation agreement.[16] Fortunately, she had turned over to the seminary trustees much of her property as a trust fund before her marriage, which prevented its becoming her husband's property. She went to live with a sister in Berlin, Connecticut, feeling disgraced and embarrassed, and a few years later successfully petitioned the Connecticut legislature for a divorce and the right to use her former name.

While living in Connecticut, Emma Willard became acquainted with

Henry Barnard, who was secretary of the State Board of Commissioners for the Common Schools. Barnard asked her to prepare an address on education, and after hearing it, citizens of the town of Kensington in 1840 elected her superintendent of common schools. Willard was probably the first woman to hold such a position, and it marked a new phase in her career in education. She actively supervised the four schools, organizing their activities and curriculum. She selected new textbooks, introduced public examinations, organized a Female Common School Association, and published articles in the *Connecticut Common School Journal*. Still concerned with teacher training, she held classes for the district's teachers on alternate Saturdays and introduced normal classes in the schools. She hoped to head a state normal school or a system of teachers' institutes to reach those already teaching, but Barnard's position was abolished. Willard's reputation as an educator had grown with her work in Connecticut, however, and now included common schools. Though she considered starting an educational journal for women teachers, her sister Almira warned that it would not make money, though it "might benefit the school at Troy and aid in the business of sending out teachers."[17]

In 1844, after her marriage had been dissolved, Emma Willard returned to Troy, where she lived in a house on the seminary grounds with a favorite niece. She attended the examinations and was an inspiration to the students, whom she called her "granddaughters." Willard was frequently asked to speak and write on education and aided in teacher institutes, particularly in upstate New York. She made an extensive tour of over 8,000 miles through the West and South in 1846, during which she visited many of her former students and spoke on women's education. Willard received a gold medal at the London World's Fair in 1851 for her "Temple of Time Chart," a visual aid she devised for teaching history. In her later years, she continued to revise her textbooks, wrote a text on astronomy (1853), and attended the World's Educational Convention in London in 1854.

Willard also continued her investigations in medical subjects and, in 1846, published a paper on her theory of circulation of the blood by respiration and another on cholera a few years later. Although her scientific work has not held up, she did help pave the way for women to be taken seriously in medicine.

Throughout her life, Emma Willard focused her attention on improving women's education and teacher education and did not want to jeopardize her success in these areas by involvement in controversial issues of the day, such as woman's suffrage. Willard basically accepted the concept of women's separate sphere but sought to enlarge it from the domestic to encompass the schoolhouse. She was aware of the discrimination women faced, urged economic independence for women (which school teaching could provide), but believed "education rather than agitation would solve woman's problems." Willard herself was both a "prime exemplar of 'true womanhood'" and a role model of a "new woman" for her students. As Anne Firor Scott has shown, Troy Female Seminary with its "subversive attention to women's intellectual development" had a significant role in the "diffusion of feminist values" in the nineteenth century.[18]

Willard died on April 15, 1870. In its obituary, the *New York Times* referred to Emma Willard as "the best known teacher in America, who has well been termed the pioneer of female education, who founded the first scientific female seminary in the country, [and] wrote books of note."[19] This was a sound judgment. Other leaders followed in the paths Emma Willard first blazed. Catharine Beecher and Mary Lyon had some personal contact with her, and certainly they were aware of her work at Troy. In a fitting tribute to its founder, the Troy Female Seminary was renamed the Emma Willard School in 1895.

Willard's *Plan for Female Education* was a seminal document, its impact enhanced because Willard successfully implemented many of her ideas in the Troy Female Seminary. A "model of female respectability," she embodied traditional values but expanded women's sphere to include teaching and intellectual pursuits. She broadened the curriculum for women, insisted on solid studies, and inspired, as well as educated, hundreds of teachers who spread her influence throughout the country.[20] Her pioneering work in teacher education, both in her seminary and in teacher institutes, helped improve the quality of education in nineteenth-century America and earned her the designation "apostle of normal schools."[21] Willard's lifelong commitment to women's education meant that she and much of her work were outside the mainstream of public education and coeducational instruction. She has been unjustly neglected by traditional historians of education and is eminently deserving of recognition. Emma Willard was a crusader for improving women's education and teachers' education in the important formative years of their development.

NOTES

1. Henry Fowler, "Educational Services of Mrs. Emma Willard," in Henry Barnard, ed., *Memories of Teachers and Educators*, New York: F. C. Brownell, 1861, reprint, New York: Arno Press, 1969), quoting Emma Willard, 128. (Willard is the only woman included.)

2. Ibid., 129.

3. Ibid., 133.

4. Alma Lutz, *Emma Willard: Daughter of Democracy* (Boston: Houghton Mifflin, 1929, reprint, Washington, DC: Zenger, 1975), quoting Willard, 55.

5. Fowler, quoting Willard, 134, 135.

6. Ibid., 134.

7. Emma Willard, *A Plan for Improving Female Education* (1819, reprint, Marietta, GA: Larlin, 1987), 7. Fowler includes fairly extensive excerpts of the plan in "Educational Services," 137–42, and the plan is reprinted in a slightly abridged form in

Willystine Goodsell, *Pioneers of Women's Education* (New York: McGraw-Hill, 1931, reprint, New York, 1970), 45–81.

    8. Anne Firor Scott, *Making the Invisible Woman Visible* (Urbana: University of Illinois Press, 1984), 69; see also 47, 86 n.10.

    9. Clinton quoted by Lutz, 64.

    10. Quotations from Willard, 8, 10, 12, 22, 24.

    11. Lutz, 67–68; Frederick Rudolph, "Emma Willard," in Edward T. James, eds., *Notable American Women, 1607–1950: A Biographical Dictionary* (Cambridge: Belknap Press of Harvard University Press, 1971), 3, 612; Scott, 43.

    12. Fowler, 144.

    13. J. H. French, *Gazetteer of the State of New York* (Syracuse, NY: R. P. Smith, 1860, reprint, Interlaken, NY: Heart of the Lake Publishing, 1986), 133. See also Nancy Beadie, "Willard's Idea Put to the Test: The Consequences of State Support of Female Education in New York, 1820–1870," typescript, 1992.

    14. Lutz, 98. Middlebury and Troy Seminaries also antedated Samuel Hall's teacher's course in his (private) Concord, Vermont, Academy in 1823 or at Philips Andover Academy in 1830, as well as the Lexington, Massachusetts, state normal school.

    15. Figures are not available for earlier years (Scott, 71). Most of the scholarship or charity funds in antebellum academies and colleges were limited to young men planning to become ministers.

    16. Lutz, 206.

    17. Ibid., 218.

    18. Ibid., 238; Scott, 66, 82.

    19. *New York Times*, April 18, 1870.

    20. See Anne Firor Scott, "The Ever Widening Circle," in Scott, 64–88.

    21. Willystine Goodsell, ed., *Pioneers of Women's Education in the United States* (New York: McGraw-Hill, 1931, reprint, New York: AMS, 1970), 39.

WORKS BY EMMA HART WILLARD

An Address to the Public; Particularly to the Members of the Legislature of New-York, Proposing a Plan for Improving Female Education. Albany: I. W. Clark, 1819. Reprint, *A Plan for Improving Female Education.* Marietta, GA: Larlin, 1987.

Ancient Geography. Hartford, CT: Oliver D. Cooke, 1822. Later editions were bound with William Channing Woodbridge's texts, which were published under various titles, including *A System of Universal Geography.* Hartford, CT: Oliver D. Cooke, 1824; *Woodbridge and Willard's Universal Geography.* Hartford, CT: Hartford, Beach and Beckwirth, 1833.

Geography for Beginners; or The Instructor's Assistant. Hartford, CT: Oliver D. Cooke, 1826.

History of the United States or Republic of America. New York: White, Gallaher and White, 1828.

Abridged History of the United States. Philadelphia: Barnes, 1843.

WORKS ABOUT EMMA HART WILLARD

Brainerd, Ezra. *Life and Work in Middlebury, Vermont of Emma Willard.* New York: Evening Post Job Printing House, 1893. Under title "Mrs. Emma Willard's

Life and Work in Middlebury," in U.S. Bureau of Education, *Circular of Information*, no. 4 (1900) no. 265, vol. 29: 130–37. Reprint, Marietta, GA: Larlin, 1987.

Calhoun, Daniel H. "Eyes for the Jacksonian World: William C. Woodbridge and Emma Willard." *Journal of the Early Republic* 4 (Spring 1984): 1–26.

Fowler, Henry. "Educational Services of Mrs. Emma Willard." In Henry Barnard, ed. *Memories of Teachers and Educators*, 125–68. New York: F. C. Brownell, 1861. Reprint, New York: Arno Press, 1969.

Goodsell, Willystine, ed. *Pioneers of Women's Education in the United States.* New York: McGraw-Hill, 1931. Reprint, New York: AMS, 1970. Includes slightly abridged version of Willard's *Plan for Improving Female Education* and prefaces to several of her textbooks.

Lord, John. *Life of Emma Willard.* New York: D. Appleton, 1873.

Lutz, Alma. *Emma Willard: Daughter of Democracy.* Boston: Houghton Mifflin, 1929. Reprint, Washington, DC: Zenger, 1975. Lutz's *Emma Willard: Pioneer Educator of American Women* (Boston: Beacon Press, 1964) is a condensed version of her 1929 biography but omits the bibliographies and illustrations.

Scott, Anne Firor. "What, Then, Is the American: This New Woman?" *Journal of American History* 65 (December 1978): 679–703.

———. "The Ever-Widening Circle: The Diffusion of Feminist Values from the Troy Female Seminary, 1822–72." *History of Education Quarterly* 19 (Spring 1979): 3–25. Both of Scott's essays are reprinted with an introduction in her book *Making the Invisible Woman Visible*, 34–88. Urbana: University of Illinois Press, 1984, 34–88.

Sister Mary Madeleva Wolff

Susan Williamson

Sister Mary Madeleva Wolff (Mary Evaline) (1887–1964) achieved national distinction as president of Saint Mary's College in Notre Dame, Indiana, a position that she held from 1934 to 1961. She was an accomplished and well-known poet, as well as a recognized literary essayist. Her belief that women should play an active and vital role in the shaping of society formed the basis for her advocacy of the value and importance of education for women.

Mary Evaline Wolff ("Eva") was born May 24, 1887, in Cumberland, Wisconsin, to August and Lucy (Arntz) Wolff. She was the second of their four children and their only daughter. Her mother was born in Wisconsin to parents who had emigrated from Germany in the 1840s. August Wolff came to Wisconsin from Germany at age nine. There he became a harness maker, a trade he valued as both a "craft and an art." Lucy had been a schoolteacher prior to her marriage.

Eva's childhood was enriched by both the cultural and geographical features of its setting. She made friends among the Chippewa Indians. The local pastor spoke from the altar in several languages to serve worshipers from German, French, and Italian colonies. Eva's deep and abiding occupation with the mystery and beauty of nature was rooted in the landscape of the Cumberland area.

Eva attended local public schools. After graduating from high school in 1904, she spent a year at home to ease the burden of educational costs upon her father before entering the University of Wisconsin in the fall of 1905. There her life was rich with social and cultural activity. She participated in the development of a Catholic student center that served as the prototype for the Newman Clubs later formed for Catholic students on campuses throughout the nation. In a quest for "certitudes," she chose mathematics for a major, but a course in medieval history was to be of more lasting importance to her.

After learning of Saint Mary's College through an "advertisement" in a magazine during the summer of 1906, she transferred to the school, run by the Sisters of the Holy Cross, in the fall of that year. There her major interest shifted to English. Under the teaching of Sister Rita Heffernan, she discovered her ability to write. In the person of Sister Rita, she found the idol of her life.

For a long time, Eva had felt the need for the presence in her life of an older woman whose wise counsel would provide direction. Sister Rita fulfilled her dream. Described as beautiful and charming, Sister Rita was both a teacher par excellence and a published poet, well connected to literary circles.

Soon Eva came to see religious life as the way to fulfill her spiritual needs, well aware of the apparent incongruity of this calling with her independent way. Eva entered the novitiate of the Sisters of the Holy Cross on September 14, 1908, and on December 10 of that year she became Sister Mary Madeleva. After the completion of her formal religious training, she made perpetual vows on August 14, 1915.

Shortly after receiving the Holy Habit on December 10, 1908, Sister Madeleva was assigned to teach at the academy run by the sisters on the Saint Mary's campus. In 1909 she received a B.A. in English from Saint Mary's College, and in 1910 she began teaching at both the academy and the college. Through a program of summer study that began in 1909, she received an M.A. in English from the University of Notre Dame in 1918.

From 1919 to 1922, Sister Madeleva taught and served as principal of Sacred Heart Academy in Ogden, Utah, in the West that she loved for its mountains, deserts, and sagebrush. The academy served mostly Mormon children who were attracted by its emphasis on the arts. Among her students there were Bernard DeVoto, the only boy to be admitted to the school, and future Pulitzer Prize–winning poet Phyllis McGinley.

Sister Madeleva began her studies at Berkeley in the summer of 1922. She was assigned to Holy Rosary Academy in Woodland, California, from which she commuted to Berkeley for the next two years. Her work at Berkeley led to the publication of many critical essays, of which "Chaucer's Nuns" is the most well known. Her dissertation, "Pearl: A Study in Spiritual Dryness" (1925), was published by Appleton-Century. The originality of her work on both Chaucer and the "Pearl" lay in the use of her own religious experience as a tool of literary interpretation. Thus she carried out in her own scholarship the role that she envisioned for the educated Christian woman as an interpreter of cultural heritage. The first doctor's degree awarded to a sister by the University of California was conferred upon Sister Madeleva Wolff in 1925.

Poetry was the major focus of her lifetime writing efforts, and for this she is best known as a writer. As a student of Sister Rita, she had discovered that poetry was her "medium" of expression. Poet-teacher Father Charles O'Donnell encouraged the publication of her work. To combat the issue of mediocrity often associated with the poetry of Catholic writers, Sister Madeleva decided to begin by submitting her work to secular magazines and to use her religious name. Thus her verse appeared in *Bookman, American Mercury, Saturday Review of Literature*, and the *New York Times*, as well as in *America, Ave Maria, Catholic World, Spirit*, and *Commonweal.*

Her first two published collections of verse, *Knights Errant* (1923) and *Penelope* (1927), show her ability to exploit human emotion in the expression of passionate love of God. By writing in this controversial way, Sister Madeleva altered and expanded the legitimate domain of future religious women poets by reclaiming for them the tradition of mystical religious writing exemplified by Teresa of Avila. The range of Sister Madeleva's work includes poems without clearly religious subject matter, such as those that convey the mystery and beauty of nature. By such writing, she served to liberate future religious women from the unwritten but understood rule that prohibited writing on purely secular topics.

As a poet, Sister Madeleva was driven by creative necessity. Her efforts were severely limited and frustrated by the duties and responsibilities of the administrative positions that she held during most of her adult life, so she wrote in periods of insomnia, during recuperation from illness, and during periods of required religious silence.

The Four Last Things (1959) was the last of her twelve books of poetry published during her lifetime. A collection of Christmas poems was published posthumously in 1964.

Sister Madeleva is regarded as a leading religious poet of her own time and beyond. She served as president of the Catholic Poetry Society of America from 1942 to 1947. Her awards for poetry include the Champion Award of the Catholic Book Club in 1959 and the Poet's Corner Award, also in 1959.

In 1926, after her doctoral studies had been completed, Sister Madeleva became the first president of Saint Mary-of-the-Wasatch, a new college for women opened by the Sisters of the Holy Cross in Salt Lake City.

The challenge of building a new school was accompanied by difficult problems of enrollment, debt, and accreditation. A rule of religious community in force at that time prevented her from making the public appearances that were necessary for public relations and institutional development.

Nevertheless, Wasatch provided the advantages of a small college of academic quality. It emphasized the arts and culture and encouraged learning beyond ordinary classroom walls. The college's location in the Wasatch mountains provided a continuous display of nature's mystery, strength, and splendor, as changes of light, weather, and season played over the landscape. The environment, including the four nearby western parks, served as nature's classroom for a course in beauty.

Sister Madeleva continued to write during her seven years at Wasatch. Some of her major ideas on the role of women in society and the need for their proper education are set forth in "Scholarship for Catholic Women" (1932).

A trip to Europe for the year 1933–1934 provided her with opportunities for study, travel, and enrichment. At Oxford she attended lectures of C. S. Lewis, Martin D'Arcy, and J.R.R. Tolkien. Her travels included visits to the Riviera, Rome and the Holy Land, Paris and LeMans, Dublin and Donegal. Friendships were formed or renewed with such literary figures as Edith Wharton, William Butler Yeats, and Seumas MacManus.

After returning to the United States, Sister Madeleva was informed in August 1934 that she would be the next president of Saint Mary's College. To this position she brought her reputation as a teacher, scholar, and poet, her spirit of independence, and her abilities to "dream" and "work."

As the third president of Saint Mary's College, Sister Madeleva achieved national stature as a leading educator for her contributions both to the college and to education in general.

During her presidency, Saint Mary's grew into a modern, dynamic institution. Figures for the year 1936–1937 show a student enrollment of less than 300 students and a faculty consisting almost entirely of Sisters of the Holy Cross with graduate degrees from the University of Notre Dame. By 1961, the enrollment had increased to over 1,100 students, the faculty had become predominantly lay, and the credentials of faculty, both religious and lay, included degrees from many of the finest American and foreign universities.

Sister Madeleva oversaw the development of a modern physical plant at the college. Several major buildings were added to the landscape, including a library in 1942, a science building in 1955, and a fine arts center in 1956. For these, she dreamed, planned, and dealt with architects. The campus stands as a monument to women's ability to achieve.

But Sister Madeleva did more than construct and populate buildings. She built an environment—a setting for the nourishment and sustenance of intellectual life.

Sister Madeleva wanted students for whom the classics and other literary works breathed in their lives, students who could think both originally and creatively. She wanted students to see beauty in all its forms—in music and in the details of nature. She wanted students to embrace the universe with their full humanity—with their senses as well as their intellects. She wanted students to know that the universe contains the spiritual and to experience the silence of profound reverence. She wanted students to be aware of their Christian heritage and to prepare them for their roles as "makers and keepers" of it. From dreams such as these, the intellectual and cultural life of Saint Mary's grew.

Visits to the campus by such prominent figures as Barbara Ward, Clare Boothe Luce, Jacques Maritain, Dorothy Day, and Mortimer Adler provided a continual source of enrichment to the campus. The Trapp family gave concerts and sang mass and Benediction. Student performances of Shakespearean comedies, as well as the York Cycle Mystery plays, were produced under British direction.

Sister Madeleva describes beauty as "God's visibility." After many years of planning, her dream of a "home for beauty" was fulfilled with the completion of a center for the arts. Moreau Hall was dedicated in 1956 at an event featuring the premier of the NBC Opera Company, which drew national attention. Thus the stage was set for future performances not only by the NBC Opera Company but also by such artists as Helen Hayes, Duke Ellington and Marian Anderson.

Academic programs, as well as cultural activities, incorporated her educational ideas. Her view that "thinking" is the fundamental activity of the college student was made real in 1935 by the introduction of the Trivium— a course for freshmen that provided an integrated approach to grammar, rhetoric, and logic and stressed the dependence of writing upon thinking.

The Christian Culture Program (which later became Humanistic Studies) was introduced in 1956 to show the importance of Christianity as a historical force in Western civilization. This major program was rooted in the ideas of Christopher Dawson and offered an innovative approach within the framework of orthodox religious belief. Interdisciplinary in nature, it combined the study of such fields as literature, theology, and the arts and thereby called upon the student to engage in challenging processes of thought. Instruction was provided through the cooperative or "team" teaching of professors from Saint Mary's, University of Notre Dame, and other institutions.

Just as she enriched Saint Mary's by bringing the world to it, her work based at the college served to benefit the larger world. Sister Madeleva was an active participant in professional organizations. She served on the advisory board of *Jubilee*, chaired the committee on college faculty of the National Catholic Education Association (NCEA), and served as president of the Indiana Conference of Higher Education in 1957. As a recognized authority on higher education and a champion for the cause of women's education, she brought her message to the nation through her many speaking engagements.

For all her various contributions, she was awarded honorary degrees from Manhattan College in 1939, Mount Mary College in 1940, University of Notre Dame in 1953, Manhattanville College of the Sacred Heart in 1957, Indiana University in 1958, and Creighton and Marquette universities in 1959. She received the Siena Medal in 1948 for distinctive contribution to Catholic life in the United States and the Woman of Achievement Award in 1950 from the Women's International Institute.

Sister Madeleva initiated two major projects that had national consequences for Catholic education. In 1942, the NCEA finally recognized the problem of the shortage of qualified teachers of religion in college. At that time, both women and laypersons in general were denied access to advanced study in theology at American Catholic institutions. In 1943, with the opening of the Graduate School of Sacred Theology at Saint Mary's, women were offered a unique opportunity to pursue master's and doctor's degrees in theology. The consequences of this program were many. It led to the establishment of a theology major for undergraduates at Saint Mary's—the first such program at a women's college in the United States; it served as a model for a similar program for women begun in Rome in 1953; and, more generally, it brought theology into the legitimate domain of study by women. The program at Saint Mary's ended in 1969, following the establishment of a program open to women at the University of Notre Dame in 1966.

A second project dealt with Catholic grade school education. In order to meet the urgent need for teachers in parochial schools, sisters were often assigned to the classroom after a year in the novitiate, without having received adequate teacher preparation. At a meeting of the NCEA in 1948, Sister Madeleva requested that this serious problem be addressed. She then served as chair of a committee whose members drew up model programs by which a sister could complete both her religious training and her academic education before being assigned to teach. The work of the committee was enthusiastically received at the 1949 meeting of the NCEA and was published shortly thereafter as "The Education of Sister Lucy." The effort initiated by Sister Madeleva culminated in the establishment of a national Sister-Formation Program, which undertook the implementation of needed changes.

Sister Madeleva's vision is neither framed nor partitioned by boundaries. She sees women's potential as vast. She speaks of education for "eternity"[1] and states that "infinity is our proper dimension."[2] Horizons can be redefined and extended. Traditional ways of dividing subject matter dissolve in her interdisciplinary approach to education, which anticipates the later popularity of this instructional mode. Before ecumenism became fashionable, Sister Madeleva was already thriving in a world of varied religious views. She was sought out by non-Catholic groups to speak on spiritual matters; she spoke in Quaker chapels and in the Mormon bishop's house. She was awarded the Brotherhood Citation from the National Conference of Christians and Jews in 1957. As a student at Saint Mary's she refused membership in an honor society that excluded non-Catholics. As president of the college in 1941, she admitted the first black student known to apply, because it was "right," and handled the resulting controversy with both courage and dexterity. Walls that had previously separated worshipers at the college by constituency disappeared early in her administration, as she brought together students, sisters, and lay faculty at the same chapel service.

The form that shapes the women's college is seen as necessary to provide identity, to nourish growth, to prepare and strengthen for action in the world—rather than to simply separate. In Sister Madeleva's view, the proper role of women is not only to serve but also to transform society—to explore and create a new world rooted in the ways of the spirit and the intellect. For this, the college must prepare women to go forth with the courage, holiness, and learning shown by St. Helena and St. Paula in the fourth century and St. Hilda in the sixth. Sister Madeleva speaks of the "supernatural stature" of women, for which Mary of Nazareth provides the ultimate role model.[3] In anticipation of future feminist arguments, she asserts that women's colleges are uniquely capable of developing women fully, because they educate women "as" and "with" women.[4]

Many of Sister Madeleva's views on the higher education of women that were presented at student convocations have been published in *Addressed to Youth* (1944) and *Conversations with Cassandra* (1961). The general story of her life is given in an autobiographical work, *My First Seventy Years* (1959).

The untimely death of Sister Rita Heffernan in 1910, while Sister Madeleva was still in the novitiate, defeated her dream of their friendship as sisters and left a void in her life that could not be filled. Sister Madeleva accepted this deprivation as evidence that God wanted her to have no "props," and thus she went forward with renewed independence.

Sister Madeleva valued the sisters with whom she lived in community and had special admiration for Mother Angela, who founded the college, and Mother Pauline, who served as its first president from 1895 to 1931. When Sister Madeleva assumed its presidency, Saint Mary's already had a long tradition of commitment to academic excellence and the arts. But it was essentially her own ingenuity and insight that guided her as she shaped a modern institution from a small college born of a convent school. She, who had no role models, as the term is commonly understood, became herself a role model for the type of woman that she wanted to send out into the world as a graduate of Saint Mary's College.

The enduring legacy of Sister Madeleva may very well be the value that she places upon women, as articulated in her spoken and her written word and demonstrated by her extraordinary efforts and achievements on their behalf.

In *Conversations with Cassandra*, Sister Madeleva discusses the classical concept of poet—as "a seer, a maker, a singer." For her dreams and for the exquisite manner in which she brought her dreams to realization, both in verse and in the area of the education of women, Sister Madeleva is a poet indeed, in the full classical sense of the word.

After her retirement from the presidency of Saint Mary's in 1961, Sister Madeleva served as a consultant to her successor.

During a trip to Boston in 1964, it became necessary for her to undergo surgery on July 23 at the New England Baptist Hospital for a nonmalignant condition, from which she developed a postoperative complication.

In her poem, "Patrins," written in a setting of departure, Sister Madeleva invites others to follow her "wild and wistful way" that "leads but to peace." Sister Madeleva Wolff died on July 25, 1964.

NOTES

1. Sister M. Madeleva Wolff, C.S.C., *Conversations with Cassandra* (New York: Macmillan, 1961), 118.

2. Ibid., 10.

3. Sister M. Madeleva Wolff, C.S.C., *My First Seventy Years* (New York: Macmillan, 1959), 128.

4. Ibid., 127.

WORKS BY SISTER MARY MADELEVA WOLFF

Chaucer's Nuns and Other Essays. New York: D. Appleton, 1925.
Pearl: A Study in Spiritual Dryness. New York: D. Appleton, 1925.
"Scholarship for Catholic Women." *The Catholic Educational Review* 30 (January 1932): 21–32.
Addressed to Youth. Paterson, NJ: St. Anthony Guild Press, 1944.
Collected Poems. New York: Macmillan, 1947.
"The Education of Our Young Religious Teachers." ["The Education of Sister Lucy."] *National Catholic Educational Association Bulletin* 46 (August 1949): 253–56.
The Four Last Things. New York: Macmillan, 1959.
My First Seventy Years. New York: Macmillan, 1959.
Conversations with Cassandra. New York: Macmillan, 1961.

WORKS ABOUT SISTER MARY MADELEVA WOLFF

Creek, Sister Mary Immaculate. *A Panorama: 1844–1977, Saint Mary's College, Notre Dame, Indiana*. Notre Dame, IN: Saint Mary's College, 1977.
———. "A Poet for One Season Only?" *Courier* 52 (Summer 1978): 11–16.
Jegen, Carol Frances. "Women in Theology." *Listening: Journal of Religion and Culture* 13 (Spring 1978): 134–47.
Jencks, Barbara C. *The Sister Madeleva Story*. South Bend, IN: McClave, 1961.
Kilmer, Kenton. "Contemporary Catholic Authors: Sister M. Madeleva, C.S.C., Pioneer Poet." *Catholic Literary World* 12 (December 1940): 67–71.
Klein, Mary Ellen. "Sister M. Madeleva Wolff, C.S.C., Saint Mary's College, Notre Dame, Indiana: A Study of Presidential Leadership 1934–1961." Ph.D. diss., Kent State University, 1983.

Martha Beulah Mann Yallup

Margaret Connell Szasz

Martha Beulah Mann Yallup (b. 1942) is a Yakima Indian educator and tribal administrator who has contributed in a wide variety of ways to the education of Yakima Indian youth, of students enrolled at Heritage College, which is located on the Yakima Indian Nation Reservation, and of American Indian university students across the nation. She is one of the most important American Indian educators in the United States.[1]

As an American Indian, Yallup should be viewed through the cultural framework of her tribe and its past. Born in 1942 in Toppenish, Washington, shortly after the United States entered World War II, Martha Yallup grew up in the heart of the Yakima Indian Nation. Her heritage was both Yakima and Nez Perce. Her mother, Ellen Kash Kash, was the daughter of James and Julia Williams Kash Kash of Kamiah, Idaho, located in Nez Perce country. Her father, Jacob Mann, Sr., was the son of Moses and Ellen Buchanan Mann of White Swan, Washington, located on Yakima lands. Hence, her family background represented two of the strongest cultural traditions maintained by the native people of the Columbia River Plateau: the Nez Perce and the groups that now make up the Confederated Tribes and Bands of the Yakima Indian Nation. From their ancient past to the present, the Nez Perces and the Yakimas have shared many common cultural traits. These include the Sahaptian languages (Sahaptin and Nez Perce), "whose genetic relationship is close."[2] They also shared a common economic base—salmon fishing, hunting, and gathering—similar patterns of living, and spiritual and ceremonial traditions. Although they were not immediate neighbors, these groups met at annual gatherings and were linked through ties of marriage, as well.

In June 1855, the Nez Perces and the tribes and bands that came to be known as the Yakimas gathered in Walla Walla, where some of their leaders signed the controversial Treaty of 1855, negotiated between Plateau tribes and the United States. In accordance with treaty provisions, the Yakimas ceded over 10 million acres of ancestral homeland, or one-third of the area of what is now Washington state, retaining the 1,371,918 acres that now constitute the Yakima Indian Reservation. Simultaneously, they secured

The exclusive right of taking fish in all the streams, where running through or bordering said reservation . . . as also the right of taking fish at all usual and accustomed places, in common with citizens of the Territory, and of erecting temporary buildings for curing them, together with the privilege of hunting, gathering roots and berries, and pasturing their horses and cattle upon open and unclaimed land.[3]

At the Walla Walla Council the Nez Perce leader, Lawyer, had urged the whites "to act toward them in good faith."[4] Nonetheless, the Yakimas, like most American Indians, learned that paper agreements offer no guarantee of their rights. Consequently, from 1855 to the present, the Yakimas have defended their treaty rights through warfare, in Congress, by way of the Bureau of Indian Affairs (BIA) and the numerous other federal agencies that deal with Indian affairs, in the public schools, at the state and local levels of government, and in the courtroom. Among the victories they have won, one of the most symbolic gains was the 1972 return of 21,000 acres of Yakima lands, including a major part of Pahto (Mt. Adams), the snow-covered 12,000-foot volcanic peak that forms part of the western boundary of the Yakima Reservation.[5]

From World War II to the present, a time span matching Yallup's life, the Yakima Indian Nation has undergone vast change. Shortly before the war the Yakimas, like many other federally recognized tribes, were offered the right to accept or reject the Indian Reorganization Act (IRA), the centerpiece legislation of the "Indian New Deal," which provided for a limited form of tribal self-government. When the Yakimas chose to reject the IRA, they were informing the federal government that they intended to carve out their own path of governing themselves. As one member noted, "There has never been a time when the speeches of officials as explained to us Indians have been carried out."[6] Some of those tribes that accepted the IRA also voted to adopt a written constitution. The Yakima Indian Nation does not operate under a constitution; it relies on resolutions.

In 1947, a resolution established a Yakima Tribal Council, which is composed of fourteen elected members, symbolically representing the fourteen tribes and bands of 1855. The Tribal Council relies heavily on an administrative staff to implement its policies and procedures. At the turn of the twenty-first century, tribal government is often the equivalent of a big business, as sophisticated as a corporation and encompassing vast sums of money and a complex personnel operation. This is especially true for tribes with abundant natural resources or other forms of significant income (such as Bingo) and a large membership, as well. The Yakima Nation has both.

Its multimillion-dollar annual operating budget relies heavily on income from timber harvested from the forested lands that lie at the base of Pahto. In December 1991, the enrolled Yakima Indian membership was 8,146, the majority of whom lived on the reservation. The Yakima Indian Nation is responsible for a tribal court system, a tribal police force, the tribal cultural heritage center, a tribal school, an annual rodeo and other community tribal events, and many other programs for the people, such as housing, job training, and chemical dependency treatment. These responsibilities place a heavy burden on the administrative staff serving the Tribal Council and enrolled members. The staff includes three departments: Natural Resources, Law and Justice, and Human Services, which, cumulatively, employ over 600 people. The Department of Human Services, which supervises all Yakima programs in the areas of health, social services, employment, training, education, and housing, is currently headed by Martha Yallup, who serves as deputy director. In five decades Yallup has moved a considerable distance from her childhood in a nation that little resembled the multimillion-dollar tribe of today.

Yallup has traveled and, on occasion, lived away from the Yakima Reservation, but at heart, she has never traveled very far. Perhaps unlike many of the educators depicted in this volume, Yallup is, above all, a tribal person. Her concerns lie first with the Yakimas; second, with other Indians; third, with the disadvantaged in general. Her commitments to education, as well as other social services, reflect these concerns.

Much of Yallup's schooling was fairly standard for a child growing up on the reservation in the 1940s and 1950s. She attended the reservation public schools that had opened at the turn of the century when the allotment and subsequent leasing of Yakima lands (following the passage of the General Allotment Act in 1887) brought a flood of outsiders who demanded schools for their children. During her secondary school years, however, she and her sister received scholarships through the Christian church to attend a private, all-girls high school and junior college located in central Kentucky. At an impressionable age, therefore, she learned that stereotypes mold most opinions of other cultures. We do not wear feathers every day, she taught her white school friends, nor do contemporary Yakima Indians live in tepees. Importantly, however, the stereotype that "Indians could not learn" was always present.[7] The cultural translation moved in dual directions, however. On her return, she interpreted the Midwest experiences to students at White Swan High School, where she graduated in 1960.

Yallup began college at the local community college in the town of Yakima, a fruit-growing center located just a few miles from the reservation boundary. In order to complete a bachelor's degree, she then commuted to Central Washington State College (now CWSU), located about sixty miles from the reservation, where she majored in physical education and health, with a minor in education. Few of her high school classmates had progressed to that level. She was already moving beyond the average expectation for her Yakima peers. A decade later, in 1978, when she completed an M.Ed. in adult education with a multicultural focus, her education level well exceeded that of other Yakimas, many of whom had not moved beyond the eighth grade.

Yallup's college years coincided directly with the American Indian activism of the 1960s. She was completing her studies when the Red Power movement, the occupation of Alcatraz, "The Trail of Broken Treaties," and the "Second Wounded Knee" dominated the news media, and the thrust for Indian rights and self-determination led to the legislation of the 1970s. These events traced some of their roots to the civil rights movement and turmoil of the 1960s, but they were spurred by President Lyndon B. Johnson's Great Society programs, supported by Congress. Martha Yallup's involvement in education placed her in the forefront of this tumultuous era.

Only three years after she had received her bachelor's degree, Yallup became director of the Head Start Program for the Yakimas, one of the creative ideas spawned by the Economic Opportunity Act. Immediately, she encountered the reality of the reservation's comparatively low level of schooling. Aware that few Yakimas had acquired sufficient training to serve as Head Start teachers, she crafted a program in cooperation with her colleague, Violet Rau, and Dr. Kathleen Ross at Fort Wright College (where Yallup and Rau would receive their master's degrees) to provide that training. The program was designed to circumvent the daunting conditions for these Indian college students, challenges that included poverty, distance, transportation, competition with outsiders who were neither Indian nor specifically Yakima, and the expanding academic bureaucracy. A journalist later described the project as "a splendid example of how a private college and a community group could work together."[8]

At about the same time, Yallup was also gaining direct experience with Yakima Indian children in a public school environment. In 1970–1971, she served as a Johnson-O'Malley (J-O'M) tutor in a school located in Toppenish, the largest town on the reservation and the hub for tribal government. By the 1970s, the J-O'M program was a venerable institution created in 1934 during the Indian New Deal and initially intended to provide special services for American Indian students. In practice, however, J-O'M had come under the thumb of state departments of education, which arbitrarily channeled the well-intentioned federal dollars into general state school funds. Not until the mid-1970s, with the passage of the Indian Education Act, would this funding become more accountable to Indians themselves.

By 1975, when Congress passed the Indian Education Act, Yallup had moved into tribal administration. Her experience in the classroom and as Head Start director, plus her bachelor's degree and graduate school course work, had prepared her for serving as the Yakimas' Division of Education director. Yallup held this position for a decade, from 1976 to 1986. In addition, for the last seven years of this period, she also served as chief school administrator for the Yakima Tribal School, a private school founded by the Tribal Council in response to her urging.

The tribal school reflected the 1970s era of Indian self-determination. Founded in 1988, it has provided a unique junior and senior high school experience for Yakima children who do not attend the reservation public schools. Although it relies on the basic curriculum required in the public schools, it also includes aspects of tribal culture. Yakima elders offer a link with the past through storytelling and teaching of arts and crafts; instruction in the Yakima language, history, and tribal government is integral to learning. The school provides a sense of belonging that appeals to a segment of Yakima families.

When Yallup moved into the position of deputy director of the Department of Human Services in 1986, once again, her administrative experience and her graduate studies in education had guided her steps. Her goal, which was "to implement comprehensive human services for the people of the Yakima Indian Nation," required a large staff.[9] Since this department encompassed many areas of Yakima life, it required a large staff, which by 1991 had grown to 249 employees. With the transfer, Yallup adopted a much wider range of responsibilities, adding health, welfare, and other programs to her previous specialty in education. The change also intensified the level of stress. Although she had negotiated with state and federal bureaucracies in education in the preceding decade, she now dealt with these multilevel bureaucracies in employment, housing, health, and several other social services. The new assignment was a formidable one.

By 1986, however, Yallup was already involved in working toward another advanced degree, and the added demands of her new position did not deter her. Enrolled in the Ed.D. program at Seattle University, she completed her doctorate in education leadership, with a cognate in public service two years later. When the *Yakima Nation Review* reported the story, it editorialized:

Congratulations to you, Dr. Martha B. Yallup. Your support, knowledge and multicultural skills will continue to assist and develop many more professional and career oriented programs for life and work in the rural communities of the Yakima Indian Nation and Yakima Valley.[10]

Within the tribal membership of the Yakima Indian Nation, Yallup was the first woman to earn a doctorate, a distinction that could have set her apart from other tribal members. As the *Yakima Nation Review* suggested, however, she had viewed her previous degrees as catalysts to assist both Yakimas and other rural residents of the region; it was likely that she would regard the Ed.D. in an equally pragmatic fashion.

From the degree-awarding ceremony held at Seattle University in June 1988 to the present, Yallup has expanded her commitment to education for American Indians, minorities, and the disadvantaged, while, at the same time, directing the Yakimas' Human Service Department. Despite her tribal and regional commitments, she has moved into national service as well. In the last decade she has become a nationally known leader in American Indian and minority education. In 1981 the National Education Association presented Yallup with the Leo Reano Memorial Award for outstanding leadership in education for American Indians and Alaska Natives; by 1991 Seattle University had honored her at its centennial celebration as one of its one hundred living outstanding alumni. In the interim years, Yallup has served on a number of national boards that represent Indian educational needs. She was a member of the Board of Regents for Haskell Indian Junior College, which is located in Lawrence, Kansas, and which has evolved from its founding in 1884 as one of the first off-reservation BIA boarding schools to one of two "BIA operated post-secondary institutions" serving American Indian and Alaska Native students.[11] She also served as secretary for the American Indian Graduate Center, an organization based in Albuquerque and providing financial assistance to American Indian and Alaska Native graduate students throughout the United States. Among American Indians and those Americans involved in education for the disadvantaged, Yallup has gained a stature shared by few.

These widespread commitments have also enabled her to gain a perspective on the educational issues that dominate the Yakima Reservation and surrounding lands of the Yakima Valley. Simultaneously, Yallup has acquainted the national organizations with the specific educational challenges faced by her own region. Her successes, combined with her humanitarian concern, have enhanced her reputation. When she attends national conferences, such as the National Indian Education Association, an organization committed to "an effort to attack the problems of Indian education on a national level," she greets and converses with innumerable friends and acquaintances who have shared in the struggle.[12]

Yallup's most innovative educational endeavor has enabled her to combine all of her skills as educator and administrator and has demonstrated her singular ability to combat the bureaucracy. The story of this endeavor is not only a tribute to her skills and perseverance but also a classic encounter between central and peripheral power bases. From the Yakima Indian perspective, it also evokes the skills and shrewdness of Speel-yi. Appearing most often in the guise of a coyote, Speel-yi used "daring and humor" to teach humans "how to survive and live harmoniously with nature in all its forms and moods."[13] Speel-yi's presence long antedated that of Europeans and other outsiders; his heritage lingers today.

By 1980, the program developed by Yallup and Ross to train Head Start teachers was almost a decade old, and it had achieved many of the goals of its founders. When the two educators learned of the imminent closure of Fort Wright College, therefore, they anticipated that it would also force their program to close. Ross recalled later how Yallup responded to the news: "I remember she just looked at me and said: 'No, it's not closing.' "[14]

This determination carried the alternative plan devised by Yallup, Violet

Rau, and Ross to fruition. As academic vice president of Fort Wright College, Ross was able to provide the three educators with a little interim time by persuading the college's officials to postpone closure until the summer of 1982. This granted them a reprieve of less than two years to create a college that would carry on the Head Start teacher training and offer other college course work, as well. Through skillful negotiation among the Yakimas, with the leadership in nearby communities, and with federal bureaucrats, the three women carried out an imaginative campaign that led to the founding of Heritage College. In 1982, Fort Wright College was closed, and its academic programs were transferred to the new Board of Directors that had incorporated as Heritage College in the summer of 1981. Violet Rau served as the first chair of the board; she was followed by Martha Yallup.

The opening of Heritage College and its subsequent expansion to include a student body that in 1991 included 1,000 retain strong parallels with the history of the tribally controlled colleges. Begun in the late 1960s with the founding of Navajo Community College and expanding across the American West in the 1970s and 1980s, by the early 1990s these colleges included twenty-four, largely reservation-based postsecondary institutions. The tribally controlled colleges, like Heritage, are designed to meet the needs of the rural poor. Their students are generally older than the average 18- to 21-year-old college student: at Heritage, the average age of students is 34 or 35. The students are often married or coping with the problems faced by single parents, the majority receive some type of financial aid, and more than half of the students hold at least a part-time job. Heritage, like the tribally controlled colleges, attracts students who probably would not have attended other colleges. Although Heritage does not receive either federal or tribal funding, like its tribally controlled counterparts, it has struggled to survive.

The stringent budget at Heritage means that the teaching staff is dedicated. Begun with a handful of faculty who taught in a three-room cottage, by 1991 the number of faculty had grown to thirty full-time and eighty part-time teachers whose classes were offered in a former elementary school complex located near Toppenish. The undergraduate students at Heritage, over half of whom are American Indian, Mexican-American, or of international origin, have been described as "place-bound."[15] By 1990, over 400 of them had graduated, and many of these planned to teach. Others, however, went into business, encouraged by the establishment of the college's Center for Minority Entrepreneurship, which opened in 1990. Still others worked for social agencies, aided by the college's extensive internship program.

Heritage College represents the dedication of many educators who have struggled to stabilize the institution during its first decade. Without its founders, however, it would not have materialized. Yallup once noted in a tribute to Ross, "It was a dream that needed someone with vision."[16] Yallup, like her counterparts, has persisted in the fulfillment of that vision. From 1982 to the present, she has served on the Board of Directors as chairperson, vice-chairperson, and secretary. Her ongoing commitment to the goals of Heritage College suggests that it epitomizes her views of education. Through her own achievements in undergraduate and graduate programs and in her teaching and administrative leadership for the Yakima Indian Nation, Yallup has demonstrated her faith in the values of higher education and, more important, in the need to adapt that education to the circumstances and unique cultures of American Indian/Alaska Native and other students from disadvantaged backgrounds.

A tribute by one of her colleagues in the field of American Indian education suggests her contributions:

Martha Yallup is best recognized by some as a founder of the Heritage College on the Yakima Indian reservation, and with that, a recognition of the mounting scores of success stories, of ordinary tribal people achieving their personal dreams of greatness. Her leadership in early childhood education is legend. Her accomplishments in the field of Indian education are numerous. Her guidance to the American Indian Graduate Center for eight years has led to financial support to hundreds of needy university students. But, true to her Yakima heritage, she has sought humility. And in so doing, Indian people throughout the land have modeled her ways. Perhaps Martha Yallup's real contribution to American Indians, is her living example of character.[17]

NOTES

1. The author would like to thank Martha Yallup for her warm cooperation in the preparation of this chapter.

2. Bruce Rigsby, "An Anthropological Linguistic View of Sahaptian/Interior Salishan Relations," unpublished paper, 2.

3. "Treaty Between the United States and the Yakima Nation of Indians," in Click Relander, ed., *Treaty Centennial, 1855–1955, the Yakimas* (Yakima: Republic Press, 1955), 22.

4. Col. Lawrence Kip, "The Indian Council at Walla Walla, May and June, 1855, a Journal" (San Francisco: Whitton, Towne, 1855); reprinted in *Sources of the History of Oregon* (Eugene: Star Job Office, 1897), vol. 1, part 2, 19.

5. *Yakima Treaty Land, "Not For Sale"* (Washington, DC: Jim Thomas Associates, n.d.).

6. General meeting, Wapato Longhouse, November 23, 1934. Records of the Confederated Tribes and Bands of the Yakima Indian Nation, Toppenish, WA.

7. Communication from Yallup to author, August 25, 1992.

8. Michael Ryan, "Don't Tell Us It Can't Be Done," *Albuquerque Journal* "Parade," March 31, 1991, 24.

9. Department of Human Services, Annual Report, FY 1991, 1.

10. *Yakima Nation Review* 20 (June 20, 1988): 5.

11. Margaret Connell Szasz, "Listening to the Native Voice, American Indian Schooling in the Twentieth Century," *Montana, The Magazine of Western History* 39 (Summer 1989): 44.

12. "Control-Change-Choose: Indian Education," brochure for the Third National Indian Education Conference, November 4–6, 1971, Albuquerque, NM.

13. "The Challenge of Spil yay" (Toppenish, WA: Yakima Nation Museum Program, 1984); see also *Yakima Indian Nation* (Toppenish, WA: Center for the Study of Migrant and Indian Education, n.d.).

14. Ryan, 24.

15. *Yakima Nation Review* 21 (February 9, 1990): 5.

16. *Yakima Herald Republic*, January 1, 1987.

17. Rick St. Germaine, Ojibwa, personal communication to author, February 21, 1992.

WORK BY MARTHA BEULAH MANN YALLUP

"A Treatise on the Philosophy of Education for Yakima Indian Children." Ed.D. diss., Seattle University, 1988. (EDD Publication Number AAC8810166)

WORKS ABOUT MARTHA BEULAH MANN YALLUP

Garretson, Margaret Ann Connell. "The Yakima Indians, 1855–1935, Background and Analysis of the Rejection of the Indian Reorganization Act." M.A. thesis, University of Washington, 1968.

Guie, H. Dean. *Tribal Days of the Yakimas*. Yakima, WA: Republic, 1937.

Mays, Theo, ed. *100 Years—100 Women, Yakima County Washington*. Yakima, WA: Print Masters, 1989.

Relander, Click. *Drummers and Dreamers*. Caldwell, ID: Caxton, 1956.

———, ed. *Treaty Centennial, 1855–1955. The Yakimas*. Yakima, WA: Republic, 1955.

Ryan, Michael. "Don't Tell Us It Can't Be Done." *Albuquerque Journal*, "Parade," March 31, 1991, 29–25.

Schuster, Helen H. *The Yakima*. New York: Chelsea House, 1990.

Splawn, Andrew J. *Ka-Mi-Akin. The Last Hero of the Yakimas*. Portland, OR: Kiham Stationery and Printing, 1917. Reprint, Portland, OR: Binfords and Mort, 1944; Caldwell, ID: Caxton, 1980.

Ella Flagg Young

Joan K. Smith

Ella Flagg Young (1845–1918) was the first female superintendent of a major city school system—Chicago—from 1909 to 1915. She spent most of her life working in some educational setting. At the age of seventeen she graduated from the normal department of the Chicago high school and began teaching in the early grades of one of the city's elementary schools. For the next thirty-six years she was a high school teacher, principal of two grammar schools, and a district superintendent. By 1900 she had returned to school to earn her Ph.D. under John Dewey at the University of Chicago. In 1902 she joined that university's education faculty, and when Dewey left in 1904 she resigned her faculty position to become principal of the Chicago Normal, where she remained until her appointment to the superintendency in 1909. Her administration was regarded as one in which many progressive reforms were achieved.[1]

Ella Flagg's parents, of Scottish ancestry, were living in Buffalo when she, the youngest of their three children, was born in 1845. Her father, Theodore, had little formal education, having been apprenticed to the sheet metal trades at the age of ten. Her mother, Jane, had married at age sixteen or seventeen and had borne a daughter, Cecilia Sarah, then a son, Charles Theodore, and finally Ella. Although her sister and brother went to school at the appropriate ages, Ella stayed home until the age of ten. Her mother thought her sickly and delicate, in need of a mother's protection and lots of sunshine.

At the age of eight or nine, Ella had not learned to read or write. One morning at the breakfast table her parents were reading an account of a school fire in which young children had to jump from upper-story windows. Ella asked her mother to read the story to her. Then, crying for the fate of children her age, the little girl took the newspaper into another room. Remembering how her mother had started the story, she matched that up with the words in print. When she got stuck, she asked the maid, until finally, she had worked her way through the whole article. Then she began reading other books in the house. Most of these were related to Presbyterian doctrines. One day she expounded on some of her religious knowledge when an aunt and some other women were visiting. Her aunt asked her what she had been reading; it was Baxter's *Call to the Unconverted*. While her aunt was amused, her mother was not. Mrs. Flagg calmly but sternly told her daughter to remove herself to the backyard to garden. In a couple of days, Mother Goose stories replaced Baxter.

By the time she was ten, Ella had taught herself how to write, and soon after this, her mother finally allowed her to enter the grammar department of the nearby school that her brother and sister attended. She found school intriguing. She had an aptitude for math, as did her father. The teacher made her a monitor (helper) in math. This meant that her desk was moved next to the teacher's. Mr. Flagg thought he noticed a rather "priggish" attitude on the part of his younger daughter, and he blamed it on the new location of her desk. He told Ella that she could continue to help the teacher if she moved her desk back with the rest of the class.

When Ella was thirteen, the Flaggs moved to Chicago. Ella had finished the grammar grades in Buffalo; therefore, she was ready for high school. Before she could take the entrance exams for Chicago's high school, she had to complete one year in a Chicago grammar school. The course of study at the Brown School was one Ella had already completed in Buffalo, so she found little challenge. Her parents had never really encouraged her to go to school, and it was not particularly common for girls to attend high school anyway. After a few months, she dropped out.

In 1860, when she was fifteen, Ella found a chance to further her education. A friend was going to take a teacher certification test and asked Ella to go along. She took the exam, too, and passed it but was told that she was too young to teach. With the encouragement of the superintendent of the city's schools, William H. Wells, she enrolled in the normal department of the Chicago high school.

Ella Flagg was entering her second year of training when her mother told her that she would not make a good teacher. She was not accustomed to young children and knew nothing of their nature and capabilities. Ella was too hard on herself and would be the same way with children, her mother explained. Determined to test herself under teaching circumstances, Ella looked for, and found, a classroom where the children were friendly and the teacher was good. She arranged to help the teacher on a weekly basis, thus setting up her own student teaching situation.

After a year's practice-teaching experience, her mother admitted that her daughter seemed to thrive on the experience. In the spring of 1862 Miss Ella Flagg graduated from the normal department of the Chicago high school; she was seventeen. The following fall, she began her long teaching career in the primary department of a Chicago ghetto school. Two weeks to the day after Ella started teaching, her mother died.

By 1863 Flagg was an assistant to the principal of the old Brown School, where she had felt bored five years earlier. From there she went to another grammar school as head of the two practice-teaching rooms. In the next seventeen years, Ella Flagg experienced other aspects of public education: she taught math at the high school level; she devised an "object" curriculum based on Pestalozzi's methods; and she became principal, first of the Scammon School and next of the largest school in Chicago, the Skinner. She remained at the Skinner as principal until 1887, when she was called to a newly created assistant superintendent's position.

The years paralleling Flagg's climb to the assistant superintendency were mixed with happiness and pain. In 1868 her brother, Charles, was the sole victim killed in a freak train accident. That same year she married a much older friend of the family named William Young. Little is known of the circumstances surrounding her marriage. Mr. Flagg may have encouraged the marriage. He was getting older, and with Charles gone, there would be no male to look after his younger daughter. At any rate, she married Young in December 1868, but his health was failing. He went west to recuperate and died there in 1873. That same year her sister and father succumbed to pneumonia. At the age of twenty-eight, Ella Flagg Young was widowed and without any living members in her immediate family. She turned her familial affections to the teachers and children of the Chicago schools.

From 1887 to 1899 Young worked as an assistant or district superintendent. This period also witnessed one of the most rapid growth periods for the Chicago schools. Even with the erection of 271 school buildings between 1884 and 1893, temporary arrangements were still necessary. Total enrollment grew from 630,000 in 1886 to about 1.5 million in 1893, and pupils attending half-day sessions rose from 6,000 to 14,000 over that same period.[2]

Curricular changes accompanied these growth patterns. Many of the progressive reforms were starting to gain attention. Manual arts, domestic science, music, art, and the kindergarten were some of the innovations that critics derogatorily called "fads and frills." In addition, many of the elementary school teachers—predominantly women—were holding meetings in order to protest their working conditions. For example, women teachers were not supposed to be married, yet they had no pension system to safeguard their retirement years. Second, whenever the city's treasury was found to be lacking, the elementary (women) teachers were the first to receive salary cuts. Finally, they wanted to have some voice in the curriculum—an activity that assistant superintendent Young allowed in her district. The outgrowth of these meetings was the organization called the Chicago Teachers' Federation (CTF). Its two powerful leaders, Catharine Goggin and Margaret Haley, had been influenced by Young's democratic policies as district superintendent.

In 1895 Ella Flagg Young was feeling the need for more academic preparation and decided to enroll in a course at the University of Chicago's newly
opened department of philosophy, psychology, and pedagogy, headed by
John Dewey. By 1898 Young was contemplating giving up the district superintendency to pursue a doctorate. She had several reasons: a new superintendent with much more autocratic and conservative policies had been
hired; even though she was fifty-four, she was not ready to retire, and she
had gone about as far as she could without an advanced degree; and Dewey
was anxious to have her come to Chicago and help him run an experimental
school that was in trouble.

In June 1899 Young submitted her resignation. The CTF planned a protest only to discover that Young did not want it. She told them that she
could not work in such a harness as the new superintendent had imposed.
She also tried to squelch the rumor that she was going on the faculty at the
University of Chicago. (No professorship had been offered her yet, but many
rumors circulated to the effect that she had resigned for such a reason.) In
pursuing a Ph.D., she was sticking to an old motto of hers: "Those who live
on the mountain have a longer day than those who live in the valley. Sometimes all we need to brighten our day is to climb a little higher." Ella Flagg
Young would climb much higher before she finished her career.

On a blistering August day in 1900, Mrs. Young became Dr. Young as
she successfully defended her dissertation entitled "Isolation in School Systems." Her dissertation embodied a philosophy of learning by experience
and of social freedoms for a school community through a democratically run
administration from superintendent to student. She was obviously pragmatic
in her views, and John Dewey was later to say that she "was a practicing
pragmatist long before the doctrine was ever in print" and that he got more
ideas from her than anyone else when it came to education.[3]

For the next four years Dr. Young served as a professor of education at
the University of Chicago. Her mission was to bring Chicago teachers to
the university and to expand Dewey's scope as a leading professor in preparing elementary teachers—something similar to what Parker had been doing. The University of Chicago had just acquired the renowned Colonel
Parker and his faculty. Dewey and his lab school were in eclipse. Even after
Parker died in 1902, the fighting continued. Dewey tried to rid himself of
the colonel's faculty. Finally, when this did not work, he resigned. The year
was 1904, and Dr. Young, who was tired of the petty politics and of playing
a middle role, left too. Rumor had it that the university's president, William
Rainey Harper, had offered her a better position if she would stay but that
she had turned it down. She left for Europe with her friend and roommate,
Laura Brayton. While she was there, the principalship of the Chicago Normal School (the old Cook County Normal where Parker had been) came
open. Friends suggested her name, and in the fall of 1905 she entered upon
the duties of principal.

Young's demonstrated leadership skills, knowledge of subject matter, familiarity with Chicago's schools, and ability to inspire made the normal school a model of pragmatic and progressive doctrines during the four years that she was its head. Young screened student applicants to determine their dedication to teaching and their understanding of children. She encouraged the faculty to interweave the new manual arts and domestic sciences with traditional subjects. She chose practice-teaching schools for their ethnic and cultural diversity because the city's population was predominantly foreign-born. But if the normal was running efficiently and effectively, it was one of the few educational institutions in the city to do so. By 1909 internal strife and factionalism were tearing the city schools apart.

The series of events that led to such divisiveness had built up over a period of ten years. The biggest single element that made Board of Education members anxious and hostile was the growth of the teachers' organizations. The CTF, especially, had gained power, independence, and publicity because of its victory in bringing tax dodging corporations under the law and thereby increasing revenues for teachers' salaries. The school board and Superintendent Edwin G. Cooley attempted to squelch this increasingly powerful teachers' organization. Superintendent Cooley tried a philosophy of divide and conquer. The result was tension and hostility throughout the school structure. The teachers discovered that their friend on the board, Jane Addams—while a great social reformer—had little stamina for confronting authority. Several times her sentiment lay with the teachers, but she cast her vote with the board. For example, she voted with the board when it removed the compulsory contribution part of the teachers' pension bill. She also supported Cooley's "merit" system for salary advancement. Opposed by teachers, this system was a secretive process whereby, sometime during the year (unbeknown to the teacher), a principal would fill out a report on each teacher's "efficiency" in the classroom. In order to advance on the salary schedule the teacher had to secure above 70 percent on the efficiency report, which was never shown to the teacher being evaluated. To move into the top levels on the schedule, teachers had to receive 80 percent efficiency marks and be reexamined for certification.

After Cooley resigned in 1909, the board took five months to interview six candidates. Finally, on July 29, they unanimously elected Ella Flagg Young on the second ballot. Apparently, the board put its trust in her because it felt that she could best handle the CTF, which had since managed to put back the compulsory contribution clause of their pension fund, along with a pension board predominantly made up of teachers and few school board members. (There was also a clause that made the board contribute some money to the fund.) Dr. Young had told the school board that she thought the CTF could be made to equalize pension board representation if it meant that the school board would match the teachers dollar for dollar.

The teachers trusted Young because most of them had had some personal encounters with her previously. It was said that she knew all 6,000 teachers in the system by name. She removed the secret marking system and began to involve the teachers in decisions that affected their professional lives. From the first she announced that her administration would be characterized by "democratic efficiency. . . . There is to be but one head," she said, "and I am it. Whenever I find that I cannot have complete charge of the educational end of the school system, I will quit. I cannot carry out my ideas unless I am given control of affairs."[4]

The first two and a half years of her superintendency were harmonious. Courses of study reflected individual differences. Grammar schools offered domestic science, and manual arts was organized along the lines she had used at the normal school. The regular high schools offered more vocational work instead of placing it in separate technical high schools. Sex hygiene— under the name personal purity—was introduced, although many parents were a little concerned about such a topic. Young got salary increases for the elementary teachers, as well as the high school teachers, in two of her first three years in office.

The various parts of the school system were united enough by 1910 to successfully "boom" her to the presidency of the National Education Association (NEA). She was the first female to ever head any large school system, and her picture made front pages of most city newspapers, including the *New York Times*. With her NEA victory she added another first, for no female had ever been elected president of this male-dominated professional organization. This presidency was not without its problems, however, because the old guard leaders William T. Harris and Nicholas Murray Butler were frightened by Young's announced intention of having the organization's permanent fund investigated. Rumors had circulated suggesting that all was not well when one of the fund's trustees—the superintendent of schools in Peoria, Illinois—went to prison for fraud and embezzlement after a bank that he had owned failed. Actually, the fund had not been tampered with, although some of the money was invested badly. The permanent fund's directors instituted a campaign of threats and mudslinging. In the end Young emerged, if not completely victorious, at least as a courageous leader in the eyes of many teachers who appreciated her efforts to make the NEA more democratic.

In 1912, with the NEA fight behind, trouble began to loom in Chicago. A new mayor, Carter Henry Harrison, Jr., had appointed a new board under different leadership, and it was changing its relationship to the superintendent, even though it had reelected her and her assistant, John D. Shoop. By early summer 1912, rumors were developing that Mayor Harrison no longer supported her. The mayor wrote, assuring her of his support and asking her to ignore the empty rumors. She acknowledged her appreciation of his support, told him that she had ignored the rumors, and wished his administration well. But her troubles were just beginning.

The next three and a half years demonstrated some of the problems of large school bureaucracies. Mayor Harrison appointed board members who reflected important political interests. Some of these members understood and agreed with what Young wanted to do. Others either did not understand or had different (often personal) agendas. For example, some board members disagreed with manual training ("fads and frills") and blocked Young's curriculum plans. One member wanted to choose the texts. Others wanted control of the teachers' pension fund. After extensive behind-the-scenes conversations about pension fund control, the CTF called an open meeting to allow interested parties to state positions and answer questions. Margaret Haley, head of the CTF, learned that William Rothmann, chair of the school board's finance committee and the man who wanted to oversee the teachers' pension fund, had absconded with interest money from the police pension fund years earlier. She documented the evidence and circulated it to the CTF membership. Young, on the other hand, was trying to convince teachers that they could get matching pension fund dollars from the board if board membership was increased.

The CTF mass meeting was scheduled for a Thursday after school. It opened in chaos. The acting chairman—William B. Owen, Young's successor at the normal school—could hardly get the meeting called to order. Both Haley and Young asked for the floor at the same time. Owen did not know whom to recognize, so he asked the pleasure of the convention. "Amidst cries of 'let her speak,' and 'no, no, no,' [the superintendent] left [the room] because she thought she had been denied the floor." Owen sent a messenger after her. Upon her return, Young explained that Rothmann would not be able to do anything underhanded with the interest from the pension fund because he would be too closely watched and also because the laws had been changed to forbid it. When the teachers voted, their preference was against the board's bill. Young lost, and, what was worse, she appeared to have been pitted against the teachers.

Up until this time her open-door policy had seemed to keep in tune with teachers' sentiment, but now she felt more isolated. She lamented this in her 1913 annual report and called for the adoption of teachers' councils. These were to meet on a monthly basis during school hours. Teachers could express their views and make suggestions. They were to start in the fall of 1913, but that spring and summer it looked as if they would be starting without her. In June, board members began openly expressing hostility toward her. Rothmann pestered her, seeking favors, including the demotion of certain CTF teachers, but she refused. Another board member, John C. Harding, was upset because she ignored his choice of spellers. In June, Mayor Harrison wrote her another letter of support. It helped, and so did the fact that the new board president, Peter Reinberg, supported her; but hostility from other board members persisted.

On June 27, under Governor Dunne, a former Chicago mayor, the Illinois women got the franchise. An article in the *Chicago Record Herald* pictured Ella Flagg Young with Jane Addams and Julia Lathrop, a social reformer. The caption read, "Three Reasons Why Illinois Women Won the Vote First," but it was little comfort to her. At the end of July, she submitted her resignation. She told newspaper reporters that she "was the victim of political intrigue among board members." The interview quoted her as saying "that her retention of the superintendency would impair the efficiency of the schools." Former member of the board Dr. Cornelia DeBey told reporters that it was due to actions "of a lot of cheap politicians and the board. We women won't stand for it." But two other board members said they were sure that the board would accept her resignation. President Reinberg said he would resign if the action was approved. Another board member, William Vincent, alluded to some of her difficulties with three of the board members. "It's too bad," said Vincent, "but it's the only thing she can do to save her self-respect."[5]

Events of the next few days, however, changed things. A delegation of women arrived at the mayor's office; the mayor wrote to the superintendent urging her to reconsider and stay as head of schools; and he apprised her of three new board appointments—Mrs. Gertrude Britton, Mrs. Florence Vosbrink, and Dr. Peter Clemenson. On July 30 the board voted fourteen to one to retain her. (Harding voted no.) She was encouraged. "I shall abide by the action of the board of education," she told newspapers. "It will still be my aim to make the Chicago public schools the embodiment of [progressive] thought. . . . The kind words of parents and teachers have touched me deeply." Mayor Harrison announced, "Her rule should be unopposed in all matters pertaining to the schools."[6]

The fall term went smoothly, but all it meant was that her antagonizers had gone underground. On December 10 the board convened to take up the reelection of superintendent and assistant. In a sudden move, Young's enemies nominated and elected her subordinate, John D. Shoop, as superintendent. Citywide protests by numerous groups pressured the mayor into making enough new board appointments to bring about Young's reelection. Rothmann was ousted from the board in this process.

Both Young and Shoop accepted their old posts, and the school administration began functioning just in time to see the schools open after the holiday break. Through a series of legal appeals, the ousted members were finally reinstated by May 1914. Their original terms, however, expired shortly after they were reseated.

The time from January 1914 to December 1915 moved along without the personal struggles of the previous year, but also without the triumphs and unity of the early two years. In December 1914 Young was reappointed by a vote of fourteen to seven. She was able to continue her policies and even managed to get a 5 percent salary increase for the teachers. The same board members who had refused to vote for her return smoldered. Her opponents on the board resented the restraint placed upon them by the mayor, and they blamed his long arm of control and the CTF for her reelection. Real estate magnate Jacob Loeb—by now a dominant force on the board—voted for Young and publicly supported her, but he resented the CTF's power. As long as Young remained in office, he was somewhat careful in his overt activities, but when the approach of her retirement became obvious, so did his motives.

Young planned to retire on July 1, 1915. She decided, however, to remain to face a new budget deficit and threat of salary decreases. She trimmed the budget so that Loeb's threatened salary cut did not go into effect. Toward the end of August 1915, she went on vacation, and while she was gone, the board met. Loeb presented a ruling to be voted on immediately. Known as the "Loeb rule," it prohibited teachers from belonging to any union-type organization such as the CTF. The board approved the "Loeb rule," some because of Loeb's autocratic control and others because business interests compelled it. When Young returned, there was little she could do. Her imminent December retirement made her a lame duck. All teachers had received contracts with clauses containing the new rulings. They had to sign these before they could get a paycheck. Young tried to get some recommendations for promotions approved. Loeb and the board refused approval until the contracts were signed. CTF attorney Greenacre secured an injunction against the board. Haley went to work for a tenure protection bill in the meantime. So CTF opposition was held at bay until Young retired in December. Before she left town, she warned the teachers that the opposition was not over—it was just lying dormant. In the spring of 1916 under Superintendent Shoop, board president Loeb refused to issue contracts to sixty-eight teachers for the following year.

Even in retirement Young kept faith with the teachers. She presented a paper at the NEA meeting in July 1916. Ironically, Jacob Loeb preceded her, defending his stand against teachers' unions. When she heard this, she discarded her prepared speech and answered his criticisms. She said, "No person should ever be on the board of education who does not send his own children, or did not send them while they were of school age, to the public schools." Loeb's children attended private schools.[7]

By the fall of 1917 the United States was involved in war. Young and some friends went to work for the second Liberty Loan Committee. This loan was one of five huge bond issues floated to finance the war and sold to citizens in small denominations. She continued to attend the NEA's conventions. At Pittsburgh, in July 1918, when she walked into the meeting hall, everyone spontaneously stood in silent ovation. She stepped up to the lectern, and as she began to speak, she glanced down at her well-worn dress and said, "Why, since the war began I haven't even thought of clothes."[8]

In the fall, Young went on another speaking tour for the fourth Liberty Loan. In Wyoming she contracted the flu but refused to go to bed. She finished the trip and was able to get to Washington to turn her money in to secretary of state William McAdoo, but by now she had pneumonia. She died on October 26. Her body was brought back to Chicago, accompanied by a military regiment. The flags in Chicago were flown at half-mast, and the Board of Education offices were draped in black. McAdoo said that she "died in the service of her country, working like a soldier." It was a fitting homage for a leader of whom Jane Addams had said, "She had more general intelligence and character than any other woman I knew."[9]

Ella Flagg Young was the archetypical progressive: intelligently altruistic, open to change, always learning, democratic, and humane. Even the war efforts that brought on her death typified the progressive notion that everyone should work for the good of the group. For women, she opened the tightly locked door to educational administration and the superintendency. For children she brought the fresh air of progressive reform into the stale and stifling classroom atmosphere of rote memorization and harsh discipline.

NOTES

1. Joan K. Smith, *Ella Flagg Young: Portrait of a Leader* (Ames, IA: Educational Studies Press, 1979). All biographical information on Young is from this source.

2. Department of Public Instruction, City of Chicago, *Thirty-Ninth Annual Report of the Board of Education for the Year Ending June 30, 1893*, 29–32; *Thirty-Second Annual Report* (1886), 39; Department of Public Instruction, City of Chicago, *Proceedings of the Board of Education for the Year Ending June 30, 1887* (Chicago: Hack and Anderson, 1888), 229.

3. John T. McManis, *Ella Flagg Young and a Half Century of the Chicago Public Schools* (Chicago: A. C. McClurg, 1916), Frontispiece, 120–21.

4. "Young at the Helm," *Chicago Record Herald*, August 1909.

5. "Mrs. Young Quits as School Head; Politics Cause," *Daily Inter-Ocean*, July 25, 1913, 1; "Mrs. Young May Reconsider Her Decision to Quit," *Chicago Record Herald*, July 26, 1913, 1.

6. "Mrs. Young to Stay as Head of Schools," *Daily Inter-Ocean*, July 31, 1913, 1.

7. Ella Flagg Young, "A Reply," *Journal of Proceedings and Addresses of the Fifty-Fourth Annual Meeting of the National Education Association Held at New York City*, July 1–8, 1916 (Chicago: University of Chicago Press, 1916), 359.

8. C. W. Bardeen, "Necrology," *Journal of Addresses and Proceedings of the Fifty-Sixth Annual Meeting of the NEA Held in Pittsburgh*, June 29–July 6, 1918 (Chicago: University of Chicago Press, 1918), 685.

9. "Flags to Fly at Half Mast Today for Mrs. Young," *Chicago Tribune*, October 28, 1918, 8; "Ella F. Young Dies," *Chicago Tribune* October 27, 1918.

WORKS BY ELLA FLAGG YOUNG

Ethics in the School. Chicago: University of Chicago Press, 1902.
Isolation in the School. Chicago: University of Chicago Press, 1902.
Some Types of Educational Theory. Chicago: University of Chicago Press, 1902.

WORKS ABOUT ELLA FLAGG YOUNG

McManis, John T. *Ella Flagg Young and a Half Century of the Chicago Public Schools.* Chicago: A. C. McClurg, 1916.
Smith, Joan K. *Ella Flagg Young: Portrait of a Leader.* Ames, IA: Educational Studies Press, 1979.

Marie E. Zakrzewska

Maureen A. Kingston

Marie E. Zakrzewska (1829–1902) was among the first cohort of women to be admitted to the all-male American medical schools of the nineteenth century. After receiving her degree, Dr. Zakrzewska found she was unable to acquire requisite clinical experience. No hospital would admit her (or any woman) for such training. Zakrzewska responded to this discrimination by devoting her career to creating clinical education opportunities for women. Her greatest achievement was the establishment of the New England Hospital for Women and Children, which she founded in Boston in 1862. For four decades, Zakrzewska presided over one of the few institutions in the United States where female physicians and nurses could obtain the clinical preparation they needed in order to practice their professions.

Marie Elizabeth Zakrzewska was born on September 6, 1829, in Berlin, Germany. She was the eldest of six children (five girls and one boy) born to Martin Ludwig Zakrzewska and Frederika C. W. Urban. Zakrzewska's father descended from an aristocratic Polish family that lost its fortune to Russian repatriation in the late 1700s. Frederika Zakrzewska's family were gypsies of the Lombardi tribe. There was a considerable tradition of medical practice on the Urban side of Dr. Zakrzewska's family. For instance, her maternal great-grandfather was a surgeon in Frederick the Great's army; her grandmother, for whom she was named (Marie Elizabeth Sauer), was a veterinary surgeon; and her mother, Frederika, was a midwife. Dr. Zakrzewska resided in Berlin until 1853, when she emigrated to the United States. She lived most of her life in the environs of Boston.

A prescient theme of Zakrzewska's childhood was her challenge of authority and authority figures. At the age of five, she had already earned the label "unruly" in school because, as she recalls, "I would not obey [teachers'] arbitrary demands."[1] In primary school, where boys and girls received separate instruction, she was placed with the boys as a punishment for her failure to abide by accepted norms of female comportment: she was often rude in manner and unkempt in appearance. Zakrzewska actually preferred this arrangement. With boys, she could be "frank and self- possessed" while she felt "shy and awkward" in the company of girls.[2]

Zakrzewska's interest in medicine began early in life. Like many little girls, she played doctor and nursed her dolls. At the age of nine, play became reality. She spent all her free time that year tending an ailing cousin in an ophthalmic hospital. Despite her youth, her immediate and extended families had great confidence in her nursing skills, and she was frequently called upon to minister to sick relatives. Ironically, Zakrzewska's desire to enter medicine was cemented by her own experience with an illness.

In 1838, Martin Zakrzewska was dismissed from his post as a military officer. His government pension proved too meager to cover the family's expenses. Frederika Zakrzewska enrolled in Berlin's prestigious School for Midwives in an attempt to rescue her family from privation. During her hospital residency in the summer of 1840 her daughter contracted a debilitating eye infection. Blind and frightened, Marie begged to join her mother at the hospital, and her mother complied.

Dr. Johannes Müller treated Zakrzewska's infection. He was so impressed with the ten-year-old's precocity that he took her on rounds with him and fondly referred to her as his "little blind doctor."[3] Listening to Dr. Müller's examinations and diagnoses convinced Zakrzewska that medicine would be her life's work. She was afraid of neither the hospital environment nor the sickness she encountered. In fact, the first thing she did when her sight returned was sneak into the hospital's morgue to view a corpse that was reputed to be in an unusual state of decay. "I examined everything," she reported, "and looked to my heart's content at the [green] poisoned young man."[4] At the end of the summer, Dr. Müller loaned Zakrzewska two history books on midwifery and surgery. From this beginning, her appetite for medical knowledge grew, and she continued to borrow books as often as she could.

Between the ages of fourteen and eighteen, Zakrzewska acquired practical medical knowledge by assisting her mother in her midwife duties. This experience also influenced her character development. For instance, the unpredictability of childbirth allowed Zakrzewska the freedom to traverse the city at all times of the day and night. She developed a sense of independence and self-reliance from this unfettered mobility. Moreover, her contact with women from various social class backgrounds led her to question prevailing stereotypes regarding women's morality. She recalls:

During these years, I learned [about] life. . . . I saw nobleness in dens, and meanness in palaces; virtue among prostitutes, and vice among so-called respectable women. I learned to . . . see goodness where the world found nothing but faults, and also to see faults where the world could see nothing but virtue.[5]

Several personality traits nascent in Zakrzewska's childhood became definitive in her adulthood. They included dogged determination, self-discipline, independence of mind, and the ability to handle tremendous responsibilities. As a child and a teen, she sought and adopted adult roles: caring for younger siblings, ailing relatives, and her mother's patients. Although she earned top honors in school, her intelligence tended to alienate peers and exasperate teachers. Leaving school permanently at the age of thirteen, she taught herself from her father's library and borrowed books. None of Zakrzewska's future achievements would have been possible, however, without the early support of her parents. While expecting her to perform traditional ("female") household tasks, they also took great pains to nurture and prize her intellect and independent spirit.

By the time she arrived at the doorstep of Dr. Joseph Herman Schmidt, Marie Zakrzewska was self-assured and ready to make her mark on the world. Following in her mother's footsteps, she applied to the Berlin School for Midwives at the age of eighteen. Her father encouraged her, believing a woman ought to be able to support herself. Surprisingly, her mother objected. Having been forced by financial need to become a midwife, she knew its hardships firsthand and wanted to spare her daughter the trauma.

Unlike in America, midwifery in Germany was formalized, had professional status, and paid well. Though competition was fierce, Zakrzewska's initial rejection by the school was more a function of her age than her qualifications. She was young, unmarried, and ambitious. Typical students were more like her mother—married, middle-aged, the wives of civil servants hoping to supplement their family's income, in short, women who would pose no threat to the male doctors-in-training with whom the student midwives shared course work.

Dr. Schmidt was a renowned professor of midwifery at the School for Midwives and the director of the Royal Hospital Charité. Zakrzewska sought his counsel after her rejection. He was extremely impressed with her talents and promised to use his influence to help her. True to his word, Dr. Schmidt appealed to the royal family on her behalf (the king held Schmidt in high esteem), and she was admitted.

Near the end of her studies, Schmidt became gravely ill. Fearing the worst, he designated Zakrzewska to be his successor as professor of midwifery at the School for Midwives, and he also recommended her for the post of chief *accoucheuse* (chief clinical midwife) at the hospital. If Zakrzewska's appointments were approved, the entire education of midwives would be under the supervision of a woman for the first time in German history. As she had passed her final exams with superior marks, Dr. Schmidt assumed his protégé's installation would be a simple formality. The raucous public debate that ensued caught both Schmidt and Zakrzewska by surprise.

For five months, Zakrzewska was *the* topic of conversation in Berlin. Apparently, few in the medical community minded women's becoming midwives so long as males controlled their education and male gynecologists and obstetricians were not obliged to take orders from them. Zakrzewska's appointments would indeed have upset this male hegemony. Debate concerning her appointments permeated the medical community and sparked citywide discussions of women's roles, rights, and abilities. "The real question at stake," Zakrzewska recalls, "was 'How shall women be educated,' and 'what is their true sphere'?"[6]

Schmidt believed women should have the same opportunities as men in life and in medicine. Though seriously ill, he called in numerous political markers to garner support for Zakrzewska's appointments. In the meantime, Zakrzewska's father, humiliated by the public scrutiny, rescinded his support and urged Marie to find a husband and return to her proper (woman's) sphere. Frederika Zakrzewska also reversed her position. Confident that her daughter was as capable as any man, she encouraged her to stand her ground.

On May 15, 1852, twenty-two-year-old Marie Zakrzewska was legally installed in both positions. The next day, her beloved mentor died. Few of Schmidt's cronies maintained their allegiance to Zakrzewska after his death. The new hospital director and several male doctors were particularly resentful of her presence and plotted to oust her. They succeeded. Friendless and exhausted by political chicanery, she resigned six months later. Throughout her life, males (e.g., her father, friends, Drs. Müller and Schmidt) had nurtured Zakrzewska and treated her as their equal. This bald encounter with sexism introduced her to the destructive side of male power, and she would be forever wary of it.

Zakrzewska was certain she would never be treated fairly in the Berlin medical community. A few months before his death, Dr. Schmidt received a positive report concerning the Female Medical College of Pennsylvania (established in 1850). "In America," he said, "women will now become physicians, like the men; this shows that only in a republic can it be proved that science has no sex."[7] Hoping Americans would be more tolerant of female doctors than Berliners, Zakrzewska decided to lend her expertise to the women's college. She and her sister Anna sailed for New York in 1853 to begin a new life.

Zakrzewska's first year in America was as bad as her last year in Berlin. She hung out her shingle but failed to entice even one patient. Upon inquiry, she discovered that many New Yorkers equated "female physicians" with Madame Restelle, an infamous abortionist. In addition, no practicing physician would take Zakrzewska on as a partner, including an old family friend who informed her that "female physicians in this country [are] of the lowest rank and . . . they [do] not hold even the position of a good nurse."[8] After a year of disappointment, she conceded she had "idealized the freedom of America and especially the reform of the position of women."[9]

In the spring of 1854, Zakrzewska experienced a change of luck. An acquaintance introduced her to Dr. Elizabeth Blackwell, the first American woman to be awarded a medical degree. Of this meeting, Elizabeth wrote her sister Emily, "I have at last found a student in whom I can take a great deal of interest."[10] Blackwell became Zakrzewska's preceptor, tutored her in English, convinced her to pursue a medical degree, and helped her to gain admittance to the Cleveland Medical College (Western Reserve) in Ohio.

The two years Zakrzewska spent earning her medical degree were pivotal. The medical education itself was tedious because, though technically a midwife, much of Schmidt's training had actually prepared her to become a doctor. The real lessons of these years occurred outside the classroom.

Zakrzewska was one of four women and 200 men to matriculate at the Cleveland Medical College in the fall of 1854. During her first term, she was lonely, isolated, and short of funds. Her father, who had hoped the trip to America would blunt his daughter's desire to become a doctor, refused to help her. In a letter, he chided, "If you were a young man, I could not find words in which to express my satisfaction and pride in respect to your acts; for I know that all you accomplish you owe to yourself: but you are a woman, a weak woman; and all that I can do for you now is to grieve."[11] Enervated by this disapproval, Zakrzewska recalled, "I resolved to follow my father's advice and give up [the] man's sphere."[12]

When word of her imminent departure became known, several women came to Zakrzewska's aid. Caroline Severance, president of the Ladies Physiological Society of Cleveland, provided free room and board; Dr. Harriet Hunt, through the Ohio Female Medical Society, paid lecture dues; and Dr. Blackwell, who had already loaned Zakrzewska medical books, promised to share her small practice once she graduated. This tangible support enabled her to complete her medical degree in 1856. The most important woman and role model in Zakrzewska's life, her mother, died at sea while en route to her graduation.

Zakrzewska was profoundly affected by the women's support. Despite personal encounters with sex discrimination, she had considered feminist movements of her day to be "ridiculous" and referred to the women involved as "crowing hens."[13] The floodgates to her consciousness were pried open, however, by the magnanimity of the "crowing hens" of Cleveland, and she began to reevaluate her thinking on many issues. Zakrzewska spent her second year attending numerous lectures, lyceums, and discussions sponsored by sundry antebellum reform movements (e.g., woman's rights, free love, abolitionism, spiritualism, temperance). "This second year," she explained, "was . . . a most valuable episode of my life, turning all my views topsy-turvy, uprooting me . . . from all [my] German conservatism and throwing me into this chaotic medley of contradictions."[14]

The one movement she did rebuff was "irregular" medicine. At this juncture, medicine was more of a healing art than a science. In terms of medical professionalization (licensure regulations, university affiliations, clinical training, and so on), the United States was about a half century behind Europe. Although some regulation existed, "doctors" could and did encompass a wide variety of individuals (e.g., both hypnotists and surgeons used the appellation "Dr."). In general, those who attended medical schools like Harvard were considered "regular" practitioners while those who apprenticed with homeopaths or herbalists were considered "irregular" practitioners.

Though a firm supporter of America's "regular" medical education establishment, Zakrzewska was appalled by its lack of clinical instruction. In Europe, the hospital had become the lecture hall. In America in the 1860s, only Harvard and the University of Pennsylvania had affiliations with hospitals that provided students with clinical practice. Zakrzewska believed it was "impossible to have a thorough medical education without actual experience at the bedside of . . . patients."[15]

The conundrum for women went as follows: they could attend a few "regular" all-male medical schools (though not the two schools offering clinical instruction) but were forbidden from entering hospitals either for clinical residency or for treatment of patients. Some women who could afford it, like Dr. Blackwell, went to Europe for instruction and returned to establish private practices. Those who could not afford it were like auto mechanics who managed to become certified to repair cars without ever having lifted a hood—useless to flesh-and-blood patients. Zakrzewska made it her mission to create clinical opportunities so that female physicians could actually practice their profession.

After receiving her medical degree, Zakrzewska joined Elizabeth Blackwell in New York. Between 1856 and 1859, they traveled around New England, raising funds and promoting the idea of women in medicine. They worked well together because, as Blackwell put it, "I work[ed] chiefly in [p]rinciples, and [Marie] in putting them into practical use; and one [was] essential to the other."[16] Each pioneer advanced the cause in her own way. Blackwell lectured and developed a social rationale for women's presence in medicine, and Zakrzewska mobilized support to build institutions for them to practice in. The fruit of this collaboration was the opening of the New York Infirmary for Women and Children (the first hospital in America run entirely by women) in the spring of 1857. Women doctors desperate for clinical experience quickly filled the small hospital, and, within a year, applicants had to be turned away.

In 1859, Zakrzewska accepted a professorship at the New England Female Medical College in Boston. Though the school was "irregular," she hoped to upgrade its standards so women might obtain quality theoretical and clinical instruction in the same place. Zakrzewska and Samuel Gregory, the school's founder, battled constantly over his slipshod certification policies.

Determined to educate women "on sound principles," she left the school three years later to open her own hospital.[17] During this career transition, Martin Zakrzewska died. He went to his grave still exhorting his daughter to abandon her "masculine" pursuits.

The New England Hospital for Women and Children opened in Boston on July 1, 1862. It was the second all-female hospital in the United States (after the New York Infirmary). The hospital owed its life to a core group of middle-class feminists who financed its launching and helped to operate it throughout its existence. Except for a brief period in the 1950s, the hospital maintained its single-sex identity until it closed in 1969.

Within fifteen years, Dr. Zakrzewska (now known simply as "Dr. Zak") had accomplished her major goals in founding the hospital: to provide female physicians and nurses with clinical training and employment and to provide poor women with medical service from female physicians. By the turn of the century, the hospital had long outgrown its initial ten-bed facility and moved to larger quarters, adding surgical, obstetric, and pediatric wings along the way.

In many ways, the hospital and its founder were products of their times. The New England was similar to other charity hospitals constructed after the 1840s to meet the needs of the urban poor. Its all-female focus was a novelty for hospitals, but other all-female institutions did exist (e.g., women's colleges). The hospital's striking feature was its symbolic and actual challenge of the status quo. The very existence of an institution owned and operated by women contradicted Victorian social mores, which insisted women were incapable of functioning outside the home.

Before she died of a stroke at her home in Jamaica Plain, Massachusetts, on May 12, 1902, Zakrzewska was beginning to experience some of the controversy that surrounds advocates of single-sex institutions today. She believed women should receive the same quality of medical education as men, but within their own institutions. This "separate but equal" philosophy offended many integration-minded interns and physicians who worked at the New England in the closing decades of the nineteenth century. They were no longer barred from many male-dominated hospitals, and some of the best schools had begun admitting women (e.g., Johns Hopkins in 1893 and Cornell in 1899). They found Zakrzewska's insistence on rigorous clinical study and social responsibility and female solidarity to be dated and unnecessary. Although the New England Hospital for Women and Children managed to survive into the twentieth century, it reached its zenith during Zakrzewska's lifetime.

Dr. Zakrzewska devoted her life to medicine and to her hospital. Like many pioneers, she never married or had children. Although never officially published, her autobiography, *A Practical Illustration of "Woman's Right to Labor"* (describing her life up to 1860), was widely circulated.[18] It earned her the respect of men and inspired women to enter medicine. Her chief contribution to the women of her time was to make it possible for them to learn and practice medicine when all other educational avenues were closed to them.

NOTES

1. Agnes C. Vietor, ed., *A Woman's Quest: The Life of Marie E. Zakrzewska, M.D.* (New York: Arno Press, 1924, reprint, 1972), 8.
2. Ibid., 9.
3. Ibid., 17.
4. Ibid., 18.
5. Ibid., 28.
6. Ibid., 47.
7. Ibid., 67.
8. Ibid., 84.
9. Ibid., 70.
10. Ibid., 109.
11. Ibid., 140.
12. Ibid., 142.
13. Ibid., 134.
14. Ibid., 159.
15. Virginia G. Drachman, *Hospital with a Heart; Women Doctors and the Paradox of Separatism at the New England Hospital, 1862–1969* (Ithaca, NY: Cornell University Press, 1984), 64.
16. Vietor, 188.
17. Ibid., 292.
18. Drachman, 49.

WORK BY MARIE E. ZAKRZEWSKA

"Report of One Hundred and Eighty-Seven Cases of Midwifery in Private Practice." *Boston Medical and Surgical Journal* 121 (December 1889): 557–60.

WORKS ABOUT MARIE E. ZAKRZEWSKA

Blake, John B. "Zakrzewska, Marie Elizabeth." In Edward T. James, ed., *Notable American Women 1607–1950*, 702–4. Cambridge, MA: Belknap Press of Harvard University Press, 1971.

Drachman, Virginia G. *Hospital with a Heart: Women Doctors and the Paradox of Separatism at the New England Hospital, 1862–1969*. Ithaca, NY: Cornell University Press, 1984.

———. "Female Solidarity and Professional Success: The Dilemma of Women Doctors in Late 19th-Century America." In Judith W. Leavitt and Ronald L. Numbers, eds., *Sickness and Health in America: Readings in the History of Medicine and Public Health*, 173–82. Madison: University of Wisconsin Press, 1985.

Greenwood, Ronald D. "Marie Zakrzewska, M.D." *New York State Journal of Medicine* 76 (August 1976): 1339–41.

Kleinert, Margaret N. "Linda Richards and the New England Hospital." *Journal of the American Medical Women's Association* 23 (September 1968): 828–30.

New England Hospital for Women and Children. *Marie Elizabeth Zakrzewska: A Memoir*. Boston: New England Hospital for Women and Children, 1903. New Haven, CT: Research Publications, 1977, microfilm, 5403.

Vietor, Agnes C., ed. *A Woman's Quest: The Life of Marie E. Zakrzewska, M.D.* New York: Arno Press, 1924. Reprint, 1972.

Walsh, Mary R. *"Doctors Wanted: No Women Need Apply": Sexual Barriers in the Medical Profession, 1835–1975*. New Haven, CT: Yale University Press, 1977.

Appendix: A Chronological List of Women Educators

This appendix attempts to place the women educators discussed in this volume in the four chronological periods described in the introduction. Some had such long careers, however, that they were professionally active beyond the period in which their name appears.

I. The Pioneers 1820–1870

Emma Hart Willard (1787–1870)

Almira Hart Lincoln Phēlps (1793–1884)

Zilpah Polly Grant Banister (1794–1874)

Mary Lyon (1797–1849)

Catharine Beecher (1800–1878)

Lydia Maria Francis Child (1802–1880)

Sarah Mapps Douglass (1806–1882)

Emily Eliza Ingham Staunton (1811–1889)

Mary Atkins Lynch (1819–1882)

Caroline F. Putnam (1826–1917)

Lucretia Crocker (1829–1886)

Marie E. Zakrzewska (1829–1902)

Caroline Elizabeth Bushyhead Quarles (1834–1909)

Fanny Marion Jackson Coppin (1837–1913)

Sarah Ann Dickey (1838–1904)

II. Expanders and Reformers 1870–1920

Julia Strudwick Tutwiler (1841–1916)
Ellen Swallow Richards (1842–1911)
Mother Mary Regis Casserly (1843–1917)
Ella Flagg Young (1845–1918)
Sister Blandina Segale (1850–1941)
Celestia Susannah Parrish (1853–1918)
Lucy Craft Laney (1854–1933)
Julia Etta Crane (1855–1923)
Alice Freeman Palmer (1855–1902)
Julia Richman (1855–1912)
Mary Carroll Craig Bradford (1856/1862?–1938)
Martha Carey Thomas (1857–1935)
Mary Adelaide Nutting (1858–1948)
Marion Talbot (1858–1948)
Mother Mary Katharine Drexel (1859–1955)
Anna Julia Cooper (1860–1964)
Laura Jane Addams (1860–1935)
Margaret Haley (1861–1939)
Mary Church Terrell (1863–1954)
Sophonisba Breckinridge (1866–1948)
Winifred Holt (1870–1945)
Elizabeth Avery Colton (1872–1924)
Harriet M. Bedell (1875–1969)
Mary McLeod Bethune (1875–1955)
Lucy Sprague Mitchell (1878–1967)
Nannie Helen Burroughs (1879–1961)

III. Losses and Gains 1920–1960

Mother Joseph Butler (1860–1940)
Willystine Goodsell (1870–1962)
Alice P. Barrows (1877–1954)
Nina Otero-Warren (1881–1965)
Lucy Diggs Slowe (1883–1937)
Fannia Mary Cohn (1885–1962)
Sister Mary Madeleva Wolff (1887–1964)
Hilda Worthington Smith (1888–1984)
Lois Meek Stolz (1891–1984)
Polingaysi Qöyawayma (1892–1990)

Helen Heffernan (1896–1987)

Katharine Kuh (b. 1904)

IV. Pursuing Equality and Excellence 1960–1993

Septima Poinsette Clark (1898–1987)

Mary Steichen Calderone (b. 1904)

Helen Mansfield Robinson (1906–1988)

Dolores "Lola" Gonzales (1917–1975)

Mari-Luci Jaramillo (b. 1928)

Miriam Colón (b. 193?)

Deborah W. Meier (b. 1931)

Peggy McIntosh (b. 1934)

Johnnetta B. Cole (b. 1936)

Joyce Sachiko Tsunoda (b. 1938)

Sucheng Chan (b. 1941)

Martha Beulah Mann Yallup (b. 1942)

Janine Pease-Windy Boy (b. 1949)

Selected Bibliography

American Association of University Women. *How Schools Shortchange Girls: The AAUW Report: A Study of Major Findings on Girls in Education*. Washington, DC: AAUW Educational Foundation, 1992.

Antler, Joyce, and Sari Knopp Biklen, eds. *Changing Education: Women as Radicals and Conservators*. Albany: State University of New York Press, 1990.

Blair, Karen. *The Clubwoman as Feminist: True Womanhood Redefined 1868–1914*. New York: Holmes and Meier, 1980.

Blandin, Isabella M. E. *History of Higher Education of Women in the South Prior to 1870*. New York: Neale, 1909.

Bowler, Mary. *A History of Catholic Colleges for Women in the United States*. Washington, DC: Catholic University Press of America, 1933.

Chamberlain, Mariam K., ed. *Women in Academe: Progress and Prospects*. New York: Russell Sage Foundation, 1988.

Clifford, Geraldine Joncich. *Lone Voyagers: Academic Women in Coeducational Institutions 1870–1937*. New York: Feminist Press, 1989.

Conrad, Susan Phinney. *Perish the Thought: Intellectual Women in Romantic America*. New York: Oxford University Press, 1976.

Degler, Carl. *At Odds: Women and the Family in America from the Revolution to the Present*. New York: Oxford University Press, 1980.

Edson, Sakre Kennington. *Pushing the Limits; The Female Administrative Aspirant*. Albany: State University of New York Press, 1988.

Giddings, Paula. *When and Where I Enter: The Impact of Black Women on Race and Sex in America*. New York: Morrow, 1984.

Gilligan, Carol. *In a Different Voice: Psychological Theory and Woman's Development*. Cambridge: Harvard University Press, 1982.

Glazer, Penina Migdal, and Miriam Slater. *Unequal Colleagues: The Entrance of Women into the Professions 1890–1940*. New Brunswick, NJ: Rutgers University Press, 1987.

Gordon, Lynn D. *Gender and Higher Education in the Progressive Era*. New Haven, CT: Yale University Press, 1990.

Harris, Barbara J. *Beyond Her Sphere: Women and the Professions in American History.* Westport, CT: Greenwood Press, 1978.

Hoffman, Nancy, ed. *Woman's "True" Profession: Voices from the History of Teaching.* Old Westbury, NY: Feminist Press, 1979.

Holmes, Lulu Haskell. *A History of the Position of Dean of Women in a Selected Group of Coeducational Colleges and Universities in the United States.* New York: Teachers College, Columbia University, 1939.

Horowitz, Helen Lefkowitz. *Alma Mater: Design and Experience in the Women's Colleges from Their Nineteenth Century Beginnings to the 1950s.* Boston: Beacon Press, 1984.

James, Janet Wilson. *Changing Ideas About Women in the United States 1776–1825.* New York: Garland, 1981.

Kaufman, Polly. *Women Teachers on the Frontier.* New Haven, CT: Yale University Press, 1984.

Lagemann, Ellen Condliffe, ed. *A Generation of Women: Education in the Lives of Progressive Reformers.* Cambridge: Harvard University Press, 1979.

Mayo, A. D. *Southern Women in the Recent Educational Movement in the South*, ed. Dan T. Carter and Amy Friedlander. Baton Rouge: Louisiana State University Press, 1978.

Morantz-Sanchez, Regina Markell. *Sympathy and Science: Women Physicians in American Medicine.* New York: Oxford University Press, 1985.

Powers, Jane Bernard. *The "Girl Question" in Education: Vocational Training for Young Women in the Progressive Era.* London: Falmer Press, 1992.

Rosenberg, Rosalind. *Beyond Separate Spheres: Intellectual Roots of Modern Feminism.* New Haven, CT: Yale University Press, 1982.

Rossiter, Margaret W. *Women Scientists in America: Struggles and Strategies to 1940.* Baltimore: Johns Hopkins University Press, 1982.

Salem, Dorothy. *To Better Our World: Black Women in Organized Reform, 1890–1920.* Brooklyn, NY: Carlson, 1990.

Scarborough, Elizabeth, and Laurel Furmoto. *Untold Lives: The First Generation of Women Psychologists.* New York: Columbia University Press, 1987.

Seller, Maxine Schwartz, ed. *Immigrant Women.* Philadelphia: Temple University Press, 1981. Rev. ed., Albany: State University of New York Press, 1994.

Solomon, Barbara Miller. *In the Company of Educated Women: A History of Women and Higher Education in America.* New Haven, CT: Yale University Press, 1985.

Sturnick, Judith, Jane Milley, and Catharine A. Tisinger, eds. *Women at the Helm: Pathfinding Presidents at State Colleges and Universities.* Washington, DC: AASCU Press, 1991.

Tobin, McLean. *The Black Female PhD: Education and Career Development.* Washington, DC: University Press of America, 1981.

Tyack, David, and Elizabeth Hansot. *Learning Together: A History of Coeducation in American Public Schools.* New Haven, CT: Yale University Press and Russell Sage Foundation, 1990.

Warren, Donald, ed. *American Teachers: Histories of a Profession at Work.* New York: Macmillan, 1989.

Woody, Thomas. *A History of Women's Education in the United States.* 2 vols. New York: Science Press, 1929. Reprint, New York: Octagon Books, 1966.

Index

Note: page numbers in *italics* indicate main entries in the text.

About the Editor and Contributors

LINDA D. ADDO is Assistant Professor of History and Social Science Education at North Carolina A. and T. State University in Greensboro, North Carolina. She is the coauthor of *To Be Faithful to Our Heritage: A History of Black United Methodism in North Carolina* and Secretary of the Commission on Archives and History of the Western North Carolina Conference of the United Methodist Church. She has been the recipient of a Woodrow Wilson Fellowship and a Charles B. Dana United Negro College Fund Fellowship.

JOYCE ANTLER is Associate Professor of American Studies at Brandeis University and Cochair of the Graduate Consortium in Women's Studies at Radcliffe College. She is the author of *Lucy Sprague Mitchell: The Making of a Modern Woman* and *The Educated Woman and Professionalization: The Struggle for a New Feminine Identity, 1890–1920* and coauthor of the historical drama *Year One of the Empire: A Play of American Politics, War and Protest*. Among her edited books are *Change in Education: Women as Radicals and Conservators, The Challenge of Feminist Biography: Writing the Lives of Modern American Women*, and *America and I: Short Stories by American Jewish Women Writers*.

ROGER W. ARMSTRONG is Professor of Chemistry at Russell Sage College and does research in environmental chemistry. He has also been active in recent years in teaching hands-on chemistry to elementary school teachers.

JANE BERNARD-POWERS is Assistant Professor of Elementary Education at San Francisco State University. Her recent publications include *The Girl Question in Education, Vocational Education for Young Women in the Progressive Era*, "Gender Differences in Educational Achievement" in *Multicultural Education for the 21st Century*, and "Women, Gender and the California History Social Science Framework" (coeditor) in *Social Studies Review*. She is on the Editorial Board for *Theory and Research in Social Education* and is currently working on a curriculum biography of Fannie Shaftel and Hilda Taba.

SELMA BERROL is Professor of History at Baruch College. She has published extensively in the field of history of education, particularly in the education of immigrants in the United States in the late nineteenth and early twentieth centuries. Her books include *Immigrants at School, Getting Down to Business: A History of Baruch College*, and *Julia Richman*. Her most recent project is a comparative study of Jewish immigrants in New York City and London.

SARI KNOPP BIKLEN is Associate Professor at Syracuse University in the Department of Cultural Foundations of Education. She has written a number of articles about women as teachers, women's education, and feminist scholarship and has written a book (with Robert Bogdan), *Qualitative Research for Education*. She has edited (with Joyce Antler) *Changing Education: Women as Radicals and Conservators* and (with Diane Pollard) the National Society for the Study of Education yearbook, *Gender and Education*, and is finishing *School Work: Gender and the Cultural Construction of Teaching*. She also received the Willystine Goodsell Award from the American Educational Research Association.

BARBARA BRENZEL is Professor of Education and Department Chair at Wellesley College. She wrote *Daughters of the State: A Social Portrait of the First Reform School of Girls in North America, 1856–1905*. She has been the author of many articles and book reviews, most of them concerning the lives of women, their education, and work. She is presently beginning new research on dependent children and orphanages.

MARY LYNN McCREE BRYAN is associated with Duke University as the editor of the Jane Addams Papers project and is currently preparing a selected, printed edition of the Jane Addams Papers. She is the editor of the microfilm edition of *The Jane Addams Papers* and *The Jane Addams Papers: A Comprehensive Guide*. Between 1966 and 1983, Bryan was curator of the Jane Addams Hull House, University of Illinois at Chicago. She coedited *100 Years at Hull House*, with Allen F. Davis.

RONALD E. BUTCHART is a historian and the Director of the Education Program at the University of Washington Tacoma campus. He is author of *Northern Schools, Southern Blacks, and Reconstruction: Freedmen's Education, 1862–1875*, *Local Schools: Exploring Their History*, and a number of articles and papers on the history of education and related issues. He has served in a variety of offices in the History of Education Society, the American Educational Research Association, and the American Educational Studies Association.

SUCHENG CHAN is Professor and Chair of Asian American Studies at the University of California (UC), Santa Barbara. The recipient of a Distinguished Teaching Award at UC, Berkeley in 1978, Chan was the first Asian-American woman to become a provost in the system when she served in that capacity at UC, Santa Cruz. She has held postdoctoral fellowships from the National Endowment for the Humanities, the Institute for American Cultures at UC, Los Angeles, and the John Simon Guggenheim Foundation. Three of her books—*This Bittersweet Soil: The Chinese in California Agriculture, 1860–1910, Quiet Odyssey: A Pioneer Korean Woman in America*, and *Asian Americans: An Interpretive History*—as well as her article "Chinese Livelihood in Rural California, 1860–1880: The Impact of Economic Change" have received awards for outstanding scholarship.

C. H. EDSON is Associate Professor of Education in the Division of Educational Policy and Management at the University of Oregon. He was former Director of the American Studies Program and received the university's Burlington Northern Foundation Award for Teaching Excellence in 1985. His research and publications focus on late nineteenth-century educational and social history. Edson is a past president of the American Educational Studies Association and currently serves as secretary/treasurer of the History of Education Society.

LINDA EISENMANN is Assistant Director of the Mary Ingraham Bunting Institute of Radcliffe College and is working on a history of the institute. She has contributed chapters on women's education, graduate training for women, and teacher education for *The Search for Equity: Women at Brown University, 1891–1991*, edited by Polly W. Kaufman, and *Places Where Teachers Are Taught*, edited by John I. Goodlad, Roger Soder, and Kenneth Sirotnik. She has taught at Bowdoin and Wellesley colleges and Harvard University.

JANICE COOKE FEIGENBAUM is Associate Professor of Nursing and the Coordinator of the Community Addictions Nursing component of the graduate program in Community Health Nursing at D'Youville College, Buffalo, New York. She is a member of the American Association of the History of Nursing.

BERNARDO P. GALLEGOS is currently Associate Professor in the Division of Educational Foundations and Interdisciplinary Studies at the California State University at Los Angeles. He is the author of *Literacy, Education, and Society in New Mexico 1693–1821*.

LYNNE MARIE GETZ is Assistant Professor of History at Appalachian State University in Boone, North Carolina. She has written articles on education in New Mexico for the *Teachers College Record* and the *History of Higher Education Annual*.

JULIA GRANT is Assistant Professor at James Madison College, Michigan State University. She is currently completing a monograph on motherhood in twentieth-century America that investigates the impact of the child development profession on mothers' thinking and childrearing practices.

BEVERLY GUY-SHEFTALL is founding director of the Women's Research and Resource Center at Spelman College and Anna Julia Cooper Professor of Women's Studies. She is also founding coeditor of *SAGE: A Scholarly Journal on Black Women*, coeditor of *Sturdy Black Bridges: Visions of Black Women in Literature*, coeditor (with the SAGE editorial group) of *Double Stitch: Black Women Write About Mothers and Daughters*, and author of *Daughters of Sorrow: Attitudes Toward Black Women, 1880–1920*.

ELIZABETH L. IHLE is Professor of Secondary Education and Affirmative Action Officer at James Madison University in Harrisonburg, Virginia. She recently edited an anthology, *Black Women in Higher Education*, and developed brochures designed to encourage minority women to consider teaching.

EMILY C. JONES is a labor educator for the Texas State Employees Union/Communications Workers of America, Local 6186, in Austin, Texas. Her research and publications are in the areas of education history and labor history.

POLLY WELTS KAUFMAN teaches women's history at the University of Massachusetts in Boston. She is the author of *Women Teachers on the Frontier* and the editor of *The Search for Equity, Women at Brown University, 1891–1991*. She has published articles and reviews on women's history and the history of women's education and is currently working on a book about women and national parks.

MAUREEN A. KINGSTON is a doctoral student in the Social Foundations program in the Graduate School of Education at the State University of New York at Buffalo. Her primary research focus is the sociohistorical development of knowledge and identity constructions.

SUSAN McINTOSH LLOYD is Instructor in History and Music at Phillips Academy, Andover, and coordinates the Lawrence High School/Andover Urban Studies Institute, an intensive ten-week program engaging students from both schools in course work, research, and community service. Her publications include *A Singular School: Abbott Academy, 1828–1973* and *The Putney School: A Progressive Experiment*. She has served since 1987 on the National Board for Professional Teaching Standards as a "distinguished teacher" and representative for private schools.

KOFI LOMOTEY is currently Chair and Associate Professor in the Department of Administrative and Foundational Services in the College of Education at Louisiana State University. He has written several articles, book chapters, and books on urban education in general and African-American education in particular. He is also the editor of the journal *Urban Education*.

RUTH JACKNOW MARKOWITZ's major publication is *My Daughter, the Teacher: Jewish Teachers in the New York City Schools*. She has taught history at the State University of New York at Stony Brook, Adelphi University, and the State University of New York/College at Oswego.

ROSA LUISA MÁRQUEZ is Professor at the University of Puerto Rico's Theater Department, a theater director, and an actress. She has published several articles on Augusto Boal, the Bread and Puppet Theatre, popular and educational theater, and Latin American and Puerto Rican theater in Latin American and English theater journals. Her book, *Brincos y Saltos: el juego como disciplina teatral*, was published while she was an artist-in-residence at Massachusetts Institute of Technology, Department of Music and Drama.

THEODORA PENNY MARTIN is Assistant Professor of Education at Bowdoin College. She is the author of *The Sound of Our Own Voices: Women's Study Clubs, 1860–1910*.

AMY THOMPSON McCANDLESS is Associate Professor of History at the College of Charleston in Charleston, South Carolina. She has published articles on southern women's higher education in *Southern Studies*, *The Journal of Thought*, *The History of Higher Education Annual*, *Mississippi Quarterly*, and *The National Women's Studies Association Journal*. She is currently finishing a manuscript on the higher education of women in the twentieth-century South.

KAREN K. McKELLIPS is Professor of Education at Cameron University in Lawton, Oklahoma, where she teaches graduate and undergraduate courses in social foundations of education. Her primary research interest is in the educational history of the Plains Indians.

DORIS MARGUERITE MEADOWS teaches History and Humanities in the City School District, Rochester, New York. She is a community activist as well as historian and author of *Neighborhood as Community: The Nineteenth Ward in Rochester*. Her current work is *Creed of Caste: Journalism and the Race Question During the Progressive Era, 1900–1914*.

TRACY MITRANO has taught at Ithaca College, SUNY-Buffalo, and Cornell University. A revised manuscript from her dissertation is entitled "A Century of Catholic Women's Higher Education: The Colleges in New York State, 1890–1990." She is currently in her first year of law school at Cornell University.

RAYMOND A. MOHL is Professor of History at Florida Atlantic University. He is the author or editor of nine books, including *The Paradox of Progressive Education: The Gary Plan and Urban Schooling*, *The New City: Urban America in the Industrial Age, 1860–1920*, and *Urban Policy in Twentieth-Century America*. He has held Fulbright lectureships at Tel Aviv University, the University of Gottingen, and the University of Western Australia. He is currently completing a book on the history of race relations in the Miami metropolitan area.

KATHLEEN A. MURPHEY is Assistant Professor of Social Foundations of Education in the School of Education at Indiana University-Purdue University at Fort Wayne. She taught as a Foreign Expert in Beijing, the People's Republic of China. Her research interests are in educational history and policy, with a special focus on race and gender issues, and comparative education.

NATALIE A. NAYLOR is Professor of Foundations of Education, teaching Fellow in History in New College, and Director of the Long Island Studies Institute at Hofstra University. She is coauthor of *Teaching Today and Tomorrow*, editor of *Exploring African-American History*, and coeditor of *Theodore Roosevelt: Many-Sided American* and has published articles in *History of Education Quarterly*. She was a Director of the History of Education Society and was on the Editorial Board of *History of Education Quarterly*, and is coeditor of the *Nassau County Historical Society Journal*.

MARY J. OATES is Professor of Economics at Regis College, Weston, Massachusetts, and is the editor of *Higher Education for Catholic Women* and the author of *The Role of the Cotton Textile Industry in the Economic Development of the American Southeast*. She has published numerous articles and chapters on American economic history and on the occupational history of Catholic women. At present, she is completing a book on the Catholic philanthropic tradition in America since 1790.

LINDA M. PERKINS is Associate Professor of Educational Foundations at Hunter College, City University of New York. Her research areas are the history of African-American and women's higher education. She has published widely in the areas of African-American and women's educational histories in various journals. She is the author of *Fanny Jackson Coppin and the Institute for Colored Youth, 1837–1902*. She is currently completing a manuscript entitled *The Black Female Talented Tenth: A History of Black Women's Higher Education*. She has served on the Program Committee for the History of Education Society and Division F of the American Educational

Research Association (AERA). She has also served as Secretary of Division F of AERA, Secretary of the Association of Black Women Historians, and Associate Editor, Dictionary of American Biography, and is coeditor of a special issue on the history of women's education for the *History of Education Quarterly.*

F. MICHAEL PERKO, S.J., is Professor of Educational Leadership and Policy Studies and of History at Loyola University, Chicago. Among his publications are *A Time to Favor Zion: Religion and Schooling on the Urban Frontier, To Enlighten the Rising Generation,* and *Catholic and American: A Popular History.* He is a past president of the Midwest History of Education Society and the International Society for Educational Biography.

JON REYHNER is currently Associate Professor of Education at Eastern Montana College, where he teaches education and Native American studies classes. He has worked over the past two decades as a teacher, school administrator, and consultant with a variety of tribes, including the Apaches, Navajos, and Blackfeet. He cowrote *A History of Indian Education* and was a commissioned author for the U.S. Secretary of Education's Indian Nations at Risk Task Force. His most recent edited book is *Teaching American Indian Students.* He has published a number of articles on American Indian education and is currently working on a Phi Delta Kappa Fastback on Indian education.

CLARK ROBENSTINE is Assistant Professor in the Department of Educational Foundations and Leadership at the University of Southwestern Louisiana. His most recent publications include an article on education reform and at-risk students in *Educational Foundations* and research on French colonial political policy and the education of women and minorities in early Louisiana, published in the *History of Education Quarterly.*

SUSAN F. ROSSEN has been Executive Director of Publications at the Art Institute of Chicago since 1981. Her career began at the Detroit Institute of Arts, where she founded and headed Detroit's first Publications Department. She organized an exhibition of the Detroit museum's collection of women artists in conjunction with the first course on the history of women artists to be offered in Michigan, which she cotaught. She has been active in the Women's Caucus for Art and in Chicago Women in Publications, has lectured widely on women artists and women as patrons of the arts, and has worked for the professionalization of museum publishing.

JOHN L. RURY teaches social history and research methods at the School for New Learning, an alternative liberal arts college for adults at DePaul University in Chicago. He is the author of *Education and Women's Work: Female Schooling and the Division of Labor in Urban America 1870–1930.*

RITA S. SASLAW is the Head of the Department of Educational Foundations and Leadership in the College of Education at the University of Akron. Her field is the history of education in America with emphasis on the higher education of women. She has done extensive research on pre–Civil War students of Oberlin and Western Reserve Colleges. She is currently compiling biographical material on the 2,063 female students who attended Oberlin College between 1836 and 1860 to discover the impact a college education had on their future lives. Saslaw is also working on an oral history of twentieth-century students at Lake Erie College, a former nineteenth-century seminary. Her publications have appeared in *Educational Horizons, Educational Studies, Journal of Midwest History of Education, History of Education,* and *Ohio History.* She has been active in many professional organizations and currently serves as President of the Society of Professors of Education.

B. D. SAUNDERS' research interests focus on identity formation and career development of women in American society, women in the history of higher education, and the training and development of women as administrators.

MAXINE SCHWARTZ SELLER is Professor in the Department of Educational Organization, Administration, and Policy and Adjunct Professor in the Department of History at the State University of New York at Buffalo. A past president of the History of Education Society, she has published extensively on the history of education in the United States and on the history of women and ethnic minorities. Her books include *To Seek America: A History of Ethnic Life in the United States, Ethnic Theater in the United States,* and *Immigrant Women.*

BARBARA SHIRCLIFFE has an M.A. in American Studies. She is currently working towards her Ph.D. in Social Foundations at the University of New York at Buffalo.

OLGA SKORAPA is an independent scholar living and working in Cincinnati, Ohio. Her interests include feminism and educational history. She is presently working to complete a biography of Mary McLeod Bethune.

NANCY G. SLACK is Professor of Biology at Russell Sage College. She does research in plant ecology and history of science, including women in ecology and botany. She has just published a book on Adirondack ecology and is currently co-editing a book on scientific couples.

JOAN K. SMITH is Professor of Education and History and Associate Dean of the Graduate School at Loyola University, Chicago. She is the author of several books, including a biography of Ella Flagg Young, and numerous articles dealing with the history of education in Chicago. She presents papers regularly at national and international conferences and is currently President-Elect of the Society of Professors of Education, a Special Interest Group within the American Educational Research Association.

NANCY L. STEWART wrote her dissertation on the American composer and teacher Marion Bauer. She has contributed to *Women in Music: A History* and the forthcoming edition of *Die Musik in Geschichte und Gegenwart* and has done research on Julia Crane and other American women musicians of the nineteenth and twentieth centuries.

MARCIA G. SYNNOTT is Associate Professor in the History Department of the University of South Carolina in Columbia. She has previously published *The Half-Opened Door: Discrimination and Admissions at Harvard, Yale, and Princeton, 1900–1970* and several articles on ethnic and racial discrimination in higher education. She is currently examining the process of educational desegregation in South Carolina and other southern states.

MARGARET CONNELL SZASZ teaches American Indian/Alaska Native History at the University of New Mexico. She has published extensively in this field, particularly in the area of American Indian education.

MARY TREMBLAY is Associate Professor in the School of Occupational Therapy and Physiotherapy, McMaster University, Hamilton, Ontario, Canada. Her research interests are in the area of disability history, particularly the development of historical accounts about life experiences of individuals with disability.

OLGA VASQUEZ, is Assistant Professor in the Department of Communication at the University of California, San Diego. As an ethnographer of education, her work focuses primarily on language and literacy of bilingual populations in the United States. She is coauthor of *Pushing Boundaries: Language in a Mexicano Community* and author of "A Look at Language as Resource: Lessons from La Clase Magica," published in the ninety-second yearbook of the National Society for the Study of Education.

MARILYN WATT is a Cherokee who lives in the Adair County community of Baron, just a few miles south of where Carrie Bushyhead taught at Baptist Mission. Watt has extensive experiences in Indian education and in various tribal projects. She has worked as a director of educational programs for the American Indian Resource Center and is at present an Assistant Professor at Northeastern State University, both located in Tahlequah, Oklahoma.

KATHLEEN WEILER teaches in the Education Department at Tufts University. She is the author of *Women Teaching for Change* and coeditor (with Candace Mitchell) of *Rewriting Literacy* and *What Schools Can Do: Critical Pedagogy and Practice*, and (with Madeleine Arnot) of *Education, Gender, and Social Justice*. She has written on feminist pedagogy and the history of women teachers and is currently engaged in writing a history of women teachers in rural California in the period 1850–1950.

SAM WEINTRAUB is Professor at the State University of New York at Buffalo. He has served on the faculties at the University of Chicago and Indiana University. He is the editor and major author of the *Annual Summary of Investigations Relating to Reading*. He is a member of the Reading Hall of Fame and a past president of the National Conference for Research in English. In 1987, he was awarded the International Reading Association's Special Service Award.

SALLY H. WERTHEIM is Professor of the History of Education and Dean of the Graduate School at John Carroll University in Cleveland, Ohio. She has been involved in many professional organizations, and has published in *Education Digest*, *Intellect*, *The School Review*, *Educational Studies*, among other journals.

SUSAN WILLIAMSON is Professor of Mathematics at Regis College in Weston, Massachusetts, where she has also served as Academic Dean. Her work in algebra has been published in the *Nagoya Mathematical Journal*. As an outgrowth of her interest in the nature and structure of institutions of higher education, she coauthored, with Mary J. Oates, "Women's Colleges and Women Achievers." She has held several offices in the Massachusetts Conference of the American Association of University Professors.

RICHARD L. WING holds a joint appointment as faculty member (writing) and administrator at Houghton College in western New York.